The 1986 Bedford Prizes in Student Writing

Student, (Instructor), *School, State*

Mary Benner, (Louise Deutsch), *Cape Cod Community College, Massachusetts*
Richard Clinkscales, (Deborah Barrett), *Houston Baptist University, Texas*
Larry W. Earl, (Virginia Tinsley Johnson), *North Idaho College, Idaho*
Christopher Ford, (Edward Miller), *Harvard University, Massachusetts*
Donald B. Foster, (Matthew A. Crow), *California State University–Fresno, California*
Connie Hailey, (Wayne P. Hubert), *Chaffey Community College, California*
Mark David Harris, (Holly Weeks), *Harvard University, Massachusetts*
Peter Carl Krause, (Felicia Lamport), *Harvard University, Massachusetts*
Gregg Landis, (Natalie Brown), *University of Delaware, Delaware*
Rebecca Lester, (Marie E. Foley), *University of California at Santa Barbara, California*
Thomas Leyba, (Martha Connolly), *University of Texas, El Paso, Texas*
Deborah Lielasus, (Joey Wauters), *University of Alaska–Juneau, Alaska*
Kathleen Ann McNeil, (Laura Caruso Grannan), *University of North Carolina, Chapel Hill, North Carolina*
An-thu Quang Nguyen, (George S. Fayen), *Yale University, Connecticut*
Peter Schwartz, (Douglas Bauer), *Harvard University, Massachusetts*
Xiao Mei Sun, (Rebecca K. Mlynarczyk), *Hunter College, New York*
Walter Thies, (Ina E. Lipkowitz), *Columbia University, New York*
Toi Valenza, (John Elder), *Middlebury College, Vermont*
David M. Wang, (Fred Strebeigh), *Yale University, Connecticut*

STUDENT WRITERS AT WORK

and in the company
of other writers

JUDGES OF THE 1986 AND THE 1987 BEDFORD PRIZES IN STUDENT WRITING

Hans P. Guth
Richard Marius
Nell Ann Pickett
Elaine P. Maimon
Donald A. McQuade
Nancy Sommers

JUDGES OF THE 1985 BEDFORD PRIZES IN STUDENT WRITING

Frederick Crews
Janet Emig
Donald McQuade
Donald M. Murray
Nancy Sommers
Lynn Quitman Troyka
William Zinsser

JUDGES OF THE 1983 BEDFORD PRIZES IN STUDENT WRITING

Wayne Booth
Edward P. J. Corbett
Ellen Goodman
Maxine Hairston
Donald McQuade
Nancy Sommers
Alice Trillin
Calvin Trillin

STUDENT WRITERS AT WORK

and in the company of other writers

The Bedford Prizes

THIRD EDITION

Edited by

Nancy Sommers & Donald McQuade

Harvard University   University of California, Berkeley

in collaboration with

Michael Tratner

University of California, Berkeley

A Bedford Book
ST. MARTIN'S PRESS · NEW YORK

For Bedford Books

Publisher: Charles H. Christensen
Associate Publisher: Joan E. Feinberg
Managing Editor: Elizabeth M. Schaaf
Developmental Editor: Stephen A. Scipione
Production Editor: Kathryn S. Daniel
Copyeditor: Barbara G. Flanagan
Text Design: Anna Post
Cover Design: Richard Emery Design, Inc.

Library of Congress Catalog Card Number: 88 – 70420
Copyright © 1989 by St. Martin's Press, Inc.
3 2 1 0 9
f e d c b

For information, write: St. Martin's Press, Inc.
175 Fifth Avenue, New York, NY 10010

Editorial Offices: Bedford Books of St. Martin's Press
29 Winchester Street, Boston, MA 02116

ISBN: 0 – 312 – 00247 – 5

Acknowledgments

James Baldwin, from *Notes of a Native Son.* Copyright © 1955, renewed 1983 by James Baldwin.
  Reprinted by permission of Beacon Press.
Emily Dickinson, "To make a prairie it takes a clover and one bee." Reprinted by permission of the
  publishers and the Trustees of Amherst College from *The Poems of Emily Dickinson,* edited by

(*Acknowledgments and copyrights are continued at the back of the book on pages 705–706, which constitute
an extension of the copyright page.*)

PREFACE

The third series of *Student Writers at Work* strengthens our commitment to making student writing the *primary* text in a composition course. This new edition reflects what we have learned from the Bedford Prize winners, from their instructors, from our own students, and from instructors who have used the first two editions. We are pleased with the continued success of *Student Writers at Work*; it remains the most widely used collection of student writing ever published. We take this as confirmation that a steadily increasing number of freshman composition instructors see *students* as *writers* and place student writing at the center of their composition courses.

In the first series of *Student Writers at Work*, we celebrated the writing of first-year college students. Yet the principles guiding our development of the book have always been more than simply celebratory. We designed *Student Writers at Work* to accord student writing the sustained attention and high regard it deserves, not only by publishing it but also by focusing the same critical attention on it that is reserved for professional writing in the most useful composition readers. In each edition of *Student Writers at Work*, we have acted on this conviction by preparing specific, process-oriented instructional activities to highlight the accomplishments of the more than one hundred student writers to date who have won Bedford Prizes in Student Writing. Our commitment to understanding the excellence that is both visible and embedded in the essays students write has also been expressed in the pedagogical principles that govern our work with student writing: each of the three editions explores the distinctive nature of the composing processes of prize-winning student writers, encouraging them to speak in their own voices about their purposes and strategies, their hopes and anxieties, their struggles and satisfactions as writers.

In the second series of *Student Writers at Work*, we continued to celebrate as well as to work vigorously and informatively with student writing, but we also made an additional effort: we placed the prize-winning essays of student writers in the company of other writers' work. We juxtaposed the work of student and professional writers not as an occasion to draw unfair comparisons between the two kinds of writing but as an opportunity to observe and comment on the similarities in their subjects and purposes. Combining collections of student and professional essays in a single, coordinated collection offers a powerful pedagogical alternative to the typical practice of reprinting professional essays in a separate volume and encourages the wider use of student writing in composition courses.

In developing this third edition of the book, we have not only reinforced our commitment but also refined our original idea. In all three editions, we have attempted to demonstrate that student writing is worthy of all the analysis, appreciation, and imitation that has been restricted to more "serious" and more obviously "literary" writing. But more specifically, we have set out in this new edition to offer a detailed response to a simple and direct question: what are the specific compositional features of each student essay that earned it a Bedford Prize in Student Writing? One of the most useful ways to deal with this question is to ask a related one: what specific compositional techniques and strategies can we identify in the prize-winning essays that other student writers can master in their own work?

An Added Emphasis on the Literary Elements of Student Writing

As we reread these Bedford Prize–winning essays and worked with them in class, we repeatedly found ourselves returning to literary terms when we tried to describe what makes these student essays both excellent and memorable. This new collection highlights—and encourages other student writers to work effectively with—such literary elements as voice, tone, irony, metaphor, symbol, character, conflict, and structure. The Bedford Prize–winning essays demonstrate that these literary elements can be created through specific compositional techniques. We have highlighted one such technique in each student essay and use it as the basis of an extended instructional unit. This edition thereby provides a compendium of successful techniques for bringing literary qualities into student essays.

The particular literary elements—and the compositional techniques that achieve them—that we identify and work with in this new edition are derived inductively from the particular student essays included. A different list of prize-winning essays would have led to a different list of features and techniques. In this respect, the thirty essays included in this edition are not meant to represent "the best of" the Bedford Prize–winning essays. These essays suggest the range of pedagogical options available to teachers who want not only to place student essays at the center of their writing courses but also to encourage sustained attention to specific successful features and effective techniques. As in previous editions, the student essays are arranged alphabetically by author to emphasize that the book need not be used in a particular instructional sequence and that the Bedford Prize winners, not the editors, are the source of the literary qualities and compositional techniques presented.

Following each student essay is a fairly brief but detailed analysis (entitled "An Effective Technique") of what the editors regard to be *one* of the essay's most effective techniques. This analysis not only examines the ways in which the distinctive technique contributes to the essay's effectiveness but also suggests how other student writers can adapt the technique to their own writing. The analysis also identifies the kinds of writing topics and purposes for which the technique seems most suited. By serving as an instructional bridge to the professional essay or story that follows, the analysis also prepares students for the specific ways in which the effective compositional technique used by the student writer is employed in a professional writer's work. In presenting this new feature, we trust that the analysis will serve several interrelated pedagogical purposes: it will provide a model of effective reading as well as analytic writing; it will encourage students to expand their own repertoires of successful reading and writing strategies; it will demonstrate that student writing is often distinguished by the same compositional techniques and literary qualities—the same verbal richness and depth—previously attributed only to professional examples of composition. In effect, we hope that the brief analysis following each student essay will prompt other student writers to reach for their own distinctive versions of complexity, intensity, and originality.

We have paired each student essay with a professional essay because our classroom experience has convinced us that it is easier to recognize a particular compositional technique when it appears in two different essays. Focusing on the same technique used by two different writers also enables student writers to recognize more readily that they are members of a community of writers, that the specific techniques they use are shared with other, professional writers. The professional essays also provide students with abundant and rich opportunities to engage in their own analyses of effective writing techniques. We have included some well-known and justly celebrated professional essays and stories. This is no accident: the same qualities that distinguish professional essays as excellent also distinguish student writing.

Each example of professional writing is accompanied by a headnote, which introduces students to the distinctive intellectual character, personality, and accomplishments of each writer as well as to his or her special approach to composition, often in the writer's own words. Discussion questions follow each professional essay and focus exclusively on the specific compositional technique that links the professional essay to the student essay. Each instructional unit (matching the work of a student and professional writer) concludes with "Working with the Technique in Your Own Writing." Each of these writing exercises invites students to practice the particular effective technique in their own compositional efforts and to adapt the technique to their own, often quite different, compositional purposes.

Our own experience in the classroom has led us to another conclusion: students write most effectively when they aim beyond competence at excellence. A pedagogy focused only on competence in student writing leads students and teachers to think largely about features that are *common* to all essays, with the result that students often work to efface their distinctive personalities, to eliminate emotion, to make their writing conform to a preset pattern despite their special topics or purposes, and to believe that their essays would be better written by someone else, presumably the teacher. In marked contrast, a pedagogy focused on the literary elements of student essays and the techniques that produce them leads students to discover and to exercise mastery over their own distinctive voices, to play with words and images, to create patterns and structures to suit their topics and purposes, and to believe that their essays could not be written by anyone else.

A Continued Emphasis on Process and Revision

In addition to the new features included in the third edition of *Student Writers at Work*, we have strengthened and refined the five special chapters ("Student Writers on Writing: An Overview" and the four chapters in Part II, "Student Writers at Work") from the previous editions. Our effort in each instance has been to emphasize further our attention to the actualities of the writing process and more especially to the specifics of revising.

Moreover, the material surrounding the student essays is unprecedented in a reader. Because the Bedford Prize contest rules stipulated that all entries be accompanied by preliminary notes and drafts and because all the winning essayists and their instructors completed detailed questionnaires, the headnotes and discussion questions explore the writers' composing processes as well as their finished products. The headnotes provide not only biographical information about the writers but also quotations from them about their intentions and their writing habits.

We have developed five unique chapters to help students in their writing and in their working with other students' writing:

Student Writers on Writing. This introduction provides an overview of the writing process through the voices of the winning essayists. They discuss their satisfactions and frustrations as writers and their specific strategies for getting started, drafting, and revising. In this third edition we have included more student comments on invention and revision, along with an example of brainstorming.

Revising Drafts. This chapter focuses on the composing processes of two prize-winning essayists. Guided by editorial comments, students can examine the complete notes and the rough draft of one of the prize-winning essays, along with the writer's own explanations of her intentions. Then, guided by questions, students can analyze the choices of another prize-winning writer as he develops his essay from rough drafts to a final version.

Peer Editing. This chapter prepares students to be effective peer editors and to respond as writers to the editing of their fellow students. We begin with an explanation of the principles and procedures of peer editing. Next, students see the comments of four composition students on one of the winning essays. Through questions, they are then guided to analyze the peer editors' comments and to evaluate the essay on their own. We present the writer's response to the peer editors' comments and his revision of his essay, and students are again invited by questions to examine the results. Further exercises in peer editing with a second example of peer editing are also included.

Moving from Personal Experience to Exposition and Argument. This chapter guides students step by step from writing firsthand accounts of their own experience to broader and more objective approaches to the same material. Two Bedford Prize winners, Beverly Dipo and Curtis Chang, developed new essays from the ones they had originally submitted to their instructors. The chapter records their progress: Dipo's from narration to argument, Chang's from narration to exposition and argument. These writers kept detailed notes on their writing processes, from brainstorming to outlining and then to drafting and revising. Reinforcing these examples is specific advice on how to make the transition from personal to expository or argumentative writing and exercises to help students get started.

Responding to Professional Editing. The final chapter demonstrates what happens to writing when it is prepared for publication. We found that many users of previous editions appreciated this demonstation of close critical reading and editing as an example of the kinds of comments professional editors make to encourage writers to revise. Observing a professional editor at work also illustrates and emphasizes how even first-rate essays written by professional writers can be revised. After an introduction explaining the goals and procedures of editing, the professional editor offers specific recommendations for one of the winning essays, focusing on how to improve communication between the writer and the reader. We then present the writer's revision of his essay, with his comments on the revision and on the experience of being edited. Through a series of questions, we help students examine the editing of each essay and the writer's response to it.

Each of the distinctive parts as well as the special features of *Student Writers at Work and in the company of other writers* receives thoughtful and imaginative attention in the complementary *Instructor's Manual* prepared with the expertise of Miriam Baker of Dowling College. The manual thoroughly discusses each part as well as each essay and offers teaching suggestions, discussion questions, and writing topics. It also provides an arrangement by compositional elements to help generate ideas for using *Student Writers at Work and in the company of other writers* throughout a semester.

Our most recent work on this project continues to be influenced by the more than two hundred members of the Council of Writing Program Administrators who responded a few years ago to our survey on the uses of student writing in the classroom. Among many other ideas, the respondents shared their almost unanimous belief that the students' own writing should be the primary text in the composition class; as one teacher put it, no book can replace "the living, breathing student in the class who is there to speak up, to argue, to defend, to explain, to accept, and to reject." *Student Writers at Work and in the company of other writers* does not attempt such replacement. Instead, the book offers a collection of essays that are both worthy of emulation and possible to emulate. *Student Writers at Work and in the company of other writers* supplements the work of students in the class with the work of their peers across the nation, giving them an opportunity to sharpen their critical skills, to study how successful writers make the composing process work for them, and to see themselves as members of a community of writers that extends well beyond the classroom walls.

Acknowledgments

Sherwood Anderson once said that "the whole glory of writing lies in the fact that it forces us out of ourselves and into the lives of others." Behind this third edition of *Student Writers at Work* stands a large—and steadily increasing—number of colleagues and friends who graciously allowed us into their already crowded lives to seek advice, encouragement, and assistance.

Before we could prepare this new edition, we conducted two additional national contests to determine the winners of the Bedford Prizes in Student Writing. And before there could be a contest, there were rules to be checked and written. For their counsel during this phase of the project, we would like to thank David Kaye, Paul Slevin, and Hans Smit, Esq. Most important, we would like to acknowledge both the instructors across the country who supported the contest by submitting their students' work and the nearly five thousand students who wrote essays worthy of submission.

We are indebted to the kind people who kept track of the essays as they were submitted and who prepared them to be read anonymously by our judges: Jane Betz, Matthew Carnicelli, and Julie Shevach. The generosity of Rutgers University and of Joe McDermott, of Local 237 of the Teamsters Union in New York, and Ed Quinn, the former Director of the Center for Worker Education in the City University of New York, provided us with a comfortable place to read and reread essay after essay.

We are also grateful to the writers, editors, and teachers of writing who served as judges in the first rounds of reading: Abby Attias, Agnes Azzolino, Joan Baranow, Philip Beichtman, Pat Bellanca, Peter Bowen, Mollie Brodsky, Lyall Bush, Mary Ellen Byrne, Cheryl Calletta, John Canaday, Eleanor Carducci, Michael Conlin, Jacqueline Costello, Walter Cummins, Karen D'Agostino, Phebe E. Davidson, Leonard Deen, Rosemary Deen, Hugh Dignon, Dennis Donahue, Hugh English, David Evans, Kathy Fedorko, Beverly Fenig, Deborah Gussman, Vicki Harrison, Anne Herzog, Sister Grace Hewitt, Peter Hitchcock, Sharon Jessee, Virginia Johnson, Marjorie Keyishian, Kathleen Kier, Margaret Klawunn, Mitchell Levenberg, Mary Anne Lutz, Robert Lynch, Alisha Mahaney, Maureen McFeely, Diane Menna, Thomas Murray, Andrew Nargolwala, Karin Nyenstad, Anthony O'Brien, Mary O'Reilly, Mitchell Orlowsky, Susan Osborn, Donna Perry, Marie Ponsot, Rick Poverny, Thomas Recchio, Michael Robertson, Robert Roth, Joseph C. Santora, Michael Sargent, Stephen Schmidt, Guy Shebat, John Shufelt, Jo Tarvers, Joseph Thomas, Michelle Tokarczyk, Robert Ulesky, Joyce Warren, Peter Weiss, G. Gordon Whatley, Cecilia Wilshire, Matthew Wilson, and Marion Yee.

Once again special thanks are due Deborah Asher and Susan Osborn, who helped recruit many of our first-round judges, and to Jacqueline Costello, who also helped recruit judges and then trained them and choreographed the multiple readings of each essay. Working with the distinguished panel of judges who chose the winners of the Bedford Prizes in Student Writing remains one of the special pleasures of this project. For their careful readings and thoughtful comments, we would like to thank Hans Guth, Elaine Maimon, Richard Marius, and Nell Ann Pickett.

We would also like to thank the many instructors who so generously shared with us their experience of working with *Student Writers at Work* in their classes: William Arfin, University of North Carolina, Chapel Hill; Eugene Baer, Wisconsin Lutheran College; Dennis Baeyem, Iowa State University; Carol Bamdad, Union County College; Sheila Bender, Seattle Central Community College; Daryl Coats, University of Mississippi; Terri Cook, Westmont College; Donald Daiker, Miami University, Ohio; Patricia Daire, Pima Community College; Dorothy Fillmore, Virginia Commonwealth University; Paulette Flowers, Vanderbilt University; Beth Franklin, University of Minnesota; J. L. Funston, James Madison University; Margie Garner, Freeman Junior College; Lt. Jill Garzone, United States Naval Academy; E. R. Gelber-Beechler, University of North Carolina, Charlotte; George Greenlee, Missouri Southern State College; Quay Grigg, Hamline University; Susan S. Hankins, University of Mississippi; Susanne E. Hill, Maria Regina College; John K. Hoernig, Niagara County Community College; Diane Horan, Montgomery County Community College; David Jolliffe, University of Illinois; Jim Kolsky, Western Nevada Community College; Mary Beth Lake, Normandale Community College; Sherry Mon Lidaka, Northern Illinois University; Pamela Liebing, Harper College; Darlene Lister, California State University, Dominguez Hills; Nancy G. Little, Motlow State Community College; Theresa L. McLain, University of Texas, San Antonio; Barbara C. McMillan, University of Mississippi; Adelio F. Maccentelli, Essex Community College; Harry Marks, Temple University; Vernon G. Miles, University of Arkansas, Fayetteville; Mary Frances Minton, Virginia Commonwealth University; Kathy Morris Murray, University of Mississippi; Edward M. O'Keefe, Niagara County Community College; J. Daniel Patterson, Kent State University; Paul Perry, University of Texas, San Antonio; Douglas Roycraft, Erie Community College; Joseph Sanders, Lakeland Community College; Judi Sandler, Union County College; Paul Sladky, University of Texas, Austin; Mary Ann Smith, Boston College; Cheryl A. Staunton, Mary Washington College; Mary Kathryn Stein, University of Arkansas, Little Rock; Mary Stein, Evergreen Valley College; Judith Straffin, Rock Valley College; Edward F. Sundberg, Cabrillo College; Marilynn Talal, University of Texas, San Antonio; Gilbert Tierney, W. R. Harper College; Erskine S. White, University of North Carolina, Charlotte; and Gerald C. Wood, Carson-Newman College.

We are also extremely grateful to the following colleagues for their detailed readings of various editions of *Student Writers at Work* and for their many helpful suggestions: Eleanor Agnew, Francis Marion College; Miriam Baker, Dowling College; Nancy K. Barry, University of Iowa; Richard P. Batteiger, Oklahoma State University; Carolyn Beck, Kent State University; Thomas Blues, University of Kentucky; Margaret Butler, Motlow State Community College; Kathleen Shine Cain, Merrimack College; Robert Connors, University of New Hampshire; Marie B. Czarnecky, Mohawk Valley Community College; Michele Czosnek, University of Wisconsin, Milwaukee; Connie Douglas, Louisiana College; Kathryn Fitzgerald, University of Utah; Anne Hall, University of North Carolina, Chapel Hill; Jay Jernigan, Eastern Michigan University; Janet Marting, University of Akron; Agnew M. McDonald, University of North Carolina, Wilmington; Marge McMinn, University of Arkansas, Little Rock; Thomas J. Murray, Trenton State College; Steven Rayburn, University of Mississippi; Lucinda H. Roy, Virginia Polytechnic Institute and State University; Bonnie Rudner, Boston College; John Ruszkiewicz, University of Texas, Austin; Judith Stanford; and Marilyn J. Valentino, Lorain County Community College. Rebecca Boswell, Cornelia Fleischman, Sarah Hubbard, and Frank Lortscher offered detailed as well as insightful readings of the second edition from the vantage point of accomplished student writers. For their advice and encouragement, we'd like to thank Deborah Asher, Robert DiYanni, Edward Dornan, Nancy Jones, William P. Kelly, Joyce Kinkaid, Gerry McCauley, Laura Novo, David Richter, Robert Roth, Mimi Schwartz, and William Taliaferro. Gary Goshgarian graciously consented to let us print drafts of one of his many fine essays on culture in the chapter on the professional editor. We'd also like to acknolwedge Edward P. J. Corbett. His collegiality, accomplishments in print, and intellectual integrity stand as models for our profession.

We continue to be indebted to Jane Aaron, an eloquent and encouraging voice in "Responding to Professional Editing." Miriam Baker of Dowling College has lived through three editions of this book with us, and she has been a constant friend and a limitless source of first-rate ideas and teaching strategies. Hers is the strongest voice in the Instructor's Manual, and reports of the manual's success in previous editions are a tribute primarily to her accomplishments as an outstanding teacher and writer as well as to her vision of the book's potential.

We would like to acknowledge our colleagues in England and the United States whose work helped shape the chapter on peer editing: M. L. J. Abercrombie, Lil Brannon, John Clifford, Richard Gebhardt, Thom Hawkins, Edwin Mason, Stepehen Tschudi, and especially Ken Bruffee, Rosemary Deen, and Marie Ponsot. For their invaluable help on the peer editing chapter, we would also like to thank the student writers and peer editors at Queens College,

CUNY: Nicholas Balamaci, Jason Eskenazi, Nelson Farias, and Frances Osborne. Their intelligent, sensitive readings of another, and rather distant, student's writing broadened and enriched the limits of a productive community of writers.

For helping us with "Moving from Personal Experience to Exposition and Argument," asking us difficult questions, and offering generous advice, we would like to add a special note of thanks to Ron Strahl of California State University, Long Beach, and Barbara Cambridge and her colleagues at Indiana University/Purdue University at Indianapolis. Anne Middleton pursued a similarly helpful and rigorous series of questions in conversation at the University of California, Berkeley, for which we are grateful. The work of James Moffett also proved helpful in developing this chapter.

The most important contributor to this new edition is Michael Tratner. His intelligence, imagination, energy, and accomplishments as a teacher and writer helped strengthen this edition in innumerable ways. We are grateful for his work as a collaborator.

Our continuing thanks go to the kind people at Bedford Books. For the elegant look of their work, we would like to thank Anna Post, who once again designed the book and contest poster, and Richard S. Emery, who deftly repeated his success in designing the book's cover. Barbara Flanagan copyedited the manuscript with outstanding skill, and Joan Kocsis proofread the book with great ability. Jane Betz skillfully managed assembling the permissions for the professional writing, and Sarah Royston and Erin Curtiss helped with research and manuscript preparation. Kathy Daniel skillfully managed the project through production. Nancy DeCubellis and Nancy Lyman coordinated the contest's first round of judging with great skill and intelligence. Stephen Scipione deserves an MVP award for his work on this edition; a utility infielder on previous editions, Steve batted third in the new starting line-up. Without his hard work, dedication, and patience, this book could not have gone to press. Michael Eads imaginatively designed a first-rate advertising program for this new edition. Elizabeth Schaaf, managing editor, guided the manuscript through a maze of production problems with an extraordinary amount of intelligence and energy and with an unflappable professionalism. Joan Feinberg, associate publisher, not only gave us generous, rigorous comments on every aspect of the manuscript but also repeatedly encouraged us to take the kinds of intellectual risks that made working on this book at once exhausting and yet enormously satisfying. She is the kind of editor every writer hopes to work with and the kind of reader every writer hopes to write for. And Chuck Christensen, publisher, who enticed us with the idea of the Bedford Prizes, has continued to offer us wise and genial support and the kind of confidence in his authors that makes each sentence easier to write. This new edition of *Student Writers at Work and in the company of other writers* has been a truly collaborative enterprise.

Finally, we would like to thank the friends who gave us time to work or ideas to work with or, in several cases, both: Robert Atwan; Hans Dieter, Sarah, and Amelia Batchelet; Fred, Jill, and Alexander Buell; William Harris; Janine Karoly; William P. Kelly; Helene Kessler; Robert and Bridget Lyons; Judy and Amanda Myers; and Kurt Spellmeyer. Most important, we can only hope that in this sentence Patrick, Rachel, and Alexandra Hays; Leda and Jeffrey Tratner; as well as Susanne, Christine, and Marc McQuade will know how much they have helped us and how much their help has meant to us.

CONTENTS

STUDENT WRITERS ON WRITING:
AN OVERVIEW

O NE OF THE MOST reasuring discoveries any student of writing can make is that there is no single way to write, no fail-proof formula to produce successful essays. Anyone seriously interested in learning to write can benefit from listening to what other writers have to say about the challenges and pleasures of the composing process. The pages that follow will give you a special opportunity to examine the writing process from the point of view of student writers. The thirty winners of Bedford Prizes in Student Writing whose work is reprinted here explain their successes and frustrations as writers as well as their particular methods of composition. From their detailed responses to a questionnaire on their specific habits and goals, their strategies and concerns as writers, we have drawn practical information on many aspects of writing — from how these student writers search for an idea and then develop it in a first draft to how they revise and then prepare that idea for presentation in a finished essay.

What do these student writers talk about when they are invited to discuss writing? Like all writers, they invariably speak of the problems and the pleasures of struggling to convey a clear sense of their ideas. They also talk about the purpose and structure of their essays, their use of language, and their relation to an audience. They frequently touch on their respect for and anxiety about mastering the skills required to write good prose. And they describe in detail the distinctive ways in which they compose: how they go about generating ideas for a paper, how they brainstorm and freewrite about that idea, how they organize and develop their first drafts, how they contend with the procrastination and the dead ends that threaten their progress, how they revise, and how they determine when their essays are finished and ready to be read by their peers and submitted to their instructors. Given the academic context within which they work, these students also touch on

1

their concern about grades and discuss their perceptions of the place of writing in their career goals.

The perspectives these student writers present on the composing process are as varied as their backgrounds and interests. Yet the procedures they follow when writing can be grouped into three general phases: getting started, drafting, and revising. Writers usually start by searching for and then deciding on a subject to write about, developing their ideas about the subject, clarifying their purpose in writing, organizing their thoughts, and considering the audience they want to address. In the drafting phase, they usually carry out their detailed plan in a first draft; in the revising phase, they study what they have written and determine how they can improve it. These designations are not a lockstep series of discrete stages that writers work through in exactly the same manner each time. They are simply patterns of activities that describe what happens when writers write. As every writer knows, at least intuitively, writing is not a linear but a recursive process. Writing rarely proceeds neatly from one phase to the next. Rather, the phases frequently overlap, making the process often appear messy. Many writers, for example, revise what they have written as soon as the word or the sentence appears on the page. Each writer participates in the writing process in a different way, at a different pace, and with a different result. In tracing the exact movements of a writer's mind at work on an idea, it is possible to discover and describe patterns, but the specific circumstances and the particular moves are never exactly the same every time.

Reading what other students have to say about writing should assure you that all writers—whether they are professionals, prize-winning student essayists, or classmates—grapple with many of the same basic problems. (When you turn to the professional writers whose work we have included in this volume, you will hear them talk in much the same terms as student writers about the frustrations and pleasures of writing.) You may also be surprised—and pleased—to learn that in many instances the observations and solutions of these professional and prize-winning student writers are similar to those you may have developed in your own writing. In addition, you may find that the prize-winning student writers will offer new suggestions that can help you improve your writing. Recognizing both the unique and the shared elements of the writing experience will enable you to place yourself in the company of other writers while distinguishing your own voice from theirs. What follows is not a comprehensive survey of every facet of the writing process but a detailed report on what happens when successful student writers work productively.

Getting Started

In the first of the three phases of the writing process, a writer usually chooses a subject to write about if one has not been assigned, discovers a purpose for writing about the subject, generates a thesis or a controlling idea about the subject, considers the audience to be addressed, and then develops that idea in freewriting and brainstorming exercises, in an outline, or in some other form that will be the basis of a first draft of an essay. This is the most difficult phase of writing for most people. Because they usually face so many problems and obstacles here, most writers seem to have more to say about it than about any other phase.

Procrastination

Celeste Barrus identifies what is perhaps the single most common obstacle these prize-winning students face when they write—their tendency to procrastinate, a trait they share with most other writers, students and professionals alike: "There is no one easy thing about writing, except putting it off."

Some writers apparently can produce only under great pressure, usually the looming presence of a deadline. John Clyde Thatcher takes "perverse delight in watching the time slip by until it is almost too late to begin writing." For him, getting started is "like a game of literary Russian roulette." In a similar vein, Johnna Lynn Benson notes: "I like to procrastinate, but I don't know any cute tricks for that bad habit. It usually takes a panicked glance at the calendar to make me decide to start." Bonnie Harris regularly uses the due date for an assignment and some caffeine to prompt herself to start writing: "Usually it's the impending deadline that spurs me to action. I realize that time is running out, so I make one more cup of coffee, take it to my desk, map out an introduction, and try to let it flow from there."

The stratagems these student writers draw on so freely to put off writing are often almost as ingenious as the methods they finally discover to write successfully. Bonnie Harris no doubt speaks for many student writers when she reports: "Normally I put off writing as long as I can and end up working into the wee morning hours. There's always plenty of excuses—I need to clean my room, do laundry, make phone calls, eat. . . ." The road Ann Louise Field routinely travels on her way to a first draft includes quite a few visual and gastronomic detours: "First, I make sure there is nothing on TV that I have to watch, because once I get started I can't stop. Then I make sure that my other homework is completed or can wait without putting me too far behind in my studies. Then I make sure I'm running on a full stomach and then I begin. I always eat shortly before I begin writing." As Field's comment suggests, the kitchen is an especially appealing place for student writers both to prepare for writing and to procrastinate, and eating is the most common source of pleasurable distraction for writers intent on postponing the work they need to do. Few descriptions of putting off writing match Allison Rolls's—at least in terms of putting on weight:

> I have come up with many methods to avoid writing, but the primary one is eating. It works like this: I gather up everything I need to start—pens, pencils, paper, references, etc.—and then I arrange them very neatly for maximum efficiency. After brooding about it for some time, I finally decide that writing is very tiring, so I should gather some strength. I go to the kitchen and fix myself a snack and a cup of tea. When I am through eating, I make more tea and go out for an ice cream cone and to ponder my subject. When I return, my tea is cold, so I wait for the water to boil and eat and think some more. . . . And by the time I actually sit down to write, I am exhausted.

Yet these successful student writers do manage somehow, and often rather ingeniously, to overcome the widespread tendency to delay writing.

The student writers whose essays are gathered in this book identify equally successful tactics to combat procrastination. Earnestine Johnson imposes deadlines on herself and scrupulously, if somewhat "begrudgingly," observes them. Curtis Chang relies on a more intricate but flexible schedule of work and rest: "I enjoy marking out thirty-minute breaks every two hours. It gives me a definite point to work until and, surprisingly, my best thoughts usually come right before break time. Often, I will stew in frustration for an hour and forty-five minutes and then—BAM!—begin typing continuously for the next hour, missing my break time." Brad Manning frequently puts himself in the company of other writers and depends on at least one time-honored, if somewhat aggressive, form of inspiration: "With respect to getting started, I admire these words of Jack London: 'You can't wait for inspiration; you have to go after it with a club.' I think of his words every time I sit down to write." For Heather Ashley, "Getting started is rarely a problem. . . . It is finishing that I have trouble with."

The Writing Environment

Most writers are as finicky about the circumstances of where and when they write as they are about whether they will start writing at all. Thomas Leyba, for example, explains that he "loves . . . to write just after a shower; it's always nice to have water rinse away fatigue and instill fresh thoughts." For Tor Valenza, writing depends on creating a relaxing, uncluttered environment within which to work: "Soft music in the background, a cup of coffee, and me." Ha Song Hi creates a high-tech—but equally fragile—environment for writing: "A person walking into my room while I am writing would see the back of my head outlined by my computer screen and surrounded by stacks of papers and books. They had better be very quiet, because I hate being interrupted while lost in my work. They would see me pause to think, drink sodas, eat snacks, look up words in the dictionary, laugh at my own jokes, curse when I delete a whole page by mistake, or scream when my two-year-old unplugs me and I know that Save Document never saves it all." Paula Sisler reports that she depends on people, not places: "The ideal environment to write in is not a place but an attitude of support and encouragement."

The student writers in this book seem to be divided on the question of whether writers need a quiet work space to concentrate on practicing the skills required to produce successful essays. Judy Jennings represents one extreme when she reports that she needs "total quiet" in order to write. Bonnie Harris also must "have quiet when I'm writing; I'm supersensitive to extraneous noise. Sometimes I put my clock under a pillow so I don't have to hear it ticking." Brad Manning is equally determined to eliminate any distracting sounds from his environment: "Noise kills my concentration. If there is talking in the room, I insert my yellow ear plugs and just listen to myself. The only noise that I think actually helps me when I write is rain." Ha Song Hi imagines a late-twentieth-century version of a rustic retreat for writing: "The ideal writing environment for me would be an isolated cabin deep in the woods, snowbound and alone, plenty of food, a wood fire, all my books and files around me, a modem to connect my computer terminal with the Library of Congress, unlimited funds for mainframe time, and someone to unobtrusively clean house and cook."

At the other extreme, many students need some form of sound in the background to offset the silence and solitude of writing. Some students prefer to work in front of a television set, and a few even report that they write only during the commercials. Terry Burns's sound is the stereo: "I know most people like it quiet when they write, but I just can't think when it's quiet. Crank up the stereo, and I'm in business." James Seilsopour's sound is the radio. Karen Kramer establishes more stringent requirements; her "ideal" environment for writing is "in my room, alone, with a stereo on, playing some kind of music that I won't feel inclined to sing along with, dance to, or stare out the window and reminisce with. I like it dark, too, with just one desk light on. Makes it cozier somehow." William Hill reports that finding adequate time to write is far more important to him than locating an adequate place to work. Sound seems to be a built-in, unavoidable feature of his life and work: "Some people find quiet necessary to be able to write; I don't. I have two children and live almost directly in the landing portion of the Memphis International Airport, so noises do not bother me. What I need is time, periods from two to three hours when I don't have to be bothered with anything else." John Mason relies on a more portable—and inspiring—environment within which to write; he prefers to "surround myself with pictures of people that have influenced me and that I care about."

Discarded food and packaging, half-filled coffee cups, jugs of Kool-Aid, three-liter bottles of soda, crumpled papers, mangled pencils, disgruntled expressions, furrowed brows, and lingering curtains of cigarette smoke are fairly common features of the productive writing environment many students favor. Jill Savitt describes such circumstances: "My writing habits are chewing on pens and smoking cigarettes. I never notice either. I also reread my work a lot, making me take too many breaks. If I don't stop and listen to music or get something to eat or make a phone call, I can't distance myself from what I write, and everything sounds the same." An-Thu Quang Nguyen provides an equally hair-raising account of what people would discover if they peered in on her trying to make meaning out of a half-formed idea: "They would see me clutch my hair, stare about the room vaguely from time to time, bite my nails, and sigh a lot. I would start jotting something down furiously, sit back to look at it, then furiously cross it out. I may do this several times until the right word appears, at which time I could force out a couple more sentences until I'm again blocked and need to repeat the process." Bonnie Harris reports:

> Someone watching my writing process would see a lot of starts and stops and crossing out of sentences, putting sheets of paper aside and starting over, reading through my reference materials, flipping from page to page where I've stuck note cards to mark passages, staring at my outline and deciding to revise it, or writing notes in the margins about things I've just thought of to go back and work on again. I never crumple up pages and throw them away; I might need them later. I'll go back and read what I've written dozens of times. When I get stuck I go make coffee and munch on Wheat Thins. I don't think I could do this for a living; I'd end up obese.

Yet student writers do get started on their papers, however perilously close to the deadline they may be and even if it means, as some report, using "favorite" pens or pencils, wearing "lucky" clothes, or consuming special foods while writing. Karen Kramer reports that when she writes "sometimes I do like to wear a silly hat and sunglasses." Brad Manning feels most comfortable writing when wearing a particular hat and adopting a special identity when he writes: "On my head I wear a Greek sailor's hat backward and pushed down over my forehead. It probably looks dumb to other people, but it makes me feel adventurous for a little while, as if I were an airplane pilot or a catcher behind the plate." Jill Savitt's needs as a writer are more modest: "To start a paper I use one of those yellow legal pads. Always, I scribble and doodle and eventually start thinking of what I want to say." Whatever the quirk, the ritual, the superstition, or the curious concern or costume, many writers feel that certain circumstances must be present before they can even begin to write.

Other writers find the time and circumstances of composition unimportant. Heather Ashley reports, for example, that "I write ideas down as soon as they come to me on whatever is handy—napkins, receipts, whatever—and then use them or throw them out later. Mostly I save them." Ann Louise Field offers a more confident version of this same conviction: "I can write anywhere. If I don't have a place to sit and a surface to rest the paper on, then I just write in my head. I've written brilliant essays while washing dishes, pulling weeds, and scrubbing the bathtub."

Finding a Topic

Jill Savitt speaks for many writers when she reports, "The most difficult thing is finding a topic, locating something manageable and contained. Too often I follow tangents because I like my digressions more than my topic." To help herself identify a suitable subject and topic for an essay, An-Thu Quang Nguyen repeatedly challenges both her own intelligence and her powers of retention: "I jot down anything to do on the subject before I truly start to think about it, then throw that list away. The more worthwhile ideas will be remembered." In contrast, Karen Kramer explains that "if getting started means picking a topic, then the best thing for me to do is to sit and wait. It'll come to me. If I try to think actively about it, I usually panic because I feel under the gun as the assignment deadline nears. However, after several of these intense little panic sessions, interspersed by my doing something completely unrelated to the task at hand, I usually end up with a good topic. I know it's a good topic if I get excited about it or if I just smile in anticipation of writing about it."

For many writers, ideas about subjects as well as specific topics for writing often come when they least expect them—while taking a shower, riding a bicycle, or reading a newspaper. Dianne Emminger, for example, recounts the unexpected origins of her essay "The Exhibition":

> I had a great deal of difficulty choosing my topic for this essay. I had been out of town that week and was, in fact, sitting in a plane in Atlanta, full of frustration at my failure to begin writing, when I made the decision to write about the most insignificant thing I could see there in the plane. It was raining that day, and the most insignificant thing I saw were the raindrops on the window—one looks right through the raindrops. Several days later, while reviewing the notes I had taken on the plane, I began thinking of the prismatic effect raindrops have on light and was reminded of what I had seen while visiting a gallery years earlier.

As Dianne Emminger notes, writing invariably involves a great deal of both patience and self-discipline. Barbara Seidel explains the difficulties of each: "If the subject is not of my choosing, I have to wait until an idea hits me like a ton of bricks, and I am not good at waiting. If the subject is of my choosing, I have to restrain myself to get one word at a time out, rather than one paragraph at a time, and I am not good at self-control." Celeste Barrus agrees in the following dramatic, if not anxious, terms: "Writing is waiting—unsettled waiting—for ideas to come."

Student writers rely on a seemingly limitless supply of tactics to find their topics and to get started on exploring their ideas about them—from deliberate reading and research to peer group discussions and random mental association. Jill Savitt has found that the most effective way to generate ideas to write about is to "read voraciously—everything from the backs of cereal boxes to *TV Guide* to newspapers to novels to history books." Tor Valenza begins with a seminal word or phrase and develops his ideas from that point: "I always begin not with an idea in my head, but a word or a sentence, such as 'At Diane's.' I may not use that particular phrase, but I set the mood and tone in my own mind." Paula Sisler reports that she has developed an effective strategy for finding subjects and topics for writing: "I watch people. I sit in a restaurant and wonder what the people at the table are talking about. I look at the way they are dressed, the way they move, the way they look at each other. I watch the way they hold their utensils, the way they use their eyes, the way they do or don't use manners. To write about people, one must first *see* people, must first *hear* people, must first *know* people."

Other students prefer to review the material they are studying either in their writing class or in the other courses they are taking. The assigned reading in these courses may well provide a subject on which to focus. Magazines and television news as well as documentary programs also offer ready sources of subjects that will engage a writer's interest—and a reader's. Writers need to develop practiced confidence in their ability to choose an interesting subject to focus on in an essay. As John Mason observes: "The easiest thing for me to come up with is an idea to write about. The world is filled with subjects to write about." But Mason also reminds us that writing involves a good deal of hard work: "Sitting down and explaining that idea in writing is another matter."

A journal is one excellent way to keep track of your ideas about a subject. A journal is a daily written record of your experiences and thoughts on particular subjects. Journal entries are usually more focused and related than those in a diary, which poses no restrictions on subject or focus. Beverly Dipo, for example, uses her journal to discover—and rediscover—her hopes and aspirations, her fears and anxieties: "I keep my journal hidden as if it were top secret. I feel this writing stuff bares my innermost self to the world and that is uncomfortable for me. How does one go about overcoming that? . . . Writing in a journal is a free psychiatric session that would cost upwards of $50 an hour. It recalls feelings you thought were buried long ago, returns your mistakes to haunt you, and for me, it gives me an insight into a self that I am surprised to find." Earnestine Johnson connects her journal entries more directly to her essay assignments. Keeping a journal provides her with useful starting points for writing: "What works best for me is sitting down and writing whatever comes to mind on the subject. I may write ten pages, and once I have reviewed them all I may find that only two or three pages are useful, but they give me a starting point."

Many writers find that they can discover ideas about a subject by writing down everything they know about it. Barbara Seidel relies on a technique known as *freewriting,* also called *nonstop writing.* She begins writing by "pouring out words, thoughts, feelings down on paper, without concern for grammar or punctuation or neatness. I write in a mad rush and want to be undisturbed at this point in the writing process." Seidel's work as a writer comes later, "in organizing those poured-out feelings and thoughts, in getting them to make sense to someone other than me. Words trip over each other, each demanding to be first." As Seidel implies, to use freewriting successfully it is crucial to put your pen to paper and continue writing without pausing between words or sentences to consider grammar, sentence structure, word choice, and spelling. Should you find yourself stuck along the way, repeat an important word and expand on it. Heather Ashley relies on freewriting to keep track of her initial— and instinctive—thoughts on a subject: "Often I force myself to freewrite, just put down whatever comes into my head, and then go back and revise later. That way my gut feelings are recorded."

Many writers follow up on their initial thoughts with another round of freewriting, often called focused freewriting. In focused freewriting, the writer reviews the first round of freewriting, selects what seems to be a promising lead, and then freewrites about that more limited topic. Judy Jennings offers an instructive sample. Having spent some time freewriting about her marriage and children, Jennings decided to loop back over the subject of her stepchildren to focus more deliberately on "the injustices of stepparenting" and "to make a few clarifications about a very misunderstood role."

I don't really know what to say or where to start when I try to talk (or write) a logical something about my relationship with my stepchildren. I think all the time "How did I get myself into this?" When Les and I got married, I was an extremely naive 24 and never realized that I was marrying not only a man, but a man with three kids — a package deal so to speak. The first thing I think of when I remember back to our early marriage is the second weekend after we were married. It was Les' weekend to have his children. The older son rode with him to pick up the other two. On the way back they came across an old man on the side of the road selling (or rather giving away) puppies — Mongrel dogs if ever there were such. Some awful mixture that looked like a cross between a bloodhound and a chihuahua. They stopped and took not one but two of the horrible bloodshot-eyed pups.

These notations, still in rough form, served as the basis for Jennings's first draft of her essay "Second-Class Mom."

Other writers prefer to develop ideas through brainstorming. Unlike freewriting, which produces ideas by linking or associating one thought with another, brainstorming records thoughts as they come, with no regard for their relation to one another. When writers brainstorm, they often leap from one thought to another without stopping to explore the connections between what may be two completely unrelated ideas. Margot Harrison explains the usefulness of her distinctive form of brainstorming: "My most successful method of getting started involves thinking through the subject I've chosen and taking down unorganized notes of all my ideas, which I then shape into an outline. This is useful because it allows me to explore why I was attracted to the subject—what points I might bring up about it—without having to worry yet about organization." In contrast, Thomas Leyba has developed an equally successful and personalized form of brainstorming: "I rarely freewrite, and I rarely outline. I brainstorm and organize all of my ideas mentally, then my pen becomes a medium, translating my thoughts into words."

When Barbara Seidel set out to write "A Tribute to My Father," she tried several different techniques for getting started. In this instance, she decided to brainstorm to come up with some ideas for her essay. Here is a sample of what she produced by thinking in writing for a few minutes:

— 58 years old
— parents divorced when he was young
— 1 older brother, Arthur, Mom's favorite
— young—white hair, pale skin, blue eyes
— young—brother had darker skin, brown eyes, black hair
— grew up—wore hand-me-down clothes and shoes—
    used to fold newspapers into shoes
— Mother worked early morn till after dinner
— went to corner store for meal—Mother paid $ in advance to store
— hell-raiser as a teen; didn't like school, dropped out (car and Uncle Art)
— navy man during WW II; never overseas
— loved animals; always bringing home strays
— saw little of his father, who was alcoholic, till age 19 (father dating)
— great common sense, wise man, folk sayings

— not an intellectual; doesn't read; not "learned"
— patient; calm in crisis; resigned
— very hard worker; in car business since hung around
        father's car lot in late teens
— family man, loyal, devoted, dependable
— instinctive, yet never called it that (marrying Mom)
— extremely honest

(For a complete account of the progress Barbara Seidel makes from her brain-storming notes to her final draft, see Chapter 1, "Revising Drafts.") Brain-storming, like freewriting, is a writing exercise that can be done virtually anywhere, at any time, and at any pace. Curtis Chang explains, "Some of my most creative thoughts or flashes of eloquence come to me late at night when I am lying awake in bed. I will then have to get up, stumble about for pen and paper, jot it down, and go back to bed." Most writers offer the simplest and most effective advice about this stage of thinking in writing: "Just get it down."

Exercises such as freewriting and brainstorming are excellent confidence builders, especially for relatively inexperienced writers, because they can help writers produce a great deal of writing in a very short time. These exercises also enable writers to see rather quickly just what they have to say about a subject while resisting the urge to edit their work prematurely. Whether you write in a leather-bound journal or on the inside of a matchbook, doing your thinking in writing is perhaps the best way to discover a subject. A practiced writer is usually an effective writer.

Purpose

Once they have settled on a subject, most student writers decide on a purpose for writing about that subject; they make decisions about what to say and how to say it. The first of these concerns establishes the general content and the overall goal of the essay. The second focuses on the structure and tone of the essay. Whether an essay is designed to narrate, describe, explain, convince, or persuade, a clearly stated purpose helps ensure its effectiveness. Such a purpose marks most of the essays printed in this book. In most cases, the students' motives for writing include, but are rarely restricted to, the understandable desire to earn an outstanding grade. For some student writers, the pure pleasure of working with words is an added attraction of writing. For

others, writing offers the prospect of helping change attitudes and behavior:
to defeat a prejudice or upset a stereotype, to underscore the dignity of the
oppressed or the terminally ill, to change long-standing opinion on public
issues. Curtis Chang views his "writing skills as a tool to work for justice,
especially in matters of race. In certain situations, this view leads to moralistic
rhetoric that does not appeal to the wider populace. Thus, I consciously attempt to base my writings on analytical and empirical arguments which work
from certain common assumptions." In drafting his essay "Streets of Gold: The
Myth of the Model Minority," Chang explains that his goal was "both educative and stimulative. I wished to explain to everyone the true socioeconomic
condition of Asian-Americans and expose how we are being used for ideological
reasons. I also hoped to stimulate further thought on Asian-American issues,
to interest others in subjecting our situation to intellectual scrutiny." Other
writers seem intent on positing their distinctive voices in the communities in
which they participate, whether those communities are the political, social,
economic, racial, or ethnic intersections of a neighborhood or the intellectual
expanses of a college or university.

A clear purpose need not be as public or as issue-oriented as Curtis Chang's
essay challenging the myths of minority identity. For many writers, the principal purpose for writing can be as simple as wanting to narrate or describe an
experience, record a personal anecdote, remember a family story, or recover
the pleasure of reading a book, hearing a concert, or seeing a film or play. Just
as there is no single, sure-fire way to succeed at writing, there is no single
definition of an appropriate subject or purpose in writing. Whatever your purpose, try to make it as clear as possible. An-Thu Quang Nguyen offers the
following explanation of her purpose in writing her essay: "I tried to capture
as faithfully as possible the purity of the emotions which I was trying to portray." Heather Ashley declares that her goal in writing "Leaving Vacita" was
"to remind readers what it was like to be a kid, especially in that strange period
of the late seventies. I'm certainly not pretentious enough to claim it is a
period piece; perhaps mood piece would be a better label." Paula Sisler says
that when writing her essay "The Water Lily" she quite deliberately aimed at
making her readers "taste the gasoline and grit, experience the sunburn, remember what the bottom of a lake felt like. And since I was an adult interpreting a childhood memory, I wanted to leave the reader with a taste of
wistfulness for what could have been." Brad Manning's goal was far more
personal. He explains that in focusing on his relationship with his father
through the repeated symbolic detail of arm-wrestling with him, "I also wished
that I could gain an understanding for myself of what actually had happened
and how I felt about it."

Audience

Imagining an audience looms large in the mind of every writer. David Landmann speaks for many when he says, "I could not write if I could not imagine that someone was going to read my work." The writer's view of the reader invariably helps determine the extent of an essay's success. The writer usually asks, "Who is my reader? What do I have to do to help that person to understand what I want to say about my particular subject?" The first question addresses the knowledge, background, and predispositions of the reader toward the subject. The second points to the kinds of information or appeals to which the reader is most likely to respond.

Not all writers concern themselves with the issue of audience from the beginning of their work on an essay. The primary concern of most writers, however experienced they may be, is to establish authority over their own experience, to express as clearly and as deliberately as possible a sense of control over their own ideas. Johnna Lynn Benson puts it this way: "When I start, I'm trying to find my ideas and make them meaningful to myself. I try to get a hold of what I want to say, but my ideas don't always make sense to other people in that form. Then I start trying to present the ideas, but the ideas are set." Bonnie Harris offers another perspective: "I start with the ideas or feelings that are the most important to me. Consideration of my audience is there but usually becomes more prominent during the revising process." Karen Kramer emphasizes this point when she notes: "The fact that someone is going to read my writing doesn't really influence me as far as I'm aware. . . . I don't think about my audience when I'm getting started. When I begin writing, I set out to produce something that I enjoy writing and reading, and I hope everyone else will enjoy it too." Thomas Leyba underscores this idea by distinguishing between the nature of the satisfactions involved in writing successfully: "Instructors always say consider the reader *first*. This is true for some; however, many times pleasing the reader can be a result of pleasing *yourself* first." And as Terry Burns explains, writing with an audience in mind initially "made me very nervous. But as I gained confidence, the nervousness lessened. Now I encourage people to read my writing. The influence an outsider can have on your work can be invaluable. I usually don't think much about my reader until my last couple of drafts; the first drafts are for me."

Since all student writers prepare papers to satisfy course requirements, they are also mindful of their instructor's presence in their audience. Allison Rolls deals with what many students regard as their instructor's intimidating presence by imagining herself writing for a teacher with whom she feels comfortable. Others, practiced in and encouraged by the principles of collaborative learning, write specifically for their peers. But whether they are writing for a teacher, their peers, or an audience beyond the classroom, the fact that someone is going to read their writing imposes a good deal of discipline on most student writers. Thinking about their readers helps student writers make decisions about appropriate subjects, the kinds of examples to include, the type and level of diction and tone to use, and the overall organization of the essay. Every writer wants to be clear and convincing.

Outlining

To reduce the possibility that they will be misunderstood and to maximize the likelihood that they will appreciate the implications of their own ideas, most writers find it useful to plan the scope and sequence of their ideas carefully before or during the writing of a first full draft. For many students, outlining figures prominently in that effort. Yet the point at which they turn to outlining varies greatly. Some student writers routinely outline their essays in their minds before they set pen to paper. Thomas Leyba, for example, reports, "Organizing my thoughts comes easiest for me before and during the writing process. Because I don't care too much for planning on paper, I do it all mentally." The process is equally intricate for Paula Sisler: "Once I have decided my topic, I take some time to think about it as I go about my daily activities. I mull over the conflict, the conclusion, how all the parts will fit together."

Many writers recognize that their habits of composition may well be unique. Beverly Dipo, for example, reports, "I can write, and have written, an entire outline and the first paragraphs of an essay at night, in bed, in my head. . . . I pretty well have my outline in my head before I actually start writing. I sit down at the typewriter and start typing my thoughts on paper. I'm a pretty organized person, so my first thoughts seem to organize themselves; sentences fall into paragraphs naturally for me. I sometimes use an outline to get an idea going, but I seem to outline in my head better. This was easy with the short essays we were required to do. I imagine it would be difficult for longer works." Curtis Chang describes his own method of composing: "I am most successful when I begin with an outline. An outline matches the way my mind works; it assures me that I am not wandering and am clearly headed in a particular direction. However, when I am faced with an analytical problem or cannot adequately express a thought I have, I just 'free type' for several minutes on my word processor." But he quickly adds a note of caution: "The most difficult part for me, as probably for many, is forcing myself to stop organizing and researching and to begin the physical process of writing."

Other student writers reserve outlining until their writing is well under way.

Bonnie Harris adapts the standard textbook principles of outlining to meet her own compositional needs: "Outlining usually helps but sometimes feels too confining for my thoughts, and I often have to write a bunch of paragraphs or a beginning draft and then go back and write an outline and start to fit the ideas into it." Jill Savitt creates an even more intricate system for organizing her essays: "I make a skeleton draft of the parts. Then I review and put meat on the parts. When the parts have substance, I look at the whole. Then I go back through the parts."

In contrast, many writers find outlining inhibiting. Barbara Seidel observes, for example, that "although I have learned to write down notes, points, and ideas, an actual step-by-step outline is too organized, restrictive, and proper for me. I just start writing." Johnna Lynn Benson outlines only when she is revising her essays: "Outlining encourages me to discard ideas. I use it later in revising sometimes, but never in the beginning."

As the preceding quotations underscore, the student writers whose work appears in this book probably would not agree on whether it is most helpful to outline an essay before, during, or after writing a first draft. Yet surely they would agree that all writers should develop a clear sense of the strategies for getting started that work best for them. Practicing these strategies frequently will result in increasing skill and confidence.

Drafting

It would not be practical to enumerate each of the strikingly different ways writers work during the second phase of the writing process—completing a full draft of an essay. Instead, the introduction to each essay and the questions and Suggestions for Writing that follow it include detailed information about the specific circumstances in which each essay was written. Here we present just a few general statements from the student writers on their characteristic styles of drafting.

Some writers write to discover what they want to say. In one sense, such writers must see their ideas on paper in order to explore, develop, and revise them. They must write in order to discover and shape their own meaning. Heather Ashley offers an instructive account of one such procedure: "Ideas generally come to me full-blown, and then I need to break them down on paper, in notes usually, although sometimes I just write until I can't write anymore and then try to figure out what I mean and how I am going to say it later." Brad Manning reminds writers that they ought not to be anxious about the seeming weaknesses and digressions of a first draft: "I don't mind writing badly and digressively in my first draft; I even look forward to it. Therefore, it is easy to get at least something started on paper. Only after I begin to type will the choice words and ideas come out of hiding. I can't sit back and organize in my head. It would take too long, and I would forget it all before I started." Johnna Lynn Benson describes herself as "definitely a person who needs to see her ideas on paper before she can evaluate them." Terry Burns reports that he writes as much as he can in his first draft, without paying "any attention at all to things like punctuation, spelling, and grammar. I just write whatever comes into my head and worry about the mechanics later. I guess this works for me because it frees my mind for writing what I feel, and I don't get bogged down in technicalities." Such writing works incrementally: the writer quickly produces a very rough first draft to sketch out, explore, and develop the controlling idea of the essay and then focuses in subsequent drafts on organizing and polishing that idea. Beverly Dipo makes a similar point in more figurative terms: "Writing for me now is like painting a picture. I have a painting of horses that I did hanging in my living room. It turned out fairly well, but only after much effort. Writing is also something I can accomplish fairly well, with some effort. I am not a 'natural' at anything, including writing."

Some writers proceed at a slower pace. They think carefully about what they are going to say before they commit themselves to writing it out. These writers generally are more comfortable composing in their heads than on paper. They usually regard thinking and writing as separate, and in fact sequential, intellectual activities. Celeste Barrus describes her style of composing in just such terms: "It takes me a very long time to write anything, mainly because I mull each sentence over and over in my mind, taking it apart and putting it together again in different ways, changing words, and so on before I even put it on paper." David Landmann recounts a similar method: "I generally have everything organized in my mind before I even put fingers to my typewriter. I seldom need to write more than two drafts of anything, and many times my first draft is in most respects my final draft. I don't know why this works. It does, though. In fact, it works so well that sometime it is a little scary." And as is the case with most accomplished writers, Landmann knows not to tamper with what works best for him. For Terry Burns, careful planning can sometimes produce surprising results: "Most of what I write has been carefully thought out. I can spend weeks turning an idea over and over in my head, until I know exactly what I want to write. Then I sit down and write something totally different."

Many student writers feel most comfortable creating their own distinctive blends of both the write/rewrite and think/write styles of drafting. An-Thu Quang Nguyen reports that she moves freely between the two: "I use a combination of both—composing the base idea mentally, then putting it on paper. Sometimes that will be good enough, other times seeing the black-and-white gives rise to further need of exploration." Margot Harrison reports that she is most confident writing when she is able to work out the basic ideas and direction of her essay as she proceeds: "I can't conceive an essay full-blown in my head at all; all the intermediate stages have to be in writing, where I can refer to them. A single very good insight may come at any time in the writing process, and so the essay keeps being shaped as it goes along." Not so for Ann Louise Field. Her style of composing propels her through her first draft at a rapid pace:

> I do most, if not all, of my prewriting in my head, so it looks as if I'm starting in the middle when I sit down and write. I also try to write my first draft in one sitting. Once I get to the sit-down-and-write stage I know what I want to say and how I want to try to say it. And once I get started I just can't stop. It's as if the ideas are running away, and if I don't get them down on paper in some crude form they will be lost forever. In the past I have forced myself to stop in the middle of a first draft, and when I've come back I have been unable to pick up where I left off.

Karen Kramer prepares her essay carefully enough to be able to rely confidently on writing two drafts: "Generally speaking, the body of the essay is already in my head before I sit down and start typing. Once I think up an introduction, the rest just flows naturally from there. . . . I know I'm finished with the essay when I read it and I wouldn't change, add, or delete anything." And at times, as Tor Valenza notes, the best method can be rather unmethodical: "Sometimes you write without thinking about what you're trying to say. You just write."

Most of the writers whose essays have earned Bedford Prizes continue to be aware of their audience as they write, and that awareness helps shape the ways in which they write. But for some, the anxiety about having their work read continues to haunt their efforts during the drafting phase of composing. Margot Harrison, for example, describes her tendency "to think all too much about my readers while I am getting started and all through the writing process. My best moments of insight come when I stop thinking about what would please this or that potential reader and concentrate only on how I feel about my subject." For some writers, the issue of an audience helps expedite the process of writing an essay. An equal number of others try to avoid such questions, leaving them to be dealt with during the revision phase of the writing process.

Revising

Many writers appreciate the power and permanence that revision can add to the act of writing. When writers revise, they reexamine what they have written with an eye on strengthening their control over their ideas. As they revise, they expand or delete, substitute or reorder. In some cases, they revise to clarify or emphasize. In others, they revise to tone down or reinforce particular points. And, more generally, they revise either to simplify what they have written or to make it more complex. Revising gives writers an opportunity to rethink their essays, to help them accomplish their intentions more clearly and fully. Revising also includes such larger concerns as determining whether the essay is logically consistent, whether its main idea is supported adequately, whether it is organized clearly enough, and whether it satisfies its audience's needs or demands in engaging and accessible terms. Revising enables writers to make sure that their essays are as clear, precise, and effective as possible.

Although revising is often the most painstaking phase of the writing process (James Seilsopour, for example, equates revising with "cutting yourself with a hot blade"), it is crucial to successful writing. The student writers whose work is included in this volume value the opportunity that revising provides to clarify their ideas, sharpen their purpose in writing, tighten and strengthen the structure of their paragraphs and sentences, and refine their selection of examples and word choices. Ha Song Hi expresses the point vividly: "To me revision means the evolution and growth of a work of art from its crude beginnings to something which approaches perfection, much as a sculptor changes with her mind and hands an unformed lump of clay into an entity that needs no further alteration, that says exactly what she wants it to say and begs to be left alone." Margot Harrison sees revision in similarly artistic terms: "I like to think of revising in terms of a metaphor of painting: after filling in the whole canvas with broad strokes you go back, fill up empty spaces, create connections and subtleties, achieve an effect of finesse." Brad Manning, more practically, thinks of revising as "a chance to improve the sound of my essay. If I already have the body of the essay, I love going over it sentence after sentence, testing for clarity and beat."

Each of the writers in this gathering of prize-winning essays provides a distinctive account of the procedures and underpinnings of the revising process. Jill Savitt, for example, refuses to grant the assumption that there is a creditable difference between writing and revising: "Revising is writing. I can't call the beginning stages of putting words to paper writing. It's spewing. Revising is when all the papers around me are replaced by printouts of what I've spewed.

These printouts are cut up and rearranged. The red pen wages war against paper. Arrows. Exes. Carets. Riders are added and taped or clipped. Changes are made. This process goes on and on. Writing, printing, cutting, adding, revising." Heather Ashley describes a procedure for revising aimed at once at sharpening the focus of her essay, pruning its diction, and strengthening its structure:

> I wrote four drafts of my essay. The first was a lot of freewriting, just trying to get my memories and emotions down on paper. It was, to say the least, maudlin. In the first revision I eliminated some of the saccharine sweetness in the writing and put in more of my interpretation of the events from my current perspective as an adult. In the second revision I tried to clarify some description and events that were unclear to the reader. In the final revision I cleaned up the wording and tightened the structure a little to make it easier and clearer to read.

Paula Sisler casts the revision process she follows in more assertive—and slightly moralistic—terms: "I slash and cut, save the good, eliminate the bad when I am rewriting. Then I think the piece through, give it time to age, then go through the process again. And again. And again, until I am satisfied."

Revising also provides writers with the occasion to distance themselves from their work and to see more clearly its strengths and weaknesses, helping them to make constructive, effective decisions about the best ways to produce a final draft. As Barbara Seidel observes: "Revising means taking my emotional likes and dislikes out of the writing process and looking at my work objectively. This is truly difficult to do because, like most creative people, I am insecure and therefore uncertain of what should stay and what should go." Heather Ashley recognizes the tensions that must be balanced when writers revise: "The easiest thing is knowing what I am not happy with. . . . The hardest is figuring out what I want instead. It is also hard to revise something which I personally like but I know is ineffective." As Curtis Chang moves from one draft to the next, he forces himself to think "otherwise." He does this by grappling with the point of view and the reservations he anticipates his opponents will adopt when responding to what he has written. For Chang, revising means "acting as a devil's advocate and trying to pick apart my paper's argument. Then I have to answer to those criticisms." For An-Thu Quang Nguyen, "revising is the act of rereading the piece of work from another perspective than the one with which I had written it, searching for clarity, for faithfulness to the idea, and technical errors."

Some writers revise after they have written a very quick and usually very rough draft. Once they have something on paper, they revise for as long as they have time and energy. Patrick Kinder Lewis accentuates this point: "Length and overall development of structure seem the first factors which I weigh. Then I move slowly through the text actually listening to how it sounds to me. Sometimes I just have to take a breather, or I lapse into verbose stiltedness." Beverly Dipo's method of revision produces numerous drafts, each less messy than the preceding: "I take my typewritten rough draft with its double or triple spacing and wide margins and a red pencil. Then I proceed to thoroughly mess up the rough draft with slashes, marks, underlines, parentheses, arrows, exclamation points, secret codes, doodles, and assorted expletives. I will then retype what is left and repeat the procedure until I produce a whole essay without one single red mark!" Dianne Emminger offers another view of revising: "I revise as I go along, writing two or three paragraphs, going back to revise the first, and then continuing. By the time I finish composing the essay, I will have completed most of the essay."

Still other student writers require more distance from their first draft to revise effectively. Earnestine Johnson reports, "I try to give myself several days between my first draft and my revision. The several days allow me to return to my writing, after what I call putting my work in 'cold storage.' I can review it later with a more critical eye." An-Thu Quang Nguyen recounts a somewhat more ethereal process of revision: "I try to elevate myself as far as possible from the work, almost pretending that I were another mind. And then I reach out with an imaginary finger and poke at it until I feel weakness, some part which may cave in or does not cohere." Proximity to her own work became Paula Sisler's greatest obstacle to revising her award-winning essay: "I had trouble with certain areas where I found myself getting too close, feeling too much. My greatest problem was pulling back to be objective and to just observe from the outside." As the reports of these student writers suggest, distance, perspective, and objectivity are the crucial factors in producing first-rate revisions. As Ann Louise Field notes, distance from a first draft enables her to "see the essay as if I were not the one who wrote it. Passages that are unclear or unnecessary are easier to see. And sometimes I have thought of new things to write or new ways to write the old things."

Many student writers mention the value of reading their work aloud as an aid to revision. Jill Savitt offers just such a solution to the problems of revising: "The most difficult aspect is writing the rewrite—fine-tuning the work, creating a cadence and style and tone. It is at this stage that I think of the intended audience. This is when I begin to revise aloud. Seeing how the work sounds and hearing how the words look." Karen Kramer enumerates the benefits of reading essays aloud:

I read the paper *out loud*. This is very important. I could
read a paper a hundred times to myself and never catch
something, but if I read it out loud, I'll catch it. Sometimes
you have to actually *hear* what you wrote before you realize
that it sounds like something a fourth grader wrote. So I
read it aloud and change what doesn't sound right. Clumsily constructed sentences, weak words, questionable modifiers, etc., all come to light when I read it aloud to myself.

Other students remind themselves of an audience for their writing by asking
family or friends to read their essays aloud to them. Johnna Lynn Benson
reports, "I recruit people who live on my floor, members of study groups, and
anyone I can get to read my drafts. I have my victims read for the sense of it,
not for grammar, though many cannot help but comment on grammar. I also
ask them to read aloud. That way I can tell if they get the jokes, understand
the phrases, etc., without asking them if they noticed it. This technique really
helps me . . . because I knew my readers were mainly unwilling, and that
forced me to rework anything boring or technical or that sounded like dead
space." Brad Manning explains that he thinks of his readers "mostly when I
am revising. At that time, it is most productive for me to read through a piece
with an outside perspective, imagining the audience's reaction to every sentence. This is when I make many of my changes for clarity and effect." Heather
Ashley reinforces this point with some detailed procedural advice: "Identify
specifically what you are trying to say, and then ask yourself or somebody else
whether that is what is conveyed by the piece you have written."

Thinking about an audience for their writing also helps many writers revise,
edit, and proofread their essays. When writers and publishers edit a piece of
writing, they read it with an eye to preparing it for publication, whether that
occurs literally in a newspaper, magazine, or a book or figuratively in the
exchange of essays within the community of a classroom, department, college,
or university. When writers proofread, they reread their final drafts to detect
any errors—misspellings, omitted lines, inaccurate information, and the like.
Several student writers recommend what they call a "fail-safe" method for
proofreading their essays: read the essay backward. Doing so enables writers to
see the words more clearly outside the context of the sentence.

In general, more experienced writers concentrate on the larger concerns of
writing—their purpose, ideas, evidence, structure—before they give attention
to such matters as strengthening syntax and searching for the right word. The
student writers here tend to be interested in both when they revise. And they
revise well because they are both practiced writers and readers.

An increasing number of students use word processors when preparing their essays. Some go right to the keyboard, while others prefer to make that move after beginning with longhand drafts. For some writers, the computer serves as a tool and the physical medium of their work. And for many students, using a word processor makes revising simpler and less time-consuming. As Ann Louise Field observes, a word processor eliminates the drudgery of retyping and offers an added attraction: "The hardest part of revising is cutting out unnecessary parts. It feels like I'm throwing away something important. Now that I have a word processor, I can save all the unnecessary parts and use them someday somewhere else."

When asked to offer some final, general advice to first-year college students to help them improve their writing, the thirty Bedford Prize winners gave responses as varied as their descriptions of the distinctive ways in which they compose. Common responses were such good-natured imperatives as "Trust your own experience," "Write about what you know or about what you are interested in learning," "Don't be too critical of yourself," "Don't fear failure," "Listen to your teachers," and "Keep it simple!" Jill Savitt reminds writers that one of the most difficult aspects of writing is knowing when to give up a sentence, even a well-crafted one: "Be willing to sacrifice a seemingly great sentence for content. You can always create a new and probably better sentence, but brilliance ain't always easy. A great sentence stinks unless it fits into the paper as a whole. Remember the whole while working on the parts." "Don't forget the poetics of language, its rhythms, its nuances: you can't write like an AP ticker tape and expect it to matter." Perhaps not surprisingly, "Write and write and write" and "Rewrite, again and again" are the most frequent refrains in the advice these Bedford Prize winners offer their peers. As Thomas Leyba notes, "What does an amateur pianist do to become an expert composer? He practices." For Paula Sisler, perseverance no doubt will produce effective results: "Keep trying. If you want to be a writer, then you must write and write and rewrite." Brad Manning reminds other writers that they don't have to be born literary virtuosos to write well. "I had a really slow start on writing, unlike the big-time writers whose biographies portray them dictating from the crib to their enthusiastic parents."

These student writers also urge their peers to read as widely, voraciously, and rigorously as possible. Earnestine Johnson underscores this advice when she says, "Read as much and often as possible. I would also encourage other student writers to take as many writing courses, labs, and workshops as possible. I believe growth is through knowledge, be it in life experience or in writing experience."

These student writers apparently heard—and acted on—similar advice; they enjoy reading—for knowledge *and* pleasure. As Margot Harrison explains,

"What I like most about reading is reading itself." It is, she says, "the very essence of the process" that draws her so repeatedly to reading, yet that process is, in her terms, "something so basic I can't describe it." Heather Ashley makes a similar point more directly: "I hate having to put down a good book. 'So many books, so little time.' "

Yet Heather Ashley and so many other student writers often distinguish between reading for pleasure and reading in response to an assignment. For her, "reading for an assignment means you have to pay attention to important points, remember names and dates, and try to figure out what this piece has to do with what you are supposed to be learning. Reading for pleasure means you get to eat up what the author is saying and understand and feel whatever you naturally do." Terry Burns draws the distinction in slightly more wry terms: "The main difference is that reading for pleasure can keep me up late; reading for an assignment can put me to sleep early." Brad Manning discovers a special joy in reading for pleasure; "by doing this, I can discover a writer for myself. Afterwards, I feel privileged, like a kid with an extra marble in his pocket."

Patrick Kinder Lewis describes himself as *not* being a "reader in the traditional sense in which writers seem to be. That is not to say I don't read: I read voraciously—I can almost never be caught anywhere without a book in my possession. But the habit is more a thirst for wisdom than from any learned pleasure of reading for its own sake. I didn't grow up reading, but thinking and doing instead." Yet he explains that he recognizes in reading the opportunity to "look out of a different window onto the same wonderfully complex world. Like learning a new language, reading is truly liberating." Todd Unruh recognizes the literal and the metaphorical values of reading often and carefully: "Good books are read just like a person thinks, and I've learned that in order to write well a person has to write like people think." "Reading," Barbara Seidel explains, "relaxes me, teaches me, reaches my heart, makes me think about people and lifestyles different from me and mine. It expands my limits of tolerance and makes me realize how fortunate I am in life. I could not think of a life without words."

The motivations for writing vary widely among these student writers—from the reasonable desire to earn a good grade to the understandable need to discover more about themselves and their relation to the world that is larger than the self. Karen Kramer is fully aware that writing can sometimes be a "chore," but she also regards it as "an incredibly enjoyable experience. I know no greater pleasure than when I have written something I really like. Writing is also one of the easiest ways I know of obtaining a sense of accomplishment. Besides," she quickly adds, "someone has to keep the Liquid Paper people in business." For Barbara Seidel, writing is "an emotional release, a very selfish pleasure. It is the only time in my life I am totally selfish. I write for my own sanity."

Most important, these writers are all students who write because they have something to say. Paula Sisler uses writing to respond to the stubborn itch to have her ideas understood: "The better you write, the better you can communicate your ideas to others." "Be a person when you write," Johnna Lynn Benson urges. "The more you write what you think, the better you think." Tor Valenza sees a fundamental connection between writing and daily experience: "Writing is living and observing and manipulating those experiences and observations. You can't observe the world from your dorm room."

Perhaps the most enduring satisfaction that writing affords is gaining authority over the ideas and states of consciousness writers value and want to express to others. Margot Harrison summarizes this point most succinctly, if slightly irreverently: "The more you can make the essay yours—even if it means breaking some of the rules you learned in high school—the better." Despite the personal frustrations, writing can also be an enormously satisfying experience.

Many writers finally have faith in their own ability to surprise themselves, to be able to express something that they did not previously think they knew or could express. Margot Harrison extends that point when she observes: "You should believe—whether it be true or not—that you have something original to contribute not only to the class, but to the world at large." The possibility of expressing their originality in writing prompts many students to make writing an enduring satisfaction in their lives, both within and beyond an academic environment. These student writers recognize the power of composition to transform the world of actuality—the world already formed by the words of others—into a world of possibility—the world they create with the words they craft on a blank page. Writing offers that opportunity.

Questions for Thinking and Writing

This exercise gives you an opportunity to examine your own attitudes toward writing in general and, more specifically, toward each stage of the composing process outlined in this overview. Respond in writing to each of the following questions in as much detail as possible.

1. What are your earliest recollections of writing?

2. Have any members of your family, teachers, or anyone else encouraged you to write? Explain the circumstances.

3. What is the easiest thing for you to do when you write an essay?

4. What is the most difficult aspect of writing for you?

5. What method of getting started is most successful for you? Why do you think that method works for you?

6. If someone walked into your room and observed you trying to get started writing, what would this person see? Write your answer in a paragraph or two.

7. Do you try to avoid writing? If so, what do you do to avoid it?

8. What special habits do you have when you write?

9. What is the ideal environment for you as a writer?

10. How does the fact that your writing has an *audience* influence the way you write? How do you take an audience into account when you are writing an essay?

11. Describe in detail the specific procedures you follow when writing the first draft of an essay.

12. What does revising mean to you? Describe your methods of revision. How many drafts do you usually write? How do you decide when a paper is finished and there is nothing more that you can do with it?

13. How would you describe yourself as a writer? As a reader?

14. What do you like most about reading? What do you like least? What have you learned about writing as a result of your reading? Identify what you do when you read that helps you when you write.

15. What general advice would you offer other first-year students to help them improve their writing?

16. Add any comments on or clarifications of any aspect of your writing that was not addressed adequately in these questions.

STUDENT WRITERS IN THE COMPANY OF OTHER WRITERS

Part I

HEATHER ASHLEY

Cornell University
Ithaca, New York
JoElaine Retzler Wasson, instructor

Heather Ashley reports that she forces herself to freewrite: "I just put down whatever comes into my head and then go back and revise later. . . . I also write ideas down as soon as they come to me on whatever is handy—napkins, receipts, whatever—and then use them or throw them out later. Mostly I save them."

Born in Poughkeepsie, New York, Heather Ashley grew up in an environment she characterizes as "white, upper middle class, Jewish, and typically suburban—mom, dad, two kids, and a dog. The only interest I practice religiously is reading, anything and everything." She attended Spackenhill High School, where she participated in, to use her terms, "almost too many extracurricular activities: softball, volleyball, newspaper, International Thespian Society, National Honor Society, and Students Against Drunk Driving." A National Merit Scholarship finalist when she graduated in 1986, Heather Ashley also received a Thomas J. Watson Memorial Scholarship from IBM as well as the senior class award in English. Now an undergraduate at Cornell University, she has participated in a peer counseling group called EARS (Empathy, Assistance, and Referral Service), contributed to a feminist newspaper, and decided to major in human development and family studies "with the expectation that it will be helpful in one of many prospective careers, clinical or research psychology."

Heather Ashley describes "Leaving Vacita" as "a story about the loss of innocence," but her ambition in the essay transcends the conventional expectations of that traditional literary subject: "The goal was to remind readers what it was like to be a kid, especially in that strange period of the late seventies. I'm certainly not pretentious enough to claim it is a period piece; perhaps mood piece would be a better label."

Leaving Vacita

". . . rage, rage against the dying of the light."
—Dylan Thomas

It was the year of the Iran hostage crisis. The year before the summer that my parents had my dog put to sleep because of epilepsy. The year they elected an old B-grade movie actor to the presidency. It was the year I started taking karate lessons, and the year after the Vander Veer family moved into the house with the backyard shortcut to Hagen Elementary School that only the big kids knew about. It was two years after they bulldozed half the Vacant Lot to build the Bass's house. It was the year of Vacita.

The Shens had moved out of their black-and-white house in the middle of   2
Old Mill Drive in the fall of fifth grade. In the spring, when the SOLD sign went up, kids from the four blocks around rode past the house on their bikes, trying to catch a glimpse of the new family's children.

There were three of them: Daria, the oldest, Tina, in the middle, and   3
Hilary, one year behind. They transferred to our school just in time for Tina, who was in my grade, to go to the fifth grade picnic. The final events of the school year rushed by: the Science Fair, Field Day, summer. I sang the Carpenters' "On Top of the World" walking home on the last day of school, dribbling pebbles through my fingers.

That summer before sixth grade was muggy and sweet with fresh cut grass.   4
Daria was our leader, going into her freshman year in high school, and my brother Mark was in love with her. Most days I was torn between wanting to wade in the Creek with Tina and Hilary and watching Mark and Daria make out on the sofa.

Sometimes we would play boxball in the street when it would stay light   5
forever and then, when it grew dark, under the streetlight, clouds of gnats hovering in the air.

Tina and I read the Great Brain books, *The Phantom Tollbooth, Bridge to*   6
Terabithia, and the Narnia Chronicles. I remember that my first impression of her was that she was an incredible liar: she told me that a couple of years before, she had received an answer to a message she had sent in a bottle from her beach house in Madison, Connecticut. I don't know why I didn't believe her at the time. Her first impression of me was that I was a braggart—she was right. We became best friends that summer.

Vacita did not emerge over the course of a lazy fall afternoon, nor did it   7
bloom overnight like the apple blossoms. Instead it descended slowly, filling our lives like the red-orange autumn leaves flooded our yards.

Tina and I had evolved into amateur survivalists, in tune with a world   8
threatened by nuclear war. We would have run off to live in the wilderness if we could have, like the boy in *My Side of the Mountain.* We read botany books and learned to identify the poisonous and edible plants that grew in the Vacant Lot and near the Creek. We picked the mint leaves that grew on the damp

clay banks of the Creek and made bitter-tasting tea. We nibbled the soft cinnamon ends of the timothy stalks that grew in the field behind the Bass's house.

Sometimes we would fish in the Creek, knowing that everything we caught 9 we would have to throw back; the fish were tiny and their bodies polluted by the sewage dumped by the factories far upstream. I hated to fish even then; the sport seemed pointless and cruel.

We went for long walks or rode our bikes in the Vacant Lot and in back of 10 the golf course. We had to slip through a hole in the fence that the high school kids had cut in order to get to the course. IBM owned all the property on and around the greens; the trees were littered with paper signs reading "No Trespassing: Violators Will Be Prosecuted."

When we walked, we found sticks—broken, tall saplings—to bring home. 11 We made them into spears, shaving the ends with jackknives bought in the Boy Scout department of Schwartz's. We wanted to hunt and practiced hurling our weapons at helpless trees and rocks. The animals we sometimes stumbled on—groundhogs, chipmunks, rabbits—were too fast and too enchanting to be killed.

Vacita was real, as real as America or France. It never struck us as odd to 12 discuss Vacitian laws and Mideast wars with exactly the same seriousness. We had that ability, to know and yet not know; we were at an age at which being aware of strife did not yet throw us into it. Perhaps unconsciously, we chose not to let ourselves be concerned. We dug our heels in at the borders of Vacita.

Tina and I sat in my kitchen eating Breyer's strawberry ice cream from the 13 container. Breyer's was still the best you could get—Frusen Glädjé and Häagen Dazs weren't even on the market. We had just come back from playing in the Vacant Lot.

"You know what's weird?" I said. "When you said I'll meet you in the 14 Quarry, I knew where it was. Like we have these names for things and stuff but we both know where we're talking about."

"Yeah," Tina said, digging a spoonful of ice cream from the container. "Like 15 the Quarry, the Field, the Glen, the Plateau—"

"Wait," I interrupted. "Where's the Glen?" 16

"You know, those trees—" She put the ice cream in her mouth and slid it 17 out, leaving half of it in a smooth mound on the spoon. "—at the top of the hill."

"Which ones?" I licked a sticky dribble off the back of my thumb.   18

"The ones near the ditch. Here, wait." She opened the "everything   19 drawer," sorted through the cards, rubber bands, old receipts, keys, paper clips, yarmulkes, candles, and pulled out a pencil and a scrap of paper.

"OK, here," she said, sitting back down. "Here's the edge of the Vacant   20 Lot." She began to draw as she spoke. "And here's the Field. And this is the fence, and all this is IBM." She scribbled, shading the area on one side of the fence line. "This is the Plateau." It was actually tee 7 of the IBM golf course. "The Quarry's here, and the big tree . . . y'know?" She looked at me, and I nodded, knowing which tree she meant. We climbed in it and could survey all of Hagen Town. The whole world. "And here," she said triumphantly, drawing a circle near the Field and poking it with her pencil a few times, "is the Glen."

I looked down at the sketch and began to add features to it. The ditch we   21 jumped over, the hole in the fence, a grove of poison sumac trees we sometimes played in.

I don't remember if it was then or later that we officially named our land   22 "Vacita." We debated over names, searching for an appellation both proud and magical, ethereal and yet concrete. I can't remember any of the names we discarded, but I know that no prefabricated word in any language would do.

We elaborated and drew maps of Vacita. A tiny patch of land, perhaps an   23 acre square, contained landmarks, monuments to nature: the wonders of the Vacant Lot.

The expanse of the golf course and beyond, owned by International Business   24 Machines Corporation, was ours, simply by carving our names in a tree.

We took lofty names, à la astronomy Latin. Draco, the dragon, was mine.   25 I don't remember Tina's, except that it was after an obscure constellation that was visible in the Northern Hemisphere only in late spring.

We had a secret code, a written language looking like a combination of   26 Aramaic and Morse code. Tina became "fluent" much faster than I and quickly scribbled messages in cramped dots and dashes. I carried a crib sheet of our alphabet for weeks, which I used to laboriously reply to her notes.

Tina, who was still taking piano lessons at the time, and I made up a   27 national anthem. I think I made up most of the words, while Tina plunked out a tune on her upright Steinway. We both eventually learned how to play it on her harmonica.

It became a ritual to stand, side by side, with eleven-year-old seriousness,   28 watching the sun set, at the highest point of the mountain that was Vacita.

As the sun touched the horizon, we would hold short spears in the air, crossed, like swords en garde, and sing.

> Vacita, my home, my beautiful country,   29
> Land of the children, land of the free.
> Full of love and bravery,
> Oh grand Vacita we cherish thee.

I was always off-key, but neither of us ever seemed to mind. Then we would put our spears away in the secluded Glen and race home to meat loaf, mashed potatoes, and Sara Lee frozen cheesecake.

When I was eight, my aunt gave me a small wooden box, a souvenir from 30 her trip to Israel. It was red with gold inlay, and tiny, hand-painted flowers decorated the outside. The inside was crushed red velvet. Now it sits on my bureau, holding jewelry and loose change.

But when I was eleven, it was mine and Tina's treasure box. It held a blue 31 jay feather, a stream-smoothed quartz pebble, a piece of rabbit fur, and all of our Vacitian documents—the map, the alphabet, the constitution, which consisted of an elaborate list of qualifications for citizenship. One had to know our alphabet, recognize several edible plants, build a fire, and know how to fish (phrased in such a way that I, personally, never had to bait a hook).

I lived in three worlds then: one consisted of Chinese jump rope and Town 32 of Poughkeepsie Junior Soccer League; another was Vacita; and the third was full of protests, elections, and the federal deficit. I jumped from one to the other with no culture shock, all three like jobs that I could leave at the office.

I still wonder what caused me to begin seeing Vacita as trivial. Perhaps I 33 looked and really *saw* it for the first time. Perhaps I simply stopped believing the magic for just one moment, and the spell was broken.

It was almost Christmas. Although there was no snow on the ground, the 34 air was bitter cold, and Tina and I hunched our shoulders deeper into our insulated parkas. She was carrying her sleeping bag, and I, her pajamas and clothes in a plastic Teepeedashery bag. It was almost inevitable that one of us would sleep over the other's house at least one night out of the weekend.

That Saturday, after raiding the kitchen for Fritos and Coke and watching 35 Saturday Night Live (which we found mostly unamusing, except for Mr. Bill), we went to bed.

"It's too bad you have to go to Hebrew school on Tuesdays and Thursdays," 36 said Tina into the darkness.

"Yeah, it sucks. I hate it," I said.   37

"And we don't get to see each other because by the time you get home, it's 38
almost dinnertime."

"Yeah." 39

"Heather, what's going to happen to Vacita when it's really winter?" I got 40
a sudden knot in my stomach at her mention of Vacita.

"What do you mean?" 41

"It's gonna be hard to walk around up there with the ice, and it'll be too 42
cold to stay outside long."

"Yeah, I guess," I said. 43

"Maybe we could make snowshoes," Tina mused. I didn't answer. I didn't 44
want to talk about Vacita, but Tina rambled on about snowshoes and tracking
animals after a fresh fall. I realized that I didn't really care about what she was
saying, that, suddenly, I didn't want to track animals or throw spears or go ice
fishing. I almost winced at her enthusiasm. Listening to her, I realized that I
had done those things, willingly and excitedly, and I was embarrassed.

"Tina," I interrupted. 45

"What?" she asked. 46

I took a deep breath, hesitated, let it out, took another, and said: 47

"I don't think we should do Vacita anymore." 48

"What?" she said. I don't believe that Tina ever thought of Vacita as being 49
"done." It just was.

"I don't . . . Vacita just isn't . . . *real* anymore." 50

"What," she paused, "are you talking about?" 51

"You know," I said. "You know it's just a game. It's just a game, Tina!" 52

"No," she said abruptly. "Yes. No. What about our pact? To buy that land 53
and live there? What about being friends forever?"

"Jesus, Tina, this has nothing to do with our being friends," I said. 54

"What *does* it have to do with?" 55

"Tina, we're too old for this." 56

She exploded air from her lungs in disgust. 57

"Old. Old? Since when have you been so *mature?*" 58

"Since now," I said defensively. 59

"Oh bullshit." 60

"Bullshit yourself. It's true. I'm sorry, Tina, but it just feels dumb now." 61

"Dumb. Vacita's dumb." Only her tightened jaw belied the lack of emotion 62
on her face.

I shook my head. Nodded. "Yeah," I said. 63

"Fuck you. *Fuck you!*" Tina yelled, crying. 64

"Tina—" 65

"Shut up! Just shut up!" She got up and began to gather her clothes and bag. 66

"What are you doing?" I said. "What are you going to do, go home now? 67 It's two o'clock in the morning."

Tina stopped, her back turned, refusing to look at me. 68

"Tina," I said softly. 69

"Shut up," she said flatly. She knelt back down, throwing her face into her 70 pillow. I sighed and stared at the ceiling. I knew this wouldn't end our friendship, but I wondered how long it would take for Tina to accept that Vacita was over for both of us.

Recently, Tina told me that she tried for a few days to keep Vacita alive. 71 But it felt silly to hold up a sword with no one to cross it with, useless to write notes that would go unread, lonely to sing an anthem to a winter-barren mountain. She showed me the diary she kept during that year. Us becoming friends, creating Vacita, my leaving it, her attempts to stay. There is a break of a few weeks in the diary after her last trip to Vacita. The next entry reads, "Today, Heather and I tried smoking for the first time."

It was the year of the sixth grade Washington trip. The year of my first kiss, 72 the year they tied yellow ribbons around trees, the year my father sold our big station wagon. It was the year before the first summer I went away to camp. It had been the year of Vacita.

Focusing on Heather Ashley's Techniques and Revisions

1. In paragraph 32, Heather Ashley reports, "I lived in three worlds then: one consisted of Chinese jump rope and the Town of Poughkeepsie Junior Soccer League; another was Vacita; and the third was full of protests, elections, and the federal deficit." Reread Ashley's essay and focus on the writing strategies she uses to create effective distinctions between and among these "three worlds." More specifically, discuss the shifts in tone Ashley makes to emphasize the distinctiveness of each world.

2. One of the most successful features of Ashley's description of Vacita is her effective use of details. As you reread her essay, identify as many of these details as possible and explain what they illustrate and emphasize about the "three worlds" Ashley lived in.

3. How is the return to reality underscored in the changes in the speaker's tone of voice and diction during her discussion with Tina about abandoning the reverie that is Vacita? Consider, for example, the obscenities shouted near the

end of the essay. What dramatic purpose do they serve? What other changes in tone and diction perform a similar function?

4. Heather Ashley wrote four drafts of her essay: "The first was a lot of freewriting, just trying to get my memories and emotions down on paper. It was, to say the least, maudlin. In the first revision [the second draft], I eliminated some of the saccharine sweetness in the writing and put in more of my interpretation of the events from my current perspective as an adult." Read the following excerpt from Ashley's second draft and compare and contrast it with the final version.

> "I don't think we should have Vacita anymore." I could almost feel Tina blinking at me in disbelief.
>
> "What?" she said. The word sounded utterly different and foreign, though she had uttered the same question just a moment before.
>
> "I don't . . . Vacita just isn't . . . *real* anymore." Why are you saying this? I thought. The words seemed to tumble out my mouth from my gut, bypassing my brain.
>
> "What . . . are you talking about?" Tina sounded as if she couldn't decide whether to laugh, scream, or cry.
>
> "Oh, God, you know!" I said. "You know, you know. You know it's just a game. It's just a game, Tina!"

How would you characterize the changes Ashley made? Which version do you prefer? Why?

5. In paragraph 33, Ashley begins her account of "seeing Vacita as trivial." In paragraph 34, she describes the setting for the decision not "to do Vacita anymore." In the second draft of her essay, Ashley decided to drop the next paragraph. It read:

> We would stay up late, talking about things eleven-year-olds shouldn't: conformity, war, religion, prejudice. And things we should: friends, or lack thereof, UFOs, Billy Joel, soccer, our parents and siblings. Surprisingly, we didn't usually talk about Vacita. Vacita was for doing, not talking.

What response(s) would this paragraph have elicited from her readers? What did Ashley gain or lose by eliminating this paragraph?

6. In her second revision (her third draft), Heather Ashley tried, as she reports, "to clarify some description and events that were unclear." Consider the second paragraph from her third draft and compare and contrast it with the final version.

> The Shens moved out of their black-and-white house in the middle of Old Mill Drive in the fall of fifth grade. In

the spring, when the SOLD sign went up, every kid strained puppy-like, against the leashes of their newly learned child manners, happily and excitedly anticipating the new family's children.

Identify each of the revisions Ashley makes in her final version and comment on the effectiveness of each.

7. In her final revision (her fourth draft), Ashley "cleaned up the wording and tightened the structure a little to make it easier and clearer to read." Reread the final two paragraphs of Ashley's essay. What function does the white space before each of these paragraphs serve? What stylistic and structural parallels do you notice between the first and final paragraphs of "Leaving Vacita"?

Suggestions for Writing

1. Each of us might well be able to remember—and to re-create—the pleasure of putting off, however temporarily, the responsibilities of adult awareness. Consider your own experience in this respect. Write an essay in which you recount one such experience. Be as specific as possible in re-creating this imaginary childhood world. What prompted you to abandon that vision? Describe in detail the moment when you decided to abandon reverie for reality. What were the effects of doing so?

2. The British writer W. Somerset Maugham once defined reverie as "the groundwork of creative imagination; it is the privilege of the artist that with him it is not as with other men an escape from reality, but the means by which he accedes to it." Write an essay in which you draw on your own experience to endorse—or to challenge—the validity of Maugham's assertion.

3. Read the following poem by the American poet Emily Dickinson:

> To make a prairie it takes a clover and one bee,
> One clover, and a bee,
> And revery.
> The revery alone will do,
> If bees are few.
> —Poem 1755, from *The Complete Poems of Emily Dickinson*

Use this poem as the basis for writing another poem, a prose fable, or an expository essay in which you discuss the pleasures and the risks of returning from reverie to reality.

AN EFFECTIVE TECHNIQUE

The strongest feelings are set up by contrasts: a tragedy is saddest if it happens immediately after a moment of great joy; sudden good fortune is sweetest if it comes in the midst of a disaster. Relying on this trait of human psychology, Heather Ashley has developed a technique for maintaining strong feelings throughout her essay: she keeps shifting back and forth between contrasting tones. She takes her readers into a happy imaginary world created by two children, but repeatedly interrupts this reverie to remind us of the unpleasant reality of hostage crises and nuclear war awaiting these children when they grow up and have to leave their imaginary kingdom behind. By contrasting the reverie and the reality, Ashley causes our feelings about both to become stronger: the fantasy is made sweeter by our sense that it cannot last; the real world seems all the uglier for destroying such childhood fantasies. Moreover, the contrast makes Ashley's essay much more than a pleasant indulgence in reminiscence. She is criticizing the world of politicians and large corporations and suggesting that maturity with its cigarette smoke and "bullshit" may be considerably less sane than immature fantasies.

Though the central tension in this essay is between reverie and reality, between Vacita and politics, Ashley actually creates three "worlds" and three tones in this essay, the third being the world of childhood before the split between reality and reverie arises. Childhood joins with Vacita in opposition to adult reality, increasing our sense of what is lost as the two children grow up. Ashley presents childhood in amusing, sweet passages; it is a world where "it would stay light forever" (paragraph 5) while she licks "a sticky dribble off the back of my thumb" (paragraph 18). Vacita is formed of lyrical words, like its name, "proud and magical, ethereal and yet concrete" (paragraph 22). Politics enters in ironic and angry sentences uttered by the adult author ("they elected an old B-grade movie actor to the presidency" [paragraph 1]; "the fish were tiny and their bodies polluted by the sewage dumped by the factories" [paragraph 9]). At the end of the essay, the nastiness of reality finally replaces everything else; tensions become a permanent part of daily life, and with them a new and violent language of obscene curses enters the essay. To be an adult, Ashley seems to be saying, is to become part of the obscenities of nuclear war and hostages. She is also making us aware that the passage out of reverie is always shocking; the two girls are slapping themselves into consciousness with their violent language. The climactic curse "Fuck you!" also foreshadows that element of the adult world that will most directly transform childhood friendships: sex. The curse is the dark side of the "first kiss" that ends the essay.

This essay shows us one way to turn our fantasies into powerful commentaries on the real world: consider what is making the fantasy so appealing, what real events we want to escape from. By weaving together fantasy and reality, we can bring our readers to share our sense of the evils that we want to escape. Such an essay need not be written about adolescence; adults indulge in reveries as much as children do. We could also write an essay that contrasts fantasy and reality in a person's life to criticize the fantasy rather than the reality (perhaps showing how dreaming keeps a person from doing anything worthwhile).

More generally, Ashley shows us the interesting effects that can be created by mixing sentences written in different tones in one essay. This technique can be adapted to other kinds of essays. For example, if we were using a sharp, ironic tone in an essay about the greed motivating American industry, we might switch to a sweet, even sentimental, style for a short passage presenting a utopian vision of moral businessmen, thereby indicating that we are not mean-spirited critics, but rather disappointed dreamers.

In the next selection, "Once More to the Lake," E. B. White draws us into a dream of stopping or even reversing the flow of time. In Ashley's essay, the reality that drives her to fantasy is one she has yet to experience; in White's essay, it is a world he knows all too well.

ANOTHER ILLUSTRATION OF THE TECHNIQUE

E. B. WHITE

Once More to the Lake

E. B. White has written witty, urbane columns for The New Yorker *magazine, two children's classics (*Charlotte's Web *and* Stuart Little*), parodies of literary works and sex manuals, sweet reminiscences, idealistic political tracts, and an updated version of the most popular and briefest guide to writing,* The Elements of Style. *Though few writers have gained recognition in as many fields, his career began with failure. After graduating college in 1921, he went to work for United Press, but, he recalls, "As a reporter I was a flop because I always came back laden not with facts about the case, but with a mind full of the little difficulties and amusements I had encountered in my* *travels. Not till* The New Yorker *came along did I ever find any means of expressing these impertinences and irrelevancies."*

All of White's essays display a gentle humor; he has tried to explain why: "There is a deep vein of melancholy running through everyone's life and . . . a humorist, perhaps more sensible of it than some others, compensates for it actively and positively." Compensating for the deficiencies of the world is, for White, the basic task of all writers, not only humorists. "I have always felt," he states, "that the first duty of a writer was to ascend—to make flights, carrying others along if he could manage it. To do this takes courage. . . . Today, with so much of earth damaged and endangered, with so much of life dispiriting or joyless, a writer's courage can easily fail him. I feel this daily. . . . But despair is not good—for the writer, for anyone. Only hope can carry us aloft. . . . Only hope, and a certain faith . . . for writing itself is an act of faith, nothing else. And it must be the writer, above all others, who keeps it alive—choked with laughter, or with pain."

August 1941

One summer, along about 1904, my father rented a camp on a lake in   1
Maine and took us all there for the month of August. We all got ringworm
from some kittens and had to rub Pond's Extract on our arms and legs night
and morning, and my father rolled over in a canoe with all his clothes on; but
outside of that the vacation was a success and from then on none of us ever
thought there was any place in the world like that lake in Maine. We returned
summer after summer—always on August 1 for one month. I have since become
a salt-water man, but sometimes in summer there are days when the restlessness
of the tides and the fearful cold of the sea water and the incessant wind that
blows across the afternoon and into the evening make me wish for the placidity
of a lake in the woods. A few weeks ago this feeling got so strong I bought
myself a couple of bass hooks and a spinner and returned to the lake where
we used to go, for a week's fishing and to revisit old haunts.

I took along my son, who had never had any fresh water up his nose and   2
who had seen lily pads only from train windows. On the journey over to the
lake I began to wonder what it would be like. I wondered how time would
have marred this unique, this holy spot—the coves and streams, the hills that
the sun set behind, the camps and the paths behind the camps. I was sure
that the tarred road would have found it out and I wondered in what other
ways it would be desolated. It is strange how much you can remember about
places like that once you allow your mind to return into the grooves that lead
back. You remember one thing, and that suddenly reminds you of another
thing. I guess I remembered clearest of all the early mornings, when the lake

was cool and motionless, remembered how the bedroom smelled of the lumber it was made of and of the wet woods whose scent entered through the screen. The partitions in the camp were thin and did not extend clear to the top of the rooms, and as I was always the first up I would dress softly so as not to wake the others, and sneak out into the sweet outdoors and start out in the canoe, keeping close along the shore in the long shadows of the pines. I remembered being very careful never to rub my paddle against the gunwale for fear of disturbing the stillness of the cathedral.

The lake had never been what you would call a wild lake. There were cottages sprinkled around the shores, and it was in farming country although the shores of the lake were quite heavily wooded. Some of the cottages were owned by nearby farmers, and you would live at the shore and eat your meals at the farmhouse. That's what our family did. But although it wasn't wild, it was a fairly large and undisturbed lake and there were places in it that, to a child at least, seemed infinitely remote and primeval.

I was right about the tar: it led to within half a mile of the shore. But when I got back there, with my boy, and we settled into a camp near a farmhouse and into the kind of summertime I had known, I could tell that it was going to be pretty much the same as it had been before—I knew it, lying in bed the first morning, smelling the bedroom and hearing the boy sneak quietly out and go off along the shore in a boat. I began to sustain the illusion that he was I, and therefore, by simple transposition, that I was my father. This sensation persisted, kept cropping up all the time we were there. It was not an entirely new feeling, but in this setting it grew much stronger. I seemed to be living a dual existence. I would be in the middle of some simple act, I would be picking up a bait box or laying down a table fork, or I would be saying something, and suddenly it would be not I but my father who was saying the words or making the gesture. It gave me a creepy sensation.

We went fishing the first morning. I felt the damp moss covering the worms in the bait can, and saw the dragonfly alight on the tip of my rod as it hovered a few inches from the surface of the water. It was the arrival of this fly that convinced me beyond any doubt that everything was as it always had been, that the years were a mirage and that there had been no years. The small waves were the same, chucking the rowboat under the chin as we fished at anchor, and the boat was the same boat, the same color green and the ribs broken in the same places, and under the floorboards the same fresh-water leavings and debris—the dead helgramite, the wisps of moss, the rusty discarded fishhook, the dried blood from yesterday's catch. We stared silently at the tips of our rods, at the dragonflies that came and went. I lowered the tip of mine into the water, tentatively, pensively dislodging the fly, which darted two feet

away, poised, darted two feet back, and came to rest again a little farther up
the rod. There had been no years between the ducking of this dragonfly and
the other one—the one that was part of memory. I looked at the boy, who
was silently watching his fly, and it was my hands that held his rod, my eyes
watching. I felt dizzy and didn't know which rod I was at the end of.

We caught two bass, hauling them in briskly as though they were mackerel,   6
pulling them over the side of the boat in a businesslike manner without any
landing net, and stunning them with a blow on the back of the head. When
we got back for a swim before lunch, the lake was exactly where we had left
it, the same number of inches from the dock, and there was only the merest
suggestion of a breeze. This seemed an utterly enchanted sea, this lake you
could leave to its own devices for a few hours and come back to, and find that
it had not stirred, this constant and trustworthy body of water. In the shallows,
the dark, water-soaked sticks and twigs, smooth and old, were undulating in
clusters on the bottom against the clean ribbed sand, and the track of the
mussel was plain. A school of minnows swam by, each minnow with its small
individual shadow, doubling the attendance, so clear and sharp in the sunlight.
Some of the other campers were in swimming, along the shore, one of them
with a cake of soap, and the water felt thin and clear and unsubstantial. Over
the years there had been this person with the cake of soap, this cultist, and
here he was. There had been no years.

Up to the farmhouse to dinner through the teeming, dusty field, the road   7
under our sneakers was only a two-track road. The middle track was missing,
the one with the marks of the hooves and the splotches of dried, flaky manure.
There had always been three tracks to choose from in choosing which track
to walk in; now the choice was narrowed down to two. For a moment I missed
terribly the middle alternative. But the way led past the tennis court, and
something about the way it lay there in the sun reassured me; the tape had
loosened along the backline, the alleys were green with plantains and other
weeds, and the net (installed in June and removed in September) sagged in
the dry noon, and the whole place steamed with midday heat and hunger and
emptiness. There was a choice of pie for dessert, and one was blueberry and
one was apple, and the waitresses were the same country girls, there having
been no passage of time, only the illusion of it as in a dropped curtain—the
waitresses were still fifteen; their hair had been washed, that was the only
difference—they had been to the movies and seen the pretty girls with the
clean hair.

Summertime, oh, summertime, pattern of life indelible, the fade-proof lake,   8
the woods unshatterable, the pasture with the sweetfern and the juniper forever
and ever, summer without end; this was the background, and the life along

the shore was the design, the cottagers with their innocent and tranquil design, their tiny docks with the flagpole and the American flag floating against the white clouds in the blue sky, the little paths over the roots of the trees leading from camp to camp and the paths leading back to the outhouses and the can of lime for sprinkling, and at the souvenir counters at the store the miniature birch-bark canoes and the postcards that showed things looking a little better than they looked. This was the American family at play, escaping the city heat, wondering whether the newcomers in the camp at the head of the cove were "common" or "nice," wondering whether it was true that the people who drove up for Sunday dinner at the farmhouse were turned away because there wasn't enough chicken.

It seemed to me, as I kept remembering all this, that those times and those 9 summers had been infinitely precious and worth saving. There had been jollity and peace and goodness. The arriving (at the beginning of August) had been so big a business in itself, at the railway station the farm wagon drawn up, the first smell of the pine-laden air, the first glimpse of the smiling farmer, and the great importance of the trunks and your father's enormous authority in such matters, and the feel of the wagon under you for the long ten-mile haul, and at the top of the last long hill catching the first view of the lake after eleven months of not seeing this cherished body of water. The shouts and cries of the other campers when they saw you, and the trunks to be unpacked, to give up their rich burden. (Arriving was less exciting nowadays, when you sneaked up in your car and parked it under a tree near the camp and took out the bags and in five minutes it was all over, no fuss, no loud wonderful fuss about trunks.)

Peace and goodness and jollity. The only thing that was wrong now, really, 10 was the sound of the place, an unfamiliar nervous sound of the outboard motors. This was the note that jarred, the one thing that would sometimes break the illusion and set the years moving. In those other summertimes all motors were inboard; and when they were at a little distance, the noise they made was a sedative, an ingredient of summer sleep. They were one-cylinder and two-cylinder engines, and some were make-and-break and some were jump-spark, but they all made a sleepy sound across the lake. The one-lungers throbbed and fluttered, and the twin-cylinder ones purred and purred, and that was a quiet sound, too. But now the campers all had outboards. In the daytime, in the hot mornings, these motors made a petulant, irritable sound; at night, in the still evening when the afterglow lit the water, they whined about one's ears like mosquitoes. My boy loved our rented outboard, and his great desire was to achieve single-handed mastery over it, and authority, and he soon learned the trick of choking it a little (but not too much), and the adjustment of the needle valve. Watching him I would remember the things you could do with the old one-cylinder engine with the heavy flywheel, how you could have it eating out of your hand if you got really close to it spiritually. Motorboats in those days didn't have clutches, and you would make a landing by shutting off the motor at the proper time and coasting in with a dead rudder. But there was a way of reversing them, if you learned the trick, by cutting the switch and putting it on again exactly on the final dying revolution of the flywheel, so that it would kick back against compression and begin reversing. Approaching a dock in a strong following breeze, it was difficult to slow up sufficiently by the ordinary coasting method, and if a boy felt he had complete mastery over his motor, he was tempted to keep it running beyond its time and then reverse it a few feet from the dock. It took a cool nerve, because if you threw the switch a twentieth of a second too soon you would catch the flywheel when it still had speed enough to go up past center, and the boat would leap ahead, charging bull-fashion at the dock.

We had a good week at the camp. The bass were biting well and the sun 11 shone endlessly, day after day. We would be tired at night and lie down in the accumulated heat of the little bedrooms after the long hot day and the breeze would stir almost imperceptibly outside and the smell of the swamp drift in through the rusty screens. Sleep would come easily and in the morning the red squirrel would be on the roof, tapping out his gay routine. I kept remembering everything, lying in bed in the mornings—the small steamboat that had a long rounded stern like the lip of a Ubangi, and how quietly she ran on the moonlight sails, when the older boys played their mandolins and the girls sang and we ate doughnuts dipped in sugar, and how sweet the music was on the water in the shining night, and what it had felt like to think about girls then. After breakfast we would go up to the store and the things were in the same place—the minnows in a bottle, the plugs and spinners disarranged and pawed over by the youngsters from the boys' camp, the Fig Newtons and the Beeman's gum. Outside, the road was tarred and cars stood in front of the store. Inside, all was just as it had always been, except there was more Coca-Cola and not so much Moxie and root beer and birch beer and sarsaparilla. We would walk out with the bottle of pop apiece and sometimes the pop would backfire up our noses and hurt. We explored the streams, quietly, where the turtles slid off the sunny logs and dug their way into the soft bottom; and we lay on the town wharf and fed worms to the tame bass. Everywhere we went I had trouble making out which was I, the one walking at my side, the one walking in my pants.

One afternoon while we were there at that lake a thunderstorm came up. 12 It was like the revival of an old melodrama that I had seen long ago with childish awe. The second-act climax of the drama of the electrical disturbance over a lake in America had not changed in any important respect. This was the big scene, still the big scene. The whole thing was so familiar, the first feeling of oppression and heat and a general air around camp of not wanting to go very far away. In mid-afternoon (it was all the same) a curious darkening of the sky, and a lull in everything that had made life tick and then the way the boats suddenly swung the other way at their moorings with the coming of a breeze out of the new quarter, and the premonitory rumble. Then the kettle drum, then the snare, then the bass drum and cymbals, then crackling light against the dark, and the gods grinning and licking their chops in the hills. Afterward the calm, the rain steadily rustling in the calm lake, the return of light and hope and spirits and the campers running out in joy and relief to go swimming in the rain, their bright cries perpetuating the deathless joke about how they were getting simply drenched, and the children screaming with delight at the new sensation of bathing in the rain, and the joke about getting drenched linking the generations in a strong indestructible chain. And the comedian who waded in carrying an umbrella.

When the others went swimming, my son said he was going in, too. He 13 pulled his dripping trunks from the line where they had hung all through the shower and wrung them out. Languidly, and with no thought of going in, I watched him, his hard little body, skinny and bare, saw him wince slightly as he pulled up around his vitals the small, soggy, icy garment. As he buckled the swollen belt, suddenly my groin felt the chill of death.

Focusing on E. B. White's Use of Tone

1. White lets his readers know in the first paragraph that he is going to the lake in an effort to escape, but he identifies the sea as what he is trying to escape. How do White's descriptions of the sea and the lake suggest that they represent more than just bodies of water? What kind of lifestyle does "the sea" represent? What kind of lifestyle does "the lake" represent?

2. The first three paragraphs end with quite evocative phrases: "old haunts," "the stillness of the cathedral," and "infinitely remote and primeval." If all you knew of this essay was that it contained these three phrases, what sort of tone would you expect the essay to have? Despite these phrases, what seems to be the dominant tone of the first few paragraphs?

3. How does White make us feel in the first few paragraphs that he is partly seeing reality and partly indulging in a reverie, a daydream? How does White let us know in the fifth paragraph that he is trying to escape reality? What is it about the real world that he wishes he could alter? Why does he feel dizzy?

4. White begins paragraph 8, "Summertime, oh summertime, pattern of life indelible, the fade-proof lake. . . ." What kind of language is this? Why does he
   use this kind of language? In the middle of this paragraph, he speaks of "postcards that showed things looking a little better than they looked." How is this
   paragraph in particular, and much of the whole essay, a "postcard"? In paragraph 10, the sound of outboard motors disrupts his reverie. Why doesn't this
   sound fit in his postcard world?

5. How does the last sentence break the tone of the whole essay? Why does White
   draw attention to his son's "vitals" and his own "groin"? Why are such references surprising in this essay? Throughout the essay White has referred to
   feeling an identity with his son because they share the same experiences. How
   does this last line suggest another way that father and son are linked, and how
   is death a part of that linkage?

WORKING WITH THE TECHNIQUE IN YOUR OWN WRITING

1. Write an essay about a time in your life when you found a particular reverie
   or daydream especially appealing. Include in the essay references to what was
   really happening in your life at that time. Try to make your readers feel how
   the reverie and reality were different; you might try to use different tones to
   describe the two parts of your life at that time. Why was the daydream important to you? Were you trying to escape painful events? Did the reverie serve a
   function in your life—say, to allow you to pass through a confusing transition
   or to avoid a dangerous confrontation?

2. Write an essay criticizing some institution or group; you might write about your
   school, a group of friends, or a government agency. Include in the essay a
   fantasy or a vision of what that institution or group could be. Try to develop
   two different but equally strong tones in the two parts of the essay, in the
   utopian fantasy as well as in the critique.

CELESTE L. BARRUS

Boise State University
Boise, Idaho
Karen S. Thomas, instructor

Celeste Barrus, the mother of seven children, decided to enroll in college in 1982 along with her oldest son, Marc. In fact, they enrolled in the same composition class. She describes writing as "waiting, unsettled waiting. Waiting for ideas to come; staring into space a lot." She has written stories and essays for her church's monthly paper under the name Heppsaba Hepplewhite. "In case my writing was bad I didn't want the church congregation to know who wrote the articles. If they were good the people didn't need to know anyway."

Born in Nampa, Idaho, Celeste Barrus has always enjoyed writing, singing, and playing musical instruments. In addition to piano, she taught herself to play an old violin her aunt resurrected from the hayloft of a barn: "Even though nicotine fly spray had been spilt on it, giving it a strong, unforgettably pungent odor, I learned to play on it," she recalls.

Asked to write a personal essay, Barrus immediately thought of writing about her son Todd. She reports: "Our teacher read some sample essays to the class. All were humorous. I changed my mind, thinking that my original subject wasn't what the teacher wanted. I tried to write something funny about the dating habits of my teenage daughter. It just didn't work. I needed to write about Todd."

In the years since earning a Bedford Prize for her essay "Todd," Celeste Barrus continued to pursue a degree in English as a part-time student at Boise State University. "Winning the Bedford Prize told me that I, too, could DO IT! Though I have gotten very few Bs on college papers, writing does not come easily. I work for it, and I work hard." After graduating in 1988, Barrus must decide whether to devote herself to full-time teaching. If she does, it will be with the hope, as she put it, "that in some way I can make a difference in a student's life."

Whatever career she chooses, writing no doubt will continue to make a difference in her own life: "I still write my Heppsaba Hepplewhite column for our church newspaper, and I try to keep up in my personal journal." Her interest in genealogical research also prompts her to write numerous letters and to "piece together" family histories.

When asked if she had taken any risks when she wrote "Todd," Barrus modestly responded: "When I wrote my essay, I was too ignorant about writing in general. How could I break rules I didn't even know? The only risk I took was in baring my emotions." Little in her essay was premeditated, she reported: "The words just came. They were just there. They had been lived. I wrote and arrived at the end result because it 'felt right.'"

Todd

Trauma comes to every life. It can leave us helpless. But finally we realize   1
that the world still turns and life goes on. We keep living and doing, although
many times automatically and without feeling. Then, when the crisis is over,
we find we have more understanding, a greater depth of feeling, and a sparkle
of love that enriches life.

It began in August, the month Bill and I started preparations for our move   2
to Biloxi, Mississippi. Bill was assigned, by the Idaho Air National Guard, to
an eleven-month radio-electronics school at Keesler Air Force Base.

All three of our children were small. Marc was barely three; Todd would   3
turn two in a month; and Kelly had just had her first birthday a few days
before. I loved all three dearly, but even in normal circumstances it was sometimes trying, dealing with three "almost" babies. Their demands were greater
than my energy.

The problem was Todd. I was at my wit's end trying to cope with him. He   4
cried all the time and when he wasn't crying he would toddle into his bedroom,
crawl onto the lower bunk and lie there, listless and apathetic. Then he would
get up, cry again while he clung to my leg, demanding that I pick him up.
Every week I took him to the doctor and after each visit I came home with a
"new" medicine to try for the ear infection that just wouldn't clear up.

I remembered what a good baby he had always been. With an imp-like smile   5
he would gather my cheeks between both tiny hands, grinning widely as he
forced a pucker from my lips. As he grew, he looked like a broad-shouldered
football player, but in miniature.

I felt despair at the total change in him. Wild thoughts clouded my mind: 6
"Is his personality changing? Why is he so different all of a sudden? Why does
he cry constantly? What more can I do for him? How can I be a good mother
when I am so tired?"

Night after night I put Todd beside me on the couch, trying not to disturb   7
Bill as he slept in the bedroom. Night after night I sang and talked softly to
him, all the while gently brushing his back with the palm of my hand as I
tried to quiet the cries and groans that emitted from his thinning frame.

Somehow, though the nightmare continued, the month of August passed.   8
The trailer Bill was building was finally finished. With our furniture loaded
and with tearful good-byes from parents, we left, heading for the Mississippi
Gulf Coast.

One event stands in my memory of our seven-day car ride. One evening   9
after a day of fussy babies and long miles, we stopped at a motel in Arkansas.
We ate our supper, then bathed, diapered, and pajamaed the little ones. That

night I had such a hard time getting Todd to settle down. He seemed to hurt all over. Even as I held him in my arms he cried out if I moved wrong. His cries turned to screams as he flailed by my side on the bed. As tears of worry and frustration clouded my eyes, a knock sounded at the door. I opened the door to see a balding, paunchy man leaning sleepily against the door frame.

"Hey folks," he drawled, "I'm sorry, but if you can't keep that kid quiet, 10 you're gonna hafta find another place. I got other customers that wanna get some sleep." Murmuring assurances, I closed the door, then folded into a sobbing heap on the bed.

That night we did something purposely that we never had done before or 11 have done since to any of our children. In our anguish, we literally drugged Todd with aspirin, orange flavored, that we dissolved and poured down his throat. I held him for the rest of the night, watching as his body began to limply relax, petting him, listening closely with my ear to his mouth, feeling the pulse in his neck, afraid to sleep for fear he wouldn't wake. That was the first night in over a month that he was quiet.

In the days that followed, everything improved. We moved into a rental 12 house in Biloxi; Bill enjoyed his radio-electronics classes; and little Todd was smiling, though still not active.

One muggy morning about a month later, as I sat on the front step watching 13 Marc and Kelly play in the sand, I noticed Todd walk slowly from the house, taking small, plodding steps on the line where the sand of the front yard joined the pebbly surface of the pavement. Suddenly he tripped, striking the crown of his head on the hard asphalt. I rushed to him and scooped him up. Holding him close, I brushed the sand from his face. A knot was beginning to rise on his forehead. Whimpering, he was limp in my arms as though the plug to his energy had been pulled, leaving him drained.

I carried him into the backyard where Bill was mowing the lawn. Turning 14 off the motor, he took Todd from me and carried him into the house, questioning me on the way. We began to notice that Todd's head was turning black and blue, not just around the lump, but continuing down to his neck.

Almost sure he had a skull fracture, we dropped everything and took him 15 to the hospital on base. The only doctor available at the time was a Dr. White. He was of medium height, in his early thirties, and of an arrogant disposition. A feeling of distrust came to me, of immediate dislike.

We waited in his 10 × 10 foot cubicle. Without saying one word to us, he 16 strode into the room, took a pocket flashlight and tongue depressor from his pocket, and proceeded to examine Todd from the neck up.

"Okay, parents," he challenged indifferently, leaning against the wall with 17 his arms folded and legs crossed, "What's the problem?"

I began. "Well, doctor, about an hour ago Todd tripped on the asphalt in 18
front of our house and fell. He hit his head pretty hard; then he started turning
black and blue. We thought maybe he had a skull fracture."

"I'm sure anyone would turn black and blue if they fell on the asphalt," he 19
returned, looking quite bored.

"But look at him! He's really black and blue," I said, shocked at his indif- 20
ference.

"It must have been a pretty hard fall. Just let him rest and he'll be fine." 21

Enraged at his arrogance and complete lack of compassion, I was at a loss 22
for words. I could feel Bill stiffen with indignation as he stood up from his
chair, facing this "doctor" who militarily outranked him.

"Sir, you need to know also that Todd has had a fever lately and seems 23
very tired and listless all the time."

"I noticed, sergeant," clipped the doctor, "that this child has a slight ear 24
infection, his tonsils also being somewhat enlarged, all of which would account
for the fever. This penicillin ought to do the trick."

As he ripped the prescription from the pad, he began again. "We doctors 25
like to follow up on the same patients. The second paper there is for one week
from today. Come any time of the day; first come, first served basis." Then
without a smile he lifted Todd from the table and stood him on the floor.
With that, he started toward the door.

Tears of rage and disgust and smoldering dislike began coursing down my 26
cheeks. Standing quickly, I blocked his path to the door. With my arms locked
stiffly to my sides and my hands clenched tightly into balled fists, I began
spitting the words out slowly, my enunciation perfect.

"Doctor White," I began in a soft hiss, "something is wrong with this child. 27
I watch him day after day and I know from the changes I've seen that something
is wrong. Look at him! Look at his arm!" My voice was rising. "Look at my
hand print on his arm!"

I had taken my hand from around Todd's tiny arm and there was an almost 28
perfect five-fingered print, turning black and blue. Looking up at the doctor
with icy eyes, I continued.

"This child is sick! I want a blood test done and if you won't do it, I'll find 29
someone in this hospital who will!"

"Okay, mother. Okay. Don't get upset," he acquiesced as he jerked a paper 30
from another pad. "Here, just to satisfy you," he said in a condescending tone.
"Take this to the lab. They'll do the rest. Come back in a week." And with
that he strode, steely eyed, from the room.

After the exhaustion of the blood test, Todd slept heavily in my arms as 31
we drove home. Walking into the house, Bill took the appointment slip and

stuck it between the switch plate of the living room light and the wall—an instant bulletin board. Then after eating an early lunch he left for his six hours of school.

While washing dishes about one and a half hours later, I was startled to see 32 Bill walk in the front door. He took the appointment slip from behind the switch plate, ripped it in two, and said, "We won't need this anymore." Noticing an indignant protest rising in my throat, he quickly added. "The hospital just called me out of school. We are to get Todd there right away."

A knot immediately tied in my stomach. I felt my eyes enlarge with fear 33 and could feel the whine in my ears as the blood rushed to my head. Even so, I knew my face was chalky white. Without saying anything more, Bill handed me my purse, picked Todd gently from the couch, and walked to the car, knowing that even in my stupor I would follow.

Riding in the car with Todd in my arms I felt a consuming love for him, 34 along with overwhelming fear; and I knew. The ugly word of the disease came to my mind without my consciously ever before thinking about it. I could never remember reading or hearing the word before—but I knew. It was like someone beyond myself whispering the word in my mind.

Todd was a very independent little spirit even in those months of lethargy. 35 Getting out of the car, Bill reached for him to carry him up the hill to the hospital.

"No Daddy," he said, pushing Bill's hand aside, "I walk." 36

So we walked. Todd began with two steps. Then rest. Another step. Rest. 37 But still he would not be carried.

Looking toward the hospital I saw a man standing outside the door in the 38 same type of tan air force dress pants and white calf-length smock that Dr. White had worn, but this man had a heavier build. He stood there and watched us for the full ten minutes it took to walk the one block from the car to the hospital emergency entrance.

Taking a step forward he said knowingly, "Sergeant Barrus, Mrs. Barrus, 39 I'm Dr. Haney. I'm sorry we had to call you out of school, but we felt a few more tests were needed." And then bending, he ever so gently picked Todd up, cuddled him over his shoulder, reassured him in a quiet voice, and said to the two of us, "Follow me, please," as he walked in the door and down the hall.

Pediatrics was on the third floor. After getting off the elevator, the doctor 40 took us to a room that already had Todd's name on the door.

"Now, Mrs. Barrus," he stated kindly, "if you would get Todd undressed 41 please and slip this hospital gown on him. Sergeant, there's a wheelchair right behind the door there." Handing Bill two pieces of paper he explained, "There

are three tests we must do. First he has to be X-rayed totally. Next take him
to the lab for more blood tests. While you're gone, I'll set up down the hall
for the third test, which I'll do myself. Give those papers to the people in
charge. They'll know what to do."

Turning, he started briskly down the hall only to stop in midstep. "Oh, 42
Sergeant Barrus," he called back, "it is imperative that you hurry." With that
he was gone.

Riding the elevator was the first chance we had to look at the papers shaking 43
in my hand. On both, scrawled across the bottom, were those dreaded words,
those words I knew already—"possible leukemia." As we rushed from test to
test, the words reverberated in my mind, bringing pictures of a tiny pain-
racked body and possible death, because death was all I knew of those horrible
words.

After the attending orderlies finished each test, they would always say, 44
"Sergeant, it's extremely necessary that you hurry."

I was acutely aware of things going on around me that day, but as if I were 45
watching from outside my body. I could see myself as I felt—staring vacantly,
yet not seeing, knowing what was happening but not participating. And yet
it was me. I was there, clinging to hope as hard as I was clinging to Bill's
hand, all the while tears streaming down my face.

When we got back upstairs Dr. Haney and Captain Shiller, the head nurse, 46
were waiting for us by the elevator. As she hurried off, pushing Todd, the
doctor explained to us what would happen next.

"Mrs. Barrus," he began, "this last test is one we do only when absolutely 47
necessary. It is very painful and hard on the patient but we have no other
choice." Apologetically, he went on. "I cannot give him an anesthetic." He
waited for the statement to sink in.

"We take a syringe with a hollow screw-type bit on the end of it and drill 48
either into the breastbone or in one of the vertebra in the back. We'll probably
do the breastbone. After we are in the marrow of the bone, instead of injecting
into it, I'll suck the marrow into the syringe, then unscrew the drill and it will
be over." He paused, anticipating a question from us. There was none. I was
too numb and hollow to reply. Bill, also, was silent.

Then Dr. Haney looked at me. "Mrs. Barrus, I'd like you to go to the far 49
end of the hall where you can't hear. Mr. Barrus, if you'll follow me please,
you can be one of the four people we need to hold him down."

They left me then, standing solitary, alone in the middle of a crashing 50
world. Crying silently, with my face pressed to the hard comfort of the wall,
I heard Todd scream. Five, ten, fifteen minutes of constant screaming seemed
an eternity. Then, silence. It was over. The door opened. Bill, his usually dark

face now a pallid white, came out first, taking me gently in his arms. Dr. Haney came next, pushing Todd on an ambulatory stretcher across the hall to his room. Nurses and orderlies converged through the open door bringing IV stands, glucose, and plasma drips, tubing, and needles necessary for the next step.

Bill and I clung together in numb amazement in the corner. This time there 51 were no screams from Todd as they strapped him to the bed, no screams as the transfusion needles entered his unconscious body.

The rest of the day was a haze to me. Dr. Haney, always so thoughtful, 52 explained everything he was going to do and why. He explained the reason for the rush; Todd's hemoglobin level was so low that total heart failure could have occurred at any time; thus the necessity for blood transfusions as quickly as possible.

Every day for thirty days I left Marc and Kelly with a babysitter and walked 53 up the hospital hill. Little by little I saw a change in Todd. It was very slow at first; from his unconscious state, to smiling slightly as he lay in bed, then to clapping and laughing as he saw me come down the hall for our daily visit. On the thirtieth day he ran the length of the corridor, waving his discharge papers as he tackled my legs.

In the next nine months as Todd made his daily and then weekly visit to 54 the hospital outpatient clinic, I watched a love develop between him and every nurse, orderly, and doctor that he came in contact with. They gave him candy and gum constantly. Whatever he asked for he got. Dr. Haney even gave Todd his tiny flashlight and an unopened box of tongue depressors. Because of this affection for him, Todd never had to wait in line, always getting preferential "stat" treatment.

The day before our return trip to Idaho they all gathered to give a small 55 tow-headed boy, who sparkled with mischief, a send-off, knowing most likely they would never see him again.

Todd died one year later on September 3, 1964, three days before his fourth 56 birthday.

Focusing on Celeste Barrus's Techniques and Revisions

1. Barrus focuses on the day she found out about Todd's illness rather than trying to cover all of Todd's life, the entire course of his disease, or even the day of his death. What does she gain by limiting her focus in this way? Consider Barrus's purpose. Is it principally to narrate a traumatic event in her life or to reflect on or examine its effect on her now? How does her focus serve that purpose?

2. When asked in a recent interview to reread her essay several years after writing it and to comment on its effectiveness, Barrus replied: "Perhaps the greatest strengths of this story are my way of portraying the emotion of the moment and my feeling for those around me through the use of descriptive words—for example, in paragraphs 26 and 27, 'balled fists,' 'spitting,' 'soft hiss,' etc. There are also some word combinations that work nicely, such as in paragraph 26—'spitting' and 'slowly.' One cannot 'spit slowly.' " Reread her essay carefully and identify as many additional features of its success as you can. Be as specific as possible.

3. Barrus also identifies another successful strategy: "Keeping the reader in suspense, not disclosing Todd's affliction immediately." How does Barrus raise her readers' concern that something dreadful will happen to Todd? Consider, for example, paragraph 4, where Barrus writes, "The problem was Todd." The question of what is wrong with Todd is repeated throughout the essay, but it is not until paragraph 43 that we learn what the exact problem is. What effect does this delay have? What other strategies does Barrus use to heighten her readers' sense of suspense, to keep her readers reading? Comment, for example, on the role of the doctors in her essay.

4. Barrus writes about a difficult subject, the death of her child. This essay could become sentimental or maudlin, but it never does. How does Barrus avoid sentimentality? Comment on the effectiveness of Barrus's last line. What would have been the effect of returning at the end of her essay to the generalities of its opening?

5. Part of this essay's success comes from Barrus's use of effective images. She describes Todd after his fall, "as though the plug to his energy had been pulled" (paragraph 13). Identify other specific images and details that you find especially effective.

6. Barrus uses dialogue effectively to catch the nuances of style and the manner of speaking of her characters, such as the Arkansas motel owner in paragraph 10 and the arrogant Dr. White beginning in paragraph 17. Identify specific instances of dialogue that you find effective and explain what you learn about the character from each dialogue.

7. How does the structure of Barrus's essay add to or detract from the overall effect of her essay? Barrus added the introductory paragraph in her final draft in response to her teacher's suggestion. Reread the essay without this paragraph. Which version is more effective? Why? Which introduction best suits Barrus's purpose?

Suggestions for Writing

1. Barrus writes: "Trauma comes to every life. It can leave us helpless. But finally we realize that the world still turns and life goes on." Write a narrative essay about a time when trauma came to your life and about the realizations it prompted.

2. If a member of your family has had a long or serious illness, write an essay describing the effects of this illness on the rest of the family.

3. Celeste Barrus describes her conflicts with doctors, one of the most formidable of contemporary America's authority figures. Drawing on her experiences and your own, analyze the indifferent or arrogant behavior of these or similar figures and suggest possible causes for their behavior. What did the person look like? How was his or her attitude reflected in a posture or in a gesture? What did he or she say? How would you characterize his or her tone?

AN EFFECTIVE TECHNIQUE

Suspenseful movies and books are popular but rarely taken seriously. Celeste Barrus's essay shows how a writer can use the technique of building suspense to create a serious, moving, and thought-provoking essay. Barrus sets up her essay in the first paragraph, by giving her readers only vague hints of what is to come. She says she will talk about trauma and about surviving a crisis with "more understanding" than she had before. Yet the insights she promises remain undefined; some even read like clichés. We can not tell much, for example, about what it means to discover "a sparkle of love." Even though we know we are going to learn about a trauma, we wonder, with some dread, "How great a trauma are we going to see?" Barrus leaves that question hanging throughout the entire essay. The uncertainties of Barrus's first paragraph propel us to read further. The suspense she creates is more important than what she tells us about her son's illness, because she is not writing about illness but about what it is like to have one's world rendered utterly uncertain.

To bring her readers to share the fears and hopes of a parent with a very sick child, Barrus carefully controls the information she feeds us about the illness. After mentioning "trauma," she says, "It began in August," without any identification of "it." Then we read, "The problem was Todd," whose constant crankiness suggests that he is suffering a personality change. When Barrus finally presents strong evidence that Todd has a terrible disease, a doctor steps in to state quite authoritatively and for several paragraphs that Barrus is wrong. At that point, Barrus has brought us to a classic moment of suspense: we feel on the verge of a calamity, as if a bomb is about to explode, and we are being hindered by incompetent people as we try to find the bomb. We share Barrus's anger and frustration as the essay moves ever so slowly toward the final diagnosis, toward the "trauma" we have been expecting. Not until paragraph 43 do we finally read, "those dreaded words, those words I knew already—'possible leukemia.' " Barrus has brought us to the same state she was in; we hear that some such words are coming, and they appear in the essay as they did in life, merely as confirmation of our horrible suspicions.

Diagnosis does not end the suspense; it intensifies it. We are plunged into a world where "it's extremely necessary that you hurry," a world of terrible medical procedures. Then, miraculously, Todd gets better and better, until he can be sent away from the hospital with the extremely ambiguous words "most likely they would never see him again." We hope that it is because he won't need any hospitals again. Instead, the last line flatly dates his death. Finally, we know the extent of the trauma.

It might seem odd that we do not see anything of Barrus's life after Todd's death, but she is not going to spell out what she gained from "trauma"; she only puts us through the trauma ourselves. We feel the difficulty of watching someone we love in extreme pain. We see the terrible necessity of resisting the only authority—doctors—that could stop the pain. We experience the slowing and speeding up of time as uncertainty grows and wanes. We see the "sparkle of mischief" return to a limp body (and finally know what a "sparkle of love" means). The feelings created by the essay provide us with the understanding of how trauma can enrich life.

Barrus demonstrates how to make suspense carry the meaning of an essay. Her whole tale is structured to sustain the suspense from the first word to the last sentence, to leave questions hanging intensely in our minds. She carefully places her information to provide us with the sense of gradually increasing "understanding." She shows us the power that can be derived from purposely using vague phrases to tantalize readers. (We might even wonder if her essay would have been more powerful if she had dropped her first paragraph and started with the utterly ambiguous phrase "It began.") Her techniques are especially useful in essays about uncertainty, about trying to make sense of confusing and unwanted parts of life. But every essay has some suspense in it, because an effective beginning always sets up questions in the readers' minds that are not answered until much later. Even when we decide to state a thesis at the beginning of an essay, we want to set readers up for the rest of our argument and not give everything away. Barrus's opening paragraphs are a model of how to propel readers into our essays, how to make them eager to find out what we are going to say.

William Carlos Williams in "The Use of Force" also writes a tale about trying to discover how sick a child is, but he makes his readers share the suspense and uncertainty of the doctor's experience rather than the parents'.

ANOTHER ILLUSTRATION OF THE TECHNIQUE

WILLIAM CARLOS WILLIAMS

The Use of Force

*In his Autobiography, William Carlos Williams describes how he first became inter-
ested in writing: "It began with a heart attack. I was 16 or 17. There was a race. They
said we had to run one more lap. . . . [After it] I was sick, vomiting, my head hurt.
. . . Doc said 'heart murmur.' It meant a complete change in my life. I had lived for
sports, like any other kid. . . . No more baseball. No more running. Not being with the
others after school. I was forced back on myself. I had to think about myself, look into
myself, and I began to read." He turned to poetry because, he says, "I never thought I
was a very good prose writer." Feeling he would not make a living as a poet, he went
straight from high school to the School of Medicine at the University of Pennsylvania
(not an unusual transition in 1900) and eventually returned to Rutherford, New Jersey,
his hometown, to become a general practitioner. He published more than forty volumes
of poetry and several collections of essays and short stories but remained fairly obscure
until the 1950s. His subsequent fame, including many literary prizes, did not disrupt his
medical practice; until his death in 1963, his neighbors still knew him as William C.
Williams, M.D., the doctor who occasionally did readings at the high school and at
nearby Fairleigh Dickinson University.*

*When he started writing, Williams reported, "I didn't know what I was doing but I
knew what I wanted to do . . . to protest against the blackguardy and beauty of the
world, my world." But the first thing he learned was "that it isn't so easy to let yourself
go. I had learned too much already, even before I started to write. I ran into good safe
stereotypes everywhere. Perfectly safe, that's why we cling to it. If I ducked out of that
I ran into chaos." He began experimenting with breaking the traditional forms of English
poetry and eventually found a voice in his writing that was angrily defiant of all conventions (literary, political, and religious) and self-consciously American, building on the
nonliterary idioms and traditions of industrial New Jersey. According to Williams, a
writer is like a doctor, in rebellion against the diseases of his world, trying "to represent
exactly what he has to say CLEAN of the destroying, falsifying, besmutching agencies
with which he is surrounded."*

They were new patients to me, all I had was the name, Olson. Please come   1
down as soon as you can, my daughter is very sick.

When I arrived I was met by the mother, a big startled-looking woman,   2 very clean and apologetic who merely said, Is this the doctor? and let me in. In the back, she added. You must excuse us, doctor, we have her in the kitchen where it is warm. It is very damp here sometimes.

The child was fully dressed and sitting on her father's lap near the kitchen 3 table. He tried to get up, but I motioned for him not to bother, took off my overcoat and started to look things over. I could see that they were all very nervous, eyeing me up and down distrustfully. As often, in such cases, they weren't telling me more than they had to, it was up to me to tell them; that's why they were spending three dollars on me.

The child was fairly eating me up with her cold, steady eyes, and no expres- 4 sion to her face whatever. She did not move and seemed, inwardly, quiet; an unusually attractive little thing, and as strong as a heifer in appearance. But her face was flushed, she was breathing rapidly, and I realized that she had a high fever. She had magnificent blond hair, in profusion. One of those picture children often reproduced in advertising leaflets and the photogravure sections of the Sunday papers.

She's had a fever for three days, began the father and we don't know what 5 it comes from. My wife has given her things, you know, like people do, but it don't do no good. And there's been a lot of sickness around. So we tho't you'd better look her over and tell us what is the matter.

As doctors often do I took a trial shot at it as a point of departure. Has she 6 had a sore throat?

Both parents answered me together, No . . . No, she says her throat don't 7 hurt her.

Does your throat hurt you? added the mother to the child. But the little 8 girl's expression didn't change nor did she move her eyes from my face.

Have you looked?   9

I tried to, said the mother, but I couldn't see.   10

As it happens we had been having a number of cases of diphtheria in the 11 school to which this child went during that month and we were all, quite apparently, thinking of that, though no one had as yet spoken of the thing.

Well, I said, suppose we take a look at the throat first. I smiled in my best 12 professional manner and asking for the child's first name I said, come on, Mathilda, open your mouth and let's take a look at your throat.

Nothing doing.   13

Aw, come on, I coaxed, just open your mouth wide and let me take a look. 14 Look, I said opening both hands wide, I haven't anything in my hands. Just open up and let me see.

Such a nice man, put in the mother. Look how kind he is to you. Come 15 on, do what he tells you to. He won't hurt you.

At that I ground my teeth in disgust. If only they wouldn't use the word 16 "hurt" I might be able to get someplace. But I did not allow myself to be hurried or disturbed but speaking quietly and slowly I approached the child again.

As I moved my chair a little nearer suddenly with one cat-like movement 17 both her hands clawed instinctively for my eyes and she almost reached them too. In fact she knocked my glasses flying and they fell, though unbroken, several feet away from me on the kitchen floor.

Both the mother and father almost turned themselves inside out in embar- 18 rassment and apology. You bad girl, said the mother, taking her and shaking her by one arm. Look what you've done. The nice man . . . .

For heaven's sake, I broke in. Don't call me a nice man to her. I'm here to 19 look at her throat on the chance that she might have diphtheria and possibly die of it. But that's nothing to her. Look here, I said to the child, we're going to look at your throat. You're old enough to understand what I'm saying. Will you open it now by yourself or shall we have to open it for you?

Not a move. Even her expression hadn't changed. Her breaths however 20 were coming faster and faster. Then the battle began. I had to do it. I had to have a throat culture for her own protection. But first I told the parents that it was entirely up to them. I explained the danger but said that I would not insist on a throat examination so long as they would take the responsibility.

If you don't do what the doctor says you'll have to go to the hospital, the 21 mother admonished her severely.

Oh yeah? I had to smile to myself. After all, I had already fallen in love 22 with the savage brat, the parents were contemptible to me. In the ensuing struggle they grew more and more abject, crushed, exhausted while she surely rose to magnificent heights of insane fury of effort bred of her terror of me.

The father tried his best, and he was a big man but the fact that she was 23 his daughter, his shame at her behavior and his dread of hurting her made him release her just at the critical moment several times when I had almost achieved success, till I wanted to kill him. But his dread also that she might have diphtheria made him tell me to go on, go on though he himself was almost fainting, while the mother moved back and forth behind us raising and lowering her hands in an agony of apprehension.

Put her in front of you on your lap, I ordered, and hold both her wrists. 24

But as soon as he did the child let out a scream. Don't, you're hurting me. 25 Let go of my hands. Let them go I tell you. Then she shrieked terrifyingly, hysterically. Stop it! Stop it! You're killing me!

Do you think she can stand it, doctor! said the mother.   26

You get out, said the husband to his wife. Do you want her to die of 27 diphtheria?

Come on now, hold her, I said.   28

Then I grasped the child's head with my left hand and tried to get the 29 wooden tongue depressor between her teeth. She fought, with clenched teeth, desperately! But now I also had grown furious—at a child. I tried to hold myself down but I couldn't. I know how to expose a throat for inspection. And I did my best. When finally I got the wooden spatula behind the last teeth and just the point of it into the mouth cavity, she opened up for an instant but before I could see anything she came down again and gripping the wooden blade between her molars she reduced it to splinters before I could get it out again.

Aren't you ashamed, the mother yelled at her. Aren't you ashamed to act 30 like that in front of the doctor?

Get me a smooth-handled spoon of some sort, I told the mother. We're 31 going through with this. The child's mouth was already bleeding. Her tongue was cut and she was screaming in wild hysterical shrieks. Perhaps I should have desisted and come back in an hour or more. No doubt it would have been better. But I have seen at least two children lying dead in bed of neglect in such cases, and feeling that I must get a diagnosis, now or never I went at it again. But the worst of it was that I too had got beyond reason. I could have torn the child apart in my own fury and enjoyed it. It was a pleasure to attack her. My face was burning with it.

The damned little brat must be protected against her own idiocy, one says 32 to one's self at such times. Others must be protected against her. It is social necessity. And all these things are true. But a blind fury, a feeling of adult shame, bred of a longing for muscular release are the operatives. One goes on to the end.

In a final unreasoning assault I overpowered the child's neck and jaws. I 33 forced the heavy silver spoon back on her teeth and down her throat till she gagged. And there it was—both tonsils covered with membrane. She had fought valiantly to keep me from knowing her secret. She had been hiding that sore throat for three days at least and lying to her parents in order to escape just such an outcome as this.

Now truly she *was* furious. She had been on the defensive before but now 34 she attacked. Tried to get off her father's lap and fly at me while tears of defeat blinded her eyes.

Focusing on William Carlos Williams's Use of Suspense

1. What details in the first few paragraphs make us think that the child may be very sick? What details make it seem that she is quite healthy? At what points in the story does Williams give us further information about her illness? What is the effect of Williams's gradually releasing information?

2. How do the parents' actions interfere with Williams's efforts to diagnose the child? How do their actions increase the suspense of the essay?

3. What elements of Williams's portrayal of himself make him seem like the hero of an adventure tale? How does Williams make the girl into a worthy opponent to test his power?

4. Williams says, "It was a pleasure to attack her [the child]." How does he make us share this pleasure? How does he make us share his "longing for . . . release" from the tension of the story? How does he turn our own pleasure in reading this story against us at the end, making us share his "adult shame" at the love of violence?

WORKING WITH THE TECHNIQUE IN YOUR OWN WRITING

1. Write an essay about a time in your life when you felt quite uncertain about what the future would bring. You might write about the fears that arose when you or someone close to you became ill or about the hopes and desires that grew from some good news or an impending change in your life. You need not focus on months of uncertainty; you could write about an hour's intense doubt and concern. Build the suspense in your essay to make your readers share the hopes and fears that you experienced. What could someone learn from your experience? Barrus believes that living through a trauma, a period of fear and hope, enriches life. Your experience might lead you to a similar—or a very different—conclusion.

2. William Carlos Williams and Celeste Barrus both show us the effects of suspenseful experiences on people, but they differ in their sense of the value of such experiences. Barrus says that her life was enriched, and she shows that her character becomes stronger from having shared her son's trauma. Williams shows a doctor reduced to a dangerous "blind fury" in reaction to his inability to help. Write an essay about how people change when they are placed in situations beyond their control. What makes such experiences valuable or harmful? Structure at least part of your essay to give your readers an experience of suspense (perhaps by using an introductory anecdote that breaks off at a crucial point and is not finished until later).

JOHNNA LYNN BENSON

Brigham Young University
Provo, Utah
Brian S. Best, instructor

Johnna Lynn Benson reports that she drafts most of her papers late at night in her dorm room, a place that "has privacy and yet is near people who will listen to drafts and make comments. . . . I wouldn't recommend my method for writing papers. I need more time to write a paper than most of my friends would. I have to start soon after an assignment is given, and I need time between drafts for my ideas to soak down. I like writing this way because I end up with papers no one else would write—papers that sound like me. And even though I agonize over my papers, I enjoy working at them more than throwing together forgettable papers I never thought about. Some people don't like my kind of paper, and some people includes some professors. It's a choice I made."

Benson's choice to express her own distinctive voice marks virtually every aspect of her life. The eldest of six children, she was born in Santa Monica, California. She explains that the "biggest influence on me was my name, Johnna. It's a combination of my Dad's little-used first name and an unrecognizable portion of my Mom's first name. I always felt like I could take the components of my life and put them together in my own new way." A 1984 graduate of El Camino Real High School in Woodland Hills, California, she has earned two academic scholarships—the Mattel Foundation Scholarship and the Presidential Scholarship at Brigham Young University. "I don't have a career goal," she notes, "except to have a career and be able to write in it."

Benson explains that the assignment for her paper was "basically to pick any topic we'd studied in the writing colloquium and talk about it. In a class that jumped from evolution to psychology to philosophy, . . . I should have felt like I was at a topic banquet. But I didn't feel like I had anything to say. In connection with the class, I had an adviser who had the title 'writing lab instructor,' whom I was supposed to meet by such-and-such a date, topic in hand, to plan my paper. I mixed up my appointments and showed up without a subject as my adviser, Chris, was leaving for work. She sat on her moped and made suggestions for topics—all ideas I had looked at and discarded in disgust. I tried to explain to her that I needed a topic I could 'soapbox' on, yell and scream about injustice and ignorance. (My previous paper had been on homosexuality.) She asked me why, and I tried to explain that I was different, that I couldn't present an idea someone else might have thought of. In groping for an example of how I am unique, I remembered a book we had been reading, George Kelly's A Theory of Personality. Chris said, 'Look at you, you're yelling at me. I think you'd better do your paper on Kelly.' And she buzzed off to work.

"By now," Benson reports, "I had not only made my writing lab instructor late for work but I had also made myself late to math. I found an empty seat in the back of the class, but I have a weakness in not paying attention to a teacher when more than one hundred people separate us. I turned over my homework and started writing about Kelly, or, more accurately, about the things I wanted to say to Chris when she had escaped. I

ended up with a page and a half of sarcasm and jokes, mainly about myself. Later I . . . ended up showing a friend what I wrote. . . . He said he also felt different than everyone else. . . . He showed me that he understood what was under the sarcasm. From then on, I wanted to write the paper using Kelly's Theory of Personality only for what light Kelly threw on the topic of myself. I wanted to make my sometimes abstract sense of uniqueness understandable.''

Three years after writing her prize-winning essay and changing her major from me-chanical engineering (with a minor in modern dance) to physics, classics, and comparative literature, Johnna Lynn Benson left Brigham Young University to establish, as she ex-plains, ''some distance from and a clearer perspective on'' school. Currently working in a medical lab where she writes witty and entertaining memos, Benson plans to return to a university—perhaps UCLA—to ''work on a degree in linguistics.''

For an exercise in peer editing, see Johnna Lynn Benson's essay in Part II.

Rotten at the Core

George A. Kelly's *Theory of Personality* has scrubbed me on a washboard and put me through the wringer. Discovering what I actually am under the dirt and debris has been bewildering and has left me wondering if I would be better off blissfully ignorant. I had thought "to know thyself " an admirable pursuit, especially since I believed truth was beauty. Now I see I have been beautifully wrong about who I am and who everybody else is.

When the colloquium introduced me to *Theory of Personality*, I was sure we would get along great. I have always loved dabbling in psychology. My friends and I would make Freudian jokes or play shrink-games, using those little tests in women's magazines designed to save on psychoanalysis costs. You could say I won those games; my free associations were always more bizarre than anyone else's. I wasn't even trying to be shocking or clever. That is just a bad habit. My only feud with psychology was that I aspired to be more than a product of my environment, a multiplication of Mormonism by a materialistic middle-class suburb. *Theory of Personality* eliminated that limitation for me.

I loved it instantly. Kelly's treatise holds that people create their own per-sonalities. As a person tries to make sense of the circus around him, he picks up on recurring themes in his life and makes deductions about what is going on. The individual creates these explanations, called "constructs," for his con-venience in anticipating what the world is going to hit him with next. As a person construes, he builds an inner road map of himself, of life, and of what he can expect from it. The psychology I had been exposed to before treated man like an organism poked and prodded into reactions. I found the concept of deciding for yourself who you are and what you can expect from life far more palatable. Claiming total responsibility for my outlook on life filled me with satisfaction.

Theory of Personality created a little garden paradise in the corner for me,   4
but it also unearthed something upsetting. As part of our colloquium study of constructs, we were asked to write about our core roles, or how we viewed ourselves. I kept putting the assignment off because every time I started it, my query led me down the same path. If you do not want to go to Rome, finding that all roads go there is rather dismaying. Suddenly it was the day to hand in the assignment, and I discovered, as I frantically wrote the thing in the Harris Fine Arts Center an hour before class, that I had spent enough time trying not to think about it that I knew exactly what I didn't want to know.

With Fresh, Original, and Bizarre as my highest ideals, my core role seems   5
to be that I must be different. And I am different, which makes me exceptional, though not in a way the general population appreciates. This arrogant idea actuates my every thought and emotion, a realization that makes me shudder. Exploring the fact that I'm rotten at the core reduced me to tears.

Yet I can't seem to get around it. I look at how I hate get-acquainted parties.   6
To adhere "Hello, my name is . . ." on my lapel is to assume common ground exists between these strangers and me. But my core role says my lifeline runs geometrically askew to theirs. Kelly defines guilt as an awareness of contradicting one's core role structure, and "guilty" well describes the uncomfortable feeling I get pretending such parties aren't futile. I forget that I actually do share significant parallels and intersections with family and friends. I like the differences. By the time I was six I introduced myself by saying, to the consternation of my playmates, that I did not like chocolate cake or soda pop. For years my favorite color was chartreuse, sienna, or puce. My favorite number is 3.02875×10^{14}. I took up origami because I thought no one had heard of it. In short, anything popular was not worth my time, while anything obscure or new was mine by right.

Moreover, I felt unique enough to assume that although rules were necessary   7
to keep the regulars in line, they did not apply to me. Because rules were necessary, I never quite broke them but found interpretations to suit me. For example, when an elementary class punishment to copy five pages from the dictionary was handed down, my paper always included a few words outside the assigned alphabetical range, like "despot," "toupee," or "maltreatment." Lights-out at camp meant it was dark enough to leave the cabin unnoticed and go for a moonlight walk. Going to parties where friends were too drunk to really notice my abstinence was showing my love and understanding for people with problems, not to mention making them aware of the Mormon Church. And of course, as long as my boyfriend and I didn't go all the way,

whatever we wanted to do was fine. We were toying with the idea of marriage anyway. Other people needed rules. I did not.

I have been carried away with my own individuality enough to hypothesize 8 that when I was a zygote, some stray cosmic ray zapped my DNA, making me a daughter of chance and not of Terry and Dianna Benson. On a similar note, I latched onto the idea that I have always existed, that before I was a spirit I was an entity, an intelligence bobbing out somewhere like a chartreuse soap bubble. I did not want to be someone else's creation. I figured God recognized the special and distinctive thing I was and handpicked me to be his child.

Being Mormon has been convenient in other ways. It is a guaranteed way 9 to stick out like a sore thumb. I always felt a swell of pride as I answered astonished cries of "You've never done such and such?" I could spend hours elaborating on LDS precepts with the sole intent of blowing an innocent Protestant mind. I have had so much fun being Mormon that I have to wonder how much of my testimony is based on faith and how much on the attention it garners. I created my outlook on life according to my convenience, says Kelly. My convenient testimony thus becomes as meaningful as my green argyle earrings; I would probably join any group that boasted of being a peculiar people.

Yet my testimony of the gospel encapsulates some of my strongest emotions 10 and most important rational convictions. I founded my belief on study, contemplation, and prayer, not whim. If such a testimony is invalid, there is little I think or feel that is valid. But I must consider I may have forced my personality to grow in unnatural and indirect ways because I wanted to be different, cultivating a taste for mustard on my french fries and a taste for LDS doctrine. I have created my personality and maybe I could have done a better job. Yet the thought of supplanting myself with a new and improved model based on different criteria scares me. It would be personality suicide; although someone would be here named Johnna, I would cease to exist.

And what about all these other people? I always pictured my intelligence 11 as a chartreuse bubble in contrast with their monochromatic assembly of lemon yellow bubbles. If Kelly gives me the right to be self-made, he also extends that right to all those dumb slobs. Besides, I doubt Kelly was lemon yellow. If he and I can be different, then probably everyone else is on a slightly different wavelength, can be a slightly different color. This means I probably don't stand out at all. I have always understood why people were worried that God might not know them specifically. There was no reason for him to bother when they were all the same. But if everyone is a unique individual, how does Heavenly Father remember which fingerprint I am? In my place in the sun, I did not notice all those stars out there, each one shining bright for someone. I do not feel important or special while gazing at billions of stars.

For the first time in my life I feel truly lost, an electron carrying practically 12
no weight, fairly indistinguishable from any other electron, whose orbit is an
unknown in a probability cloud. I am looking at life in a new and startling
way, and this is the ultimate test of my taste for the new and startling. I find
myself attempting to straddle the importance of my uniqueness and the existence of 4.5 billion other unique individuals. I do not like wondering who I
am. I could always tell before by the stark contrast between me and anyone
else. I had three dimensions and the other person only had two. Now I see
that I just had no depth perception.

How everyone can be different intimidates and amazes me. Without its 13
former base, my sense of identity has become as fragile as the chartreuse soap
bubble I imagine as its beginnings. I fear the existence of all the variegated
personalities that might crowd and pop it. Yet in returning to that sense of
fragile newness, I see the world freshly. I have bemoaned the fact that no one
could appreciate my special outlook. Now I see there are countless other outlooks for me to explore, each a world as strange and wonderful as mine. For
the first time there is an impetus for me to get to know people. This potential
soothes my battered psyche and fills me with wonder in proportion to my fear.

Focusing on Johnna Lynn Benson's Techniques and Revisions

1. Johnna Lynn Benson's instructor, Brian Best, reports that his interdisciplinary
   writing colloquium had been reading George Kelly's A *Theory of Personality*,
   "which discusses the roles, or 'constructs,' people adopt and stresses that all
   of us have alternative possibilities if we are willing to reexamine our constructs
   and experiment with other ways of going about creating our self-identity. We
   had also read Lao-tse, the *Tao Te Ching*, and the *Book of the Hopi*, with the
   intent of getting some idea of how other cultures view their world. All of this
   apparently worked for Johnna, and she found herself in something of an
   identity crisis. Her journal and her rough drafts of this paper became her
   personal battleground with some long-held personal constructs which she began to question." Outline the major points that Johnna Benson makes in her
   essay. How is each of these points specifically connected to her analysis of
   George Kelly's book A *Theory of Personality*? How does Benson use Kelly's
   book to help organize her essay?
2. What assumptions does Benson seem to make about her audience's familiarity
   with A *Theory of Personality*? Where and how does Benson provide her readers
   with information about Kelly's theory? Consider, for example, paragraph 6.
   In writing it, Benson notes that she "spent a great deal of time trying to find
   concrete examples to back up the connection between Kelly's theories and
   my own." How successful is she in this paragraph at accomplishing that goal?

What overriding point does she make about herself in this essay? What examples does she offer to support it? How does she connect it to Kelly's theory? What exactly does she mean when she judges herself to be "rotten at the core"? How does she expect her *audience* to react to her use of this phrase?

3. Benson reports that one of the goals of her essay is "to make my sometimes abstract sense of uniqueness understandable." What specific examples does Benson use to make this abstract notion understandable to her audience? Do these examples suggest that her self-awareness increased gradually or occurred suddenly in a moment of revelation while reading Kelly? Point to specific words and phrases to verify your response.

4. Benson also relies on metaphor to make her "uniqueness understandable" in concrete terms. Reread Benson's essay and identify as many metaphors as you can. Assess the effectiveness of each metaphor. What characteristics and features do these metaphors share? What pattern seems to emerge from these metaphors? With what effect?

5. Another of the many strengths of Benson's essay is the lively, honest voice she uses to address her readers. Figurative language helps make this voice memorable. See, for example, paragraph 1, where she begins, "Kelly's *Theory of Personality* has scrubbed me on a washboard and put me through the wringer." What is the nature of this metaphor? Why is it particularly appropriate to Benson's overall *purpose* in writing? Point to other metaphors with similar effects.

6. In describing how she writes, Benson notes: "I . . . cram initial drafts with jokes and cynical parenthetical comments. They keep me entertained and sometimes evolve into relevant subtopics." For example, in paragraph 2 she says, "My friends and I would make Freudian jokes or play shrink-games, using those little tests in women's magazines designed to save on psychoanalysis costs." What is the nature of Benson's cynicism here? Reread Benson's essay and identify other moments when her voice seems to be marked by lingering traces of "jokes and cynical parenthetical comments." What does each contribute to the overall effectiveness of her essay?

7. Benson explains that she drafted this essay "in sections rather than just plodding through the whole paper. I spent a lot of time on the third paragraph, trying to explain Kelly without getting overtechnical or breaking the tone." Reread that paragraph carefully and evaluate how successful she has been. What writing strategies does she use to avoid being "overtechnical"? How successful is she in maintaining the overall *tone* of her essay in this particular paragraph? Point to specific words and phrases to support your response.

8. In discussing the satisfactions and frustrations of writing this essay, Benson observes: "Finding a way to say what I really mean plagued me in the paragraphs on religious attitudes. I would draft and ask myself, 'Is that what I think?'" Reread paragraphs 7–10. What role have her religious beliefs and

practices played in her increasing self-awareness? What exactly does she mean at the end of paragraph 10 when she talks about "personality suicide"?

9. Benson explains that she worked her way through "one package of notebook paper and half a package of typing paper" as she prepared the multiple drafts of this essay. "I write on every other line in drafts and then cross most everything out. I'm hard on trees." Here is one of Benson's earliest drafts of what became paragraph 6:

> Yet I can't seem to get around it. Kelly defines guilt as "awareness of dislodgement of the self from one's core role structure," a realization that you've contradicted your core role. Guilt can act as a trailmaker pointing to the core role maligned. No wonder I feel guilty at parties where everyone runs around with "Hello, my name is." It's not right for me to act that way, anxious to meet and make friends because people are not my peer group. My lifeline runs geometrically skew, no parallels and no intersections. Of course a logical voice in the back of my head will intone that for me to be so alien to the human race is simply not true. Interactions with family and friends deny the possibility. Logic is thereby, however, ignored. Since I believed I was so set apart, I set myself apart; the conviction was a self-fulfilling prophecy.

Compare and contrast this very early version of paragraph 6 with the final draft of Benson's essay. Which points from this early draft does Benson preserve in the final version and how is each developed? What are the choices she makes as a writer in moving from one draft to another? In what specific ways does Benson's revised version more successfully support the overriding point of her essay? How might her final draft of this paragraph be strengthened further?

10. The conclusion of Benson's essay posed special problems for her. "Some parts were only worked about three times, but the ending had at least twenty attempts. . . . Ending the essay was difficult because I felt I had really reached no conclusions; I had a diagnosis but no prescription." Reread Benson's essay carefully, with special emphasis on the relationship between the final paragraph and the rest of the essay. Show how she is—or is not—accurate in her assessment that her essay provides a "diagnosis but no prescription." Point to specific words and phrases to support your response. If Benson had the opportunity to revise her essay, what specific recommendations would you offer her to help strengthen her final paragraph?

Suggestions for Writing

1. Each of us has had one or more experiences that have fundamentally changed our perceptions of ourselves and of our relationships with those around us. This

changed perception might well have also led to substantial changes either in our way of doing something or in our relationships. Often such changed perceptions can be expressed in metaphorical terms, as Benson uses the image of a "chartreuse soap bubble" to express much of what she thinks of herself. Write an essay in which you use a metaphor to re-create or summarize such an experience. Use the metaphor to reveal your changed perception of yourself and your behavior as well as changes in your relationships.

2. In paragraph 7, Benson notes: "I felt unique enough to assume that although rules were necessary to keep the regulars in line, they did not apply to me. Because rules were necessary, I never quite broke them but found interpretations to suit me." She offers as an example an anecdote about "an elementary class punishment to copy five pages from the dictionary," in which she included several words "outside the alphabetical range." Write an expository essay recounting an incident in your own experience in which you thought that rules did not apply to you. What "lesson" did you learn about yourself—and rules—as a result of this experience?

3. One of the effective features of Benson's essay is her deft use of humor. Psychology and psychiatry have often been the subjects of both cynical and good-spirited humor. Gather as many "professional" jokes about one occupation as you can. What traits do the jokes have in common? Write an *expository* essay using these jokes to illustrate what you take to be the general public's prevailing perception of this profession.

AN EFFECTIVE TECHNIQUE

In developing her essay, Johnna Lynn Benson faced a problem with which every writer is familiar: how to make a vague, abstract concept both understandable and interesting to her readers. She wanted to write about having a "unique personality." She came up with some examples of actions that contribute to her uniqueness, but those examples did not directly define the "spirit" and "intelligence" that she felt were the essential parts of her personality. She might have floundered for many sentences trying to help us understand, but instead she developed a strategy that lets us see at a glance what she means. She thought about a familiar object that her unique personality might be *like* and settled on a "chartreuse soap bubble." This delightful metaphor summarizes much of what she thinks about herself. It certainly presents a picture of "uniqueness," but it also suggests that she views her personality as a fragile container, possibly with nothing inside it. It conveys a tone as well; Benson is lightly mocking herself by using such a lowly, humorous image. The metaphor helps keep her from appearing pretentious when she says she is proud of being "unique." How proud can she be of being a chartreuse soap bubble?

Finding the right *metaphor* can do much more than clarify a vague idea; Benson's metaphoric chartreuse soap bubble ends up coloring her whole essay. Not only does she mention it three times to describe her uniqueness, but she uses variations of its elements—soap, bubbles, and chartreuse—as images to convey other ideas. For example, when she wants to describe everyone else's lack of uniqueness, she speaks of "their monochromatic assembly of lemon yellow bubbles" (paragraph 11). When her sense of how wonderful she is for being unique is destroyed by her realization that every person is also unique, her chartreuse bubble turns into "an electron carrying practically no weight, fairly indistinguishable from any other electron, whose orbit is an unknown in a probability cloud" (paragraph 12). This might seem a completely new image, but many elements of the original bubble are retained: electrons are usually visualized as little spheres, like bubbles, and are light and easily blown about. We can imagine that Benson has simply found a perspective far enough away from her bubbles that their colors can no longer be distinguished and the total collection appears to be a "cloud."

Even Benson's opening sentence touches on her soap metaphors: she says, "Kelly's *Theory of Personality* scrubbed me on a washboard and put me through the wringer." We might think this opening metaphor contradicts the bubble one used later; we cannot scrub a soap bubble and put it through a wringer. The clash between the two images would have been a problem only if she had put them both in the same paragraph; her readers would have mixed up the two pictures and been a bit confused. Although some writers build an entire essay on a single metaphor, most writers do not expect their readers to hold metaphorical images in their minds for much more than one paragraph, and so metaphors need not be consistent in different sections of an essay. Using metaphorical imagery in different ways in different parts of an essay as Benson does even adds a sense of playfulness to an essay; we can see that she is having fun with her words.

By bringing in ordinary objects as metaphors, we can add to our abstract discussions the immediate and varied emotional connotations such objects carry with them. It is easier to make readers laugh at silly soap bubbles than at "uniqueness." Metaphors can also help us discover and clarify our own ideas; they can help extricate us from the dullness of repeating the tired and often meaningless phrases that come to mind when we think about a topic. For example, if we are assigned an essay about the president's defense policy, we might find that all we can think of are the ideas we have read in the papers, and our own feelings about the man and his policy might be lost. We might try making a list of possible terms we could use to end the sentences "The current defense policy is like a. . . ." or "The President is like a. . . ." Political columnists use this technique all the time, and the metaphorical images they invent often have such power that they end up becoming more familiar than the original issue or person they were describing. More people are familiar with the derisive label "Star Wars," taken from a fantasy movie, than with the official name of the government's space-based antimissile program, the Strategic Defense Initiative. During the latter years of the Reagan administration, columnists and cartoonists repeatedly described Ronald Reagan as "the Teflon president" because the numerous scandals involving his aides never seemed to stick to him; he remained a popular and trusted public figure. Besides putting new life into the old phrase "slippery politician," the image of a Teflon man was easy to elaborate into complete satiric essays against Reagan.

Probably the realm that uses metaphors most extensively is science; scientific theories are nothing but elaborately developed metaphors. For example, the image of atoms as little solar systems is a metaphor, as is the image of the retina in the eye as a movie screen. In the next essay, "The World's Biggest Membrane," Lewis Thomas shows one of the basic ways scientists develop their ideas, by borrowing the metaphors or theories from one branch and applying them to another.

ANOTHER ILLUSTRATION OF THE TECHNIQUE

LEWIS THOMAS
The World's Biggest Membrane

"We have language and can build metaphors as skillfully and precisely as ribosomes make proteins," writes Lewis Thomas, a medical researcher who started a new career as an essayist at age fifty-seven. He was worried when he began his first essay because, as he puts it, "the only other writing I'd done was scientific papers, around two hundred of them, composed in the relentlessly flat style required for absolute unambiguity in every word, hideous language as I read it today." He has succeeded in "breaking free of that kind of prose" to become one of the most widely read essayists in the country, though he still thinks of himself as writing mainly for scientists. Now his writing often exploits ambiguity, as he seeks to encourage scientific workers to ponder the broad and uncertain implications of their theories.

The change in Thomas's writing mirrors a change he would like to bring about in the way science is viewed and taught. In this century, he says, "the hard facts have softened, melted away and vanished under the pressure of new hard facts." Scientists have begun to realize that "the conclusions reached in science are always, when looked at closely, far more provisional and tentative than are most of the assumptions arrived at by our colleagues in the humanities. But we do not talk much in public about this, nor do we teach this side of science." Thomas proposes "a new set of courses dealing systematically with ignorance in science. . . . Part of the intellectual equipment of every educated person, however his or her time is going to be spent, ought to be a feel for the queernesses of nature, the inexplicable thing, the side of life for which informed bewilderment will be the best way of getting through the day."

Viewed from the distance of the moon, the astonishing thing about the earth, catching the breath, is that it is alive. The photographs show the dry, pounded surface of the moon in the foreground, dead as an old bone. Aloft, floating free beneath the moist, gleaming membrane of bright blue sky, is the rising earth, the only exuberant thing in this part of the cosmos. If you could look long enough, you would see the swirling of the great drifts of white cloud, covering and uncovering the half-hidden masses of land. If you had been looking for a very long, geologic time, you could have seen the continents themselves in motion, drifting apart on their crustal plates, held afloat by the fire beneath. It has the organized, self-contained look of a live creature, full of information, marvelously skilled in handling the sun.

It takes a membrane to make sense out of disorder in biology. You have to be able to catch energy and hold it, storing precisely the needed amount and releasing it in measured shares. A cell does this, and so do the organelles inside. Each assemblage is poised in the flow of solar energy, tapping off energy from metabolic surrogates of the sun. To stay alive, you have to be able to hold out against equilibrium, maintain imbalance, bank against entropy, and you can only transact this business with membranes in our kind of world.

When the earth came alive it began constructing its own membrane, for the general purpose of editing the sun. Originally, in the time of prebiotic elaboration of peptides and nucleotides from inorganic ingredients in the water on the earth, there was nothing to shield out ultraviolet radiation except the water itself. The first thin atmosphere came entirely from the degassing of the earth as it cooled, and there was only a vanishingly small trace of oxygen in it. Theoretically, there could have been some production of oxygen by photodissociation of water vapor in ultraviolet light, but not much. This process would have been self-limiting, as Urey showed, since the wavelengths needed for photolysis are the very ones screened out selectively by oxygen; the production of oxygen would have been cut off almost as soon as it occurred.

The formation of oxygen had to await the emergence of photosynthetic cells, and these were required to live in an environment with sufficient visible light for photosynthesis but shielded at the same time against lethal ultraviolet.

Berkner and Marshall calculate that the green cells must therefore have been about ten meters below the surface of water, probably in pools and ponds shallow enough to lack strong convection currents (the ocean could not have been the starting place).

You could say that the breathing of oxygen into the atmosphere was the result of evolution, or you could turn it around and say that evolution was the result of oxygen. You can have it either way. Once the photosynthetic cells had appeared, very probably counterparts of today's blue-green algae, the future respiratory mechanism of the earth was set in place. Early on, when the level of oxygen had built up to around 1 percent of today's atmospheric concentration, the anaerobic life of the earth was placed in jeopardy, and the inevitable next stage was the emergence of mutants with oxidative systems and ATP. With this, we were off to an explosive developmental stage in which great varieties of respiring life, including the multicellular forms, became feasible.

Berkner has suggested that there were two such explosions of new life, like vast embryological transformations, both dependent on threshold levels of oxygen. The first, at 1 percent of the present level, shielded out enough ultraviolet radiation to permit cells to move into the surface layers of lakes, rivers, and oceans. This happened around 600 million years ago, at the beginning of the Paleozoic era, and accounts for the sudden abundance of marine fossils of all kinds in the record of this period. The second burst occurred when oxygen rose to 10 percent of the present level. At this time, around 400 million years ago, there was a sufficient canopy to allow life out of the water and onto the land. From here on it was clear going, with nothing to restrain the variety of life except the limits of biologic inventiveness.

It is another illustration of our fantastic luck that oxygen filters out the very bands of ultraviolet light that are most devastating for nucleic acids and proteins, while allowing full penetration of the visible light needed for photosynthesis. If it had not been for this semipermeability, we could never have come along.

The earth breathes, in a certain sense. Berkner suggests that there may have been cycles of oxygen production and carbon dioxide consumption, depending on relative abundances of plant and animal life, with the ice ages representing periods of apnea. An overwhelming richness of vegetation may have caused the level of oxygen to rise above today's concentration, with a corresponding depletion of carbon dioxide. Such a drop in carbon dioxide may have impaired the "greenhouse" property of the atmosphere, which holds in the solar heat otherwise lost by radiation from the earth's surface. The fall in temperature would in turn have shut off much of living, and, in a long sigh, the level of oxygen may have dropped by 90 percent. Berkner speculates that this is what happened to the great reptiles; their size may have been all right for a richly oxygenated atmosphere, but they had the bad luck to run out of air.

Now we are protected against lethal ultraviolet rays by a narrow rim of   9
ozone, thirty miles out. We are safe, well ventilated, and incubated, provided
we can avoid technologies that might fiddle with that ozone, or shift the levels
of carbon dioxide. Oxygen is not a major worry for us, unless we let fly with
enough nuclear explosives to kill off the green cells in the sea; if we do that,
of course, we are in for strangling.

It is hard to feel affection for something as totally impersonal as the at-   10
mosphere, and yet there it is, as much a part and product of life as wine or
bread. Taken all in all, the sky is a miraculous achievement. It works, and for
what it is designed to accomplish it is as infallible as anything in nature. I
doubt whether any of us could think of a way to improve on it, beyond maybe
shifting a local cloud from here to there on occasion. The word "chance" does
not serve to account well for structures of such magnificence. There may have
been elements of luck in the emergence of chloroplasts, but once these things
were on the scene, the evolution of the sky became absolutely ordained.
Chance suggests alternatives, other possibilities, different solutions. This may
be true for gills and swim-bladders and forebrains, matters of detail, but not
for the sky. There was simply no other way to go.

We should credit it for what it is: for sheer size and perfection of function,   11
it is far and away the grandest product of collaboration in all of nature.

It breathes for us, and it does another thing for our pleasure. Each day,   12
millions of meteorites fall against the outer limits of the membrane and are
burned to nothing by the friction. Without this shelter, our surface would long
since have become the pounded powder of the moon. Even though our receptors are not sensitive enough to hear it, there is comfort in knowing that the
sound is there overhead, like the random noise of rain on the roof at night.

Focusing on Lewis Thomas's Use of Metaphor

1. In the first sentence, Thomas says that the earth is "alive." How does he build on
   this metaphor in the rest of the essay? How does Thomas qualify his metaphor,
   backing off from claiming that the earth is actually a living creature (consider, for
   example, the last sentence of paragraph 1 and the first sentence of paragraph 8)?

2. In paragraph 2, Thomas seems to be using "membrane" literally; he describes
   how membranes work in cells. He goes on in paragraph 3 to say that the earth
   has "its own membrane." Which of the properties of actual membranes match
   properties of the earth's "membrane"? How does Thomas's summary of the
   properties of a membrane in paragraph 2 serve to organize the rest of the essay?
   In paragraph 9, Thomas summarizes what he has said about the working of the
   atmosphere. How does he restate the concepts developed in paragraph 2?

3. In paragraphs 5 and 8 Thomas uses "breathing" in its literal sense, to refer to exchange of oxygen and carbon dioxide via lungs. In what sense does the atmosphere literally "breathe"? In what other, metaphorical ways does the atmosphere "breathe"?

4. In paragraph 10, Thomas implies that we should feel "affection" for the atmosphere. How do Thomas's metaphors help us develop feelings about "something as totally impersonal as the atmosphere"? Consider in particular the feelings Thomas creates by saying that the earth is "exuberant" (paragraph 1) and by saying that the earth does things "for our pleasure" (paragraph 12).

WORKING WITH THE TECHNIQUE IN YOUR OWN WRITING

1. Each of us uses certain words fairly often because they seem to capture some qualities that we care about. Some people talk about how "nice" things are; others repeatedly talk about being "free"; some are always complaining about how "limited" most people's thinking is. Johnna Benson obviously thinks often about being "different" and "unique." We usually select for this purpose rather vague terms because they leave us free to develop our own distinctive meanings. Write an essay about a word or phrase that is important to you or to someone you know well. Try to make clear to readers the distinctive meaning that you (or the person you choose) have given the word or phrase. Find some familiar images that you can use as metaphors to specify the meaning; in other words, look for things you could use to finish sentences such as "Being free is like. . . ." or "Limited people are like. . . ." You might make a long list of such comparisons to find one or two that will help your essay. You might make your essay humorous or ironic, mocking the kind of person who would always try to be "nice" or "unique," or you might write seriously, perhaps explaining how everyone should try to remain as "free" as you or your subject.

2. Write an essay about how your view of your own personality has changed. You might write about something that caused such a change, as Benson does, or you might just describe how you gradually revised your sense of yourself. See if you can find some familiar image to represent how you visualized your personality before and after the change. Benson says she changed from seeing herself as a bubble to seeing herself as an electron. A football player might change from thinking of himself as an efficient, self-contained machine to seeing himself as merely a cog in a much larger machine. Try to use the metaphor you decide on—and variations on it—throughout your essay.

3. Practice Lewis Thomas's strategy for developing an unusual view: take a bit of scientific theory that you know and apply it to some entirely unrelated realm. To give you some idea of the possibilities, consider these examples: What is revealed if you consider cell division as a metaphor for the breakup of a friendship? How is the way a skyscraper is built similar to the growth of a crystal?

TERRY L. BURNS

Canisius College
Buffalo, New York
Robert Durante, instructor

Born in Buffalo, New York, Terry Burns is the youngest of nine children. "Being the youngest in a large family made it hard to be taken seriously. I always had things to say, but it was difficult to get anyone to listen. I find writing a better way to say what is on my mind. If I get words just right, I can make people listen." Terry Burns needs no special circumstances or environment to write. "I can write just about anywhere," he notes, "at work, on the bus, in a bar, anywhere but at my desk. . . . All I need is a pen, some paper, and a very large ashtray." Given the size of his family, Burns has no difficulty writing in the midst of commotion: "I know most people like it quiet when they write, but I just can't think when it's quiet. Crank up the stereo and I'm in business." He writes his drafts in longhand and then types only his final version: "I don't type well, and I can lose a thought before I can put it on paper."

A self-described apathetic student in his "younger" years, Burns has become increasingly interested in writing. He majors in English and intends to pursue a career as a freelance writer. Reading a great deal of fiction occupies much of his time away from classes, and he includes Edgar Allan Poe, Dick Francis, Stephen King, Ayn Rand, and Kurt Vonnegut among his favorite writers. "The main difference between reading for pleasure and reading for an assignment," he observes, "is that reading for pleasure can keep me up late and reading for an assignment can put me to sleep early."

Asked to write "a narrative essay from an omniscient point of view," Burns chose, as he reports, "to write about an inspection in basic training. After using almost all of the allotted time, I decided to change the subject to a different aspect of basic training. This essay was started the day before and was finished just hours before it was due." In it, Burns re-creates the response of "a scared eighteen-year-old, far from home," to a violent initiation into military life and ritual.

The Blanket Party

Crickets chirped in the grass surrounding the compound as four men, dressed 1 only in white government issue underwear, made their way through the dark barracks. Airman Goodrich woke as the rough military blanket settled over his head and chest. He tried to move, but the four men held the blanket securely, pinning him to his bunk. His feet kicked as a fifth man rose from his neighboring bunk and began to pummel him to unconsciousness. Goodrich's screams shattered the night, yet no one moved a muscle to help. Though the

76

snoring, which was incessant at night, had stopped abruptly and completely, everyone pretended to sleep. When the screaming and pleading had finally died away, Goodrich was motionless. The moonlight poured through the windows, casting unearthly shadows across his body.

After ten minutes of total silence, the taps on Sgt. Siat's shoes could be 2 heard echoing in the long tile hallway. The fluorescent overhead lights blinked on, momentarily blinding the entire flight. Everyone was standing at "Attention" as Sgt. Siat, perfectly creased and polished, walked the length of the barracks, the taps on his shoes adding an exclamation point to each step. He stopped at Goodrich's bunk and pulled the blood-soaked blanket from his face. As he turned and surveyed the entire flight, Sgt. Siat's lips bent to form a smile that didn't quite reach his eyes. If any concern showed on his face it was certainly not for Goodrich. Why should he waste his concern on Goodrich? He couldn't march, he couldn't make his bed, he couldn't even shine his shoes right. The Sergeant threw the blanket on the foot of Goodrich's bunk, turned on his heel, and headed toward his office to call the base ambulance.

The ambulance arrived, along with two Military Police officers. As the 3 ambulance attendants piled the broken, battered body of Goodrich onto a stretcher, the MPs finished their cursory investigation and left, thinking nothing of the fact that a man could be mercilessly beaten as one hundred men slept on in the same room.

The "Blanket Party" was a rarely mentioned, but highly encouraged method 4 of dealing with malingerers and incompetents. It was the favorite method of some of the "best" instructors. Give extra duty to everyone when one man consistently made mistakes, and eventually some of his peers would visit him in the night. The training missed while in the hospital would cause him to be recycled into a younger flight and then he was someone else's problem. The "Blanket Party" seemed to work just fine when a man could do the work but wouldn't. Airman Goodrich, a meek, nervous, unhealthy-looking young man, just could not do the work. He was easily shaken and seemed on the verge of tears anytime anyone raised his voice. But the men who are your comrades and buddies can easily become your enemies when deprived of even a few of the already meager privileges.

The young men who had joined this organization with the dream of becoming "men" had been betrayed by the people they had trusted. They had in 5 reality become a mob, skulking in the darkness, preying on people as they slept, always making sure to cover their victim's face, not so much to avoid being seen as to avoid seeing. The act of felonious assault is much easier when your victim is faceless. Back at the barracks, life went on as usual, but not for

Goodrich; two flights and two "Blanket Parties" later, Goodrich was discharged for a defective attitude. The men who had assaulted him, as well as those who had looked on, went on to graduate. But Goodrich, his face still swollen and his hair just a shadow on his head, was sent home to face his family.

Focusing on Terry Burns's Techniques and Revisions

1. Terry Burns's advice to other students in first-year writing courses is to "get a good first sentence. A reader can decide if he likes a story very quickly, and you have to hook him as soon as possible." Reread the opening sentence of Burns's essay carefully. In what specific ways does that sentence demonstrate the soundness of his own advice? What features of the sentence encourage— and even impel—his readers to continue reading?

2. Characterize Burns's *point of view* in this essay: Is he detached and objective? Involved and subjective? Some other combination? Where and how is his point of view established? Does it remain consistent throughout the essay? If not, when and how does it change, and with what effect? Support your responses with an analysis of specific words and phrases from the essay.

3. What larger significance does Burns find in the ritual of beating Airman Goodrich? When and how does he signal this significance to his readers? What overall point does he try to make in his essay?

4. What specific strategies does Burns use to broaden the scope of his anger— from the small group of men who beat Goodrich to the larger chain of command that tolerates such methods of discipline? What techniques does Burns employ to condemn both the young men who beat Goodrich and the military system that condones their actions?

5. One of the strengths of Burns's essay is his choice of phrasing and details. Reread Burns's first two paragraphs. How does his choice of phrasing reinforce the ominous story he tells? What, for example, is the effect of his repeating "taps" in paragraph 2? In what other ways is this an effective word choice? Point out additional examples of phrasing and details in these two paragraphs that heighten the effect Burns tries to create.

6. Consider Burns's final paragraph. What is the effect of using the word "organization" in sentence 1? What attitude toward the military does this word choice express? Toward Airman Goodrich? Does Burns's attitude toward the military and toward Goodrich remain the same throughout this paragraph? What issue is embedded in the final sentence? Why would Goodrich's facing his family be an issue, either for him or for Burns? What does the last sentence tell his readers about Burns's attitude toward Goodrich?

7. Burns wrote several drafts of this essay. The following is his first draft of the opening paragraph:

Screams shattered the sleep of one hundred men in the dark barracks as Airman Goodrich pleaded for help. Everyone knew what was happening. Three men were holding a blanket over Goodrich's upper torso and head as the fourth pummeled him into unconsciousness, yet no one moved a muscle to help. Everyone pretended to be asleep, though the snoring, which was incessant at night, had stopped abruptly and completely. When the screaming finally stopped the room was deadly silent. The only sounds to be heard were the chirping of the crickets in the grass surrounding the compound and the ominous buzz of the locust in the trees. Goodrich lay still on his bunk, the moonlight pouring through the windows, casting eerie shadows across his body.

Compare the two drafts of the opening paragraph of this essay. What specific changes do you notice? Comment on the effectiveness of each change. Which version do you prefer? Why?

8. Burns notes that, "while revising is not the easiest part of writing, I find it to be the most satisfying part. Rearranging sentences and searching for just the right word or phrase until I have a clear and concise finished product is very gratifying to me." Here is Burns's last sentence as it stood *before* the final draft: "Airman Goodrich was sent home to face his family, discharged, according to his separation papers, for a 'Defective Attitude.' " Reread the final-draft last sentence and consider the revisions Burns made as he prepared the final draft. Which version do you prefer? Why? How well do the terms *clear* and *concise* apply to his revisions?

Suggestions for Writing

1. The world we live in is filled with various rituals: hazing for fraternities and sororities, joining a team, preparing to jog, studying for exams, and the like. Choose a ritual that is part of your own life and write an essay in which you tell a story about your participation in and reaction to this ritual. Build your essay to lead to a generalization about this ritual.

2. In the final paragraph of his essay, Burns notes that the soldiers who beat Airman Goodrich acted like a mob, "preying on people as they slept, always making sure to cover their victim's face, not so much to avoid being seen as to avoid seeing." Choose a contemporary example of such "faceless" violence and write an essay in which you re-create the nature of the incident and use the incident to draw a generalization about the effects of this incident on those involved and on American society.

3. In an earlier draft of his essay, Terry Burns added a series of sentences to his final paragraph that read, in part: "Goodrich, as well as the rest of these young men, had been betrayed by a group of people they had trusted to show the way to adulthood, to lead them away from the simple world of childhood to the complex world of men." Write an essay in which you argue that the "way to adulthood" should (or should not) include experience with violence. What role should violence play in the move from "the simple world of childhood to the complex world" of adulthood? Support your position with evidence from your own experience and from contemporary world events.

AN EFFECTIVE TECHNIQUE

Terry Burns uses a simple two-part structure for his essay: he tells a story and then states several general points illustrated by that story. He shows us how effective this structure can be, allowing him to combine in five short paragraphs an intense tale of horror and a complex critique of the workings of military organizations. Burns is able to compress so much into his essay because he carefully tailors his story and his generalizations to each other; every detail drives us forward to the conclusions he wants us to draw.

Burns's story moves relentlessly from the particular to the general, taking us from the opening small detail of crickets chirping through wider and wider perspectives, much like a movie camera pulling back farther and farther. At first, we are watching what seems to be the cruelty of a small group of men. In the second and third paragraphs, we realize, however, that these men are part of a conspiracy that involves a whole military base, including the sergeant and the military police. Burns then announces that the actions on this base are typical of a general "method" of discipline in the entire military system.

By the end of the fourth paragraph, Burns has made us angry at a whole institution, not just a few men. Burns then turns his essay back on itself, taking the specific elements of his first four paragraphs and interpreting them in general terms. He returns to the young men we saw in the first paragraph; now he indicts them and all other young men who take part in the military's violent system of discipline, calling them a "mob, skulking in the darkness." The sergeant and MPs of the second and third paragraph are condemned as representative of the entire "organization" that has "betrayed" the "trust" of the youngsters who joined up dreaming of becoming men. Finally, in a subtle last sentence, Burns suggests that much more than the military might be at fault; the families who teach their sons that the military makes men also contribute to the horrible system by shaming the "weaklings" like Airman Goodrich who are driven out of the armed forces.

In his last paragraph, Burns explicitly guides us in how to read his story; he lets us know that it is not simply a macabre tale, but a dramatic illustration, an example that provides insight into the entire military system and the society that supports that system. Burns's tale and his generalizations depend on each other. Without the generalizations, we might dismiss the story as a tale about strange people unlike us; we might not have to think about how our family would treat a young man discharged from the army for "defective attitude" or whether we belong to any organizations that occasionally turn into mobs, perhaps in more subtle ways than vicious night raids. And without the story, the anger in Burns's generalizations would make him seem out of control, a malcontent. Burns needs the intensity of his story to make us accept his description of a standard practice of the military as "felonious assault" on "faceless" victims by a "skulking" mob.

The two-part structure Burns uses is a variant of the most common form for essays. We are used to thinking of essays as composed of generalizations (a "thesis" and "topic sentences") and supporting evidence. Often we think of intertwining these two parts, stating a generalization, then giving evidence, then moving to another generalization and further evidence. Burns shows us the power of arranging all our "evidence" into one intense, long scene and then drawing several generalizations from different parts of that scene. Such a structure is especially useful for essays that grow from a particular experience that we feel gave us broad insights. We could, for example, build a similar essay based on an incident at school that we suddenly realize is typical of the unfeeling nature of the educational system or based on an incident on the tennis court that we realize happens every time we play a sport with middle-aged people who refuse to age gracefully.

Burns's structure can also be reversed, putting the generalization first. If we put the generalization at the beginning, we risk boring readers who are confident that they know what is coming next. George Orwell, in the next selection, shows a way to use a generalization as a kind of foreshadowing, to direct readers to the point of a story without giving it away. He tells his readers that his tale will reveal the "basis of imperialism," but he leaves it to the reader to figure out how the story does so. His general statement merely invites readers to consider every element in the story as possibly having broad significance, and in doing so he adds a secondary pleasure to our enjoyment of his tale, that of figuring out a secret, hidden message.

ANOTHER ILLUSTRATION OF THE TECHNIQUE

GEORGE ORWELL

Shooting an Elephant

Eric Blair (who took the pen name George Orwell) believed that events in his adult life, not his natural inclinations, determined the kind of writer he became: "In a peaceful age I might have written ornate or merely descriptive books, and might have remained almost unaware of my political loyalties. As it is I have been forced into becoming a sort of pamphleteer. First I spent five years in an unsuitable profession (the Indian Imperial Police, in Burma) and then I underwent poverty and the sense of failure." Orwell's first few books, published in the early 1930s, were full of his anger at the English government but also full, he says, "of purple passages in which words were used partly for the sake of their sound." Then he fought in the Spanish civil war in 1936 and discovered both the subject and the style he would explore for the rest of his life. He says, "Every line of serious work that I have written since 1936 has been written, directly or indirectly, against totalitarianism and for democratic socialism. . . . What I have most wanted to do . . . is to make political writing into an art." He succeeded, producing two of the best known and most influential twentieth-century books on politics, the satiric fable Animal Farm *and the science fiction novel* Nineteen Eighty-Four. *Orwell fought as much for clear language as against totalitarianism, and he felt the two goals were intimately tied together. To write well, in any form, was in Orwell's view a political act, an effort to counter the "mass of lies, evasions, folly, hatred, and schizophrenia" that is too often the language of politics.*

In Moulmein, in lower Burma, I was hated by large numbers of people — the only time in my life that I have been important enough for this to happen to me. I was sub-divisional police officer of the town, and in an aimless, petty kind of way anti-European feeling was very bitter. No one had the guts to raise a riot, but if a European woman went through the bazaars alone somebody would probably spit betel juice over her dress. As a police officer I was an obvious target and was baited whenever it seemed safe to do so. When a nimble Burman tripped me up on the football field and the referee (another Burman) looked the other way, the crowd yelled with hideous laughter. This happened more than once. In the end the sneering yellow faces of young men that met me everywhere, the insults hooted after me when I was at a safe distance, got badly on my nerves. The young Buddhist priests were the worst of all. There were several thousands of them in the town and none of them seemed to have anything to do except stand on street corners and jeer at Europeans.

All this was perplexing and upsetting. For at that time I had already made up my mind that imperialism was an evil thing and the sooner I chucked up my job and got out of it the better. Theoretically—and secretly, of course—I was all for the Burmese and all against their oppressors, the British. As for the job I was doing, I hated it more bitterly than I can perhaps make clear. In a job like that you see the dirty work of Empire at close quarters. The wretched prisoners huddling in the stinking cages of the lock-ups, the gray, cowed faces of the long-term convicts, the scarred buttocks of the men who had been flogged with bamboos—all these oppressed me with an intolerable sense of guilt. But I could get nothing into perspective. I was young and ill educated and I had had to think out my problems in the utter silence that is imposed on every Englishman in the East. I did not even know that the British Empire is dying, still less did I know that it is a great deal better than the younger empires that are going to supplant it. All I knew was that I was stuck between my hatred of the empire I served and my rage against the evil-spirited little beasts who tried to make my job impossible. With one part of my mind I thought of the British Raj as an unbreakable tyranny, as something clamped down, in *saecula saeculorum*, upon the will of prostrate peoples; with another part I thought that the greatest joy in the world would be to drive a bayonet into a Buddhist priest's guts. Feelings like these are the normal by-products of imperialism; ask any Anglo-Indian official, if you can catch him off duty.

One day something happened which in a roundabout way was enlightening. It was a tiny incident in itself, but it gave me a better glimpse than I had had before of the real nature of imperialism—the real motives for which despotic governments act. Early one morning the sub-inspector at a police station the other end of the town rang me up on the phone and said that an elephant was ravaging the bazaar. Would I please come and do something about it? I did not know what I could do, but I wanted to see what was happening and I got on to a pony and started out. I took my rifle, an old .44 Winchester and much too small to kill an elephant, but I thought the noise might be useful *in terrorem*. Various Burmans stopped me on the way and told me about the elephant's doings. It was not, of course, a wild elephant, but a tame one which had gone "must." It had been chained up, as tame elephants always are when their attack of "must" is due, but on the previous night it had broken its chain and escaped. Its mahout, the only person who could manage it when it was in that state, had set out in pursuit, but had taken the wrong direction and was now twelve hours' journey away, and in the morning the elephant had

suddenly reappeared in the town. The Burmese population had no weapons
and were quite helpless against it. It had already destroyed somebody's bamboo
hut, killed a cow, and raided some fruit-stalls and devoured the stock; also it
had met the municipal rubbish van and, when the driver jumped out and took
to his heels, had turned the van over and inflicted violences upon it.

The Burmese sub-inspector and some Indian constables were waiting for me   4
in the quarter where the elephant had been seen. It was a very poor quarter,
a labyrinth of squalid bamboo huts, thatched with palm-leaf, winding all over
a steep hillside. I remember that it was a cloudy, stuffy morning at the beginning of the rains. We began questioning the people as to where the elephant
had gone and, as usual, failed to get any definite information. That is invariably
the case in the East; a story always sounds clear enough at a distance, but the
nearer you get to the scene of events the vaguer it becomes. Some of the
people said that the elephant had gone in one direction, some said that he
had gone in another, some professed not even to have heard of any elephant.
I had almost made up my mind that the whole story was a pack of lies, when
we heard yells a little distance away. There was a loud, scandalized cry of "Go
away, child! Go away this instant!" and an old woman with a switch in her
hand came round the corner of a hut, violently shooing away a crowd of naked
children. Some more women followed, clicking their tongues and exclaiming;
evidently there was something that the children ought not to have seen. I
rounded the hut and saw a man's dead body sprawling in the mud. He was an
Indian, a black Dravidian coolie, almost naked, and he could not have been
dead many minutes. The people said that the elephant had come suddenly
upon him round the corner of the hut, caught him with its trunk, put its foot
on his back and ground him into the earth. This was the rainy season and the
ground was soft, and his face had scored a trench a foot deep and a couple of
yards long. He was lying on his belly with arms crucified and head sharply
twisted to one side. His face was coated with mud, the eyes wide open, the
teeth bared and grinning with an expression of unendurable agony. (Never tell
me, by the way, that the dead look peaceful. Most of the corpses I have seen
looked devilish.) The friction of the great beast's foot had stripped the skin
from his back as neatly as one skins a rabbit. As soon as I saw the dead man
I sent an orderly to a friend's house nearby to borrow an elephant rifle. I had
already sent back the pony, not wanting it to go mad with fright and throw
me if it smelt the elephant.

The orderly came back in a few minutes with a rifle and five cartridges, and   5
meanwhile some Burmans had arrived and told us that the elephant was in
the paddy fields below, only a few hundred yards away. As I started forward
practically the whole population of the quarter flocked out of the houses and

followed me. They had seen the rifle and were all shouting excitedly that I was going to shoot the elephant. They had not shown much interest in the elephant when he was merely ravaging their homes, but it was different now that he was going to be shot. It was a bit of fun to them, as it would be to an English crowd; besides they wanted the meat. It made me vaguely uneasy. I had no intention of shooting the elephant—I had merely sent for the rifle to defend myself if necessary—and it is always unnerving to have a crowd following you. I marched down the hill, looking and feeling a fool, with the rifle over my shoulder and an ever-growing army of people jostling at my heels. At the bottom, when you got away from the huts, there was a metaled road and beyond that a miry waste of paddy fields a thousand yards across, not yet plowed but soggy from the first rains and dotted with coarse grass. The elephant was standing eight yards from the road, his left side toward us. He took not the slightest notice of the crowd's approach. He was tearing up bunches of grass, beating them against his knees to clean them, and stuffing them into his mouth.

I had halted on the road. As soon as I saw the elephant I knew with perfect 6 certainty that I ought not to shoot him. It is a serious matter to shoot a working elephant—it is comparable to destroying a huge and costly piece of machinery—and obviously one ought not to do it if it can possibly be avoided. And at that distance, peacefully eating, the elephant looked no more dangerous than a cow. I thought then and I think now that his attack of "must" was already passing off; in which case he would merely wander harmlessly about until the mahout came back and caught him. Moreover, I did not in the least want to shoot him. I decided that I would watch him for a little while to make sure that he did not turn savage again, and then go home.

But at that moment I glanced round at the crowd that had followed me. It 7 was an immense crowd, two thousand at the least and growing every minute. It blocked the road for a long distance on either side. I looked at the sea of yellow faces above the garish clothes—faces all happy and excited over this bit of fun, all certain that the elephant was going to be shot. They were watching me as they would watch a conjurer about to perform a trick. They did not like me, but with the magical rifle in my hands I was momentarily worth watching. And suddenly I realized that I should have to shoot the elephant after all. The people expected it of me and I had got to do it; I could feel their two thousand wills pressing me forward, irresistibly. And it was at this moment, as I stood there with the rifle in my hands, that I first grasped the hollowness, the futility of the white man's dominion in the East. Here was I, the white man with his gun, standing in front of the unarmed native crowd— seemingly the leading actor of the piece; but in reality I was only an absurd puppet pushed to and fro by the will of those yellow faces behind. I perceived in this moment that when the white man turns tyrant it is his own freedom that he destroys. He becomes a sort of hollow, posing dummy, the conventionalized figure of a sahib. For it is the condition of his rule that he shall spend his life in trying to impress the "natives," and so in every crisis he has got to do what the "natives" expect of him. He wears a mask, and his face grows to fit it. I had got to shoot the elephant. I had committed myself to doing it when I sent for the rifle. A sahib has got to act like a sahib; he has got to appear resolute, to know his own mind and do definite things. To come all that way, rifle in hand, with two thousand people marching at my heels, and then to trail feebly away, having done nothing—no, that was impossible. The crowd would laugh at me. And my whole life, every white man's life in the East, was one long struggle not to be laughed at.

But I did not want to shoot the elephant. I watched him beating his bunch   8
of grass against his knees with that preoccupied grandmotherly air that elephants have. It seemed to me that it would be murder to shoot him. At that age I was not squeamish about killing animals, but I had never shot an elephant and never wanted to. (Somehow it always seems worse to kill a *large* animal.) Besides, there was the beast's owner to be considered. Alive, the elephant was worth at least a hundred pounds; dead, he would only be worth the value of his tusks, five pounds, possibly. But I had got to act quickly. I turned to some experienced-looking Burmans who had been there when we arrived, and asked them how the elephant had been behaving. They all said the same thing: he took no notice of you if you left him alone, but he might charge if you went too close to him.

It was perfectly clear to me what I ought to do. I ought to walk up to within,   9
say, twenty-five yards of the elephant and test his behavior. If he charged, I could shoot; if he took no notice of me, it would be safe to leave him until the mahout came back. But also I knew that I was going to do no such thing. I was a poor shot with a rifle and the ground was soft mud into which one would sink at every step. If the elephant charged and I missed him, I should have about as much chance as a toad under a steamroller. But even then I was not thinking particularly of my own skin; only of the watchful yellow faces behind. For at that moment, with the crowd watching me, I was not afraid in the ordinary sense, as I would have been if I had been alone. A white man mustn't be frightened in front of "natives"; and so, in general, he isn't frightened. The sole thought in my mind was that if anything went wrong those two thousand Burmans would see me pursued, caught, trampled on, and reduced to a grinning corpse like that Indian up the hill. And if that happened it was quite probable that some of them would laugh. That would never do.

There was only one alternative. I shoved the cartridges into the magazine and lay down on the road to get a better aim.

The crowd grew very still, and a deep, low, happy sigh, as of people who see the theater curtain go up at last, breathed from innumerable throats. They were going to have their bit of fun after all. The rifle was a beautiful German thing with cross-hair sights. I did not then know that in shooting an elephant one would shoot to cut an imaginary bar running from ear-hole to ear-hole. I ought, therefore, as the elephant was sideways on, to have aimed straight at his ear-hole; actually I aimed several inches in front of this, thinking the brain would be further forward.

When I pulled the trigger I did not hear the bang or feel the kick—one never does when a shot goes home—but I heard the devilish roar of glee that went up from the crowd. In that instant, in too short a time, one would have thought, even for the bullet to get there, a mysterious, terrible change had come over the elephant. He neither stirred nor fell, but every line of his body had altered. He looked suddenly stricken, shrunken, immensely old, as though the frightful impact of the bullet had paralyzed him without knocking him down. At last, after what seemed a long time—it might have been five seconds, I dare say—he sagged flabbily to his knees. His mouth slobbered. An enormous senility seemed to have settled upon him. One could have imagined him thousands of years old. I fired again into the same spot. At the second shot he did not collapse but climbed with desperate slowness to his feet and stood weakly upright, with legs sagging and head drooping. I fired a third time. That was the shot that did for him. You could see the agony of it jolt his whole body and knock the last remnant of strength from his legs. But in falling he seemed for a moment to rise, for as his hind legs collapsed beneath him he seemed to tower upward like a huge rock toppling, his trunk reaching skyward like a tree. He trumpeted, for the first and only time. And then down he came, his belly toward me, with a crash that seemed to shake the ground even where I lay.

I got up. The Burmans were already racing past me across the mud. It was obvious that the elephant would never rise again, but he was not dead. He was breathing very rhythmically with long rattling gasps, his great mound of a side painfully rising and falling. His mouth was wide open—I could see far down into caverns of pale pink throat. I waited a long time for him to die, but his breathing did not weaken. Finally I fired my two remaining shots into the spot where I thought his heart must be. The thick blood welled out of him like red velvet, but still he did not die. His body did not even jerk when the shots hit him, the tortured breathing continued without a pause. He was dying, very slowly and in great agony, but in some world remote from me where not even a bullet could damage him further. I felt that I had got to put an end to that dreadful noise. It seemed dreadful to see the great beast lying there, powerless to move and yet powerless to die, and not even to be able to finish him. I sent back for my small rifle and poured shot after shot into his heart and down his throat. They seemed to make no impression. The tortured gasps continued as steadily as the ticking of a clock.

In the end I could not stand it any longer and went away. I heard later that 13 it took him half an hour to die. Burmans were bringing dahs and baskets even before I left, and I was told they had stripped his body almost to the bones by the afternoon.

Afterward, of course, there were endless discussions about the shooting of 14 the elephant. The owner was furious, but he was only an Indian and could do nothing. Besides, legally I had done the right thing, for a mad elephant has to be killed, like a mad dog, if its owner fails to control it. Among the Europeans opinion was divided. The older men said I was right, the younger men said it was a damn shame to shoot an elephant for killing a coolie, because an elephant was worth more than any damn Coringhee coolie. And afterward I was very glad that the coolie had been killed; it put me legally in the right and it gave me a sufficient pretext for shooting the elephant. I often wondered whether any of the others grasped that I had done it solely to avoid looking a fool.

Focusing on George Orwell's Use of Generalizations

1. Orwell's first two paragraphs form a kind of mini-essay that seems to give the standard reasons why imperialism is bad. What examples does Orwell provide in these paragraphs of what is wrong with imperialism? What criticisms of imperialism does he state? How does he indicate that his view is more complicated than these criticisms?

2. In the third paragraph Orwell promises that the "tiny" incident he is going to relate will give a glimpse of "the real nature of imperialism—the real motives for which despotic governments act." What do you expect him to reveal as those real motives?

3. As you read the story, almost everything in it could be interpreted in the light of Orwell's promised generalization as giving insight into imperialism. It is possible to develop several different interpretations; here are some questions that could lead you to two different ones. After considering these two possibilities, see if you can put the two interpretations together into a complex generalization about the real nature of imperialism.

   a. How is Orwell's relationship to the Burmese in the crowd like the relationship of England to its colonies? How does Orwell treat the crowd tyrannically? What are his feelings about the crowd (look especially at the last line)? How could you generalize Orwell's feelings about the crowd into an insight about what motivates imperialism?

b. How is Orwell's relationship to the elephant like the relationship of an imperial power to a colony? What despotic act does Orwell perform in relation to the elephant? What are Orwell's feelings about the elephant? How could you generalize Orwell's feelings about the elephant into an insight about what motivates imperialism?

WORKING WITH THE TECHNIQUE IN YOUR OWN WRITING

1. Write a narrative essay about a specific incident that you either participated in or observed that seemed to you to reveal some general truth. You might write about something that happened at school or during a sporting event that led you to a fresh insight into school or sports. Or you might write about comments you heard people make while watching a TV news broadcast as a way of leading up to a conclusion about how most Americans live in a world of fantasy. You might begin with the story and then move to generalizations at the end, or you might indicate in the beginning what you feel the incident reveals in general and then leave it to your readers to draw the appropriate conclusions.

2. Write a fable, that is, a story designed to prove a point that you state as a "moral" at the end. Fables often use very simple stories, usually with animals representing humans. You can make your story as much a fantasy as you wish (perhaps even science fiction). Try to make every detail of the story contribute to leading the readers to your moral, but without allowing readers to guess too readily what is to come.

CURTIS CHANG

Harvard University
Cambridge, Massachusetts
Judith Cohen, instructor

Curtis Chang immigrated to the United States from Taiwan with his parents and two older sisters in 1971. He attended school in the Chicago area, and it was there that he was first encouraged to write well: "My teachers were probably the biggest factor in encouraging me to write. In elementary school, they often assigned creative writing assignments, and my teachers usually enjoyed my stories and, more importantly, told me so." After enrolling in Harvard University, Chang founded the Harvard Minority Student Alliance. A government major with a special interest in political philosophy, Chang also serves as a member of both the Asian-American Association and the Harvard Parliamentary Debate Society, contributes to the Harvard Political Review, coordinates Investigative Bible Studies for the Harvard-Radcliffe Christian Fellowship, and works as a volunteer at the University's Lutheran Homeless Shelter. "While I have no definite career plans," Chang reports, "I would like to be connected with public policy and to work at a job which would concentrate on public speaking and writing skills."

"The easiest thing for me to do when I write is to organize the structure of my thought. My mind works in a very analytical fashion, and with every paper my mind will immediately break a topic down into its constituent parts." Chang relies on an outline to begin his essays: "I compose the outline on a paper in my head. But after that point, I must see my thoughts on the computer screen. I find it difficult to manipulate thoughts unless I can physically manipulate the words that represent them." Like many writers, Chang identifies the most difficult part of writing as "forcing myself to stop organizing and researching." He tries to overcome this tendency by, as he puts it, "setting imaginary deadlines for myself."

Asked to write a "convincing, well documented, engaging essay in support of a clearly defined proposition," Curtis Chang drew his topic, as he reports, "mostly from my personal dealings with black, radical Christians at Harvard. As I listened to them discuss the issue of race in America, I realized that it wasn't clear to them (or to me) where Asian-Americans fit into the picture." His goal in writing "Streets of Gold: The Myth of the Model Minority" was "both educative and stimulative. I wished to explain to everyone the true socio-economic condition of Asian-Americans and expose how we are being used for ideological reasons. I also hoped to stimulate further thought on Asian-American issues, to interest others in subjecting our situation to intellectual scrutiny."

For another view of Curtis Chang's essay, see Part II.

Streets of Gold:
The Myth of the Model Minority

Over 100 years ago, an American myth misled many of my ancestors. Seek- 1
ing cheap labor, railroad companies convinced numerous Chinese that American streets were paved with gold. Today, the media portrays Asian-Americans
as finally mining those golden streets. Major publications like *Time, Newsweek,*
U.S. News and World Report, Fortune, the *New Republic,* the *Wall Street Journal,*
and *The New York Times* have all recently published congratulatory "Model
Minority" headline stories with such titles:

> America's Super Minority
> An American Success Story
> A Model Minority
> Why They Succeed
> The Ultimate Assimilation
> The Triumph of the Asian Americans

But the Model Minority is another "Streets of Gold" tale. It distorts Asian- 2
Americans' true status and ignores our racial handicaps. And the Model Minority's ideology is even worse than its mythology. It attempts to justify the
existing system of racial inequality by blaming the victims rather than the
system itself.

The Model Minority myth introduces us as an ethnic minority that is finally 3
"making it in America" (*Time,* July 8, 1985). The media consistently defines
"making it" as achieving material wealth, wealth that flows from our successes
in the workplace and the schoolroom. This economic achievement allegedly
proves a minority can "lay claim to the American dream" (*Fortune,* Nov. 24,
1986).

Trying to show how "Asian-Americans present a picture of affluence and 4
economic success" (*N.Y. Times Magazine,* Nov. 30, 1986), 9 out of 10 of the
major Model Minority stories of the last four years relied heavily on one statistic: the family median income. The median Asian-American family income,
according to the U.S. Census Survey of Income and Education data, is $22,713
compared to $20,800 for white Americans. Armed with that figure, national
magazines have trumpeted our "remarkable, ever-mounting achievements"
(*Newsweek,* Dec. 6, 1982).

Such assertions demonstrate the truth of the aphorism "Statistics are like a 5
bikini. What they reveal is suggestive, but what they conceal is vital." The
family median income statistic conceals the fact that Asian-American families
generally (1) have more children and live-in relatives and thus have more

mouths to feed; (2) are often forced by necessity to have everyone in the family work, averaging *more* than two family income earners (whites only have 1.6) (Cabezas, 1979, p. 402); and (3) live disproportionately in high cost of living areas (i.e., New York, Chicago, Los Angeles, and Honolulu) which artificially inflate income figures. Dr. Robert S. Mariano, professor of economics at the University of Pennsylvania, has calculated that

> When such appropriate adjustments and comparisons are made, a different and rather disturbing picture emerges, showing indeed a clearly disadvantaged group. . . . Filipino and Chinese men *are no better off than black men with regard to median incomes.* (Mariano, 1979, p. 55)[1]

Along with other racial minorities, Asian-Americans are still scraping for the crumbs of the economic pie.

Throughout its distortion of our status, the media propagates two crucial   6 assumptions. First, it lumps all Asian-Americans into one monolithic, homogeneous, yellow skinned mass. Such a view ignores the existence of an incredibly disadvantaged Asian-American underclass. Asians work in low income and low status jobs 2 to 3 times more than whites (Cabezas, 1979, p. 438). Recent Vietnamese refugees in California are living like the Appalachian poor. While going to his Manhattan office, multimillionaire architect I. M. Pei's car passes Chinese restaurants and laundries where 72% of all New York Chinese men still work (U.S. Bureau of the Census, 1977, Table 7).

But the media makes an even more dangerous assumption. It suggests that   7 (alleged) material success is the same thing as basic racial equality. Citing that venerable family median income figure, magazines claim Asian-Americans are "obviously nondisadvantaged folks" (*Fortune*, May 17, 1982). Yet a 1979 United States Equal Employment Opportunity Commission study on Asian-Americans discovered widespread anti-Asian hiring and promotion practices. Asian-Americans "in the professional, technical, and managerial occupations" often face "modern racism—the subtle, sophisticated, systemic patterns and practices . . . which function to effect and to obscure the discriminatory outcomes" (Nishi, 1979, p. 398). One myth simply does not prove another: neither our "astonishing economic prosperity" (*Fortune*, Nov. 24, 1986) nor a racially equal America exist.

An emphasis on material success also pervades the media's stress on Asian-   8 Americans' educational status at "the top of the class" (*Newsweek on Campus*, April 1984). Our "march into the ranks of the educational elite" (*U.S. News*, April 2, 1984) is significant because "all that education is paying off spectacularly" (*Fortune*, Nov. 24, 1986). Once again, the same fallacious assumptions plague this "whiz kids" image of Asian-Americans.

The media again ignores the fact that class division accounts for much of   9 the publicized success. Until 1976, the U.S. Immigration Department only admitted Asian immigrants that were termed "skilled" workers. "Skilled" generally meant college educated, usually in the sciences since poor English would not be a handicap. The result was that the vast majority of pre-1976 Asian immigrants came from already well-educated, upper-class backgrounds—the classic "brain drain" syndrome (Hirschman and Wong, 1981, pp. 507–510).

The post-1976 immigrants, however, come generally from the lower, less 10 educated classes (Kim, 1986, p. 24). A study by Professor Elizabeth Ahn Toupin of Tufts University matched similar Asian and non-Asian students *along class lines* and found that Asian-Americans "did not perform at a superior academic level to non-Asian students. Asian-Americans were more likely to be placed on academic probation than their white counterparts . . . twice as many Asian American students withdrew from the university" (Toupin, 1986, p. 12).

Thus, it is doubtful whether the perceived widespread educational success 11 will continue as the Asian-American population eventually balances out along class lines. When 16.2% of all Chinese have less than 4 years of schooling (*four times* that of whites) (Azores, 1979, p. 73), it seems many future Asian-Americans will worry more about being able to read a newspaper rather than a Harvard acceptance letter.

Most important, the media assumes once again that achieving a certain 12 level of material or educational success means achieving real equality. People easily forget that to begin with, Asians invest heavily in education since other means of upward mobility are barred to them by race. Until recently, for instance, Asian-Americans were barred from unions and traditional lines of credit (Yun, 1986, pp. 23–24).[2] Other "white" avenues to success, such as the "old boy network," are still closed to Asian-Americans.

When *Time* (July 8, 1985) claims "as a result of their academic achievement 13 Asians are climbing the economic ladder with remarkable speed," it glosses over an inescapable fact: there is a white ladder and then there is a yellow one. Almost all of the academic studies on the *actual returns Asians receive* from their education point to prevalent discrimination. A striking example of this was found in a City University of New York research project which constructed resumes with equivalent educational backgrounds. Applications were then sent to employers, one group under an Asian name and a similar group under a Caucasian name. Whites received interviews 5 times more than Asians

(Nishi, 1979, p. 399). The media never headlines even more shocking data that can be easily found in the U.S. Census. For instance, Chinese and Filipino males only earned respectively 74 and 52 percent as much as their *equally educated* white counterparts. Asian females fared even worse. Their salaries were only 44 to 54 percent as large as equivalent white males' paychecks (Cabezas, 1979, p. 391). Blacks suffer from this same statistical disparity. We Asian-Americans are indeed a Model Minority—a perfect model of racial discrimination in America.

Yet this media myth encourages neglect of our pressing needs. "Clearly,   14 many Asian-Americans and Pacific peoples are invisible to the governmental agencies," one state agency reported. "Discrimination against Asian-Americans and Pacific peoples is as much the result of omission as commission" (California State Advisory Committee, 1975, p. 75). In 1979, while the president praised Asian-Americans' "successful integration into American society," his administration revoked Asian-Americans' eligibility for minority small business loans, devastating thousands of struggling, newly arrived small businessmen. Hosts of other minority issues, ranging from reparations for the Japanese American internment to the ominous rise of anti-Asian violence, are widely ignored by the general public.

The media, in fact, insist to the general populace that we are not a true   15 racial minority. In its attack on affirmative action, the *Boston Globe* (Jan. 14, 1985) pointed out that universities, like many people, "obviously feel that Asian-Americans, especially those of Chinese and Japanese descent, are brilliant, privileged, and wrongly classified as minorities." Harvard Dean Henry Rosovsky remarked in the same article that "It does not seem to me that as a group, they are disadvantaged. . . . Asian-Americans appear to be in an odd category among other protected minorities."

The image that we Asians aren't like "other minorities" is fundamental to   16 the Model Minority ideology. Any elementary school student knows that the teacher designates one student the model, the "teacher's pet" in order to set an example for others to follow. One only sets up a "model minority" in order to communicate to the other "students," the blacks and Hispanics, "Why can't you be like that?" The media, in fact, almost admit to "grading" minorities as they headline Model Minority stories, "Asian-Americans: Are They Making the Grade?" (*U.S. News*, April 2, 1984). And Asians have earned the highest grade by fulfilling one important assignment: identifying with the white majority, with its values and wishes.

Unlike blacks, for instance, we Asian-Americans have not vigorously as-   17 serted our ethnic identity (a.k.a. Black Power). And the American public has historically demanded assimilation over racial pluralism.[3] Over the years,

Newsweek has published titles from "Success Story: Outwhiting the Whites" (*Newsweek*, June 21, 1971) to "Ultimate Assimilation" (*Newsweek*, Nov. 24, 1986), which lauded the increasing number of Asian-White marriages as evidence of Asian-Americans' "acceptance into American society."

Even more significant is the public's approval of how we have succeeded in 18 the "American tradition" (*Fortune*, Nov. 24, 1986). Unlike the blacks and Hispanics, we "Puritan-like" Asians (*N.Y. Times Magazine*, Nov. 30, 1986) disdain governmental assistance. A *New Republic* piece, "America's Greatest Success Story" (July 15, 1985), similarly applauded how "Asian-Americans pose no problems at all." The media consistently compares the crime-ridden image of other minorities with the picture of law abiding Asian parents whose "well-behaved kids" (*Newsweek on Campus*, April 1984) hit books and not the streets.

Some insist there is nothing terrible about whites conjuring up our "tre- 19 mendous" success, divining from it model American traits, then preaching, "Why can't you Blacks and Hispanics be like that?" After all, one might argue, aren't those traits desirable?

Such a view, as mentioned, neglects Asian-Americans' true and pressing 20 needs. Moreover, this view completely misses the Model Minority image's fundamental ideology, an ideology meant to falsely grant America absolution from its racial barriers.

David O. Sears and Donald R. Kinder, two social scientists, have recently 21 published significant empirical studies on the underpinnings of American racial attitudes. They consistently discovered that Americans' stress on "values, such as 'individualism and self-reliance, the work ethic, obedience, and discipline' . . . can be invoked, however perversely, to feed racist appetites" (Kennedy, 1987, p. 88). In other words, the Model Minority image lets Americans' consciences rest easy. They can think: "It's not our fault those blacks and Hispanics can't make it. They're just too lazy. After all, look at the Asians."[4] Consequently, American society never confronts the systemic racial and economic factors underlying such inequality. The victims instead bear the blame.

This ideology behind the Model Minority image is best seen when we ex- 22 amine one of the first Model Minority stories, which suddenly appeared in the mid 1960s. It is important to note that the period was marked by newfound, strident black demands for equality and power.

> At a time when it is being proposed that hundreds of bil-
> lions be spent to uplift Negroes and other minorities, the
> nation's 300,000 Chinese Americans are moving ahead on
> their own—with no help from anyone else . . . few
> Chinese-Americans are getting welfare handouts—or even

want them . . . they don't sit around moaning. (*U.S. News*, Dec. 26, 1966)

The same article then concludes that the Chinese American history and accomplishment "would shock those now complaining about the hardships endured by today's Negroes" (*U.S. News*, Dec. 26, 1966).

Not surprisingly, the dunce-capped blacks and Hispanics resent us apple 23 polishing, "well-behaved" teacher's pets. Black comedian Richard Pryor performs a revealing routine in which new Asian immigrants learn from whites their first English word: "Nigger." And Asian-Americans themselves succumb to the Model Minority's deceptive mythology and racist ideology.[5] "I made it without help," one often hears among Asian circles, "why can't they?" In a 1986 nationwide poll, only 27% of Asian-American students rated "racial understanding" as "essential." The figure plunged 9% in the last year alone (a year marked by a torrent of Model Minority stories) (Hune, 1987). We "whitewashed" Asians have simply lost our identity as a fellow, disadvantaged minority.

But we don't even need to look beyond the Model Minority stories themselves to realize that whites see us as "whiter" than blacks — but not quite white enough. For instance, citing that familiar median family income figure, *Fortune* magazine of May 17, 1982, complained that Asian-Americans are in fact "getting *more* than its share of the pie." For decades, when white Americans were leading the nation in every single economic measure, editorials arguing that whites were getting more than *their* share of the pie were rather rare.

No matter how "well behaved" we are, Asian-Americans are still excluded 25 from the real pie, the "positions of institutional power and political power" (Kuo, 1979, p. 289). Professor Harry Kitano of UCLA has written extensively on the plight of Asian-Americans as the "middleman minority," a minority supposedly satisfied materially but forever racially barred from a true, *significant* role in society. Empirical studies indicate that Asian-Americans "have been channeled into lower-echelon white-collar jobs having little or no decision making authority" (Suzuki, 1977, p. 38). For example, in *Fortune*'s 1,000 largest companies, Asian-American nameplates rest on a mere half of one percent of all officers' and directors' desks (a statistical disparity worsened by the fact that most of the Asians founded their companies) (*Fortune*, Nov. 24, 1986). While the education of the upper-class Asians may save them from the bread lines, their race still keeps them from the boardroom.

Our docile acceptance of such exclusion is actually one of our "model" traits. 26 When Asian-Americans in San Francisco showed their first hint of political activism and protested Asian exclusion from city boards, the *Washington*

Monthly (May 1986) warned in a long Asian-American article, "Watch out, here comes another group to pander to." The *New Republic* (July 15, 1985) praised Asian-American political movements because

> Unlike blacks or Hispanics, Asian-American politicians have the luxury of not having to devote the bulk of their time to an "Asian-American agenda," and thus escape becoming prisoners of such an agenda. . . . The most important thing for Asian-Americans . . . is simply being part of the process.

This is strikingly reminiscent of another of the first Model Minority stories:

> As the Black and Brown communities push for changes in the present system, the Oriental is set forth as an example to be followed—a minority group that has achieved success through adaptation rather than confrontation. (*Gidra*, 1969)

But it is precisely this "present system," this system of subtle, persistent 27 racism that we all must confront, not adapt to. For example, we Asians gained our right to vote from the 1964 Civil Rights Act that blacks marched, bled, died, and in the words of that original Model Minority story, "sat around moaning for." Unless we assert our true identity as a minority and challenge racial misconceptions and inequalities, we will be nothing more than techno-coolies—collecting our wages but silently enduring basic political and economic inequality.

This country perpetuated a myth once. Today, no one can afford to dreamily 28 chase after that gold in the streets, oblivious to the genuine treasure of racial equality. When racism persists, can one really call any minority a "model"?

Notes

1. The picture becomes even more disturbing when one realizes that higher income figures do not necessarily equal higher quality of life. For instance, in New York Chinatown, more than 1 out of 5 residents work more than 57 hours per week, almost 1 out of 10 elderly must labor more than 55 hours per week. (Nishi, 1979, p. 503).

2. For further analysis on the role racism plays in Asian-Americans' stress on education and certain technical and scientific fields, see Suzuki, 1977, p. 44.

3. A full discussion of racial pluralism vs. assimilation is impossible here. But suffice it to say that pluralism accepts ethnic cultures as equally different; assimilation asks for a "melting" into the majority. An example of the assimilation philosophy is the massive "Americanization" programs of the late 1800s which successfully erased Eastern European immigrants' customs in favor of Anglo-Saxon ones.

4. This phenomenon of blaming the victim for racial inequality is as old as America itself. For instance, Southerners once eased their consciences over slavery by labeling blacks as animals

lacking humanity. Today, America does it by labeling them as inferior people lacking "desirable" traits. For an excellent further analysis of this ideology, actually widespread among American intellectuals, see *Iron Cages: Race and Culture in 19th-Century America* by Ronald T. Takaki.

5. America has a long history of playing off one minority against the other. During the early 1900s, for instance, mining companies in the west often hired Asians solely as scabs against striking black miners. Black versus Asian hostility and violence usually followed. This pattern was repeated in numerous industries. In a larger historical sense, almost every immigrant group has assimilated, to some degree, the culture of anti-Black racism.

List of Sources

Azores, Fortunata M., "Census Methodology and the Development of Social Indicators for Asian and Pacific Americans," *U.S. Commission on Civil Rights: Testimony on Civil Rights Issues of Asian and Pacific Americans* (1979), pp. 70–79.

Boston Globe, "Affirmative Non-actions," Jan. 14, 1985, p. 10.

Cabezas, Dr. Armado, "Employment Issues of Asian Americans," *U.S. Commission on Civil Rights: Testimony on Civil Rights Issues of Asian and Pacific Americans* (1979), pp. 389–399, 402, 434–444.

California State Advisory Committee to the U.S. Commission on Civil Rights, *Asian American and Pacific Peoples: A Case of Mistaken Identity* (1975) (quoted in Chun, 1980, p. 7).

Chun, Ki-Taek, "The Myth of Asian American Success and Its Educational Ramifications," *IRCD Bulletin* (Winter/Spring 1980).

Dutta, Manoranjan, "Asian/Pacific American Employment Profile: Myth and Reality—Issues and Answers," *U.S. Commission on Civil Rights: Testimony on Civil Rights Issues of Asian and Pacific Americans* (1979), pp. 445–489.

Fortune: "America's Super Minority," Nov. 24, 1986, pp. 148–149; "Working Smarter," May 17, 1982, p. 64.

Gidra (1969), pp. 6–7 (quoted in Chun, p. 7).

Hirschman, Charles, and Wong, Morrison, "Trends in Socioeconomic Achievement Among Immigrant and Native-Born Asian-Americans, 1960–1976," *The Sociological Quarterly* (Autumn 1981), pp. 495–513.

Hune, Shirley, keynote address, East Coast Asian Student Union Conference, Boston University, Feb. 14, 1987.

Kahng, Dr. Anthony, "Employment Issues," *U.S. Commission on Civil Rights: Testimony on Civil Rights Issues of Asian and Pacific Americans* (1979), pp. 411–413.

Kennedy, David M., "The Making of a Classic, Gunnar Myrdal and Black-White Relations: The Use and Abuse of An *American Dilemma*," *The Atlantic* (May 1987), pp. 86–89.

Kiang, Peter, professor of sociology, University of Massachusetts, Boston, personal interview, May 1, 1987.

Kim, Illsoo, "Class Division Among Asian Immigrants: Its Implications for Social Welfare Policy," *Asian American Studies: Contemporary Issues, Proceedings from East Coast Asian American Scholars Conference* (1986), pp. 24–25.

Kuo, Wen H. "On the Study of Asian-Americans: Its Current State and Agenda," *Sociological Quarterly* (1979), pp. 279–290.

Mariano, Dr. Robert S., "Census Issues," *U.S. Commission on Civil Rights: Testimony on Civil Rights Issues of Asian and Pacific Americans* (1979), pp. 54–59.

New Republic, "The Triumph of Asian Americans" (July 15–22, 1985), pp. 24–31.

The New York Times Magazine, "Why They Succeed" (Nov. 30, 1986), pp. 72 +.

Newsweek: "The Ultimate Assimilation" (Nov. 24, 1986), p. 80; "Asian-Americans: A 'Model Minority' " (Dec. 6, 1982), pp. 39–51; "Success Story: Outwhiting the Whites" (June 21, 1971), pp. 24–25.

Newsweek on Campus: "Asian Americans, the Drive to Excel" (April 1984), pp. 4–13.

Nishi, Dr. Setsuko Matsunaga, "Asian American Employment Issues: Myths and Realities," *U.S. Commission on Civil Rights: Testimony on Civil Rights Issues of Asian and Pacific Americans* (1979), pp. 397–399, 495–507.

Sung, Betty Lee, *Chinese American Manpower and Employment* (1975).

Suzuki, Bob H., "Education and the Socialization of Asian Americans: A Revisionist Analysis of the 'Model Minority' Thesis," *Ameriasia Journal,* vol. 4, issue 2 (1977), pp. 23–51.

Time, "To America with Skills" (July 8, 1985), p. 42.

Toupin, Dr. Elizabeth Ahn, "A Model University for A 'Model Minority,' " *Asian American Studies: Contemporary Issues, Proceedings from East Coast Asian American Scholars Conference* (1986), pp. 10–12.

U.S. Bureau of the Census, *Survey of Minority-Owned Business Enterprises* (1977) (as quoted in Cabezas, p. 443).

U.S. News & World Report: "Asian-Americans, Are They Making the Grade?" (April 2, 1984), pp. 41–42; "Success Story of One Minority Group in U.S." (Dec. 26, 1966), pp. 6–9.

Washington Monthly, "The Wrong Way to Court Ethnics" (May 1986), pp. 21–26.

Yun, Grace, "Notes from Discussions on Asian American Education," *Asian American Studies: Contemporary Issues, Proceedings from East Coast Asian American Scholars Conference* (1986), pp. 20–24.

Focusing on Curtis Chang's Techniques and Revisions

1. What is the "clearly defined proposition" Curtis Chang was expected to present in this essay? Where is it stated? Outline the principal points Chang uses to support the proposition. Assess the effectiveness of each point.

2. Among Chang's many achievements in this essay is his ability to move so readily from the abstract to the concrete and to summarize facts into tightly constructed, highly memorable images. Point to specific examples of Chang's ability to move effectively from the abstract to the concrete. Point also to as many examples as possible of highly memorable images that Chang has created in this essay. Comment, for example, on the effectiveness of such images as "statistics are like a bikini. What they reveal is suggestive, but what they conceal is vital" (paragraph 5). Explain how such images are essential components in building the structure—and the persuasiveness—of Chang's essay.

3. Consider the qualities of and the discernible patterns in Chang's research. What strategies, for example, does he use to lead his readers beyond the stereotypical images of Asian-Americans in this nation's mass-circulated weekly magazines? How does Chang employ stereotypical images of Asian-Americans in the print and electronic media not only to challenge—and clarify—the assumptions of these images but also to complicate the matter of Asian-American identity?

4. Curtis Chang reports that he envisioned two distinct audiences for his essay: "(1) Asian-Americans who were unaware of their own people's true condition, and (2) the wider, white audience who may have unknowingly accepted the ideology inherent in the Model Minority image." As you reread Chang's essay,

identify and comment on the effectiveness of the specific strategies Chang uses to address both groups. Which group, for example, does he seem to spend more time addressing? Point to specific passages to support your response.

5. Chang explains that he approached both audiences as "skeptics, since many Asian-Americans are just as ignorant and just as 'white' in attitude as Caucasians. Thus, I knew I had to avoid the rhetoric and catchphrases which often typify my end of the political spectrum. . . . I tried to work from their beginning assumptions and avoid alienating the reader from the outset. For instance, my argument superficially begins as an argument against a media stereotype. However, I tried to weave in the idea that what was at stake was not just a simple media mistake, but the definite racial ideology of the entire nation." Reread the opening of Chang's essay and trace how he develops this argument. Comment on its effectiveness.

6. For Curtis Chang, revising means "more than just the usual forms of correcting grammar and spelling and using one adjective instead of another. For myself, revising means acting as a devil's advocate and trying to pick apart my paper's argument. Then I have to answer to those criticisms." In reviewing the revisions he made in the multiple drafts of his essay, Chang observed, "I think perhaps that I used a bit too many empirical arguments (to convince the audience of Asian-Americans' true situation) at the expense of further developing the ideological implications of the Model Minority." Do you agree with Chang's assessment of his revisions? Point to specific passages to support your response.

7. Compare Curtis Chang's essay with Johnna Lynn Benson's and Karen Kramer's. How does each writer use images to present his or her point? Which writer most clearly and effectively relates these images to the purpose of the essay?

Suggestions for Writing

1. Read through several past issues of your favorite weekly or monthly magazine. Examine carefully the advertisements, the articles, and the editorial content of that magazine. What collective image(s) of Asian-Americans can you identify in those pages? Write an essay in which you (1) make an assertion about the current image of Asian-Americans in that magazine and (2) assess the racial and ideological implications of that image. If you prefer, you may substitute contemporary American films or television shows for a magazine.

2. Go to the reference section of the library and choose a popular American magazine that has published continuously from the late nineteenth century to the present (*Saturday Evening Post*, *Harper's*, and *Ladies' Home Journal* are but three of numerous possibilities). Choose a year between 1890 and 1920 and follow the basic procedure outlined in the first suggestion for writing. Do the same for a year between 1980 and the present. Write an expository essay in

which you document what changes, if any, occurred in the depiction of Asian-Americans in the popular magazine.

3. Consider the many myths about minority groups and sports that continue to be passed from the occupant of one bar stool to another—or of one living room chair to another—during the viewing of television's seemingly marathon fall weekend sports coverage. Choose one such media stereotype and write an argumentative essay in which you (1) document the nature and the extent of the stereotype of a minority group's identity and performance in a particular sport and (2) draw some conclusions about the limitations of that stereotype.

AN EFFECTIVE TECHNIQUE

We can feel Curtis Chang's confidence from the beginning of his essay: he is even willing to stack the odds against himself by giving in his first paragraph a formidable list of major news publications that stand opposed to what he is going to prove. We can imagine that his confidence grows not only from his belief that he is ready to dissect every detail of the opposing arguments but also from his impressive collection of evidence to balance the weight of those authoritative journals. However, he takes risks with the very subtlety of his arguments and the weight of his own evidence; he could swamp his readers in waves of facts and figures and make them dizzy with intricate swirls of logic. Chang has developed a superb strategy for keeping the emotional center of his argument alive through all the formal evidence: he repeatedly summarizes his main points in powerful small images. These images translate the generalities and statistics of the debate into familiar scenes that we can understand immediately. For example, after presenting three long paragraphs full of numbers that show that the economic situation of Asian-Americans cannot be accurately assessed by merely looking at their average income, Chang summarizes what he has proved by saying, "While going to his Manhattan office, multimillionaire architect I. M. Pei's car passes Chinese restaurants and laundries where 72% of all New York Chinese men still work." We see at a glance Chang's point.

Once Chang has developed an image to summarize one of his arguments, he builds on it later in his essay. For example, in paragraph 16, he compares those who speak of a "model minority" to unfair teachers: "Any elementary school student knows that the teacher designates one student the model, the 'teacher's pet' in order to set an example for others to follow." At that point, he is explaining how the ideology of the "model minority" leads politicians to conclude that Asians do not suffer from discrimination at all. Seven paragraphs later, he uses his image again to explain how talk of model minorities sets one minority against another: "Not surprisingly, the dunce capped blacks and Hispanics resent us apple polishing, 'well behaved' teacher's pets."

Chang's images reveal the passionate and personal consequences of the statistics he has assembled. We can imagine that Chang has been in classrooms where he has felt the resentment of blacks and Hispanics. Yet it does not seem that Chang is distorting his facts due to his personal bias, principally because his images are tied so tightly to the facts and figures he uses in his arguments. Chang shows us that to be "objective" does not require that writers have no feelings, but rather that they examine all the facts to decide what to be passionate about. Chang's images show a very deep understanding of both sides of the issue he is considering. Especially powerful is the way that Chang turns the very words of his opponents against them. He structures the entire essay to expose a myth, to uncover an illusion propagated by others. His images are a crucial part of his exposure; they translate the formal praise of respectable journalists into familiar terms to make visible the hidden meanings buried within those formal words.

It takes confidence to allow yourself to put your own images in the midst of detailed statistics and subtle analyses of public issues and especially to claim that your images reveal the truth behind the complex words used by others. You have to believe that your own way of understanding issues is as important as the words of the authorities you quote. But if you do not believe that, if you hope that facts and figures can speak on their own while you hide offstage because you do not belong in the world of impressive persons who debate real issues, you will simply not be arguing; you will be giving a report on what others have said or collecting numbers for other people to argue about. Curtis Chang does not merely examine intellectual patterns; he argues for something about which he cares passionately.

Aldous Huxley, in "Words and Behavior," also translates some of the words of public discourse into vivid images so that we can see the kinds of lies and evasions that allow politicians and ordinary citizens to "enjoy the luxury of behaving badly with a good conscience."

ANOTHER ILLUSTRATION OF THE TECHNIQUE

ALDOUS HUXLEY

Words and Behavior

Huxley intended as a youth to enter the medical profession, but a disease of the eyes left him temporarily blind at sixteen, so he instead studied English literature at Oxford. He went on to become a renowned and prolific man of letters, writing essays, fiction, and poetry, as well as criticism of painting, music, and literature. Huxley wrestled all his life with one problem: how "to transform a detached intellectual skepticism into a way of harmonious all-round living." Skepticism dominated his early writings (until 1930), in which he wittily dissected British society; the search for harmony dominated his later works (until his death in 1963), in which he created visions of mystical worlds, sometimes produced under the influence of hallucinogenic drugs. His early love of science colored all his works, producing a precision of analysis and a desire for order that often conflicted with an equally strong desire to free the human mind (and society) from all inhibiting rules. Huxley's description of the ideal essay reflects this conflict: "Free association artistically controlled—this is the paradoxical secret of . . . [the] best essays. One damned thing after another—but in a sequence that in some miraculous way develops a central theme and relates it to the rest of human experience."

Words form the thread on which we string our experiences. Without them 1 we should live spasmodically and intermittently. Hatred itself is not so strong that animals will not forget it, if distracted, even in the presence of the enemy. Watch a pair of cats, crouching on the brink of a fight. Balefully the eyes glare; from far down in the throat of each comes bursts of a strange, strangled noise of defiance; as though animated by a life of their own, the tails twitch and tremble. With aimed intensity of loathing! Another moment and surely there must be an explosion. But no; all of a sudden one of the two creatures turns away, hoists a hind leg in a more than fascist salute and, with the same fixed and focused attention as it had given a moment before to its enemy, begins to make a lingual toilet. Animal love is as much at the mercy of distractions as animal hatred. The dumb creation lives a life made up of discreet and mutually irrelevant episodes. Such as it is, the consistency of human characters is due to the words upon which all human experiences are strung. We are purposeful because we can describe our feelings in remembrable words, can justify and rationalize our desires in terms of some kind of argument. Faced by an enemy we do not allow an itch to distract us from our emotions; the mere word "enemy" is enough to keep us reminded of our hatred, to convince us that we do well to be angry. Similarly the word "love" bridges for us those chasms of momentary indifference and boredom which gape from time to time between even the most ardent lovers. Feeling and desire provide us with our motive power; words give continuity to what we do and to a considerable extent determine our direction. Inappropriate and badly chosen words vitiate thought and lead to wrong or foolish conduct. Most ignorances are vincible, and in the greater number of cases stupidity is what the Buddha pronounced it to be, a sin. For, consciously, or subconsciously, it is with deliberation that we do not know or fail to understand—because incomprehension allows us, with a good conscience, to evade unpleasant obligations and responsibilities, because ignorance is the best excuse for going on doing what one likes, but ought not, to do. Our egotisms are incessantly fighting to preserve themselves, not only from external enemies, but also from the assaults of the other and better self with which they are so uncomfortably associated. Ignorance is egotism's most effective defense against that Dr. Jekyll in us who desires perfection; stupidity, its subtlest stratagem. If, as so often happens, we choose to give continuity to our experience by means of words which falsify the facts, this is because the falsification is somehow to our advantage as egotists.

Consider, for example, the case of war. War is enormously discreditable to those who order it to be waged and even to those who merely tolerate its existence. Furthermore, to developed sensibilities the facts of war are revolting and horrifying. To falsify these facts, and by so doing to make war seem less evil than it really is, and our own responsibility in tolerating war less heavy, is doubly to our advantage. By suppressing and distorting the truth, we protect our sensibilities and preserve our self-esteem. Now, language is, among other things, a device which men use for suppressing and distorting the truth. Finding the reality of war too unpleasant to contemplate, we create a verbal alternative to that reality, parallel with it, but in quality quite different from it. That which we contemplate thenceforward is not that to which we react emotionally and upon which we pass our moral judgments, is not war as it is in fact, but the fiction of war as it exists in our pleasantly falsifying verbiage. Our stupidity in using inappropriate language turns out, on analysis, to be the most refined cunning. 2

The most shocking fact about war is that its victims and its instruments are individual human beings, and that these individual human beings are condemned by the monstrous conventions of politics to murder or be murdered in quarrels not their own, to inflict upon the innocent and, innocent themselves of any crime against their enemies, to suffer cruelties of every kind. 3

The language of strategy and politics is designed, so far as it is possible, to 4
conceal this fact, to make it appear as though wars were not fought by individuals drilled to murder one another in cold blood and without provocation,
but either by impersonal and therefore wholly nonmoral and impassible forces,
or else by personified abstractions.

Here are a few examples of the first kind of falsification. In place of "cav- 5
alrymen" or "foot-soldiers" military writers like to speak of "sabres" and "rifles."
Here is a sentence from a description of the Battle of Marengo: "According to
Victor's report, the French retreat was orderly; it is certain, at any rate, that
the regiments held together, for the six thousand Austrian sabres found no
opportunity to charge home." The battle is between sabres in line and muskets
in echelon—a mere clash of ironmongery.

On other occasions there is no question of anything so vulgarly material as 6
ironmongery. The battles are between Platonic ideas, between the abstractions
of physics and mathematics. Forces interact; weights are flung into scales;
masses are set in motion. Or else it is all a matter of geometry. Lines swing
and sweep; are protracted or curved; pivot on a fixed point.

Alternatively the combatants are personal, in the sense that they are per- 7
sonifications. There is "the enemy," in the singular, making "his" plans, striking "his" blows. The attribution of personal characteristics to collectivities, to
geographical expressions, to institutions, is a source, as we shall see, of endless
confusions in political thought, of innumerable political mistakes and crimes.
Personification in politics is an error which we make because it is to our
advantage as egotists to be able to feel violently proud of our country and of
ourselves as belonging to it, and to believe that all the misfortunes due to our
own mistakes are really the work of the Foreigner. It is easier to feel violently
toward a person than toward an abstraction; hence our habit of making political
personifications. In some cases military personifications are merely special instances of political personifications. A particular collectivity, the army or the
warring nation, is given the name and, along with the name, the attributes of
a single person, in order that we may be able to love or hate it more intensely
than we could do if we thought of it as what it really is: a number of diverse
individuals. In other cases personification is used for the purpose of concealing
the fundamental absurdity and monstrosity of war. What is absurd and monstrous about war is that men who have no personal quarrel should be trained
to murder one another in cold blood. By personifying opposing armies or
countries, we are able to think of war as a conflict between individuals. The
same result is obtained by writing of war as though it were carried on exclusively
by the generals in command and not by the private soldiers in their armies.
("Rennenkampf had pressed back von Schubert.") The implication in both

cases is that war is indistinguishable from a bout of fisticuffs in a bar room.
Whereas in reality it is profoundly different. A scrap between two individuals
is forgivable; mass murder, deliberately organized, is a monstrous iniquity. We
still choose to use war as an instrument of policy; and to comprehend the full
wickedness and absurdity of war would therefore be inconvenient. For, once
we understood, we should have to make some effort to get rid of the abominable
thing. Accordingly, when we talk about war, we use a language which conceals
or embellishes its reality. Ignoring the facts, so far as we possibly can, we imply
that battles are not fought by soldiers, but by things, principles, allegories,
personified collectivities, or (at the most human) by opposing commanders,
pitched against one another in single combat. For the same reason, when we
have to describe the processes and the results of war, we employ a rich variety
of euphemisms. Even the most violently patriotic and militaristic are reluctant
to call a spade by its own name. To conceal their intentions even from themselves, they make use of picturesque metaphors. We find them, for example,
clamoring for war planes numerous and powerful enough to go and "destroy
the hornets in their nests"—in other words, to go and throw thermite, high
explosives and vesicants upon the inhabitants of neighboring countries before
they have time to come and do the same to us. And how reassuring is the
language of historians and strategists! They write admiringly of those military
geniuses who know "when to strike at the enemy's line" (a single combatant
deranges the geometrical constructions of a personification); when to "turn his
flank"; when to "execute an enveloping movement." As though they were
engineers discussing the strength of materials and the distribution of stresses,
they talk of abstract entities called "man power" and "fire power." They sum
up the long-drawn sufferings and atrocities of trench warfare in the phrase, "a
war of attrition"; the massacre and mangling of human beings is assimilated to
the grinding of a lens.

A dangerously abstract word, which figures in all discussions about war, is   8
"force." Those who believe in organizing collective security by means of military pacts against a possible aggressor are particularly fond of this word. "You
cannot," they say, "have international justice unless you are prepared to impose
it by force." "Peace-loving countries must unite to use force against aggressive
dictatorships." "Democratic institutions must be protected, if need be, by
force." And so on.

Now, the word "force," when used in reference to human relations, has no   9
single, definite meaning. There is the "force" used by parents when, without
resort to any kind of physical violence, they compel their children to act or
refrain from acting in some particular way. There is the "force" used by at-

tendants in an asylum when they try to prevent a maniac from hurting himself or others. There is the "force" used by the police when they control a crowd, and that other "force" which they used in a baton charge. And finally there is the "force" used in war. This, of course, varies with the technological devices at the disposal of the belligerents, with the policies they are pursuing, and with the particular circumstances of the war in question. But in general it may be said that, in war, "force" connotes violence and fraud used to the limit of the combatants' capacity.

Variations in quantity, if sufficiently great, produce variations in quality. 10 The "force" that is war, particularly modern war, is very different from the "force" that is police action, and the use of the same abstract word to describe the two dissimilar processes is profoundly misleading. (Still more misleading, of course, is the explicit assimilation of a war, waged by allied League-of-Nations powers against an aggressor, to police action against a criminal. The first is the use of violence and fraud without limit against innocent and guilty alike; the second is the use of strictly limited violence and a minimum of fraud exclusively against the guilty.)

Reality is a succession of concrete and particular situations. When we think 11 about such situations we should use the particular and concrete words which apply to them. If we use abstract words which apply equally well (and equally badly) to other, quite dissimilar situations, it is certain that we shall think incorrectly.

Let us take the sentences quoted above and translate the abstract word 12 "force" into language that will render (however inadequately) the concrete and particular realities of contemporary warfare.

"You cannot have international justice, unless you are prepared to impose 13 it by force." Translated, this becomes: "You cannot have international justice unless you are prepared, with a view to imposing a just settlement, to drop thermite, high explosives and vesicants upon the inhabitants of foreign cities and to have thermite, high explosives and vesicants dropped in return upon the inhabitants of your cities." At the end of this proceeding, justice is to be imposed by the victorious party—that is, if there is a victorious party. It should be remarked that justice was to have been imposed by the victorious party at the end of the last war. But, unfortunately, after four years of fighting, the temper of the victors was such that they were quite incapable of making a just settlement. The Allies are reaping in Nazi Germany what they sowed at Versailles. The victors of the next war will have undergone intensive bombardments with thermite, high explosives and vesicants. Will their temper be better than that of the Allies in 1918? Will they be in a fitter state to make a just settlement? The answer, quite obviously, is: No. It is psychologically all but impossible that justice should be secured by the methods of contemporary warfare.

The next two sentences may be taken together. "Peace-loving countries 14 must unite to use force against aggressive dictatorships. Democratic institutions must be protected, if need be, by force." Let us translate. "Peace-loving countries must unite to throw thermite, high explosives and vesicants on the inhabitants of countries ruled by aggressive dictators. They must do this, and of course abide the consequences, in order to preserve peace and democratic institutions." Two questions immediately propound themselves. First, is it likely that peace can be secured by a process calculated to reduce the orderly life of our complicated societies to chaos? And, second, is it likely that democratic institutions will flourish in a state of chaos? Again, the answers are pretty clearly in the negative.

By using the abstract word "force," instead of terms which at least attempt 15 to describe the realities of war as it is today, the preachers of collective security through military collaboration disguise from themselves and from others, not only the contemporary facts, but also the probable consequences of their favorite policy. The attempt to secure justice, peace and democracy by "force" seems reasonable enough until we realize, first, that this noncommittal word stands, in the circumstances of our age, for activities which can hardly fail to result in social chaos; and second, that the consequences of social chaos are injustice, chronic warfare and tyranny. The moment we think in concrete and particular terms of the concrete and particular process called "modern war," we see that a policy which worked (or at least didn't result in complete disaster) in the past has no prospect whatever of working in the immediate future. The attempt to secure justice, peace and democracy by means of a "force," which means, at this particular moment of history, thermite, high explosives and vesicants, is about as reasonable as the attempt to put out a fire with a colorless liquid that happens to be, not water, but petrol.

What applies to the "force" that is war applies in large measure to the 16 "force" that is revolution. It seems inherently very unlikely that social justice and social peace can be secured by thermite, high explosives and vesicants. At first, it may be, the parties in a civil war would hesitate to use such instruments on their fellow-countrymen. But there can be little doubt that, if the conflict were prolonged (as it probably would be between the evenly balanced Right and Left of a highly industrialized society), the combatants would end by losing their scruples.

The alternatives confronting us seem to be plain enough. Either we invent 17 and conscientiously employ a new technique for making revolutions and settling international disputes; or else we cling to the old technique and, using "force" (that is to say, thermite, high explosives and vesicants), destroy ourselves. Those who, for whatever motive, disguise the nature of the second alternative under inappropriate language, render the world a grave disservice. They lead us into one of the temptations we find it hardest to resist—the temptation to run away from reality, to pretend that facts are not what they are. Like Shelley (but without Shelley's acute awareness of what he was doing) we are perpetually weaving

> A shroud of talk to hide us from the sun
> Of this familiar life.

We protect our minds by an elaborate system of abstractions, ambiguities, metaphors and similes from the reality we do not wish to know too clearly; we lie to ourselves, in order that we may still have the excuse of ignorance, the alibi of stupidity and incomprehension, possessing which we can continue with a good conscience to commit and tolerate the most monstrous crimes:

> The poor wretch who has learned his only prayers
> From curses, who knows scarcely words enough
> To ask a blessing from his Heavenly Father,
> Becomes a fluent phraseman, absolute
> And technical in victories and defeats,
> And all our dainty terms for fratricide;
> Terms which we trundle smoothly o'er our tongues
> Like mere abstractions, empty sounds to which
> We join no meaning and attach no form!
> As if the soldier died without a wound:
> As if the fibers of this godlike frame
> Were gored without a pang: as if the wretch
> Who fell in battle, doing bloody deeds,
> Passed off to Heaven translated and not killed;
> As though he had no wife to pine for him,
> No God to judge him.

The language we use about war is inappropriate, and its inappropriateness 18 is designed to conceal a reality so odious that we do not wish to know it. The language we use about politics is also inappropriate; but here our mistake has a different purpose. Our principal aim in this case is to arouse and, having aroused, to rationalize and justify such intrinsically agreeable sentiments as pride and hatred, self-esteem and contempt for others. To achieve this end we speak about the facts of politics in words which more or less completely misrepresent them.

The concrete realities of politics are individual human beings, living to- 19
gether in national groups. Politicians—and to some extent we are all politicians—substitute abstractions for these concrete realities, and having done
this, proceed to invest each abstraction with an appearance of concreteness
by personifying it. For example, the concrete reality of which "Britain" is the
abstraction consists of some forty-odd millions of diverse individuals living on
an island off the west coast of Europe. The personification of this abstraction
appears, in classical fancy-dress and holding a very large toasting fork, on the
backside of our copper coinage; appears in verbal form, every time we talk
about international politics. "Britain," the abstraction from forty millions of
Britons, is endowed with thoughts, sensibilities and emotions, even with a
sex—for, in spite of John Bull, the country is always a female.

Now, it is of course possible that "Britain" is more than a mere name—is 20
an entity that possesses some kind of reality distinct from that of the individuals
constituting the group to which the name is applied. But this entity, if it
exists, is certainly not a young lady with a toasting fork; nor is it possible to
believe (though some eminent philosophers have preached the doctrine) that
it should possess anything in the nature of a personal will. One must agree
with T. H. Green that "there can be nothing in a nation, however exalted
its mission, or in a society however perfectly organized, which is not in the
persons composing the nation or the society. . . . We cannot suppose a national spirit and will to exist except as the spirit and will of individuals." But
the moment we start resolutely thinking about our world in terms of individual
persons we find ourselves at the same time thinking in terms of universality.
"The great rational religions," writes Professor Whitehead, "are the outcome
of the emergence of a religious consciousness that is universal, as distinguished
from tribal, or even social. Because it is universal, it introduces the note of
solitariness." (And he might have added that, because it is solitary, it introduces the note of universality.) "The reason of this connection between universality and solitude is that universality is a disconnection from immediate
surroundings." And conversely the disconnection from immediate surroundings, particularly such social surrounding as the tribe or nation, the insistence
on the person as the fundamental reality, leads to the conception of an all-
embracing unity.

A nation, then, may be more than a mere abstraction, may possess some 21
kind of real existence apart from its constituent members. But there is no
reason to suppose that it is a person; indeed, there is every reason to suppose
that it isn't. Those who speak as though it were a person (and some go further
than this and speak as though it were a personal god) do so, because it is to
their interest as egotists to make precisely this mistake.

In the case of the ruling class these interests are in part material. The personification of the nation as a sacred being, different from and superior to its constituent members, is merely (I quote the words of a great French jurist, Léon Duguit) "a way of imposing authority by making people believe it is an authority *de jure* and not merely *de facto.*" By habitually talking of the nation as though it were a person with thoughts, feelings and a will of its own, the rulers of a country legitimate their own powers. Personification leads easily to deification; and where the nation is deified, its government ceases to be a mere convenience, like drains or a telephone system, and, partaking in the sacredness of the entity it represents, claims to give orders by divine right and demands the unquestioning obedience due to a god. Rulers seldom find it hard to recognize their friends. Hegel, the man who elaborated an inappropriate figure of speech into a complete philosophy of politics, was a favorite of the Prussian government. *"Es ist,"* he had written, *"es ist der Gang Gottes in der Welt, das der Staat ist."* The decoration bestowed on him by Frederick William III was richly deserved.

Unlike their rulers, the ruled have no material interest in using inappropriate language about states and nations. For them, the reward of being mistaken is psychological. The personified and deified nation becomes, in the minds of the individuals composing it, a kind of enlargement of themselves. The superhuman qualities which belong to the young lady with the toasting fork, the young lady with plaits and a brass *soutien-gorge*, the young lady in a Phrygian bonnet, are claimed by individual Englishmen, Germans and Frenchmen as being, at least in part, their own. *Dulce et decorum est pro patria mori.* But there would be no need to die, no need of war, if it had not been even sweeter to boast and swagger for one's country, to hate, despise, swindle and bully for it. Loyalty to the personified nation, or to the personified class or party, justifies the loyal in indulging all those passions which good manners and the moral code do not allow them to display in their relations with their neighbors. The personified entity is a being, not only great and noble, but also insanely proud, vain and touchy; fiercely rapacious; a braggart; bound by no considerations of right and wrong. (Hegel condemned as hopelessly shallow all those who dared to apply ethical standards to the activities of nations. To condone and applaud every iniquity committed in the name of the State was to him a sign of philosophical profundity.) Identifying themselves with this god, individuals find relief from the constraints of ordinary social decency, feel themselves justified in giving rein, within duly prescribed limits, to their criminal proclivities. As a royal nationalist or party-man, one can enjoy the luxury of behaving badly with a good conscience.

The evil passions are further justified by another linguistic error—the error 24
of speaking about certain categories of persons as though they were mere em-
bodied abstractions. Foreigners and those who disagree with us are not thought
of as men and women like ourselves and our fellow-countrymen; they are
thought of as representatives and, so to say, symbols of a class. In so far as
they have any personality at all, it is the personality we mistakenly attribute
to their class—a personality that is, by definition, intrinsically evil. We know
that the harming or killing of men and women is wrong, and we are reluctant
consciously to do what we know to be wrong. But when particular men and
women are thought of merely as representatives of a class, which has previously
been defined as evil and personified in the shape of a devil, then the reluctance
to hurt or murder disappears. Brown, Jones and Robinson are no longer thought
of as Brown, Jones and Robinson, but as heretics, gentiles, Yids, niggers,
barbarians, Huns, communists, capitalists, fascists, liberals—whichever the
case may be. When they have been called such names and assimilated to the
accursed class to which the names apply, Brown, Jones and Robinson cease to
be conceived as what they really are—human persons—and become for the
users of this fatally inappropriate language mere vermin or, worse, demons
whom it is right and proper to destroy as thoroughly and as painfully as possible.
Wherever persons are present, questions of morality arise. Rulers of nations
and leaders of parties find morality embarrassing. That is why they take such
pains to depersonalize their opponents. All propaganda directed against an
opposing group has but one aim: to substitute diabolical abstractions for concrete persons. The propagandist's purpose is to make one set of people forget
that certain other sets of people are human. By robbing them of their personality, he puts them outside the pale of moral obligation. Mere symbols can
have no rights—particularly when that of which they are symbolical is, by
definition, evil.

Politics can become moral only on one condition: that its problems shall 25
be spoken of and thought about exclusively in terms of concrete reality; that
is to say, of persons. To depersonify human beings and to personify abstractions
are complementary errors which lead, by an inexorable logic, to war between
nations and to idolatrous worship of the State, with consequent governmental
oppression. All current political thought is a mixture, in varying proportions,
between thought in terms of concrete realities and thought in terms of depersonified symbols and personified abstractions. In the democratic countries the
problems of internal politics are thought about mainly in terms of concrete
reality; those of external politics, mainly in terms of abstractions and symbols.
In dictatorial countries the proportion of concrete to abstract and symbolic
thought is lower than in democratic countries. Dictators talk little of persons,

much of personified abstractions, such as the Nation, the State, the Party, and much of depersonified symbols, such as Yids, Bolshies, Capitalists. The stupidity of politicians who talk about a world of persons as though it were not a world of persons is due in the main to self-interest. In a fictitious world of symbols and personified abstractions, rulers find that they can rule more effectively, and the ruled, that they can gratify instincts which the conventions of good manners and the imperatives of morality demand that they should repress. To think correctly is the condition of behaving well. It is also in itself a moral act; those who would think correctly must resist considerable temptations.

Focusing on Aldous Huxley's Use of Images

1. What is the function of the simple images that appear in the first few paragraphs? Why does Huxley "translate" political phrases in paragraph 8? What is the function of the simple images in paragraph 9? How does Huxley convey his antiwar sentiments in this paragraph?

2. What is the effect of Huxley's "translations" of typical statements of formal political diplomacy in paragraphs 13 and 14? What is the effect on his readers of the comparison to a familiar scene that ends paragraph 15?

3. What kinds of language does Huxley object to and what kinds of language does he advocate? What does he say are the consequences of "linguistic error" (see especially paragraphs 23 and 24)? Why is the technique he uses, of translating other people's words, particularly useful in revealing the consequences of linguistic error?

WORKING WITH THE TECHNIQUE IN YOUR OWN WRITING

1. Chang writes about beliefs about Asians that seem plausible and even flattering. Chang argues not only that these beliefs are false but that they are actually insulting. Write an essay like Chang's dealing with a belief about a group that seems on the surface to be believable and complimentary, or at least not insulting; show that the belief is a "myth" (i.e., is not true) and that believing it causes harm. You might want to focus on stereotypes about ethnic groups, as Chang did, or you might want to write about some other kind of group, such as baseball players, teachers, or students (you could expose the myth that teachers work because they love children, or the myth that students' grades reflect their intelligence). Include in your essay some "translations" of the myth to show how it is actually not just a "nice" belief (for example, "teachers work for love" could translate into "teachers are happy no matter how much they

are paid"). If you can find facts and figures to back up your arguments, use
them, but see if you can summarize your formal arguments in familiar images
that convey the emotional power of your facts and figures.

2. Select some phrases that people use that offend you. You might be bothered
   by words of politicians and journalists, as Chang and Huxley are, or you might
   dislike expressions teenagers use, such as "awesome" or "like," or expressions
   waiters in fancy restaurants use, such as "Would Madam like. . . ." Write an
   essay explaining why these phrases are offensive. To show what is wrong with
   the phrases, "translate" them into terms that express directly the implied meanings that bother you. You might even "translate" the tone with which a phrase
   is said, explaining for example that the brusqueness with which waiters answer
   questions is a way of saying to customers, "You have just asked the stupidest
   question I have ever heard. You probably have the taste buds of an earthworm."

BEVERLY P. DIPO

Utah State University
Logan, Utah
Joyce Kinkead, instructor

Beverly Dipo can recall with remarkable detail and winsome irony the first day she worked on cursive writing:

> I was in the third grade. My wooden desk was, even then, ancient and bore the history of previous academic scholars and shirkers. The glossy surface had acquired its glow more from the sweaty palms of test takers and greasy elbows of second-base sliders than from wood polish. The dark embedded pencil scratches attested to the fact that Shirley had once sat here; Patrick was a lousy speller; J.K. did unspeakable things to S.D.; and much to my relief, someone had kindly left me the seven times table.

With her feet wrapped around what she describes as the desk's "de-painted metal legs," Beverly Dipo spent hours practicing large, wire-thin, continuous circles, impelled by her teacher's well-intentioned cautioning: " 'Be sure to use your whole arm to glide evenly over the paper; do not use just your wrist,' she warned, 'or you will have a sloppy slinky.' "

Born in Hayward, California, and graduated from Sky View High School in Smithfield, Utah, in 1984, Beverly Dipo writes these days on an old, water-stained bathroom door that has "no pencil marks or times tables to entertain or inform me." It is cluttered, she reports, "with books, cans of pencils and colored pens, paint brushes, a vase of ugly brown and yellow flowers, a recipe file, a clock, a basket of scissors, tape, paper clips, and other assorted junk, all of which I pay little attention to until they come up missing." Such painstakingly careful observations reflect the strength of her work both as a licensed practical nurse and as a writer at Utah State University, where she is pursuing a degree as a registered nurse.

Asked to write a narrative that focuses on an experience in which she gained some insight, Beverly Dipo responded with what is at once an incisive description and a moving account of the personal and clinical routines that attend the quietly dignified death of an elderly victim of cancer. "Death happens in my profession," Beverly Dipo observes. "It is not uncommon. I think it is difficult for nurses to remember sometimes that these experiences are special and that we need to cherish them more than we do."

For a more detailed discussion of Dipo's essay, see Part II.

No Rainbows, No Roses

I have never seen Mrs. Trane before, but I know by the report I received 1
from the previous shift that tonight she will die. Making my rounds, I go from
room to room, checking other patients first and saving Mrs. Trane for last,
not to avoid her, but because she will require the most time to care for.
Everyone else seems to be all right for the time being; they have had their
medications, backrubs and are easily settled for the night.

At the door to 309, I pause, adjusting my eyes to the darkness. The only 2
light in the room is coming from an infusion pump, which is flashing its red
beacon as if in warning, and the dim hall light that barely confirms the room's
furnishings and the shapeless form on the bed. As I stand there, the smell hits
my nostrils, and I close my eyes as I remember the stench of rot and decay
from past experience. In my mouth I taste the bitter bile churning in the pit
of my stomach. I swallow uneasily and cross the room in the dark, reaching
for the light switch above the sink, and as it silently illuminates the scene, I
return to the bed to observe the patient with a detached, medical routineness.

Mrs. Trane lies motionless: the head seems unusually large on a skeleton 3
frame, and except for a few fine wisps of gray hair around the ears, is bald from
the chemotherapy that had offered brief hope; the skin is dark yellow and sags
loosely around exaggerated long bones that not even a gown and bedding can
disguise; the right arm lies straight out at the side, taped cruelly to a board to
secure the IV fluid its access; the left arm is across the sunken chest, which
rises and falls in the uneven waves of Cheyne-Stokes respirations; a catheter
hanging on the side of the bed is draining thick brown urine from the bladder,
the source of the deathly smell.

I reach for the long, thin fingers that are lying on the chest. They are ice 4
cold, and I quickly move to the wrist and feel for the weak, thready pulse.
Mrs. Trane's eyes flutter open as her head turns toward me slightly. As she
tries to form a word on her dry, parched lips, I bend close to her and scarcely
hear as she whispers, "Water." Taking a glass of water from the bedside table,
I put my finger over the end of the straw and allow a few droplets of the cool
moisture to slide into her mouth. She makes no attempt to swallow; there is
just not enough strength. "More," the raspy voice says, and we repeat the
procedure. This time she does manage to swallow and weakly says, "Thank
you." I touch her gently in response. She is too weak for conversation, so
without asking, I go about providing for her needs, explaining to her in hushed
tones each move I make. Picking her up in my arms like a child, I turn her
on her side. She is so very small and light. Carefully, I rub lotion into the
yellow skin, which rolls freely over the bones, feeling perfectly the outline of

each vertebrae in the back and the round smoothness of the ileac crest. Placing a pillow between her legs, I notice that these too are ice cold, and not until I run my hand up over her knees do I feel any of the life-giving warmth of blood coursing through fragile veins. I find myself in awe of the life force which continues despite such a state of decomposition.

When I am finished, I pull a chair up beside the bed to face her and, taking her free hand between mine, again notice the long, thin fingers. Graceful. There is no jewelry; it would have fallen off long ago. I wonder briefly if she has any family, and then I see that there are neither bouquets of flowers, nor pretty plants on the shelves, no brightly crayon-colored posters of rainbows, nor boastful self-portraits from grandchildren on the walls. There is no hint in the room anywhere that this is a person who is loved. As though she has been reading my mind, Mrs. Trane answers my thoughts and quietly tells me, "I sent . . . my family . . . home . . . tonight . . . didn't want . . . them . . . to see. . . ." She cannot go on, but knowingly, I have understood what it is she has done. I lower my eyes, not knowing what to say, so I say nothing. Again she seems to sense my unease, "You . . . stay. . . ." Time seems to have come to a standstill. In the total silence, I noticeably feel my own heartbeat quicken and hear my breathing as it begins to match hers, stride for uneven stride. Our eyes meet and somehow, together, we become aware that this is a special moment between us, a moment when two human beings are so close we feel as if our souls touch. Her long fingers curl easily around my hand and I nod my head slowly, smiling. Wordlessly, through yellowed eyes, I receive my thank you and her eyes slowly close.

Some unknown amount of time passes before her eyes open again, only this time there is no response in them, just a blank stare. Without warning, her breathing stops, and within a few moments, the faint pulse is also gone. One single tear flows from her left eye, across the cheekbone and down onto the pillow. I begin to cry quietly. There is a tug of emotion within me for this stranger who so quickly came into and went from my life. Her suffering is done, yet so is the life. Slowly, still holding her hand, I become aware that I do not mind this emotional tug of war, that in fact, it was a privilege she has allowed me, and I would do it again, gladly. Mrs. Trane spared her family an episode that perhaps they were not equipped to handle and instead shared it with me, knowing somehow that I would handle it and, indeed, needed it to grow, both privately and professionally. She had not wanted to have her family see her die, yet she did not want to die alone. No one should die alone, and I am glad I was there for her.

Two days later, I read Mrs. Trane's obituary in the paper. She had been a widow for five years, was the mother of seven, grandmother of eighteen, an active member of her church, a leader of volunteer organizations in her community, college-educated in music, a concert pianist, and a piano teacher for over thirty years.

Yes, they were long and graceful fingers.   8

Focusing on Beverly Dipo's Techniques and Revisions

1. Beverly Dipo reports that in writing this essay, "I just sat down and typed up a rough draft, made some minor working changes, typed a second draft, and turned in that." This second draft was "critiqued" by the peer editors in her class: "I was worried about its needing some sort of introduction, like 'I'm a nurse and I work the night shift,' or something like that. I couldn't come up with anything that didn't sound like Jack Webb" of *Dragnet* fame ("I'm a nurse and I work the night shift"). What choices does Dipo make to increase the effectiveness of her opening paragraph?

2. "No Rainbows, No Roses" begins with the first-person pronoun. When and how does that *point of view* shift in the first paragraph? Reread each of the subsequent paragraphs. Is the emphasis in each paragraph personal? Impersonal? Some blend of the two? Support your response with specific examples. Dipo notes that one of her readers suggested she revise paragraph 3 by adding personal pronouns. As a writer, however, she exercised her authority over her own work and resisted, explaining: "As a nurse I frequently observe *things* before I ever speak to a patient or get to know them as human beings. Right or wrong, it's the way we are trained." What do you think are the "things" Dipo has in mind here? What reasons would you offer to support or to challenge her decision that her essay ought "to remain impersonal at that point"?

3. Dipo describes outlining in her head as the most effective method of getting started: "I sit down at the typewriter and start typing my thoughts on paper. I'm a pretty organized person, so my first thoughts seem to organize themselves; sentences fall into paragraphs for me." Which paragraphs in this essay strike you as well organized? Why? Less well organized? Why? What would you suggest that she do to strengthen those you judged less organized?

4. How does Dipo's careful attention to detail in the first two paragraphs reinforce the atmosphere she seeks to create in her *narrative*? At the end of the second paragraph, she announces that she will "observe the patient with a detached, medical routineness." Point to specific examples of her "detached" point of view. What is the effect in each instance?

5. In the final sentence of paragraph 4, Dipo shifts the focus of her essay from the woman to her own reaction to rubbing lotion on the woman's frail body: "I find myself in awe of the life force which continues despite such a state of decomposition." Comment on the effectiveness of this sentence. How does it

either add to or detract from the overall point of this paragraph and of the essay as a whole?

6. One of the appreciable strengths of Dipo's essay is its use of evocative *diction*. Identify at least three instances where Dipo chooses an especially effective word or phrase to underscore the effect she aims to create. Explain why each is so effective.

7. Identify the contending forces in the "emotional tug of war" the writer describes in paragraph 6. Why does Dipo note that she "needed" this experience "to grow, both privately and professionally"? Our familiarity with superficially similar scenes in movies and soap operas threatens to reduce the painful intensity and emotional integrity of a woman's dignified death. At what moments does the essay come closest to melodrama, and how does Dipo prevent her essay from slipping into it?

8. Dipo explains that she knew her essay was finished "when I remembered [Mrs. Trane's] obituary and recalled thinking then how appropriate that she had played the piano; her hands were the hands of a piano player." When and how does she introduce the detail of Mrs. Trane's hands in the essay? With what effect? Explain whether you think she should have given more attention to Mrs. Trane's hands throughout her essay. Explain whether you think her title ought to reflect this controlling image.

Suggestions for Writing

1. Beverly Dipo's account of Mrs. Trane's death exemplifies the medical profession at its best: well-trained people who can display both rigorous objectivity and generous compassion. Consider other careers that require such seemingly paradoxical qualities as objectivity and compassion. Choose one and write an expository essay using concrete examples to explain why such qualities are necessary in that particular line of work and how one can create a proper balance between them. You may find it useful to explore not only the external but also the psychological aspects of the job.

2. Part of the success of Dipo's essay depends on the element of surprise—both at how Mrs. Trane responds to her own impending death and the reaction this elicits from the professional who cares for her. Write a narrative essay recounting in detail how someone you know behaved in ways that defeated the expectations of those around him or her.

3. As a nurse, Dipo notes that she sees "human suffering, weakness, triumphs, and tragedies on a daily basis." Write an essay describing the ways in which someone you know has had to deal with a serious illness, a family member's death, or an awareness of his or her own impending death. What changes has this knowledge brought about in both the person most directly affected and in

those around him or her? What insight have you gleaned from this experience? Recalling what Beverly Dipo has accomplished in her essay, include as many evocative details as possible.

AN EFFECTIVE TECHNIQUE

Beverly Dipo uses one of the most common techniques of essay writers— first-person point of view—in a particularly effective way, to draw her readers very close to an experience we often avoid looking at or thinking about: death. We are carried so close because the voice speaking, the "I," is so open, so honest, and so trustworthy that we are pleased to let down our guard, to be carried along and share her emotions. The person speaking is both "just like us" and the kind of person we would most like to be. From Dipo's essay, we can learn how to create the most intimate point of view, one that can serve as a bridge to allow readers to share experiences that they might be unwilling or unable to have themselves.

One small but important way that Dipo brings us to share her point of view is to write consistently in the present tense. We feel we are seeing each detail at the same moment that Dipo sees it; she is not censoring her thoughts but rather is taking the risk of letting us know whatever passes through her mind. Her first few thoughts establish that she is quite professional; she knows how to calmly face death. We can relax somewhat; we are not going to be put through the uncomfortable experience of watching people make mistakes or panic in a moment of crisis. We are with someone who can recognize "infusion pumps" and "Cheyne-Stokes respirations," someone who can react to horrors with "detached, medical routineness."

Dipo is not, however, an unfeeling medical robot. She smells the "stench of rot and decay," tastes "bitter bile churning in the pit of" her own stomach, and sees "thick brown urine" draining from the body. Part of what makes us trust Dipo is her willingness to admit her disgust; she does not want to be where she is any more than we do, yet she recognizes that she must be there, and we accept her judgment that we must as well.

Gradually, a change occurs in Dipo's feelings. She moves from disgust to "awe of the life force which continues despite such a state of decomposition." The warmth of Mrs. Trane's blood reveals there is more here than a skeleton. We can feel the warmth of Dipo's feelings slowly overcoming her disgust, and this warmth grows steadily until the "two human beings are so close" that for a moment Dipo is no longer writing from her own point of view alone, but rather from a joint point of view: "we feel as if our souls touch." The readers are included in this "we," and we feel as Dipo does the "tug of emotion" at having part of "us" die.

Dipo has carried us into the center of a powerful, disturbing experience, and she does not just leave us there; she shows us a way out, a way back to everyday reality. First there is a moment of appreciation, a recognition that we have shared with Dipo a "privilege," something that we "needed" as much as she did, "to grow." Finally, Dipo transforms this intense scene into another kind of story: an obituary, a formal way to honor the dead and distance ourselves from them. There is no narrator of an obituary, no person having a relationship to the dying, just a life objectively reported, sounding fairly pleasant.

This essay shows that to bring readers to understand the importance of a powerful experience, we need to do more than simply describe the experience; we have to create a believable point of view. We must try to win the readers' trust very quickly—not an easy task. Imagine being introduced to a stranger, and having him or her immediately tell you about some intense experience. You probably would mentally distance yourself from the person, thinking, "This person's imposing on me; he must be weird or lonely." Dipo shows us a way to overcome such natural reserve very quickly: present ourselves as persons who have nothing to hide, who are willing to admit to some flaws but are basically decent and humane. We have to convince our readers that we will not play with their emotions if they let themselves react strongly to what we say. And Dipo shows us how to carry through on that promise: once we have brought our readers to have strong feelings, we do not just leave them, especially when the feelings are partly painful; we have to let them know why the experience was worth going through, to give them something to take back to everyday life.

The author of the next selection, Oliver Sacks, is also a medical professional, a neurosurgeon, and he also writes about an incomprehensible and frightening experience, like death, that no one could react to "objectively." Sacks uses the first person to carry his readers with him as he goes beyond "impersonal psychology" to care for and get close to a patient who has quite literally lost his mind.

ANOTHER ILLUSTRATION OF THE TECHNIQUE

OLIVER SACKS

The Lost Mariner

Oliver Sacks is a neurosurgeon whose writing has evolved as his conception of his profession has changed. He began his career as a "fairly orthodox" neurologist after receiving his M.D. in 1960. His first book, on migraine headaches, was, as he put it, "well within the established medical canon." He began veering outside standard practices when he became convinced that the effects of the drugs he was administering to patients were determined by the patients' personalities and lifestyles, their entire "being-in-the-world." He tried to write up his research as a collection of "human dramas," but his articles were summarily rejected by medical journals as unscientific. He stopped writing for a time, feeling confused about what he should be doing in his profession. Sacks finally developed a new view of medicine and a new way to write about his cases as a result of a mountaineering accident that temporarily paralyzed his leg. For the first time in his life, he was a patient in a hospital, and he felt he was treated as a "pigmy, an inmate, a prisoner." He had strange difficulties bringing his brain to reconnect to his leg, difficulties that the doctor treating him tried to ignore. His painful experiences led him to write a book about himself for the first time (A Leg to Stand On, 1984). Since then, he has returned to writing about neurological cases, but in a new way, bringing in his own personal reactions as well as his patients' characters. The new point of view in his writing is part of his effort to create a "new" neurology, one that goes beyond the bounds of empirical science, "to assert and affirm the living subject, to escape from a purely objective or 'robotic' science, to find and establish what was missing—a living 'I.' "

> You have to begin to lose your memory, if only in bits and
> pieces, to realize that memory is what makes our lives. Life
> without memory is no life at all. . . . Our memory is our co-
> herence, our reason, our feeling, even our action. Without it,
> we are nothing. . . . (I can only wait for the final amnesia, the
> one that can erase an entire life, as it did my mother's. . . .)
> —Luis Buñuel[1]

This moving and frightening segment in Buñuel's recently translated mem-   1
oirs raises fundamental questions—clinical, practical, existential, philosophi-

---

[1]Luis Buñuel (1900–1983), Spanish filmmaker.

cal: what sort of a life (if any), what sort of a world, what sort of a self, can be preserved in a man who has lost the greater part of his memory and, with this, his past, and his moorings in time?

It immediately made me think of a patient of mine in whom these questions 2 are precisely exemplified: charming, intelligent, memoryless Jimmie G., who was admitted to our Home for the Aged near New York City early in 1975, with a cryptic transfer note saying, "Helpless, demented, confused, and disoriented."

Jimmie was a fine-looking man, with a curly bush of gray hair, a healthy 3 and handsome forty-nine-year-old. He was cheerful, friendly, and warm.

"Hiya, Doc!" he said. "Nice morning! Do I take this chair here?" He was 4 a genial soul, very ready to talk and to answer any questions I asked him. He told me his name and birth date, and the name of the little town in Connecticut where he was born. He described it in affectionate detail, even drew me a map. He spoke of the houses where his family had lived—he remembered their phone numbers still. He spoke of school and school days, the friends he'd had, and his special fondness for mathematics and science. He talked with enthusiasm of his days in the navy—he was seventeen, had just graduated from high school when he was drafted in 1943. With his good engineering mind he was a "natural" for radio and electronics, and after a crash course in Texas found himself assistant radio operator on a submarine. He remembered the names of various submarines on which he had served, their missions, where they were stationed, the names of his shipmates. He remembed Morse code, and was still fluent in Morse tapping and touch-typing.

A full and interesting early life, remembered vividly, in detail, with affec- 5 tion. But there, for some reason, his reminiscences stopped. He recalled, and almost relived, his war days and service, the end of the war, and his thoughts for the future. He had come to love the navy, thought he might stay in it. But with the GI Bill, and support, he felt he might do best to go to college. His older brother was in accountancy school and engaged to a girl, a "real beauty," from Oregon.

With recalling, reliving, Jimmie was full of animation; he did not seem to 6 be speaking of the past but of the present, and I was very struck by the change of tense in his recollections as he passed from his school days to his days in the navy. He had been using the past tense, but now used the present—and (it seemed to me) not just the formal or fictitious present tense of recall, but the actual present tense of immediate experience.

A sudden, improbable suspicion seized me. 7

"What year is this, Mr. G.?" I asked, concealing my perplexity under a 8 casual manner.

"Forty-five, man. What do you mean?" He went on, "We've won the war, 9
FDR's dead, Truman's at the helm. There are great times ahead."

"And you, Jimmie, how old would you be?"   10

Oddly, uncertainly, he hesitated a moment, as if engaged in calculation. 11

"Why, I guess I'm nineteen, Doc. I'll be twenty next birthday."   12

Looking at the gray-haired man before me, I had an impulse for which I 13
have never forgiven myself—it was, or would have been, the height of cruelty
had there been any possibility of Jimmie's remembering it.

"Here," I said, and thrust a mirror toward him. "Look in the mirror and 14
tell me what you see. Is that a nineteen-year-old looking out from the mirror?"

He suddenly turned ashen and gripped the sides of the chair. "Jesus Christ," 15
he whispered. "Christ, what's going on? What's happening to me? Is this a
nightmare? Am I crazy? Is this a joke?"—and he became frantic, panicked.

"It's okay, Jimmie," I said soothingly. "It's just a mistake. Nothing to worry 16
about. Hey!" I took him to the window. "Isn't this a lovely spring day. See
the kids there playing baseball?" He regained his color and started to smile,
and I stole away, taking the hateful mirror with me.

Two minutes later I reentered the room. Jimmie was still standing by the 17
window, gazing with pleasure at the kids playing baseball below. He wheeled
around as I opened the door, and his face assumed a cheery expression.

"Hiya, Doc!" he said. "Nice morning! You want to talk to me—do I take 18
this chair here?" There was no sign of recognition on his frank, open face.

"Haven't we met before, Mr. G?" I asked casually.   19

"No, I can't say we have. Quite a beard you got there. I wouldn't forget 20
you, Doc!"

"Why do you call me 'Doc'?"   21

"Well, you are a doc, ain't you?"   22

"Yes, but if you haven't met me, how do you know what I am?"   23

"You *talk* like a doc. I can *see* you're a doc."   24

"Well, you're right, I am. I'm the neurologist here."   25

"Neurologist? Hey, there's something wrong with my nerves? And 'here'— 26
where's 'here'? What is this place anyhow?"

"I was just going to ask you—where do you think you are?"   27

"I see these beds, and these patients everywhere. Looks like a sort of hospital 28
to me. But hell, what would I be doing in a hospital—and with all these old
people, years older than me. I feel good, I'm strong as a bull. Maybe I *work*
here. . . . Do I work? What's my job? . . . No, you're shaking your head, I
see in your eyes I don't work here. If I don't work here, I've been *put* here.
Am I a patient, am I sick and don't know it, Doc? It's crazy, it's scary. . . .
Is it some sort of joke?"

"You don't know what the matter is? You really don't know? You remember 29
telling me about your childhood, growing up in Connecticut, working as a
radio operator on submarines? And how your brother is engaged to a girl from
Oregon?"

"Hey, you're right. But I didn't tell you that, I never met you before in my 30
life. You must have read all about me in my chart."

"Okay," I said. "I'll tell you a story. A man went to his doctor complaining 31
of memory lapses. The doctor asked him some routine questions, and then
said, 'These lapses. What about them?' 'What lapses?' the patient replied."

"So that's my problem," Jimmie laughed. "I kinda thought it was. I do find 32
myself forgetting things, once in a while—things that have just happened. The
past is clear, though."

"Will you allow me to examine you, to run over some tests?"   33

"Sure," he said genially. "Whatever you want."   34

On intelligence testing he showed excellent ability. He was quick-witted, 35
observant, and logical, and had no difficulty solving complex problems and
puzzles—no difficulty, that is, if they could be done quickly. If much time was
required, he forgot what he was doing. He was quick and good at tic-tac-toe
and checkers, and cunning and aggressive—he easily beat me. But he got lost
at chess—the moves were too slow.

Homing in on his memory, I found an extreme and extraordinary loss of 36
recent memory—so that whatever was said or shown to him was apt to be
forgotten in a few seconds' time. Thus I laid out my watch, my tie, and my
glasses on the desk, covered them, and asked him to remember these. Then,
after a minute's chat, I asked him what I had put under the cover. He remembered none of them—or indeed that I had even asked him to remember. I
repeated the test, this time getting him to write down the names of the three
objects; again he forgot, and when I showed him the paper with his writing
on it he was astounded, and said he had no recollection of writing anything
down, though he acknowledged that it was his own writing, and then got a
faint "echo" of the fact that he had written them down.

He sometimes retained faint memories, some dim echo or sense of famil- 37
iarity. Thus five minutes after I had played tic-tac-toe with him, he recollected
that "some doctor" had played this with him "a while back"—whether the
"while back" was minutes or months ago he had no idea. He then paused and
said, "It could have been you?" When I said it *was* me, he seemed amused.
This faint amusement and indifference were very characteristic, as were the
involved cogitations to which he was driven by being so disoriented and lost
in time. When I asked Jimmie the time of the year, he would immediately
look around for some clue—I was careful to remove the calendar from my

desk—and would work out the time of year, roughly, by looking through the window.

It was not, apparently, that he failed to register in memory, but that the memory traces were fugitive in the extreme, and were apt to be effaced within a minute, often less, especially if there were distracting or competing stimuli, while his intellectual and perceptual powers were preserved, and highly superior.

Jimmie's scientific knowledge was that of a bright high school graduate with a penchant for mathematics and science. He was superb at arithmetical (and also algebraic) calculations, but only if they could be done with lightning speed. If there were many steps, too much time, involved, he would forget where he was, and even the question. He knew the elements, compared them, and drew the periodic table—but omitted the transuranic elements.

"Is that complete?" I asked when he'd finished.

"It's complete and up-to-date, sir, as far as I know."

"You wouldn't know any elements beyond uranium?"

"You kidding? There's ninety-two elements, and uranium's the last."

I paused and flipped through a *National Geographic* on the table. "Tell me the planets," I said, "and something about them." Unhesitatingly, confidently, he gave me the planets—their names, their discovery, their distance from the sun, their estimated mass, character, and gravity.

"What is this?" I asked, showing him a photo in the magazine I was holding.

"It's the moon," he replied.

"No, it's not," I answered. "It's a picture of the earth taken from the moon."

"Doc, you're kidding! Someone would've had to get a camera up there!"

"Naturally."

"Hell! You're joking—how the hell would you do that?"

Unless he was a consummate actor, a fraud simulating an astonishment he did not feel, this was an utterly convincing demonstration that he was still in the past. His words, his feelings, his innocent wonder, his struggle to make sense of what he saw, were precisely those of an intelligent young man in the forties faced with the future, with what had not yet happened, and what was scarcely imaginable. "This more than anything else," I wrote in my notes, "persuades me that his cut-off around 1945 is genuine. . . . What I showed him, and told him, produced the authentic amazement which it would have done in an intelligent young man of the pre-Sputnik era."

I found another photo in the magazine and pushed it over to him.

"That's an aircraft carrier," he said. "Real ultramodern design. I never saw one quite like that."

"What's it called?" I asked. 54

He glanced down, looked baffled, and said, "The *Nimitz!*" 55

"Something the matter?" 56

"The hell there is!" he replied hotly. "I know 'em all by name, and I *don't* 57
know a *Nimitz*. . . . Of course there's an Admiral Nimitz, but I never heard
they named a carrier after him."

Angrily he threw the magazine down. 58

He was becoming fatigued, and somewhat irritable and anxious, under the 59
continuing pressure of anomaly and contradiction, and their fearful implications, to which he could not be entirely oblivious. I had already, unthinkingly,
pushed him into panic, and felt it was time to end our session. We wandered
over to the window again, and looked down at the sunlit baseball diamond;
as he looked his face relaxed, he forgot the *Nimitz*, the satellite photo, the
other horrors and hints, and became absorbed in the game below. Then, as a
savory smell drifted up from the dining room, he smacked his lips, said
"Lunch!," smiled, and took his leave.

And I myself was wrung with emotion—it was heartbreaking, it was absurd, 60
it was deeply perplexing, to think of his life lost in limbo, dissolving

"He is, as it were," I wrote in my notes, "isolated in a single moment of 61
being, with a moat or lacuna of forgetting all round him. . . . He is a man
without a past (or future), stuck in a constantly changing, meaningless moment." And then, more prosaically, "The remainder of the neurological examination is entirely normal. Impression: probably Korsakov's syndrome, due
to alcoholic degeneration of the mammillary bodies." My note was a strange
mixture of facts and observations, carefully noted and itemized, with irrepres-
sible meditations on what such problems might "mean," in regard to who and
what and where this poor man was—whether, indeed, one could speak of an
"existence," given so absolute a privation of memory or continuity.

I kept wondering, in this and later notes—unscientifically—about "a lost 62
soul," and how one might establish some continuity, some roots, for he was a
man without roots, or rooted only in the remote past.

"Only connect"—but how could he connect, and how could we help him 63
to connect? What was life without connection? "I may venture to affirm,"
Hume[2] wrote, "that we are nothing but a bundle or collection of different
sensations, which succeed each other with an inconceivable rapidity, and are
in a perpetual flux and movement." In some sense, he had been reduced to a
"Humean" being—I could not help thinking how fascinated Hume would have

[2]David Hume (1711–1776), British philosopher.

been at seeing in Jimmie his own philosophical "chimera" incarnate, a gruesome reduction of a man to mere disconnected, incoherent flux and change.

Perhaps I could find advice or help in the medical literature—a literature which, for some reason, was largely Russian, from Korsakov's original thesis (Moscow, 1887) about such cases of memory loss, which are still called "Korsakov's syndrome," to Luria's *Neuropsychology of Memory* (which appeared in translation only a year after I first saw Jimmie). Korsakov wrote in 1887: 64

> Memory of recent events is disturbed almost exclusively; recent impressions apparently disappear soonest, whereas impressions of long ago are recalled properly, so that the patient's ingenuity, his sharpness of wit, and his resourcefulness remain largely unaffected.

To Korsakov's brilliant but spare observations, almost a century of further research has been added—the richest and deepest, by far, being Luria's. And in Luria's account science became poetry, and the pathos of radical lostness was evoked. "Gross disturbances of the organization of impressions of events and their sequence in time can always be observed in such patients," he wrote. "In consequence, they lose their integral experience of time and begin to live in a world of isolated impressions." Further, as Luria noted, the eradication of impressions (and their disorder) might spread backward in time—"in the most serious cases—even to relatively distant events." 65

Most of Luria's patients, as described in this book, had massive and serious cerebral tumors, which had the same effects as Korsakov's syndrome, but later spread and were often fatal. Luria included no cases of "simple" Korsakov's syndrome, based on the self-limiting destruction that Korsakov described—neuron destruction, produced by alcohol, in the tiny but crucial mammillary bodies, the rest of the brain being perfectly preserved. And so there was no long-term follow-up of Luria's cases. 66

I had at first been deeply puzzled, and dubious, even suspicious, about the apparently sharp cut-off in 1945, a point, a date, which was also symbolically so sharp. I wrote in a subsequent note: 67

> There is a great blank. We do not know what happened then—or subsequently. . . . We must fill in these "missing" years—from his brother, or the navy, or hospitals he has been to. . . . Could it be that he sustained some massive trauma at this time, some massive cerebral or emotional trauma in combat, in the war, and that *this* may have affected him ever since? . . . was the war his "high

point," the last time he was really alive, and existence since
one long anti-climax?*

We did various tests on him (EEG, brain scans), and found no evidence of
massive brain damage, although atrophy of the tiny mammillary bodies would
not show up on such tests. We received reports from the navy indicating that
he had remained in the navy until 1965, and that he was perfectly competent
at that time.

Then we turned up a short nasty report from Bellevue Hospital, dated 1971,   68
saying that he was "totally disoriented . . . with an advanced organic brain-
syndrome, due to alcohol" (cirrhosis had also developed by this time). From
Bellevue he was sent to a wretched dump in the Village, a so-called "nursing
home" whence he was rescued—lousy, starving—by our Home in 1975.

We located his brother, whom Jimmie always spoke of as being in accoun-   69
tancy school and engaged to a girl from Oregon. In fact he had married the
girl from Oregon, had become a father and grandfather, and been a practicing
accountant for thirty years.

Where we had hoped for an abundance of information and feeling from his   70
brother, we received a courteous but somewhat meager letter. It was obvious
from reading this—especially reading between the lines—that the brothers had
scarcely seen each other since 1943, and gone separate ways, partly through
the vicissitudes of location and profession, and partly through deep (though
not estranging) differences of temperament. Jimmie, it seemed, had never
"settled down," was "happy-go-lucky," and "always a drinker." The navy, his
brother felt, provided a structure, a life, and the real problems started when
he left it, in 1965. Without his habitual structure and anchor Jimmie had
ceased to work, "gone to pieces," and started to drink heavily. There had been
some memory impairment, of the Korsakov type, in the middle and especially
the late sixties, but not so severe that Jimmie couldn't "cope" in his nonchalant
fashion. But his drinking grew heavier in 1970.

Around Christmas of that year, his brother understood, he had suddenly   71
"blown his top" and become deliriously excited and confused, and it was at

---

*In his fascinating oral history *The Good War* (1985) Studs Terkel transcribes countless stories
of men and women, especially fighting men, who felt World War II was intensely real—by far
the most real and significant time of their lives—everything since was pallid in comparison. Such
men tend to dwell on the war and to relive its battles, comradeship, moral certainties and
intensity. But this dwelling on the past and relative hebetude towards the present—this emotional
dulling of current feeling and memory—is nothing like Jimmie's organic amnesia. I recently had
occasion to discuss the question with Terkel: "I've met thousands of men," he told me, "who
feel they've just been 'marking time' since '45—but I never met anyone for whom time termi-
nated, like your amnesiac Jimmie."

this point he had been taken into Bellevue. During the next month, the excitement and delirium died down, but he was left with deep and bizarre memory lapses, or "deficits," to use the medical jargon. His brother had visited him at this time—they had not met for twenty years—and, to his horror, Jimmie not only failed to recognize him, but said, "Stop joking! You're old enough to be my father. My brother's a young man, just going through accountancy school."

When I received this information, I was more perplexed still: why did 72 Jimmie not remember his later years in the navy, why did he not recall and organize his memories until 1970? I had not heard then that such patients might have a retrograde amnesia. "I wonder, increasingly," I wrote at this time, "whether there is not an element of hysterical or fugal amnesia—whether he is not in flight from something too awful to recall," and I suggested he be seen by our psychiatrist. Her report was searching and detailed—the examination had included a sodium amytal test, calculated to "release" any memories which might be repressed. She also attempted to hypnotize Jimmie, in the hope of eliciting memories repressed by hysteria—this tends to work well in cases of hysterical amnesia. But it failed because Jimmie could not be hypnotized, not because of any "resistance," but because of his extreme amnesia, which caused him to lose track of what the hypnotist was saying. (Dr. M. Homonoff, who worked on the amnesia ward at the Boston Veterans Administration hospital, tells me of similar experiences—and of his feeling that this is absolutely characteristic of patients with Korsakov's, as opposed to patients with hysterical amnesia.)

"I have no feeling or evidence," the psychiatrist wrote, "of any hysterical 73 or 'put-on' deficit. He lacks both the means and the motive to make a façade. His memory deficits are organic and permanent and incorrigible, though it is puzzling they should go back so long." Since, she felt, he was "unconcerned . . . manifested no special anxiety . . . constituted no management problem," there was nothing she could offer, or any therapeutic "entrance" or "lever" she could see.

At this point, persuaded that this was, indeed, "pure" Korsakov's, uncom- 74 plicated by other factors, emotional or organic, I wrote to Luria and asked his opinion. He spoke in his reply of his patient Bel,* whose amnesia had retroactively eradicated ten years. He said he saw no reason why such a retrograde amnesia should not thrust backward decades, or almost a whole lifetime. "I can only wait for the final amnesia," Buñuel writes, "the one that can erase an entire life." But Jimmie's amnesia, for whatever reason, had erased memory

*See A. R. Luria, *The Neuropsychology of Memory* (1976), pp. 250–52.

and time back to 1945—roughly—and then stopped. Occasionally, he would recall something much later, but the recall was fragmentary and dislocated in time. Once, seeing the word "satellite" in a newspaper headline, he said offhandedly that he'd been involved in a project of satellite tracking while on the ship *Chesapeake Bay*, a memory fragment coming from the early or mid-sixties. But, for all practical purposes, his cut-off point was during the mid- (or late) forties, and anything subsequently retrieved was fragmentary, unconnected. This was the case in 1975, and it is still the case now, nine years later.

What could we do? What should we do? "There are no prescriptions," Luria 75 wrote, "in a case like this. Do whatever your ingenuity and your heart suggest. There is little or no hope of any recovery in his memory. But a man does not consist of memory alone. He has feeling, will, sensibilities, moral being— matters of which neuropsychology cannot speak. And it is here, beyond the realm of an impersonal psychology, that you may find ways to touch him, and change him. And the circumstances of your work especially allow this, for you work in a Home, which is like a little world, quite different from the clinics and institutions where I work. Neuropsychologically, there is little or nothing you can do; but in the realm of the individual, there may be much you can do."

Luria mentioned his patient Kur as manifesting a rare self-awareness, in 76 which hopelessness was mixed with an odd equanimity. "I have no memory of the present," Kur would say. "I do not know what I have just done or from where I have just come. . . . I can recall my past very well, but I have no memory of my present." When asked whether he had ever seen the person testing him, he said, "I cannot say yes or no, I can neither affirm nor deny that I have seen you." This was sometimes the case with Jimmie; and, like Kur, who stayed many months in the same hospital, Jimmie began to form "a sense of familiarity"; he slowly learned his way around the home—the whereabouts of the dining room, his own room, the elevators, the stairs, and in some sense recognized some of the staff, although he confused them, and perhaps had to do so, with people from the past. He soon became fond of the nursing sister in the Home; he recognized her voice, her footfalls, immediately, but would always say that she had been a fellow pupil at his high school, and was greatly surprised when I addressed her as "Sister."

"Gee!' he exclaimed, "the damnedest things happen. I'd never have guessed 77 you'd become a religious, Sister!"

Since he's been at our Home—that is, since early 1975—Jimmie has never 78 been able to identify anyone in it consistently. The only person he truly recognizes is his brother, whenever he visits from Oregon. These meetings are

deeply emotional and moving to observe—the only truly emotional meetings
Jimmie has. He loves his brother, he recognizes him, but he cannot understand
why he looks so old: "Guess some people age fast," he says. Actually his brother
looks much younger than his age, and has the sort of face and build that
change little with the years. These are true meetings, Jimmie's only connection
of past and present, yet they do nothing to provide any sense of history or
continuity. If anything they emphasize—at least to his brother, and to others
who see them together—that Jimmie still lives, is fossilized, in the past.

All of us, at first, had high hopes of helping Jimmie—he was so personable,   79
so likable, so quick and intelligent, it was difficult to believe that he might be
beyond help. But none of us had ever encountered, even imagined, such a
power of amnesia, the possibility of a pit into which everything, every experience, every event, would fathomlessly drop, a bottomless memory-hole that
would engulf the whole world.

I suggested, when I first saw him, that he should keep a diary, and be   80
encouraged to keep notes every day of his experiences, his feelings, thoughts,
memories, reflections. These attempts were foiled, at first, by his continually
losing the diary: it had to be attached to him—somehow. But this too failed
to work: he dutifully kept a brief daily notebook but could not recognize his
earlier entries in it. He does recognize his own writing, and style, and is always
astounded to find that he wrote something the day before.

Astounded—and indifferent—for he was a man who, in effect, had no "day   81
before." His entries remained unconnected and unconnecting and had no
power to provide any sense of time or continuity. Moreover, they were trivial—
"Eggs for breakfast," "Watched ballgame on TV"—and never touched the
depths. But were there depths in this unmemoried man, depths of an abiding
feeling and thinking, or had he been reduced to a sort of Humean drivel, a
mere succession of unrelated impressions and events?

Jimmie both was and wasn't aware of this deep, tragic loss in himself, loss   82
of himself. (If a man has lost a leg or an eye, he knows he has lost a leg or an
eye; but if he has lost a self—himself—he cannot know it, because he is no
longer there to know it.) Therefore I could not question him intellectually
about such matters.

He had originally professed bewilderment at finding himself amid patients,   83
when, as he said, he himself didn't feel ill. But what, we wondered, did he
feel? He was strongly built and fit, he had a sort of animal strength and energy,
but also a strange inertia, passivity, and (as everyone remarked) "unconcern";
he gave all of us an overwhelming sense of "something missing," although this,
if he realized it, was itself accepted with an odd "unconcern." One day I asked

him not about his memory, or past, but about the simplest and most elemental feelings of all:

"How do you feel?"   84

"How do I feel," he repeated, and scratched his head. "I cannot say I feel   85
ill. But I cannot say I feel well. I cannot say I feel anything at all."

"Are you miserable?" I continued.   86

"Can't say I am."   87

"Do you enjoy life?"   88

"I can't say I do. . . ."   89

I hesitated, fearing that I was going too far that I might be stripping a man   90
down to some hidden, unacknowledgeable, unbearable despair.

"You don't enjoy life," I repeated, hesitating somewhat. "How then *do* you   91
feel about life?"

"I can't say that I feel anything at all."   92

"You feel alive though?"   93

"Feel alive? Not really. I haven't felt alive for a very long time."   94

His face wore a look of infinite sadness and resignation.   95

Later, having noted his aptitude for, and pleasure in, quick games and   96
puzzles, and their power to "hold" him, at least while they lasted, and to allow,
for a while, a sense of companionship and competition—he had not complained of loneliness, but he looked so alone; he never expressed sadness, but
he looked so sad—I suggested he be brought into our recreation programs at
the Home. This worked better—better than the diary. He would become
keenly and briefly involved in games, but soon they ceased to offer any challenge: he solved all the puzzles, and could solve them easily; and he was far
better and sharper than anyone else at games. And as he found this out, he
grew fretful and restless again, and wandered the corridors, uneasy and bored
and with a sense of indignity—games and puzzles were for children, a diversion.
Clearly, passionately, he wanted something to do: he wanted to do, to be, to
feel—and could not; he wanted sense, he wanted purpose—in Freud's words,
"Work and Love."

Could he do "ordinary" work? He had "gone to pieces," his brother said,   97
when he ceased to work in 1965. He had two striking skills—Morse code and
touch-typing. We could not use Morse, unless we invented a use; but good
typing we could use, if he could recover his old skills—and this would be real
work, not just a game. Jimmie soon did recover his old skill and came to type
very quickly—he could not do it slowly—and found in this some of the challenge and satisfaction of a job. But still this was superficial tapping and typing;
it was trivial, it did not reach to the depths. And what he typed, he typed

mechanically—he could not hold the thought—the short sentences following one another in a meaningless order.

One tended to speak of him, instinctively, as a spiritual casualty—a "lost soul": was it possible that he had really been "desouled" by a disease? "Do you think he *has* a soul?" I once asked the Sisters. They were outraged by my question, but could see why I asked it. "Watch Jimmie in chapel," they said, "and judge for yourself."

I did, and I was moved, profoundly moved and impressed, because I saw here an intensity and steadiness of attention and concentration that I had never seen before in him or conceived him capable of. I watched him kneel and take the Sacrament on his tongue, and could not doubt the fullness and totality of Communion, the perfect alignment of his spirit with the spirit of the Mass. Fully, intensely, quietly, in the quietude of absolute concentration and attention, he entered and partook of the Holy Communion. He was wholly held, absorbed, by a feeling. There was no forgetting, no Korsakov's then, nor did it seem possible or imaginable that there should be; for he was no longer at the mercy of a faulty and fallible mechanism—that of meaningless sequences and memory traces—but was absorbed in an act, an act of his whole being, which carried feeling and meaning in an organic continuity and unity, a continuity and unity so seamless it could not permit any break.

Clearly Jimmie found himself, found continuity and reality, in the absoluteness of spiritual attention and act. The Sisters were right—he did find his soul here. And so was Luria, whose words now came back to me: "A man does not consist of memory alone. He has feeling, will, sensibility, moral being. . . . It is here . . . you may touch him, and see a profound change." Memory, mental activity, mind alone, could not hold him; but moral attention and action could hold him completely.

But perhaps "moral" was too narrow a word—for the aesthetic and dramatic were equally involved. Seeing Jim in the chapel opened my eyes to other realms where the soul is called on, and held, and stilled, in attention and communion. The same depth of absorption and attention was to be seen in relation to music and art: he had no difficulty, I noticed, "following" music or simple dramas, for every moment in music and art refers to, contains, other moments. He liked gardening, and had taken over some of the work in our garden. At first he greeted the garden each day as new, but for some reason this had become more familiar to him than the inside of the Home. He almost never got lost or disoriented in the garden now; he patterned it, I think, on loved and remembered gardens from his youth in Connecticut.

Jimmie, who was so lost in extensional "spatial" time, was perfectly orga- 102
nized in Bergsonian[3] "intentional" time; what was fugitive, unsustainable, as
formal structure, was perfectly stable, perfectly held, as art or will. Moreover,
there was something that endured and survived. If Jimmie was briefly "held"
by a task or puzzle or game or calculation, held in the purely mental challenge
of these, he would fall apart as soon as they were done, into the abyss of his
nothingness, his amnesia. But if he was held in emotional and spiritual attention—in the contemplation of nature or art, in listening to music, in taking
part in the Mass in chapel—the attention, its "mood," its quietude, would
persist for a while, and there would be in him a pensiveness and peace we
rarely, if ever, saw during the rest of his life at the Home.

I have known Jimmie now for nine years—and neuropsychologically, he has 103
not changed in the least. He still has the severest, most devastating Korsakov's,
cannot remember isolated items for more than a few seconds, and has a dense
amnesia going back to 1945. But humanly, spiritually, he is at times a different
man altogether—no longer fluttering, restless, bored, and lost, but deeply at-
tentive to the beauty and soul of the world, rich in all the Kierkegaardian[4]
categories—the aesthetic, the moral, the religious, the dramatic. I had wondered, when I first met him, if he was not condemned to a sort of "Humean"
froth, a meaningless fluttering on the surface of life, and whether there was
any way of transcending the incoherence of his Humean disease. Empirical
science told me there was not—but empirical science, empiricism, takes no
account of the soul, no account of what constitutes and determines personal
being. Perhaps there is a philosophical as well as a clinical lesson here: that
in Korsakov's, or dementia, or other such catastrophes, however great the
organic damage and Humean dissolution, there remains the undiminished possibility of reintegration by art, by communion, by touching the human spirit:
and this can be preserved in what seems at first a hopeless state of neurological
devastation.

Focusing on Oliver Sacks's Use of First-Person Point of View

1. Why does Sacks only slowly reveal what Jimmie's problem is? How does
   Sacks present himself in this essay? How does his willingness to admit to an
   "impulse for which I have never forgiven myself" in paragraph 13 make us
   think of him?

[3]Henri Bergson (1859–1941), French philosopher.
[4]Søren Kierkegaard (1813–1855), Danish philosopher.

2. When does Sacks first introduce the official diagnosis, "Korsakov's syndrome"? How does he work into his essay references to the previous research on this syndrome? How would this essay begin differently if it were a "scientific" report on a patient?

3. In paragraphs 60–62, Sacks speaks of being "wrung with emotion" and "unscientifically" including comments about "a lost soul" in his official notes on the case. In paragraph 65, Sacks comments that in another researcher's formal account of a similar case, "science became poetry." What is it about cases such as Jimmie's that make it impossible for scientists studying them to remain "scientific"? Why is poetry, or the kind of personal narration that Sacks uses, a more appropriate way to report such cases than the language of science?

4. Sacks asks in paragraph 75, "What could we do? What should we do?" to help Jimmie. He quotes Dr. Luria's reply, that "it is here, beyond the realm of an impersonal psychology, that you may find ways to touch him, and change him." At the end of the essay (in the last five paragraphs), Sacks tells of how he finally finds a way to touch and change Jimmie. What realms outside of "impersonal psychology" does Sacks find? How is Jimmie touched and changed in those realms? Why is the point of view of Sacks's essay necessary to bring us to appreciate these "personal" realms?

5. In the last paragraph, Sacks says that "empirical science, empiricism, takes no account of the soul." How does Sacks's essay take account of the soul? How does Sacks manage to combine in his essay "empirical science" and "the soul"?

WORKING WITH THE TECHNIQUE IN YOUR OWN WRITING

1. Write a narrative essay about an encounter you have had with an "untouchable" subject, either one that is awful, such as death, insanity, or child abuse, or one that is awe-inspiring, such as birth or religious revelation. See if you can structure your essay to carry your readers with you as you get close to the "untouchable"; you might set up your essay as Dipo and Sacks do to move from a fairly "objective" and distant perspective to a much more personal one. All these subjects bring out strong and quite contradictory reactions when we really get close to them. Try to honestly reveal your ambivalent feelings, even ones that you are not particularly proud of. Use the first-person point of view, and try to create a trustworthy, sincere narrator.

2. Write an essay about what science or medicine overlooks in its insistence on objectivity. Use the first-person point of view and draw on personal experience,

but you do not necessarily have to deal with awesome subjects such as death or insanity. You might try to arrange your essay so that for at least part of it you move from a "distant," objective, scientific point of view to a closer, more personal one. Your essay need not be a critique of science or medicine; both Dipo and Sacks show us how they went beyond scientific objectivity, but both writers clearly have great respect for science.

DIANNE EMMINGER

Point Park College
Pittsburgh, Pennsylvania
James Rosenberg, instructor

"The most important thing to me as a writer is to encourage criticism of my work and to accept it gracefully," Dianne Emminger reports. "I have done my best work when my children have shown me that my writing lacks clarity and I have revised the work until I got it right. Thinking of someone reading and understanding my writing makes me enthusiastic about my subject. It doesn't make much sense to write if my readers don't understand my ideas."

Born in Pittsburgh, Pennsylvania, in 1948, Dianne Emminger enrolled in Point Park College when her children entered elementary school. A part-time computer science major and a full-time data processing supervisor while an undergraduate, she learned "to juggle job, family, and college." In the several years since winning a Bedford Prize, Emminger has earned a B.S. degree in computer science from Point Park College and has enrolled in evening classes in the University of Pittsburgh's M.B.A. program. At the same time she has continued to work at her career in data processing. She currently holds the position of director of information systems in the construction division of the Cyclops Corporation.

Dianne Emminger identifies "increased confidence in my writing ability" as the principal benefit of having won a Bedford Prize in Student Writing: "After winning the Prize, I stated that I didn't like to write. Perhaps that was more a reflection of a lack of confidence than a disliking for the task because I would not make that same statement today. The only change that I am aware of, though, is my own attitude. Where I was once a bit timid about writing, I now feel comfortable with just about any written assignment." Emminger reports that she currently spends "about 20 to 30 hours a week writing. Much of that writing is business correspondence and business presentations. Business school requires me to write term papers, essays, and issue briefs."

Winning a Bedford Prize has also produced some charming anecdotes: "Since Student Writers at Work was widely used in Pennsylvania colleges and universities, I received comments from nieces and nephews who were surprised to find their aunt's name in their freshman composition textbook. My daughter's boyfriend was a freshman the year the book was published. He visited our home last Christmas and noticed the book on the shelf. When my daughter told him her mother's essay was published there, he related his recollection of reading it in class. I still chuckle at his comment. He said he remembers liking it because it was short."

The assignment that produced Dianne Emminger's prize-winning essay required her to write an essay about something insignificant that at one time caught her attention. Emminger reports that she was sitting on a plane in Atlanta "full of frustration at my failure to begin writing" when she decided to write about the most insignificant thing she could see—the raindrops on the plane window. Several days later, while reviewing the notes she had written on the plane, she began thinking of the prismatic effect of raindrops on light and was reminded of something she had seen a few years earlier while visiting a local art gallery.

The Exhibition

It was on a dismal, rainy Sunday afternoon in a local art gallery that I   1
learned how a conscious attempt at art appreciation can, at times, render one
unaware of simple, gentle things. A large exhibition was being presented, and
the gallery was crowded. Some rather good local artists exhibited their works
there, and this was a particularly fine collection, one of the most diverse
exhibitions the gallery had ever hosted. It also drew a very diverse crowd, and
as I strolled through the spacious halls, I alternately found my attention on
patrons and paintings.

Pearl-draped elderly women, reeking of perfume, promenaded the halls, at   2
times speaking of art, at times of their bridge games. On the wall, an extravagant ballroom scene hung, displaying aristocratic beauties in flowing silk gowns.
Unkempt, long-haired men and sandal-footed women, with toddlers clinging
to their hips, nodded appreciatively at the contemporary selections. Above
them, bold brush strokes and shapeless forms brought an artist's thunderstorm
to life. A few middle-aged men in golf attire slumped dejectedly on marble
benches, while their scooting children made a game out of sliding on polished
floors. On a pillar hung a solitary painting of stern-faced Dutchmen, staring
down from their austere meeting room, as if distracted by the commotion
below.

Now, I don't profess to know anything about painting, so I like to follow   3
close behind those who do. Thus, I followed that day, hoping to learn something about art appreciation. I studied each canvas intently, trying hard to
comprehend what genius there was behind the bold, blue streak transecting
the yellow circle and to understand why my favorite ocean scene was unimag-
inative. By the time I reached the end of the fourth hall, I no longer knew
what I liked and disliked, and, perhaps, I didn't care.

But as I turned the corner, there appeared a small child, a girl of about six,   4
crouched near one of the walls, playing quietly. The rain had decreased to a
drizzle, and the sun had come out. The window opposite her was dotted with
tiny raindrops, and each prismatic one refracted the sunlight and sent dancing,
rainbow-colored lights bouncing on the gallery wall. Each clinging drop shim-
mied when struck by falling drizzle, and the light on the wall darted out, then
back. Some droplets sent out tiny armlike appendages that touched others,
and the rainbow colors kissed and parted. The heavier drops crept down the
window pane, pulling others within, until their combined weight became so
great that they would race, helter-skelter, down the glass. On the wall, small
rainbows scurried and darted, changing speeds, changing shapes.

The group I had been following moved farther down the hall, praising a   5
nearby painting—"Such color! Such form! Such movement!" They didn't no-

tice the child or the lights, nor did the child notice them. She was holding out a small hand watching the speckles of color scurry down a finger, up a thumb, across her palm. She removed her hat and tried to catch a rainbow inside. She twisted her head sideways and upside down to see the colors from another angle. Her eyes gleamed like the lights. Such innocence was in this child. She didn't know how the brush danced in the hand of the artist, only how the colors danced on the wall.

The crowd of connoisseurs could still be heard. "Look at this one! The   6
colors seem alive! The artist has such imagination!" The entranced child didn't look; her fingers merely traced circles around the tiny specks of color on the wall. And so she remained until, having been located by her mother, she was quickly rushed away to look at paintings, the reason for which she had been brought to the gallery.

If I could paint, I would have painted those rainbow lights, that child, the   7
wall. I would have permanently preserved the lively exhibition of colored lights that dwarfed great works of art in one young mind. And I would hang that canvas in that very same gallery for the art connoisseurs, for the sandal-footed mothers, for the perfumed bridge players, and especially for the little girl, that she might never let sophistication in art appreciation prevent her from seeing unsophisticated beauty.

Focusing on Dianne Emminger's Techniques and Revisions

1. Dianne Emminger came to the art gallery to see one exhibition but saw some-thing very different from what she expected. What does the child teach Em-minger about art and beauty? How would Emminger answer the question "What is art?" Describe how Emminger learns this lesson.

2. What is Emminger's purpose in this essay? Is it to describe the exhibition, the crowd of connoisseurs, the child, or all three? Is it to tell us about her own insights from her experience? Is it to argue for a particular view of art? Explain. How do Emminger's introduction and conclusion reinforce her purpose?

3. What strategies does Emminger use to bring the reader closer to her experience? For instance, how does she show the child, the art, and the gallery patrons as competing possibilities, competing exhibitions? One of the principal strengths of this essay is in Emminger's effective descriptions, her ability to put the reader in the art gallery. As you reread her essay, point to specific details and passages and explain why you find each especially effective.

4. What strategy does Emminger use to portray the two different views of art she discovers on "a dismal, rainy Sunday afternoon in a local art gallery"? How

does she characterize the different kinds of people who would advocate each of these views of art?

5. Which of these two views of art (unsophisticated and sophisticated) does the narrator favor? Point to specific words and phrases to support your response. What strategies does Emminger use to reinforce the narrator's attraction to one kind of art? Where—and how effectively—does the narrator state the point she makes in her essay? How would the effect differ if Emminger had presented a formal argument about art instead of creating a scene to dramatize it?

6. Emminger reports: "This was not a difficult essay to write, but I had a great deal of difficulty with the second paragraph in which I describe the people and the paintings in the gallery. It was awkward taking the readers from one subject to another without confusing them." Do you think that Emminger was successful in handling the second paragraph? How might the paragraph be revised to be more effective?

7. When invited to reread her prize-winning essay several years after having written it, Dianne Emminger responded: "The third paragraph of this essay introduces my struggle with the comments of art experts. They didn't like what I liked. I didn't understand what they liked. I don't think that conflict was presented very effectively. I should have taken more time to develop that idea." Reread the third paragraph of Emminger's essay. What specific advice would you offer to help her "develop that idea"?

8. When asked to list what changes, if any, she would now make in her essay, Emminger observed: "I would change many of the phrases. I would write 'attempt to appreciate art' rather than 'attempt at art appreciation.'" I would change 'there appeared a small child' to 'a small child appeared.' The phrase 'I alternately focused my attention on' would be entirely replaced. I have learned since that time to write in a more direct manner. I would expand paragraph 3 to strengthen the explanation of the conflict. The ending of the last sentence in that paragraph is abrupt and unsupported. The tense of the last paragraph is inconsistent and makes the sentences awkward. And I'm still not sure what I would like to do with the second paragraph." Keep Emminger's principle "to write in a more direct manner" in mind as you reread her essay. Can you identify any other instances in which she might use this principle to revise her prose?

Suggestions for Writing

1. Emminger describes a perfect moment that becomes, for her, a work of art. Try to recall such a moment in your own experience. What was it that captured your attention? Write an essay describing the details of such a moment and explain its significance.

2. We have all had experiences that have changed our perceptions so that we develop a new way of understanding something. Describe such an experience by showing not only what changed your perception but also what this change meant for you.

AN EFFECTIVE TECHNIQUE

Dianne Emminger shows us a distinctive method of developing an argument: instead of presenting facts and figures, she builds a small scene in which she shows the two sides of a debate about art by portraying the kinds of people who would be advocates for each side. Emminger wants to convince her readers to appreciate "unsophisticated beauty." To do so, she portrays, in words, sophisticates who listen to art experts and naive persons who enjoy whatever is pleasing to their eyes. Her descriptions of these two groups and of what each considers beautiful indicate clearly where she hopes we will line up.

On the sophisticated side of the debate are a "crowd of connoisseurs" composed of "elderly women, reeking of perfume, . . . unkempt, long-haired men . . . [and] a few middle-aged men in golf attire [who were] slumped dejectedly on marble benches." Not a very appealing bunch of people. Emminger shows that these people basically admire paintings that remind them of themselves, or of what they wish they were: the elderly women stand by an "extravagant ballroom scene . . . displaying aristocratic beauties"; the unkempt men "nod appreciatively at . . . shapeless forms"; the middle-aged men slump under a painting of "stern-faced Dutchmen."

On the other side of this debate about art are the child and the narrator. The child plays with the "rainbow colors" created by the sun and raindrops. The child's "eyes gleamed like the lights": she is "entranced" and "full of innocence." We cannot help but like this child, and we sense that she is truly looking at beauty. Also on this side of the debate is the narrator, who describes herself as unsophisticated as the child: "I don't profess to know anything about painting." But without any knowledge of painting, the narrator paints a picture of the beauty she can appreciate, the beauty of the child and the rainbow— and, as an integral part of the scene, the ugliness of the connoisseurs and the art on the walls. By contrast, this ugliness makes the child and the rainbow all the more beautiful.

Though Emminger directly states the point she is arguing for at the beginning and at the end of her essay, what makes her essay so convincing is her depiction of the two opposed sides of the debate. We could easily imagine a formal argument that would lead to the same conclusion, but it would be very difficult to specify what is wrong with "sophisticated" beauty and what is good about "unsophisticated" beauty. Besides, to define good and bad kinds of beauty fully would probably require the language of connoisseurs and might make the narrator appear sophisticated herself, undercutting her argument.

Essays like Emminger's may emerge from actual scenes we have witnessed, or we might invent an encounter between two opposed persons to show how one view is superior to another. It may be easier to use this technique for issues that touch our everyday lives, but we could portray the president of the United States and the Soviet general secretary conversing at lunch as a way of indicating our view of relations between the superpowers. Political satirists often create such scenes. By portraying the people who hold opinions, we evoke very powerful responses in our readers; it is much easier to care about a person than about an idea. This technique also enables us to give our writing a strong tone. Emminger's sweet, sentimental intensity contributes much to the power of her argument; she would have difficulty developing such a tone in a more formal essay. Writing about people who hold opinions is not an unfair or sneaky way to argue about an issue. Any idea worth defending must have some human consequences and generate responses in people; to explore those responses is a way to gain understanding of just what is at stake, what is at the heart of the logical tangles that often envelop issues.

Andrew Ward, in the next selection, uses a variation of Emminger's technique: he creates two scenes, two encounters between persons with opposed views. Both scenes are rather silly, and the overt point he seems to be arguing for is almost as silly, but embedded in his scenes is a subtle and serious critique of some recent trends.

ANOTHER ILLUSTRATION OF THE TECHNIQUE

ANDREW WARD

Yumbo

Andrew Ward writes, "I consider myself a humorist, a designation which performs the function of forcing my intentions out into the open. My work must pass a simple test; if it fails to get a laugh or raise a smile from my readers (meaning my wife and brother) then it fails to justify itself. This may not seem a particularly lofty test, but I'm not a very lofty fellow, and believe that laughter, at least the laughter that comes with recognition, is our surest barometer of truth." Ward prefers his barometer of truth to the ones he was subjected to in his years of schooling; he says he still dreams of taking finals for classes he never attended and remembers his teachers covering his exams with "explosions [of] red-inked exclamations expressing regret, alarm, and grave concern for my future." Ward attended Oberlin College for three semesters and then switched to the Rhode Island School of Design. He had trouble selecting a career until his stories and essays began being regularly published and he realized that "being a humorist beats being a puzzle cutter, a soda jerk, a machinist, a janitor, a teacher, a photographer, or any of the other professions I've given a try." At present, Ward is a commentator for "All Things Considered" on National Public Radio.

I was sitting at an inn with Kelly Susan, my ten-year-old niece, when she   1
was handed the children's menu. It was printed in gay pastels on construction paper and gave her a choice of a Ferdinand Burger, a Freddie the Fish Stick, or a Porky Pig Sandwich. Like most children's menus, it first anthropomorphized the ingredients and then killed them off. As Kelly read it her eyes grew large, and in them I could see gentle Ferdinand being led away to the stockyard, Freddie gasping at the end of a hook, Porky stuttering his entreaties as the ax descended. Kelly Susan, alone in her family, is a resolute vegetarian and has already faced up to the dread that whispers to us as we slice our steaks. She wound up ordering a cheese sandwich, but the children's menu had ruined her appetite, and she spent the meal picking at her food.

Restaurants have always treated children badly. When I was small, my   2
family used to travel a lot, and waitresses were forever calling me "Butch" and pinching my cheeks and making me wear paper bibs with slogans on them. Restaurants still treat children badly; the difference is that restaurants have lately taken to treating us all as if we were children. We are obliged to order an Egg McMuffin when we want breakfast, a Fishamajig when we want a fish sandwich, a Fribble when we want a milkshake, a Whopper when we want a hamburger with all the fixings. Some of these names serve a certain purpose. By calling a milkshake a Fribble, for instance, the management need make no promise that it contains milk, or even that it was shaken.

But the primary purpose is to convert an essentially bleak industry, mass-   3
marketed fast foods, into something festive. The burger used to be a culinary last resort; now resorts are being built around it. The patrons in the commercials for burger franchises are all bug-eyed and goofy, be they priests or grandmothers or crane operators, and behave as if it were their patriotic duty, their God-given right, to consume waxy buns, translucent patties, chewy fries, and industrial strength Coca-Cola.

Happily, the patrons who actually slump into these places are an entirely   4
different matter. I remember with fond admiration a tidy little man at the
local Burger King whom I overheard order a ham and cheese sandwich.

"A wha'?" the eruptive girl at the counter asked, pencil poised over her   5
computer card.

"I wish to order a ham and cheese sandwich," the man repeated.   6

"I'm sorry, sir," the girl said, "but we don't carry ham and cheese. All we   7
got is what's on the board up there."

"Yes, I know," the man politely persisted, "but I believe it is up there. See?   8
The ham and cheese?"

The girl gaped at the menu board behind her. "Oh," she finally exclaimed.   9
"You mean a *Yumbo*. You want a *Yumbo*."

"The ham and cheese. Yes."   10

"It's called a *Yumbo*, sir," the girl said. "Now, do you want a Yumbo or   11
not?"

The man stiffened. "Yes, thank you," he said through his teeth, "the *ham*   12
and *cheese*."

"Look," the girl shouted, "I've got to have an order here. You're holding   13
up the line. You want a *Yumbo*, don't you? You want a *Yumbo*?"

But the tidy man was not going to say it, and thus were they locked for a   14
few more moments, until at last he stood very straight, put on his hat, and
departed intact.

Focusing on Andrew Ward's Use of Scenes

1. How does Andrew Ward make us side with Kelly Susan and himself against
   everyone in the fast food industry (waiters, managers, and even the menus)?

2. The essay starts off with what seems to be a rather small complaint about some
   words. What larger issues does Ward raise in paragraphs 2 and 3? How would
   the essay be different if he had started with his large points? If he had placed
   them at the end of the essay? What is the effect of starting and ending the
   essay with scenes?

3. How does Ward make us side with the man in the scene at the end of the
   essay? How does he make the girl at the counter unlikable? How does this scene
   contribute to his overall argument?

WORKING WITH THE TECHNIQUE IN YOUR OWN WRITING

1. Write an argumentative essay in which you create an extended scene (or several scenes) that portray people who are on opposite sides of the issue you are writing about. Use your descriptions of the people, and any dialogue, to support your position in the debate. Let your readers see how phony, silly, nasty, evil, or simply bad the people are who would oppose you; and let them see how decent, sweet, kind, intelligent, or otherwise good those on your side are. You might include some indications of what sort of person you are as well, perhaps through the tone and voice you use to write the scene. You might find a topic for this essay by watching people around you for a few days, waiting until you observe a scene worth commenting on—some behavior that seems immoral or silly. You can also just invent a scene that can show the contrast between the two sides of an issue.

2. Using a scene to make your case, write an essay that argues against either Emminger's or Ward's essay. You might try to retell the very scenes they use but change the descriptions and the dialogue so that the scenes prove the opposite points. Or you might build an entirely different scene that argues against their points. You might even create a scene in which Emminger or Ward appears as a character and has to change her or his mind.

ANN LOUISE FIELD

University of Iowa
Iowa City, Iowa
Nancy Jones, instructor

"When I was about three, I packed all of my clothes in a paper sack and informed my parents that I was running away to an alligator farm and could they please tell me where to find one. Ever since then I've been making up all kinds of stories in my head. Many of the stories were based on things that my brother Brett and I had done or wanted to do. Those stories never left my head or ended up on paper until after Brett died in 1977. It was in remembering all that Brett and I had shared that I realized the stories in my head about our youth were interesting even without the parts I made up. I felt as if I had something to say that others might be interested in reading."

Asked to write an essay on some aspect of her hometown or childhood, Field reports that she knew she would write about Brett and herself. "Brett was my childhood. We spent every minute together. He taught me how to climb trees, how to peel an orange in one continuous piece, how to spit, how to throw dirt clods, and how to shoot rubber bands across the room."

Ann Louise Field was born in Ukiah, California, spent the first sixteen years of her life in Redlands, and now calls Salem, Oregon, her hometown. Field worked as a manager for McDonald's, as a seamstress in a drapery business, and as a maid in a motel to help pay for her college education. Married to a graduate student in telecommunications in August 1986, Ann Field–Stidham completed her degree in nursing at the University of Iowa in 1988 before returning to the Pacific Northwest.

Invited to reread her prize-winning essay and to identify its most memorable features several years after having written it, Field–Stidham readily responded: "The essay remains successful for me because it is so real. I can close my eyes and be there. I hope it has the same effect on others."

The Sound of Angels

When I was nine I lived in Southern California. Redlands was a small town, as California towns go, and not an exciting place to live. My life in Redlands was as predictable as the fact that we always had tacos for dinner on Saturday, chili on Sunday, and tamale pie on Monday. Every day was a carbon copy of all the previous days. Nothing ever seemed to change. But in spite of this sameness I wasn't unhappy. My brother Brett and the orange groves at the top of our street were both a big part of the sameness and the source of happiness. 1

Brett had an afternoon paper route in the summer of 1969. The route and 2

147

the money he earned were something that he and I shared. Every afternoon at two he'd deliver *The Daily Facts* to 107 paying customers and I would ride with him on the last half of the route. I didn't really help deliver any of the papers on the paper route. I was still too new at riding a bike to hold the bike steady with one hand and heave a rolled-up paper onto the porch of a house with the other, but I don't think Brett wanted the help—he wanted the company. Brett never let me go with him to the newspaper office to pick up the papers because some of the other boys would say nasty things to me. He didn't want me to hear the things these boys would say, and he was concerned that the long uphill ride home would be too much for me, so Brett did the first half of the route alone. And I would wait, in the front yard if it wasn't too hot, for Brett to come riding around the corner on his new orange ten-speed.

Brett's bike was the most beautiful bike I had ever seen. It was much too 3 expensive for Mom and Dad to buy so Brett had helped pay for it by selling greeting cards. It was nicer than my bike. My bike was blue and it didn't have any speeds, just stop and go. It was the first bike I had ever owned and I had finally gotten it for Christmas when I was eight after having wished for a bike since I was six. The bike was used and had been painted over and the purple basket on the handlebars was faded, but I didn't care. Brett liked my bike almost as much as I liked his. He never treated my bike as if it were any less valuable than the one he had. He took good care of his own bike, washing and waxing it on the weekends, and he helped me do the same to mine.

Brett bought things for the two of us with the money he made from his 4 paper route. He bought things that we never seemed to get enough of at home: a dozen doughnuts that we didn't have to share with anyone, plastic vampire teeth and fake blood at Halloween, toys from the five- and ten-cent machines just inside the door of the store, and a note pad of pink paper with matching envelopes that he had seen me admiring. When I saw these things in the store I never asked Brett to buy them for me. He just did. Whenever he chose something for himself he chose one for me too. But the doughnuts were the best of all. I can remember getting up early on cool Saturday mornings in the fall or spring and riding with Brett two miles to the Winchell's doughnut house. We would spend thirty minutes just looking in the window at all the different shapes and sizes and kinds of doughnuts. Then, when we had decided which twelve we wanted, Brett would buy them. We would bicycle two blocks over to the high school and eat them there on the lawn in front of one of the buildings. I would eat four and he would eat the rest. They were just for us. If we decided that we didn't like one of the doughnuts that we chose we just left it there for the birds. They were our doughnuts and we could do with them whatever we pleased.

Brett and I also spent a lot of time in the orange groves at the top of our   5
street. Running through these groves were sankies, open drainage ditches
that caught the runoff from the groves. When the groves ended the sankies
went underground and continued, for miles sometimes, until they reached
the next grove. The sankies were lined on the sides and bottom with rock
and cement. Sometimes they had a few inches of water in the bottom and
sometimes they were dry. We weren't supposed to play in the orange groves
but we did anyway. The orange groves supplied us with rotten oranges that
we liked to throw at passing cars. It was into the sankies that we dove for
cover when an angry motorist stopped to locate the source of the rotten orange, but not even the most ardent pursuer could catch us once we went
underground.

The orange groves were always a pleasant place, winter or summer. In   6
summer we had the shade of the trees and the dust rising from the dry dirt to
fill our nostrils and stick to our sweaty skin. We could sit in the sankies with
our feet in the water and feel the coolness of the rock wall against our backs
as we ate sweet, stolen oranges. In the winter the wind whispered through the
leaves bringing with it the pungent odor of oil from the smudge pots burning
nearby to keep the trees and their fruit warm. There was a crispness to the
cold that could carry the smell of a chimney fire a mile away and bring the
stars in the sky within reach.

It was in this cold that Brett and I would steal Christmas lights off of houses.   7
We would go out after dark for a walk to look at the houses decorated for the
holiday and we would steal the lights. Never very many though. Only one or
two from each house and never more than a handful each trip. It was a
challenge for Brett to sneak up to the front of a well-lit house and take the
bulbs without getting caught. I was too chicken to leave the safety of the
shadows so I was always the lookout. Once we had the bulbs we would return
to the orange grove at the top of our street and break them. As they struck
the ground there was a hollow POP! followed by the tinkling of colored glass.
It was such a pretty sound. Brett said it was the sound of angels. That sound
put me at peace and made me happy in a way I had never known. By the
smile in his eyes and the way he held my hand as we walked home, I knew it
made Brett feel the same way.

We loved our orange groves, our bicycles, the dozens of doughnuts we   8
shared, and the carefree life they gave us. It was the only side of life we knew.
I figured that one morning I would wake up and find that I had grown up
during the night, but I didn't think that it would change things. Nothing could
possibly matter more than paper routes, climbing trees, eating oranges, and
crawling around on our bellies in the sankies under the streets.

It was sometime during the latter half of 1969 that I realized we were poor. 9
It was 6:15 one fall evening and the sun would be setting in about an hour. I
was standing on a footstool in front of the kitchen sink doing the dinner dishes
and I could see Dad and Brett out of the window. Dad was talking and Brett
was shaking his head and saying "no" with an intensity I had never seen before.
I thought Brett might be crying. After a few moments they both came in the
house and my dad handed Brett two empty grocery sacks.

"Go with your brother, please," was all my dad said.   10

Something in his voice frightened me so I went without asking why. Word- 11
lessly, Brett and I left the house and climbed over the back fence. We crossed
the dirt field of the junior high school and passed the buildings until we came
to an orange grove on the other side of the school. We climbed this fence too
and went back into the trees. I wondered what we were doing there because
we never played in this orange grove. Brett opened his sack and began picking
oranges and dropping them into it.

"What are you doing?" I screeched. "Dad will kill us if we steal oranges!" 12

Brett looked at me with tears running down his cheeks. "Dad said to take 13
them."

"Why? Dad would never let us steal."   14

"Just shut up and do it!" Brett yelled at me.   15

I stomped my foot. "Not until you tell me why."   16

"Because we're poor!" he shouted. "If we don't steal these oranges we won't 17
have anything for lunch tomorrow." With that he threw the two oranges in
his hands at me. They hit me on the head and the arm and I gave a startled
cry. Brett wiped his eyes and nose with the sleeve of his shirt and said more
quietly, "Just pick the damn oranges."

As our house came into view on the walk home I saw it as if for the first 18
time. The paint was peeling and the yard was overgrown with bushes and ivy.
The run-down condition embarrassed me. From inside the house I could hear
two people yelling at each other. I saw my whole life in that frame; my hand-
me-down clothes that had been Brett's before mine and somebody else's before
his, and my used and shabby bike with rust and dents under the cheap blue
paint. I remembered a time when I was six and we had "camped out" in front
of the fireplace for a week. It had been fun sleeping on the floor, pretending
we were pioneers and cooking over the fire. I also remember trying to turn the
bathroom light on and my mother's strange look when I asked her why it
wouldn't work. I knew now why it wouldn't—the electricity had been shut
off. That same year a box of food and some presents appeared on the front
porch Christmas morning. My mother cried when I scolded her for not leaving
the door unlocked for Santa.

We were poor. I had three oranges as my lunch the next day to remind me.   19

The days went on and so did Brett and I. We continued to play the way   20 we always had, but I think it was easier for me than for him. Sometimes I felt that he was simply going through the motions of play for my sake. At times he would grow tired of our games and want to just sit quietly in one of the trees. I sensed that things weren't the same because the more we did the things we once loved to do, the more withdrawn Brett became. I didn't like seeing him this way so I was glad when we drifted away from the orange grove. I knew that something had taken the fun out of our orange grove, but I wasn't sure what it was or what it meant.

I'm not sure exactly when it happened, but my brother and I drifted apart.   21 We occasionally went for doughnuts on Saturdays and stole Christmas lights each year, but we weren't as close as we had been. And then puberty came along and gave Brett longer legs and me wider hips and I could no longer wear his old clothes and that somehow set us farther apart. The unpleasant memories associated with that day in the orange grove faded and were almost forgotten until I was fourteen and in the ninth grade. I came home one afternoon to find that my mother had tried to kill herself. I was angry at her for doing it. Not so much because she had almost died but because she had brought reality back into my life once and for all. I didn't want to see what reality had to show me. I didn't want to see the shabbiness of the blue bike or the hand-me-down clothes that filled my closet. I didn't want to grow up if it was going to be so complicated that it made some people want to die so bad that they could cut their own wrists. I wanted camping in front of the fireplace to be just camping, not keeping warm because the electricity had been shut off. I wanted to eat an orange without remembering that week when they were all we had to eat. I wanted to share a dozen doughnuts with Brett on a Saturday morning and disappear laughingly into the sankies where reality, like the angry motorist, wouldn't follow. I wanted to close my eyes and hear the hollow POP! and the tinkling of colored glass. I wanted the sound of angels to mask the fact that life wasn't always as easy as orange groves and sankies and a dozen doughnuts.

But the sound of angels couldn't help me anymore. As my mother lay in   22 the hospital and my life went on I said goodbye to the magic, the predictability, and the simplicity of a life filled with paper routes, colored Christmas lights, and a dozen doughnuts to share with Brett. These things were gone, and with their going came the knowledge that they could never return.

Focusing on Ann Louise Field's Techniques and Revisions

1. Ann Louise Field tells us that when she was nine her life was as predictable as the fact that "we always had tacos for dinner on Saturday, chili on Sunday, and tamale pie on Monday. Every day was a carbon copy of all the previous days. Nothing ever seemed to change. But in spite of this sameness I wasn't unhappy" (paragraph 1). What are the happy memories that Field remembers about this time in her life? How did she think of these events as a child? How does she think of these events now?

2. How many different stories does Field tell about her childhood? Why does Field choose to tell a number of stories and present a number of memories to her readers instead of just one? How does this strategy serve her *purpose?*

3. What do we learn about Brett in paragraph 2? How is this impression of him maintained throughout the rest of the essay? How did he react to the stealing of oranges?

4. Field writes with tremendous care and detail in describing her relationship with Brett: "Brett bought things for the two of us with the money he made from his paper route. He bought things that we never seemed to get enough of at home: a dozen doughnuts that we didn't have to share with anyone, plastic vampire teeth and fake blood at Halloween, toys from the five- and ten-cent machines just inside the door of the store, and a note pad of pink paper with matching envelopes that he had seen me admiring" (paragraph 4). Identify details that you found vivid and evocative in the essay. How does Field use these details to create the picture we have of her younger self and her relationship with Brett?

5. Describe Field's *tone* in the first part of her essay. How does she achieve this effect? Point to specific words and phrases to support your response. Where and how does this tone change? To what? With what effect? What strategies does Field use to avoid indulging in self-pity or sentimentality in writing about her childhood? What effect does this have on your reading of her essay?

6. The center of Ann Louise Field's essay is the moment when she revises her view of her childhood world. Where, exactly, is this revelation presented? What specific terms does she use to describe the nature of this revelation? What was the major event that caused her to see her life differently? How did this event change her life? How does Field foreshadow the revelation of her family's poverty?

7. Field presents a number of recurring *images*—the orange groves, the paper route, eating doughnuts, the sound of angels. What strategies does Field use to keep these images alive in her readers' minds throughout the essay? How do these images change in meaning for her readers as Field's understanding changes? What is the effect of repeating these images in the last two paragraphs?

8. Field's first draft began this way:

> I grew up in southern California. When I tell this to people their next comment is always along the lines of how nice it must have been to live near a beach. Redlands, California, was far enough away from any beach for adults to say "inconvenient" or "too much driving involved" whenever we asked to go. Sun and sand and surfers were not a part of my life. Nor was much of anything else in the summer of 1969.

What are the advantages and the disadvantages of Field's deleting this paragraph as her introduction? Why is her revised introduction more effective?

9. Field reports: "The biggest problem I had in writing this essay was cutting unnecessary parts out of the essay. To me everything belonged in the essay and I wanted to find some way to work it all in. Normally I can revise essays with no problems, but revising this paper was like cutting off bits of my arms and legs."

Field wrote and revised her conclusion many times before she was satisfied with it. Here are two earlier versions:

From draft 1:
> I was growing up, but not overnight. It had been happening little by little for I didn't know how long. The sameness of my life that I hoped to leave behind was partly responsible for my maturity. And as my mother lay in the hospital and my life went on I was comforted in knowing that the sameness would never leave me completely.

From draft 2:
> Five years before I had tried to leave the orange groves because everything Brett and I did there seemed to remind us that we were poor. The sameness and the peace that I knew there had been everything to me once. That sameness that I had hoped to forget was now what I wanted most. As my mother lay in the hospital and my life went on I was comforted in knowing that the sameness would never leave me completely.

Compare these two conclusions with the conclusion in the final draft. What are the differences between the conclusions in these rough drafts and the conclusion in the final draft? How does the revised conclusion more successfully tie together the various ideas in the essay?

Suggestions for Writing

1. Field's essay illustrates the idea that life looks a lot different to a child than to an adult. Do you think that Field's parents should have told her that she was poor and explained to her what that meant? Should children be protected and sheltered from the realities of life? Write an argumentative essay to support your point of view on this issue.

2. Field successfully writes about the vivid edges of experience that children know and the small pleasures that give childhood its meaning. Select an experience or a series of experiences from your childhood and reflect on their meaning.

AN EFFECTIVE TECHNIQUE

We do not usually think of revision as a feature *within* an essay; we think of it as something that occurs between drafts. But an essay can be structured to take readers through a revision in their thinking, simply by first convincing them of one view of something and then giving them a different view. Ann Louise Field uses this technique to take her readers through a particularly painful revision that she experienced, a change in her thinking that utterly transformed her childhood world. From her essay we can discover some of the subtleties involved in evoking the powerful feelings of discovering a new truth and being forced to abandon an old one.

A revision is not merely a change; what is revealed in the revised view must exist as potential that has been overlooked in the earlier one. There is a tricky balance to be maintained in the presentation of the early view: we have to include sufficient information about what is to come in order to make the "revision" plausible. We must be careful not to provide too many hints that would allow readers to see that the first view is merely an illusion.

Ann Louise Field quite carefully selects the details that she includes in the first part of her essay: she points to the poverty that will be revealed later, but only in ambiguous terms that could easily be overlooked. For example, she describes things her parents could not afford, but only things that seem un-necessary: an expensive bicycle, a dozen doughnuts, fake vampire teeth. We can easily think that her parents simply refused to buy her these things. Even her "used" and "painted over" bicycle could just be a sign that her parents were thrifty, not that they were poor. So too, Field does not mention until the second half of her essay that her family "camped out" for a week in front of the fireplace. If she had tried to tell us in the first part about the "fun" she had "pretending we were pioneers and cooking over the fire," she knows we might have seen through that description and realized that what we were seeing was a child's distorted view of things.

Field's revelation in the middle of the essay is powerfully surprising and yet believable because she has so carefully prepared her readers for it. Suddenly we see, as she does, her house's "run-down condition," the yard "overgrown with bushes and ivy." We might for a moment think that she had deceived us in the first part, because we had envisioned a decent house. Now we realize that all she had mentioned of the house was that it had a "front yard." She relied on us to fill in an image of a nice front yard because the world she was describing was so pleasant. She has made us create illusions as we read, just as she had created illusions, and so we share with her the shock of realizing our errors.

The most shocking revelation in Field's essay is that the tone of the first part, the peace and happiness, was such an illusion. With the revelation of poverty comes a scene of her father and brother intensely arguing; then her parents are heard yelling at each other; finally, her mother attempts suicide. Field is careful not to tell us much at all about the personalities of her family members, so that we cannot dismiss these tensions as individual psychological problems. Instead, these pains simply become reactions to the whole world Field grew up in. Because Field reveals these tensions at exactly the same point in her essay that she reveals her family's poverty, she makes us think that these tensions are directly a result of that poverty. The essay thereby becomes much broader than a paper about one family; it causes us to ponder the whole social issue of poverty and its psychological costs.

The ending of Field's essay also leads us to think in general about how everyone has to face up to the horrors of the "real world." Field creates the frightening impression that there might be suicidal pains lurking in the over-looked details of all our lives. We are led to these broad thoughts partly because the revision we have been taken through shows us so powerfully the surprises that might accompany expanding our view; we are left a bit fearful that we might even now have a limited view that needs to be revised to a broader one.

Field's essay follows a classic principle for building dramatic effects: take an audience through a reversal of feeling. By moving from happiness to sadness so suddenly, Field creates a tragic and intense sense of loss. We could also take our readers through a revision that moves in the opposite direction, from viewing life as horrible to viewing it as delightful, and thus we would create a strong feeling of humor or joy at the surprising reversal. For example, we could show how a summer camp that seemed painful from beginning to end actually was fun, if only because we discovered the pleasures of complaining and being grumpy. James Baldwin, in "Notes of a Native Son," takes his readers through a very complicated revision in his view of his father and of himself, a revision that involves both painful and joyful discoveries.

ANOTHER ILLUSTRATION OF THE TECHNIQUE

JAMES BALDWIN

Notes of a Native Son

"It's not possible to overstate the price a Negro pays to climb out of obscurity," wrote James Baldwin, describing his early life. Born in Harlem in 1924, he graduated from high school and worked as a preacher, handyman, dishwasher, waiter, and office boy while writing essays and novels that very quickly made him famous. He found himself honored and reviled for his race and his views. At twenty-four he moved to France, "hoping through exile in Europe to escape from a suffocating society that . . . seemed to lock every black writer into the crude simplicities of propaganda and protest."

In 1957, Baldwin returned to the United States and became active in the civil rights movement. His fiery voice led him to be identified as a spokesman, but he preferred to call himself a "witness to whence I came, where I am. . . . A spokesman assumes he is speaking for others. I never assumed that." He stated in an interview in 1984, three years before he died, that the task facing black writers is "to make the question of color obsolete." To accomplish this task, he felt, requires "first of all realizing that the world is not white" and then developing a new language in which to write because "a language is a frame of reference. I say a new language. I might say a new morality, which, in my terms, comes to the same thing. And that's on all levels—the level of color, the level of identity, the level of sexual identity, what love means, especially in a consumer society, for example. Everything is in question, according to me. One has to forge a new language to deal with it."

I

On the 29th of July, in 1943, my father died. On the same day, a few hours   1
later, his last child was born. Over a month before this, while all our energies were concentrated in waiting for these events, there had been, in Detroit, one of the bloodiest race riots of the century. A few hours after my father's funeral, while he lay in state in the undertaker's chapel, a race riot broke out in Harlem. On the morning of the 3rd of August, we drove my father to the graveyard through a wilderness of smashed plate glass.

The day of my father's funeral had also been my nineteenth birthday. As   2
we drove him to the graveyard, the spoils of injustice, anarchy, discontent,
and hatred were all around us. It seemed to me that God himself had devised,
to mark my father's end, the most sustained and brutally dissonant of codas.
And it seemed to me, too, that the violence which rose all about us as my
father left the world had been devised as a corrective for the pride of his eldest
son. I had declined to believe in that apocalypse which had been central to
my father's vision; very well, life seemed to be saying, here is something that
will certainly pass for an apocalypse until the real thing comes along. I had
inclined to be contemptuous of my father for the conditions of his life, for the
conditions of our lives. When his life had ended I began to wonder about that
life and also, in a new way, to be apprehensive about my own.

I had not known my father very well. We had got on badly, partly because   3
we shared, in our different fashions, the vice of stubborn pride. When he was
dead I realized that I had hardly ever spoken to him. When he had been dead
a long time I began to wish I had. It seemes to be typical of life in America,
where opportunities, real and fancied, are thicker than anywhere else on the
globe, that the second generation has no time to talk to the first. No one,
including my father, seems to have known exactly how old he was, but his
mother had been born during slavery. He was of the first generation of free
men. He, along with thousands of other Negroes, came North after 1919 and
I was part of that generation which had never seen the landscape of what
Negroes sometimes called the Old Country.

He had been born in New Orleans and had been a quite young man there   4
during the time that Louis Armstrong, a boy, was running errands for the dives
and honky-tonks of what was always presented to me as one of the most wicked
of cities—to this day, whenever I think of New Orleans, I also helplessly think
of Sodom and Gomorrah. My father never mentioned Louis Armstrong, except
to forbid us to play his records; but there was a picture of him on our wall for
a long time. One of my father's strong-willed female relatives had placed it
there and forbade my father to take it down. He never did, but he eventually
maneuvered her out of the house and when, some years later, she was in trouble
and near death, he refused to do anything to help her.

He was, I think, very handsome. I gather this from photographs and from   5
my own memories of him, dressed in his Sunday best and on his way to preach
a sermon somewhere, when I was little. Handsome, proud, and ingrown, "like
a toe-nail," somebody said. But he looked to me, as I grew older, like pictures
I had seen of African tribal chieftains: he really should have been naked, with
war-paint on and barbaric mementos, standing among spears. He could be
chilling in the pulpit and indescribably cruel in his personal life and he was

certainly the most bitter man I have ever met; yet it must be said that there was something else in him, buried in him, which lent him his tremendous power and, even, a rather crushing charm. It had something to do with his blackness, I think—he was very black—with his blackness and his beauty, and with the fact that he knew that he was black but did not know that he was beautiful. He claimed to be proud of his blackness but it had also been the cause of much humiliation and it had fixed bleak boundaries to his life. He was not a young man when we were growing up and he had already suffered many kinds of ruin; in his outrageously demanding and protective way he loved his children, who were black like him and menaced, like him; and all these things sometimes showed in his face when he tried, never to my knowledge with any success, to establish contact with any of us. When he took one of his children on his knee to play, the child always became fretful and began to cry; when he tried to help one of us with our homework the absolutely una-bating tension which emanated from him caused our minds and our tongues to become paralyzed, so that he, scarcely knowing why, flew into a rage and the child, not knowing why, was punished. If it ever entered his head to bring a surprise home for his children, it was, almost unfailingly, the wrong surprise and even the big watermelons he often brought home on his back in the summertime led to the most appalling scenes. I do not remember, in all those years, that one of his children was ever glad to see him come home. From what I was able to gather of his early life, it seemed that this inability to establish contact with other people had always marked him and had been one of the things which had driven him out of New Orleans. There was something in him, therefore, groping and tentative, which was never ex-pressed and which was buried with him. One saw it most clearly when he was facing new people and hoping to impress them. But he never did, not for long. We went from church to smaller and more improbable church, he found himself in less and less demand as a minister, and by the time he died none of his friends had come to see him for a long time. He had lived and died in an intolerable bitterness of spirit and it frightened me, as we drove him to the graveyard through those unquiet, ruined streets, to see how pow-erful and overflowing this bitterness could be and to realize that this bitter-ness now was mine.

When he died I had been away from home for a little over a year. In that 6 year I had had time to become aware of the meaning of all my father's bitter warnings, had discovered the secret of his proudly pursed lips and rigid car-riage. I had discovered the weight of white people in the world. I saw that this had been for my ancestors and now would be for me an awful thing to live with and that the bitterness which had helped to kill my father could also kill me.

He had been ill a long time—in the mind, as we now realized, reliving 7 instances of his fantastic intransigence in the new light of his affliction and endeavoring to feel a sorrow for him which never, quite, came true. We had not known that he was being eaten up by paranoia, and the discovery that his cruelty, to our bodies and our minds, had been one of the symptoms of his illness was not, then, enough to enable us to forgive him. The younger children felt, quite simply, relief that he would not be coming home anymore. My mother's observation that it was he, after all, who had kept them alive all these years meant nothing because the problems of keeping children alive are not real for children. The older children felt, with my father gone, that they could invite their friends to the house without fear that their friends would be insulted or, as had sometimes happened with me, being told that their friends were in league with the devil and intended to rob our family of everything we owned. (I didn't fail to wonder, and it made me hate him, what on earth we owned that anybody else would want.)

His illness was beyond all hope of healing before anyone realized that he 8 was ill. He had always been so strange and had lived, like a prophet, in such unimaginably close communion with the Lord that his long silences which were punctuated by moans and hallelujahs and snatches of old songs while he sat at the living-room window never seemed odd to us. It was not until he refused to eat because, he said, his family was trying to poison him that my mother was forced to accept as a fact what had, until then, been only an unwilling suspicion. When he was committed, it was discovered that he had tuberculosis and, as it turned out, the disease of his mind allowed the disease of his body to destroy him. For the doctors could not force him to eat, either, and, though he was fed intravenously, it was clear from the beginning that there was no hope for him.

In my mind's eye I could see him, sitting at the window, locked up in his 9 terrors; hating and fearing every living soul including his children who had betrayed him, too, by reaching towards the world which had despised him. There were nine of us. I began to wonder what it could have felt like for such a man to have had nine children whom he could barely feed. He used to make little jokes about our poverty, which never, of course, seemed very funny to us; they could not have seemed very funny to him, either, or else our all too feeble response to them would never have caused such rages. He spent great energy and achieved, to our chagrin, no small amount of success in keeping us away from the people who surrounded us, people who had all-night rent parties to which we listened when we should have been sleeping, people who cursed and drank and flashed razor blades on Lenox Avenue. He could not understand why, if they had so much energy to spare, they could not use it to make their lives better. He treated almost everybody on our block with a most uncharitable asperity and neither they, nor, of course, their children were slow to reciprocate.

The only white people who came to our house were welfare workers and 10 bill collectors. It was almost always my mother who dealt with them, for my father's temper, which was at the mercy of his pride, was never to be trusted. It was clear that he felt their very presence in his home to be a violation: this was conveyed by his carriage, almost ludicrously stiff, and by his voice, harsh and vindictively polite. When I was around nine or ten I wrote a play which was directed by a young, white schoolteacher, a woman, who then took an interest in me, and gave me books to read and, in order to corroborate my theatrical bent, decided to take me to see what she somewhat tactlessly referred to as "real" plays. Theatergoing was forbidden in our house, but, with the really cruel intuitiveness of a child, I suspected that the color of this woman's skin would carry the day for me. When, at school, she suggested taking me to the theater, I did not, as I might have done if she had been a Negro, find a way of discouraging her, but agreed that she should pick me up at my house one evening. I then, very cleverly, left all the rest to my mother, who suggested to my father, as I knew she would, that it would not be very nice to let such a kind woman make the trip for nothing. Also, since it was a schoolteacher, I imagine that my mother countered the idea of sin with the idea of "education," which word, even with my father, carried a kind of bitter weight.

Before the teacher came my father took me aside to ask *why* she was coming, 11 what *interest* she could possibly have in our house, in a boy like me. I said I didn't know but I, too, suggested that it had something to do with education. And I understood that my father was waiting for me to say something—I didn't quite know what; perhaps that I wanted his protection against this teacher and her "education." I said none of these things and the teacher came and we went out. It was clear, during the brief interview in our living room, that my father was agreeing very much against his will and that he would have refused permission if he had dared. The fact that he did not dare caused me to despise him: I had no way of knowing that he was facing in that living room a wholly unprecedented and frightening situation.

Later, when my father had been laid off from his job, this woman became 12 very important to us. She was really a very sweet and generous woman and went to a great deal of trouble to be of help to us, particularly during one awful winter. My mother called her by the highest name she knew; she said she was a "christian." My father could scarcely disagree but during the four or five years of our relatively close association he never trusted her and was always trying to surprise in her open, Midwestern face the genuine, cunningly hidden, and hideous motivation. In later years, particularly when it began to be clear that this "education" of mine was going to lead me to perdition, he became more explicit and warned me that my white friends in high school were not really my friends and that I would see, when I was older, how white people would do anything to keep a Negro down. Some of them could be nice, he admitted, but none of them were to be trusted and most of them were not even nice. The best thing was to have as little to do with them as possible. I did not feel this way and I was certain, in my innocence, that I never would.

But the year which preceded my father's death had made a great change in 13 my life. I had been living in New Jersey, working in defense plants, working and living among southerners, white and black. I knew about the south, of course, and about how southerners treated Negroes and how they expected them to behave, but it had never entered my mind that anyone would look at me and expect *me* to behave that way. I learned in New Jersey that to be a Negro meant, precisely, that one was never looked at but was simply at the mercy of the reflexes the color of one's skin caused in other people. I acted in New Jersey as I had always acted, that is as though I thought a great deal of myself—I had to *act* that way—with results that were, simply, unbelievable. I had scarcely arrived before I had earned the enmity, which was extraordinarily ingenious, of all my superiors and nearly all my co-workers. In the beginning, to make matters worse, I simply did not know what was happening. I did not know what I had done, and I shortly began to wonder what *anyone* could possibly do, to bring about such unanimous, active, and unbearably vocal hostility. I knew about jim-crow but I had never experienced it. I went to the same self-service restaurant three times and stood with all the Princeton boys before the counter, waiting for a hamburger and coffee; it was always an extraordinarily long time before anything was set before me; but it was not until the fourth visit that I learned that, in fact, nothing had ever been set before me: I had simply picked something up. Negroes were not served there, I was told, and they had been waiting for me to realize that I was always the only Negro present. Once I was told this, I determined to go there all the time. But now they were ready for me and, though some dreadful scenes were subsequently enacted in that restaurant, I never ate there again.

It was the same story all over New Jersey, in bars, bowling alleys, diners, 14 places to live. I was always being forced to leave, silently, or with mutual imprecations. I very shortly became notorious and children giggled behind me when I passed and their elders whispered or shouted—they really believed that

I was mad. And it did begin to work on my mind, of course; I began to be afraid to go anywhere and to compensate for this I went places to which I really should not have gone and where, God knows, I had no desire to be. My reputation in town naturally enhanced my reputation at work and my working day became one long series of acrobatics designed to keep me out of trouble. I cannot say that these acrobatics succeeded. It began to seem that the machinery of the organization I worked for was turning over, day and night, with but one aim: to eject me. I was fired once, and contrived, with the aid of a friend from New York, to get back on the payroll; was fired again, and bounced back again. It took a while to fire me for the third time, but the third time took. There were no loopholes anywhere. There was not even any way of getting back inside the gates.

That year in New Jersey lives in my mind as though it were the year during 15 which, having an unsuspected predilection for it, I first contracted some dread, chronic disease, the unfailing symptom of which is a kind of blind fever, a pounding in the skull and fire in the bowels. Once this disease is contracted, one can never be really carefree again, for the fever, without an instant's warning, can recur at any moment. It can wreck more important things than race relations. There is not a Negro alive who does not have this rage in his blood—one has the choice, merely, of living with it consciously or surrendering to it. As for me, this fever has recurred in me, and does, and will until the day I die.

My last night in New Jersey, a white friend from New York took me to the 16 nearest big town, Trenton, to go to the movies and have a few drinks. As it turned out, he also saved me from, at the very least, a violent whipping. Almost every detail of that night stands out very clearly in my memory. I even remember the name of the movie we saw because its title impressed me as being so patly ironical. It was a movie about the German occupation of France, starring Maureen O'Hara and Charles Laughton and called *This Land Is Mine.* I remember the name of the diner we walked into when the movie ended: it was the "American Diner." When we walked in the counterman asked what we wanted and I remember answering with the casual sharpness which had become my habit: "We want a hamburger and a cup of coffee, what do you think we want?" I do not know why, after a year of such rebuffs, I so completely failed to anticipate his answer, which was, of course, "We don't serve Negroes here." This reply failed to discompose me, at least for the moment. I made some sardonic comment about the name of the diner and we walked out into the streets.

This was the time of what was called the "brown-out," when the lights in 17 all American cities were very dim. When we re-entered the streets something happened to me which had the force of an optical illusion, or a nightmare. The streets were very crowded and I was facing north. People were moving in every direction but it seemed to me, in that instant, that all of the people I could see, and many more than that, were moving toward me, against me, and that everyone was white. I remember how their faces gleamed. And I felt, like a physical sensation, a *click* at the nape of my neck as though some interior string connecting my head to my body had been cut. I began to walk. I heard my friend call after me, but I ignored him. Heaven only knows what was going on in his mind, but he had the good sense not to touch me—I don't know what would have happened if he had—and to keep me in sight. I don't know what was going on in my mind, either; I certainly had no conscious plan. I wanted to do something to crush these white faces, which were crushing me. I walked for perhaps a block or two until I came to an enormous, glittering, and fashionable restaurant in which I knew not even the intercession of the Virgin would cause me to be served. I pushed through the doors and took the first vacant seat I saw, at a table for two, and waited.

I do not know how long I waited and I rather wonder, until today, what I could possibly have looked like. Whatever I looked like, I frightened the waitress who shortly appeared, and the moment she appeared all of my fury flowed towards her. I hated her for her white face, and for her great, astounded, frightened eyes. I felt that if she found a black man so frightening I would make her fright worthwhile.

She did not ask me what I wanted, but repeated, as though she had learned it somewhere, "We don't serve Negroes here." She did not say it with the blunt, derisive hostility to which I had grown so accustomed, but, rather, with a note of apology in her voice, and fear. This made me colder and more murderous than ever. I felt I had to do something with my hands. I wanted her to come close enough for me to get her neck between my hands.

So I pretended not to have understood her, hoping to draw her closer. And she did step a very short step closer, with her pencil poised incongruously over her pad, and repeated the formula: ". . . don't serve Negroes here."

Somehow, with the repetition of that phrase, which was already ringing in my head like a thousand bells of a nightmare, I realized that she would never come any closer and that I would have to strike from a distance. There was nothing on the table but an ordinary water-mug half full of water, and I picked this up and hurled it with all my strength at her. She ducked and it missed her and shattered against the mirror behind the bar. And, with that sound, my frozen blood abruptly thawed, I returned from wherever I had been, I *saw*, for the first time, the restaurant, the people with their mouths open, already, as it seemed to me, rising as one man, and I realized what I had done, and where I was, and I was frightened. I rose and began running for the door. A round, potbellied man grabbed me by the nape of the neck just as I reached the doors and began to beat me about the face. I kicked him and got loose and ran into the streets. My friend whispered, *"Run!"* and I ran.

My friend stayed outside the restaurant long enough to misdirect my pursuers 22 and the police, who arrived, he told me, at once. I do not know what I said to him when he came to my room that night. I could not have said much. I felt, in the oddest, most awful way, that I had somehow betrayed him. I lived it over and over and over again, the way one relives an automobile accident after it has happened and one finds oneself alone and safe. I could not get over two facts, both equally difficult for the imagination to grasp, and one was that I could have been murdered. But the other was that I had been ready to commit murder. I saw nothing very clearly but I did see this: that my life, my *real* life, was in danger, and not from anything other people might do but from the hatred I carried in my own heart.

II

I had returned home around the second week in June—in great haste be- 23 cause it seemed that my father's death and my mother's confinement were both but a matter of hours. In the case of my mother, it soon became clear that she had simply made a miscalculation. This had always been her tendency and I don't believe that a single one of us arrived in the world, or has since arrived anywhere else, on time. But none of us dawdled so intolerably about the business of being born as did my baby sister. We sometimes amused ourselves, during those endless, stifling weeks, by picturing the baby sitting within in the safe, warm dark, bitterly regretting the necessity of becoming a part of our chaos and stubbornly putting it off as long as possible. I understood her perfectly and congratulated her on showing such good sense so soon. Death, however, sat as purposefully at my father's bedside as life stirred within my mother's womb and it was harder to understand why he so lingered in that long shadow. It seemed that he had bent, and for a long time, too, all of his energies towards dying. Now death was ready for him but my father held back.

All of Harlem, indeed, seemed to be infected by waiting. I had never before 24 known it to be so violently still. Racial tensions throughout this country were exacerbated during the early years of the war, partly because the labor market brought together hundreds of thousands of ill-prepared people and partly be- cause Negro soldiers, regardless of where they were born, received their military training in the south. What happened in defense plants and army camps had repercussions, naturally, in every Negro ghetto. The situation in Harlem had grown bad enough for clergymen, policemen, educators, politicians, and social workers to assert in one breath that there was no "crime wave" and to offer, in the very next breath, suggestions as to how to combat it. These suggestions always seemed to involve playgrounds, despite the fact that racial skirmishes were occurring in the playgrounds, too. Playground or not, crime wave or not, the Harlem police force had been augmented in March, and the unrest grew—perhaps, in fact, partly as a result of the ghetto's instinctive hatred of policemen. Perhaps the most revealing news item, out of the steady parade of reports of muggings, stabbings, shootings, assaults, gang wars, and accusations of police brutality is the item concerning six Negro girls who set upon a white girl in the subway because, as they all too accurately put it, she was stepping on their toes. Indeed she was, all over the nation.

I had never before been so aware of policemen, on foot, on horseback, on 25 corners, everywhere, always two by two. Nor had I ever been so aware of small knots of people. They were on stoops and on corners and in doorways, and what was striking about them, I think, was that they did not seem to be talking. Never, when I passed these groups, did the usual sound of a curse or a laugh ring out and neither did there seem to be any hum of gossip. There was certainly, on the other hand, occurring between them communication extraordinarily intense. Another thing that was striking was the unexpected diversity of the people who made up these groups. Usually, for example, one would see a group of sharpies standing on the street corner, jiving the passing chicks; or a group of older men, usually, for some reason, in the vicinity of a barber shop, discussing baseball scores, or the numbers or making rather chilling observations about women they had known. Women, in a general way, tended to be seen less often together—unless they were church women, or very young girls, or prostitutes met together for an unprofessional instant. But that summer I saw the strangest combinations: large, respectable, churchly matrons standing on the stoops or the corners with their hair tied up, together with a girl in sleazy satin whose face bore the marks of gin and the razor, or heavyset, abrupt, no-nonsense older men, in company with the most disreputable and fanatical "race" men or these same "race" men with the sharpies, or these sharpies with the churchly women. Seventh Day Adventists and Methodists and Spiritualists seemed to be hobnobbing with Holyrollers and they were all, alike, entangled with the most flagrant disbelievers; something heavy in their stance seemed to indicate that they had all, incredibly, seen a common vision, and on each face there seemed to be the same strange, bitter shadow.

The churchly women and the matter-of-fact, no-nonense men had children 26 in the Army. The sleazy girls they talked to had lovers there, the sharpies and the "race" men had friends and brothers there. It would have demanded an

unquestioning patriotism, happily as uncommon in this country as it is unde-
sirable, for these people not to have been disturbed by the bitter letters they
received, by the newspaper stories they read, not to have been enraged by the
posters, then to be found all over New York, which described the Japanese as
"yellow-bellied Japs." It was only the "race" men, to be sure, who spoke
ceaselessly of being revenged—how this vengeance was to be exacted was not
clear—for the indignities and dangers suffered by Negro boys in uniform; but
everybody felt a directionless, hopeless bitterness, as well as that panic which
can scarcely be suppressed when one knows that a human being one loves is
beyond one's reach, and in danger. This helplessness and this gnawing uneasiness does something, at length, to even the toughest mind. Perhaps the best
way to sum all this up is to say that the people I knew felt, mainly, a peculiar
kind of relief when they knew that their boys were being shipped out of the
south, to do battle overseas. It was, perhaps, like feeling that the most dangerous part of a dangerous journey had been passed and that now, even if death
should come, it would come with honor and without the complicity of their
countrymen. Such a death would be, in short, a fact with which one could
hope to live.

It was on the 28th of July, which I believe was a Wednesday, that I visited 27
my father for the first time during his illness and for the last time in his life.
The moment I saw him I knew why I had put off this visit so long. I had told
my mother that I did not want to see him because I hated him. But this was
not true. It was only that I *had* hated him and I wanted to hold on to this
hatred. I did not want to look on him as a ruin: it was not a ruin I had hated.
I imagine that one of the reasons people cling to their hates so stubbornly is
because they sense, once hate is gone, that they will be forced to deal with
pain.

We traveled out to him, his older sister and myself, to what seemed to be 28
the very end of a very Long Island. It was hot and dusty and we wrangled, my
aunt and I, all the way out, over the fact that I had recently begun to smoke
and, as she said, to give myself airs. But I knew that she wrangled with me
because she could not bear to face the fact of her brother's dying. Neither
could I endure the reality of her despair, her unstated bafflement as to what
had happened to her brother's life, and her own. So we wrangled and I smoked
and from time to time she fell into a heavy reverie. Covertly, I watched her
face, which was the face of an old woman; it had fallen in, the eyes were
sunken and lightless; soon she would be dying, too.

In my childhood—it had not been so long ago—I had thought her beautiful. 29
She had been quick-witted and quick-moving and very generous with all the
children and each of her visits had been an event. At one time one of my

brothers and myself had thought of running away to live with her. Now she could no longer produce out of her handbag some unexpected and yet familiar delight. She made me feel pity and revulsion and fear. It was awful to realize that she no longer caused me to feel affection. The closer we came to the hospital the more querulous she became and at the same time, naturally, grew more dependent on me. Between pity and guilt and fear I began to feel that there was another me trapped in my skull like a jack-in-the-box who might escape my control at any moment and fill the air with screaming.

She began to cry the moment we entered the room and she saw him lying 30 there, all shriveled and still, like a little black monkey. The great, gleaming apparatus which fed him and would have compelled him to be still even if he had been able to move brought to mind, not beneficence, but torture; the tubes entering his arm made me think of pictures I had seen when a child, of Gulliver, tied down by the pygmies on that island. My aunt wept and wept, there was a whistling sound in my father's throat; nothing was said; he could not speak. I wanted to take his hand, to say something. But I do not know what I could have said, even if he could have heard me. He was not really in that room with us, he had at last really embarked on his journey; and though my aunt told me that he said he was going to meet Jesus, I did not hear anything except that whistling in his throat. The doctor came back and we left, into that unbearable train again, and home. In the morning came the telegram saying that he was dead. Then the house was suddenly full of relatives, friends, hysteria, and confusion and I quickly left my mother and the children to the care of those impressive women, who, in Negro communities at least, automatically appear at times of bereavement armed with lotions, proverbs, and patience, and an ability to cook. I went downtown. By the time I returned, later the same day, my mother had been carried to the hospital and the baby had been born.

III

For my father's funeral I had nothing black to wear and this posed a nagging 31 problem all day long. It was one of those problems, simple, or impossible of solution, to which the mind insanely clings in order to avoid the mind's real trouble. I spent most of that day at the downtown apartment of a girl I knew, celebrating my birthday with whiskey and wondering what to wear that night. When planning a birthday celebration one naturally does not expect that it will be up against competition from a funeral and this girl had anticipated taking me out that night, for a big dinner and a night club afterwards. Sometime during the course of that long day we decided that we would go out anyway, when my father's funeral service was over. I imagine I decided it, since, as the funeral hour approached, it became clearer and clearer to me that I would not know what to do with myself when it was over. The girl, stifling her very lively concern as to the possible effects of the whiskey on one of my father's chief mourners, concentrated on being conciliatory and practically helpful. She found a black shirt for me somewhere and ironed it and, dressed in the darkest pants and jacket I owned, and slightly drunk, I made my way to my father's funeral.

The chapel was full, but not packed, and very quiet. There were, mainly, 32 my father's relatives, and his children, and here and there I saw faces I had not seen since childhood, the faces of my father's one-time friends. They were very dark and solemn now, seeming somehow to suggest that they had known all along that something like this would happen. Chief among the mourners was my aunt, who had quarreled with my father all his life; by which I do not mean to suggest that her mourning was insincere or that she had not loved him. I suppose that she was one of the few people in the world who had, and their incessant quarreling proved precisely the strength of the tie that bound them. The only other person in the world, as far as I knew, whose relationship to my father rivaled my aunt's in depth was my mother, who was not there.

It seemed to me, of course, that it was a very long funeral. But it was, if 33 anything, a rather shorter funeral than most, nor, since there were no overwhelming, uncontrollable expressions of grief, could it be called—if I dare to use the word—successful. The minister who preached my father's funeral sermon was one of the few my father had still been seeing as he neared his end. He presented to us in his sermon a man whom none of us had ever seen— a man thoughtful, patient, and forbearing, a Christian inspiration to all who knew him, and a model for his children. And no doubt the children, in their disturbed and guilty state, were almost ready to believe this; he had been remote enough to be anything and, anyway, the shock of the incontrovertible, that it was really our father lying up there in that casket, prepared the mind for anything. His sister moaned and this grief-stricken moaning was taken as corroboration. The other faces held a dark, noncommittal thoughtfulness. This was not the man they had known, but they had scarcely expected to be confronted with *him;* this was, in a sense deeper than questions of fact, the man they had not known, and the man they had not known may have been the real one. The real man, whoever he had been, had suffered and now he was dead: this was all that was sure and all that mattered now. Every man in the chapel hoped that when his hour came he, too, would be eulogized, which is to say forgiven, and that all of his lapses, greeds, errors, and strayings from the truth would be invested with coherence and looked upon with charity.

This was perhaps the last thing human beings could give each other and it was what they demanded, after all, of the Lord. Only the Lord saw the midnight tears, only He was present when one of His children, moaning and wringing hands, paced up and down the room. When one slapped one's child in anger the recoil in the heart reverberated through heaven and became part of the pain of the universe. And when the children were hungry and sullen and distrustful and one watched them, daily, growing wilder, and further away, and running headlong into danger, it was the Lord who knew what the charged heart endured as the strap was laid to the backside; the Lord alone who knew what one *would* have said if one had had, like the Lord, the gift of the living word. It was the Lord who knew of the impossibility every parent in that room faced: how to prepare the child for the day when the child would be despised and how to *create* in the child—by what means?—a stronger antidote to this poison than one had found for oneself. The avenues, side streets, bars, billiard halls, hospitals, police stations, and even the playgrounds of Harlem—not to mention the houses of correction, the jails, and the morgue—testified to the potency of the poison while remaining silent as to the efficacy of whatever antidote, irresistibly raising the question of whether or not such an antidote existed; raising, which was worse, the question of whether or not an antidote was desirable; perhaps poison should be fought with poison. With these several schisms in the mind and with more terrors in the heart than could be named, it was better not to judge the man who had gone down under an impossible burden. It was better to remember: *Thou knowest this man's fall; but thou knowest not his wrassling.*

While the preacher talked and I watched the children—years of changing their diapers, scrubbing them, slapping them, taking them to school, and scolding them had had the perhaps inevitable result of making me love them, though I am not sure I knew this then—my mind was busily breaking out with a rash of disconnected impressions. Snatches of popular songs, indecent jokes, bits of books I had read, movie sequences, faces, voices, political issues—I thought I was going mad; all these impressions suspended, as it were, in the solution of the faint nausea produced in me by the heat and liquor. For a moment I had the impression that my alcoholic breath, inefficiently disguised with chewing gum, filled the entire chapel. Then someone began singing one of my father's favorite songs and, abruptly, I was with him, sitting on his knee, in the hot, enormous, crowded church which was the first church we attended. It was the Abyssinia Baptist Church on 138th Street. We had not gone there long. With this image, a host of others came. I had forgotten, in the rage of my growing up, how proud my father had been of me when I was little. Apparently, I had had a voice and my father had liked to show me off before the members of the church. I had forgotten what he had looked like when he was pleased but now I remembered that he had always been grinning with pleasure when my solos ended. I even remembered certain expressions on his face when he teased my mother—had he loved her? I would never know. And when had it all begun to change? For now it seemed that he had not always been cruel. I remembered being taken for a haircut and scraping my knee on the footrest of the barber's chair and I remembered my father's face as he soothed my crying and applied the stinging iodine. Then I remembered our fights, fights which had been of the worst possible kind because my technique had been silence.

I remembered the one time in all our life together when we had really 35 spoken to each other.

It was on a Sunday and it must have been shortly before I left home. We 36 were walking, just the two of us, in our usual silence, to or from church. I was in high school and had been doing a lot of writing and I was, about this time, the editor of the high school magazine. But I had also been a Young Minister and had been preaching from the pulpit. Lately, I had been taking fewer engagements and preached as rarely as possible. It was said in the church, quite truthfully, that I was "cooling off."

My father asked me abruptly, "You'd rather write than preach, wouldn't 37 you?"

I was astonished at his question—because it was a real question. I answered, 38 "Yes."

That was all we said. It was awful to remember that that was all we had 39 *ever* said.

The casket now was opened and the mourners were being led up the aisle 40 to look for the last time on the deceased. The assumption was that the family was too overcome with grief to be allowed to make this journey alone and I watched while my aunt was led to the casket and, muffled in black, and shaking, led back to her seat. I disapproved of forcing children to look on their dead father, considering that the shock of his death, or, more truthfully, the shock of death as a reality, was already a little more than a child could bear, but my judgment in this matter had been overruled and there they were, bewildered and frightened and very small, being led, one by one, to the casket. But there is also something very gallant about children at such moments. It has something to do with their silence and gravity and with the fact that one cannot help them. Their legs, somehow, seem *exposed*, so that it is at once incredible and terribly clear that their legs are all they have to hold them up.

I had not wanted to go to the casket myself and I certainly had not wished 41 to be led there, but there was no way of avoiding either of these forms. One

of the deacons led me up and I looked on my father's face. I cannot say that
it looked like him at all. His blackness had been equivocated by powder and
there was no suggestion in that casket of what his power had or could have
been. He was simply an old man dead, and it was hard to believe that he had
ever given anyone either joy or pain. Yet, his life filled that room. Further up
the avenue his wife was holding his newborn child. Life and death so close
together, and love and hatred, and right and wrong, said something to me
which I did not want to hear concerning man, concerning the life of man.

After the funeral, while I was downtown desperately celebrating my birth- 42
day, a Negro soldier, in the lobby of the Hotel Braddock, got into a fight with
a white policeman over a Negro girl. Negro girls, white policemen, in or out
of uniform, and Negro males—in or out of uniform—were part of the furniture
of the lobby of the Hotel Braddock and this was certainly not the first time
such an incident had occurred. It was destined, however, to receive an unprecedented publicity, for the fight between the policeman and the soldier
ended with the shooting of the soldier. Rumor, flowing immediately to the
street outside, stated that the soldier had been shot in the back, an instantaneous and revealing invention, and that the soldier had died protecting a Negro
woman. The facts were somewhat different—for example, the soldier had not
been shot in the back, and was not dead, and the girl seems to have been as
dubious a symbol of womanhood as her white counterpart in Georgia usually
is, but no one was interested in the facts. They preferred the invention because
this invention expressed and corroborated their hates and fears so perfectly. It
is just as well to remember that people are always doing this. Perhaps many of
those legends, including Christianity, to which the world clings began their
conquest of the world with just some such concerted surrender to distortion.
The effect, in Harlem, of this particular legend was like the effect of a lit
match in a tin of gasoline. The mob gathered before the doors of the Hotel
Braddock simply began to swell and to spread in every direction, and Harlem
exploded.

The mob did not cross the ghetto lines. It would have been easy, for ex- 43
ample, to have gone over Morningside Park on the west side or to have crossed
the Grand Central railroad tracks at 125th Street on the east side, to wreak
havoc in white neighborhoods. The mob seems to have been mainly interested
in something more potent and real than the white face, that is, in white power,
and the principal damage done during the riot of the summer of 1943 was to
white business establishments in Harlem. It might have been a far bloodier
story, of course, if at the hour the riot began, these establishments had still
been open. From the Hotel Braddock the mob fanned out, east and west along
125th Street, and for the entire length of Lenox, Seventh, and Eighth avenues.

Along each of these avenues, and along each major side street—116th, 125th, 135th, and so on—bars, stores, pawnshops, restaurants, even little luncheonettes had been smashed open and entered and looted—looted, it might be added, with more haste than efficiency. The shelves really looked as though a bomb had struck them. Cans of beans and soup and dog food, along with toilet paper, corn flakes, sardines, and milk tumbled every which way, and abandoned cash registers and cases of beer leaned crazily out of the splintered windows and were strewn along the avenues. Sheets, blankets, and clothing of every description formed a kind of path, as though people had dropped them while running. I truly had not realized that Harlem *had* so many stores until I saw them all smashed open; the first time the word *wealth* ever entered my mind in relation to Harlem was when I saw it scattered in the streets. But one's first, incongruous impression of plenty was countered immediately by an impression of waste. None of this was doing anybody any good. It would have been better to have left the plate glass as it had been and the goods lying in the stores.

It would have been better, but it would also have been intolerable, for 44 Harlem had needed something to smash. To smash something is the ghetto's chronic need. Most of the time it is the members of the ghetto who smash each other, and themselves. But as long as the ghetto walls are standing there will always come a moment when these outlets do not work. That summer, for example, it was not enough to get into a fight on Lenox Avenue, or curse out one's cronies in the barber shops. If ever, indeed, the violence which fills Harlem's churches, pool halls, and bars erupts outward in a more direct fashion, Harlem and its citizens are likely to vanish in an apocalyptic flood. That this is not likely to happen is due to a great many reasons, most hidden and powerful among them the Negro's real relation to the white American. This relation prohibits, simply, anything as uncomplicated and satisfactory as pure hatred. In order really to hate white people, one has to blot so much out of the mind—and the heart—that this hatred itself becomes an exhausting and self-destructive pose. But this does not mean, on the other hand, that love comes easily: the white world is too powerful, too complacent, too ready with gratuitous humiliation, and, above all, too ignorant and too innocent for that. One is absolutely forced to make perpetual qualifications and one's own reactions are always canceling each other out. It is this, really, which has driven so many people mad, both white and black. One is always in the position of having to decide between amputation and gangrene. Amputation is swift but time may prove that the amputation was not necessary—or one may delay the amputation too long. Gangrene is slow, but it is impossible to be sure that one is reading one's symptoms right. The idea of going through life as a cripple is more than one can bear, and equally unbearable is the risk of swelling up slowly, in agony, with poison. And the trouble, finally, is that the risks are real even if the choices do not exist.

"But as for me and my house," my father had said, "we will serve the Lord." 45 I wondered, as we drove him to his resting place, what this line had meant for him. I had heard him preach it many times. I had preached it once myself, proudly giving it an interpretation different from my father's. Now the whole thing came back to me, as though my father and I were on our way to Sunday school and I were memorizing the golden text: *And if it seem evil unto you to serve the Lord, choose you this day whom you will serve; whether the gods which your fathers served that were on the other side of the flood, or the gods of the Amorites, in whose land ye dwell: but as for me and my house, we will serve the Lord.* I suspected in these familiar lines a meaning which had never been there for me before. All of my father's texts and songs, which I had decided were meaningless, were arranged before me at his death like empty bottles, waiting to hold the meaning which life would give them for me. This was his legacy: nothing is ever escaped. That bleakly memorable morning I hated the unbelievable streets and the Negroes and whites who had, equally, made them that way. But I knew that it was folly, as my father would have said, this bitterness was folly. It was necessary to hold on to the things that mattered. The dead man mattered, the new life mattered; blackness and whiteness did not matter; to believe that they did was to acquiesce in one's own destruction. Hatred, which could destroy so much, never failed to destroy the man who hated and this was an immutable law.

It began to seem that one would have to hold in the mind forever two ideas 46 which seemed to be in opposition. The first idea was acceptance, the acceptance, totally without rancor, of life as it is, and men as they are: in the light of this idea, it goes without saying that injustice is a commonplace. But this did not mean that one could be complacent, for the second idea was of equal power: that one must never, in one's own life, accept these injustices as commonplace but must fight them with all one's strength. This fight begins, however, in the heart and it now had been laid to my charge to keep my own heart free of hatred and despair. This intimation made my heart heavy and, now that my father was irrecoverable, I wished that he had been beside me so that I could have searched his face for the answers which only the future would give me now.

Focusing on James Baldwin's Use of Revision Within His Essay

1. Baldwin tells stories about his early relationship with his father in two different places in the essay. What kind of man does his father seem to be in paragraphs 3–9? What kind of relationship does Baldwin have with his father in these early paragraphs? In paragraphs 34–38, what kind of man does the father seem to be? What kind of relationship between father and son is indicated in these paragraphs? Why does Baldwin divide up his memories of his father in this way?

2. The change in Baldwin's image of his father actually occurs in several stages. For example, in paragraphs 6–15 he tells of a change that occurred in the year before his father died. How does Baldwin come to understand his father's paranoia? Baldwin says in paragraph 15 that he himself has contracted a "chronic disease"; how does this explanation change his (and our) view of his father's mental illness? In paragraphs 27 through 33, how does Baldwin's view of his father change?

3. Baldwin's essay is constructed as a series of flashbacks. It begins and ends on the day of his father's funeral, but in between it circles back through Baldwin's life leading up to that day. How does this structure contribute to the sense that Baldwin is continually revising his view of his father and of himself?

4. Much more is being revised than Baldwin's view of his father. How does Baldwin's view of himself change? How does his view of society change?

5. The first paragraph begins with personal events and then moves to a wide view of what was happening in society at the time of those personal events. How does Baldwin make the same move, expanding his view, in paragraphs 41 and 42? How does Baldwin suggest throughout the essay that his father's death is connected to social events (consider, for example, paragraph 2 and the last five paragraphs)?

WORKING WITH THE TECHNIQUE IN YOUR OWN WRITING

1. Write an essay like Field's or Baldwin's about a time when you were forced to revise your view of your life. You might want to center your essay on a distinct moment when you suddenly realized that you had been mistaken. See if you can bring your readers to share the shock of revelation; try to convince readers of your original view and then bring them to revise what you have just convinced them to believe. You might construct your essay so that it seems to move chronologically, as Field does, or you might make it circle back through time, as Baldwin's does.

2. Write an essay that brings your readers to revise their view of some events; set up your essay so that you first convince your readers of one view, then reveal

some pertinent information that requires that they change their view. For example, you could describe a riot on campus that followed a political demonstration and at first make it seem that the political leaders had incited the riot; then you could move to showing that some kind of riot had occurred every year just before spring vacation, but in previous years the riot had consisted of students cutting classes for a day and running around. You would thereby lead your readers to revise their view and conclude that the politics may have actually had little to do with the riot.

BONNIE HARRIS

University of Alaska
Juneau, Alaska
Joan Waters, instructor

Bonnie Harris is the youngest of four children in a family she describes as "friendly middle-class WASP folks, with a typically Alaskan love of the outdoors and spirit of adventure." All of her family are involved in the arts and have encouraged her love of music. "I've been a professional musician since about age fifteen, first as a church organist, later as a folk singer, club and saloon entertainer, and in concert appearances all over Alaska and occasionally in other places on the West Coast. I spent five years traveling to towns and villages in the Alaskan bush performing and teaching as an artist-in-residence, and in the process discovered that I really love teaching. So I've decided to go to school and get a degree in music education. I have built a home in the tiny rural community of Gustavus, about sixty air miles from Juneau. I plan to teach music in the bush, developing itinerant programs for remote villages and continue my performance career as well. And someday soon (I've put it off too long!) I want to record an album of my songs."

Growing up in Alaska has had a major impact on Bonnie Harris's life. "I have always cherished my independence," she reports, "which many people consider to be an Alaskan trait, and I have a deep, abiding love of nature and the wilderness. I've been fortunate, as many people are not, to have experienced many of nature's wonders firsthand. My songs and my writing often reflect images of southeast Alaska's beautiful mountains, forests, and the sea. I also believe very much in music as a way of moving people, of helping to stimulate feeling and reflection and change in the world."

Asked to write a "persuasive research paper" in which she was to formulate her own position on an issue of interest to her, Harris chose to write about the healing power of music. She describes the circumstances that led to writing her essay in these terms:

> My own intuitive sense of the power of music led to my recent
> interest in music healing, and in the fall of 1986 I attended a
> workshop on the subject taught by Kay Gardner. That experi-
> ence excited me and made me want to learn more. My personal
> interest was mostly in the physics of sound and its effects on the
> human body/psyche, rather a technical subject for a general
> essay. Writing the research paper for my English composition
> class necessitated revising my focus quite a bit. I figured my
> fellow students and the English professors who might read my
> essay would probably not be interested as I was in the technical
> aspects of music healing and in fact might need some convincing
> that there really was such a thing. I wanted them to realize that
> music really can have a positive effect on our lives, that it has

> *more value than its usual accepted cultural functions, and that
> there is a historical and scientific basis for its use in healing.*

*A deadline prevented Harris from completing a third revision of her essay. Nonetheless,
the necessarily "final" draft that follows underscores the maxim that writers write best
about subjects they know best.*

The Healing Power of Music

> In both Mexico and Peru there is a legend which tells that
> the ancient peoples were "scientists of sound." They could
> split massive stone slabs along precise harmonic lines with
> sound alone, and then "resonate" them into position. . . .
> Their religion recognized each individual as having a par-
> ticular note and pitch. With the "sound knowledge" a man
> could be "purified" and raised by vibratory mantras, or con-
> versely, slain by a single note.
> —Lawrence Blair, *Rhythms of Vision* (Laughingbird 276)

Ancient civilizations knew the healing power of music. Many tribal cultures 1
traditionally have used songs and chants for curing the sick, and mantras have
been intoned for centuries by Buddhists and Hindus for healing and enlightenment. The Bible tells the story of David the shepherd, who played his harp
for Saul and made him well (1 Sam. 16:14–23). Hippocrates, the "father of
medicine," took his mental patients to hear healing music in the Temple of
Aesculapius (Tame 156), and the Greek teacher/mathematician Pythagoras is
said to have used songs to soothe pain and calm the angry or disturbed.

Early philosophies of healing were based on the premise that harmony was 2
inherent in the universe. It followed that when a body was in discord, music—
the sounds of balanced, organized harmony—could help to bring it back to
health. Although modern Western medicine has largely diverged from this
philosophy of health and harmony, new research in human responses to music
and its medical uses has brought recognition of its unique therapeutic properties. Music is a powerful force for healing, profoundly affecting both the
human body and the psyche.

The Hindus' cosmic Om, the Pythagoreans' "Music of the Spheres," the 3
ancient Egyptians' "Word" of the Gods—all of these forms of universal vibra-
tory energy reveal the ancients' belief in sound as an underlying principle of
life. Today modern physicists in their search to discover the basis of matter
have come to the same conclusion as the early philosophers and mystics: all

matter is composed of energy in motion, in other words, vibration. Ongoing physics research actually describes the nature of atoms as harmonic systems, with subatomic particles theoretically considered as "nodes of resonance" (Murchie 76–77).

Resonance, by definition, is the phenomenon of one body in vibration 4 causing another body to vibrate at the same frequency. For example, if one tuning fork is struck to produce a tone, another near it will also begin to hum. The sound waves from the first fork are of the same frequency as the second fork's natural tendency to vibrate, setting up a "sympathetic vibration" within the second fork. The two forks are said to form a "resonant system" (Resonance 440). A more common perception of this phenomenon is that of a piercing soprano voice shattering glass. If the soprano's vocal frequency can be made to match that of the glass, the glass's tendency to vibrate can be reinforced to the point where it will shatter. This phenomenon is exploited in modern medicine in the form of sound "explosions" applied selectively within the body to shatter kidney stones (Gardner). It should be noted, however, that this natural reinforcement tendency can also be used to tune resonant systems, as in the tuning of radio frequencies.

Another universal phenomenon closely related to resonance is called "entrainment." When two or more oscillators (bodies vibrating in a regular periodic manner, such as a pendulum clock or a human heart) are vibrating at close to the same rate, they tend to shift their vibrations so that both are oscillating at exactly the same time and come "into phase" with each other. Such "in-phase" systems may also resonate, each reinforcing the vibration of the other (Halpern and Savary 44).

The human body can be considered a natural resonant system made up of 6 atoms, molecules, cells, muscles, and organs all oscillating to their own biorhythms and vibrational frequencies. In its natural relaxed state the whole body system is known to have a resonant frequency of 7.8 cycles per second, the frequency of alpha brain waves such as those produced during some kinds of meditation (Halpern and Savary 38). This is also the frequency of the cranial-sacral pulse which flows through the spinal cord. And in a phenomenon known as the "Schumann Resonance," the earth vibrates at this same 7.8 cycles per second, an "earth pulse" which resonates in the nervous systems of all life forms (Gardner). Thus evolved the concept of a body "in tune" with the world and a suggestion that this might be accomplished through the application of sounds that are in harmony with the natural rhythms of the body.

Due to their vibrational nature and the phenomenon of resonance, all of 7 the body's cells are potential sound receptors. We are affected by sounds even when they are beyond the normal range of hearing or if we unconsciously tune them out. How often have we found ourselves tapping our toes to the rhythm of piped-in Muzak, without even realizing that we heard it? Pervasive sounds in the environment (even inaudible ones such as 60-cycle electrical hum) may actually change the body's own natural rhythms and vibrational patterns (Halpern and Savary 7–8). Extended exposure to noise tends to have negative effects on the central nervous system, causing perceptual problems associated with the neural coding processes in the brain. Children living in the flight path of L.A. International Airport have been shown to have impaired mental concentration and a greater than average instance of high blood pressure, and European studies indicate that high noise levels among industrial workers are likely to contribute to abnormal heart rhythms, circulatory disease, balance disturbances, ulcers, and psychological problems (Halpern and Savary 26–27).

At the same time researchers are learning that unpleasant sound contributes   8
to stress and ill health, they are also discovering that the natural tendencies in the human body toward resonance and entrainment—the forces for harmony—can be aided by the appropriate use of music and sounds. While modern medicine treats the symptoms of disease with drugs and surgical technology, music acts on the whole person. As a natural healing agent, it can penetrate the subtle underlying causes of disease rooted in the body, mind, and spirit, which more traditional methods tend to ignore. Modern medicine has made great strides in alleviating pain and suffering and eradicating epidemic diseases like smallpox and polio. Yet the need for healing remains as strong as ever, with more and more incidences of cancer and heart disease and new epidemics like AIDS. The costs of health care continue to rise dramatically, with Americans spending over five billion dollars a year for prescription drugs alone, and an additional two billion for over-the-counter drugs like aspirin (Young 11).

Considering the lucrative nature of the drug industry and other expensive   9
treatment procedures like heart surgery and radiation therapy, it is not surprising that alternatives are often discouraged by the medical establishment. But there are other reasons for skepticism, too. Holistic healing does not conform to the training of most modern medical practitioners, and the recent malpractice controversies make it difficult for doctors to risk stepping outside of established procedures (Young 10). Yet when confronted with unexplained phenomena like "spontaneous remission" in cancer patients, doctors and researchers must admit that they don't have all the answers. Many doctors are aware of the dangerous risks and side effects of drugs and surgery. And in spite of skeptical attitudes toward nontraditional healing methods, many doctors are finding the beneficial effects of music therapy useful in their medical practices.

Psychological theories abound to explain how music works for healing. Some   10
psychologists believe that music preoccupies the conscious mind while opening

up the unconscious, stimulating buried memories and feelings. Some think, as Darwin implied, that music was used to express emotion before we had a spoken language and that it still serves as a sort of "primal language" (Brody, Ingber, and Pearson 78). Most certainly the elements of harmony and rhythm can create powerful mood changes. A Juneau workshop on music and healing conducted by musician Kay Gardner gave a convincing example. Participants listened to a powerful rendition of Maurice Ravel's *La Valse*, written upon Ravel's return from the war front of World War I. The piece has been described by music critics as "a Viennese waltz gone mad" (Gardner), and reactions to it at the workshop ranged from feeling mildly disturbed to very crazy and upset, to one woman who felt so emotionally battered that she had to leave the room. By contrast, everyone felt transported and calmed by the beautiful hymns of Hildegarde Von Bingen, a musically gifted abbess and spiritual leader of the Middle Ages.

The psychological effects of music are well known to music therapists. Some 11 use music as a sort of subliminal background to aid in detachment from pain or for soothing effect, and others require active listening or producing of music to immerse the patient in the sound and the emotions or images associated with the music. In his pioneering work *Through Music to the Self*, music therapist Peter Hamel cites examples from Europe, where behavioral scientist Johannes Kneutgen has used tape recorded music of cradle songs to aid emotionally disturbed children and mental patients in relaxation, lowering incidences of bedwetting and the need for sleeping drugs (167). Bonn therapist Georges Hengesch has used rhythm instruments for spontaneous music-making with schizophrenic psychotic patients, achieving a state of calmness which made possible a previously unsuccessful attempt at speech therapy (167). Music has been used with terminal patients in hospices to help them express their feelings about death and communicate with their families, stimulating memories and moods to aid the process. At the close of World War I in 1918 nurse/musician Margaret Anderton played music for shell-shocked veterans, stimulating memory in cases of amnesia and calming states of acute temporary insanity brought on by exposure to the horrors of war (Heline 16). And therapists have found that when other methods do not work to reach autistic children, music often will (Brody, Ingber, and Pearson 78).

Another compelling reason for the growing acceptance of music as a healing 12 agent is the evidence of physical benefits. Taking pleasure in a favorite piece of music causes people to breathe deeply and aids relaxation, a crucial factor in many illnesses. At Kaiser-Permanente Medical Center in Los Angeles doctors are using musically induced relaxation to great advantage in relieving pain for cancer patients and burn victims. "These people often can't be kept on drugs all the time," says Stephen Kilbrick, a clinical psychologist who developed special music tapes for the hospital's stress management program. "This kind of music and relaxation instruction has proven very effective in helping them stay in a relaxed, calm state while undergoing treatment" (Malesky 58). At St. Agnes Hospital in Baltimore, music therapist Helen Bonny has used classical music as a sedative to lower heart rates and blood pressure for patients in the coronary unit, prompting director of coronary care Raymond Bahr to comment that "Music therapy ranks high on the list of techniques of modern-day management of critical care patients" (Rosenfeld 54).

In a more joyful application, music used in the delivery rooms of hospitals 13
across the country helps to decrease both labor time and the need for anesthetics. Expectant mothers learn breathing-relaxation exercises to music and use the focus provided by music to distract from pain during the birth. In a particularly difficult moment during a birth at the University of Kansas Medical Center, one woman was inspired to turn down the offer of a painkiller by the rousing theme from *Rocky*. Another sang her way through delivery (Brody, Ingber, and Pearson 24).

An important factor in the use of music for healing is our innate response 14
to rhythm. The first sounds that a baby hears are the pulses of the mother's heartbeat from within the womb. A baby's own breathing and pulse tend to become synchronized with its mother's, and so later in life we find that music with a smooth rhythm and tempo of about 60–70 beats per minute relaxes us, while fast, syncopated music tends to excite us. Kay Gardner explains that rhythms which duplicate the healthy human pulses will, through the process of entrainment, aid in bringing "out-of-phase" bodies back to health. A flute player whose music is both soothing and energizing, Gardner suggests that people with respiratory diseases like asthma and emphysema listen to the music of wind instruments because of the natural rhythms of deep breathing incorporated in the sounds produced.

Entrainment works on brain wave rhythms, too, and music can help to 15
balance the neural responses in the hemispheres of the brain. Gardner relates an experience with her father who was dying of stroke and had been unable to communicate for some time. When she played recorded music with beta brain wave rhythms of 14–22 cycles per second, he became lucid and able to communicate for several minutes at a time.

New progress is being made in research on music healing and how it works. 16
At the University of Miami's music therapy department, director Dr. Frederick Times excitedly predicts that music may be able to help the immune system by balancing the body's biorhythms and reducing the level of stress-related hormones called corticosteroids (Larkin 12). Endorphins, "natural opiates"

produced by the hypothalamus during musical stimulation and believed to create mild euphoric states and analgesic effects, are also fertile ground for new research (Malesky 60). Experiments in the study of sound waves that show different organs in the body such as the heart and liver emitting different vibrational frequencies prompt sound researcher Stephen Halpern to speculate that it may soon be possible to focus music therapy on specific organs of the body (39).

Music healers emphasize that the intent, or emotional message given out 17 by composer and performer, is the most important aspect of healing music. In working directly with people, the healer must let go of the ego attachment to healing and allow the process to be aided simply by the flow of love, while using music to open up the capacities to receive healing energy. "Music raises the life energy and facilitates the forces . . . within the individual to heal himself," says John Diamond, M.D., in his book *The Life Energy in Music* (14). San Francisco harpist Diana Stork, who has used the healing vibrations of her harp to relieve the cramping pain of arthritis and facilitate deep breathing for people with asthma, agrees. "You have to give up control, become an honored guest of the energy, and make people a part of the music," she says.

Music is also suggested as preventive medicine for healthy people, to coun- 18 teract the stresses of noise pollution and emotional upheavals in daily life. Many kinds of music can be therapeutic, depending on the desired results, but most music healers caution against rock music of the heavy metal variety. Surprisingly, this is not due as much to loud volume as to the particular rhythm in this type of music, a continuous "da da DA—" pattern called the "stopped-anapestic" beat, which is counter to the normal heartbeat. Knowledgeable music healers recommend listening to classical music, Indian ragas, Zen meditation music, or even some jazz, blues, and soft rock. And some, like singer Molly Scott, recommend using your own voice to sing along. She explains that the deep breathing needed for singing and the effects of vibrating tones within the body help to ease both physical and emotional stress. "Singing is like an internal massage, cleansing and vitalizing the system," she claims. "You cannot sing and stay depressed."

Therapeutic music is becoming popular commercially as well as in appli- 19 cations for holistic health purposes. With combinations of electronic instruments, acoustic instruments like flute and harp, and sometimes sounds from nature, more and more composers are delving into the art of healing music, and the genre of "New Age Music" is catching on with music lovers and healing professionals alike.

Civilization and its healing technology have changed a great deal since 20 ancient times, yet some of the old knowledge still survives. The healing power of music has been known from antiquity, and modern students and practitioners of the healing arts would do well to investigate its past as they continue to explore new applications. Scientific research is proving music to be a valuable tool as both an adjunct and an alternative to modern medical practices, and indications are that healing uses of music will become more and more an accepted part of health care in the future.

Works Cited

Brody, Robert. "Music Medicine." *Omni*, April 1984: 24–25.

Brody, Robert, Dina Ingber, and Cliff Pearson. "Music Therapy: Tune-up for Mind and Body." *Science Digest*, January 1982: 78.

Diamond, John, M.D. *The Life Energy in Music*. Valley Cottage, NY: Archaeus Press, 1981.

Gardner, Kay. "Music and Healing." Workshop presented by Juneau Arts and Humanities Council, Juneau, Alaska, 18–19 October 1986.

Halpern, Stephen, and Louis Savary. *Sound Health: The Music and Sounds That Make Us Whole*. San Francisco: Harper and Row, 1985.

Hamel, Peter. *Through Music to the Self*. Boulder: Shambhala Press, 1979.

Heline, Corine. *Healing and Regeneration Through Music*. Los Angeles: New Age Press, 1978.

Laughingbird, Gaea. "Expressions of Unity: The Uses of Sound in Healing." *The Holistic Health Handbook*. Ed. Edward Bauman, et al. Brattleboro, VT: Stephen Greene Press, 1984.

Larkin, Marilynn. "Music and Healing." *Health*, July 1985: 12.

Malesky, Gale. "Music That Strikes a Healing Chord." *Prevention*, October 1983: 57–63.

Murchie, Guy. *The Seven Mysteries of Life: An Exploration in Science and Philosophy*. Boston: Houghton Mifflin, 1978.

"Resonance." *Encyclopedia Americana*, 1985 ed., 440.

Rosenfeld, Anne. "Music, the Beautiful Disturber." *Psychology Today*, December 1985: 48–56.

Scott, Molly. "Tuning: The Power of Sound and Song: Self-Healing with Sound." *The New Holistic Health Handbook*. Ed. Shepherd Bliss. Lexington, MA: D. C. Heath, 1985.

Stork, Diana. Personal interview. 12 November 1986.

Tame, David. *The Secret Power of Music*. New York: Destiny Books, 1984.

Young, Alan. *Spiritual Healing: Miracle or Mirage?* Marina Del Rey, CA: Devorss & Co., 1981.

Focusing on Bonnie Harris's Techniques and Revisions

1. Bonnie Harris was asked to write a "persuasive research paper" on an issue of interest to her. What is the *thesis*—the stated or implied assertion—that governs the development of her essay? Where is that proposition stated most clearly?

2. Harris describes her purpose in writing "The Healing Power of Music" in these terms: "I wanted them [her classmates and 'the English professors' who might read her essay] to realize that music really can have a positive effect on our lives, that it has more value than its usual accepted cultural functions, and that there is a historical and scientific basis for its use in healing." How does Harris go about achieving this goal? To what extent is she successful? Explain why.

3. How would you describe the structure of Harris's essay? What kind of order does she establish for the particular sequence of her ideas? Is her essay organized, for example, according to a principle of increasing complexity? Increasing importance? Chronology? Specific to general? General to specific? Something else? Point to specific passages to support your response.

4. Identify each of the specific perspectives Harris creates for looking at the healing power of music. What is the distinguishing feature of each perspective? Comment on the effectiveness of each.

5. What does Harris reveal about the ways in which the many seemingly disparate theories about the healing power of music actually overlap? Consider, for example, the specific ways in which listening to music can reflect at once a scientific process and a spiritual experience.

6. Another successful feature of Harris's essay is her effective use of metaphors. In paragraph 6, for example, Harris observes, "The human body can be considered a natural resonant system made up of atoms, molecules, cells, muscles, and organs all oscillating to their own biorhythms and vibrational frequencies." Identify other examples of metaphoric language in Harris's essay and assess the effectiveness of its use in each instance.

7. In what specific ways do you think the technical details add to or detract from the success of Harris's essay? Does her use of technical language increase or diminish the power of her essay to persuade her readers about the healing power of music? How does she make sure that her audience will not be put off or bored by what might be unfamiliar language?

8. Bonnie Harris reports that her process of revision begins as soon as she puts words on paper: "I try not to get too hung up that way, however, or it gets too slow and I lose my train of thought. Sometimes I start by revising my outline. I might write two or three sample outlines before I start the paper. Real revising, though, comes after I've typed the whole thing into the computer and start mercilessly eliminating unnecessary sections. The editing I do for smoothness

and grammar comes pretty easily; letting go of those brilliant but unnecessary ideas I've worked so hard on is much more painful." Harris also repositions her paragraphs for greater effect. Consider, for example, the next to last paragraph of Harris' essay. In an earlier draft, this paragraph followed paragraph 15. Comment on the effectiveness of this revision. What did Harris gain and lose by making this change?

9. Compare Harris's essay with Thomas Leyba's "The Marfa Lights." Examine how each writer uses shifting frames of reference to elucidate the governing idea of the essay. Which writer more effectively relates different perspectives to his or her overriding purpose in writing the essay? Explain.

Suggestions for Writing

1. American folklore is replete with anecdotes about the curative powers of various activities and objects. Choose one such activity or object and write a research essay tracing the origins of its identity as a resource for healing. What is the current perception of its curative power? In developing your essay, draw on as many different frames of reference as possible for viewing the healing power of the activity or object.

2. In an essay entitled "Notes on Music and Opera," the poet W. H. Auden observed, "A verbal art like poetry is reflective; it stops to think. Music is immediate; it goes on to become." Write an essay in which you compare and contrast the essential features of these different frames of reference for expressing one's relation to experience.

AN EFFECTIVE TECHNIQUE

Bonnie Harris transforms a part of everyday life—music—into an amazing, almost supernatural phenomenon. To do so, she uses a powerful strategy for generating new insights into a familiar subject: shifting to a perspective that we do not usually associate with that subject. The central perspective from which Harris looks at music is that of medicine: she is trying to prove that music can be a cure for illnesses. Harris does not settle, however, for only one strange perspective on music: she shows her readers what ancient legends, physicists, psychologists, spiritual healers, and finally medical workers all have to say about the subject. By shifting perspective so many times, Harris develops a whole series of surprising insights about music.

We might expect the views of these varied frames of reference to conflict: science should prove legends wrong; doctors should disdain the work of mystical healers. However, the discovery that Harris has made is that these different realms overlap: "modern physicists in their search to discover the basis of matter have come to the same conclusion as the early philosophers and mystics: all matter is composed of . . . vibration" (paragraph 3); doctors are developing technology to improve on ritual healing methods. Her essay ends up not only transforming our understanding of music but also giving us unusual views of other realms. When Harris speaks of the rhythms scientists have discovered inside the earth, or the frequencies of atoms, she makes it seem that there is music in the physical world; she gives us a musical view of science.

As Harris moves from one frame of reference to another, she gains new words to explain how music can have medical properties. After she has explained the physics term "entrainment," for example, she can mix it with the vocabulary of medicine, speaking of "the natural tendencies in the human body toward resonance and entrainment—the forces for harmony" (paragraph 8). Words such as "harmony" and "vibration" have special importance in this essay, because they belong to more than one vocabulary and so automatically mix perspectives. Harris speaks of legendary sorcerers splitting rocks along "harmonic" lines, of physicists describing atoms as "harmonic systems," and of the "harmony" of music. She thereby suggests that harmony as a property of sound waves is closely connected to harmony as a spiritual and emotional state. By the end of her essay, phrases such as "life energy" and "in tune" bring to mind both mystical and scientific meanings simultaneously.

Because Harris wants to break us out of our conventional ways of thinking of music, she begins her essay with the two frames of reference furthest from everyday life: legends and physics. She starts with a quotation that presents truly wild claims about music's power: that ancient peoples used it to split stones and "resonate" them into position. Harris then jumps into a detailed scientific explanation of "resonance" that ends up supporting the legends; she even reports that modern medicine seems to have revived the ancient art, using "sound 'explosions' ". . . to "shatter kidney stones" (paragraph 4). Further, she reports claims made by scientists that seem more mystical than the legends—that the "nervous systems of all life forms" are "in tune" with the earth (paragraph 6). Harris breaks down the rigid barriers that usually stand between different frames of reference: the science in this essay makes the legends plausible; the legends make the science wondrous; and science and legends together serve to bridge the gap between music and medicine.

We can use Harris's methods to generate insights about almost any part of everyday life. We might find that we can generate new views of professional baseball, for example, by considering it from the perspective of psychology (what happens to a man's personality when he "plays games" all his life? what do fans get from watching the sport?); of sociology (how does the arrangement of seating at a baseball stadium reflect the economic structure of the country?); or of technology (how have changes in the manufacturing of baseballs altered the relative success of batters and pitchers?). We could even mix several of these perspectives together, say by connecting the psychology of fans to their economic status. In such essays, we do not have to prove everything we say with complete rigor; we can bring in interesting speculations and possibilities. Harris never actually proves that the "harmonic system" of atoms has anything to do with musical harmony. Using unusual frames of reference is a way to open a subject up, to stimulate thinking and action in our readers. This can be as valuable a goal as providing a single, definitive explanation.

Like Harris, Joyce Carol Oates takes a familiar subject—boxing—and both explains it and reveals that it is more complex than we previously thought. Viewing boxing from several unusual frames of reference, she argues that boxing is not a sport; instead, she says, "each boxing match is a story," a play without words that speaks to its audience about father-son relations, sexuality, economics, and class warfare.

ANOTHER ILLUSTRATION OF THE TECHNIQUE

JOYCE CAROL OATES

On Boxing

"I began writing in high school, consciously training myself by writing novel after novel and always throwing them out when I completed them," recalls Joyce Carol Oates. She has continued to discipline herself all her life, writing each day regardless of how she is feeling: "One must be pitiless about this matter of 'mood.' In a sense, the writing will create the mood. If art is, as I believe it to be, a genuinely transcendental function—a means by which we rise out of limited, parochial states of mind—then it should not matter very much what states of mind or emotion we are in."

Oates has become one of the most prolific and honored American writers and has also been actively involved in the studying and teaching of literature. She received her B.A. from Syracuse University in 1960, entered a doctoral program at Rice University that she dropped out of when her writing began to provide a substantial income, and has taught at several American and Canadian universities. Her writing and teaching emphasize the importance of establishing a sense of community; she disagrees with modern artists

who believe that the only thing they can write about is themselves. Oates's writing often
leads her far from her own experience; she has published novels dealing with medicine,
law, politics, religion, and sports.

They are young welterweight boxers so evenly matched they might be 1
twins—though one has a redhead's pallor and the other is a dusky-skinned
Hispanic. Circling each other in the ring, they try jabs, tentative left hooks,
right crosses that dissolve in midair or turn into harmless slaps. The Madison
Square Garden crowd is derisive, impatient. "Those two! What'd they do,
wake up this morning and decide they were boxers?" a man behind me says
contemptuously. (He's dark, nattily dressed, with a neatly trimmed mustache
and tinted glasses. A sophisticated fight fan. Two hours later he will be crying,
"Tommy! Tommy! Tommy!" over and over in a paroxysm of grief as, on the
giant closed-circuit television screen, middleweight champion Marvelous Marvin Hagler batters his challenger, Thomas Hearns, into insensibility.)

The young boxers must be conscious of the jeers and boos in this great 2
cavernous space reaching up into the $20 seats in the balconies amid the
constant milling of people in the aisles, the smells of hotdogs, beer, cigarette
and cigar smoke, hair oil. But they are locked desperately together, circling,
jabbing, slapping, clinching, now a flurry of light blows, clumsy footwork,
another sweaty stumbling despairing clinch into the ropes that provokes a fresh
wave of derision. Why are they here in the Garden of all places, each fighting
what looks like his first professional fight? What are they doing? Neither is
angry at the other. When the bell sounds at the end of the sixth and final
round, the crowd boos a little louder. The Hispanic boy, silky yellow shorts,
damp, frizzy, floating hair, strides about his corner of the ring with his gloved
hand aloft—not in defiance of the boos, which increase in response to his
gesture, or even in acknowledgment of them. It's just something he has seen
older boxers do. He seems to be saying "I'm here, I made it, I did it." When
the decision is announced as a draw, the crowd's derision increases in volume.
"Get out of the ring!" "Go home!" Contemptuous male laughter follows the
boys in their robes, towels about their heads, sweating, breathless. Why had
they thought they were boxers?

How can you enjoy so brutal a sport, people ask. Or don't ask. 3

And it's too complicated to answer. In any case, I don't "enjoy" boxing, 4
and never have; it isn't invariably "brutal"; I don't think of it as a sport.

Nor do I think of it in writerly terms as a metaphor for something else. (For 5
what else?) No one whose interest in boxing began in childhood—as mine did
as an offshoot of my father's interest—is likely to suppose it is a symbol of

something beyond itself, though I can entertain the proposition that life is a metaphor for boxing—for one of those bouts that go on and on, round following round, small victories, small defeats, nothing determined, again the bell and again the bell and you and your opponent so evenly matched it's clear your opponent *is* you and why are the two of you jabbing and punching at each other on an elevated platform enclosed by ropes as in a pen beneath hot crude all-exposing lights in the presence of an indifferent crowd: that sort of writerly metaphor. But if you have seen five hundred boxing matches, you have seen five hundred boxing matches, and their common denominator, which surely exists, is not of primary interest to you. "If the Host is only a symbol," the Catholic writer Flannery O'Connor said, "I'd say the hell with it."

Each boxing match is a story, a highly condensed, highly dramatic story— 6 even when nothing much happens: then failure is the story. There are two principal characters in the story, overseen by a shadowy third. When the bell rings no one knows what will happen. Much is speculated, nothing known. The boxers bring to the fight everything that is themselves, and everything will be exposed: including secrets about themselves they never knew. There are boxers possessed of such remarkable intuition, such prescience, one would think they had fought this particular fight before. There are boxers who perform brilliantly, but mechanically, who cannot improvise in midfight; there are boxers performing at the height of their skill who cannot quite comprehend that it won't be enough; to my knowledge there was only one boxer who possessed an extraordinary and disquieting awareness, not only of his opponent's every move or anticipated move, but of the audience's keenest shifts in mood as well—Muhammad Ali, of course.

In the ring, death is always a possibility, which is why I prefer to see films 7 or tapes of fights already past—already crystallized into art. In fact, death is a statistically rare possibility of which no one likes to think—like your possible death tomorrow morning in an automobile crash, or in next month's airplane crash, or in a freak accident involving a fall on the stairs—a skull fracture, subarachnoid hemorrhage.

A boxing match is a play without words, which doesn't mean that it has 8 no text or no language, only that the text is improvised in action, the language a dialogue between the boxers in a joint response to the mysterious will of the crowd, which is always that the fight be a worthy one so that the crude paraphernalia of the setting—the ring, the lights, the onlookers themselves— be obliterated. To go from an ordinary preliminary match to a "Fight of the Century"—like those between Joe Louis and Billy Conn, Muhammad Ali and

Joe Frazier, most recently Marvin Hagler and Thomas Hearns—is to go from listening or half-listening to a guitar being idly plucked to hearing Bach's "Well-Tempered Clavier" being perfectly played, and that too is part of the story. So much is happening so swiftly and so subtly you cannot absorb it except to know that something memorable is happening and it is happening in a place beyond words.

The fighters in the ring are time-bound—is anything so excruciatingly long   9 as a fiercely contested three-minute round?—but the fight itself is timeless. By way of films and tapes, it has become history, art. If boxing is a sport, it is the most tragic of all sports because, more than any human activity, it consumes the very excellence it displays: Its very drama is this consumption. To expend oneself in fighting the greatest fight of one's life is to begin immediately the downward turn that next time may be a plunge, a sudden incomprehensible fall. *I am the greatest*, Muhammad Ali says. *I am the greatest*, Marvin Hagler says. You always think you're going to win, Jack Dempsey wryly observed in his old age, otherwise you can't fight at all. The punishment—to the body, the brain, the spirit—a man must endure to become a great boxer is inconceivable to most of us whose idea of personal risk is largely ego related or emotional. But the punishment, as it begins to show in even a young and vigorous boxer, is closely assessed by his rivals. After junior-welterweight champion Aaron Pryor won a lackluster fight on points a few months ago, a younger boxer in his weight division, interviewed at ringside, said: "My mouth is watering."

So the experience of seeing great fighters of the past—and great sporting 10 events are always *past*—is radically different from having seen them when they were reigning champions. Jack Johnson, Jack Dempsey, Joe Louis, Sugar Ray Robinson, Willie Pep, Rocky Marciano, Muhammad Ali—as spectators we know not only how a fight ends but how a career ends. Boxing is always particulars, second by incalculable second, but in the abstract it suggests these haunting lines by Yeats:

> Everything that man esteems
> Endures a moment or a day.
> Love's pleasure drives his love away,
> The painter's brush consumes his dreams;
> The herald's cry, the soldier's tread
> Exhaust his glory and his might:
> Whatever flames upon the night
> Man's own resinous heart has fed.
> —from "The Resurrection"

The referee, the third character in the story, usually appears to be a mere observer, even an intruder, a near-ghostly presence as fluid in motion and quick-footed as the boxers themselves (he is frequently a former boxer). But so central to the drama of boxing is the referee that the spectacle of two men fighting each other unsupervised in an elevated ring would appear hellish, obscene—life rather than art. The referee is our intermediary in the fight. He is our moral conscience, extracted from us as spectators so that, for the duration of the fight, "conscience" is not a factor in our experience; nor is it a factor in the boxers' behavior.

Though the referee's role is a highly demanding one, and it has been esti- 11 mated that there are perhaps no more than a dozen really skilled referees in the world, it seems to be necessary in the intense dramatic action of the fight that the referee have no dramatic identity. Referees' names are quickly forgotten, even as they are announced over the microphone preceding a fight. Yet, paradoxically, the referee's position is one of crucial significance. The referee cannot control what happens in the ring, but he can frequently control, to a degree, *that* it happens: he is responsible for the fight, if not for the individual fighter's performance. It is the referee solely who holds the power of life and death at certain times; whose decision to terminate a fight, or to allow it to continue, determines a man's fate. (One should recall that a well-aimed punch with a boxer's full weight behind it can have an astonishing impact—a blow that must be absorbed by the brain in its jelly sac.)

In a recent heavyweight fight in Buffalo, 220-pound Tim Witherspoon re- 12 peatedly struck his 260-pound opponent, James Broad, caught in the ropes, while the referee looked on without acting—though a number of spectators called for the fight to be stopped. In the infamous Benny Paret–Emile Griffith fight of March 24, 1962, the referee Ruby Goldstein was said to have stood paralyzed as Paret, trapped in the ropes, suffered as many as 18 powerful blows to the head before he fell. (He died ten days later.) Boxers are trained not to quit; if they are knocked down they will try to get up to continue the fight, even if they can hardly defend themselves. The primary rule of the ring—to defend oneself at all times—is both a parody and a distillation of life.

Boxing is a purely masculine world. (Though there are female boxers—the 13 most famous is the black champion Lady Tyger Trimiar with her shaved head and tiger-striped attire—women's role in the sport is extremely marginal.) The vocabulary of boxing is attuned to a quintessentially masculine sensibility in which the role of patriarch/protector can only be assured if there is physical strength underlying it. First comes this strength—"primitive," perhaps; then comes civilization. It should be kept in mind that "boxing" and "fighting," though always combined in the greatest of boxers, can be entirely different

and even unrelated activities. If boxing can be, in the lighter weights especially, a highly complex and refined skill belonging solely to civilization, fighting seems to belong to something predating civilization, the instinct not merely
to defend oneself—for when has the masculine ego ever been assuaged by so
minimal a gesture?—but to attack another and to force him into absolute
submission. Hence the electrifying effect upon a typical fight crowd when
fighting emerges suddenly out of boxing—the excitement when a boxer's face
begins to bleed. The flash of red is the visible sign of the fight's authenticity
in the eyes of many spectators, and boxers are right to be proud—if they are—
of their facial scars.

To the untrained eye, boxers in the ring usually appear to be angry. But, 14
of course, this is "work" to them; emotion has no part in it, or should not.
Yet in an important sense—in a symbolic sense—the boxers *are* angry, and
boxing is fundamentally about anger. It is the only sport in which anger is
accommodated, ennobled. Why are boxers angry? Because, for the most part,
they belong to the disenfranchised of our society, to impoverished ghetto
neighborhoods in which anger is an appropriate response. ("It's hard being
black. You ever been black? I was black once—when I was poor," Larry Holmes
has said.) Today, when most boxers—most good boxers—are black or Hispanic, white men begin to look anemic in the ring. Yet after decades
of remarkable black boxers—from Jack Johnson to Joe Louis to Muhammad
Ali—heavyweight champion Larry Holmes was the object of racist slurs and
insults when he defended his title against the over-promoted white challenger
Gerry Cooney a few years ago.

Liberals who have no personal or class reason to feel anger tend to dispar- 15
age, if not condemn, such anger in others. Liberalism is also unfairly harsh
in its criticism of all that predates civilization—or "liberalism" itself—without comprehending that civilization is a concept, an idea, perhaps at times
hardly more than fiction, attendant upon, and always subordinate to, physical strength: missiles, nuclear warheads. The terrible and tragic silence
dramatized in the boxing ring is the silence of nature before language, when
the physical *was* language, a means of communication swift and unmistakable.

The phrase "killer instinct" is said to have been coined in reference to Jack 16
Dempsey in his famous early fights against Jess Willard, Georges Carpentier,
Luis Firpo ("The Wild Bull of the Pampas"), and any number of other boxers,
less renowned, whom he savagely beat. The ninth of eleven children born to
an impoverished Mormon sharecropper and itinerant railroad worker, Dempsey
seems to have been, as a young boxer in his prime, the very embodiment of

angry hunger; and if he remains the most spectacular heavyweight champion in history, it is partly because he fought when rules governing boxing were somewhat casual by present-day standards. Where aggression must be learned, even cultivated, in some champion boxers (Tunney, Louis, Marciano, Patterson, for example), Dempsey's aggression was direct and natural: Once in the ring he seems to have wanted to kill his opponent.

Dempsey's first title fight in 1919, against the aging champion Jess Willard, 17 was called "pugilistic murder" by some sportswriters and is said to have been one of boxing's all-time blood baths. Today, this famous fight—which brought the nearly unknown twenty-four-year-old Dempsey to national prominence— would certainly have been stopped in the first minute of the first round. Badly out of condition, heavier than Dempsey by almost sixty pounds, the thirty-seven-year-old Willard had virtually no defense against the challenger. By the end of the fight, Willard's jaw was broken, his cheekbone split, nose smashed, six teeth broken off at the gum, an eye was battered shut, much further damage was done to his body. Both boxers were covered in Willard's blood. Years later Dempsey's estranged manager Kearns confessed—perhaps falsely—that he had "loaded" Dempsey's gloves—treated his hand tape with a talcum substance that turned concrete-hard when wet.

For the most part, boxing matches today are scrupulously monitored by 18 referees and ring physicians. The devastating knockout blow is frequently the one never thrown. In a recent televised junior-middleweight bout between Don Curry and James Green, the referee stopped the fight because Green seemed momentarily disabled: His logic was that Green had dropped his gloves and was therefore in a position to be hurt. (Green and his furious trainer protested the decision but the referee's word is final: No fight, stopped, can be resumed.) The drama of the ring begins to shift subtly as more and more frequently one sees a referee intervene to embrace a weakened or defenseless man in a gesture of paternal solicitude that in itself carries much theatrical power—a gesture not so dramatic as the killing blow but one that suggests that the ethics of the ring are moving toward those that prevail beyond it. As if fighter-brothers whose mysterious animosity has somehow brought them to battle are saved by their father. . . .

In the final moment of the Hagler-Hearns fight, the dazed Hearns—on his 19 feet but clearly not fully conscious, gamely prepared to take Hagler's next assault—was saved by the referee from what might well have been serious injury, if not death, considering the ferocity of Hagler's fighting and the personal anger he seems to have brought to it that night. This eight-minute fight, generally believed to be one of the great fights in boxing history, ends with

Hearns in the referee's protective embrace—an image that is haunting, in itself profoundly mysterious, as if an indefinable human drama had been spontaneously created for us, brilliantly improvised, performed one time and one time only, yet permanently ingrained upon our consciousness.

Years ago in the early 1950s, when my father first took me to a Golden 20 Gloves boxing tournament in Buffalo, I asked him why the boys wanted to fight one another, why they were willing to get hurt. My father said, "Boxers don't feel pain quite the way we do."

Gene Tunney's single defeat in an eleven-year career was to a flamboyant 21 and dangerous fighter named Harry Greb ("The Human Windmill"), who seems to have been, judging from boxing literature, the dirtiest fighter in history. Low blows, butting, fouls, holding and hitting, using his laces on an opponent's eyes—Greb was famous for his lack of interest in the rules. He was world middleweight champion for three years but a presence in the boxing world for a long time. After the first of his several fights with Greb, the twenty-four-year-old Tunney had to spend a week in bed, he was so badly hurt; he'd lost two quarts of blood during the fifteen-round fight. But as Tunney said years afterward: "Greb gave me a terrible whipping. He broke my nose, maybe with a butt. He cut my eyes and ears, perhaps with his laces. . . . My jaw was swollen from the right temple down the cheek, along under the chin and part way up the other side. The referee, the ring itself, was full of blood. . . . But it was in that first fight, in which I lost my American light-heavyweight title, that I knew I had found a way to beat Harry eventually. I was fortunate, really. If boxing in those days had been afflicted with the commission doctors we have today—who are always poking their noses into the ring and examining superficial wounds—the first fight with Greb would have been stopped before I learned how to beat him. It's possible, even probable, that if this had happened I would never have been heard of again."

Tommy Loughran, the light-heavyweight champion from 1927 to 1929, was 22 a master boxer greatly admired by other boxers. He approached boxing literally as a science—as Tunney did—studying his opponents' styles and mapping out ring strategy for each fight. He rigged up mirrors in his basement so that he could see himself as he worked out—for, as Loughran realized, no boxer ever sees himself quite as he appears to his opponent. But the secret of Loughran's career was that he had a right hand that broke so easily he could use it only once in each fight: It had to be the knockout punch or nothing. "I'd get one shot, then the agony of the thing would hurt me if the guy got up. Anybody I ever hit with a left hook, I knocked flat on his face, but I would never take a chance for fear if my left hand goes, I'm done for."

Both Tunney and Loughran, it is instructive to note, retired from boxing 23
before they were forced to retire. Tunney was a highly successful businessman
and Loughran a successful sugar broker on the Wall Street commodities market—
just to suggest that boxers are not invariably illiterate, stupid, or punch-drunk.

One of the perhaps not entirely acknowledged reasons for the attraction of 24
serious writers to boxing (from Swift, Pope, Johnson to Hazlitt, Lord Byron,
Hemingway, and our own Norman Mailer, George Plimpton, Wilfrid Sheed,
Daniel Halpern, et al.) is the sport's systematic cultivation of pain in the
interests of a project, a life-goal: the willed transposing of the sensation called
"pain" (whether physical or psychological) into its opposite. If this is maso-
chism—and I doubt that it is, or that it is simply—it is also intelligence,
cunning, strategy. It is the active welcoming of that which most living beings
try to avoid and to flee. It is the active subsuming of the present moment in
terms of the future. Pain now but control (and therefore pleasure) later.

Still, it is the rigorous training period leading up to the public appearance 25
that demands the most discipline. In this, too, the writer senses some kinship,
however oblique and one-sided, with the professional boxer. The brief public
spectacle of the boxing match (which could last as little as sixty seconds), like
the publication of the writer's book, is but the final, visible stage in a long,
arduous, fanatic, and sometimes quixotic, subordination of the self. It was
Rocky Marciano who seems to have trained with the most monastic devotion,
secluding himself from his wife and family for as long as three months before
a fight. Quite apart from the grueling physical training of this period and the
constant preoccupation with diet and weight, Marciano concentrated on only
the upcoming fight, the opening bell, his opponent. Every minute of the
boxer's life was planned for one purpose. In the training camp the name of
the opponent was never mentioned and Marciano's associates were careful
about conversation in his presence: They talked very little about boxing.

In the final month, Marciano would not write a letter. The last ten days 26
before a fight he saw no mail, took no telephone calls, met no new acquaintances. The week before the fight he would not shake hands with anyone. Or
go for a ride in a car. No new foods! No envisioning the morning after the
fight! All that was not *the fight* was taboo: When Marciano worked out punching the bag he saw his opponent before him, when he jogged early in the
morning he saw his opponent close beside him. What could be a more powerful
image of discipline—madness?—than this absolute subordination of the self,
this celibacy of the fighter-in-training? Instead of focusing his energies and
fantasies upon Woman, the boxer focuses them upon the Opponent.

No sport is more physical, more direct, than boxing. No sport appears more 27
powerfully homoerotic: the confrontation in the ring—the disrobing—the

sweaty, heated combat that is part dance, courtship, coupling—the frequent urgent pursuit by one boxer of the other in the fight's natural and violent movement toward the "knockout." Surely boxing derives much of its appeal from this mimicry of a species of erotic love in which one man overcomes the other in an exhibition of superior strength.

Most fights, however fought, lead to an embrace between the boxers after 28 the final bell—a gesture of mutual respect and apparent affection that appears to the onlooker to be more than perfunctory. Rocky Graziano, often derided for being a slugger rather than a "classic" boxer, sometimes kissed his opponents out of gratitude for the fight. Does the boxing match, one almost wonders, lead irresistibly to this moment: the public embrace of two men who otherwise, in public or in private, could not approach each other with such passion. Are men privileged to embrace with love only after having fought? A woman is struck by the tenderness men will express for boxers who have been hurt, even if it is only by way of commentary on photographs: the startling picture of Ray ("Boom Boom") Mancini after his second losing fight with Livingstone Bramble, for instance, when Mancini's face was hideously battered (photographs in *Sports Illustrated* and elsewhere were gory, near-pornographic); the much-reprinted photograph of the defeated Thomas Hearns being carried to his corner in the arms of an enormous black man in formal attire—the "Hit Man" from Detroit now helpless, only semiconscious, looking precisely like a black Christ taken from the cross. These are powerful, haunting, unsettling images, cruelly beautiful, very much bound up with the primitive appeal of the sport.

Yet to suggest that men might love one another directly without the violent 29 ritual of combat is to misread man's greatest passion—for war, not peace. Love, if there is to be love, comes second.

Boxing is, after all, about lying. It is about cultivating a double personality. 30 As José Torres, the ex-light-heavyweight champion who is now the New York State Boxing Commissioner, says: "We fighters understand lies. What's a feint? What's a left hook off the jab? What's an opening? What's thinking one thing and doing another . . . ?"

There is nothing fundamentally playful about boxing, nothing that seems 31 to belong to daylight, to pleasure. At its moments of greatest intensity it seems to contain so complete and so powerful an image of life—life's beauty, vulnerability, despair, incalculable and often reckless courage—that boxing *is* life, and hardly a mere game. During a superior boxing match we are deeply moved by the body's communion with itself by way of another's flesh. The body's dialogue with its shadow-self—or Death. Baseball, football, basketball—these quintessentially American pastimes are recognizably sports because they in-volve play: They are games. One *plays* football; one doesn't *play* boxing.

Observing team sports, teams of adult men, one sees how men are children 32
in the most felicitous sense of the word. But boxing in its elemental ferocity cannot be assimilated into childhood—though very young men box, even professionally, and numerous world champions began boxing when they were hardly more than children. Spectators at public games derive much of their pleasure from reliving the communal emotions of childhood, but spectators at boxing matches relive the murderous infancy of the race. Hence the notorious cruelty of boxing crowds and the excitement when a man begins to bleed. ("When I see blood," says Marvin Hagler, "I become a bull." He means his own.)

The boxing ring comes to seem an altar of sorts, one of those legendary 33
magical spaces where the laws of a nation are suspended: Inside the ropes, during an officially regulated three-minute round, a man may be killed at his opponent's hands but he cannot be legally murdered. Boxing inhabits a sacred space predating civilization; or, to use D. H. Lawrence's phrase, before God was love. If it suggests a savage ceremony or a rite of atonement, it also suggests the futility of such rites. For what atonement is the fight waged, if it must shortly be waged again . . . ?

All this is to speak of the paradox of boxing—its obsessive appeal for many 34
who find in it not only a spectacle involving sensational feats of physical skill but an emotional experience impossible to convey in words; an art form, as I have suggested, with no natural analogue in the arts. And of course this ac-counts, too, for the extreme revulsion it arouses in many people. ("Brutal," "disgusting," "barbaric," "inhuman," "a terrible, terrible sport"—typical com-ments on the subject.)

In December 1984, the American Medical Association passed a resolution 35
calling for the abolition of boxing on the principle that it is the only sport in which the *objective* is to cause injury. This is not surprising. Humanitarians have always wanted to reform boxing—or abolish it altogether. The 1896 heavyweight title match between Ruby Robert Fitzsimmons and Peter Maher was outlawed in many parts of the United States, so canny promoters staged it across the Mexican border four hundred miles from El Paso. (Some three hundred people made the arduous journey to see what must have been one of the most disappointing bouts in boxing history—Fitzsimmons knocked out his opponent in a mere ninety-five seconds.)

During the prime of Jack Dempsey's career in the 1920s, boxing was illegal 36
in many states, like alcohol, and like alcohol, seems to have aroused a hys-

terical public enthusiasm. Photographs of jammed outdoor arenas taken in the 1920s with boxing rings like postage-sized altars at their centers, the boxers themselves scarcely visible, testify to the extraordinary emotional appeal boxing had at that time, even as reform movements were lobbying against it. When Jack Johnson won the heavyweight title in 1908 (he had to pursue the white champion Tommy Burns all the way to Australia to confront him), the special "danger" of boxing was also that it might expose and humiliate white men in the ring. After Johnson's victory over the "White Hope" contender Jim Jeffries, there were race riots and lynchings throughout the United States; even films of some of Johnson's fights were outlawed in many states. And because boxing has become a sport in which black and Hispanic men have lately excelled, it is particularly vulnerable to attack by white middle-class reformers, who seem uninterested in lobbying against equally dangerous but "establishment" sports like football, auto racing, and thoroughbred horse racing.

There is something peculiarly American in the fact that, while boxing is 37 our most controversial sport, it is also the sport that pays its top athletes the most money. In spite of the controversy, boxing has never been healthier financially. The three highest paid athletes in the world in both 1983 and 1984 were boxers; a boxer with a long career like heavyweight champion Larry Holmes—forty-eight fights in thirteen years as a professional—can expect to earn somewhere beyond $50 million. (Holmes said that after retirement what he would miss most about boxing is his million-dollar checks.) Dempsey, who said that a man fights for one thing only—money—made somewhere beyond $3,500,000 in the ring in his long and varied career. Now $1.5 million is a fairly common figure for a single fight. Thomas Hearns made at least $7 million in his fight with Hagler while Hagler made at least $7.5 million. For the first of his highly publicized matches with Roberto Duran in 1980—which he lost on a decision—the popular black welterweight champion Sugar Ray Leonard received a staggering $10 million to Duran's $1.3 million. And none of these figures takes into account various subsidiary earnings (from television commercials, for instance) which in Leonard's case are probably as high as his income was from boxing.

Money has drawn any number of retired boxers back into the ring, very 38 often with tragic results. The most notorious example is perhaps Joe Louis, who, owing huge sums in back taxes, continued boxing well beyond the point at which he could perform capably. After a career of seventeen years he was stopped by Rocky Marciano—who was said to have felt as upset by his victory as Louis by the defeat. (Louis then went on to a degrading second career as a professional wrestler. This, too, ended abruptly when 300-pound Rocky Lee stepped on the forty-two-year-old Louis's chest and damaged his heart.) Ezzard Charles, Jersey Joe Walcott, Joe Frazier, Muhammad Ali—each continued fighting when he was no longer in condition to defend himself against young heavyweight boxers on the way up. Of all heavyweight champions, only Rocky Marciano, to whom fame and money were not of paramount significance, was prudent enough to retire before he was defeated. In any case, the prodigious sums of money a few boxers earn do not account for the sums the public is willing to pay them.

Though boxing has long been popular in many countries and under many 39 forms of government, its popularity in the United States since the days of John L. Sullivan has a good deal to do with what is felt as the spirit of the individual—his "physical" spirit—in conflict with the constrictions of the state. The rise of boxing in the 1920s in particular might well be seen as a consequence of the diminution of the individual vis-à-vis society; the gradual attrition of personal freedom, will, and strength—whether "masculine" or otherwise. In the Eastern bloc of nations, totalitarianism is a function of the state; in the Western bloc it has come to seem a function of technology, or history—"fate." The individual exists in his physical supremacy, but does the individual matter?

In the magical space of the boxing ring so disquieting a question has no 40 claim. There, as in no other public arena, the individual as a unique physical being asserts himself; there, for a dramatic if fleeting period of time, the great world with its moral and political complexities, its terrifying impersonality, simply ceases to exist. Men fighting one another with only their fists and their cunning are all contemporaries, all brothers, belonging to no historical time. "He can run, but he can't hide"—so said Joe Louis before his famous fight with young Billy Conn in 1941. In the brightly lighted ring, man is *in extremis*, performing an atavistic rite or agon for the mysterious solace of those who can participate only vicariously in such drama: the drama of life in the flesh. Boxing has become America's tragic theater.

Focusing on Joyce Carol Oates's Use of Frames of Reference

1. In the beginning of her essay, Oates shifts our perspective about boxing, denying that it is a sport, claiming instead that "each boxing match is a story" (paragraphs 4, 6). What terms that we usually associate with literature and drama does she use to describe boxing in paragraphs 5–8? Which of these terms recur throughout her essay? What different kinds of stories does she say boxing matches tell?

2. We do not usually speak of a sport as being "about" anything, but we often say stories are "about" things such as death or love. What different things does Oates say boxing is about (consider, for example, paragraphs 13 and 28)?

3. What frames of reference besides sports and literature does Oates turn to (for some examples, you might look at paragraphs 12, 13, 25, and 35)? How do these other frames of reference help her describe the kinds of stories that boxing matches tell?

4. One of Oates's frames of reference, the archeological view of the world before civilization, appears in paragraphs 12, 14, 31, and 38. In paragraph 14, she says that boxing uses a type of communication that predates language. How does this concept help explain how boxing can be a "play without words." How is the boxing ring like an "altar" (paragraph 14)? How is boxing like a "rite" (paragraph 38)? How is a rite performed on an altar like a drama?

WORKING WITH THE TECHNIQUE IN YOUR OWN WRITING

---

1. Select a subject with which you are familiar and a frame of reference that is not often applied to that subject but touches on it in some way. Use that frame of reference to generate an unusual view of your familiar subject. What insights can you derive from considering, for example, the economics of tennis, the ecology of schools, or the psychology of baseball?

2. Oates's unusual perspective on boxing can be applied to almost any other spectator sport. Select a professional sport and write an essay like Oates's, explaining how each time the sport is played a story is being enacted for the spectators. What kinds of stories are told by the sport you select? Is baseball, for example, a family drama about "home" and "visitors"? You might think about how your sport differs from boxing to help you determine how the stories your sport enacts might differ from the kinds of stories Oates describes.

3. Write an essay about a myth, a legend, or an element of folklore that contains an insight that modern science might support. You might, for example, explore the idea that people need a balance of yin and yang, or that certain foods operate like magic potions to alter people's thinking. You might find it useful in developing your essay to bring in some other frames of reference besides legend and science.

MARGOT HARRISON

Harvard University
Cambridge, Massachusetts
Leonard Cassuto, instructor

Margot Harrison traces her abiding interest in reading to the encouragement of her parents and the circumstances of her childhood: "A degree of isolation from the outside world when I was young (living in rural New York State without a TV) and the efforts of parents who were constantly giving me books and reading me books combined to make me into someone who often felt that the world within the pages was more real than the one outside. People who love to read often say that they don't like to 'dissect' books, but with me it has been almost the opposite; I have always enjoyed criticism, perhaps mainly because it gives me a chance to analyze my experience as a reader."

The older of two daughters, Margot Harrison was born in New York City but has lived in several different parts of the country, most recently in Bloomington, Indiana, where her father is a composer and professor of composition at Indiana University, while her mother works as a court clerk in Vermont and studies toward a degree in family therapy. Reading and writing have always figured prominently in Harrison's life, both in and out of school:

> My interests and activities, both academic and extracurricular,
> have generally centered around writing and reading: writing fic-
> tion, writing criticism (and, recently, attempting to write social
> commentary), reading fiction and literary theory. In high school
> I was active in theater, and I still have an interest in acting.
> What I think of as my accomplishments usually relate to things
> I've written. In high school I won the Brown Book Award, first
> prize for a short story in a Purdue University Department of
> English contest, and honorable mention for a short story in the
> National Arts Recognition and Talent Search; in college I've
> won the Detur Prize for a high academic average during fresh-
> man year.

She describes herself as someone without "meaningful work experience—so far [her jobs] have only been in libraries and at a fast food place." Now a literature major in college, Harrison plans to "go on to graduate school and hopefully someday be a professor, writing critical articles and perhaps fiction on the side."

Harrison's method of writing involves, as she reports, "putting various stages in the development of my ideas down on paper. I can't conceive an essay full-blown in my head at all; all the intermediate stages have to be in writing, where I can refer to them. A single very good insight may come at any time in the writing process, and so the essay keeps being shaped as it goes along. Basically, those ideas and insights are the foundation of the essay and what matter the most in it; logical transitions and appropriate wordings have to be 'draped' over them after the fact." Harrison's impressionistic view of her own writing process is extended in the analogy she draws between revising and painting: "after filling in the whole canvas with broad strokes, you go back, fill up empty spaces, create connections and subtleties, achieve an effect of finesse."

Asked to write an essay comparing and contrasting two essays from the course reader, Harrison decided to compare Virginia Woolf's "The Death of the Moth" and Annie Dillard's "Death of a Moth" principally, as she explains, "because the similarities of title and subject interested me." She reports that the goals of her essay were "to carry out an effective comparison, specifically to prove that the two essays, written in different time periods by very different authors, deserved to be compared at all. It was also my goal to elucidate the methods used in each individual essay, especially the narrative methods, which seemed to me in one case to run the risk of leaving too much unsaid and, in the other, of saying too much."

Virginia Woolf's "The Death of the Moth" is reprinted on pages 397–400, Annie Dillard's "Death of a Moth" on pages 330–332.

Creative Transfiguration from the Death of a Moth

At first glance, Virginia Woolf's essay "The Death of the Moth" and Annie   1 Dillard's "Death of a Moth" seem to demand comparison. But for one small article, after all, the titles are identical, and a reading reveals general similarities in the essays themselves. Each uses the death of a moth as its focus, and in each this small, normally unnoticed incident—about which, as Woolf says, there is "nobody to care or to know" (59)—becomes a concentrated moment of pure insight for the author, something comparable to what Wordsworth calls a "spot of time." It arouses philosophical reflection and religious awe; to Woolf, it is a dramatization of the struggle between life and death, to Dillard, a "transfiguration."

Yet although both essays are centered around a "spot of time," they vary   2 substantially in the way this moment is framed and depicted. A difference is suggested already in the small distinction between the titles: Woolf's "*the* moth" is emphasized and definite, indicating the moth's importance as a symbol (just as "The Rape of *the* Lock" sets Pope's mock-heroic mood better than "The Rape of *a* Lock" would have done), while Dillard's "*a* moth" is vaguer, more equivocal about this particular moth's significance. Woolf, as her title implies, makes the moth's death very clearly her focus and states its symbolic meaning to us: the moth is "dancing and zigzagging to show us the true nature of life" (58), then illustrates the fact that "nothing, I knew, had any chance against death" (59). The incident inspires "wonder" because it is a display in microcosm of "an oncoming doom which could, had it chosen, have submerged an entire city . . . masses of human beings" (59). The author exists purely to observe, to feel and record this wonder. There is an "I," a first-person narrator, but her reasons for sitting at the window with a book are unimportant and she is often eclipsed by impersonal forms: "the eyes strictly turned upon the book" (57) rather than "my eyes" and "my book," the frequent use of "one." This impersonality seems to serve to point out the moth's universal significance, the implication being that, although Woolf is the only one on hand to witness this particular death, any one of us would have seen it as she does. When she writes, "Nothing, I knew, had any chance against death" (59) or "One's sympathies, of course, were all on the side of life" (59), she uses the assumption that each of us accepts these facts to invite us to step into her place before the window and become ourselves the observer.

In dealing with "universal" concepts and telling us directly that she is doing   3
so, Woolf runs the risk of making a simplified, self-evident statement—"nothing has a chance against death"—and nothing more. But, almost as if in disdain of subtlety and concealment, she says what she means and then digs deeper into the "self-evident," using images to give concrete, perceptible form to the abstract concepts which otherwise might have become meaningless catch words. She states flatly that the entire landscape is "inspired" by "energy," that the moth is "a tiny bead of pure life" (58), but she shows us at the same time what she means by "energy" and "life" in descriptions such as that of the rising and settling of a flock of rooks. Here there are evocations of motion ("soaring . . . sank . . . thrown into the air"), sound ("utmost clamor and vociferation"), and emotion ("tremendously exciting") (57). Perhaps most graphic is the description of life in its diluted and less energetic form: "humped and bossed and garnished and cumbered so that it has to move wth the greatest circumspection and dignity" (58). In this image an abstract, general quality becomes concrete—"life" appears before the mind's eye as a ponderous, ornate piece of machinery, the spontaneity of its movement crushed by the weight of human custom. When this machine image is opposed to that of the tiny, flitting moth, the contrast between everyday life and "pure life" is as sharply visible to us as it is to Woolf's narrator, visible in terms of shape, size, and motion. Death becomes equally concrete and visible when it is depicted in terms of a loss of motion, the sudden relaxation and stiffening of a corpse. Woolf's aim thus seems less to make new philosophical observations about mortality than to give us a vivid, sensual experience of the abstract.

While Woolf makes abstractions concrete, Dillard begins with concrete   4
objects—a moth, a candle—and draws from them the abstract concept of transfiguration. Since Woolf also takes the concrete body of the moth and gives it symbolic significance, one could say that this is generally true for both

essays. The difference lies primarily in structure: Woolf states the significance
of the moth almost immediately, while Dillard brings it in as a revelation,
literally a sudden burst of light as the moth sizzles and the candle flares. Unlike
Woolf's speaker, Dillard's has a definite identity, and this revelatory moment
is framed by descriptions of her daily life which bear no obvious relation to it.
The essay begins with the statement that she lives alone ("I live alone with
two cats, who sleep on my legs" [107]) and ends with a return to that fact
("Sometimes I think it is pretty funny that I sleep alone" [109]). Nowhere in
this prologue or epilogue to the description of the moth's death does there
seem to be any of its emotion. The speaker claims that she is only telling the
story of the moth in order to explain her ability to identify moth corpses left
by a spider, but this is clearly an excuse for a striking image which becomes
the essay's centerpiece. The descriptions up to this point, such as the catalogue
of the spider's victims, have been detached and emotionless, carrying the
implication that chance rather than any master-plan determines acts of nature:
"I wondered on what fool's errand an earwig, or a moth, or a sow bug, would
visit that clean corner of the house" (107). As the moth burns, however,
Dillard's imagery and tone become passionate and religious; the moth is "like
an immolating monk," "like a hollow saint, like a flame-faced virgin gone to
God" (109). While Woolf calmly reflects on the moth's vitality and its struggle
against death, Dillard is carried away by the force of the moment she describes,
her imagery becoming more and more lyrical until, like a poet rather than an
essayist, she is no longer responsible for telling us why the corpse should
resemble a "flame-faced virgin"; we sense that the image is appropriate and
understand intuitively. We have the sense that it is actually the author who
is being transfigured in this passage, baring to us the deep significance which
the burning moth holds for her as an individual.

    After a series of fiery religious images, it is jarring to be returned abruptly   5
at the end of the essay to a discussion of the pros and cons of living alone. Is
this an unintentional anticlimax? Or is there an implicit connection between
the moth's transfiguration and the author's life? Dillard's narrator clearly establishes such a connection when, in a deadpan tone which suggests a kind of
compulsive coyness, a reluctance to point, as Woolf does, directly to symbolic
meaning, she calls the reader's attention to the "three candles here on the
table" which echo the image of immolation (109). Why should it matter to
us that Dillard's house contains candles? Perhaps living alone itself is seen here
as a sort of death and transfiguration. Celibacy ("sleeping alone") represents
death in that it involves a removal of oneself from the normal flow of social
life and the continuance of that life which sexual reproduction ensures. The

"flame-faced virgin" and the "immolating monk" are, like Dillard's narrator, celibate, and their death is at the same time a transfiguration, a rebirth as light which is made possible by their purity, their sacrifice of earthly concerns. Death, literal or symbolic, becomes a way of achieving sainthood.

Dillard herself undergoes no literal transfiguration in flames, but the mentions of Rimbaud in the essay strongly suggest that a transfiguration of analogous nature is available to her. The camping trip on which the moment of the moth's immolation occurs is a quest for artistic inspiration: Dillard takes with her "a novel about Rimbaud that had made me want to be a writer when I was sixteen; I was hoping it would do it again" (108). The connection between art and transfiguration is later made more explicit: "Rimbaud in Paris burnt out his brain in a thousand poems," just as the moth burns out its husk in the candle-flame. Neither art nor light is born without a sacrifice of the more earthly elements. Thus the transfiguration which Dillard shows us is also that of her own life as a writer, and it is made all the more startling and dramatic by the impassive descriptions of everyday life which surround it. Dillard seems almost to carry off a quiet deception on us, beginning her essay with what appears to be earthy realism—close description of cats, a house, a spider—and showing within the essay that writing itself provides an abstract way to transcend the earth and life altogether.

The tone of Dillard's essay is generally deadpan, with one sudden burst of emotion in sharp contrast, while Woolf's is constant throughout, tranquil and yet quietly awed. There is a corresponding difference in their visual styles. Woolf's moth is a day moth, and her setting is suffused with light and energy. She focuses in on the moth as a harmonious part of this setting which contains its essence in miniature, including the inevitable tendency—not directly shown but perhaps implied in the landscape—of life to end in death. Dillard's moth is a night moth and lights up the darkness with its burning; rather than emphasizing detail of a harmonious picture, she describes one of the most potent images of creation: light out of darkness. From the death of a moth comes rebirth, the creation of a new being and transfiguration of the old.

A basic difference between Woolf and Dillard seems to be between close observation and creation, reflection and transfiguration. A revelation, a transcendence of the ordinary, occurs in both essays, but while Woolf's revelation seems to come naturally and calmly from her observations of what is around her, Dillard's is born of a violent combination of elements—her own mind, the flaming moth, Rimbaud. And yet on another, deeper level the two essays are alike, for Woolf's redefining of familiar concepts in terms of sensual imagery also has a subjective, creative component. She makes us, as Shelley wrote about the role of a poet, "imagine what we know," while Dillard implicitly takes the abstract, imagined idea of transfiguration and assimilates it into the reality of her own life, suggesting that, even in the twentieth century, the eternal and transcendent are not beyond our reach.

Works Cited

Dillard, Annie. "Death of a Moth." *Elements of Literature.* Ed. Carl H. Klaus. New York: Oxford University Press, 1986. 107–109.
Woolf, Virginia. "The Death of the Moth." *Elements of Literature.* Ed. Carl H. Klaus. New York: Oxford University Press, 1986. 57–59.

Focusing on Margot Harrison's Techniques and Revisions

1. What is the *thesis*—the controlling idea—of Margot Harrison's essay? Where does she state it most explicitly? What is the nature of the "creative transfiguration" referred to in the title of the essay? How is this term applied to Virginia Woolf and Annie Dillard as writers as well as to their essays?

2. Margot Harrison was asked to write an essay comparing two works of literature. List each of the major points of comparison she discusses. Show how each paragraph supports and extends her thesis. What principal themes and stylistic features of each essay does she analyze? How does Harrison organize this comparison? Does she, for example, compare each writer point by point, or does she treat each essay separately? Or does she organize her comparison by combining the two approaches? Explain.

3. What order—what sense of sequence—does Harrison establish for the specific points she makes about Woolf's and Dillard's essays: from simple to complex? From the first paragraph of each essay to the last? Something else? Explain. What specific compositional strategies does she use to create effective transitions?

4. Identify the specific strengths of Harrison's literary analysis. Where does she draw on evidence from Woolf's and Dillard's essays most effectively to support the points she makes? What other strategies does she use well? Where and how, for example, does Harrison effectively work into her paragraphs her own views on the death of a/the moth?

5. In what specific ways does Harrison reveal her own attitude toward Woolf and Dillard as writers? Where, for example, does she state, either directly or indirectly, her attitude toward each writer's style? Which parts of speech—verbs, adjectives, adverbs—does she rely on to express her attitude toward each writer's style? How, in effect, does Harrison maintain a sense of her own in-

tellectual identity and dignity in the company of these other, far more celebrated writers?

6. Harrison reports that in drafting this essay, she "tried to appeal to my readers by being clear and simple, yet brilliant, surprising, and always logical—the usual impossible-to-achieve combination." As you reread Harrison's essay, point to specific examples where she succeeded at "being clear and simple." What compositional elements, what stylistic features of Harrison's essay did you find "surprising"? Comment on whether her essay was "always logical."

7. What compositional strategies does Harrison rely on to create an element of suspense in her essay? What, for example, are the "revelations" that Harrison analyzes? What kinds of distinctions does she draw between the paths Woolf and Dillard take to these revelations?

8. Margot Harrison reports that she prepared two drafts of her essay.

> In the second draft I expanded my analysis of the Dillard essay; where originally I had touched on the idea that a "transfiguration" might have occurred in the author's life, [in the second draft] I explained the nature of that transfiguration. I wrote only two drafts because only two were assigned and I didn't have time to revise anymore; although I'm satisfied with the essay, I think that the part about Woolf and her impersonal narration might have been expanded and the whole thing polished up.

Explain why you agree or disagree with Harrison's assessment of "the part about Woolf and her impersonal narration." If you agree with Harrison's view of the weaknesses of that section of her essay, what specific advice would you offer her about how to strengthen it?

Suggestions for Writing

1. Read the following poem by Robert Frost carefully.

Design
I found a dimpled spider, fat and white,
On a white heal-all, holding up a moth
Like a white piece of rigid satin cloth—
Assorted characters of death and blight
Mixed ready to begin the morning right,
Like the ingredients of a witches' broth—
A snow-drop spider, a flower like a froth,
And dead wings carried like a paper kite.

What had that flower to do with being white,
The wayside blue and innocent heal-all?
What brought the kindred spider to that height,
Then steered the white moth thither in the night?
What but design of darkness to appall?
If design govern in a thing so small.

"Design" was published in 1936. In 1912, Frost had written the first version of this poem; he titled it "In White." Read it carefully.

In White

A dented spider like a snow drop white
On a white Heal-all; holding up a moth
Like a white piece of lifeless satin cloth—
Saw ever curious eye so strange a sight?
Portent in little, assorted death and blight
Like the ingredients of a witches' broth?—
The beady spider, the flower like a froth,
And the moth carried like a paper kite.

What had that flower to do with being white,
The blue prunella every child's delight.
What brought the kindred spider to that height?
(Make we no thesis of the miller's plight.)
What but design of darkness and of night?
Design, design! Do I use the word aright?

Write an essay comparing these two drafts, especially with respect to how the different voice in each poem invites the reader to a different response. Point to particular changes in diction and metaphor that help to characterize the alterations in voice evident in the second version. You might want to speculate about why Frost might have preferred the second version. (He never published the first version.)

2. When asked to offer other first-year college students some general advice to help them improve their writing, Margot Harrison responded generously and incisively, although not in essay form:

> It's hard to offer general advice, of course, because everyone's skills and needs are different, but one thing I think is essential to good writing is to write about something you *like*—"like" in the sense that it generally interests you, that you want to examine it in detail. Nor should you feel like a slave to your topic; you should believe—whether true or not—that you have something original to contribute not only to the class but to the world at large. It's depressing to be modest and feel as if you're only saying

what professors of English have said or can say better, and I don't think that this kind of modesty contributes to good writing, however "realistic" it may be. It pays to think hard about what you are going to write about and to make it something that you can individualize, although the topic shouldn't quite become a slave to your personal expression, either. A balance has to be achieved. Another general rule, which I am still straining to follow myself, is that it helps incredibly to get rid of stock phrases and clichés, to express things in energetic and original language. The more you can make the essay yours—even if it means breaking some of the rules you learned in high school—the better.

Consider Harrison's advice on writing. How consistent is her advice with the advice you would offer other first-year students of writing? If it is consistent, then write an essay in which you recount when and how you applied such advice to your own writing. What results did it produce? If your advice about writing differs from Harrison's, write an essay in which you present, in as much detail as possible, your own advice about the composing process. Based on your experience as a writer, what advice would you offer to other first-year students of writing?

AN EFFECTIVE TECHNIQUE

Often when we try to analyze a published piece of writing, we feel stifled by the sense that the work is already complete and states its points much better than we could. Margot Harrison shows us a way to escape this trap when we write criticism. Instead of trying to restate the ideas in the works she is writing about, she sets out to build her own essay. She extracts from Woolf's and Dillard's essays the pieces that strike her as intriguing, weaves those pieces together with her own words explaining why she finds the pieces intriguing, adds her own conclusions, and ends up with a work that has its own structure, its own tone, its own surprises and pleasures. Reading Harrison's essay is not like reading Woolf's or Dillard's essays; rather it is like following a map to discover treasure buried in the thicket of those writers' words. We could say that Harrison revises Woolf's and Dillard's works, because she gives us a new vision, a re-vision, of the texts she analyzes.

Harrison begins by noting that the two essays she is writing about "demand comparison" because of their similar topics and structures: both are about death, moths, and both show writers undergoing "transfigurations" or "reve-lations." But Harrison wants to draw our attention away from such obvious features of the two essays; she is fascinated by subtle differences between them. Elements that would not seem interesting in either Woolf's or Dillard's essay alone—such as the articles "the" and "a" in the titles—become intriguing when set against each other. By examining such differences, Harrison draws our attention away from the powerful "revelations" that Woolf and Dillard each describe and leads us to her own provocative insight: revelations can come in different forms. Harrison structures her essay to gradually reveal some of the possible forms of revelations. At first, basing her conclusions entirely on the difference between "the" and "a" in the titles, she can only say that Woolf's revelation is "definite" while Dillard's is "more equivocal." By the end of the essay, however, Harrison can speak of a much sharper contrast, between revelations that come "naturally and calmly" from observation and those that are "born of a violent combination of elements." Neither Woolf nor Dillard would have led us to think that calm observation and violent emotions might be equally good paths to "the eternal and transcendent," and neither writer would have left us wondering whether we ourselves tend more toward calm revelations, violent ones, or some other type. Harrison's essay offers its own original and memorable insights.

Harrison finds her own distinctive ideas not only by comparing the two texts; she also searches through each one separately for small, intriguing elements that suggest points that the author has not completely laid out. For example, she draws our attention to two sentences in Dillard's essay that mention the French poet Rimbaud, especially one where Dillard says that Rimbaud "burnt out his brain in a thousand poems." Harrison makes explicit what Dillard left implied: that Rimbaud is like the moth burning in the candle flame that is at the center of Dillard's essay. But then Harrison goes further. She builds a lovely sentence of her own based on the idea of poets and moths burning up: "Neither art nor light is born without a sacrifice of the more earthly elements." This sentence could be considered just an "explanation" of what Dillard implies, but it seems more a new insight of Harrison's inspired by her reading of Dillard. Harrison gains the freedom to create her own complex sentences because she builds on small details in Dillard's essay. It is as if Dillard's essay were a tapestry with a few strands left dangling, and Harrison has woven a new image using those strands. A critic can extensively embroider small, odd details before we will feel that she is tampering with the main picture.

From critics such as Margot Harrison, we can learn several ways to develop our own ideas from analyses of other people's writing. We can use her techniques even on essays that seem much less "literary" than Dillard's and Woolf's. If we were to compare two politicians' speeches arguing for the same position or even two scientists' explanations of the same theory, we might be surprised at what we could discover. In the ways the speeches and explanations were written, even in the differences between words such as "a" and "the," we might uncover fascinating things we could use to build effective essays.

If we have a single piece of writing to analyze, we can read through it for ideas that other readers might overlook. If we simply follow whatever fascinates and puzzles us about a book, we will usually end up developing a view unlike anyone else's. We can even find elements that the writer himself or herself has overlooked. The greatest writers all say that they could have revised their published works further; critics can try to decide where the writer has left elements undeveloped. We could also adapt Harrison's basic strategy and use comparisons to develop ideas for a paper about a single work: we could compare it to other works by the same author or other works of the same type. We might not even mention these other works in the final essay we write, using them only to help us discover what is distinctive or unusual in the work we are analyzing.

The next selection is an example of one of the most common types of criticism: a review published in a newspaper to help people decide whether to buy and read a new book. Newspapers often try to enlist as the reviewer of a new book an author who has written books like it. The newspaper hopes readers will be as interested in the mind of the reviewer as in the book being reviewed; often readers enjoy reading reviews without ever being inspired to pick up the books reviewed. Patricia Hampl, the reviewer of Christopher Nolan's autobiography, has herself written an autobiography. Hampl does not directly refer to her own work in her review, but she compares Nolan's book to what is "usually" done in autobiographies. Throughout her review we see *her* vision of what an autobiography should be.

ANOTHER ILLUSTRATION OF THE TECHNIQUE

PATRICIA HAMPL

Defying the Yapping Establishment:
Under the Eye of the Clock

After getting her B.A. at the University of Minnesota in 1968 and an M.F.A. at the University of Iowa in 1970, Patricia Hampl worked as a sales clerk, telephone operator, and editor before returning to the University of Minnesota to become a professor of English. She has published several volumes of poetry and two autobiographical memoirs, A Romantic Education and Spillville. Her memoirs seem to her to continue the impulse behind her poetry; she says that she always writes about "all the things I intended to leave behind, to grow out of, or deny: being a Midwesterner, a Catholic, a woman." Her writing bears many similarities to the writing of Christopher Nolan, whose book she reviews in this selection: he, too, published poetry focused on the region where he grew up, on his Catholicism, and on his body; and he, too, turned at a young age to writing his memoirs. Her comments on her own autobiography may shed some light on what she is looking for in reviewing Nolan's: "The self-absorption that seems to be the impetus and embarrassment of autobiography . . . begins as a hunger for a world, one gone or lost, effaced by time or a more sudden brutality. But in the act of remembering, the personal environment expands, resonates beyond itself, beyond its 'subject,' into the endless and tragic recollection that is history."

"How do I overcome my muteness?" This question, posed by Christopher 1 Nolan in his extraordinary autobiography, might usually be taken metaphorically. Frustration is implicit in any attempt to express the deepest self.

But Mr. Nolan's question is exact: he survived birth trauma with severe 2 brain damage. He can see and hear perfectly, but he is paralyzed, spastic, and unable to speak. He describes himself at the beginning of his slender book as "castrated by crippling disease, molested by scathing mockery, silenced by paralysed vocal muscles yet ironically blessed with a sense of physical well-being."

He is blessed as well with a radiant intelligence. Mr. Nolan, who is 22, was 3 born and lives in Ireland. *Under the Eye of the Clock* is his second book. The first, *Dam-Burst of Dreams*, was a collection of poems published in his teens that received wide attention and earned him comparisons with Joyce, Yeats, and Dylan Thomas.

His stylistic hallmark has been a linguistic virtuosity that, at its best, is 4
heady and acrobatic. It may be a style better suited to the compression of lyric
poetry than to the discursive tendencies of narrative prose. But his prose has
moxie, though it rushes and stumbles from a pent-up surge: "Crying hurrah
for lilysweet knowledge he frowned at the greatness of Joyce; wanting to emulate him for boyhood's fame, he nadir-aspired to mould his only gift into briny,
bastardized braille so that fellows following never had to nod yes to mankind's
gastric view that man speechless and crippled must forever be strolling as
underlings to the yapping establishment."

A further eccentricity (one Henry Adams also chose for *The Education*) is 5
that Mr. Nolan has written his life story in the third person; he appears always
as Joseph Meehan. Like so much about Mr. Nolan's style, it is a risk. The
third person works most effectively when it gives his autobiography the fresh,
jaunty tone of a picaresque novel: "Baffled by beauty, slow to worry, able only
to think, Joseph continued on his lively path through life."

One of the abiding pleasures of the book, in fact, is that while the reader 6
is never allowed to forget Joseph's extreme disability and physical dependence,
the story reads like an adventure, not a meditation. It is busy, active—and
young even when it is wise.

A second, simpler style seems also to be emerging in Mr. Nolan's prose, 7
more precise and immediate, less contorted than his "Joycean" manner. There
is a tour-de-force rhapsody about his mother killing and cleaning a turkey on
the family farm in which Nora, "wielding a sharp knife . . . cut off the lone-
some, guilty-looking head, then she cut off the scaled-skin legs." Describing
the layout of his new school, he says, "Great long corridors blossomed between
the various school sections."

The act of writing itself is, for him, not simply laborious; it is heroic, and 8
requires someone (usually his mother) to cup his chin in her hands while he
attempts, amid spastic lurches he cannot control, to aim a head-mounted
pointer at the keyboard. "As he typed he blundered like a young foal strayed
from his mother," he says. "Sometimes his head shot back on his shoulders
crashing like a mallet into his mother's face."

He is aware of the vast ambition before him: "to find a voice for the voice- 9
less." After all, "century upon century saw crass crippled man dashed, branded
and treated as dross in a world offended by their appearance." Mr. Nolan has
a sense of his historical importance; he maintains his sly, appealing good humor
as he makes his contract with the able-bodied: "Accept me for what I am and
I'll accept you for what you're accepted as."

But the sign that Mr. Nolan is a true writer comes not from his ability to 10
describe his own locked world, compelling as that report is. Rather, it is the

lasting portraits of his family and, to a lesser degree, of rural Ireland that makes his firmest claim.

And what a family! Nora and Matthew, his mother and father, and his 11 older sister, Yvonne, display a relentless faith in Joseph. Their faith is clearly the buoyant wave he "crests"—to use a favorite Nolan verb. Yvonne, "nimble of wit, could never understand how folk failed to capture the mind hinting from her brother's eyes." And when Joseph's spastic arm lurches out to a passing stranger and the "hand flew in between the man's legs while his fingers tickled all before them," Yvonne is there. Her comment at such moments: "Let go, you sex mechanic!"

And the greatest compliment from son to devoted mother: "Nora never 12 gobbled up her son." As for Matthew: "Placing his wobbling son on his knee he recited poetry, told nursery rhymes and later on bawdy vulgar stories. Joseph's mind was wallowing in his father's mire of memories." His father gave him "musical notation, intricate thought patterns and a merry love of writing. Literature was never mentioned."

The driving plot of Mr. Nolan's autobiography is Joseph's assault on the 13 world of the able-bodied. The citadel Joseph rushes is the educational system. He makes one effort after another, moving from a school for handicapped children to a regular high school and then to Dublin's Trinity College itself.

The book's ironic triumph comes when Joseph decides to leave Trinity after 14 all, although he's won the day and has been invited to work for a degree. "The grim rigours of his family" to see him through strike him, finally, as too high a price. He graciously liberates them, as their constant assistance has, earlier, liberated him.

It is the right, the honest, finish. Mr. Nolan does not pretend to conquer 15 the province of the able-bodied. He knows he is outside. But this knowledge isn't a defeat. It is a choice, that most adult thing.

What is left is the truth of his testimony. His voice speaks, as a writer must, 16 from the margin, the solitude where detachment encounters all the jangled emotions it must serve.

Focusing on Patricia Hampl's Method of Criticism

1. What is Hampl trying to achieve in her opening paragraph? Does she make you want to hear more about Nolan's book? Does she make you interested in hearing *her* say more? In other words, do you find *her* personality engaging? Explain your answers.

2. In paragraphs 2, 3, and 4, Hampl uses words that are also used in quotations from Nolan's book. What is the effect of this repetition?

3. How do the first eight paragraphs let us know what is distinctive about Nolan's styles? Hampl gives many quotes to illustrate Nolan's writing, but she also describes his styles in her own words (for example, she says in paragraph 4 that his writing is "heady and acrobatic" and "rushes and stumbles"; in paragraph 7 she says that Nolan sometimes is "more precise and immediate"). Do you find her descriptions or the quoted examples more effective at giving you a sense of Nolan's book? Why? What does she praise about Nolan? What does she criticize?

4. What qualities of writers does Hampl appreciate most? What qualities does she like least? Do you agree with her values? Why or why not?

5. What is the effect of the last four paragraphs? The last paragraph is entirely in Hampl's voice and states *her* ideas, not Nolan's. How has she prepared us for this conclusion?

WORKING WITH THE TECHNIQUE IN YOUR OWN WRITING

1. Find two essays on the same subject, read them carefully, and then write an essay about how the two writers approach the subject differently. You can use pairs of essays in this book, such as "Returning Home" by William Hill and "On Going Home" by Joan Didion; or "Arm-Wrestling with My Father" by Brad Manning and "The Inheritance of Tools" by Scott Sanders; "The Blanket Party" by Terry Burns and "On Killing the Man" by John Clyde Thatcher; or "Tâi Con" by An-Thu Quang Nguyen and the selection from *The Woman Warrior* by Maxine Hong Kingston. You might also use two articles on the same political issue; it might be especially interesting to compare and contrast two articles arguing the same position. See if you can comment not only on the attitudes expressed by the two authors but also on the specific strategies the writers use in developing their essays.

2. Write a review of a book you have read; you might examine Patricia Hampl's review of Christopher Nolan's book for some sense of what readers expect to find in a review. Remember that the most important part of a review is *your* evaluation of the book. You want to give your readers a sense of what the author does especially well and what he or she does less successfully. You also want to make your review interesting to read on its own; you might borrow some small humorous or poignant moments from the book to enliven your review. If there is anything about the author's life that contributes to your interest in the book, you might also mention that. Above all, try to make your review memorable.

HA SONG HI

Texas Tech University
Lubbock, Texas
Constance Kuriyama, instructor

Asked in her freshman English class to write an essay describing life on this planet as seen through an individual whose only knowledge came from reading a newspaper, Ha Song Hi reports that "viewing my world through the eyes of an alien comes easily to me. . . . I feel a bit alienated because, although I am Oriental and am interested in things Oriental, I cannot speak the language of my birthplace and have no ties there other than vague memories."

> My earliest memory is of hearing the sound of howling dogs and shivering with fear and cold with several other children beneath a single blanket on the floor of the Star of the Sea Orphanage in Choon Chon, South Korea. I was brought to the United States, age five, by the Catholic Charities to become the foster child of a family in Cincinnati. I lost my Korean name and was known as Mary Clare. Unfortunately, mine was not an entirely happy childhood. . . . My foster parents put me in an orphanage for two years when I was in the third grade. They took me back but never did treat me very well. The second time I ran away from home, age sixteen, I went to the police for help on the advice of my school counselor. They placed me in detention for not attending school. After a court battle, I was made a ward of the state, rather like Iolanthe, and was sent to Girls' Town to finish my senior year of high school. After another year in a foster home and an unsuccessful try at college, I struck out on my own and took my real name again.

After a brief stint living in a commune of radical anarchists and working as a file clerk, a nurse's aide, and as a hemodialysis technician, Ha Song Hi married, settled in Lubbock, Texas, and returned to college. An honor student at Texas Tech University, she was awarded the freshman English prize for excellence in essay writing in 1987. She plans to major in history and to either teach or go to law school.

Ha Song Hi envisions an ideal environment for writing as "an isolated cabin deep in the woods, snowbound and alone, plenty of food, a wood fire, all my books and files around me, a modem to connect my computer terminal with the Library of Congress, unlimited funds for mainframe time, and someone to unobtrusively clean house and cook." But the tranquillity of such circumstances remains quite alien from the reality of her conditions for writing: "A person walking into my room while I am writing would see the back of my head outlined by my computer screen and surrounded by stacks of papers and books. . . . They would see me pause to think, drink sodas, eat snacks, look up words in the dictionary, laugh at my own jokes, curse when I delete a whole page by mistake, or scream when my two-year-old unplugs me and I know that 'Save Document' never saves at all."

Ha Song Hi *reports that the idea for her English assignment came to her "instantly": "I did not need to write an outline, because all I had to do was read a newspaper, take notes on articles that caught my eye, and turn each one around as if being literally interpreted by an intelligent cockroach from the Andromeda Galaxy. The irony wrote itself."*

From Xraxis to Dzreebo

[*Begin Vocorder Transcription*]

HYPERSPACE TELEX

FROM: Xraxis-1227q, Supreme Hive-Queen Commander
First Solarian Expeditionary Force
Sol-III, Milky Way Galaxy

TO: Dzreebo-87004884w, Imperial High-Secretary for Defense
Hive Central
Homeworld, Andromeda Galaxy

RE: Report of semi-intelligent life on the planet Sol-III (called "Terra")

Greetings, my nest-sister. It seems that ages have passed since last we crossed antennae, and much has happened, of which I must report. We have determined since my first, overly optimistic transmission that the remarkable Terran organisms, which through parallel evolution have come so closely to resemble us, are not the dominant species on this planet as we had naturally assumed. Actually, they possess a rather low order of intelligence and are themselves the victims of systematic oppression and extermination by semi-intelligent life forms many thousands of times their own mass (and ours). It is with these huge brutes, not our primitive little sisters-under-the-chiton, that this report is concerned. 1

My xenocommunication teams have been misapprehended by these enormous creatures to be mere variants of our Terran analogues. We have utterly failed to establish communication with, or even attract the notice of, the dominant Terran species known as "Americans," while suffering an appalling loss of life in the attempt. Though we have been scurrying among them for over three circumsolar orbitals, our total knowledge of the mores, psychology, and lifestyle of Americans has, unfortunately, been thus far confined to 2 inferences derived exclusively through a laborious translation of a massive Terran American tome we managed to pilfer page by page, entitled *The New York Times, Sunday, October 19, 1986: All the News That's Fit to Print.* The effort of this colossal undertaking has caused considerable Andromeda eyestrain among many of our more nearsighted worker clones. A loose translation of the *Times* in Andromedan, with editorial inferences and my recommendations for a Final Terran Solution, follow:

The planet Terra has been parceled by its gigantic inhabitants into hundreds 3 of disparate sovereign nations, each jealously safeguarding its territory and amassing as much as it can of the planet's resources, while attempting to pollute and degrade the environment of its neighbors. The two most powerful nations, commonly known as "America" and "Russia," have for some time been cautiously maneuvering for advantage at the "bargaining table" [possibly an inexpensive feeding platform, see *McDonald's: Behind the Arches,* below] during negotiations for a nuclear arms limitation treaty, while secretly endeavoring feverishly to develop the technology which will assure military superiority in space immediately adjacent to the planetary atmosphere. Each uses fear of the other's tactical advantage to manipulate its own citizens economically and politically while squandering an enormous proportion of its own wealth, as well as the potential wealth of lesser nations, to amass vast stockpiles of military hardware and armies that number in the millions. As a result, the less fortunate among their citizens as well as most of the other denizens of Terra suffer appalling and needless privation.

America has so neglected and sapped the resources of the land (called 4 "Mexico") abutting its southern border that America itself has now become saddled with the problems of this debtor nation with which it is inextricably linked by economic and social ties. There seems to be a glimmering of hope, however, for Mexicans and other "aliens" from "South of the Border" who have had the temerity to cross over illegally into America. A new American law mandates that those illegal aliens who have resided here for more than five years be granted amnesty and regarded henceforth as American citizens. Those who enter by this route in future, however, will continue to be officially harassed, disregarded, and neglected by the American government, as they have always been. In addition, they will from now on be unable to secure gainful employment. That must be good news for the American taxpayers who support the unemployed and destitute of other lands who seek refuge from oppression and poverty by passing through their Golden Door [see *McDonald's: Behind the Arches,* below]. Somehow, with six American Blackhawk helicopters harrying Bolivian farmers in their poppy and cocoa fields [plants which provide addicting euphoric substances, see below and attached map] and with CIA operatives [agents of America's secret police] being shot down over Nicaragua [see map], I fear this latest pious act of American magnanimity may be misinterpreted by South and Central [i.e., Lesser and Alien] Americans as yet another attempt to humiliate them by further abrogating the human rights and dignity of migrant farm workers. In any case, we Andromedans arrived too late to find jobs here.

Living under constant threat of total annihilation, currently from ballistic 5 missiles and in future from particle beams reflected or projected from space, Americans are embracing in ever greater numbers the chemical oblivion of addicting alkaloids, most of which are grown, processed, and exported by their poorer neighbors to the South. The Drug Trade has become the largest growth industry in the history of the nation. Thousands are getting rich from trafficking in it while millions are getting stoned [a euphoric state of helplessly intoxicated martyrdom?] from the traffic. In a futile effort to stem this pharmaceutical tidal wave, the American government proposes to test the excretory fluids of its employees for traces of these substances, with the implied purpose of subjecting proven users to additional indignities and loss of income. Naturally, American citizens are objecting much more vociferously to this law than ever they did to the law concerning illegal aliens.

Fearful of slipping, even imperceptibly, from the apex of Terran economic 6 and technological supremacy (not realizing that their rate of infant mortality has already declined to seventeenth place worldwide) and eager to obfuscate, even from themselves, the true origins of their anxieties, some Americans have stooped to reviving old hostilities toward and mistrust for those innocent fellow citizens whose ancestry is rooted in the far side of Terra, known as "Asia." The *Times* reports "anti-alienism, re-emergence of white supremacist groups, scapegoating of Asians for failures of the domestic economy, and heightened tensions between minorities over competition for jobs." This xenophobia bodes ill for our diplomatic mission. At the heart of Americans' insecurity seems to lie their deep and abiding sense of greed.

Every aspect of American culture is for sale and carries a price tag. A great 7 amount of money and effort is expended by some Americans in an egregious attempt to induce other Americans to relinquish a portion of their assets, while the duped seem content to receive a minimum in return. For example, the "Fun Ships of the Carnival Cruise Lines" promise an eleven-day journey up the Amazon [the largest river South of the Border] on the good ship "Stella Solaris" (Greek Reg.) for only $2,695.00, double occupancy, subject to availability and additional port tax. In other words, for the price of feeding a thousand starving Ethiopian children [sorely deprived young Terrans dwelling on a distant, drought-stricken continent] for six months, gullible Americans are enticed to enjoy, from the isolated splendor of their air-conditioned Promenade Deck, the wholesale destruction (some 85,000 acres per day) of the greatest ecostabilizing rain forest on the face of the planet, for purposes of "reclaiming" the land to grow cash crops. For $455,000.00, the price of feeding 3,672 Ethiopian children for three years, one can "read the Sunday Times in a poolside solarium, play peek-a-boo on our wrap-around balcony, have neighbors who are our kind of people—successful, wordly, and fun—[and] be whisked 45 stories in high-speed elevators in just seconds at the Monarch, where nothing stands taller for East Side living." For $3,950,000.00, the price of housing, busing, educating, clothing, feeding, and employing 52,374 Ethiopian children for the rest of their lives, one can "entertain in the fire-lit sunken living room, browse in the sun-lit library, relax in the lush projection room, or revel in the breathtakingly manicured grounds of a classic Mediterranean estate in Old Bel Air."

The mentally, morally, and physically impoverished, laughably malleable   8
female of the species is irresistibly lured to "shape her bust [a glandular protuberance alleged to possess both nutritive and hedonistic values] . . . while every inch of her is cuddled and caressed elegantly in very feminine, all-lace Lycra Spandex" at Macy's. She is urged to display "Argenti" on her buttock, to read YM and learn "what guys love (and hate) about girls," to "fondle the world's finest dark ranch mink in the Black Diamond Collection," and to "express a newfound vitality in the clothes she wears, the food she eats, and even in the people she loves and marries" by reading ULTRAsport.

What entertains Americans? A Panasonic, AM/FM stereo cassette recorder   9
[a primitive electromagnetic device], your cost $45.95, lists at $65.95 at J&R Music World. Rosa Bonheur's "Flowing Fields," oil on canvas, sells for $25,000/$45,000, est., at Butterfield and Butterfield. Christopher Hogwood's new compact disc of Beethoven's Eroica symphony [a well-regarded composition of auditory vibrations] is $2.00 off at Sam Goody's. Tickets to Die Fledermaus [during which we endured much singing and posturing on stage while we awaited in vain the arrival of the top-billed small, furry flying creature] are selling for $250.00 at the Metropolitan Opera. Orchestra seats [the most advantageous position] to see Les Misérables [much talking and even more posturing] at the Broadway Theatre go for $47.50. The Magnificent Christmas Spectacular [a traditional religious observance that turns a great profit in America], starring the Rockettes [a large aggregate of female clones who alternately elevate their hind extremities in clockwork-like unison while clad in traditionally scanty costumes], sponsored by Maxwell House [a semi-addicting beverage, known to predispose to atherosclerosis, made of roasted beans grown

South of the Border] and Entenmann's (Since 1898) [a local baker of athero-
genic confections], can be viewed from an orchestra seat for only $25.00 after
standing in line for three hours in the snow. We have learned that $250.00
will purchase a "scalped" [resold] ticket at the door.

Speaking of religion, the Baptist Church of North Carolina is battling that 10
State to preserve its divine right to flout a law which expressly forbids its
employees to "shake, push, shove, pinch, slap, bite, kick, or spank" children
in its Daycare Centers. The church is citing a "higher law," which is to be
found in Proverbs 13:24 [from the first and largest-selling book in the history
of Terran printing]: "He that spareth his rod hateth his son." Having sampled
television Prime Time fare [when most children sit with optic sensors glued to
their sets], with its incessant glorification of violence, it would seem that the
state of North Carolina's belated attempt to halt the systematic corporal punishment of preschool children is fated to be an exercise in futility.

What are Americans reading for entertainment and education? The *Times* 11
Book Review tells us that *The Silent Twins* ($16.95) "explores the shocking
world of Broadmoor Prison for the Criminally Insane." *God's Snake* ($15.95)
"is stark, vivid, heroic, and haunting." *Liberace* (major credit cards accepted)
describes "all the many splendid things that make him America's best-loved
entertainer." *McDonald's: Behind the Arches* (Macmillan Book Club Alternate
Selection) "discloses the real inside story of how a single hamburger stand was
transformed into a multibillion dollar alliance." In *Unspeakable Acts: A True
Story* (at all bookstores) "the crime was unspeakable, the criminal was untouchable . . . until a five year old child. . . ." The best-selling book for the
past six weeks has been *It* ($22.95), which purveys [all-too-familiar] "childhood
horrors."

Americans enjoy sublimating their killer instincts through the ritualized 12
warfare known as "baseball." The largest headline in the newspaper shouts,
"2 CITIES IN COMBAT: IT'S MORE THAN BASEBALL." America is currently
caught up in the fever of city/state rivalry known as the "World Series." Almost
everyone is strongly partisan. Whether they live in Boston, New York, or
Lubbock, baseball is the topic on every lip during World Series week, while
business slackens, industry sags, and the economy slumps. Humankind is split
into the camps of Disinterested Outsiders, who are oblivious [the Nerds], and
the Great Vocal Majority, who remain glued to their television sets and think
of nothing else but bets, scores, players, and beer [an intoxicating carbonated
beverage made of fermented grain].

Two-wheeled conveyances known as "bicycles" are used for sport in America 13
and for transportation elsewhere. The mystery of disappearing Miami bicycles
was recently solved when police confiscated three boatloadsful bound for Haiti,

one of the most impoverished islands to nestle in the Caribbean arm of the Atlantic Ocean [see map], also considered by most Americans as their private lake. A triumphant Mayor of Miami was quoted as saying, "Let them ride Lear Jets." [This may be apocryphal.]

In summary, my dear nest-sister Dzreebo, Americans (and, by inference, *all* Terrans) are, by the evidence of their own greatest [?] newspaper, a bigoted, querulous, vapid, shortsighted, self-absorbed, oft-intoxicated, chauvinistic, and avaricious gang of child abusers. They seem bent on a course of self-annihilation which is almost sure to devastate their entire biosphere. They are cruel, wily, impetuous, xenophobic, and insular—and they seem to take a perverse delight in squashing Andromedan ambassadors! From all this one can only conclude that, if Americans are any example, Terrans are unfit to take their place among the civilized species of the Universe. It is with the greatest regret, tempered by the keenest sense of justice, that I must, therefore, strongly recommend the total and immediate sterilization of this entire Solar Syst . . . RAID'S HERE!! [cough, cough]   14

[*End Vocorder Transcription*]

MEMO:
   This tiny scrap of paper (plastic?) was found clutched in the forelimb of a heretofore undescribed variant of the domestic cockroach. Allegations that the undecipherable scribbles and faint traces of pheromones thereon bear even the slightest resemblance to a written language are totally unfounded and purely speculative.   15
Signed,

H. Rabinowitz, M.S.
Asst. Instructor in Entomology
Hunter College, NYC

Focusing on Ha Song Hi's Techniques and Revisions

1. A prominent feature of the success of Ha Song Hi's essay is her use of a clear *point of view*. Characterize the narrator's point of view in this essay. Is it detached and objective? Involved and subjective? Some other combination? Support your response with an analysis of specific words and phrases from the

essay. Follow the same procedure in characterizing Ha Song Hi's own point of view in the essay.

2. Ha Song Hi explains that she aimed at simultaneously amusing and instructing the reader of her essay: "I wanted the reader to be amused by my essay and to gain a new slant (my slant) on humanity, Americans, newspapers, and the world we live in." What specific strategies does she use to integrate these goals for her essay?

3. How does Ha Song Hi organize her essay: From simple to complex ideas? From geography to politics? From economics to entertainment? Something else? What principles—what pattern of ideas—seem to underpin the sequence of ideas presented in this essay?

4. Why is Ha Song Hi's *satiric* approach—her efforts at ridicule—more effective than if she had presented the same information in a straightforward, less venturesome tone?

5. Ha Song Hi also uses a great deal of *irony*—that is, she uses words to suggest a different meaning then their literal meaning. Find as many instances of irony in Hi's essay as you can and comment on the effectiveness of each. How does Hi's use of irony add to or detract from the success of her essay?

6. When asked to describe the special strengths of Ha Song Hi's essay, her instructor, Constance Kuriyama, observed: "I have had students write modest proposals, but Ha Song Hi is the first of my students to produce an essay that might be described as Swiftian in its force and incisive intelligence. More specifically, one might point to the novel point of view she creates in the essay, the sustained irony (difficult for inexperienced writers), and the clever use of climax and anticlimax at the end. Since this was a research assignment, one might also point to her remarkable and authoritative command of her research material, to the rich detail with which she documents contemporary American attitudes and values. Somehow she makes this alluvia and detritus of American culture speak a far more revealing language than it was ever intended to speak, mainly by placing it in the intellectual context of the ultimate outsider." Select two paragraphs from Ha Song Hi's essay and analyze their success based on the features identified here.

7. Ha Song Hi offers the following general advice to other first-year students of writing: "When you get a writing assignment, try to think of some new wrinkle, a different viewpoint—use humor, irony, metaphor, simile, hyperbole, a mood, a nuance no one else could (or would) express." Apply Hi's advice to her own essay. In light of her own criteria described above, how successful would you judge Hi's essay to be? Point to a specific passage to support each point you make.

8. Ha Song Hi reports that the most difficult aspect of revision is "to recognize

those parts which are irrelevant or redundant, especially when I have sweated over them and have fallen in love with my own words." Consider, for example, the first paragraph in Hi's original draft:

> Tragically, the organisms which, through the vagaries of parallel evolution, have come to superficially most resemble us possess a low order of intelligence and have been oppressed and systematically exterminated by semi-intelligent creatures thousands of times their own mass (and ours). It is these huge brutes, not our primitive brothers-under-the-chiton, that this report concerns. Since our arrival on Terra, some three circumsolar orbitals ago, we have been either overlooked or casually squashed by the huge denizens of this strange planet. Being regarded as variants of our domestic analogues, we have utterly failed to attract the notice of or established communication with the dominant species known as "Americans," while suffering heavy loss of life in the attempt. Our total knowledge of the mores, psychology, and lifestyle of Americans has been inferred through transliteration of a massive tome entitled "*The New York Times*, Sunday, October 19, 1986— All the News That's Fit to Print." A loose transliteration in Andromedan follows.

List the changes Ha Song Hi has made in her final draft. Which version do you prefer? Why?

9. Ha Song Hi wrote three drafts of her essay. The following is the final paragraph of her first draft:

> In summary, Americans (and by inference, all Terrans) are querulous, vapid, shortsighted, self-absorbed, and avaricious. Their lives are brutish, mean, and short. They seem bent upon a course of self-annihilation which may also devastate the biosphere. They are cruel, wily, impetuous, xenophobic, and insular. From this, held to be their greatest daily newspaper, one can only conclude that Terrans are unfit to take their rightful place among the civilized species of the Universe. It is with the greatest regret that I must strongly recommend the total and immediate sterilization of their Solar Sys. . . . RAID'S HERE!!

Compare the conclusion in this draft with the final version. What specific changes do you notice? Comment on the effectiveness of each change.

10. Compare Ha Song Hi's essay with Allison Rolls's "Lady Diana: He Married the Wrong Woman." Examine how each writer uses irony and satire to present her point. Which writer most clearly and effectively relates her ironic and satiric tone to her purpose?

Suggestions for Writing

1. Ha Song Hi successfully blends humor, satire, irony, sensitivity to human nature, and careful research to present her view of contemporary American life. Choose one of the following laws, research it, take a position on the issues it evokes, and argue either for or against its retention: (1) local or state "blue laws" (which require that stores close on Sundays or that bars close at a certain hour); (2) laws on gambling; (3) laws regulating highway speed limits; (4) some other controversial statute. Be sure to establish a distinctive identity and point of view for the narrator of your essay.

2. Ha Song Hi has written an essay highly critical of contemporary American life and culture. Identify each of Hi's criticisms and write an essay responding — either positively or negatively — to Hi's critique of America.

AN EFFECTIVE TECHNIQUE

Ha Song Hi uses one of the oldest devices for making readers enjoy being insulted: she creates an unusual identity, making it seem as if an animal is speaking to us. Readers always find it amusing to imagine what a fox (in Aesop's fables), a chicken (in Chaucer's tales), a naive flightless waterfowl (in Berke Breathed's "Bloom County"), or an insect from another planet would say to or about us. We can blithely accept that these animals view us as "enormous creatures" with disgusting habits; after all, what can a cockroach teach us? However, while we are laughing at the silly errors Hi's insect makes (such as mistaking "getting stoned" for a form of "martyrdom"), Hi slips in a powerful condemnation of the American way of life.

Paradoxically, Hi's use of an animal's voice to narrate her essay not only allows us to dismiss her attacks, but also to break through what may be our jaded response to criticism. Everyone has heard about the plight of "illegal aliens" who suffer "appalling and needless privation"; many people have tired of such appeals and no longer listen. But Hi presents a brilliant new image of what it means to be an alien illegally entering the United States and to be "squashed" in an "appalling" way. Hi at least captures our attention; at best, she reveals what has been hidden in our use of the word "alien" to describe immigrants. By presenting an insect's view of humans, she makes us aware that we have been viewing humans as insects for a long time.

Hi's essay would have been merely a cute gag if her analysis of American society were not so incisive. By relentlessly satirizing everything in the newspaper, from headlines to back-page advertisements, Hi reveals connections between such things as "laughably malleable" women, who can change the shape of their "glandular protuberances" according to the latest fashions, and the Baptist Church of North Carolina, which wants to "shake, push, shove, pinch, slap, bite, kick, or spank" children. Hi's unusual perspective allows her to see that women, children, aliens, and third world countries are all treated as less than human, as mere material to be processed to increase the wealth of this nation. And if they complain, then "let them ride Lear Jets," as Dzreebo reports the apocryphal mayor of Miami said.

It is easy to see the fun of writing such essays. All we need do is assume a strange identity, one that is appropriate to the point we want to make. To help our readers recognize our strange identity, we might develop a distinctive style of writing, a "personality" and a point of view that fit the strange identity we have adopted. So, too, we could invent bits of an imaginary culture and language if we wish, and mix them into "normal" English. We need not limit ourselves to becoming animals; we could present a timid car's perspective on human driving, the bored playground's perspective on students at recess, or an ambitious fat molecule's perspective on dieting. Mark Twain, in the next selection, shows us that we can also create an effective voice by making an exotic creature, in his case an angel, sound very ordinary, like an officious clerk. Twain thereby achieves a double purpose, mocking both religion and the subject the angel is talking about—business on earth.

ANOTHER ILLUSTRATION OF THE TECHNIQUE

MARK TWAIN

Letter to the Earth

"Seriously scribbling to excite the laughter of God's creatures" was Mark Twain's description of his chosen vocation, found after working for years as a printer, a riverboat

pilot, and a *prospector. He attended school only until he was twelve, but, as he put it later, "I never let my schooling interfere with my education." By his fiftieth birthday, with the publication of* Huckleberry Finn, *his life seemed blessed with everything: creative energy, world fame, a happy family, and wealth. But in the next ten years bad investments, the death of his favorite daughter from meningitis, and a sense that he was living in "an era of incredible rottenness" nearly drove him mad. He began writing bitter diatribes against Christianity, God, imperialism, racism, and "corn-pone opinions" in general. Even the humor drained from much of his fiction; his tales become eerie and symbolic, and he never finished most of them.*

Twain described the subject matter of his major works when he said, with characteristic irony, "I confine myself to life with which I am familiar when pretending to portray life." The tales he was working on at the end of his life might seem to indicate he was moving away from such realistic writing, but we could also say that they reveal his awareness that "realism" is a very flexible style; even in his early works he includes lyrical and dreamlike passages. In the "rules" for writers that Twain wrote early in his career, he suggested that supernatural events could be "realistic": "The personages in a tale shall confine themselves to possibilities and let miracles alone; or, if they venture a miracle, the author must so plausibly set it forth as to make it look possible and reasonable." Twain recognized at least one miracle all his life: the magic of the right word. As he explained and illustrated that magic, "The difference between the right word and the almost right word is the difference between lightning and the lightning bug."

Office of the Recording Angel
Department of Petitions, Jan. 20

Andrew Langdon, Coal Dealer
Buffalo, New York

I have the honor, as per command, to inform you that your recent act of 1
benevolence and self-sacrifice has been recorded upon a page of the Book called
Golden Deeds of Men: a distinction, I am permitted to remark, which is not
merely extraordinary, it is unique.

As regards your prayers, for the week ending the 19th, I have the honor to 2
report as follows:

1. For weather to advance hard coal 15 cents a ton. Granted.
2. For influx of laborers to reduce wages 10 percent. Granted.
3. For a break in rival soft-coal prices. Granted.
4. For a visitation upon the man, or upon the family of the man, who has
set up a competing retail coal-yard in Rochester. Granted, as follows: diphtheria, 2, 1 fatal; scarlet fever, 1, to result in deafness and imbecility. NOTE:
This prayer should have been directed against this subordinate's principals,
The N. Y. Central R. R. Co.
5. For deportation to Sheol of annoying swarms of persons who apply daily

for work, or for favors of one sort or another. Taken under advisement for later decision and compromise, this petition appearing to conflict with another one of same date, which will be cited further along.

6. For application of some form of violent death to neighbor who threw brick at family cat, whilst the same was serenading. Reserved for consideration and compromise because of conflict with a prayer of even date to be cited further along.

7. To "damn the missionary cause." Reserved also—as above.

8. To increase December profits of $22,230 to $45,000 for January, and perpetuate a proportionate monthly increase thereafter—"which will satisfy you." The prayer granted; the added remark accepted with reservations.

9. For cyclone, to destroy the works and fill up the mine of the North Pennsylvania Co. NOTE: Cyclones are not kept in stock in the winter season. A reliable article of firedamp can be furnished upon application.

Especial note is made of the above list, they being of particular moment. 3 The 298 remaining supplications classifiable under the head of Special Providences, Schedule A, for the week ending 19th, are granted in a body, except that 3 of the 32 cases requiring immediate death have been modified to incurable disease.

This completes the week's invoice of petitions known to this office under 4 the technical designation of Secret Supplications of the Heart, and which for a reason which may suggest itself, always receive our first and especial attention.

The remainder of the week's invoice falls under the head of what we term 5 Public Prayers, in which classification we place prayers uttered in Prayer Meeting, Sunday School, Class Meeting, Family Worship, etc. These kinds of prayers have value according to classification of Christian uttering them. By rule of this office, Christians are divided into two grand classes, to wit: 1, Professing Christians; 2, Professional Christians. These, in turn, are minutely subdivided and classified by size, species, and family; and finally, standing is determined by carats, the minimum being 1, the maximum 1,000.

As per balance-sheet for quarter ending Dec. 31, 1847, you stood classified 6 as follows:

Grand Classification, Professing Christian.

Size, one-fourth of maximum.

Species, Human-Spiritual.

Family, A of the Elect, Division 16.

Standing, 322 carats fine.

As per balance-sheet for quarter just ended—that is to say, forty years later— 7 you stand classified as follows:

Grand Classification, Professional Christian.
Size, six one-hundredths of maximum.
Species, Human-Animal.
Family, W of the Elect, Division 1547.
Standing, 3 carats fine.

I have the honor to call your attention to the fact that you seem to have 8
deteriorated.

To resume report upon your Public Prayers—with the side remark that in 9
order to encourage Christians of your grade and of approximate grades, it is
the custom of this office to grant many things to them which would not be
granted to Christians of a higher grade—partly because they would not be
asked for:

Prayer for weather mercifully tempered to the needs of the poor and the 10
naked. Denied. This was a Prayer-Meeting Prayer. It conflicts with Item 1 of
this report, which was a Secret Supplication of the Heart. By a rigid rule of
this office, certain sorts of Public Prayers of Professional Christians are forbidden to take precedence of Secret Supplications of the Heart.

Prayer for better times and plentier food "for the hard-handed son of toil 11
whose patient and exhausting labors make comfortable the homes, and pleasant
the ways, of the more fortunate, and entitle him to our vigilant and effective
protection from the wrongs and injustices which grasping avarice would do
him, and to the tenderest offices of our grateful hearts." Prayer-Meeting Prayer.
Refused. Conflicts with Secret Supplication of the Heart No. 2.

Prayer "that such as in any way obstruct our preferences may be generously 12
blessed, both themselves and their families, we here calling our hearts to
witness that in their worldly prosperity we are spiritually blessed, and our joys
made perfect." Prayer-Meeting Prayer. Refused. Conflicts with Secret Supplications of the Heart Nos. 3 and 4.

"Oh, let none fall heir to the pains of perdition through words or acts of 13
ours." Family Worship. Received fifteen minutes in advance of Secret Supplication of the Heart No. 5, with which it distinctly conflicts. It is suggested
that one or the other of these prayers be withdrawn, or both of them modified.

"Be mercifully inclined toward all who would do us offense in our persons 14
or our property." Includes man who threw brick at cat. Family Prayer. Received
some minutes in advance of No. 6, Secret Supplications of the Heart. Modi-
fication suggested, to reconcile discrepancy.

"Grant that the noble missionary cause, the most precious labor entrusted 15
to the hands of men, may spread and prosper without let or limit in all heathen
lands that do as yet reproach us with their spiritual darkness." Uninvited prayer
shoved in at meeting of American Board. Received nearly half a day in advance

of No. 7, Secret Supplications of the Heart. This office takes no stock in missionaries, and is not connected in any way with the American Board. We should like to grant one of these prayers but cannot grant both. It is suggested that the American Board one be withdrawn.

This office desires for the twentieth time to call urgent attention to your 16 remark appended to No. 8. It is a chestnut.

Of the 464 specifications contained in your Public Prayers for the week, 17 and not previously noted in this report, we grant 2, and deny the rest. To wit: Granted, (1), "that the clouds may continue to perform their office; (2), and the sun his." It was the divine purpose anyhow; it will gratify you to know that you have not disturbed it. Of the 462 details refused, 61 were uttered in Sunday School. In this connection I must once more remind you that we grant no Sunday School Prayers of Professional Christians of the classification technically known in this office as the John Wanamaker grade. We merely enter them as "words," and they count to his credit according to number uttered within certain limits of time; 3,000 per quarter-minute required, or no score; 4,200 in a possible 5,000 is a quite common Sunday School score among experts, and counts the same as two hymns and a bouquet furnished by young ladies in the assassin's cell, execution-morning. Your remaining 401 details count for wind only. We bunch them and use them for head-winds in retarding the ships of improper people, but it takes so many of them to make an impression that we cannot allow anything for their use.

I desire to add a word of my own to this report. When certain sorts of people 18 do a sizable good deed, we credit them up a thousand-fold more for it than we would in the case of a better man—on account of the strain. You stand far away above your classification-record here, because of certain self-sacrifices of yours which greatly exceed what could have been expected of you. Years ago, when you were worth only $100,000, and sent $2 to your impoverished cousin the widow when she appealed to you for help, there were many in heaven who were not able to believe it, and many more who believed that the money was counterfeit. Your character went up many degrees when it was shown that these suspicions were unfounded. A year or two later, when you sent the poor girl $4 in answer to another appeal, everybody believed it, and you were the talk here for days together. Two years later you sent $6, upon supplication, when the widow's youngest child died, and that act made perfect your good fame. Everybody in heaven said, "Have you heard about Andrew?"—for you are now affectionately called Andrew here. Your increasing donation, every two or three years, has kept your name on all lips, and warm in all hearts. All heaven watches you Sundays, as you drive to church in your handsome carriage; and when your hand retires from the contribution plate, the glad shout is heard even to the ruddy walls of remote Sheol, "Another nickel from Andrew!"

But the climax came a few days ago, when the widow wrote and said she 19 could get a school in a far village to teach if she had $50 to get herself and her two surviving children over the long journey; and you counted up last month's clear profit from your three coal mines—$22,230—and added to it the certain profit for the current month—$45,000 and a possible fifty—and then got down your pen and your check-book and mailed her *fifteen whole dollars!* Ah, Heaven bless and keep you forever and ever, generous heart! There was not a dry eye in the realms of bliss; and amidst the hand-shakings, and embracings, and praisings, the decree was thundered forth from the shining mount, that this deed should out-honor all the historic self-sacrifices of men and angels, and be recorded by itself upon a page of its own, for that the strain of it upon you had been heavier and bitterer than the strain it costs ten thousand martyrs to yield up their lives at the fiery stake; and all said, "What is the giving up of life, to a noble soul, or to ten thousand noble souls; compared with the giving up of fifteen dollars out of the greedy grip of the meanest white man that ever lived on the face of the earth?"

And it was a true word. And Abraham, weeping, shook out the contents 20 of his bosom and pasted the eloquent label there, "RESERVED"; and Peter, weeping, said, "He shall be received with a torchlight procession when he comes"; and then all heaven boomed, and was glad you were going there. And so was hell.

[Signed]
The Recording Angel [Seal]

By command.

Focusing on Mark Twain's Use of an Unusual Voice

1. How does the language and arrangement of the first few paragraphs create the sense that the person writing this letter is a clerk of the courts? How does the angel's style of writing change in paragraph 17? How does his style change again in the next-to-last paragraph? What sort of a person does the angel seem to be by the end of the essay? What seems to be Mark Twain's opinion of the angel in the beginning of the essay? What seems to be Twain's opinion of the angel at the end?

2. What sort of man does Andrew Langdon seem to be, based on the first nine prayers? How does the style of Langdon's public prayers differ from the style of his secret supplications? What is Mark Twain's attitude toward Langdon?

3. What seems to be the recording angel's attitude in the first few paragraphs toward Andrew Langdon's prayers? What seems to be the angel's attitude toward Langdon at the end of the essay?
4. What is the effect of the last sentence?

WORKING WITH THE TECHNIQUE IN YOUR OWN WRITING

---

1. Write an essay about an issue (either public or private) by creating a speaker with an unusual identity, perhaps an animal, and having that speaker discuss the issue. Try to make the narrator's "personality" and style of speech or writing contribute to making your point. You might put your essay into the form of a letter, as both Ha Song Hi and Mark Twain have done, or you might have the narrator delivering a monologue about the issue to a patient listener or talking to himself.
2. Tell a story from the point of view of some unusual narrator. Select the narrator and the tale to make a point. You might, for example, tell of a corrupt congressional representative's week from the view of his pocket. Or you might present a polar bear's experiences during a nuclear war and the subsequent nuclear winter.

WILLIAM G. HILL

Northwest Mississippi Junior College, DeSoto Center
Senatobia, Mississippi
Sally A. Askew, instructor

William Hill believes that "a writer needs to write from his own experiences and know what he is writing about." Asked to write a description of a place, Hill chose a place he knows well—the pool hall in his hometown, Ripley, Mississippi. Although the pool hall no longer exists, Hill didn't want the place to be forgotten, and he wanted his readers to understand something about the culture of rural Mississippi: "The goal of the essay was to help the people who knew the place to remember it and to show the people who didn't what it was like. The effect that I wanted it to have on the reader was to be able to understand a small part of the culture that I grew up in."

In the years before attending college, Hill worked as a factory laborer, a printer, an insurance agent, and a security guard at an Internal Revenue Service center. He has two sons, coaches Pop Warner football, and intends to write and teach. About the conditions necessary for writing, Hill reports: "Some people find quiet necessary to be able to write; I don't. I have two children and live almost directly in the landing pattern of the Memphis International Airport, so noises do not bother me. What I need is time, periods from two to three hours when I don't have to be bothered with anything else. Of course, with work, school, and raising a family, time is sometimes difficult to find."

Returning Home

1   The front door was always propped open in the summertime with a doorstop made from a split two-by-four. Thus it was always difficult to say for sure whether the loafers congregated around the checkerboard were inside or out on the seventy-five-year-old sidewalk that circled the town square.

2   The windows were washed every year or two, but they were usually tinted with a residue of nicotine from too much smoke in a closed room. They were painted with a sign that read, "RECREATIONAL CLUB ROOM." We all figured that the sign painter was paid by the letter and made more from that sign than if he had painted "Pool Hall."

3   Whenever I walked in the door, I usually first saw old man Hall and Mr. Monroe playing checkers. Sometimes other people played, but if they did, they usually played one of them. Mr. Hall never took his hat off, and he always had a filter-tipped Kool in one side of his mouth and a toothpick in the other. Mr. Monroe was a little man who wore thick glasses. He usually beat most of the people he played checkers with, but no one really ever kept count.

On the other side of the room was a counter with a glass case on top. From 4
behind the counter, J.M. Holly, the man who owned the place, sold candy
and cold drinks. He had the widest selection of cigarettes in town. It was the
only place I knew of that sold Picayunes. It was also a handy place to stop if
one needed a can of lighter fluid, a fishing reel, razor blades, or a hunting
license.

The pool tables were in a line side by side from the front to the back of the 5
long, narrow building. The first one was the biggest, and the best snooker
players used it. Beyond it were the other tables used by lesser players, except
for the last one. This was the bank's pool table, used only by the best players
in the country.

The place had an atmosphere of its own. The smell was a mixture of stale 6
smoke, oil from the floor, and, in the winter, fumes from the heater. It didn't
smell bad exactly, but it was as unique as the sound. On Friday and Saturday
nights the jukebox blasted out Buck Owens, Creedence Clearwater Revival,
and Ace Cannon. It was beer-drinking music played in a place that sold no
beer.

The people were always friendly except for an occasional drunk who got 7
mean. They were an odd lot of folks. Some college students home for the
weekend from Ole Miss were there, and also a few rednecks with their blue
jeans tucked in the tops of their boots—cowboy boots with gold and white
eagles. Old men came in in the early afternoon to cuss the Republicans and
stain the walls behind the spittoons with tobacco juice.

There were never many fights. Every time one got started, J.M. would call 8
Possum. When Possum got there, J.M. would say, "Possum, pick up that pool
table." Possum would lift one end of the table off the floor with one arm. J.M.
would then tell the boys who were about to fight that Possum did not like
violence. As a rule, the boys found a more peaceable way to settle their
differences.

The last time I was back in Ripley, the place was closed down. Some 9
carpenters were working in the building. I was told that it was being remodeled
into a restaurant, one of those fancy places where people wear ties. I couldn't
get very sad about my old hangout not being there anymore; I had left first. I
did wonder what happened to Possum. And I wondered where high school
boys went to warm up after a snowball fight when school was out because of
snow. I would like to know where people go now to listen to Cardinals' baseball
games on hot summer afternoons and where people who want them get Pic-
ayune cigarettes.

I had heard the expression "You can't go home again" all my life. I didn't 10
understand it until the last time I tried.

Focusing on William Hill's Techniques and Revisions

1. William Hill pictures his hometown by focusing on its pool hall. He reports: "The original intent of this essay was to describe a place, a building and what was in it. In the course of the writing, however, it changed to a description of not only a place but also a time." Reread Hill's essay carefully. What did the pool hall represent to Hill as a teenage boy growing up in Ripley, Mississippi? What does the pool hall represent to him now as an adult returning to his hometown?

2. We learn a great deal about the pool hall from Hill's description. Point to specific details in Hill's description and explain what they tell his readers about both the place and the people who congregated there. To which specific senses do these details appeal?

3. It is very easy to be sentimental and romantic about places and people from one's childhood. How does Hill avoid sentimentality in writing about his past? What words does Hill repeat in his essay? With what effect?

4. Hill begins his essay by describing the front door and "the loafers congregated around the checkerboard." What is the effect of beginning immediately with such a description, without any introductory comment or assertion?

5. Describe the overall structure of Hill's essay. How does he distinguish between the present and the past in his essay? What attitude does Hill express toward the pool hall as he knew it as a child? As an adult? Which view does he seem to favor? Point to specific words and phrases that express his attitude(s).

6. What is the significance of Hill's title? How does the phrase "Returning Home" signal his mixed emotions? In what specific parts of the essay is Hill's bittersweet tone most evident? Point to particular words and phrases to support your response.

7. What compositional strategies does Hill use to suspend the sense that time has passed in the pool hall? What specific words and phrases does he use to forestall this sense of time's passing? You might want to consider the effects of his choice of verbs and adverbs.

8. William Hill defines revision as "what you have to do when you get to a point in telling a story and can't go any further, and the story isn't finished yet. Revision takes different forms. Sometimes it is the rewriting of an individual paragraph within a story; sometimes the entire paragraph has to be redone. I have had to, at times, start over before the story was finished because the direction it was taking was all wrong. Also, there is always room for improved grammar and sentence structure." Apply Hill's sense of revision to the changes he made in paragraph 6. Here is the original version of the first three sentences in that paragraph:

> The place had a smell of its own. It was a mixture of stale
> smoke, oil from the floor, and, in the winter, fumes from
> the heater. It didn't smell bad exactly, but it was unique.

Characterize the changes Hill made in his final draft. Which version do you prefer? Why?

9. Hill wrote the following conclusion in his rough draft:

> I heard the expression "You can't go home again" all my
> life. I didn't understand it until the last time I tried. If it
> has been torn down and replaced with a restaurant, then
> it is true that you can never go home again.

Hill revised his conclusion by dropping the last sentence. Did Hill improve his conclusion by deleting the last sentence? What effect does the revised conclusion elicit from you as a reader?

Suggestions for Writing

1. William Hill's essay gains its special effects by comparing and contrasting his recollections of a place in his youth with his view of that place as an adult. What do you think he means in his last sentence when he says that he didn't understand the expression "You can't go home again" "until the last time I tried"? Consider your own relation to the expression "You can't go home again." Write an essay in which you reflect on the expression's meaning for you. What is there about your recollection of places and people in your youth that changes as you grow older? You might want to consider Hill's statement "I couldn't get very sad about my old hangout not being there anymore; I had left first" (paragraph 9). What are the implications of "leaving first"?

2. Choose a place in your hometown that captures its special textures and local color. Draft an essay in which you describe this place and show how it represents what the town once was and perhaps no longer is. Practice using a bittersweet tone in writing about the place.

3. Observe a place—a street corner, bar, park, pool hall, or the like—where people "hang out." Describe what it is about the place that encourages people to congregate there. What special meaning do people invest in the place? Write a description of the place from the point of view of someone who is returning after many years.

AN EFFECTIVE TECHNIQUE

We usually speak of the "tone," not the "tones," of a piece of writing, as if there were only one feeling or attitude throughout, but often a writer will mix several different feelings in one work. William Hill uses the technique of changing tone part-way through his essay: at the ninth paragraph, he moves from sweet recollections of his childhood world where everyone was "always friendly" to the bitter realization that he has left this world and can never return. The poignancy of Hill's essay derives from his not resolving the tension between the two feelings; he brings his readers to share his impossible, contradictory desires to be at once an adult and a child, to live simultaneously in the present and the past. From Hill, we can learn how to avoid simplifying our ambivalent feelings about a subject when we write; he shows us some ways to allow our essays to have complex, even somewhat contradictory, tones.

Hill distinguishes the two tones in his essay in an unusual way—by a subtle manipulation of the flow of time. In the first part of his essay, he places his readers in a time that never seems to really move. He creates this effect by avoiding speaking about actual events that occurred on specific days; instead he speaks of what "always" and "usually" happened "whenever" he walked into the pool hall: the doors were "always open," the people "always friendly." As the words "always" and "usually" are repeated in sentence after sentence, we begin to feel that no event Hill describes is precisely over; it is going to "always" occur again, just as the word "always" is going to keep recurring in the essay itself. Hill has created a distinctive sense of time by speaking of what "always happened"; we are watching many years all at once in each sentence, a whole way of life in unchanging perfection frozen in memory. The stability of this world adds much to its sweetness.

The scenes of the pool hall are not purely sweet, however; a touch of bitterness enters because the word "always" keeps being connected to verbs in the past tense. "The people *were* always friendly" suggests that they no longer are. We feel the present, the adult who bitterly knows the world of the pool hall is gone, in the background haunting this sweet, never-ending past.

The adult perspective finally breaks into the foreground, and with it Hill's unusual verb tense disappears. In paragraph 9 Hill jumps suddenly from reminiscing to describing one specific visit to the pool hall, the day he saw it being converted into a restaurant. We can feel time start moving in its "normal" way again; the carpenters he describes are not going to "always" tear down the pool hall "whenever" he tries to return to it. These events can occur only once.

Hill could have made the change more gradual, describing the evolution of the neighborhood or the decline of the pool business, but that was not his experience: he left when nothing had changed, and he returned after it was all gone. The jump in his essay leaves a gap in his tale, a mystery that the ending makes us ponder—the mystery of waking up one day and suddenly noticing that things aren't as they once were. With the closing of the building, the passing beyond the last time he was there, Hill has taken us through a change in time itself, the passage out of the eternally stable time of childhood into the constant flux of adulthood.

We might say Hill's essay does not provide much insight, since it leaves us pondering a mystery. But keeping a mystery alive is a valuable function of writing; we can explore Hill's essay for clues to questions perplexing us about our own lives. We can also write essays like it, essays about our own childhood and its mysterious and sudden ending. Hill shows us how to manipulate our sentences to create the stable, "timeless" experiences of childhood; we can also invent other ways to describe what "always happened" or to bring our readers to share a child's view of the world. And we can develop our own ways of representing the shift into the adult world; our experience may not have been as jarring as Hill's.

Hill turns at the end of his essay to questioning himself to try to understand the change in tone that his life underwent. He writes as much to connect with a different self as with a different time. The bittersweetness in Hill's essay results not only from the loss of the past but also from his recognition that he sought the changes that destroyed his childhood; he wanted to get beyond his sweet little world. We, too, can write to bridge the mystery of being different than we once were.

Eudora Welty, in "The Little Store," uses a different and equally unusual tense to create much the same effect that Hill does in his essay. She, too, carries us back to the timeless world of childhood and makes us wonder about its disappearance.

ANOTHER ILLUSTRATION OF THE TECHNIQUE

EUDORA WELTY

The Little Store

*"I think I became a writer because I love stories," says Eudora Welty. "I never had
any idea that I could be a professional writer. I'm now realizing, maybe the reason I
first sent stories out to magazines was that I was too shy to show them to anybody I
knew." As the following essay demonstrates, Welty's subject matter and her context are
the people she has known since childhood, moving in the landscape around Jackson,
Mississippi, where she grew up. Welty still lives and works in the house her parents
bought in 1925. She believes that "Southerners have such an intimate sense of place.
We grew up in the fact that we live here with people about whom we know almost
everything that can be known as a citizen of the same neighborhood or town. . . . We
have a sense of continuity, and that, I think comes from place. It helps to give the
meaning—another meaning—to a human life that such life has been there all the time
and will go on. Now that people are on the move a lot more, some of that sense of
continuity is gone."*

*Welty did leave her hometown as a teenager and a young adult: she attended Missis-
sippi State College for Women, finished her B.A. at the University of Wisconsin, and
then went to business school at Columbia University. During the Depression she worked
for newspapers and radio stations and as a publicity agent photographing Mississippi towns
for the Works Progress Administration. Since the 1940s, she has been able to devote
herself entirely to writing and has published collections of stories and essays as well as
novels. One of contemporary America's most celebrated writers, Welty continues to
appreciate the "independence of range and habit" that being a writer provides, the freedom
to choose the "time and place in which to work." However, she dislikes that the "income
is variable and uncertain."*

*When Welty is not writing, she is usually reading. "In fact," she says, "the only
advice I give to young writers . . . is to read." But she cautions that writing "has to
start from an internal feeling of your own and an experience of your own . . . each
reality like that has to find and build its own form."*

Two blocks away from the Mississippi State Capitol, and on the same street   1
with it, where our house was when I was a child growing up in Jackson, it was
possible to have a little pasture behind your backyard where you could keep a
Jersey cow, which we did. My mother herself milked her. A thrifty homemaker,

wife, mother of three, she also did all her own cooking. And as far as I can recall, she never set foot inside a grocery store. It wasn't necessary.

For her regular needs, she stood at the telephone in our front hall and   2 consulted with Mr. Lemly, of Lemly's Market and Grocery downtown, who took her order and sent it out on his next delivery. And since Jackson at the heart of it was still within very near reach of the open country, the blackberry lady clanged on her bucket with a quart measure at your front door in June without fail, the watermelon man rolled up to your house exactly on time for the Fourth of July, and down through the summer, the quiet of the early morning streets was pierced by the calls of farmers driving in with their plenty. One brought his with a song, so plaintive we would sing it with him:

> "Milk, milk,
> Buttermilk;
> Snap beans—butterbeans—
> Tender okra—fresh greens . . .
> And buttermilk."

My mother considered herself pretty well prepared in her kitchen and pantry   3 for any emergency that, in her words, might choose to present itself. But if she should, all of a sudden, need another lemon or find she was out of bread, all she had to do was call out, "Quick! Who'd like to run to the Little Store for me?"

I would.   4

She'd count out the change into my hand, and I was away. I'll bet the   5 nickel that would be left over that all over the country, for those of my day, the neighborhood grocery played a similar part in our growing up.

Our store had its name—it was that of the grocer who owned it, whom I'll   6 call Mr. Sessions—but "the Little Store" is what we called it at home. It was a block down our street toward the capitol and half a block further, around the corner, toward the cemetery. I knew even the sidewalk to it as well as I knew my own skin. I'd skipped my jumping-rope up and down it, hopped its length through mazes of hopscotch, played jacks in its islands of shade, serpentined along it on my Princess bicycle, skated it backward and forward. In the twilight I had dragged my steamboat by its string (this was homemade out of every new shoebox, with a candle in the bottom lighted and shining through colored tissue paper pasted over windows scissored out in the shapes of the sun, moon and stars) across every crack of the walk without letting it bump or catch fire. I'd "played out" on that street after supper with my brothers and friends as long as "first-dark" lasted; I'd caught its lightning bugs. On the first

Armistice Day (and this will set the time I'm speaking of) we made our own parade down that walk on a single velocipede—my brother pedaling, our little brother riding the handlebars, and myself standing on the back, all with arms wide, flying flags in each hand. (My father snapped that picture as we raced by. It came out blurred.)

As I set forth for the Little Store, a tune would float toward me from the 7 house where there lived three sisters, girls in their teens, who ratted their hair over their ears, wore headbands like gladiators, and were considered to be very popular. They practiced for this in the daytime; they'd wind up the Victrola, leave the same record on they'd played before, and you'd see them bobbing past their dining-room windows while they danced with each other. Being three, they could go all day, cutting in:

> "Everybody ought to know-oh
> How to do the Tickle-Toe
> (how to do the Tickle-Toe)"—

they sang it and danced to it, and as I went by to the same song, I believed it.

A little further on, across the street, was the house where the principal of 8 our grade school lived—lived on, even while we were having vacation. What if she would come out? She would halt me in my tracks—she had a very carrying and well-known voice in Jackson, where she'd taught almost every-body—saying, "Eudora Alice Welty, spell OBLIGE." OBLIGE was the word that she of course knew had kept me from making 100 on my spelling exam. She'd make me miss it again now, by boring her eyes through me from across the street. This was my vacation fantasy, one good way to scare myself on the way to the store.

Down near the corner waited the house of a little boy named Lindsey. The 9 sidewalk here was old brick, which the roots of a giant chinaberry tree had humped up and tilted this way and that. On skates, you took it fast, in a series of skittering hops, trying not to touch ground anywhere. If the chinaberries had fallen and rolled in the cracks, it was like skating through a whole shooting match of marbles. I crossed my fingers that Lindsey wouldn't be looking.

During the big flu epidemic he and I, as it happened, were being nursed 10 through our sieges at the same time. I'd hear my father and mother murmuring to each other, at the end of a long day, "And I wonder how poor little *Lindsey* got along today?" Just as, down the street, he no doubt would have to hear his family saying, "And I wonder how is poor *Eudora* by now?" I got the idea that a choice was going to be made soon between poor little Lindsey and poor

Eudora, and I came up with a funny poem. I wasn't prepared for it when my father told me it wasn't funny and my mother cried that if I couldn't be ashamed for myself, she'd have to be ashamed for me

> There was a little boy and his name was Lindsey.
> He went to heaven with the influinzy.

He didn't, he survived it, poem and all, the same as I did. But his chinaberries could have brought me down in my skates in a flying act of contrition before his eyes, looking pretty funny myself, right in front of his house.

Setting out in this world, a child feels so indelible. He only comes to find 11 out later that it's all the others along his way who are making themselves indelible to him.

Our Little Store rose right up from the sidewalk; standing in a street of 12 family houses, it alone hadn't any yard in front, any tree or flowerbed. It was a plain frame building covered over with brick. Above the door, a little railed porch ran across on an upstairs level and four windows with shades were looking out. But I didn't catch on to those.

Running in out of the sun, you met what seemed total obscurity inside. 13 There were almost tangible smells—licorice recently sucked in a child's cheek, dill-pickle brine that had leaked through a paper sack in a fresh trail across the wooden floor, ammonia-loaded ice that had been hoisted from wet croker sacks and slammed into the icebox with its sweet butter at the door, and perhaps the smell of still-untrapped mice.

Then through the motes of cracker dust, cornmeal dust, the Gold Dust of 14 the Gold Dust Twins that the floor had been swept out with, the realities emerged. Shelves climbed to high reach all the way around, set out with not too much of any one thing but a lot of things—lard, molasses, vinegar, starch, matches, kerosene, Octagon soap (about a year's worth of octagon-shaped coupons cut out and saved brought a signet ring addressed to you in the mail. Furthermore, when the postman arrived at your door, he blew a whistle). It was up to you to remember what you came for, while your eye traveled from cans of sardines to ice cream salt to harmonicas to fly-paper (over your head, batting around on a thread beneath the blades of the ceiling fan, stuck with its testimonial catch).

Its confusion may have been in the eye of its beholder. Enchantment is cast 15 upon you by all those things you weren't supposed to have need for, it lures you close to wooden tops you'd outgrown, boy's marbles and agates in little net pouches, small rubber balls that wouldn't bounce straight, frazzly kite-string, clay bubble-pipes that would snap off in your teeth, the stiffest scissors.

You could contemplate those long narrow boxes of sparklers gathering dust while you waited for it to be the Fourth of July or Christmas, and noisemakers in the shape of tin frogs for somebody's birthday party you hadn't been invited to yet, and see that they were all marvelous.

You might not have even looked for Mr. Sessions when he came around 16 his store cheese (as big as a doll's house) and in front of the counter looking for you. When you'd finally asked him for, and received from him in its paper bag, whatever single thing it was that you had been sent for, the nickel that was left over was yours to spend.

Down at a child's eye level, inside those glass jars with mouths in their sides 17 through which the grocer could run his scoop or a child's hand might be invited to reach for a choice, were wineballs, all-day suckers, gumdrops, peppermints. Making a row under the glass of a counter were the Tootsie Rolls, Hershey Bars, Goo-Goo Clusters, Baby Ruths. And whatever was the name of those pastilles that came stacked in a cardboard cylinder with a cardboard lid? They were thin and dry, about the size of tiddlywinks, and in the shape of twisted rosettes. A kind of chocolate dust came out with them when you shook them out in your hand. Were they chocolate? I'd say rather they were brown. They didn't taste of anything at all, unless it was wood. Their attraction was the number you got for a nickel.

Making up your mind, you circled the store around and around, around the 18 pickle barrel, around the tower of Cracker Jack boxes; Mr. Sessions had built it for us himself on top of a packing case, like a house of cards.

If it seemed too hot for Cracker Jacks, I might get a cold drink. Mr. Sessions 19 might have already stationed himself by the cold-drinks barrel, like a mind reader. Deep in ice water that looked black as ink, murky shapes that would come up as Coca-Colas, Orange Crushes, and various flavors of pop, were all swimming around together. When you gave the word, Mr. Sessions plunged his bare arm in to the elbow and fished out your choice, first try. I favored a locally bottled concoction called Lake's Celery. (What else could it be called? It was made by a Mr. Lake out of celery. It was a popular drink here for years but was not known universally, as I found out when I arrived in New York and ordered one in the Astor bar.) You drank on the premises, with feet set wide apart to miss the drip, and gave him back his bottle.

But he didn't hurry you off. A standing scales was by the door, with a stack 20 of iron weights and a brass slide on the balance arm, that would weigh you up to three hundred pounds. Mr. Sessions, whose hands were gentle and smelled of carbolic, would lift you up and set your feet on the platform, hold your loaf of bread for you, and taking his time while you stood still for him, he would make certain of what you weighed today. He could even remember what you weighed the last time, so you could subtract and announce how much you'd gained. That was goodbye.

Is there always a hard way to go home? From the Little Store, you could go 21 partway through the sewer. If your brothers had called you a scarecat, then across the next street beyond the Little Store, it was possible to enter this sewer by passing through a privet hedge, climbing down into the bed of a creek, and going into its mouth on your knees. The sewer—it might have been no more than a "storm sewer"—came out and emptied here, where Town Creek, a sandy, most often shallow little stream that ambled through Jackson on its way to the Pearl River, ran along the edge of the cemetery. You could go in darkness through this tunnel to where you next saw light (if you ever did) and climb out through the culvert at your own street corner.

I was a scarecat, all right, but I was a reader with my own refuge in story- 22 books. Making my way under the sidewalk, under the street and the streetcar track, under the Little Store, down there in the wet dark by myself, I could be Persephone entering into my six-month sojourn underground—though I didn't suppose Persephone had to crawl, hanging onto a loaf of bread, and come out through the teeth of an iron grating. Mother Ceres would indeed be wondering where she could find me, and mad when she knew. "Now am I going to have to start marching to the Little Store for *myself?*"

I couldn't picture it. Indeed, I'm unable today to picture the Little Store 23 with a grown person in it, except for Mr. Sessions and the lady who helped him, who belonged there. We children thought it was ours. The happiness of errands was in part that of running for the moment away from home, a free spirit. I believed the Little Store to be a center of the outside world, and hence of happiness—as I believed what I found in the Cracker Jack box to be a genuine prize, which was as simply as I believed in the Golden Fleece.

But a day came when I ran to the store to discover, sitting on the front 24 step, a grown person, after all—more than a grown person. It was the Monkey Man, together with his monkey. His grinding-organ was lowered to the step beside him. In my whole life so far, I must have laid eyes on the Monkey Man no more than five or six times. An itinerant of rare and wayward appearances, he was not punctual like the Gipsies, who every year with the first cool days of fall showed up in the aisles of Woolworth's. You never knew when the Monkey Man might decide to favor Jackson, or which way he'd go. Sometimes you heard him as close as the next street, and then he didn't come up yours.

But now I saw the Monkey Man at the Little Store, where I'd never seen 25 him before. I'd never seen him sitting down. Low on that familiar doorstep, he was not the same any longer, and neither was his monkey. They looked just like an old man and an old friend of his that wore a fez, meeting quietly together, tired, and resting with their eyes fixed on some place far away, and not the same place. Yet their romance for me didn't have it in its power to waver. I wavered. I simply didn't know how to step around them, to proceed on into the Little Store for my mother's emergency as if nothing had happened. If I could have gone in there after it, whatever it was, I would have given it to them—putting it into the monkey's cool little fingers. I would have given them the Little Store itself.

In my memory they are still attached to the store—so are all the others. 26 Everyone I saw on my way seemed to me then part of my errand, and in a way they were. As I myself, the free spirit, was part of it too.

All the years we lived in that house where we children were born, the same 27 people lived in the other houses on our street too. People changed through the arithmetic of birth, marriage, and death, but not by going away. So families just accrued stories, which through the fullness of time, in those times, their own lives made. And I grew up in those.

But I didn't know there'd ever been a story at the Little Store, one that 28 was going on while I was there. Of course, all the time the Sessions family had been living right overhead there, in the upstairs rooms behind the little railed porch and the shaded windows; but I think we children never thought of that. Did I fail to see them as a family because they weren't living in an ordinary house? Because I so seldom saw them close together, or having anything to say to each other? She sat in the back of the store, her pencil over a ledger, while he stood and waited on children to make up their minds. They worked in twin black eyeshades, held on their gray heads by elastic bands. It may be harder to recognize kindness—or unkindness, either—in a face whose eyes are in shadow. His face underneath his shade was as round as the little wooden wheels in the Tinker Toy box. So was her face, I didn't know, perhaps didn't even wonder: were they husband and wife or brother and sister? Were they father and mother? There were a few other persons, of various ages, wandering singly in by the back door and out. But none of their relationships could I imagine, when I'd never seen them sitting down together around their own table.

The possibility that they had any other life at all, anything beyond what 29 we could see within the four walls of the Little Store, occurred to me only when tragedy struck their family. There was some act of violence. The shock to the neighborhood traveled to the children, of course; but I couldn't find out from my parents what had happened. They held it back from me, as they'd already held back many things, "until the time comes for you to know."

You could find out some of these things by looking in the unabridged dic- 30
tionary and the encyclopedia—kept to hand in our dining room—but you
couldn't find out there what had happened to the family who for all the years
of your life had lived upstairs over the Little Store, who had never been
anything but patient and kind to you, who never once had sent you away. All
I ever knew was its aftermath: they were the only people ever known to me
who simply vanished. At the point where their life overlapped into ours, the
story broke off.

We weren't being sent to the neighborhood grocery for facts of life, or death. 31
But of course those are what we were on the track of, anyway. With the loaf
of bread and the Cracker Jack prize, I was bringing home the intimations of
pride and disgrace, and rumors and early news of people coming to hurt one
another, while others practiced for joy—storing up a portion for myself of the
human mystery.

Focusing on the Bittersweet Tone of Eudora Welty's Essay

1. What details in paragraphs 2–5 establish a convincing child's-eye viewpoint?
   What details emphasize that Welty is writing about her childhood from an
   adult's perspective many years later? Are there places in these first few paragraphs where you cannot tell whether a child or an adult is speaking? How
   would the essay's impact be different if Welty used a child's present-tense voice
   instead of an adult's reminiscence to tell her story? How would it be different
   if she made her adult self a character in the narrative and turned her childhood
   scenes into flashbacks?

2. Welty uses an unusual verb form throughout her account of a trip to the store,
   attaching the auxiliary *would* or *might* to verbs in paragraphs 3–5, 7–9, 16, 17,
   and 21. Why does Welty speak of what "would" or "might" happen when she
   went to the store, instead of simply telling us what *did* happen? How do the
   verb forms help create a child's sense of living in a time when nothing really
   changes? How does the ending break us out of this stable time?

2. In paragraphs 23, 26, and 27, Welty steps back from her child to her adult
   persona. What do these paragraphs tell you about Welty's adult perception of
   her childhood? How do these paragraphs function in the essay?

3. How does Welty's tone shift toward the end of the essay? Look back through
   the essay and find details that foreshadowed this change of tone.

4. Which passages at the end of the essay show that Welty is sad or bitter about
   the way her childhood ended? What passages suggest that Welty sees something
   good about the end of her childhood?

WORKING WITH THE TECHNIQUE IN YOUR OWN WRITING

1. Welty and Hill end their essays pondering the mystery of how the stable world of childhood ever ended. They seem to have ambivalent feelings about growing up; their childhoods were sweet, but they actively sought out the experiences and knowledge that destroyed their naive views of the world. Write an essay about a time in your own life when you realized that the world and you seemed different than they used to be. If you have ambivalent feelings about the change, try to bring your readers to share your ambivalence.

2. Eudora Welty compresses many trips to the store into one generalized description, writing of what "might" have happened on any given day. William Hill uses a similar technique, writing of what "always" happened at the pool hall in his hometown. Both writers give us a sense of a place and a time that is now gone. Write an essay in which you try to capture the spirit of a past time in your life. You might try using one of the distinctive verb forms Welty and Hill use, or you might invent your own way of making us feel that you are writing about the general experience of a whole period, not just about specific events. Try to make your readers aware of how this period differs from your life now.

JUDY JENNINGS

Richland College
Dallas, Texas
Rica Garcia, instructor

At the time she wrote her prize-winning essay, "Second-Class Mom," Judy Jennings explained, "I suppose my present lifestyle affects my writing more than anything. I am twenty-nine years old, married to Les Jennings, and have one son, Christopher. Les's two children, Nikki and Phillip, live with us as well. Les and I have a design firm specializing in large aircraft interiors, primarily corporate clients and heads of state. I have been attending college on a part-time basis. I tend to write about things that happen in everyday living—my children and their antics, my husband, the plight of the average housewife, etc. It is important for writers to write about things they know about." Asked to write an essay in which she explained a situation in her life, Jennings decided to write about her experience as a stepmother. "My husband's two children live with us and I feel very strongly about the injustices of stepparenting. I wanted to clarify a misunderstood role."

Judy Jennings is a Texan by birth and preference; she has always lived in the Lone Star State. Born in Fort Worth, she was raised in Greenville and graduated from its high school. After her marriage, she settled with her family in Plano, Texas. Juggling the demands of working and caring for her family leaves little time for her major hobby, reading. Her favorite authors include Danielle Steele, Jackie Collins, and Thomas Thompson—"anyone exciting and easy to read."

Rather than subsiding, the pressures of tending to work and family have increased in the three years since Judy Jennings earned a Bedford Prize: "I am still working with my husband in our design business. I've also started working part-time for a local law firm. I no longer attend college because of time limitations." Her crowded schedule continues to allow little, if any, time to read and especially to write for herself: "I find it difficult to find the time and the 'push' to do much creative writing. I do think, however, that I do well in utilizing the techniques I learned in composing for business purposes."

Second-Class Mom

On March 22, 1980, I married Leslie Floyd Jennings, Jr. On that same clear spring evening, I also married Daniel Brian Jennings (age seventeen), Lesley Nicole Jennings (age six), and Phillip Timothy Jennings (age two), Les's children by two previous marital failures. I had been warned by everyone I knew about the pitfalls of marrying a man with two failed marriages and three children in tow. But marry him I did, and in that dubious deed, settled upon my youthfully naive shoulders the burdens of the label of "stepmother" that history, mythology, ignorance, and misunderstanding allow our society to dictate.

During the first months of our marriage, I wrestled with having to rearrange 2
our schedules to accommodate weekend visits as well as with my resentment of the amount of child support my husband was paying and the hardships it imposed on our already stretched-to-the-limit budget. These factors (and others) made me often wonder if we would ever be able to have a child of our own because of these financial and emotional commitments to my husband's children. Yes, I had considered all these things before making a permanent commitment to this man, but day-to-day reality is quite different, I found, from the dreams we spin when we are blinded by love's passions.

After only five short months of marriage, Les's two younger children came 3
to live with us, and within thirty days, I was expecting a child of my own. Learning about the trials of motherhood from both Les's children and my own child virtually at the same time has certainly proven to be a unique and unpredictable experience. I feel that in the last four years, I have learned more about patience, compromise, sacrifice, and endurance than I ever thought possible.

I have never wanted to give anyone the impression that I dislike my step- 4
children, or even that I have no feelings for them at all, but they are not mine. There are times when I want to grab Les by the knot of his tie, pulling him down to my level until the tips of our noses touch and we're looking each other straight in the eye, and then snarl at him through clenched teeth, "THEY'RE NOT MINE." Everyone understands the theories of how difficult it would be to live with someone else's children, but they really never do understand the realities of it. Les's mother is always spouting endless streams of well-meant advice on "raising and disciplining Les's children just like they were my own." Yet, even though she will sit nodding her head in approval while I criticize and correct my own child, she will purse her lips and sometimes burst into tears if I get into a shouting match with one of her grandchildren who is not mine. Even after almost five years, I have never ceased to be amazed and appalled at the injustice of it all. I am expected to perform with perfect precision, but without a single trace of prejudice or partiality, all the mothering rituals, but I am also expected to stop just short of throwing any stones at their characters or past disciplinary guidelines. I'm not supposed to show the slightest bit of distaste or nausea or even say "Yuk" when cleaning up the bathroom after a "didn't-quite-make-it-to-the-toilet" bout of diarrhea or vomiting, but heaven forbid that I should criticize their clothes or hairstyles or friends, a privilege, I presume, reserved for "real" mothers.

One of the things that makes stepmothering somewhat less a joy than moth-   5
ering your "children by choice" is that it is such a thankless job. Even after
I've spent an endless day in unfruitful toilet training sessions or sore throat
crankiness, my own child will make it up to me by climbing onto my lap and
snuggling his baby head up underneath my chin, making goose bumps run up
and down my arms. I've endured countless times, after days of driving car
pools, organizing school bake sales and carnivals, soccer practices, ballet lessons, and dental appointments, having one of my stepchildren run out to get
in the car holding up some crudely fashioned trinket made in school and saying,
"Look! Look what I made for Mommy." "Mommy" being their "real" mother.
The mother they see maybe four or five times a year, and who rarely so much
as buys them a pair of shoes.

The role of a stepmother is unlike that of any other kind of mother, whether   6
it be foster mother, adoptive mother, or birth mother. Stepmothering is the
only type of mothering we do without choice. All children, certainly, are not
"planned" children, but even with an unwanted pregnancy, the mother *chooses*
not to abort the baby, or give it up for adoption, or something. And certainly,
adoptive mothers and foster mothers have a definite choice in the decision to
mother or not. The stepmother does not choose the children, she chooses the
father. He just comes as a package deal.

Stepchildren also come with an uncanny radar or sixth sense that enables   7
them to zero in with pinpoint accuracy on our vulnerabilities and fire torpedos
with deadly insensitivity. Every year, when our whole family assembles to
decorate the family Christmas tree, one of my stepchildren will take this one
certain ornament out of the box and hold it up for all the rest to see. This
particular ornament came with them when they came to live with us. I have
always presumed that it was a gift from their natural mother, so I suppose that's
why I've never found it in me to throw it away. This ornament is a small pair
of very ugly gorillas with toboggans and neck scarves with their arms around
each other looking at a book of Christmas carols. They hold it up to everyone
in the room (including me) and then announce triumphantly, "This is Mommy
and Daddy." Every year I tell myself that they're only children and that they
don't know what they're saying, but my face still gets hot and my stomach
still flipflops. I don't like being reminded of the "Mommy and Daddy" that
used to be. These children are reminder enough. Their very presence seems
to almost be a rubber stamp that says, "Your husband used to be in love with
someone else," and some things are better left unthought.

I have a very deep sense of responsibility toward these children and a great   8
deal of affection. I will probably never love them the way I love my own son—
sometimes I don't love them at all, but they are as much a part of my life as

their father or my own child. Just as I am sure about the way I feel about them, I am quite certain that they feel pretty much the same way about me. We have been thrown together by virtue of the mistakes of other people. I can't help the fact that their mother and father couldn't make a go of their marriage, and neither can they, but here we are. We have grown to accept our lives together, and even to depend upon each other somewhat. I am really the only mother they know, and neither I nor they can change that fact.

I would lay down my own life for *any* of my children. For Christopher, I 9 would do it without a backward glance and probably even with a smile on my face. For Nikki and Phillip, I would gripe all the way.

Focusing on Judy Jennings's Techniques and Revisions

1. Judy Jennings writes with honesty about a subject many people are unwilling to discuss openly. She tells us that she and her stepchildren "have been thrown together by virtue of the mistakes of other people." What does Jennings see as the injustices of being a stepmother?

2. Jennings writes: "I am expected to perform with perfect precision, but without a single trace of prejudice or partiality, all the mothering rituals, but I am also expected to stop just short of throwing any stones at their characters or past disciplinary guidelines." What details of the mothering ritual does Jennings present to illustrate her thesis? Select details you found effective and explain how these details are used in the essay.

3. Part of the success of Judy Jennings's essay is her ability to resist using the conventional language associated with stereotypical images of stepmothers. Her view of her children, her husband, and her mother-in-law is quite realistic. What terms—and, more generally, what writing techniques—does she use to depict them so even-handedly? Even though she confesses to resenting her stepchildren, most readers are drawn to Jennings. How do the examples in paragraphs 5 and 7 influence her readers' attitude toward her?

4. When invited to reread her prize-winning essay several years after having written it and to assess its strengths, Jennings quickly responded: "This piece tends to bring out feelings and thoughts that I usually try to push to the back. However, I'm quite happy with its tone, and I think I was pretty successful in getting on paper what was inside my head." How would you describe the tone of her essay? Point to specific words and phrases to support your response.

5. In a recent interview, Judy Jennings observed that one of the successful features of her essay was its comic elements: "I feel that this piece took a look at a very serious subject without being too somber. I like its somewhat comical overtones." Reread her essay. Where do these "comical overtones" surface

most visibly? With what effect(s)? What writing techniques does Jennings use to introduce these comic elements?

6. As readers, we have a strong sense of a writer who cares deeply about her subject and who has taken great care to make her essay lively. What techniques does Jennings use to make her ideas interesting to her readers?

7. Jennings begins her essay in a very direct way: "On March 22, 1980, I married Leslie Floyd Jennings, Jr. On that same clear spring evening, I also married Daniel Brian Jennings (age seventeen), Lesley Nicole Jennings (age six), and Phillip Timothy Jennings (age two), Les's children by two previous marital failures." Do you find this an effective hook for pulling the reader into the world of her essay? Why? In an earlier draft, Jennings's title was "Number Two Mom." How does her revised title better introduce her essay?

8. In her conclusion, Jennings tells us of her willingness to sacrifice herself for any of her children but says that she would be "griping all the way" in sacrificing for her stepchildren. How does her conclusion effectively tie together all the various ideas in her essay?

9. Jennings reports that she envisions her readers as "stepmother/persons about to become stepmothers." What evidence is there that she is writing for this *audience*? What evidence is there that she is writing for a more general audience? How would paragraphs 4 and 5, for instance, differ if they were written for a different group of readers?

10. Jennings *generalizes* about the role of the stepmother from her own experience, that is, she makes general statements about stepmothers and stepmothering that are based on her own particular experience. In paragraph 6, for instance, she tells us, "Stepmothering is the only type of mothering we do without choice." Why does Jennings generalize about the role of the stepmother? How does this strategy help strengthen her essay?

Suggestions for Writing

1. Jennings illustrates the burdens of the label "stepmother." Consider a role you have chosen for yourself or have been thrust into and write an essay illustrating what it is like to be cast in that role.

2. Write an essay explaining your attitude toward an event or situation in your life that might surprise your readers.

3. Write an essay responding to Jennings's complaints from a stepchild's *point of view.*

AN EFFECTIVE TECHNIQUE

From Judy Jennings's essay, we can learn how to create an uncompromisingly realistic portrayal of a subject. Her method involves more than simply telling the truth: it requires adopting a tough, hard-edged tone, demanding that readers face up to the unpleasant fact that life will never conform to the conventional stories we all like to tell. Jennings identifies herself as a realist when she begins her essay by promising to destroy two illusions: she says she will show that stepmothers do not conform to "mythology" and that the "day-to-day reality" of married life is "quite different from the dreams we spin when we are blinded by love's passions." Angry that she is treated unfairly because she is a stepmother, she nonetheless resists merely inverting the clichés by presenting herself as an angel. She complains about her life without creating heroes or villains. The success of her essay derives from her ability to paint her children, her husband, her mother-in-law, and especially herself as people who are thoughtless, even cruel, yet still lovable. She creates a realistic world that cannot be reduced to easy and conventional moral dichotomies.

Essential to a hard-edged view is an awareness of the unpleasant parts of everyone's day-to-day existence, regardless of whether they are princesses or wicked witches. Jennings writes about her "nausea" when "cleaning up the bathroom" after one of her children's " 'didn't-quite-make-it-to-the toilet' bout[s] of diarrhea or vomiting." Merely by mentioning toilets, Jennings violates one of the conventions of most writing, and what she says shows why the subject is usually left out. If writers talk about the toilet, they remind readers that people must occasionally give up control of their actions to their bodies; bodies can make everyone seem fairly disgusting. Jennings focuses quite directly on the way bodies can overrule the best of intentions: she is quite as unable to control her own disgust as her children are unable to control their intestines. We might not want to mention diarrhea in our essays, but focusing on bodies and their imperfections is an effective way to establish a realistic view. If we describe how a character combs his hair to cover his bald spot or how he hiccups a lot, we will create a character who seems to be an ordinary person, neither an angel nor a devil.

When trying to establish a realistic view, we should resist making our characters seem ridiculous. Hard-edged realism often skirts the edge of black comedy. When Jennings reports that her stepchildren pulled out a "small pair of very ugly gorillas with toboggans and neck scarves" and announced, " 'This is Mommy and Daddy,' " we have to laugh. But Jennings cuts our laughter short by reminding us of the pain she feels when her children make such statements. In the world of realistic writers, there are no uncomplicated emotions, no simple humor or simple pain or simple anger. Even in Jennings's strongest complaints, when she speaks of the "deadly insensitivity" of her stepchildren, she does not allow us to feel only anger; she does not simply paint her children as monsters. Instead, she reveals that their cruelest words and deeds are actually expressions of love for their "real" mother, expressions of their dreams of having an ideal family that would never have broken up. We can sense that Jennings does not truly want to condemn her stepchildren for such dreams. She understands their pain and their broken dreams; all she wants is equal sympathy for her pain and her broken dreams.

Showing that everyone suffers pain brings hard-edged realism close to bitter fatalism. But Jennings distances herself from hopelessness. There is clearly room for much love in her family. And her last line creates an image of a "realistic" heroism that might be possible in this confusing world: laying down one's life for others but griping all the way.

Jennings shows that we have to fight our tendency to simplify the world if we want to write realistic essays. Rather than showing people as simply good or bad, we might show how the best and worst emotions are intertwined. Rather than showing people as responsible for their acts, we might show them as out of control, making mistakes, at the mercy of their bodies. Rather than distinguishing clearly between humorous and serious moments, we might make our characters appear ridiculous but suffer real pains. Whether writing about moms and dads, the president, or a thief holding up a drugstore, we can focus on the "realistic," complicated, and amoral details that make the world disturbing and fascinating.

In the next selection, Joan Didion packs a few paragraphs with complicated and amoral details to utterly destroy all the conventional assumptions she was taught about "home." The only relief from her hard-edged tone is a light touch of humor, as she realizes how absurd it is that after thirty years of disillusionment she still expects to find a conventional "home" every time she visits her parents.

ANOTHER ILLUSTRATION OF THE TECHNIQUE

JOAN DIDION

On Going Home

Joan Didion describes Sacramento, where she grew up, as "a very extreme place. It was very flat, flatter than most people can imagine. Winter was cold rain and tulle fog. Summer was 110 degrees. Those extremes affect the way you deal with the world. It so happens that if you're a writer the extremes show up. They don't if you sell insurance." From the age of five, Didion has felt compelled to keep a notebook; she still has her first Big Five tablet, in which is recorded what she regards as her first "extreme" and "ironic" tale: an account of a woman who believed herself to be freezing to death in the Arctic night, only to find, when day broke, that she was dying of heat in the Sahara.

Didion's compulsion to write served her well as an English major at the University of California, Berkeley, and led her to find work as a columnist and magazine editor right out of college. She soon turned successfully to writing novels, but she has continued to write essays and nonfiction throughout her career. Whether she is inventing facts or reporting them, she regards writing as "the act of saying I, of imposing oneself upon other people, of saying listen to me, see it my way, change your mind. It's an aggressive, even a hostile act. . . . I write entirely to find out what I'm thinking."

Each piece Didion writes begins, she says, with "pictures in my mind, . . . images that shimmer around the edges. You can't think much about these pictures that shimmer. You just lie low and let them develop." By looking carefully at these pictures, she eventually finds what she calls "the grammar in the picture. . . . I mean grammar literally. . . . The arrangement of the words matters, and the arrangement you want can be found in the picture in your mind. The picture dictates whether this will be a sentence with or without clauses, a sentence that ends hard or a dying-fall sentence, long or short, active or passive. The picture tells you how to arrange the words, and the arrangement of the words tells you, or tells me, what's going on in the picture."

I am home for my daughter's first birthday. By "home" I do not mean the house in Los Angeles where my husband and I and the baby live, but the place where my family is, in the Central Valley of California. It is a vital although troublesome distinction. My husband likes my family but is uneasy in their house, because once there I fall into their ways, which are difficult, oblique, deliberately inarticulate, not my husband's ways. We live in dusty houses ("D-U-S-T," he once wrote with his finger on surfaces all over the house, but no one noticed it) filled with mementos quite without value to him (what 1

could the Canton dessert plates mean to him? how could he have known about
the assay scales, why should he care if he did know?), and we appear to talk
exclusively about people we know who have been committed to mental hospitals, about people we know who have been booked on drunk-driving charges,
and about property, particularly about property, land, price per acre and C-2
zoning and assessments and freeway access. My brother does not understand
my husband's inability to perceive the advantage in the rather common real-
estate transaction known as "sale-leaseback," and my husband in turn does
not understand why so many of the people he hears about in my father's house
have recently been committed to mental hospitals or booked on drunk-driving
charges. Nor does he understand that when we talk about sale-leasebacks and
right-of-way condemnations we are talking in code about the things we like
best, the yellow fields and the cottonwoods and the rivers rising and falling
and the mountain roads closing when the heavy snow comes in. We miss each
other's points, have another drink and regard the fire. My brother refers to my
husband, in his presence, as "Joan's husband." Marriage is the classic betrayal.

Or perhaps it is not anymore. Sometimes I think that those of us who are   2
now in our thirties were born into the last generation to carry the burden of
"home," to find in family life the source of all tension and drama. I had by all
objective accounts a "normal" and a "happy" family situation, and yet I was
almost thirty years old before I could talk to my family on the telephone
without crying after I had hung up. We did not fight. Nothing was wrong.
And yet some nameless anxiety colored the emotional charges between me
and the place that I came from. The question of whether or not you could go
home again was a very real part of the sentimental and largely literary baggage
with which we left home in the fifties; I suspect that it is irrelevant to the
children born of the fragmentation after World War II. A few weeks ago in a
San Francisco bar I saw a pretty young girl on crystal take off her clothes and
dance for the cash prize in an "amateur-topless" contest. There was no particular sense of moment about this, none of the effect of romantic degradation,
of "dark journey," for which my generation strived so assiduously. What sense
could that girl possibly make of, say, *Long Day's Journey into Night*? Who is
beside the point?

That I am trapped in this particular irrelevancy is never more apparent to   3
me than when I am home. Paralyzed by the neurotic lassitude engendered by
meeting one's past at every turn, around every corner, inside every cupboard,
I go aimlessly from room to room. I decide to meet it head-on and clean out
a drawer, and I spread the contents on the bed. A bathing suit I wore the
summer I was seventeen. A letter of rejection from *The Nation*, an aerial
photograph of the site for a shopping center my father did not build in 1954.

Three teacups hand-painted with cabbage roses and signed "E.M.," my grand-mother's initials. There is no final solution for letters of rejection from *The Nation* and teacups hand-painted in 1900. Nor is there any answer to snapshots of one's grandfather as a young man on skis, surveying around Donner Pass in the year 1910. I smooth out the snapshot and look into his face, and do and do not see my own. I close the drawer, and have another cup of coffee with my mother. We get along very well, veterans of a guerrilla war we never understood.

Days pass. I see no one. I come to dread my husband's evening call, not 4 only because he is full of news of what by now seems to me our remote life in Los Angeles, people he has seen, letters which require attention, but because he asks what I have been doing, suggests uneasily that I get out, drive to San Francisco or Berkeley. Instead I drive across the river to a family graveyard. It has been vandalized since my last visit and the monuments are broken, over-turned in the dry grass. Because I once saw a rattlesnake in the grass I stay in the car and listen to a country-and-Western station. Later I drive with my father to a ranch he has in the foothills. The man who runs his cattle on it asks us to the roundup, a week from Sunday, and although I know that I will be in Los Angeles I say, in the oblique way my family talks, that I will come. Once home I mention the broken monuments in the graveyard. My mother shrugs.

I go to visit my great-aunts. A few of them think now that I am my cousin, 5 or their daughter who died young. We recall an anecdote about a relative last seen in 1948, and they ask if I still like living in New York City. I have lived in Los Angeles for three years, but I say that I do. The baby is offered a horehound drop, and I am slipped a dollar bill "to buy a treat." Questions trail off, answers are abandoned, the baby plays with the dust motes in a shaft of afternoon sun.

It is time for the baby's birthday party: a white cake, strawberry-marshmal- 6 low ice cream, a bottle of champagne saved from another party. In the evening, after she has gone to sleep, I kneel beside the crib and touch her face, where it is pressed against the slats, with mine. She is an open and trusting child, unprepared for and unaccustomed to the ambushes of family life, and perhaps it is just as well that I can offer her little of that life. I would like to give her more. I would like to promise her that she will grow up with a sense of her cousins and of rivers and of her great-grandmother's teacups, would like to pledge her a picnic on a river with fried chicken and her hair uncombed, would like to give her *home* for her birthday, but we live differently now and I can promise her nothing like that. I give her a xylophone and a sundress from Madeira, and promise to tell her a funny story.

Focusing on the Hard-Edged Tone of Joan Didion's Essay

1. What kinds of conversations are supposed to take place when grown-up children visit their parents? What is unconventional about the conversations that take place at Didion's family gatherings? What is Didion's attitude toward these conversations?

2. Didion puts the word "home" in quotes in paragraphs 1 and 2 and in italics in paragraph 6, indicating that she is using the word in some unusual way. What does Didion seem to think is the conventional meaning of "home" (consider, for example, what she says in paragraphs 2 and 6)? What is unconventional about the two homes she writes about (her parents' and her own)? Why is "a young girl on crystal" taking off her clothes for money a demonstration of how "home" has lost its meaning? What does Didion mean by "the ambushes of family life" in paragraph 6?

3. In paragraph 4, Didion mentions visiting the "broken monuments" in a family graveyard. How is this essay like a collection of broken monuments? How is it like a graveyard?

4. What passages suggest that Didion is sad that "home" in its conventional sense has been broken up and buried? What passages suggest that she is happy, or at least feels some positive emotion? How would you summarize her complex feelings about the disappearance of conventional "homes"?

WORKING WITH THE TECHNIQUE IN YOUR OWN WRITING

---

1. Write an essay about a word or phrase that has a strong conventional meaning, such as "home," "mother," "well educated," or "masculinity." Show that the conventional meaning of the word is an illusion by presenting descriptions of the reality of home, mothers, educated people, truly masculine men, or whatever you have decided to write about. Try to convey how complicated reality is, neither "nice" nor "evil."

2. Write a *descriptive* or *narrative* essay presenting a realistic, unconventional view of some fairly ordinary experience, such as dating, waiting for a bus, or washing clothes. Focus on odd little details, trying to undermine what we typically expect to be mentioned in talk about that kind of experience. To select an experience, you might try to think of something that you have always felt odd about, something you have never been able to enjoy or hate or ignore quite the way other people do. Or you might think about something that TV ads or movies portray in a way that seems foreign to your experience.

EARNESTINE JOHNSON

George Mason University
Fairfax, Virginia
Lois Cucullu, instructor

Earnestine Johnson's advice to first-year students interested in improving their writing is to "read as much and as often as possible." Her earliest recollections of her own childhood reading include "my mother's telling me stories at bedtime about Brer Rabbit and Brer Fox. Even though my mother never went beyond the second grade, I never tired of listening to her versions of those stories. I remember to this day the way she made those stories real for me. As a result of that enjoyment I read as much as possible."

Johnson was born in Williamsburg, South Carolina, and raised in Philadelphia, where she worked as a volunteer in a local hospital (her activities included reading to patients) while studying at John Bartram High School. After graduating, she settled in Woodbridge, Virginia, and enrolled at George Mason University. Her academic interests include the humanities and the social sciences. She continues to pursue a degree in social work as a part-time student at George Mason and to work full-time for the U.S. Army's Community and Family Support Center in Alexandria, Virginia. The writing she does now consists principally of papers for her major courses as well as "7–12 pieces of business correspondence a day for my job."

Asked to write a three-to-five-page paper responding to Alice Walker's The Color Purple, Johnson discovered in that book "an example of the influence my mother had on my writing." Johnson recognized similarities to the circumstances of her own childhood in the characters and lifestyles depicted in The Color Purple. "The guidance and interpretations of my mother taught me to rise above the circumstances of our life then and now, in my personal life. I wrote the paper because I knew those characters, and it awoke my own lessons of survival." Winning a Bedford Prize has had a greater personal impact than it has "jobwise": "there is a great deal of personal satisfaction—even a trace of immortality. Your writing appears in a book, and other people will be able to read it for as long as the book survives. It was also satisfying to give a kind of immortality to those in my memory whose own chance for earthly recognition and acclaim was long gone. And then there's the continuity—your experience, your past eventually becomes part of someone else's future."

Thank You Miss Alice Walker: The Color Purple

I was required to read the book *The Color Purple* by my English course   1
professor. I enjoy reading and therefore I did not mind the assignment. I read

the first page and closed the book. I was ashamed of the ignorant definitions given to the parts of the body. I was embarrassed by the explicitness of the sex act. I opened and closed the book many times before I could go beyond the first page. But I did read beyond the first page. I understood the lack of communication between Celie and her mother. Celie was fourteen years old and did not understand or appear to know the functions of her body.

A few days after starting to read this book, I was listening to a news report 2 and heard ". . . ten-year-old mother and baby both doing fine. The young girl and her family did not know she was pregnant until she was ready to give birth, after complaining of severe stomach pains." The newscaster went on to say the authorities were questioning two male acquaintances of the family. Celie's circumstance, like that of the child-mother's, is ageless. Miss Walker, you brought the situation out into the open, awakening my senses. I did not want to see it, read it, feel it, or be a part of it. This was no longer "just a reading assignment." I was enthralled. I had to read on. How else would you shock me, embarrass me, and shame me?

My class is comprised of a mixture of nationalities, but only four of us are 3 black and female. I, embarrassingly, thought of all of them reading the lines of shame and ignorance of my people. I listened as one male classmate disassociated himself from the males in the story. I wondered if it was because the characters were black, or was he so naive that he believed such things did not happen? As a contemporary black female, I have buried the Celies of my past. Then why, Miss Walker, do you awaken those emotions? What do you expect to accomplish by telling me how it was, or is? Why, of all the subjects to write about, do you choose one which hurts me so deeply? I am furious with you.

I knew a lot of Celies in my teenage years. I met a few Sofias. I heard about 4 one or two Shug Averys too. I left them behind along with the old neighborhood. Those encounters were during an impoverished and ignorant period of growth. I chose to forget them. I have grown and expanded from the narrowness of my childhood and developed through the heritage passed on to me. I have also risen through the classes of the ruling society. I speak like them, dress like them, yet I know that I am but a shadow of them.

Miss Walker, I was compelled to go on with the reading of The Color Purple. 5 It was the language usage you gave your characters that held my interest this time. My mind's voice spoke the words by Celie so clearly that I could hear Mrs. Brown, from my youth, "Baby, run across to the store. . . ." Sofia became Mama Liz, big boned, dark complected, mammoth breasted, and as stubborn as the day was long, but oh what a heart. She was full of compassion and empathy for all who encountered her. It's the wonderful memories like those that made the reading of your book painful. Celie and Sofia's language was so familiar to me that in spite of the pain, I settled into the good memories the dialogues conjured up. I was also interested in what Nettie had to say, but Nettie's dialogue had connotations of my own language, educated and refined. I heard it every day. It catalyzed no images. But the other characters' dialect brought memories of faces and voices that had long ceased to exist. Those faces had diminished to just a flicker until your book revived them. Those good memories came with the people you portrayed, along with their examples of survival. Some of the people I knew were very much like Shug Avery and many were like Sofia.

Your message was subtle, Miss Walker. Now after the shame, anger, and　6 memories, I continued to read to the end of the story. Your characters came full circle. They survived. They matured and became wiser from their experiences. You showed me how they accomplished that. Sofia's way was that of self-reliance and stubbornness. She was not just physically strong, but she had a strong nature as well. She was also patient and long suffering. I cannot say that Sofia's way was successful because she lost so much. She lost her husband and children to another woman. She lost her freedom to the ruling society, first jail and then to the mayor's family. Shug Avery was independent and worldly. She learned to stroke the egos of the people she could not easily maneuver. Shug was a free spirit, her own person. Celie developed and escaped to a future of her own making by learning another method of survival than the one she lived. Celie took a portion of Sofia's stubbornness and self-reliance and mixed that with a little of Shug's independence and literally walked with a survival plan of her own.

I have read your message, Miss Walker, and anguished through the learning·　7 of it. This teaching of survival will not soon be forgotten because it was too painful an experience to relearn. It is for the lesson learned that I thank you.

Focusing on Earnestine Johnson's Techniques and Revisions

1. One of the distinguishing features of Earnestine Johnson's essay is her honest and intense response to Alice Walker's *The Color Purple*. Reread Johnson's essay carefully aloud. How would you characterize the sound of her *voice?* Does she sound, for example, tough-minded or sentimental, strident or intimidated? Young and impetuous, or experienced and worldly? Some combination of these? None of them? Do you notice any changes in Johnson's voice as the essay proceeds? Support your response by pointing to specific words and phrases.

2. At the beginning of paragraphs 6 and 7 Johnson talks about coming to un-

derstand Alice Walker's "message" in *The Color Purple*. Based on your reading of Johnson's essay only, summarize that "message." With which character in *The Color Purple* does she identify? How can you be sure? How did reading Alice Walker's novel help Johnson come to terms with—to understand better—her own past? What "message" does Johnson's essay offer about the truth of human relationships?

3. What recognition prompts Johnson to regard *The Color Purple* as much more than a "reading assignment"? What impels her to continue reading the novel after her initial reaction to Walker's explicit depiction of sexual experience? Johnson notes that she "had to read on" and proceeds to address Alice Walker directly: "How else would you shock me, embarrass me, and shame me?" How does the evidence of her essay suggest that Johnson answered her own question? What is "the lesson learned" for which she thanks Alice Walker?

4. One of the most striking features of Johnson's essay is her use of direct address. By adopting the second-person point of view, she creates the effect that her readers are privy to a conversation between her and Alice Walker. What are the advantages and disadvantages of this strategy? Be as specific as possible. Initially, what relationship does Earnestine Johnson establish between herself and Alice Walker? When and how does that relationship change as the essay unfolds?

5. Consider Johnson's explanation of the stages in her personal transformation as a result of reading *The Color Purple*: "Upon completing the book, I was able to see the message Ms. Walker conveyed. I found I had a beginning, my anger, a middle, life experiences, and an ending, my expressed gratitude, for my paper." Reread Johnson's essay and identify where each of these three sections begins and ends. List the points Johnson makes in each section.

6. How would you characterize Johnson's relationship to her audience? To what extent does her audience seem to be a presence in her essay? What specific words and phrases indicate who Johnson thinks her readers are (their probable level of intelligence, color, age, social and economic class, etc.)? To what extent must Johnson's readers be acquainted with Walker's novel to appreciate each of her points about the book?

7. One of the unusual features of Johnson's essay is her apparent resistance to being specific. She notes that "being specific . . . was exactly what I was trying to avoid." What do you suspect she hopes to gain by this strategy? What are the advantages and disadvantages of this decision?

8. Johnson explains one of the problems she had writing her essay: "trying to describe the ruling society without actually saying 'white race.' I became so frustrated with the revision of that particular section, I almost gave into being specific. . . . I continued to rework that section until it finally became acceptable to me and, with its connotations, understood by others." Reread paragraph 4 and explain with as much detail as possible exactly how Johnson

accomplishes her aim. What other moments in the essay seem to reflect John-son's decision to make her points indirectly rather than explicitly? What is the *purpose*—the desired effect—of her resistance to being specific in each instance? What are the advantages and disadvantages of this strategy?

9. Johnson describes the goal of her essay as trying to "induce a sense of empathy with my feelings by the examples I gave." What stylistic techniques does Johnson use to induce empathy in her readers? What exactly are the "examples" she uses? Roughly what percentage of them are drawn from *The Color Purple?* From her own experience?

10. Johnson offers the following advice to her readers: "I would have failed in the writing of my essay if I had to advise the reader how to understand or read what I had written. I will state what I use as a 'rule of thumb': begin reading with an open mind, void of any preconceived ideas. This should allow for the possibility of involvement, and then see what, if anything, has been gained from the experience." Apply this "rule of thumb" to Johnson's reading of Alice Walker. How well does Johnson's essay satisfy each of the criteria she establishes? Apply this "rule of thumb" to your reading of Johnson's essay. Identify what you have "gained from the experience."

Suggestions for Writing

1. Discovering books has allowed innumerable readers to explore the life of the mind and discover the self by identifying with the circumstances of literary characters. Richard Wright's autobiography, *Black Boy*, includes the following passage on the transformative power of reading:

> I read Dreiser's *Jennie Gerhardt* and *Sister Carrie* and they revived in me a vivid sense of my mother's suffering; I was overwhelmed. I grew silent, wondering about the life around me. It would have been impossible for me to have told anyone what I derived from these novels, for it was nothing less than life itself. . . . In buoying me up, reading also cast me down, made me see what was possible, what I had missed. My tension returned, new, terrible, bitter, surging, almost too great to be contained. I no longer *felt* that the world about me was hostile, killing; I *knew* it.

Consider your own experience as a reader. What books have you read that have had a profound effect on your sense of identity? Write an expository essay explaining how a particular book helped to transform your own sense of who you are.

2. In *Black Boy*, Richard Wright talks about reading as an addiction: "Reading

was like a drug, a dope." Consider the nature of this *comparison*. Track out as fully as possible the analogy between reading and taking a drug and then write an expository essay developing the analogy.

3. Consider the differences between reading books and watching television as addictions. In what specific ways are these possible "addictions" similar? Different? Write an expository essay in which you *compare and contrast* reading books and watching television as addictive activities.

AN EFFECTIVE TECHNIQUE

Earnestine Johnson uses a peculiar but effective technique for writing an essay about a novel: she addresses the author of the novel directly, referring to Alice Walker as "you." This essay is not a letter to Alice Walker; Johnson clearly intends it to be read by a general audience. She is playing with direct address to create an effect, to make her readers feel that they are being allowed to overhear an important and intimate conversation. Instead of directing our attention entirely to the text, as literary criticism usually does, Johnson tells us the story of her experience reading; we learn as much about Johnson as about the novel.

Direct address makes readers focus on the relationship between "I" and "you"; we see a shifting relationship in Johnson's essay. At first, she wants to avoid Alice Walker and Walker's novel, to have no relationship at all; she shuts the book, "ashamed" and "embarrassed." She is "furious" because, she says, Walker reveals the "shame and ignorance of my people" to the whole world. Johnson not only wishes she did not have to listen to Walker, she wishes her classmates would never have listened either. Yet she reads on, "enthralled."

In paragraphs 4 and 5, Johnson's attitude changes; she says the novel brings back memories that "had diminished to just a flicker" because she had chosen to forget them. We begin to see that it was not merely the book that Johnson was trying to shut at first; it was her own past. We begin to understand why she had to use "I" and "you" in this essay; she is speaking not only to Alice Walker, but also to people in her past. Reading the novel and writing her essay have revived actual personal relationships.

The borders between book and real life blur in the middle of this essay; we begin to feel, as Johnson herself feels, that she is in some ways a character in the book, that Alice Walker is describing Johnson's life. Walker tells how some characters went through painful times but learned how to survive and "walked away" from their shameful pasts. Johnson tells us how she has done the same, has "grown and expanded from the narrowness of my childhood." Moreover, the last paragraph suggests that reading the book has been itself one of the painful experiences that Johnson has survived and learned from.

Johnson is not claiming that every reader will find his or her own life described in Walker's book. Johnson uses "I" and "you" because she is not writing from a universal point of view; she is talking about the experience of a distinct group. Her essay shows that "we" black females who have in "our" lives had a painful time learning to survive in a hostile society will react quite differently to this novel than other people will. Johnson is not excluding these other people; she is actually drawing them closer by helping them understand feelings they cannot completely share.

From Johnson's essay, we can learn to make use of our personal and non-universal feelings in analyzing books (or movies or anything else). We might have a particularly strong reaction to a book written by a person very much like us and wish to write an essay like Johnson's using "I" and "you" to create the sense that we feel a close bond with the author. Or we might react strongly to a book written by a person very much *unlike* us and wish to write an essay angrily addressing the author as "you" to separate ourselves from him or her. A male might write an essay about *The Color Purple*, for example, titled "You Are Wrong, Alice Walker" and argue, "You have presented a distorted picture of men. We are not all cruel and insensitive."

We can also borrow from Johnson the device of making an essay look like a letter. To comment on a bad bill passed by Congress, we could write an essay in the form of an "open letter" to the entire U.S. Senate. Or we could explore our feelings about the death of a friend by writing an essay in the form of a letter to him or her. To see some further examples of such essays, you might look at Ha Song Hi's "From Xraxis to Dzreebo" (p. 217); Mark Twain's "Letter to the Earth" (p. 226), or Richard Selzer's "Letter to a Young Surgeon" (p. 324).

In the next selection, Alice Walker carries the device of writing an imaginary letter a step further; she creates a letter from one person to another, and she is neither of them. Without confronting her readers directly, she shows us that we are all personally involved in an issue most Americans would probably regard as far removed from their own experience: slavery.

ANOTHER ILLUSTRATION OF THE TECHNIQUE

ALICE WALKER

A Letter of the Times,
or Should This Sado-Masochism Be Saved?

Alice Walker describes herself as "preoccupied with the spiritual survival, the survival whole of my people"; she is especially concerned with "exploring the oppressions, the insanities, the loyalties and the triumphs of black women." She has worked for a Head Start program in Mississippi, in voter registration drives in Georgia, on the staff of the New York City welfare department, and as a teacher of literature and black studies in universities across the country. She finds that wherever she goes, black women have been and still are treated as "the mule of the world . . . we have been handed the burdens that everyone else—everyone else—refused to carry." She writes her tales to show that "the black woman is one of America's greatest heroes . . . who has been oppressed beyond recognition."

Walker believes that through her writing she maintains a personal relationship, a "spiritual union," with her ancestors; she seeks to bring her readers to feel the same closeness to their ancestors. As she put it in a subtitle to one of her stories, her works are not only for "you, the reader," but "for your gramma." She is joining in the passing of "the creative spark" from mother to daughter, not expressing her private and original self: "So many of the stories that I write, that we all write, are my mother's stories." After writing The Color Purple, *she experienced what she calls "extraordinary dream-visits" from people long dead who brought her "advice, always excellent and upbeat, sometimes just a hug." Since then, she says, "I have come to believe that only if I am banned from the presence of the ancestors will I know true grief."*

Dear Lucy,

You asked why I snubbed you at the Women for Elected Officials Ball. I   1
don't blame you for feeling surprised and hurt. After all, we planned the ball
together, expecting to raise our usual pisspot full of money for a good cause.
Such a fine idea, our ball: Come as the feminist you most admire! But I did
not know you most admired Scarlett O'Hara and so I was, for a moment, taken
aback.

I don't know; maybe I should see that picture again. Sometimes when I see   2
movies that hurt me as a child, the pain is minor; I can laugh at the things

that made me sad. My trouble with Scarlett was always the forced buffoonery of Prissy, whose strained, slavish voice, as Miz Scarlett pushed her so masterfully up the stairs, I could never get out of my head.

But there is another reason I could not speak to you at the ball that had   3 nothing to do with what is happening just now between us: this heavy bruised silence, this anger and distrust. The day of the ball was my last class day at the University, and it was a very heavy and discouraging day.

Do you remember the things I told you about the class? Its subject was God.   4 That is, the inner spirit, the inner voice; the human compulsion when deeply distressed to seek healing counsel within ourselves, and the capacity within ourselves both to create this counsel and to receive it.

(It had always amused me that the God who spoke to Harriet Tubman and   5 Sojourner Truth told them exactly what they needed to hear, no less than the God of the Old Testament constantly reassured the ancient Jews.)

Indeed, as I read the narratives of black people who were captured and set   6 to slaving away their lives in America, I saw that this inner spirit, this inner capacity for self-comforting, this ability to locate God within that they expressed, demonstrated something marvelous about human beings. Nature has created us with the capacity to know God, to experience God, just as it has created us with the capacity to know speech. The experience of God, or in any case the possibility of experiencing God, *is innate!*

I suppose this has all been thought before; but it came to me as a revelation   7 after reading how the fifth or sixth black woman, finding herself captured, enslaved, sexually abused, starved, whipped, the mother of children she could not want, lover of children she could not have, crept into the corners of the fields, among the haystacks and the animals, and found within her own heart the only solace and love she was ever to know.

It was as if these women found a twin self who saved them from their abused   8 consciousness and chronic physical loneliness; and that twin self is in all of us, waiting only to be summoned.

To prepare my class to comprehend God in this way, I requested they read   9 narratives of these captured black women and also write narratives themselves, as if they *were* those women, or women like them. At the same time, I asked them to write out their own understanding of what the inner voice, "God," is.

It was an extraordinary class, Lucy! With women of all colors, all ages, all   10 shapes and sizes and all conditions. There were lesbians, straights, curveds, celibates, prostitutes, mothers, confuseds, and sundry brilliants of all persuasions! A wonderful class! And almost all of them, though hesitant to admit it at first—who dares talk seriously of "religious" matters these days?—immediately sensed what I meant when I spoke of the inner, companion spirit, of "God."

But what does my class on God have to do with why I snubbed you at the 11 ball? I can hear you wondering. And I will get on to the point.

Lucy, I wanted to teach my students what it felt like to be captured and 12 enslaved. I wanted them to be unable, when they left my class, to think of enslaved women as exotic, picturesque, removed from themselves, deserving of enslavement. I wanted them to be able to repudiate all the racist stereotypes about black women who were enslaved: that they were content, that they somehow "chose" their servitude, that they did not resist.

And so we struggled through an entire semester, during each week of which 13 a student was required to imagine herself a "slave," a mistress or a master, and to come to terms, in imagination and feeling, with what that meant.

Some black women found it extremely difficult to write as captured and 14 enslaved women. (I do not use the word "slaves" casually, because I see enslavement from the enslaved's point of view: there is a world of difference between being a slave and being enslaved). They chose to write as mistress or master. Some white women found it nearly impossible to write as mistress or master, and presumptuous to write as enslaved. Still, there were many fine papers written, Lucy, though there was also much hair tugging and gnashing of teeth.

Black and white and mixed women wrote of captivity, of rape, of forced 15 breeding to restock the master's slave pens. They wrote of attempts to escape, of the sale of their children, of dreams of Africa, of efforts at suicide. No one wrote of acquiescence or of happiness, though one or two, mindful of the religious spirit often infusing the narratives studied, described spiritual ecstasy and joy.

Does anyone want to be a slave? we pondered.   16

As a class, we thought not.   17

Imagine our surprise, therefore, when many of us watched a television spe- 18 cial on sado-masochism that aired the night before our class ended, and the only interracial couple in it, lesbians, presented themselves as mistress and slave. The white woman, who did all the talking, was mistress (wearing a ring in the shape of a key that she said fit the lock on the chain around the black woman's neck), and the black woman, who stood smiling and silent, was— the white woman said—her slave.

And this is why, though we have been friends for over a decade, Lucy, I 19 snubbed you at the ball.

All I had been teaching was subverted by that one image, and I was incensed   20
to think of the hard struggle of my students to rid themselves of stereotype, to
combat prejudice, to put themselves into enslaved women's skins, and then to
see their struggle mocked, and the actual enslaved *condition* of literally millions
of our mothers trivialized—because two ignorant women insisted on their right
to act out publicly a "fantasy" that still strikes terror in black women's hearts.
And embarrassment and disgust, at least in the hearts of most of the white
women in my class.

One white woman student, apparently with close ties to our local lesbian   21
S&M group, said she could see nothing wrong with what we'd seen on TV.
(Incidentally, there were several white men on this program who owned white
women as "slaves," and even claimed to hold legal documents to this effect.
Indeed, one man paraded his slave around town with a horse's bit between
her teeth, and "lent" her out to other sado-masochists to be whipped.) It is
all fantasy, she said. No harm done. Slavery, real slavery, is over, after all.

But it isn't over, Lucy, and Kathleen Barry's book on female sexual slavery   22
and Linda Lovelace's book on *being* such a slave are not the only recent indications that this is true. There are places in the world, Lucy, where human
beings are still being bought and sold! And so, for that reason, when I saw
you at the ball, all I could think was that you were insultingly dressed. No,
that is not all I thought: once seeing you dressed as Scarlett, I could not see
you. I did not *dare* see you. When you accuse me of looking through you, you
are correct. For if I had seen you, Lucy, I'm sure I would have struck you, and
with your love of fighting this would surely have meant the end of our ball.
And so it was better *not* to see you, to look instead at the woman next to you
who had kinked her hair to look like Colette.

A black student said to the S&M sympathizer: I feel abused. I feel my privacy   23
as a black woman has been invaded. Whoever saw that television program can
now look at me standing on the corner waiting for a bus and not see *me* at
all, but see instead a slave, a creature who *would* wear a chain and lock around
my neck for a white person—in 1980!—and accept it. *Enjoy* it.

Her voice shook with anger and hurt.   24

And so, Lucy, you and I will be friends again because I will talk you out of   25
caring about heroines whose real source of power, as well as the literal shape
and condition of their bodies, comes from the people they oppress. But what
of the future? What of the women who will never come together because of
what they saw in the relationship between "mistress" and "slave" on TV? Many
black women fear it is as slaves white women want them; no doubt many white
women think some amount of servitude from black women is their due.

But, Lucy, regardless of the "slave" on television, black women do not want 26
to be slaves. They never wanted to be slaves. We will be ourselves and free,
or die in the attempt. Harriet Tubman was not our great-grandmother for
nothing; which I would advise all black and white women aggressing against
us as "mistress" and "slave" to remember. We understand when an attempt is
being made to lead us into captivity, though television is a lot more subtle
than slave ships. We will simply resist, as we have always done, with ever
more accurate weapons of defense.

As a matter of fact, Lucy, it occurs to me that we might plan another ball 27
in the spring as a benefit for this new resistance. What do you think? Do let
us get together to discuss it, during the week.

Your friend,
Susan Marie

Focusing on Alice Walker's Use of the Second Person

1. What do we learn about Susan Marie and Lucy in the first two paragraphs?
   What do we learn about the two of them by the end of the essay? Which of
   them do we end up knowing best? What seems to be their relationship? How
   do Susan Marie's feelings about Lucy change during the letter?

2. Questions are particularly important in letters; they emphasize the relationship
   between the writer and person he or she is writing to. What is the question
   that Susan Marie is answering in this letter? How do the questions that Susan
   Marie asks in paragraphs 4, 11, 16, 25, and 27 function in the letter? Which
   of these questions seem to be addressed to a wide audience, not merely to Lucy?

3. In paragraph 12, Susan Marie says she wanted her students "to be unable, when
   they left my class, to think of enslaved women as exotic, picturesque, removed
   from themselves, deserving of enslavement." How does this essay function for
   us readers as a similar class; in other words, how does it bring "enslaved women"
   close to our lives? What is Alice Walker saying to us about our everyday lives
   (about such things as how we dress)?

4. In what sense is this letter "of the times" rather than merely of Susan Marie
   and Lucy? "Sado-masochism" in the title refers to much more than the specific
   incident reported on TV. What kinds of sadism (hurting of others) and mas-
   ochism (hurting of oneself) does this letter suggest are parts of "the times" and
   of the lives of ordinary people like us, the readers of this essay?

WORKING WITH THE TECHNIQUE IN YOUR OWN WRITING

1. Write a commentary on a book, a short story, a poem, or a play in the form of a letter to the author. You probably will find it easier to write this essay if you choose a work to which you had a strong reaction. You might make your essay a narrative like Johnson's essay, a story of the experience you had reading the work. Try to analyze why you reacted as you did. Do you think that your reaction was in part due to the similarities or differences between your life and the author's life? You might also be able to write an effective essay about a book that you did not have much reaction to, perhaps humorously complaining to the author about boring you or suggesting how the author could have written a better book.

2. Write an essay about the portrayal of persons like you (teenagers, Asian-Americans, black females, or parents, for example) in a movie, a book, an advertisement, or a series of advertisements for one product. Write the essay in the form of a letter to the director of the movie, the author of the book, or the president of the advertising agency.

3. Write an essay about an attitude or behavior of some people you know that you wish they would change. Write your essay in the form of a letter to one person, perhaps focusing on one incident that you think was especially revealing of what is wrong with the attitude or behavior. See if you can use this one incident to make a general point, as Alice Walker does in her essay.

DIANE KOCOUR

University of Arizona
Tucson, Arizona
Marvin Diogenes, instructor

Diane Kocour describes herself as "an extroverted introvert": "I very much value my time to myself—private time to think and reflect. . . . Curiously, without a time to be by myself for a while, I don't think I would have as much to offer to others." Throughout her years in school, Diane Kocour has "found great joy in getting as involved as possible." The list of her extracurricular activities during her first year at the University of Arizona includes "participating in the honors program, being secretary of Preludes (the freshmen women's honorary society), serving on the promotions committee for the university's Spring Fling, being a member and scholarship deputy of my sorority, Kappa Alpha Theta, and a Goldenheart Little Sister to Sigma Phi Epsilon fraternity, . . . and, most recently, being president of Arizona Ambassadors (a student recruitment organization)." Her community service activities include volunteer work on the Larry Smith Cancer Run, the Campus Cleanup Program, the Arthritis Foundation, and the Saint Luke's Women's Home. Her academic honors range from receiving several scholarships to being named to the Dean's List and gaining a finalist's ranking in the Freshman Greek Woman of the Year competition. She has also earned numerous writing awards, among them first prize in the 1986 Scottsdale Board of Realtors Association Essay Contest for an essay entitled "What Home Means to Me."

Although she has not yet declared a major, she reports that "I am very seriously considering a general studies major, which would enable me to concentrate on three different areas—communications, creative writing, and media arts. . . . I am looking for a career that will involve dealing with and speaking to people, utilizing creativity and writing skills, and will offer variety and challenge."

Writing serves Diane Kocour as "a way for me to keep in touch with myself—in a sense, to get to know myself better. My parents have always encouraged me to express my feelings on paper, with diaries, as well as with letters. Soon I realized that by writing things down, I could make my whole outlook on life better. I could purge myself of emotion and at the same time seem to clarify things and put life in perspective." The easiest part of writing for Kocour is to write about something about which she cares deeply: "When the words begin to flow, I feel like I am in my own world. . . . This state of writing is almost hypnotic to me, and it gives me quite a high. . . . The big challenge for me in writing is to make the readers experience the same feeling that I did. When this is accomplished, I consider my paper a success."

Diane Kocour wrote "The Diet Industry Knows Best—Or Does It?" in response to an assignment that, as she recalls, required her to write "a documented argumentative essay which would be interesting, controversial, factual, and, above all, one which I had strong opinions on or some type of background in." After a period of uncertainty, she decided to draw on the personal struggle she was then in the process of battling: "a compulsive eating disorder" that had carried her "dangerously close to bulimia." After some hesitancy about how to proceed, she made rapid progress:

> Initially I wasn't quite sure of how to put something so emotional into a category that could be factual and argumentative. This question was answered when I took the time to sit down and assess exactly what it was that had gotten me into such a dangerous situation. . . . It became clear that I was just one of many who had become obsessed with an industry that promised quick and effective results and imprisoned helpless people to lives of food dependency and self-blame. I realized that I held within myself tremendous anger for this industry and also realized that it could be a subject which would be capable of being researched and reported on. I had stumbled on a topic that satisfied all the [course] requirements, and one which I could hardly wait to begin researching.

The Diet Industry Knows Best— Or Does It?

Strolling down the aisles of a local supermarket in search of low-cal salad dressing, reusable coffee filters, or perhaps some other item on her shopping list, a customer may be distracted for a moment by a large, attention-getting sign that says something to the effect of "Lose Weight Fast," "Lose Weight Without Going Hungry," or even "Lose Weight Deliciously." At this point, the shopper may become sidetracked and, throwing a critical glance downward over her figure, may casually meander toward the aisle where the colorful sign broadcasts the attractive proposition. Suddenly she is bombarded with name brands of appetite-suppressing drugs such as maximum strength Thinz-Span, Prolamine, Dex-a-Diet, Dexatrim, Acutrim, Fibre-Trim, Appendrine, Dietene, Diurex, and Ayds Candies. Scanning further down the shelf, she is confronted by various formula diets including Slender Diet Meal, Ensure, Sego Lite, Nutrament, and Slim Fast. Later, when pushing her cart down the frozen-food aisle, she notices such low-calorie dinners as Weight Watchers and Lean Cuisine. And of course driving home with her groceries while listening to the radio, there's a good chance that her favorite tunes will be interrupted with advertisements for clinics like Diet Center, Nutri-System, or Weight Watchers. But society's emphasis on the perfect body doesn't even end there, because between the pages of popular magazines, a new fad diet is published every week, and on the shelves of bookstores and libraries all over the United States various diet books broadcast titles made up by a myriad of diet authorities, each proclaiming that his approach to losing weight is the right one.

An observer from another culture may see this multimillion dollar industry 2 as madness, and rightly so, but in our culture it reflects an aspect of life that has been emphasized throughout the history of mankind: the pursuit of thinness and the fear of and disgust toward body fat. This pursuit of thinness began as early as Greek and Roman times, when Socrates was reported to dance every morning to keep his figure, and Roman women would swallow sand to ruin their stomachs. It continued with the corset in the mid-1800s, was exemplified by the flat-chested, lean, angular flapper of the 1920s, and in the 1960s was portrayed again by a 5'7", 92-pound teenage idol known as "Twiggy." In a study done by Canadian investigators of *Playboy* centerfolds from 1959 to 1978, it was found that average weight in relation to height declined by 8% (Irwin 10). On top of all this, the Miss America contestants and winners have been getting much thinner. Yet, despite this current emphasis on the necessity of thinness, the average American woman has become fatter (Irwin 10). So has the average American man. Daniel Cappon, author of *Eating, Loving, and Dying,* points out that four in ten North Americans are overweight, and one in three is obese (Cappon 58).

In addition to the increasing numbers of overweight people, there has been 3 increasing fear of and disgust toward body fat. In the April 1986 issue of *Psychology Today,* three Old Dominion University psychologists report that roughly half of all Americans are afraid of becoming fat. In a survey of 30,000 readers, 63% of women and 44% of men reported being afraid of being fat (Zaslow 1). The reason? Just as thinness is associated with beauty, fitness, and success, obesity is equated with failure, laziness, and dishonesty, and obese persons are often the object of discrimination (Zaslow 1). In fact, a 1979 study in the *Journal of Sociology of Work and Occupations* revealed that obese persons are considered less desirable employees. Similarly, *Industry Week* magazine reports that each pound of fat could cost an executive $1000 a year in salary. As a result of society's emphasis on the beauty of thinness and the attendant consequences of not being thin, America's obsession to be thin has become a $10-billion-a-year diet and exercise industry ("Fear of Fat" WH14). It is this obsession to be thin that completely imprisons people, making them victims of an industry that capitalizes on the impatience and nutritional ignorance of people who are in search of the perfect body at the same time that it claims to be helping them.

Marketing diet aids and ideas seems to fall into three basic categories: fad 4 and crash diets, formulas, and drugs. Each of them may be successful for a short time but in the long run proves to be ineffective, actually contributing to obesity, or even potentially dangerous. Virtually all of them trap the dieter in a vicious cycle of obsessive and dependent behavior. Edward E. Abramson, author of *Behavioral Approaches to Weight Control,* summed it up when he said, "The average American diet has been estimated to last between sixty to ninety days, but the dieter is off the diet approximately half the time. The typical weight watcher will go through this ritual approximately one to twenty-five times per year. Whatever weight is lost is regained" (13). Similarly, statistics show that only three percent of those who take off weight keep it off, and Dr. Maria Simonsen, a former director of the Johns Hopkins University health, weight, and stress clinic, reports, "Less than 6% of existing diets are effective, and 13% are downright hazardous." (Burros C1)

Examples of fad or crash diets are those that appear in magazines or books, 5 such as the "grapefruit diet," "the rice diet," "the drinking man's diet," "the ice cream and bananas diet," "the amazing-new-you diet," and the "no will-power diet" (Jeffrey and Katz 31). They are attractive to those wishing to lose weight because they are unusual, some of them appetizing, and all of them promise quick results. But the appearance and disappearance of so many diets over the years, months, weeks, and even days should say something about the effectiveness of all of them. Most of them fail simply because they fail to teach the dieter anything about changing eating habits for good. Therefore when the diet is stopped, the dieter will gain all the weight back when he resumes his normal eating habits (Jeffrey and Katz 29). Michael H. K. Irwin, M.D., M.P.H., noted that asthma and other illnesses become worse when a person is on a crash diet (11). Obviously fad and crash diets are not the answer.

Similarly, both formula diets and appetite-suppressing drugs are ineffective, 6 habit-forming, and dangerous as well. Just as formula diets have been linked with various side effects such as nausea, dehydration, electrolyte imbalance, hair loss, constipation, and cramps, diet drugs have been known to cause dangerously high blood pressure, kidney failure, stroke, and psychotic reactions (Burros C1). Furthermore, in 1978 it was reported that 58 people, each limited to 300 calories daily by formula diets for two months or longer, died from cardiac arrhythmia (Burros C1). The risks involved in turning to the diet industry definitely outweigh the benefits—especially since there *are* no proven benefits! All of the diet industry's methods of reducing install a false sense of security in the dieter, thus causing him to place all of his confidence in ready-made fad diet, pill-form methods, rather than searching himself for the answers.

In addition to the solid evidence that proves the various diet industry at- 7 tempts at losing weight are ineffective, both nutritional experts and psychol-

ogists have their own theories of *why* these methods don't work. They also
have theories on what *will* work, and the differences between the schemes
proposed by the diet industry as compared to the solutions given by nutritionists and psychologists show that the diet industry is basically leading its
customers farther and farther away from safe, effective, and permanent
weight loss.

With nutritionists, the major premise is simple: being overweight is the   8
result of too much eating and too little exercise. With this assumption in
mind, weight control experts point out that no diet pill can take weight off
unless calories consumed are less than calories expended (Brody C1). Furthermore, they say, "Hundreds of studies have shown that the faster [a person]
loses weight, the faster [that person is] likely to regain it, and a few pounds
extra besides" (Brody C1). They also maintain that fasting and dieting go
against the body's built-in defense mechanism. In times of starvation, for example, the body burns off fewer calories, and when extra calories are consumed,
the body burns off more. Therefore, reducing calorie intake by more than 500
calories a day may actually cause weight loss to stop, and even worse, when
the diet is over, previously sustaining amounts of food may become fattening.
So dieting actually ruins a person's metabolism, thus contributing, once again,
to obesity (Brody C1). Nutritionists believe that exercise is most beneficial to
weight loss, as it not only permanently increases metabolic rate, but also de-
presses the appetite and makes a person feel better about himself. They encourage wishful reducers to combine exercise with a slightly lower intake of
well-balanced meals. The results here, they say, come slowly and are permanent
(Wills 29).

Nutrition experts explain that one reason an uninformed dieter may become   9
a customer to the diet industry can be attributed to the industry's ability to
fool a dieter into thinking its weight loss methods are safe and even healthy.
Marian Burros, in her article "The Diet Game, Where Chances of Winning
Are Slim," said, "Most diet book authors [and the diet industry as well] prey
on a basic ignorance of nutrition. They sound scientific, scattering such words
as metabolism, immunology, and amino acids through their texts. But they do
not play on the one indisputable fact of weight loss—that success requires the
dieter to expend more calories than are consumed" (C1). This is easily exemplified by the once popular "Rice Diet," which promises a loss of 25 pounds
in two weeks. Upon taking the time to sit down and figure out how this could
possibly be true, one will discover that the promise of quick weight loss could
be legitimate only if a person reduces caloric intake by 5000 calories a day.
Obviously this is impossible when the average person eats only 1500 to 3000
calories daily (Brody C1).

Psychologists, in contrast to nutritionists, assume a slightly different ap- 10
proach to losing weight. Most psychologists don't believe in dieting at all,
whether it be by using diet industry attempts or following the advice of doctors
and nutritionists. One problem they pinpoint in dieting is the involved factor
of deprivation. Edward E. Abramson, in his book *Behavioral Approaches to
Weight Control*, explains that dieting makes food a reinforcer and that deprivation makes reinforcers more powerful. He goes on to say that "If you deprive
yourself of foods which you especially like, soon they will be so powerful a
reinforcer that they will overcome your willpower" (82). Three psychologists,
who conducted an "Anti-Diet Approach to Weight Loss in a Group Setting,"
likened dieting to a parental concept. In an article published in the *Transactional Analysis Journal*, they explained that deprivation represses the "free
child," brings on a temptation to cheat, and causes the "child" to rebel by
binging. They say that the more restrictive the "parent" is, the more the
"child" binges, and that furthermore, the "child" always wins (Lister et al.
69–70).

Stop and think about that for a moment. When a person diets, by crash 11
diet, pills, or formula, he is telling his body as he would tell a child, "I don't
trust you enough to know how to choose healthy, low calorie foods for yourself,
so I'm going to force you to do what this diet expert says." According to these
psychologists, sooner or later the body is going to rebel, craving foods that
aren't supplied by the diet and making up for all it has been deprived of. The
typical person will feel guilty after this binge and impose even more pressure
on the body. But the body will continue to win, thus creating an internal
struggle, corrupting a dieter's natural instincts, and causing the victim to completely lose confidence in himself and his instincts. Soon people end up putting
all their trust in an industry that capitalizes on the very weaknesses it has
created in them. These psychologists believe that eliminating deprivation will
result in a permanent change in eating habits, followed by a healthy and
effortless loss of weight.

Other psychologists attribute overeating to underlying emotional conflicts. 12
In a study of 500 overweight people, Dr. Charles Freed found that 470 of them
definitely ate more when they were nervous, worried, or idle (Irwin 5). In
addition, food is often used to express love, hate, control, hunger, and hurt.
It is used as a pacifier, a reward, punishment, stress reliever, and in celebration.
Hunger is confused with being tired, lonely, or bored ("Fear of Fat" WH14).
As Edward E. Abramson suggests, "eating serves as an anxiety-reducing mech-
anism for the obese" (7). This explains why psychologists resent diets imposed
on patients—whether they be self-imposed or recommended by doctors. Daniel
Cappon, in his book *Eating, Loving and Dying*, states, "Any diet, whether

obtained in mimeographed form from a doctor's secretary on the way out of his office, or from the latest best-selling paperback, treats symptoms only, and that simply is not good enough." If the overeating is a result of an emotional problem, it follows that the problem must be treated, rather than the symptom alone. Therefore, these psychiatrists believe that a person who is trying to reduce should forget about losing weight, discover the underlying emotional problem, and take care of that. They believe that the symptoms will take care of themselves (Cappon 58). Barbara Sternberg, Ph.D., explains, "learning to handle stress and other negative feelings without turning to food is the diet dropout's biggest challenge" (59).

But "diet dropout" doesn't come so easily to those who have become en- 13 tangled in the web of the diet industry. The ironic thing about this industry is that although fad diets, formulas, and appetite suppressants obviously have little or no long-term effect, people don't seem to realize it and definitely tend to overlook the dangers involved in using them as well. Statistics from a book called *Nutrition and Obesity Management* show that 53% of the adult population surveyed in 1980 reported efforts to lose weight and that furthermore, at any given time, 20% of the population are on some kind of weight program. These facts could be attributed to the obsessive and vicious circle that dieting creates. Judith Wills, editor of the FDA's drug bulletin, a publication for health professionals, said, "Some of these products can produce quick weight loss. But they rarely have any permanent effect and often send dieters into a cycle of quick weight loss, rebound weight gain when normal eating is resumed, and even more difficulty losing weight when the next diet is attempted" (26).

The unfortunate thing is that when a dieter regains lost weight because of 14 purely natural reasons, he often ends up blaming himself for a lack of willpower or a failure to stick to the diet. His self-image suffers a dangerous blow, he loses confidence in his ability to trust himself, and he becomes even more submissive to the commands of an industry that promises instant and painless results. Barbara Sternberg points out that "feeling bad about themselves is probably the single most important reason that people stay fat" (58). But fat people are what the diet industry thrives on, so why *not* lead the customers into an endless cycle of weight loss and weight gain?

Another thing that many people tend to overlook is the ignorance of the 15 diet industry on nutritional matters and the lack of approval by not only doctors and nutritionists but the Food and Drug Administration as well. For example, consider herbal blends, which are powdered or other mixtures that are supposed to be taken with meals. These are usually promoted by "independent counselors" who have had no nutritional or medical training. They are usually sold through various quick-profit incentive programs (Wycoff 22). In addition to this, the First Amendment to the Constitution protects claims and opinions cited in articles or books in dietary regimens (Wycoff 23). This means that the authors of the popular best selling books on how to take off weight or reduce inches aren't even required to have any nutritional or educational background, let alone medical expertise.

Besides lack of nutritional familiarity, many attempts of the diet industry 16 lack FDA approval as well. Not only does the FDA recommend against the use of amphetamines and laxatives used in weight loss clinics, it also never approved other popular methods of weight loss like the grapefruit diet pill or HCG, a hormone extracted from the urine of pregnant women, which is supposed to enable a person to lose weight without eating less (Wycoff 20). One drug, called PPA (phenylpopanolamine), similar to amphetamines, was put on the market after an advisory panel to the FDA, based on what it admitted was a "scientifically deficient, unpublished, unnamed study," said it was safe and effective for over-the-counter sale. Before the FDA even endorsed the panel's report, diet sales doubled to $200 million in 1980. It's interesting to note that reports of adverse effects like high blood pressure, dizziness, headache, heart palpitations, rashes, nausea, and chest tightness multiplied as well (Brody C1).

It seems that the diet industry is not only ignorant when it comes to nu- 17 tritional matters, it is uncaring and indifferent to the dangers and obsessive behaviors that it is subjecting its customers to but also ultimately unconcerned with actually helping people lose weight. Therefore, its main motive must be to make money, and to make lots of it, at that. Statistical reports show that each week over one million people participate in group weight loss programs (Storlie and Jordan 3) and that more than ten million Americans, 90% of them women, swallow diet pills daily (Brody C1). Of the $10 billion yearly generated by the diet industry, $800 million alone goes for frozen diet dinners and entrees, and $400 million goes for services and products carrying the Weight Watchers name. By the same token, $200 million worth of nonprescription diet pills are sold annually, as well as $150 million worth of low calorie powders. With all this money coming in, why would any "diet officials" want to admit that the diet industry didn't have the answers to permanently losing weight? Those diet experts that do acknowledge the weaknesses of the diet industry are outnumbered by the increasing multitude of others who continue to make their livings from it.

Even though the diet industry won't admit its weaknesses, it's surprising 18 that after failing so many times with so many different industry attempts to help people lose weight, dieters don't realize for themselves that this industry is nothing but a corrupt, insensitive, unjust attempt at making money from people who are frantically in search of a foolproof way of losing weight for good. Or should it really be all that astonishing? Why do people turn to the diet industry in the first place? After seeing stick-thin models strut across fashion pages, svelte, fit dancers leap across the stage, and sexy, lean actresses charm their way through soap operas and movies, the average woman might take one disgusted look at her own body and say, "I want to look like that. I need to lose weight. And I need to lose it now." And after observing what effects obesity has on the job, on health and the average life span, and on happiness in general, the male in addition to the female might be feeling something similar.

In their frantic and desperate attempts for a weight-loss solution, many 19 people seem to overlook the proven facts that it takes six months or longer to make lasting changes on eating behavior (Brody C1) and that lasting weight loss is a lifetime endeavor rather than an overnight success (Wills 29). When strolling down that supermarket aisle they are enthralled by the sign that shouts "Lose weight fast, effortlessly, and deliciously" and ignorantly place all of their faith in the product that is being advertised. As Susan Wycoff asserts in her article "Diet Fads Waste Money, Not Pounds," "Many of the estimated 50 million overweight Americans dream of losing weight quickly and painlessly without changing basic dietary and exercise habits. And numerous promoters of weight loss products and techniques have sought to capitalize on this paradox" (20). It's as simple as that.

The unfortunate thing is that not only are we fooling ourselves in believing 20 that dieting is the answer, but we are also handing down our insecurities, mistrust of our bodily instincts, and obsessive behaviors to our children, who will carry on the tradition of supporting the dieting industry until it generates enough money to feed all the starving children in Ethiopia. Studies already show that 80% of fourth grade girls are dieting. Darryl Pure, a Chicago psychologist, explains, "Kids pick up on our insecurities. We need to teach them healthy eating habits without going crazy over it" (Zaslow 1). But first we need to learn them ourselves.

The answer, obviously, lies not in the hands of the diet industry. This 21 multimillion dollar industry has been successful in causing deaths with its dangerous, habit-forming, untested formula diets and pill-form solutions. It has been successful in showing people how to center their lives around the manipulation of food. Most importantly, it has been successful in causing people to lose touch with their bodily instincts and to sacrifice their self-confidence and trust of themselves. It has thrown them into a prison of obsessive behaviors that has left them crying out for a new and improved formula for instant weight loss. All of this it has been successful in, but very rarely has it been successful in helping people to achieve the weight loss that it supposedly set out to help people do. All of this is a very sad thing, for just as the great Roman statesman Seneca said very long ago, "No one is free who is a slave to the body" (Vincent 5), it can be said in modern times, "No one is free who is a slave to the diet industry."

Works Cited

Abramson, Edward E. *Behavioral Approaches to Weight Control.* New York: Springer Publishing Co., 1977, pp. 7, 8, 10, 12, 13, 82.

Brody, Jane E. "Pills to Aid the Dieter: How Safe Are They?" *New York Times,* November 9, 1983, p. C1.

Burros, Marian. "The Diet Game, Where Chances of Winning Are Slim." *New York Times,* July 16, 1986, p. C1.

Cappon, Daniel. *Eating, Loving and Dying.* Toronto: University of Toronto Press, 1973, pp. 58, 88, 93, 97.

"Fear of Fat—Does Obsession with Weight Reflect a Distorted Self-Image?" *Washington Post,* April 30, 1986, p. WH14.

Irwin, Michael H. K., M.D., M.P.H. "Overweight a Problem for Millions." Public Affairs Pamphlet No. 364, Public Affairs Committee, Inc., 1964, pp. 5, 10, 11, 18.

Jeffrey, D. Balfour, and Katz, Roger C. *Take It Off and Keep It Off.* Englewood Cliffs, NJ: Prentice-Hall, 1977, pp. xi, 1, 12, 14, 15, 29–33.

Lister et al. "An Anti-Diet Approach to Weight Loss in a Group Setting." *Transactional Analysis Journal* (January 1985), pp. 69–70.

Sternberg, Barbara, Ph.D. "How to End Diet Failure." *Ladies' Home Journal* (June 1986), pp. 58, 59, 164.

Storlie, Jean, and Jordan, Henry A., M.D. *Nutrition and Exercise in Obesity Management.* New York: Spectrum Publications, 1984, pp. 1–3, 13.

Vincent, L. M., M.D. *Competing with the Sylph.* New York: Andrews and McMeel, 1979, pp. 5, 12.

Wills, Judith. "The Fad-Free Diet: How to Take Weight Off (and Keep It Off) Without Getting Ripped Off." *FDA Consumer* (July/August 1985), pp. 26, 27, 29.

Wycoff, Susan. "Diet Fads Waste Money, Not Pounds." *Consumers' Research* (April 1986), pp. 20–23.

Zaslow, Jeffrey. "Fourth Grade Girls These Days Ponder Weighty Matters; They Join the Dieting Craze Even if They Are Thin." *Wall Street Journal,* February 11, 1986, p. 1.

Focusing on Diane Kocour's Techniques and Revisions

1. Summarize the main points of Diane Kocour's argument. On behalf of what *thesis*—what controlling idea—are these points summoned? Where does Kocour state her thesis?

2. Diane Kocour explains that the goal of her essay quickly became "a quest" for her: "to expose the dieting industry for what it really is, to inform people of the dangers involved in depending on it, and to persuade them to abandon it and to look to themselves for the answers the diet industry prides itself on

telling people it possesses." Explain why you do or do not find Kocour's argument convincing. What do you think a representative of the diet industry would say in response to each of Kocour's major points?

3. Consideration of opposing views is an essential feature of a convincing argument. Where and how does Kocour explain and then refute opposing arguments?

4. One of the outstanding features of Diane Kocour's essay is her ability to synthesize large amounts of information and to present it clearly. Review the structure of her essay. What principle of organization does she establish for the points she makes: increasing complexity? increasing importance? increasing emotion? something else? Explain. Kocour's artful blend of so much information depends on her successful use of transitions. Reread her essay and identify the most effective of these transitions. In this respect, comment on the contribution of paragraph 8 to the overall plan of her essay.

5. Diane Kocour's essay offers an example of a research paper that has its origins in the writer's strong reaction to a subject. What evidence reveals Kocour's strong reaction to the diet industry? To what extent is Kocour able and willing to restrain her passionate response to this subject?

6. How would you characterize Kocour's *tone*—her attitude toward her subject, expressed in her choice of words and sentence structure—in this essay? What does her tone contribute to her essay's overall impact? Does her tone remain consistent throughout her essay? Point to specific words and phrases to support your response.

7. Kocour reports that the readers she imagined for her essay included not only her instructor and classmates but also "a multitude of average people, like myself, who were relying on this industry for some type of beneficial result—especially teenagers, who are so obsessed with looking and feeling the way today's society demands through the media and fashion industry: THIN. I imagined my audience as either people who hadn't yet realized the struggle they were about to throw themselves into or people who were already involved in it, who were so plagued with insecurity and self-doubt that they were too blind to see the real cause of their problems." How successfully does Kocour balance her attention to these two, quite different audiences? Point to specific passages to support your response.

8. Characterize the nature and the extent of the background information Kocour provides for her readers. How useful do you find this information? Explain. What, for example, is the effect of Kocour's having provided historical information on dieting in paragraph 2? What does this information contribute to her essay? How does this information advance her argument and help establish her purpose?

9. Diane Kocour's method of revision produces "pages of messy corrections and

a great deal of rewriting. . . . The most difficult aspect of revising is discovering that something needs to be added or deleted. . . . Rearranging ideas into a different order is by far the most complicated and tedious process of all, as it involves both adding and deleting. Even after it has been done, the paper must be read over and revised again. The most difficult aspect of rearranging ideas is that it tends to present new problems." Kocour wrote three drafts of "The Diet Industry." In her second draft, the paragraph below followed what is now paragraph 16 in the final version:

> Does this mean that the diet industry is not only ignorant when it comes to nutritional matters, but also uncaring and indifferent to the dangers and obsessive behaviors that it is subjecting its customers to? Most of the evidence gathered by the nutritional experts shows that it is. According to Marian Burros, in her article "The Diet Game, Where Chances of Winning Are Slim," "Most diet book authors [and the industry as well] prey on basic ignorance of nutrition. They sound scientific, scattering such words as metabolism, immunology, and amino acids through their texts. But they do not play on the one indisputable, and for the diet industry's customers often easily overlooked, fact of weight loss—that success requires the dieter to expend more calories than are consumed" (Burros C1). This is easily exemplified by the once popular "Rice Diet," which promises a loss of 25 pounds in two weeks. Upon taking the time to sit down and figure out how this could possibly be true, one will discover that the promise of quick weight loss could be legitimate only if a person reduces intake by 5000 calories a day. Obviously this is impossible when the average person eats only 1500 to 3000 calories daily (Brody C1).

What revisions did Kocour make in this paragraph? Where does the information in it appear in her final draft? With what effect(s)?

10. Reread the first sentence in paragraph 20 in Kocour's essay. Here is how it appeared in her previous draft:

> The unfortunate thing is that not only are we fooling ourselves in believing that dieting is the answer, but we are also handing down our insecurities, mistrust of our bodily instincts, and obsessive behaviors to our children, who will carry on the sickening traditions of supporting the ugly

dieting industry until it is generating enough money to buy
all the tea in China.

What specific changes has Kocour made in her final draft? In what ways does
her revised version more successfully support her thesis? What changes, if any,
might she make to further strengthen her final draft?

Suggestions for Writing

1. Diane Kocour cites an *Industry Week* magazine report that claims that "each
   pound of fat could cost an executive $1000 a year in salary." What are the
   "costs" of being overweight in America? Conduct some research on the literal
   and figurative costs of being overweight in this country, and write an essay
   using an impassioned tone to convince Americans that they are slowly killing
   themselves by overeating. Advocate some sensible solution to this national
   problem.
2. Kocour's argument maintains that American corporations profit from acts that
   are socially and medically irresponsible. But corporations also profit—both literally and figuratively—from socially responsible actions. Describe one such
   socially responsible action performed by an American corporation, and in a
   well-argued essay convince your readers that individuals should perform similar
   acts.

AN EFFECTIVE TECHNIQUE

Underlying most argumentative essays is a desire to attack and destroy, to
root out evils. We restrain ourselves from using the violent language that would
match our feelings because we know that if we scream curses, people will want
to eliminate us, not those at whom we are screaming. But if we just present
facts and figures "objectively," we run the risk of having our readers fail to see
the dramatic story those figures are supposed to reveal. Merely saying that 84
percent of Americans eat butter will not inspire much reaction, but if we can
establish that eating butter can be fatal, then we can use that statistic to say
"84 percent of Americans are killing themselves." An effective argument requires both the precision of the figure, 84 percent, and the drama of the phrase
"killing themselves." Diane Kocour shows us how to present evidence objectively while maintaining an impassioned tone throughout an entire essay.

Kocour begins by presenting a dramatic scene and then uses facts and figures to show that her scene is typical of what is happening all over the country every day. In her first paragraph, she creates a vignette of a person being "sidetracked" and then "bombarded" by advertising for dozens of diet aids. In the vignette, Kocour does not use particularly impassioned words, but rather puts her readers in the middle of the drama; she bombards us with brand names in three separate lists and makes us feel confused and even a bit anxious. Immediately after the opening anecdote, Kocour directly identifies and attacks the villain of her scene: she says that we should see the multimillion-dollar diet industry as "madness"; that it "imprisons" people; that it "trap[s] the dieter in a vicious cycle of obsessive and dependent behavior" (paragraph 4). She lets us know quite explicitly that her essay will tell a tale of a powerful, insidious force that manipulates the minds of unsuspecting individuals.

Kocour repeats her impassioned attacks on the diet industry throughout the essay, but only in a few words at a time, scattered across paragraphs of facts and figures. In paragraph 11, she speaks of "corrupting a dieter's natural instincts"; in paragraph 13, of people "entangled in the web of the diet industry." This impassioned language provides a framework for readers to see what all the facts and figures that fill the essay add up to. It is as if Kocour were most of the time carefully and scientifically describing some giant creature inch by inch, but occasionally stepping back so that we can see that this creature is a horrible monster, imprisoning people and driving them insane.

Toward the end of her essay, the dramatic language increases; Kocour has provided enough facts to justify getting thoroughly angry. The strong words begin piling on each other: the industry is "nothing but a corrupt, insensitive, unjust attempt at making money" (paragraph 18). She keeps the emotion building right up to her final, ringing line: "No one is free who is a slave to the diet industry." She has passed beyond merely calling the diet industry evil; she indicts it as an enemy of American democracy. It is destroying individual freedom.

Kocour shows us how to carefully control passionate language, spacing it out among calmer passages. Deciding how passionate to be in an essay is not easy; it depends on how strongly we feel, on the purpose of writing, and on the audience. Political speeches sometimes become entirely passionate rhetoric, especially when leaders are trying to inspire people who are already convinced on an issue to take strong action such as going to war or breaking laws. But even revolutionaries who seek to overthrow governments recognize that facts usually increase the effectiveness of a passionate manifesto.

In the next selection, the Declaration of Independence, Thomas Jefferson very delicately balances passionate denunciation of King George III and the presentation of objective evidence of the king's tyranny. Our reverential respect for our forefathers sometimes causes us overlook the anger in the Declaration; we imagine that it must be written in stately, formal prose. However, it is hard to miss the intensity of feeling of a sentence such as this description of King George: "He has plundered our seas, ravaged our Coasts, burnt our towns and destroyed the Lives of our people."

ANOTHER ILLUSTRATION OF THE TECHNIQUE

THOMAS JEFFERSON

The Declaration of Independence

Thomas Jefferson was a paradoxical man, an aristocrat with a strong commitment to democracy. Raised on a large Virginia estate, Jefferson studied classical language and literature in his youth, as did all upper-class boys in the eighteenth century. He first heard about the principles of republicanism in college, from a professor of mathematics, William Small. Small converted Jefferson to the Scottish Common Sense school, which is a philosophy based on the belief that the highest faculty is the moral sense, which is equally present in all people. Small guided Jefferson into the study of law and urged him to enter politics. When Jefferson, at age thirty-three, was selected to write the Declaration of Independence, he drew on the principles he had learned from Small. He did not see the task as requiring him to consult the great geniuses of the past or to exercise his own genius: "I turned to neither book nor pamphlet while writing it. I did not consider it part of my charge to invent new ideas, but merely to place before mankind the common sense of the subject."

Jefferson's colleagues did not share his "common sense." Though they had selected him because he usually wrote in a moderate tone, they found his first draft of the Declaration too inflammatory and cut a third of it. Years later, after the Revolution, after he had served as third president of the new country, he was still angry that his draft of the Declaration had been cut; he saw the trimming as an act of cowardice and compromise: "The pusillanimous idea that we had friends in England worth keeping terms with still haunted the minds of many. For this reason, those passages which conveyed censures on the people of England were struck out, lest they should give them offence. The clause, too, reprobating the enslaving the inhabitants of Africa, was struck out in complaisance to South Carolina and Georgia. . . . Our northern brethren also, I believe, felt a little tender under those censures; for though their people had very few slaves themselves, yet they had been pretty considerable carriers of them to others."

When in the course of human events, it becomes necessary for one people 1 to dissolve the political bands which have connected them with another, and to assume among the Powers of the earth, the separate and equal station to which the Laws of Nature and Nature's God entitle them, a decent respect to the opinions of mankind requires that they should declare the causes which impel them to the separation.

We hold these truths to be self-evident, that all men are created equal, that 2 they are endowed by their Creator with certain unalienable Rights, that among these are Life, Liberty and the pursuit of Happiness.

That to secure these rights, Governments are instituted among Men, de- 3 riving their just powers from the consent of the governed.

That whenever any Form of Government becomes destructive of these ends, 4 it is the Right of the People to alter or to abolish it, and to institute a new Government laying its foundation on such principles and organizing its powers in such form, as to them shall seem most likely to effect their Safety and Happiness. Prudence, indeed, will dictate that Governments long established should not be changed for light and transient causes; and accordingly all experience hath shown that mankind are more disposed to suffer, while evils are sufferable, than to right themselves by abolishing the forms to which they are accustomed. But when a long train of abuses and usurpations pursuing invariably the same Object evinces a design to reduce them under absolute Despotism, it is their right, it is their duty, to throw off such government, and to provide new Guards for their future security.

Such has been the patient sufferance of these Colonies; and such is now 5 the necessity which constrains them to alter their former Systems of Government. The history of the present King of Great Britain is a history of repeated injuries and usurpations, all having in direct object the establishment of an absolute Tyranny over these States. To prove this, let Facts be submitted to a candid world.

He has refused his Assent to laws, the most wholesome and necessary for 6 the public good.

He has forbidden his Governors to pass Laws of immediate and pressing 7 importance, unless suspended in their operation till his Assent should be obtained; and when so suspended, he has utterly neglected to attend to them.

He has refused to pass other Laws for the accommodation of large districts 8 of people, unless those people would relinquish the right of Representation in the Legislature, a right inestimable to them and formidable to tyrants only.

He has called together legislative bodies at places unusual, uncomfortable, 9 and distant from the depository of their Public Records, for the sole purpose of fatiguing them into compliance with his measures.

He has dissolved Representative Houses repeatedly, for opposing with manly 10 firmness his invasions on the rights of the people.

He has refused for a long time, after such dissolutions, to cause others to be 11 elected; whereby the Legislative Powers, incapable of Annihilation, have returned to the People at large for their exercise; the State remaining in the mean time exposed to all the danger of invasion from without, and convulsions within.

He has endeavored to prevent the population of these States; for that pur- 12 pose obstructing the Laws of Naturalization of Foreigners; refusing to pass others to encourage their migration hither, and raising the conditions of new Appropriations of Lands.

He has obstructed the Administration of Justice, by refusing his Assent to 13 Laws for establishing Judiciary Powers.

He has made Judges dependent on his Will alone, for the tenure of their 14 offices, and the amount and payment of their salaries.

He has erected a multitude of New Offices, and sent hither swarms of 15 Officers to harass our People, and eat out their substance.

He has kept among us, in time of peace, Standing Armies without the 16 consent of our Legislature.

He has affected to render the Military independent of and superior to the 17 Civil Power.

He has combined with others to subject us to jurisdictions foreign to our 18 constitution, and unacknowledged by our laws; giving his Assent to their acts of pretended Legislation:

For quartering large bodies of armed troops among us: 19

For protecting them, by a mock Trial, from Punishment for any Murders 20 which they should commit on the Inhabitants of these States:

For cutting off our Trade with all parts of the world: 21

For imposing Taxes on us without our Consent: 22

For depriving us in many cases, of the benefits of Trial by Jury: 23

For transporting us beyond Seas to be tried for pretended offenses: 24

For abolishing the free System of English Laws in a Neighbouring Province, 25 establishing therein an Arbitrary government, and enlarging its boundaries so as to render it at once an example and fit instrument for introducing the same absolute rule into these Colonies:

For taking away our Charters, abolishing our most valuable Laws, and al- 26 tering fundamentally the Forms of our Governments:

For suspending our own legislatures, and declaring themselves invested with 27 Power to legislate for us in all cases whatsoever.

He has abdicated Government here, by declaring us out of his Protection 28 and waging War against us.

He has plundered our seas, ravaged our Coasts, burnt our towns and de- 29
stroyed the Lives of our people.

He is at this time transporting large Armies of foreign Mercenaries to com- 30
pleat the works of death, desolation and tyranny, already begun with circumstances of Cruelty & perfidy scarcely paralleled in the most barbarous ages,
and totally unworthy the Head of a civilized nation.

He has constrained our fellow Citizens taken Captive on the high Seas to 31
bear Arms against their Country, to become the executioners of their friends
and Brethren, or to fall themselves by their Hands.

He has excited domestic insurrections amongst us, and has endeavored to 32
bring on the inhabitants of our frontiers, the merciless Indian Savages, whose
known rule of warfare is an undistinguished destruction of all ages, sexes and
conditions.

In every stage of these Oppressions We Have Petitioned for Redress in the 33
most humble terms. Our repeated petitions have been answered only by repeated injury. A Prince, whose character is thus marked by every act which
may define a Tyrant, is unfit to be the ruler of a free People.

Nor have We been wanting in attention to our British brethren. We have 34
warned them from time to time of attempts by their legislature to extend an
unwarrantable jurisdiction over us. We have reminded them of the circumstances of our emigration and settlement here. We have appealed to their
native justice and magnanimity and we have conjured them by the ties of our
common kindred to disavow these usurpations, which would inevitably inter-
rupt our connections and correspondence. They too have been deaf to the
voice of justice and of consanguinity. We must, therefore, acquiesce in the
necessity, which denounces our Separation, and hold them, as we hold the
rest of mankind, Enemies in War, in Peace Friends.

We, therefore, the Representatives of the United States of America, in 35
General Congress, Assembled, appealing to the Supreme Judge of the world
for the rectitude of our intentions, do, in the Name, and by Authority of the
good People of these Colonies, solemnly publish and declare, That these
United Colonies are, and of Right ought to be, Free and Independent States;
that they are Absolved from all Allegiance to the British Crown, and that all
political connection between them and the State of Great Britain, is and ought
to be totally dissolved; and that as Free and Independent States, they have
full power to levy War, conclude Peace, contract Alliances, establish Commerce, and to do all other Acts and Things which Independent States may of
right do. And for the support of this Declaration, with a firm reliance on the
protection of Divine Providence, we mutually pledge to each other our lives,
our Fortunes and our sacred Honor.

Focusing on the Impassioned Tone of Thomas Jefferson's Essay

1. What is the *tone* of the first few sentences of the Declaration of Independence? You may have difficulty answering this question because you are so familiar with some of the phrases. Why have those phrases become so well known? How does the tone change as Jefferson moves to talking about King George in the sentence beginning "But when a long train of abuses"?

2. This document is essentially a declaration of war; as such, it must keep the passions of its American readers alive even as it makes its "objective" claims to the world. In the long list of King George's abuses, which of them seem to be stated "objectively" and calmly? Which seem to be stated in impassioned or biased words (for example, consider the phrase "manly firmness" in paragraph 10)? Why does the language become so much stronger at the end of the list of abuses, in paragraphs 15 through 18?

3. What is the tone of the last sentence? What is it supposed to make its readers feel about the signers of this document?

WORKING WITH THE TECHNIQUE IN YOUR OWN WRITING

1. Select some person or group that you think deserves to be criticized. To discover what level of passion you can use most effectively to attack this opponent, try writing arguments in several different tones. First write a paragraph or two expressing your feelings in intensely angry language; you might imagine that you are trying to inspire people to violent action against this opponent. Then write a couple of paragraphs of the most reasonable arguments you can come up with, stated in a calm, objective tone; perhaps you could imagine you are trying to persuade your opponent to change his or her ways. Finally, write a paragraph of controlled emotion; imagine that you are uncertain how your words will be received, but you want people to know that you are angry. Now look over your three versions. Which seems the best written? Which seems most honestly to reflect your feelings? Can you select parts of them all and put them together? You might find that they are equally good; then you will have to decide what kind of essay you want to write, possibly based on the audience you would most like to address. Finally, write an essay that effectively makes use of your strong emotions.

2. Write a "Declaration of Independence" from someone or something that has power over you. Kocour's essay, for example, could be turned into a Declaration

of Independence from the diet industry or from dieting altogether. You could declare your independence from TV or the entire social system. You might imitate the structure of Jefferson's document, starting with a statement of ideals you believe in, then moving to a list of specific ways that the person or thing you are attacking has violated those ideals, and finishing with a ringing last line. You might, if you like, make this essay humorous, playing with passionate language.

KAREN L. KRAMER

University of Nebraska at Lincoln
Lincoln, Nebraska
Joan Griffin, instructor

"If someone walked into my room while I was trying to get started, I would probably shut off my typewriter and talk to that person for an hour or so about anything and everything except my paper. But let's suppose the person is invisible or observing me through a one-way mirror or some such thing. They would see me sit down at the typewriter, turn it on, stare at it for a minute, and then turn it off again, get up, pace around the room, return to the typewriter, turn it back on again, line up the paper, turn the typewriter off, pace around the room, sit back down again, turn it on again, type maybe a paragraph, read it, out loud of course, decide that it stinks, yank the paper out and throw it away, put in a new sheet and then just start typing away."

Karen Kramer's description of her own writing habits seems very much in keeping with her general level of energy and accomplishment. Kramer's extracurricular activities at Daniel J. Gross High School in Omaha, Nebraska, included playing in the "concert band, pep band, stage band, musical, and Dixieland band," as well as All-State Band; she was ranked fourth in her class academically, was chosen salutatorian by her classmates, and was selected to be a member of the All-State Academic Team. A Regents as well as a National Merit Scholarship winner, Kramer continued to develop her interest in music by playing in various bands both within the University of Nebraska and outside it. She plays trombone and piano, sings, enjoys drawing, and occasionally works with sculpture and computers. While at college, she has also worked part-time at, among other jobs, her dormitory food service, Ponderosa steakhouses, and a local Burger King.

Asked by her instructor to write a comparison and contrast essay, Kramer decided to write about her high school band experiences. "My years in band in high school inspired me to write my essay. . . . Music was my life then. I had ample opportunity to observe my fellow musicians. Hence, I wrote about them." As to her purpose in writing "The Little Drummer Boys," Kramer quickly adds: "The goal of my essay was to have fun, pure and simple. No earth-shattering messages here."

Karen Kramer reports that since winning a Bedford Prize for "The Little Drummer Boys" she "completed a bachelor of arts degree in English at the University of Nebraska at Lincoln. I chose this major because I enjoyed writing and because, quite frankly, I didn't know what else to do. I graduated magna cum laude and was elected to Phi Beta Kappa." Currently a graduate student in English at the University of Nebraska at Omaha, Kramer also teaches one section of freshman composition and serves as teaching assistant for another. Uncertain about her career goals, she may pursue a graduate degree in either communications or counseling.

Kramer remains equally uncertain about the effects of winning a Bedford Prize in Student Writing: "Not to demean it at all, but it's not exactly the Nobel Peace Prize. I was initially excited, but the thrill quickly faded; that's usually the way it goes for accomplishments with me. . . . It seems to impress people within the field of English and,

*of course, it looks good on a résumé or job application. . . . I remember when I won
the prize that I told myself this was a sign that I should keep writing. I sort of looked
upon it as a green light, a go-ahead, a legitimizing of my abilities as a writer. Now I
don't know."*

The Little Drummer Boys

Quick—what do you call a person who plays the trumpet? A trumpeter, of   1
course. A person who plays the flute is referred to as a flutist, or flautist, if you
prefer. Someone who plays a piano is usually known as a pianist, unless of
course he plays the player piano, in which case he is known as a player piano
player rather than a player piano pianist. Got the hang of this yet? Okay, then
what do you call someone who plays that set of instruments belonging to the
percussion family? Why, you call him a percussionist, don't you? Wrong! It's
not quite as easy as all that. There are two types of musicians who play percussion instruments, "drummers" and "percussionists," and they are as different
as the Sex Pistols and the New York Philharmonic.

You can find an initial difference even in the very names of the percussion-   2
playing musicians. If you called a percussionist a drummer, he would be highly
insulted. If you called a drummer a percussionist, he wouldn't know what you
were talking about. The two don't really think much of each other. Percussionists generally consider drummers to be what can only be described as "the
scum of the earth," two million years behind the rest of mankind in the
evolutionary process. Drummers, on the other hand, consider percussionists to
be weak, boring, effeminate individuals with questionable sexual preferences.
The differences don't end there.

Take the drummers, for example. It is their belief that all drums have to   3
come welded together in a set, not unlike Siamese twins. As for other pieces
of drum equipment, cymbals are all to come perched atop a stand and are to
be smashed with a stick and never hand-held and clashed together. Cymbals
do not ever come in pairs, except for the high hat. Triangles, sleigh bells,
woodblocks, etc., are for second-grade rhythm bands, not drummers. As for
kettle drums, as far as the drummer is concerned, they're used for boiling water.
The xylophone is merely a word in an A-B-C book. Nobody actually plays any
of those things professionally.

At least, no self-respecting drummer would because after all, drummers are   4
cool. Some drummers are so cool, they act as though they're on drugs. Some
drummers are on drugs. Regardless of the latter fact, most drummers are very

cool, hip, and laid-back kind of guys, you dig? Except, of course, for when
they play. It is then that the drummer lets the rabid, primordial Neanderthal
that lurks just beneath the surface take complete control of his very being.
When performing, the drummer throws his head around as though he were
trying to toss it from his shoulders. Sweating profusely, his face twisted into a
veritable mask of anguished, tormentuous pain, he looks not unlike a mother-
to-be who has been in labor for over nine hours. By the time a drummer
finishes a solo, he looks as though he had just come in last in the Boston
Marathon. Yet it is this very selfsame animalistic behavior that gives the drummer his appeal to the masses. Almost everybody loves the drummer. Women
love him because sweaty, hirsute, muscular guys in torn T-shirts are macho.
Men respect drummers, too. Not-so-scientific research has found that deep
down within every male of the human species there is a burning desire to beat
the hell out of a trap set, and thus men respect those members of their sex
who can do that and get paid besides.

Drummers aren't popular with everyone, however. There are those directors 5
and conductors who expect drummers to play slowly or quietly or even—
heaven forbid—with a little class. Needless to say, drummers and conductors
do not get along, but this is inevitable. The art of drumming requires a total
lack of self-control, whereas the conductor is actually trying to impose behavioral controls on the drummer, which naturally leads to confrontation. One
simply should not try to rein in a wild, crazy, drugged-out individual who
behaves as though he were raised by gorillas.

Percussionists are on the completely opposite end of the spectrum. Percus- 6
sionists always get along with their directors, as they respect them and bend
over backward to follow them and cooperate. Percussionists are *not* cool.
Rather, they are very clean-cut, square, straightforward individuals. Their hair
is always short and neat. Instead of the sweaty muscle T-shirt of the drummer,
the percussionist wears a dress shirt, sweater, and sometimes even a tie. Percussionists don't even know what drugs are. On the contrary, percussionists
don't drink or smoke, and they make a habit of attending church services
regularly. They're the basic Oral Roberts type.

Thus, percussionists don't enjoy the wide popularity of drummers. It's not 7
that people particularly dislike them. It's just that they don't particularly like
them, either. Percussionists are somewhat lacking in personality. They're
rather bland, not unlike oatmeal or unflavored soda water. They only become
somewhat animated when performing.

Whereas the drummer is merely interested in creating as much noise as 8
possible, music in the true sense of the word is of importance to the percussionist. Whether it be a well-placed cymbal crash or a tiny "ting" on the

triangle, the percussionist, with utmost precision, makes the most of it without overpowering the ensemble with which he happens to be playing. His face a mask of concentration, the percussionist's eyes bug out as he stares steadily at his lord and master, the conductor. With moves as sharp, quick, and accurate as a frog nabbing flies, the percussionist tings a triangle, whirls to whap a wood block, and with one deft, lightning-swift move, silently drops everything and seizes a pair of mallets with which he gives the tympani a resounding thump to precisely fill the gap in the music. Percussionists, who are able to create the sound illusion of a trotting horse or a babbling brook, are as subtle as a morning breeze blowing across the dew-covered grass, whereas drummers, who do their best to create the illusion of an artillery barrage, are about as subtle as a panzer division smashing through the concert hall. No one notices a percussion section. They complement the band. Drummers *are* the band as far as they are concerned. Such an attitude would appear egotistical and uncouth to a percussionist but would seem perfectly natural to a drummer.

Drummers and percussionists do have one thing in common. They both are   9 in love with their equipment. Tenderly they fondle the drumheads, cymbals, and all of their sticks, brushes, and mallets; a pair for each day of the week. They let nothing come between themselves and their equipment and woe unto the ambitious unassuming amateur who dares to sacrilegiously set sticks to the "skins" or sets of the devoted drummer or perniciously protective percussionist. Such an act is sure to ruffle the feathers of even the least temperamental drummer or percussionist.

Another sure way to ruffle them is to call a drummer a "percussionist" or a   10 percussionist a "drummer." After all, there should be no excuse for this since it is apparent that the two are as different as a piccolo and a tuba. So when addressing a player of a percussion instrument, be sure to get his name right, or at least apologize profusely for getting it wrong. Then, he'll smile at you— parum-pa-pum-pum. He and his drum.

Focusing on Karen Kramer's Techniques and Revisions

1. Karen Kramer was asked to write a *comparison and contrast* essay. List all the points Kramer makes about percussionists. How do percussionists differ from drummers? Show how Kramer organizes these points. Does she proceed point by point? Subject by subject? Some combination of the two? Support your response with detailed references to her essay.

2. Characterize Kramer's *point of view* in this essay. Is she detached and objective? Involved and subjective? Some other combination? Support your response with

an analysis of specific words and phrases from the essay. What is her attitude toward percussionists? Toward drummers? When is each attitude first expressed? Which group does Kramer seem to favor by the end of her essay? Why? Having read her essay, explain why you agree or disagree with her conclusions.

3. Karen Kramer explains her *purpose* in writing this essay in the following terms: "What I really want is for the readers to enjoy themselves and have a good laugh or at least a slight chuckle. I'd even settle for a warm smile, or a raise of the eyebrow." How would you describe "the readers" Kramer seems to have in mind here? How familiar does she assume her audience is with her subject? How familiar need they be? Describe specifically the features of Kramer's humorous essay that make it successful.

4. Make a list of the *similes* and *metaphors* Kramer uses in this essay. Which seem especially effective? Why? When asked to clarify how she intended to appeal to her readers, Kramer replied: "I appeal to the reader by using incongruous comparisons, such as that of a drummer with a Neanderthal, etc. I exaggerate like crazy, because I feel that one aspect of humor is exaggeration." Identify the moments in her essay that are marked by exaggeration and comment on the effectiveness of each.

5. Kramer has an eye for useful detail. Identify as many details as possible. What does each contribute to the sentence in which it appears? To the essay as a whole? How does Kramer's use of detail support her humorous intentions as well as some purpose beyond being humorous? What, in your judgment, might this larger purpose be? Is this essay finally about naming people? Naming things? Some combination of the two? Explain.

6. How would you describe Kramer's *tone*—her attitude toward her subject, expressed in her choice of words and sentence structure—in this essay? What specific strategies does she use to maintain that tone, or does it change as she proceeds in the essay? Comment on Kramer's *diction*, her word choice. Is it primarily informal or colloquial? Point to specific examples where Kramer has fun playing with the conventional meaning of words and phrases.

7. When describing her methods as a writer, Kramer noted: "The most difficult thing about writing a first draft is thinking of a beginning and a conclusion. I cannot begin writing from anywhere except the beginning. Some people can write the body and then tack on an intro when they're finished. I cannot. I may have the whole body written word for word in my head, but if I haven't thought of a snappy intro yet, I can't type one word of it." Consider Kramer's first draft of her opening paragraph:

> Quick—what do you call someone who plays the trumpet? A trumpeter, of course. Someone who plays the flute is known as a flutist, or flautist, if you prefer. Someone who plays the piano is usually known as a pianist, unless of

course they play the player piano, in which case he is
known as a player piano player, rather than a player piano
pianist. Got the hang of this yet? Ok, then what do you
call someone who plays that set of instruments known as
the percussion family. Why a percussionist, of course.
Wrong! It's not quite as easy as all that. Actually, there
are two types of people who play percussion instruments,
"drummers" and "percussionists," and they are as different
as the Sex Pistols and the New York Philharmonic.

What changes did Karen Kramer make as she moved from her first to her final
draft? Explain the appropriateness and the effectiveness of each change.

8. In a recent interview, Karen Kramer commented on the features that made her
essay successful: "The use of details and the exaggerated comparisons as well
as the casual, tongue-in-cheek tone are the most successful features of the essay
in my opinion. I will admit that I was surprised that I used 'you.' I've just spent
an entire semester telling my students 'As far as your papers are concerned,
"you" is just the twenty-first letter of the alphabet.' And here I slammed it
down all over the place." Comment on the effectiveness of Kramer's use of the
second-person pronoun in her essay. How appropriate is it to her style and
purpose?

9. When reviewing the procedures she follows in revising an essay, Kramer observed: "I read the paper *out loud*. This is very important. I could read a paper
a hundred times to myself and never catch something, but if I read it out loud,
I'll catch it. Sometimes you have to actually hear what you wrote before you
realize that it sounds like something a fourth grader wrote. So I read it out
loud, and I change what doesn't sound right. Clumsily constructed sentences,
weak words, questionable modifiers, etc. all come to light when I read it, and
then I correct them." Keeping in mind the criteria Kramer establishes in the
last sentence of this quotation, reread her essay *aloud*. If she had an opportunity
to revise her essay, what recommendations for revision would you offer her?
Why?

Suggestions for Writing

1. What kind of music do you most enjoy listening to? Who are some of the most
respected artists who compose and/or play that music? Write an essay in which
you *compare and contrast* the respective styles of two musicians in performance.
If you most enjoy listening to rock and roll, for example, you might want to
compare and contrast the musical styles of Elvis Presley and Bruce Springsteen.
If classical music interests you more, you might prefer to look at the styles of
violinists such as Itzhak Perlman and Isaac Stern.

2. One of the reasons Kramer's essay is successful is that she takes a relatively familiar experience (listening to a drummer and a percussionist) and exaggerates it, both to make a point and to make a lively, amusing essay. Yet Kramer does not exaggerate the differences beyond recognition. In fact, we appreciate her essay all the more because of her effective control of exaggeration. Consider a familiar experience that might be exaggerated in a similar fashion to make a point: preparing for your first date with someone; studying for final exams as opposed to quizzes; taking the road test for your driver's license. Write an account of what happened, playfully exaggerating to make a point.

3. Musicians are often asked to create *similes* to describe their compositional methods. Here are two rather celebrated, if somewhat indecorous, responses: "I produce music as an apple-tree produces apples"—Camille Saint-Saëns (1835–1921); "I write [music] as a sow piddles"—Wolfgang Amadeus Mozart (1756–1791). Here is another, somewhat more dignified comparison: "[Claude] Debussy is like a painter who looks at his canvas to see what more he can take out; [Richard] Strauss is like a painter who has covered every inch and then takes the paint he has left and throws it at the canvas"—Ernest Bloch. Analyze your method of writing and write an essay explaining your methods in terms of an analogy.

AN EFFECTIVE TECHNIQUE

Karen Kramer teaches us a method for turning an exceptionally dull topic into an exceptionally entertaining essay. She has chosen to write on the *difference* between drummers and percussionists. If she had tried to define this difference by describing in detail the techniques these musicians use, she probably would have bored most readers. Instead, Kramer produces a lively, light-hearted essay by repeatedly using the single most effective device for transforming a topic: she creates metaphors, comparing the two kinds of musicians to all sorts of strange things. Drummers are "as subtle as a panzer division smashing through the concert hall" while percussionists are as deft as "frog[s] nabbing flies." Drummers are Neanderthals while percussionists are Oral Roberts types.

By making us think about the difference between Oral Roberts and a Neanderthal, Kramer not only makes us laugh, but also makes us see the difference between drummers and percussionists quite clearly. Her comparisons, moreover, produce greater generality in her essay than a precise analysis of two types of instrumentalists would. She makes us think about two general ways of approaching life: we can imagine Neanderthals and Oral Roberts types in the classroom or on the highway.

Kramer is clearly in love with metaphors, stringing them together one after another. She is an extraordinarily energetic writer, her mind constantly transforming whatever she is thinking about into something else. Some who read her essay may think she must be having a great time writing as she does and wish to share in the fun. Others may find this kind of writing unsettling; it may seem too self-indulgent or too clever. Such reactions are useful: we begin to figure out what kind of style we want to use in our own writing.

However we react to Karen Kramer's overall style, we can learn from her essay how to use metaphors for some specific purposes. She shows us that metaphors are particularly useful when we have to distinguish between two things that seem quite similar—two shades of brown, for example, or two excellent football quarterbacks. Similarly, when we have to explain something to people who know very little about it, we might use metaphors that compare unfamiliar details to things our readers know well. Whenever we are stuck trying to decide how to explain something, we might think instead about what we could compare it to. If we come up with a good comparison, a good metaphor, we may find that it begins to exert a continuing presence throughout our essay, resolving much more than the one point on which we were stuck.

In the next selection, Richard Selzer uses metaphors much as Karen Kramer does, to make clear the subtle distinctions between different ways to perform a task—in his case, surgery. He writes of surgeons who operate like tortoises, like artists, like priests, and like swashbuckling pirates. Selzer does not simply jump from one metaphor to another as Kramer does; he builds on some of his metaphors, returning to them over and over again. He considers, for example, several ways that a surgeon is like a priest and several ways that a surgeon and a patient are like lovers. Selzer shows us how metaphors can end up structuring a whole essay.

ANOTHER ILLUSTRATION OF THE TECHNIQUE

RICHARD SELZER

Letter to a Young Surgeon

Richard Selzer is a surgeon who writes stories and essays that draw his readers into the world of disease and pain that doctors face every day, into what Selzer calls "the hell in which we wage our lives." He went through school without any doubts about his career, getting his M.D. at twenty-five from Albany Medical College in 1953. But as he practiced surgery, he felt that something was being overlooked and often lost in the mechanics of cutting and stitching the body: the souls of both the patient and the surgeon. He turned to writing to become a better doctor because, he says, "it is not the surgeon who is God's darling. It is the poet who heals with his words, stanches the flow of blood, stills the rattling breath." Selzer considers his writing as difficult as his surgery, and more often a failure, because "the events of the human body—pain, orgasm, taste, smell—are indescribable. These are events and experiences for which language offers no solution. They cannot be conveyed. The writer falls back from his assault upon these citadels of sensation and contents himself with encircling the body with an array of sentences" and an array of metaphors, comparisons to things that can be conveyed in words.

At this, the start of your surgical internship, it is well that you be told how 1 to behave in an operating room. You cannot observe decorum unless you first know what decorum is. Say that you have already changed into a scrub suit, donned cap, mask and shoe covers. You have scrubbed your hands and been helped into your gown and gloves. Now stand out of the way. Eventually, your presence will be noticed by the surgeon, who will motion you to take up a position at the table. Surgery is not one of the polite arts, as are Quilting and Illuminating Manuscripts. Decorum in the operating room does not include doffing your cap in the presence of nurses. Even the old-time surgeons knew this and operated without removing their hats.

The first rule of conversation in the operating room is silence. It is a rule 2 to be broken freely by the Master, for he is engaged in the art of teaching. The forceful passage of bacteria through a face mask during speech increases the contamination of the wound and therefore the possibility of infection in that wound. It is a risk that must be taken. By the surgeon, wittingly, and by the patient, unbeknownst. Say what you will about a person's keeping control over his own destiny, there are some things that cannot be helped. Being made use of for teaching purposes in the operating room is one of them. It is an inevitable, admirable and noble circumstance. Besides, I have placated Fate too long to believe that She would bring on wound infection as the complication of such a high enterprise.

Observe the least movement of the surgeon's hands. See how he holds out   3
his hand to receive the scalpel. See how the handle of it rides between his thumb and fingertips. The scalpel is the subtlest of the instruments, transmitting the nervous current in the surgeon's arm to the body of the patient. Too timidly applied, and it turns flabby, lifeless; too much pressure and it turns vicious. See how the surgeon applies the blade to the skin—holding it straight in its saddle lest he undercut and one edge of the incision be thinner than the other edge. The application of knife to flesh proclaims the master and exposes the novice. See the surgeon advancing his hand blindly into the abdomen as though it were a hollow in a tree. He is wary, yet needing to know. Will it be something soft and dead? Or a sudden pain in his bitten finger!

The point of the knife is called the *tang*, from the Latin word for *touch*.   4
The sharp curving edge is the *belly* of the blade. The tang is for assassins, the belly for surgeons. Enough! You will not hold this knife for a long time. Do not be impatient for it. Nor reckon the time. Ripen only. Over the course of your training you will be given ever more elaborate tasks to perform. But for now, you must watch and wait. Excessive ego, arrogance and self-concern in an intern are out of place, as they preclude love for the patient on the table. There is no room for clever disobedience here. For the knife is like fire. The small child yearns to do what his father does, and he steals matches from the man's pocket. The fire he lights in his hiding place is beautiful to him; he toasts marshmallows in it. But he is just as likely to be burned. And reverence for the teacher is essential to the accumulation of knowledge. Even a bad surgeon will teach if only by the opportunity to see what not to do.

You will quickly come to detect the difference between a true surgeon and   5
a mere product of the system. Democracy is not the best of all social philosophies in the selection of doctors for training in surgery. Anyone who so desires, and who is able to excel academically and who is willing to undergo the harsh training, can become a surgeon whether or not he is fit for the craft either manually or by temperament. If we continue to award licenses to the incompetent and the ill-suited, we shall be like those countries where work is given over not to those who can do it best, but to those who need it. That offers irritation enough in train stations; think of the result in airplane cockpits or operating rooms. Ponder long and hard upon this point. The mere decision to be a surgeon will not magically confer upon you the dexterity, compassion and calmness to do it.

Even on your first day in the operating room, you must look ahead to your 6
last. An old surgeon who has lost his touch is like an old lion whose claws
have become blunted, but not the desire to use them. Knowing when to quit
and retire from the consuming passion of your life is instinctive. It takes courage
to do it. But do it you must. No consideration of money, power, fame or fear
of boredom may give you the slightest pause in laying down your scalpel when
the first flagging of energy, bravery or confidence appears. To withdraw gracefully is to withdraw in a state of grace. To persist is to fumble your way to
injury and ignominy.

Do not be dismayed by the letting of blood, for it is blood that animates 7
this work, distinguishes it from its father, Anatomy. Red is the color in which
the interior of the body is painted. If an operation be thought of as a painting
in progress, and blood red the color of the brush, it must be suitably restrained
and attract no undue attention; yet any insufficiency of it will increase the
perishability of the canvas. Surgeons are of differing stripes. There are those
who are slow and methodical, obsessive beyond all reason. These tortoises
operate in a field as bloodless as a cadaver. Every speck of tissue in its proper
place, every nerve traced out and brushed clean so that a Japanese artist could
render it down to the dendrites. Should the contents of a single capillary be
inadvertently shed, the whole procedure comes to a halt while Mr. Clean
irrigates and suctions and mops and clamps and ties until once again the
operative field looks like Holland at tulip time. Such a surgeon tells time not
by the clock but by the calendar. For this, he is ideally equipped with an iron
urinary bladder which he has disciplined to contract no more than once a day.
To the drop-in observer, the work of such a surgeon is faultless. He gasps in
admiration at the still life on the table. Should the same observer leave and
return three hours later, nothing will have changed. Only a few more milli-
meters of perfection.

Then there are the swashbucklers who crash through the underbrush waving 8
a machete, letting tube and ovary fall where they may. This surgeon is equipped
with gills so that he can breathe under blood. You do not set foot in his room
without a slicker and boots. Seasoned nurses quake at the sight of those arms,
elbow-deep and *working*. It is said that one such surgeon entertained the other
guests at a department Christmas party by splenectomizing a cat in thirty
seconds from skin to skin.

Then there are the rest of us who are neither too timid nor too brash. We 9
are just right. And now I shall tell you a secret. To be a good surgeon does
not require immense technical facility. Compared to a violinist it is nothing.
The Japanese artist, for one, is skillful at double brushing, by which technique
he lays on color with one brush and shades it off with another, both brushes

being held at the same time and in the same hand, albeit with different fingers. Come to think of it, a surgeon, like a Japanese artist, ought to begin his training at the age of three, learning to hold four or five instruments at a time in the hand while suturing with a needle and thread held in the teeth. By the age of five he would be able to dismantle and reconstruct an entire human body from calvarium to calcaneus unassisted and in the time it would take one of us to recite the Hippocratic Oath. A more obvious advantage of this baby surgeon would be his size. In times of difficulty he could be lowered whole into the abdomen. There, he could swim about, repair the works, then give three tugs on a rope and . . . Presto! Another gallbladder bites the dust.

In the absence of any such prodigies, each of you who is full-grown must 10 learn to exist in two states—Littleness and Bigness. In your littleness you descend for hours each day through a cleft in the body into a tiny space that is both your workshop and your temple. Your attention in Lilliput is total and undistracted. Every artery is a river to be forded or dammed, each organ a mountain to be skirted or moved. At last, the work having been done, you ascend. You blink and look about at the vast space peopled by giants and massive furniture. Take a deep breath . . . and you are Big. Such instantaneous hypertrophy is the process by which a surgeon reenters the outside world. Any breakdown in this resonance between the sizes causes the surgeon to live in a Renaissance painting where the depth perception is so bad.

Nor ought it to offend you that, a tumor having been successfully removed, 11 and the danger to the patient having been circumvented, the very team of surgeons that only moments before had been a model of discipline and deportment comes loose at the seams and begins to wobble. Jokes are told, there is laughter, a hectic gaiety prevails. This is in no way to be taken as a sign of irreverence or callousness. When the men of the Kalahari return from the hunt with a haunch of zebra, the first thing everybody does is break out in a dance. It is a rite of thanksgiving. There will be food. They have made it safely home.

Man is the only animal capable of tying a square knot. During the course 12 of an operation you may be asked by the surgeon to tie a knot. As drawing and coloring are the language of art, incising, suturing and knot tying are the grammar of surgery. A facility in knot tying is gained only by tying ten thousand of them. When the operation is completed, take home with you a package of leftover sutures. Light a fire in the fireplace and sit with your lover on a rug in front of the fire. Invite her to hold up her index finger, gently crooked in a gesture of beckoning. Using her finger as a strut, tie one of the threads about it in a square knot. Do this one hundred times. Now make a hundred grannies. Only then may you permit yourself to make love to her. This method of learning will not only enable you to master the art of knot tying, both grannies and square, it will bind you, however insecurely, to the one you love.

To do surgery without a sense of awe is to be a dandy—all style and no 13 purpose. No part of the operation is too lowly, too menial. Even when suturing the skin at the end of a major abdominal procedure, you must operate with piety, as though you were embellishing a holy reliquary. The suturing of the skin usually falls to the lot of the beginning surgeon, the sights of the Assistant Residents and Residents having been firmly set upon more biliary, more gastric glories. In surgery, the love of inconsiderable things must govern your life— ingrown toenails, thrombosed hemorrhoids, warts. Never disdain the common ordinary ailment in favor of the exotic or rare. To the patient every one of his ailments is unique. One is not to be amused or captivated by disease. Only to a woodpecker is a wormy tree more fascinating than one uninhabited. There is only absorption in your patient's plight. To this purpose, willingly accept the smells and extrusions of the sick. To be spattered with the phlegm, vomitus and blood of suffering is to be badged with the highest office.

The sutured skin is all of his operation that the patient will see. It is your 14 signature left upon his body for the rest of his life. For the patient, it is the emblem of his suffering, a reminder of his mortality. Years later, he will idly run his fingers along the length of the scar, and he will hush and remember. The good surgeon knows this. And so he does not overlap the edges of the skin, makes no dog-ears at the corners. He does not tie the sutures too tightly lest there be a row of permanent crosshatches. (It is not your purpose to construct a ladder upon which a touring louse could climb from pubis to navel and back.) The good surgeon does not pinch the skin with forceps. He leaves the proper distance between the sutures. He removes the sutures at the earliest possible date, and he uses sutures of the finest thread. All these things he does and does not do out of reverence for his craft and love for his patient. The surgeon who does otherwise ought to keep his hands in his pockets. At the end of the operation, cholecystectomy, say, the surgeon may ask you to slit open the gallbladder so that everyone in the room might examine the stones. Perform even this cutting with reverence as though the organ were still within the patient's body. You cut, and notice how the amber bile runs out, leaving a residue of stones. Faceted, shiny, they glisten. Almost at once, these wrested dewy stones surrender their warmth and moisture; they grow drab and dull. The descent from jewel to pebble takes place before your eyes.

Deep down, I keep the vanity that surgery is the red flower that blooms 15 among the leaves and thorns that are the rest of Medicine. It is Surgery that, long after it has passed into obsolescence, will be remembered as the glory of Medicine. Then men shall gather in mead halls and sing of that ancient time when surgeons, like gods, walked among the human race. Go ahead. Revel in your Specialty; it is your divinity.

It is quest and dream as well.   16

The incision has been made. One expects mauve doves and colored moths 17 to cloud out of the belly in celebration of the longed-for coming. Soon the surgeon is greeted by the eager blood kneeling and offering its services. Tongues of it lap at his feet; flames and plumes hold themselves aloft to light his way. And he follows this guide that flows just ahead of him through rifts, along the edges of cliffs, picking and winding, leaping across chasms, at last finding itself and pooling to wait for him. But the blood cannot wait a moment too long lest it become a blob of coagulum, something annulled by its own puddling. The surgeon rides the patient, as though he were riding a burro down into a canyon. This body is beautiful to him, and he to it—he whom the patient encloses in the fist of his flesh. For months, ever since the first wild mitosis, the organs had huddled like shipwrecks. When would he come? Will he never come? And suddenly, into the sick cellar—fingers of light! The body lies stupefied at the moment of encounter. The cool air stirs the buried flesh. Even the torpid intestine shifts its slow coils to make way.

Now the surgeon must take care. The fatal glissade, once begun, is not to 18 be stopped. Does this world, too, he wonders, roll within the precincts of mercy? The questing dreamer leans into the patient to catch the subtlest sounds. He hears the harmonies of their two bloods, his and the patient's. They sing of death and the beauty of the rose. He hears the playing together of their two breaths. If Pythagoras is right, there is no silence in the universe. Even the stars make music as they move.

Only do not succumb to self-love. I know a surgeon who, having left the 19 room, is certain, beyond peradventure of doubt, that his disembodied radiance lingers on. And there are surgeons of such aristocratic posture that one refrains only with difficulty from slipping them into the nobility. As though they had risen from Mister to Doctor to Professor, then on to Baron, Count, Archduke, then further, to Apostle, Saint. I could go further.

Such arrogance can carry over to the work itself. There was a surgeon in 20 New Haven, Dr. Truffle, who had a penchant for long midline incisions— from sternum to pubis—no matter the need for exposure. Somewhere along the way, this surgeon had become annoyed by the presence of the navel, which, he decided, interrupted the pure line of his slice. Day in, day out, it must be gone around, either to the right or to the left. Soon, what was at first an annoyance became a hated impediment that must be got rid of. Mere circumvention was not enough. And so, one day, having arrived at the midpoint of his downstroke, this surgeon paused to cut out the navel with a neat ellipse of skin before continuing on down to the pubis. Such an elliptical incision when sutured at the close of the operation forms the continuous straight line without which this surgeon could not live. Once having cut out a navel (the first incidental umbilectomy, I suppose, was the hardest) and seeing the simple undeviate line of his closure, he vowed never again to leave a navel behind. Since he was otherwise a good surgeon, and very successful, it was not long before there were thousands of New Haveners walking around minus their belly buttons. Not that this interfered with any but the most uncommon of activities, but to those of us who examined them postoperatively, these abdomens had a blind, bland look. Years later I would happen upon one of these bellies and know at once the author of the incision upon it. Ah, I would say, Dr. Truffle has been here.

It is so difficult for a surgeon to remain "unconscious," retaining the clarity 21 of vision of childhood, to know and be secure in his ability, yet be unaware of his talents. It is almost impossible. There are all too many people around him paying obeisance, pandering, catering, beaming, lusting. Yet he must try.

It is not enough to love your work. Love of work is a kind of self-indulgence. 22 You must go beyond that. Better to perform endlessly, repetitiously, faithfully, the simplest acts, like trimming the toenails of an old man. By so doing, you will not say *Here I Am*, but *Here It Is*. You will not announce your love but will store it up in the bodies of your patients to carry with them wherever they go.

Many times over, you will hear otherwise sensible people say, "You have 23 golden hands," or "Thanks to you and God, I have recovered." (Notice the order in which the credit is given.) Such ill-directed praise has no significance. It is the patient's disguised expression of relief at having come through, avoided death. It is a private utterance, having nothing to do with you. Still, such words are enough to turn a surgeon's head, if any more turning were needed.

Avoid these blandishments at all cost. You are in service to your patients, 24 and a servant should know his place. The world is topsy-turvy in which a master worships his servant. You are a kindly, firm, experienced servant, but a servant still. If any patient of mine were to attempt to bathe my feet, I'd kick over his basin, suspecting that he possessed not so much a genuine sentiment as a conventional one. It is beneath your dignity to serve as an object of veneration or as the foil in an act of contrition. To any such effusion a simple "Thank you" will do. The rest is pride, and everyone knoweth before *what* that goeth.

Alexander the Great had a slave whose sole responsibility was to whisper 25 "Remember, you are mortal" when he grew too arrogant. Perhaps every surgeon should be assigned such a deflator. The surgeon is the mere instrument which the patient takes in his hand to heal himself. An operation, then, is a time of revelation, both physical and spiritual, when, for a little while, the secrets of the body are set forth to be seen, to be touched, and the surgeon himself is laid open to Grace.

An operation is a reenactment of the story of Jonah and the Whale. In 26 surgery, the patient is the whale who swallows up the surgeon. Unlike Jonah, however, the surgeon does not cry out *non serviam*, but willingly descends into the sick body in order to cut out of it the part that threatens to kill it. In an operation where the patient is restored to health, the surgeon is spewed out of the whale's body, and both he and his patient are healed. In an operation where the patient dies on the table, the surgeon, although he is rescued from the whale and the sea of blood, is not fully healed, but will bear the scars of his sojourn in the belly of the patient for the rest of his life.

Focusing on Richard Selzer's Use of Metaphors

1. Selzer uses metaphorical comparisons throughout his essay; though he is writing about surgery, he manages to bring in images of kids playing with fire, Japanese artists, and swashbuckling pirates. What is the overall effect of all these comparisons? Select a few of the metaphors that strike you as especially effective and explain how they work. Which ones help make his points clearer, and which of them make what he is talking about more complicated, harder to understand?

2. In paragraphs 6–9 Selzer classifies different kinds of surgeons, defining each type by a metaphorical comparison: one is like an old lion, one is a tortoise, one a swashbuckler. What is the effect of these comparisons? How do they help him define the right way he thinks surgeons should operate?

3. Selzer's writing is very "artistic" and quite different from what we would expect from a scientific writer. What features of his style make his writing seem "unscientific"? What seems to be Selzer's attitude about scientific precision; how important is it to a surgeon? Selzer brings in very unscientific professions as metaphorical models for the way surgeons should think of their work. How is being a surgeon like being a painter (paragraph 7)? A musician (paragraph 18)? A priest (paragraphs 13, 15, 17)? A hunter (paragraph 11)? How do these comparisons of surgery to nonscientific professions help explain Selzer's style of writing?

4. Selzer says that the surgeon must love his patient. How is surgery like making love? How does Selzer make surgery seem a romantic relationship in paragraph 18? What different kinds of love does Selzer discuss in this essay (look, for example, at paragraphs 4, 12, 13, and 22)? Why are all these different kinds of love important in the life and work of a surgeon?

5. In the last two paragraphs, Selzer says that the "surgeon himself is laid open" during an operation and if the patient dies on the table, the surgeon "is not fully healed." How is a surgeon himself metaphorically opened up by surgery? Of what does the surgeon need to be healed? How could writing be part of the process by which Selzer heals himself?

WORKING WITH THE TECHNIQUE IN YOUR OWN WRITING

---

1. Write an essay classifying the different ways people perform some activity that you know well, such as playing a sport, shopping, or manipulating parents. This essay might be humorous, like Kramer's, or quite serious. See if you find it useful to use metaphors to characterize some or all of the types of people you are describing, as Kramer and Selzer do. Are there Neanderthals and Oral Roberts types, or tortoises and swashbucklers, on the soccer field?

2. Write an essay in the form of a letter giving advice to a person just beginning to do something that you have done for a long time. It could be advice on how to be a waiter or a file clerk, on how to get along with the kids in your neighborhood, or on how to act on dates. Remember that the person you are writing to has never done what you are writing about, so you have to explain the subtleties of the activity in terms he or she can understand. You might find metaphorical comparisons useful ("set the plate in front of the customer the way you would place your most precious rock and roll record on the turntable").

DAVID G. LANDMANN

East Texas State University
Commerce, Texas
Richard Fulkerson, instructor

"If someone walked in the room as I was starting to write," David Landmann explains, *"he or she would see me with a coffee cup in one hand and a cigarette in the other. I would either be sitting back in my chair, staring at a spot just below the space bar of my 1928 Royal Standard, or I would be standing in the middle of the floor, looking at my feet."*

David Landmann reports that he has always been encouraged to write. His earliest recollections of writing stretch back to the third grade, when he sat in class and wrote ghost stories when he was supposed to be doing other things. He also recalls writing picture stories about an imaginary alter ego named Jim who was the athlete and adventurer he could never be. Landmann dropped out of college in the mid-1960s because he was a *"kid who enjoyed skiing more than studying."* At the age of thirty-six, with the urging of his wife, he sold his house and car and returned to school and began what he considered his last chance at formal education.

Asked to write a description, Landmann remembered an experience from nearly a decade earlier in which he was the photographer half of a reporter-photographer team covering a family he had discovered living in a cardboard shack. Landmann had always wanted to write something about the family; this assignment provided that opportunity.

In the several years since earning a Bedford Prize for "The House," David Landmann graduated from East Texas State with a degree in journalism and a minor in English. After a year's service as director of marketing and public relations at St. Joseph's Hospital in Paris, Texas, Landmann and his wife moved to Parma, Idaho—to satisfy the urge to both *"start our own publication and be near the mountains."* David Landmann is now the publisher and his wife the editor of the Parma Review, a small-town newspaper with a staff of four.

The House

The House, if you could call it that, stood in shambles just fifty feet from a major intersection. Hundreds of people passed it daily on their morning and afternoon trips between their comfortable middle-class homes two miles to the south and their comfortable white-collar jobs in the high-tech glass and steel industrial complex two miles to the north. Hundreds of times each day, The House, the cardboard and scrap wood structure that was home for Isiah Lewis and his wife and three children, was virtually not seen. If it was, its images were not allowed to register. Water-warped, refrigerator-carton walls; the single, crate-frame window; the door, made of two discarded coffee-table tops wired to a rusted iron bed frame; the cluttered yard; the ancient, one-eyed man; the odd-looking, stoop-shouldered young woman, holding an infant whose clothing was stained with its own excrement; the older children, whose hungry haunting eyes scanned the big cars on the street: If those things weren't seen, they didn't unsettle. They didn't distress. Avoidance of The House and its images became a simple matter of passersby preserving the sanctity of their to-and-from-work drives. Out of sight, out of mind.

Isiah Lewis never thought himself invisible. When he held his hand up to 2 the light, it was there, solid, black-skinned, yellow-nailed, leathery, arthritic. That hand and its twin had served him for the better part of his (as near as he could figure) seventy-three or seventy-four years. Those hands had built The House. They had fashioned the window and the door. They had kept Isiah Lewis and his wife and "babies" alive in the nearly six years since he had found "the woman" hiding in the city dump, pregnant and half-dead from malnutrition. Mute, probably retarded, "the woman," whom no one else seemed to want, stayed with the old man, who nursed her back to health, delivered her first baby, and fathered two more. The House had sheltered the oddly conceived family since the shack, in which Isiah had lived since middle age, had burned five years earlier. "Good Lawd willin'," The House would continue to keep them alive.

In summer, keeping alive meant scrounging bits of wire screen from the 3 dump—screen to cover the window and the door—to keep the "babies" from "gittin' too bad skeeta-bit."

"Dat ol' watcherman at the dump, he be blin' or sumpin'. I be walkin' in 4 there big as day, an' carryin' stuff out wid dem no trespassin' signs all 'roun', an' he don't even bat a eye. He don't be sayin' nothin'. It's jus' like I ain't there."

Summer also meant keeping the paint can that served as his family's toilet 5 outside and emptied. Lewis said he tried at the beginning of the last summer to rig a lean-to privacy screen, but his arthritis kept his hands from doing the job. Consequently, the Lewis paint can and its patrons were visible at any time to everyone driving by.

"Dey jus' look 'way," Lewis recalled. "One time dey was dis white man in 6 a big white car. He be yellin' he gonna bring the health bo'd down on me. But dey never come. I seen dat big white car. But dey never come."

Food and water were year-round problems.   7

"We usta git our water from the man who be livin' down the road. But he 8 up an' die. So we gits our wash water from the bar ditch, an' we got us a rain barrel for drinkin'. Some of the church ladies up yonder usta bring us hot foods. But the church done moved, an' we ain't got us no cookstove. Can't put no cookstove in no cardbo'd house. Den the welfare usta git us some dat commode [commodity] food. But dey done los' our card an' dey don't know we here no mo',￼" Lewis said.

When the church ladies stopped coming, Lewis began to send his two oldest 9 "babies" to fetch what food they could find in the trash bins behind the supermarket that stood a half-mile south of The House.

"Ain't never nobody 'roun' back there. If dey is, dey don't never pay no 10 mind to the babies. The babies climb right inside them big ol' hoppers and carries lots of good stuff back here. If the white folks sees them babies, dey jus' don't say nothin' nohow."

But now it was winter, and winter in The House was what Isiah Lewis called 11 "the wustest time."

There were never enough rags in the dump to stuff in the holes in the 12 makeshift walls of The House—never enough to keep the north wind out. The cold outside meant the paint can had to be brought into the comparative warmth inside, where the can sat steaming next to the pile of newspapers and rags under which the Lewis family huddled at night. The only heat came from their own bodies (because you "can't put no cookstove in no cardbo'd house").

It was winter now, and Isiah Lewis was telling the story of The House to a 13 white folks' newspaper reporter, who two days earlier had had a flat tire while driving through the intersection The House overlooked. He had overlooked The House every day for the past year, never seeing the ramshackle collection of cardboard and weathered wood until his right front tire blew and a broken jack handle forced him to go looking for a telephone. What he found was Isiah Lewis, who offered him all he had to offer—a tin can of cold rainwater and a place to sit out of the wind.

The story and pictures of Isiah Lewis, "the woman," "the babies," and The 14 House hit the streets on the day before Christmas. The following letter was published two days later:

> Dear Editor:
>
> This is to inform your readers that Isiah Lewis and his family are now being taken care of by our department. It is with regret we must admit that we were neither aware of the Lewises nor the conditions in which they lived. We didn't know they existed simply because no one ever reported their existence to us. How hundreds of people could drive past the Lewis' helplessness each day and never see there was a problem is a question for which there are only unpleasant answers. The answer, however, remains. We

simply chose not to see the Lewises. Unfortunately the old
saying is still true. Out of sight, out of mind. Now . . . the
Lewises are in our minds. Let us not forget them.

Sincerely,
County Department of Public Welfare

Focusing on David Landmann's Techniques and Revisions

1. David Landmann makes it clear that one of his purposes in writing this essay
   is to describe the house and its occupants. Yet Landmann expresses a more
   ambitious purpose. What argument does he make about society's attitude toward and treatment of the poor? How does he use his description of Isiah Lewis
   to achieve that purpose?

2. What are the advantages and the disadvantages of Landmann's decision to have
   Isiah Lewis, a destitute and uneducated person, speak at length in this essay?
   What larger audience (beyond his instructor and classmates) might Landmann
   have assumed would read his essay? What is the effect on such readers of having
   Isiah Lewis speak for himself?

3. Landmann uses dialogue to present a clear picture of Lewis and his impover-
   ishment. In effect, he allows Lewis to tell his own story in his own words.
   What does this dialogue reveal about Lewis? About Landmann? Characterize
   the nature of Isiah Lewis's dialect. Why does Landmann seem so intent on
   presenting that dialect as accurately as possible? What does he gain by doing
   so? What portrait of Isiah Lewis emerges from his own words?

4. How would you characterize Landmann's attitude toward Lewis and his family?
   Where—and how—does Landmann reveal that attitude? Point to specific words
   and phrases to support your response. What effect does Landmann's attitude
   have on his readers?

5. Can Isiah Lewis be said to represent David Landmann's position in this essay
   about society's treatment of the poor? Point to specific passages to support your
   response. If this character does represent the author in such a debate, then
   who represents the voice of the opposition? How does Landmann portray the
   people he is arguing against? Cite specific examples.

6. Why does Landmann choose to wait until nearly the end of the essay to tell
   his readers about the reporter's discovery of The House? How does this decision
   as well as the essay's overall structure heighten the effect of this description?

7. Landmann reports that the "hardest thing for me to do is to stop writing, to
   cut myself off, to keep my writing brief and to the point." Show whether
   Landmann has succeeded at being "brief and to the point."

8. Landmann's essay ends with a letter to the editor written by the county

department of public welfare. What effect does this letter have in the essay? Consider whether it is a more effective conclusion than a summary of Landmann's main points could be. Which would you prefer? Why?

9. Landmann wrote the following introduction in his rough draft:

> The house, if you could call it that, stood in shambles just fifty feet from a major intersection. Hundreds of people passed it daily on their morning and afternoon trips between their comfortable middle-class homes two miles to the south and their comfortable white-collar jobs in the high-tech glass and steel industrial complex two miles to the north. But they never saw the cardboard and scrapwood house that was shelter for Isiah Lewis and his wife and three children. Or if they saw it they didn't let it register. If they didn't see it, they didn't have to think about it. Out of sight, out of mind.

Compare and contrast the compositional strategies and effects of this rough draft with those of the final draft. Which version do you judge the more effective? Why?

Suggestions for Writing

1. David Landmann describes a house and its inhabitants who were "out of sight, out of mind." What does the expression "out of sight, out of mind" mean to you? Write an essay in which you demonstrate your understanding of the significance and the applicability of this expression.

2. Landmann discovered the cardboard shack that hundreds of people passed each day without noticing. Spend some time walking around the community in which you live, looking for as much as possible that you have never noticed before. Select one such previously unnoticed aspect of your community and draft an essay describing what you noticed and explaining why you had never noticed it before.

AN EFFECTIVE TECHNIQUE

When we choose to debate an issue and decide to write an essay to express our opinion, we usually work hard to present ourselves as respectable, intelligent people. David Landmann uses an entirely different strategy to build an argumentative essay: he introduces a rather disreputable, poorly educated man and lets that man speak at length. To understand why Landmann's strategy works, we have to consider what he is trying to prove. He is angry at "comfortable middle-class" people who believe it reasonable to ignore anyone who lives in a cardboard house, because obviously such bums are irresponsible, lazy, and stupid. If middle-class persons ever looked at the homeless, Landmann reasons, they would stop believing in such stereotypes.

Landmann does exactly what he argues his readers should do: he looks at and listens to one homeless man, Isiah Lewis. He then writes a portrait of the man so that we too can be persuaded to change our attitudes about the homeless. Lewis's "improper" dialect is important to Landmann's argument: it jars his readers out of the comfortable language of the middle class. Isiah Lewis's words may seem ungrammatical, but they have great subtlety and dignity. He does not seek pity or apologize when he says he steals from the dump; instead he insults the watchman as "blin' or sumpin' " for letting him get away with it. He mocks the welfare bureaucracy that loses his card and then can no longer recognize him. Intelligent enough to point out the hypocrisy in those who appear far better educated, Isiah Lewis is also responsible enough to keep his family alive and generous enough to share his meager supplies with others who are homeless. After hearing Isiah Lewis speak, we begin to think that those who "jus' look 'way" and dismiss him as a worthless human being because he lives in a "cardbo'd house" are the irresponsible ones. Isiah Lewis's personality and "voice" are in themselves convincing arguments against stereotypes of the homeless.

Landmann's essay demonstrates that writers do not always have to use an impersonal, objective, respectable voice to write convincing arguments. From Landmann we can learn an unusual way of thinking about an issue: instead of merely looking for reasons to be on one side or another, we can think about the kinds of persons most affected by the issue and what such persons would say about it. By thinking and writing that way, we can make a personally affecting essay about almost any issue. For example, if we wanted to argue for aid to the Contras, we could portray a refugee from Nicaragua speaking about his suffering in that country; if we wanted to argue against such aid, we could portray someone who had left the Contras because they seemed corrupt. We could also write an essay on Nicaragua by creating a person with a more distant connection to the topic—say, a person whose welfare had been cut off and felt too much money was being spent on fighting communism. If we wish to argue about more personal topics, we could draw on the persons we see every day and from them create a character with a strong voice who could argue for us. For example, if we wanted to argue that parents should not correct every little mistake their children make, we might create a teenager who has become extremely timid, docile, and can barely speak, yet still manages to express years of anger and frustration at his parents' constant carping.

In the next selection, Frances Gage proves that women are as strong as men with the most direct demonstration possible in an essay: she shows us the strength of a woman's words. She re-creates a scene she was part of, a women's rights convention in 1851, when one poor, illiterate woman's eloquence silenced a crowd of smug, well-educated, and well-heeled males.

ANOTHER ILLUSTRATION OF THE TECHNIQUE

FRANCES DANA BARKER GAGE

Sojourner Truth:
And A'n't I a Woman?

Though she was raised on the frontier of Ohio during the early 1800s and was never formally educated, Frances Gage became an influential writer and speaker on women's rights, abolition, and temperance. She began her career as an abolitionist journalist, was elected president of the Akron Convention of 1851 (the largest women's rights convention before the Civil War), wrote an advice column under the pseudonym Aunt Fanny (in which she often satirized male views of female frailty), edited two farmers' weekly newspapers, published a novel about the tragedy of marrying an intemperate husband, and wrote a volume of poems describing the position of women in farming communities. Gage used her writing to support eight children and an ailing husband.

Though she fought for fifty years without success for women's right to vote, Gage was never discouraged. As she wrote at age sixty, "We who have been mobbed, who have walked the streets of New York, with curses and vulgarisms following us as we went, only know how far we have really travelled . . . woman today is an acknowledged power." She never thought it necessary to compromise her ideals: "We would have all things at once; and we should demand all things, and get what we can."

Frances Gage was an eloquent speaker and recognized eloquence in others, as this selection from her reminiscences shows. Like all great leaders, she knew when it was time to stand in the background and let others speak for her cause. Though she was president of the Akron Convention, she recognized that the best use of her power was to overrule the objections of the other leaders of the women's movement and allow Sojourner Truth, a former domestic servant who had become an itinerant advocate of women's rights, to be heard.

The leaders of the movement trembled on seeing a tall, gaunt black woman 1
in a gray dress and white turban, surmounted with an uncouth sun-bonnet,

march deliberately into the church, walk with the air of a queen up the aisle, and take her seat upon the pulpit steps. A buzz of disapprobation was heard all over the house, and there fell on the listening ear, "An abolition affair!" "Woman's rights and niggers!" "I told you so!" . . .

I chanced on that occasion to wear my first laurels in public life as president   2 of the meeting. At my request order was restored, and the business of the Convention went on. Morning, afternoon, and evening exercises came and went. Through all these sessions old Sojourner, quiet and reticent as the "Lybian Statue," sat crouched against the wall on the corner of the pulpit stairs, her sun-bonnet shading her eyes, her elbows on her knees, her chin resting upon her broad, hard palms. At intermission she was busy selling the "Life of Sojourner Truth," a narrative of her own strange and adventurous life. Again and again, timorous and trembling ones came to me and said, with earnestness, "Don't let her speak, Mrs. Gage, it will ruin us. Every newspaper in the land will have our cause mixed up with abolition and niggers, and we shall be utterly denounced." My only answer was, "We shall see when the time comes."

The second day the work waxed warm. Methodist, Baptist, Episcopal, Pres-   3 byterian, and Universalist ministers came in to hear and discuss the resolutions presented. One claimed superior rights and privileges for man, on the ground of "superior intellect"; another, because of the "manhood of Christ; if God had desired the equality of woman, He would have given some token of His will through the birth, life, and death of the Saviour." Another gave us a theological view of the "sin of our first mother."

There were very few women in those days who dared to "speak in meeting";   4 and the august teachers of the people were seemingly getting the better of us, while the boys in the galleries, and the sneerers among the pews, were hugely enjoying the discomfiture, as they supposed, of the "strong-minded." Some of the tender-skinned friends were on the point of losing dignity, and the atmosphere betokened a storm. When, slowly from her seat in the corner rose Sojourner Truth, who, till now, had scarcely lifted her head. "Don't let her speak!" gasped half a dozen in my ear. She moved slowly and solemnly to the front, laid her old bonnet at her feet, and turned her great speaking eyes to me. There was a hissing sound of disapprobation above and below. I rose and announced "Sojourner Truth," and begged the audience to keep silence for a few moments.

The tumult subsided at once, and every eye was fixed on this almost Amazon   5 form, which stood nearly six feet high, head erect, and eyes piercing the upper air like one in a dream. At her first word there was a profound hush. She spoke in deep tones, which, though not loud, reached every ear in the house, and away through the throng at the doors and windows.

"Wall, chilern, whar dar is so much racket dar must be somethin' out o'   6
kilter. I tink dat 'twixt de niggers of de Souf and de womin at de Norf, all
talkin' 'bout rights, de white men will be in a fix pretty soon. But what's all
dis here talkin' 'bout?

"Dat man ober dar say dat womin needs to be helped into carriages, and   7
lifted ober ditches, and to hab de best place everywhar. Nobody eber helps me
into carriages, or ober mud-puddles, or gibs me any best place!" And raising
herself to her full height, and her voice to a pitch like rolling thunder, she
asked, "And a'n't I a woman? Look at me! Look at my arm! (and she bared
her right arm to the shoulder, showing her tremendous muscular power). I
have ploughed, and planted, and gathered into barns, and no man could head
me! And a'n't I a woman? I could work as much and eat as much as a man—
when I could get it—and bear de lash as well! And a'n't I a woman? I have
borne thirteen chilern, and seen 'em mos' all sold off to slavery, and when I
cried out with my mother's grief, none but Jesus heard me! And a'n't I a
woman?

"Den dey talks 'bout dis ting in de head; what dis dey call it?" ("Intellect,"   8
whispered someone near.) "Dat's it, honey. What's dat got to do wid womin's
rights or nigger's rights? If my cup won't hold but a pint, and yourn holds a
quart, wouldn't ye be mean not to let me have my little half-measure full?"
And she pointed her significant finger, and sent a keen glance at the minister
who had made the argument. The cheering was long and loud.

"Den dat little man in black dar, he say women can't have as much rights   9
as men, 'cause Christ wan't a woman! Whar did your Christ come from?"
Rolling thunder couldn't have stilled that crowd, as did those deep, wonderful
tones, as she stood there with outstretched arms and eyes of fire. Raising her
voice still louder, she repeated, "Whar did your Christ come from? From God
and a woman! Man had nothin' to do wid Him." Oh, what a rebuke that was
to that little man.

Turning again to another objector, she took up the defense of Mother Eve.   10
I can not follow her through it all. It was pointed, and witty, and solemn;
eliciting at almost every sentence deafening applause; and she ended by asserting: "If de fust woman God ever made was strong enough to turn de world
upside down all alone, dese women togedder (and she glanced her eye over
the platform) ought to be able to turn it back, and get it right side up again!
And now dey is asking to do it, de men better let 'em." Long-continued
cheering greeted this. " 'Bleeged to ye for hearin' on me, and now ole Sojourner han't got nothin' more to say."

Amid roars of applause, she returned to her corner, leaving more than one   11
of us with streaming eyes, and hearts beating with gratitude. She had taken

us up in her strong arms and carried us safely over the slough of difficulty turning the whole tide in our favor. I have never in my life seen anything like the magical influence that subdued the mobbish spirit of the day, and turned the sneers and jeers of an excited crowd into notes of respect and admiration. Hundreds rushed up to shake hands with her, and congratulate the glorious old mother, and bid her God-speed on her mission of "testifyin' agin concerning the wickedness of this 'ere people."

Focusing on Frances Gage's Use of Character

1. What sorts of personalities do the leaders of the women's right movement seem to have at the beginning of the essay? How does Gage make it seem that those who have fearful reactions about letting Sojourner Truth speak are expressing their own prejudices rather than accurately assessing the situation? How does Gage portray her own role in this controversy?

2. Gage describes the discussion as heated but quotes directly only the arguments against women's rights and against Sojourner speaking. Why would she create such a biased view of the meeting? How does Gage's presentation of the discussions help set up Sojourner's speech?

3. What impression do we have of Sojourner before she speaks? How do Sojourner's words give us a sense of her personality? Of her life? How would the effect of the essay change if Gage had transformed Sojourner's dialect into standard English?

3. How does Gage make Sojourner seem a figure out of myth or legend? Do you believe all that Gage says, or do you think she is exaggerating and perhaps distorting what really happened? Do you think this essay would be more effective if it were written more objectively? Why or why not?

WORKING WITH THE TECHNIQUE IN YOUR OWN WRITING

1. Gage and Landmann both write convincing arguments by creating characters. Write an essay like theirs by creating a scene in which a person speaks about an issue that affects him or her personally. Try to make the scene, the personality, and the voice of the speaker strengthen the arguments he or she is making. To write this essay, you might seek out and interview a person in your community whose character seems impressive, or you might create a character based on people you know.

2. Create a dialogue between a historical figure and someone alive today about

some public issue that was important when that historical figure lived and is still important today. You might, for example, write a dialogue between Sojourner Truth and a leader of the women's movement today, discussing how the issues facing women have (or have not) changed since 1851. You do not have to use famous political figures; you could write a dialogue between a farmer in Revolutionary War days and a modern farmer about East Coast intellectuals controlling the government.

PATRICK KINDER LEWIS

Wheaton College
Wheaton, Illinois
Sharon Ewert, instructor

Patrick Kinder Lewis describes himself as "not a 'reader' in the traditional sense in which writers seem to be. That is not to say I don't read. I read voraciously—I can almost never be caught anywhere without a book in my possession. But the habit is more from a thirst for wisdom than from any learned-pleasure of reading for its own sake. I didn't grow up reading, but thinking and doing instead." Lewis has spent nearly all of his life on the move. Born in Moses Lake, Washington, Lewis and his twin brother, Mike, along with an older and a younger sister, have lived as U.S. Air Force dependents in various parts of the world. A graduate of Kubasaki High School in Okinawa, Japan, Lewis grew up a "perennial traveler. I have lived in over a dozen places since I was fifteen and spent two years traveling through the United States."

Lewis's experiences on the road prompt him to characterize himself as "a people-oriented philosopher," a phrase he explains in these terms: "My folks have lent me their own brand of stoical toleration mixed with lots of love. From rather obscure sources, both I and my twin have grown into quixotic convention flouters . . . which has led us to the 'existential edge' of our lives more than once." "Five Minutes North of Redding" recounts one such experience.

In writing this essay on hobos and the saving grace of friendship while riding the rails, Lewis hoped "to create the snapshot which I never took of that epiphanic moment" on board a freight train. The lesson of that experience, Lewis suggests, is that "nothing in this life comes cheaply—nothing of value anyway—but none of us pays anywhere near the face value for what we get either: what we have, we have been given on loan."

Several years have passed since Patrick Kinder Lewis earned a Bedford Prize. During this period, he has graduated from Wheaton College, "married my most faithful friend (at least since my eighteenth birthday) within a month of graduation," worked full-time as a nurse and part-time in property management before "going the corporate route . . . as a manager in a medium-sized service industry corporation. It was not long before I learned I am not cut out for the corporate lifestyle." Most recently, Lewis has become "a partner in a property development concern." He hopes to return to graduate school "sometime in the next ten years in either business, history, or mathematics. Broad field of choices you say? True. My undergraduate degree in philosophy and mathematics has left many doors ajar."

For a revised version of Patrick Kinder Lewis's essay, see Part II.

Five Minutes North of Redding

I rolled out of the weeds into the crisp daylight of that late September 1
morning to catch the north train out of Roseville. The herder had said it would

leave about 3:00 A.M. so I had huddled in my coat for at least three hours, wishing in the predawn chill for a cup of hot anything. But the noise and lights of the train yard had filtered through the tall grass and disturbed even those harmless dreams.

Finally she came. Forty cars were in sight before the engines passed me. Moving down to the rail bed, I noticed for the first time that I had not slept alone on this stretch of tracks. Three figures were coming down to claim a rail car 150 yards up the line, and even as I cautiously watched them, two other groups of riders were claiming cars behind me. I bounded onto a flatcar, concerned that the line of empties would soon pass me by—then thought again. A solitary presence on that flat deck, instinct shouted within me warnings about such a vulnerable position. I crossed the ten-foot width and dropped down onto the ground on the other side of the car. This time I watched until everyone was on board before I picked out one of the last empty boxcars. And still there were some fifty closed cars behind mine. This train was surely big enough, I imagined, for all of us.

The line of cars came to its first stop on a siding three hours up the Sacramento Valley as we allowed another train to pass. Groves of plum trees lined the track on either side. Even so late in the season, the trees to the train's right were still full of hard purple fruit. I lay down in a splash of sun on the deck of my car. For the first time that morning warm and relaxed, the startling sound of shouts out the east door caused me to retreat into the shadows again. I peered out to find six men playing among the trees like kids as they picked plums only to pelt each other with them. I watched intently, as if it were some elaborate social experiment, until the sound of boots on gravel brought me back around. Looking to the shadow behind me, I suddenly realized that it was too late to conceal myself. The man whose crunching boots had just announced his approach was somehow already at my back door looking me over.

"There you are. I've been lookin' for you. You're travelin' alone ain't you?" All the wrong questions to ask someone who is already scared of you. Luckily the voice betrayed nothing but a desire for friendship.

"That's right, I am. What . . . are you alone, too?" I sized him up coolly as I moved toward my knapsack in the far corner. In its open front pocket I had a knife if I needed it. He had an eight-inch Bowie knife strapped frontier-style to his right shin.

"No. Couple of beaners and me pick up together in Stockton; but they ain't speakin' nothin but Spanish, man. You want sumpum to eat? They're gettin' some plums. We got cukes and and tomatoes still that they picked in the Valley yesterday. And I got a box of saltines in Roseville."

He had a ruddy face that was roughly pocked, probably from adolescence,   7
and a scraggly mustache that only became noticeable when he looked right at
you. I had reached my pack, but simply turned toward him in a crouch to look
for my next move.

If I planned to turn down his offer, standing four feet up in a boxcar was   8
the time to do it. His bony frame and large hands gave away his height: I
would be at a three- to four-inch disadvantage once down on level ground.
And he just looked tough. Shoulder-length, muddy blond hair he had tied
back with a lace of dark buckskin; it laced the seams of his chamois pants too.
(He was fond of buckskin and wore it well.) Very tough but somehow gentle.
He seemed all in all an atavism, a confusing mixture of General Custer with
a sixties flower child. I decided to trust my second inclination.

"Sounds good," I said closing my pack. "What's your name?" I grabbed my   9
jacket and hopped down onto the loose shale bed. The train was just pulling
away with a halting rumble as we neared his car. On quickening our pace, I
noticed he was limping from his hip down. I was in the car before him and
offered him a hand. But he ignored it and managed an agile roll into the car
by catching hold of a break in the floor.

Alex and the beaners were the first hobos I was to travel with. For the space   10
of a couple days we ate, drank, slept, and fought like brothers. I learned their
pasts and their plans in that short time together and laid awake to think what
it would be like to live their lives. At one point, left behind by our train
somewhere south of Red Bluff, we hiked together most of the way to the next
railhead, ducking many a curious sheriff en route. Finally Alex found us a ride
out of a truck stop with an ex-Harley biker. Ambling over the gunwales of his
pickup, we rode it all the way to Redding.

That night, we caught the last train out still on its dinner break. Ducking into   11
a store nearby, I quickly bought enough sardines, crackers, and canned sausages
for ten men. While the train sat idle we found a boxcar that was open only on its
east side. (For the cold trip into the mountains ahead, warmth was a more
important concern than a view of the scenery to the west.) We had just finished
off the sardines as the train at last began to lumber out of the yard. Our bodies
exhausted, our hunger at last abated, we sat on the dirty floor of our boxcar
enjoying the last warm breath of the evening. We were now at the northernmost
end of California's fertile basin. From here on the land would climb more steeply.
Only the Sacramento River lay between us and the Cascade mountains. As we
approached the trestle, the track took only one slow curve to the northwest. On
ahead, I was sure it would begin a series of slow switchbacks to climb Mt. Shasta's
side. But for now, because dead ahead, Shasta was out of sight.

I leaned tiredly against the back door and watched as the scene in front of 12
me began to change. Low on the horizon, a nearly full moon was rising slowly
to take its place in the center of our stage. Mt. Lassen's distant volcanic head
joined it as we rounded the last turn before the river, showing mutely through
a carpet of velvet green peaks. Inside the car, Alex stood up to blow the smoke
of his cigarette out into the crystal air. He propped himself like a caryatid
supporting the right border of our window on the world. My Mexican compadres sat nearly motionless at the door's left side. Mesmerized, I dug blindly
into my pack to find the harmonica which I had saved for just such an inspiring
moment. I sucked in a chord or two of "This Train Is Bound for Glory,"
laughing inside. Suddenly, another actor entered from stage left and I came
up to a squatting position to get a better vantage. The wild Sacramento below
us had begun to snake its way into view, illumined only by the bright moonlight.

It was all I could do to keep from walking out our door onto that stage. 13
Like something from a dream, it seemed too fantastically beautiful to be real.
And finally, unexpectedly, the train itself emerged as a player. The trestlework
not only poised the line of cars two hundred feet above the river's surface but
managed as well to bend it into a slow arc midway in the crossing. The sweep
of that northward arc turned our view to the south. And just for that instant
both the front and rear of the train were visible at once. The engines at our
head disappeared slowly into the shadow of Mt. Shasta while the cars that
trailed our coach paraded behind us across the massive trestle. And on it all
was poured the stark quiet of the moonlight reflected in the river below.

The trestle, from south to north, could not have been over a mile long. 14
The entire panorama played before us for less than two minutes. Yet, in a very
real way, it has run in my mind's eye ever since.

As that team of Southern Pacific diesels pulled us out of Redding, eternity 15
sat captive for a moment. Like a stolen glimpse of childbirth, I shared in that
peaceful feeling of something both beginning and ending at once. And like a
mother smiling at her child born at last, I found myself smiling with a similar
relief. It was joy without euphoria. I hunted again for the insights of the
moment before but found them fading with the darkness of the mountains
ahead. What race had I run to earn such rest? What was born in that moment?
I looked to my companions for an answer but found it instead full-formed in
the darkness between us. There was the sudden realization of the only bond
that we all shared: our passion for life. We were living life moment by moment.
That was our race well run. As our moonlight halos began to fade I picked up
my harmonica and found myself playing "Bound for Glory" in a different key.

Focusing on Patrick Kinder Lewis's Techniques and Revisions

1. Patrick Kinder Lewis's essay recounts a youthful adventure "on the rails." How does he organize the story he tells? Is it organized, for example, strictly according to chronology? Incident? Some other principle? Explain. What are its major parts? What is the relation of each part to the whole essay?

2. One of the strengths of Lewis's essay is the presence of an engaging narrative voice. How would you characterize the narrator? What information do you draw on to create this characterization? What does the narrator tell us about himself? In discussing his essay, Lewis notes: "I wanted to explain not only what was going on around me but also what was going on inside the narrator." How does the narrator change as the essay develops? What is your attitude toward the narrator? At the end of the essay, how has your attitude changed, if at all? Support your answer with examples from the text.

3. Characterize Lewis's *point of view*—his relation to the subject—in telling this story. Is he involved and subjective or detached and objective at the beginning of his essay? Where and how does his point of view change as the essay proceeds? Where does Lewis restrict himself to reporting his observations of incidents and where does he allow himself to draw inferences based on those observations? With what effect? Point to specific words and phrases to support your response.

4. In explaining his *purpose* in writing this essay, Patrick Lewis notes: "The experience about which I wrote was a brief but meaningful excerpt from a much longer story I hope to write about learning from life-lived-on-the-edge. 'Five Minutes North of Redding' was in a way the fulfillment of a youthful dream and the beginning of a more mature vision." Locate the moments in this essay that illustrate this point. In the final paragraph Lewis states, "I hunted again for the insights of the moment before." What, exactly, are the insights he refers to? How does the final paragraph amplify each of them?

5. Review carefully the moment when the train—with the narrator on board—crosses a curved bridge over a long valley. When the train reaches the middle of the bridge, the narrator can see the first and last cars of the train. What symbolic significance does the narrator assign to this scene?

6. This essay is rich in detail. Readers can sense the presence of a writer working hard, and consciously so, at *description*. One distinguishing feature of effective description is the use of *concrete*, sensory details. List the instances where Lewis appeals to each of his reader's senses. Another characteristic of effective description is its specificity. Consider paragraph 9, especially the last three sentences. How does the final sentence in the paragraph extend and develop the point made about Alex's "limping from his hip down"? How is Lewis's use of detail in action in this paragraph reinforced at other moments in the essay?

7. In paragraph 12 Lewis develops a compelling image of a "stage." Identify each

of the "actors" who play on this "stage." In addition to the individuals and groups you have listed, what additional "actors" does Lewis's drama depend on? Show how the *metaphor* of the stage controls the last several paragraphs of Lewis's essay. What other metaphors can you point to in the essay that further his purpose? Support your response by pointing to specific words and phrases.

8. Reread the final paragraph of this essay. What does Lewis mean when he talks about "the sudden realization . . . that we all shared: our passion for life." How does the final paragraph serve to clarify this "passion"? How has it been dramatized in each of the preceding paragraphs? If you had an opportunity to suggest revisions for improving Lewis's essay, what specific changes, if any, would you encourage Lewis to make in his final paragraph? Would you, for example, recommend that he delete it? Why? Why not?

9. When discussing how he wrote his essay, Lewis noted: "I seem to like writing introductions . . . which lead to several different beginnings. . . . I must have written six or more openings before settling on picking up in the middle of one version. Then I reworked that much shorter approach at least another six times." Here is Lewis's first draft of his opening paragraph:

> There are some memories which you need to recall on cold stormy nights. When a chilling blast begins to whisper the worst sort of misgivings about life, their inner glows can throw dark doubts in the cellar where they belong. And if ever you are sure human beings are simply perpetual self-centered trouble, it may take a real warm memory to shake free from the acid experiences with the more ignoble among us. Someone has said, "Everyone needs certain works of the literary arts to guide them through troubled times." I have expanded the rule. We can create our own art within us to carry us through storms.

Here is a much later draft of the opening paragraph:

> There are memories that chew at your insides and shorten your life. They wake you up on chilly nights and rip the blankets off. Like the time your favorite jacket was stolen from the closet at the high school dance: you shivered all the way home, convinced that the only answer to injustice was to be just as nasty and brutish as everyone else. You shivered, shook, and wanted to cry out, and none of it did any good—the doubts had been planted deep. At such times we need to recall the "angels unawares" and warm puppies in our lives. Like waking up from a bad dream, our only answer may be to hope for a good dream

to warm us again from such cold memories—from the inside out. That is when I remember Alex.

Consider Lewis's final draft of his opening. What specific differences do you notice among these three drafts? What does each emphasize? What are the connections among the three? Which version do you prefer? Why?

10. In an earlier draft of his essay, Lewis included several paragraphs recounting the "story" of Alex's life. Here, for example, is one such paragraph:

> Somewhere south of Red Bluff I confessed how new I was at running the rails. Alex wasn't running anymore. He was "tired of all that" and he was simply headed home to help out his mother. He joked that he might even settle down with a waitress who had been chasing him for some time. In any case he had begun to feel at thirty-eight that the years were wearing him away little by little. Like the Snake River near his home, he could feel time cutting its own sort of canyon. And if he was going to lay down roots, it might as well be near where he began. His father was long since dead and his mother was getting to a point where she really needed him, he said. Still, I remember thinking there was something missing from his story. It just made too much sense.

Consider the gains and the losses of Lewis's decision to delete this paragraph. How would Lewis's essay be strengthened and weakened by adding more information about Alex?

Suggestions for Writing

1. Patrick Lewis's first draft of his opening paragraph ends on this point: "Someone has said, 'Everyone needs certain works of the literary arts to guide them through troubled times.' I have expanded the rule. We can create our own art within us to carry us through storms." Examine your own experience carefully and write an essay recounting an experience to illustrate either of the "rules" Lewis mentions.

2. At the end of his essay, Lewis notes: "As that team of Southern Pacific diesels pulled us out of Redding, eternity sat captive for a moment. Like a stolen glimpse of childbirth, I shared in that peaceful feeling of something both beginning and ending at once." We have all had experiences that have symbolized our changed perceptions of ourselves and allowed us to develop a new way of understanding something. Write an essay describing such an experience to show how your perception changed and what this change in perception meant to you.

3. Lewis's essay raises questions about the nature of friendship. Montesquieu, one of the most accomplished essayists in literature, once gave the following definition: "Friendship is an arrangement by which we undertake to exchange small favors for big ones." Write an expository essay relating an anecdote that serves to verify or challenge Montesquieu's definition.

AN EFFECTIVE TECHNIQUE

We sometimes think of symbols as devices that particularly intellectual authors use in literary works to make them more complicated, to make readers work harder. However, symbols are used all the time in simple, straightforward essays, even in newspaper columns, and they often help readers understand what writers are saying. A writer might use a description of an unwashed, long-haired protester as a symbol of the turmoil of the 1960s. When a newspaper prints a picture of the president tripping as he crosses the White House lawn and uses that picture to illustrate an editorial criticizing the president for repeatedly being tripped up as he pursues his new foreign policy, the picture becomes a symbol. A symbol is simply any real object or event that conveys a larger meaning. The symbol of the unwashed protester could convey the idea that the sixties were a time of decadence, and resistance to hard work. The symbol summarizes all the complex experiences that together made up the decade. Similarly, the president's tripping might well summarize a whole series of foreign policy failures.

These symbols from newspaper columns serve as a shorthand for something that could be said another way. Sometimes, however, we find an image that seems symbolic, that seems to represent our feelings about a large part of life, without our having any clear idea what exactly it "says." Patrick Kinder Lewis shows us how to build essays out of such symbols. He tells us the story of his suddenly seeing a symbol that seems to "speak" to him about his own life. At the time, he is hopping freight trains with no particular destination, not thinking very much about "the meaning of his life." As he travels across a bridge, he is struck by a strange sight: the train has curved, so he can see the first and last cars at the same time, suspended over a beautiful wild river. He has the eerie feeling that he is watching a staged performance, with the river as an "actor" and the train itself as a "player." His description lets us know that what he sees seems to him something written by an unknown author, something that is designed to convey a meaning—a symbol. He feels that he gains "insights" as he looks at the scene.

Unfortunately, the entire "panorama played . . . for less than two minutes," and as it disappears, the meaning disappears also: "I hunted again for the insights of the moment before but found them fading." In other words, Lewis did not invent this symbol to convey some conclusions he had drawn about his life; he stumbled across it, felt it was packed with meaning, and has struggled ever since to unpack that meaning. He writes this essay to figure out for himself the "insights" he once had.

Lewis makes valiant efforts in his essay to state directly what the symbol means to him: it has something to do with "eternity," with "living life moment by moment," and with "childbirth." We can see what it is about the train curving over the valley that makes it suggest such profound thoughts: Lewis seems to be able to see the future (what is ahead of him, the front of the train) and the past (what is behind him, the last car) all at once. We can see how traveling with no particular goal could be like living in the past, the present, and the future at the same time. But we cannot quite tell how all of Lewis's explanations of his insights hang together (how is eternity like childbirth?). Even more important, Lewis himself cannot unify all the ideas he generates by thinking about the symbolic moment. Symbols rarely have one single meaning; they can summarize many experiences precisely because they mix together many ideas.

Lewis continued working on this essay after winning the Bedford Prize. In response to peer editing, he recognized that he could never fully explain all that his symbol meant to him, and so in his revision of his essay (reprinted in Chapter 2), he drops most of his abstract explanations and tells more about his life at the time he was traveling. He realizes that it is the way the symbol fits into his life that gives it its meaning, not his ability to translate it into abstract generalizations.

Lewis's revision also shows another feature of symbols: they can mean different things at different times. Lewis changed the meaning of his symbol in his revision. In the prize-winning draft, the curving train represents Lewis's "passion for life," his living "moment by moment," free of plans made in the past that determine the future. Riding the trains seems a model for what Lewis will seek all his life. In the revision, the vision on the bridge marks a moment when the narrator's life changes, when he decides to give up the life of the open road. The curving train then represents a different kind of freedom from plans: the freedom when past and future hang suspended because a person is pausing between two different paths. In this revision, riding the trains is only an interlude, a pause when Lewis steps outside the normal flow of his life.

We all have had experiences of coming upon symbols. We meander through our day and find ourselves staring intently at something—a pile of textbooks that we threw onto the desk, knocking onto the floor a postcard from a friend we haven't bothered calling for months. Suddenly what is before us seems full of meaning, seems "staged," arranged by an unknown hand to symbolize something. As we pause and stare at the books and postcard, memories from the past few days or even the past few years flit through the mind: a late-night discussion of whether one could live according to Camus's philosophy; the last visit home, when the friend looked very young. These memories seem to fit together in a pattern we had not noticed before, a pattern summarized by the textbooks and postcard. We might be able to state the insight we have in general terms, but it will probably sound vague and abstract—"I'm glad I have come to college. I guess I finally am growing up and living my own life. I am no longer clinging to the past." To communicate to other people the power of this new insight, we cannot simply state it abstractly; we have to make them feel the importance of the textbooks replacing the postcard, of school and new ideas knocking old friends and childhood into the dust. If we tell the story of coming across the symbol and of the memories that the symbol seemed to tie together, we might enable other people to share our sense of having been granted a brief but important insight.

A symbol is much more than the generalizations we derive from it, though we might have to state the generalizations to help other people see the symbol as we see it. Lewis has to tell us about "eternity" to explain why the curving train is so important to him. But we leave Lewis's essay not so much with new ideas about eternity as with a striking vision and with a sense of his life at the time.

In the next selection, Annie Dillard also retells an experience of coming upon a symbolic vision and trying to make sense of it. She describes a moth burning in a candle flame, and she uses such intense language that this ordinary event seems powerfully full of meaning. She does not try to explain the meaning explicitly, as Lewis does, but instead surrounds her description of the moth with a description of her own life, relying on the parallels between her two descriptions to reveal to us how to "read" the burning moth as she does: it is a word, a symbol, speaking to her, summarizing her life.

ANOTHER ILLUSTRATION OF THE TECHNIQUE

ANNIE DILLARD

Death of a Moth

Annie Dillard describes herself as "a poet and walker with a background in theology and a penchant for quirky facts." She studied theology and literature at Hollins College, receiving an M.A. in 1968, and then wrote nonfiction for The Living Wilderness *magazine and published several collections of poems and essays. During the last decade, she has taught creative writing at Western Washington University and Wesleyan University and has become one of the most celebrated contemporary American writers, winning a Pulitzer Prize for* Pilgrim at Tinker Creek, *her essay collection from which this selection is taken.*

Dillard regards writing and religion as alternative ways to walk into the wilderness; poets and saints explore realms beyond everyday thinking and everyday speech: "Art and religion probe the mysteries in those difficult areas where blurred and powerful symbols are the only possible speech and their arrangement into coherent religions and works of art the only possible grammar. . . . A symbol . . . is a kind of exploratory craft. It is a space probe. Although it is constructed of the planet's materials, it nevertheless leaves the planet altogether." She warns that a writer who decides to embark on such an exploratory journey by constructing a symbol cannot expect to control her travels: "Symbols outreach the span of their maker's hand; they illuminate a wider area than that which their maker ever intended. Far from being a receptacle in which you, the artist, drop your ideas . . . [a symbol] is more like an ill-trained Labrador retriever which yanks you into traffic."

I live alone with two cats, who sleep on my legs. There is a yellow one, 1
and a black one whose name is Small. In the morning I joke to the black one,
Do you remember last night? Do you remember? I throw them both out before
breakfast, so I can eat.

There is a spider, too, in the bathroom, of uncertain lineage, bulbous at 2
the abdomen and drab, whose six-inch mess of web works, works somehow,
works miraculously, to keep her alive and me amazed. The web is in a corner
behind the toilet, connecting tile wall to tile wall. The house is new, the
bathroom immaculate, save for the spider, her web, and the sixteen or so
corpses she's tossed to the floor.

The corpses appear to be mostly sow bugs, those little armadillo creatures 3
who live to travel flat out in houses, and die round. In addition to sow-bug
husks, hollow and sipped empty of color, there are what seem to be two or

three wingless moth bodies, one new flake of earwig, and three spider carcasses crinkled and clenched.

I wonder on what fool's errand an earwig, or a moth, or a sow bug, would 4 visit that clean corner of the house behind the toilet; I have not noticed any blind parades of sow bugs blundering into corners. Yet they do hazard there, at a rate of more than one a week, and the spider thrives. Yesterday she was working on the earwig, mouth on gut; today he's on the floor. It must take a certain genius to throw things away from there, to find a straight line through that sticky tangle to the floor.

Today the earwig shines darkly, and gleams, what there is of him: a dorsal 5 curve of thorax and abdomen, and a smooth pair of pincers by which I knew his name. Next week, if the other bodies are any indication, he'll be shrunk and gray, webbed to the floor with dust. The sow bugs beside him are curled and empty, fragile, a breath away from brittle fluff. The spiders lie on their sides, translucent and ragged, their legs drying in knots. The moths stagger against each other, headless, in a confusion of arcing strips of chitin like peeling varnish, like a jumble of buttresses for cathedral vaults, like nothing resembling moths, so that I would hesitate to call them moths, except that I have had some experience with the figure Moth reduced to a nub.

Two summers ago I was camped alone in the Blue Ridge Mountains of 6 Virginia. I had hauled myself and gear up there to read, among other things, *The Day on Fire*, by James Ullman, a novel about Rimbaud that had made me want to be a writer when I was sixteen; I was hoping it would do it again. So I read every day sitting under a tree by my tent, while warblers sang in the leaves overhead and bristle worms trailed their inches over the twiggy dirt at my feet; and I read every night by candlelight, while barred owls called in the forest and pale moths seeking mates massed round my head in the clearing, where my light made a ring.

Moths kept flying into the candle. They would hiss and recoil, reeling upside 7 down in the shadows among my cooking pans. Or they would singe their wings and fall, and their hot wings, as if melted, would stick to the first thing they touched—a pan, a lid, a spoon—so that the snagged moths could struggle only in tiny arcs, unable to flutter free. These I could release by a quick flip with a stick; in the morning I would find my cooking stuff decorated with torn flecks of moth wings, ghostly triangles of shiny dust here and there on the aluminum. So I read, and boiled water, and replenished candles, and read on.

One night a moth flew into the candle, was caught, burnt dry, and held. I 8 must have been staring at the candle, or maybe I looked up when a shadow crossed my page; at any rate, I saw it all. A golden female moth, a biggish one with a two-inch wingspread, flapped into the fire, drooped abdomen into the wet wax, stuck, flamed, and frazzled in a second. Her moving wings ignited like tissue paper, like angels' wings, enlarging the circle of light in the clearing and creating out of the darkness the sudden blue sleeves of my sweater, the green leaves of jewelweed by my side, the ragged red trunk of a pine; at once the light contracted again and the moth's wings vanished in a fine, foul smoke. At the same time, her six legs clawed, curled, blackened, and ceased, disappearing utterly. And her head jerked in spasms, making a spattering noise; her antennae crisped and burnt away and her heaving mouthparts cracked like pistol fire. When it was all over, her head was, so far as I could determine, gone, gone the long way of her wings and legs. Her head was a hole lost to time. All that was left was the glowing horn shell of her abdomen and thorax—a fraying, partially collapsed gold tube jammed upright in the candle's round pool.

And then this moth-essence, this spectacular skeleton, began to act as a   9 wick. She kept burning. The wax rose in the moth's body from her soaking abdomen to her thorax to the shattered hole where her head should have been, and widened into flame, a saffron-yellow flame that robed her to the ground like an immolating monk. That candle had two wicks, two winding flames of identical light, side by side. The moth's head was fire. She burned for two hours, until I blew her out.

She burned for two hours without changing, without swaying or kneeling— 10 only glowing within, like a building fire glimpsed through silhouetted walls, like a hollow saint, like a flame-faced virgin gone to God, while I read by her light, kindled, while Rimbaud in Paris burnt out his brain in a thousand poems, while night pooled wetly at my feet.

So. That is why I think those hollow shreds on the bathroom floor are 11 moths. I believe I knew what moths look like, in any state.

I have three candles here on the table which I disentangle from the plants 12 and light when visitors come. The cats avoid them, although Small's tail caught fire once; I rubbed it out before she noticed. I don't mind living alone. I like eating alone and reading. I don't mind sleeping alone. The only time I mind being alone is when something is funny; then, when I am laughing at something funny, I wish someone were around. Sometimes I think it is pretty funny that I sleep alone.

Focusing on Annie Dillard's Use of Symbolism

1. In the long description in paragraphs 6–10, what phrases make us think of things other than the moth burning? What words seem too intense, too powerful for this ordinary event and thereby suggest that Annie Dillard is seeing something much bigger than the death of a single moth here?

2. In paragraph 10, Dillard says that she herself is "kindled" by the light of the moth burning; in what sense is she burning as the moth is? She also reports that the writer Rimbaud "burnt out his brain in a thousand poems." How is Rimbaud like the moth? What is Dillard saying about herself, Rimbaud, and writers in general by comparing them to a moth?

3. Dillard surrounds her description of the moth with paragraphs describing her life written in a matter-of-fact tone. After reading the description of the moth burning up, what does her saying she has "three candles" make you think about her? She observes, in paragraph 5, that the moths on the floor of her bathroom look like "buttresses for cathedral vaults"; how does this description connect to the language she uses to describe the burning moth? She repeatedly mentions that she lives alone. How does living alone make her like the religious figures she mentions in paragraphs 9 and 10?

4. In paragraph 4, Dillard describes the spider in her house as having a "certain genius to throw things away." We often think of writers as "geniuses," and we can easily imagine a writer throwing papers on the floor like the spider who is "working on" various bugs and throwing the empty carcasses on the floor. If the spider is a symbol of the writer, what point does Dillard make about writers by using it?

WORKING WITH THE TECHNIQUE IN YOUR OWN WRITING

1. Write an essay in which you try to summarize some part of your life. See if you can find an object or event that seems centrally important to that part of your life. For example, if you were writing about your whole high school career, you might find it summarized in the view of your house out the schoolbus window. If you wanted to summarize a terrible summer vacation, you might describe a beat-up hat that you threw away with great vehemence when you finally came home. Try to make your readers see why this object or image seems to symbolize that part of your life, why you remember it so clearly. You will probably need to include some explanation of the meaning you see in the object or event, but it is equally important to surround the symbol with descriptions of what was going on in your life at the time you saw it, so your readers get the feeling that it brings together all the strands of your life at that time.

2. The hippie is repeatedly invoked as a symbol of the 1960s; the flapper represents
   the 1920s; Ozzie and Harriet, the 1950s. What kind of person would you select
   as a symbolic image of the current decade? Write an essay explaining your
   choice. If you believe something other than a person—an event, perhaps—
   would serve better as a symbol of this decade, write about that. As a slight
   variation on this topic, you might write an essay about the kind of person that
   would represent *your generation*, people going through college in this decade,
   rather than writing about the decade in general.

THOMAS LEYBA

University of Texas, El Paso
El Paso, Texas
Martha Connolly, instructor

Writing serves for Thomas Leyba as a source of pride and independence: "Instructors always say consider the reader first. This is true of some people and in some instances. However, pleasing the reader many times can be a result of pleasing yourself first. If I am not satisfied with my own work, and you can apply this to any aspect of my life, then I know those whom I am trying to please will also not be satisfied. Well, perhaps some would be, but it is always important to be the first to take pride in your work. If I have written an essay, and I am satisfied with the finished product, I have won any contest."

Thomas Leyba proudly traces his family heritage to quite different parts of the globe. His father's parents immigrated to the United States from Italy, his mother's from Mexico. His maternal grandparents' adobe home, "on a rise that creates an eroded horizon," still stands, "desolate unfortunately," as a historical landmark in San Lorenzo, New Mexico. Raised in El Paso, Texas, Thomas Leyba earned numerous honors and awards from Andress High School, including, among many others, election to the National Honor Roll and representation in Who's Who Among American High School Students. He also served as editor in chief of the school newspaper and received a scholarship from the El Paso Community Foundation to attend college.

It was during a two-year residency in the state of Washington that Leyba learned, as he explains, "the importance of race":

> I loved my stay in the Pacific Northwest, and the many beautiful
> people I met and shared life with. However, even still I was a
> raisin sharing space in a jar with other raisins, only they were
> yogurt covered—naked culture amongst a crowd whose real cul-
> ture was clothed. These people threw labels at me, at my bronze
> skin; it was an obvious attempt to create a wardrobe for me
> and the close friends I kept. I had an armoire full of clothes they
> wanted me to wear. Nevertheless, I had my own chest and my
> own clothes. It was their anger toward my own apparent culture
> that helped me to adopt a deep pride in culture Latino.

Leyba credits "my race and the lessons taught to me during the process of its adoption, coupled with my mother and her tender understanding of the art of motherhood" as the two most influential aspects of his life.

A friend pointed out the Marfa Lights to him on a trip along Highway 90 one evening. Fascinated by "any unexplained phenomenon," Leyba decided that night "to conduct some research to find out their source. The next semester I had a more specific purpose for which to conduct my research—my research project for my freshman English course." He created a simple enough goal for himself in writing "The Marfa Lights": "West Texas, hidden in a storm of dust that carries with it the aroma of stone-ground corn *tortillas and the stench of dirty river water, is the home of an extremely mysterious phenomenon. Those who know about it are proud to be hosts, and those who are not aware of it should learn." Leyba's interest in his subject prompted an unusual personal investment of his time and intelligence: "By conducting my own interviews and chasing the Lights myself, I offered the reader the opportunity to feel what I felt. After reading the completed essay, I was ready to return to Marfa and see the Lights again. After my readers read my essay, maybe they will want to do the same."*

The Marfa Lights

Space has its black hole. Bermuda has its triangle. Texas has the Marfa 1 Lights. *Texas Monthly* columnist Gary Cartwright wrote:

> I promise you, something's out there. I was with a group of writers and poets, skeptics all, who saw them in August 1983. We were parked on U.S. 90 about halfway between Marfa and Alpine, looking south across an abandoned air base toward the Chinati Mountains. When the first point of light appeared where there had been only darkness, there were some nervous giggles and a fluttering of rationalizations, and when a second came dancing above and to the right of the first, I swear something ice-cold moved across my skin. The points of light appeared one or two or sometimes three at a time, about the intensity of second-magnitude stars, moving diagonally and sometimes horizontally for ten to fifteen seconds. They would vanish and then reappear in some new location. They could have been a mile away, or twenty or thirty. True, there were some ranch houses out there in the blackness, and some unmarked roads and Santa Fe railroad track. There was even a major highway, U.S. 67, which runs from Marfa to Shafter to Presidio, but it was many miles to the west of where we saw the lights. No one spoke for a long while. Somewhere out there an animal wailed. San Antonio poet Naomi Nye told me later that she thought the experience changed her life. She said she had dreams in which the whole energy of the dream was directed at trying to figure out how to "get to the lights."[1]

Exactly one century prior to this 1983 sighting, the Mystery Lights, out- 2 side the West Texas town of Marfa, were first reported. To this day in 1986, the Lights remain a puzzle to their observers and to researchers. Although the source of the Marfa Lights stands in need of explanation, they have inspired much folklore, and while some of the legends and myths about their source have supernatural explanations, some have scientific or natural interpretations.

Marfa, located approximately 200 miles southeast of El Paso, Texas, played host to the cast of the big movie hit *Giant* in 1955. Mr. Armando Vasquez, owner of Mando's Auto Repair in Marfa, said, "I have a good friend named Pete Chavez who sold his ranch to the Art Foundation; and he told 'ole' Pete that James Dean (*Giant* cast member) asked him permission to sleep out on his land. And, for several nights Mr. Dean slept out on the ranch, just so he could stare at the Ghost Lights, all night long."[2]

Back in 1883, Robert Ellison and his wife had just moved to the Big Bend area, and on their second night upon settlement, they saw them on the horizon. They were the first to report the Marfa Lights. According to the daughter of Mr. and Mrs. Ellison, Mrs. Lee Plumbley of Marfa, "My daddy said they unloaded their cattle at what is now Alpine (Texas) and they started driving them toward Marfa. When they came through Paisano Pass and got onto the flats where you can see for a long distance, they saw the Light. He thought it was an Apache campfire, and they weren't too friendly in those times. He finally began to realize it wasn't a homeplace or a campfire. Others in the country before him told him they'd always seen it."[3] When the Lights were later explained as being automobile headlight reflections, Mr. Ellison, then aging, denounced this theory claiming there were "damned few lights, roads, or cars" in his day.[4]

The Marfa Lights are illuminated apparitions that are thought to appear near what used to be an Air Force base. (To avoid confusion in referring to the Marfa Lights as singular or plural subjects, keep in mind that while up to five Lights have been noted to appear, sometimes only one Marfa Light appears; and since their number in appearance varies, the eyewitness accounts included in this essay, indeed, will also vary as they stand as proof.) So as not to confuse the luminous gremlins with ranch lights on the horizon of Mitchell Flat, visitors are advised to view to the southwest, on or around a red light referred to as the border patrol light. According to one observer, the Lights mostly play to the right of the red light. About nine miles east of Marfa on U.S. 90 is a newly marked viewing area for tourists just passing through. A sign indicating the direction of the Marfa Lights can be found on the paved shoulder of the highway. However, "The best view of the Lights," suggests Armando Vasquez, "is on the road that has a sign that has the name of about, oh, seven ranches; it's called the Northpile road, it's a county road. . . . It's about three miles from the highway, on a little rise, beyond this small ranch—that's the best place."[5]

Mr. Vasquez, previously mentioned in this report, is an authority on the [6] Marfa Lights, at least the Texas Highway Department seems to think so. The Department contacted Mr. Vasquez to assist them in placing the "Marfa Lights viewing site" sign off of U.S. 90. They were obviously aware of his popularity among tourists and simply asked for his assistance, even though he had never worked for them before. "They (the department) thought that by taking them out there, I would show them the best area (for viewing the Ghost Lights) to place the sign," said Mr. Vasquez, whose family has resided on a ranch outside of Marfa since the beginning of the 1800s. "We drove back and forth on Highway 90, me and the Texas Highway Department head in Marfa, just so we could find the place that offered the best view of the Lights. We found it, and he (the department authority) ordered a crew to pave a small area and erect a sign that reads 'Marfa Lights Viewing Site.' "[6] According to Marfa Chamber of Commerce employee Minerva Freeman regarding the effect of weather conditions on the Lights, "They are best on a clear night, but have been seen during cloudy nights."[7]

In the same year that Mr. and Mrs. Ellison first reported the small glow- [7] ing spheres, an engineer surveying for the Southern Pacific triangulated the Lights and declared them to be kerosene lanterns on the ranch of one Jesus Rojas. Ninety years later (1973), Donald Witt, a Sul Ross State University physicist, claimed that he had solved the mystery once and for all.[8] Witt did agree with the Southern Pacific engineer that one source of light indeed originated at a ranch now know as the Mellard Ranch. U.S. 67 was the source of his second explanation. Steve Neu of Alpine was a student when Witt revealed his solution in his lab. As to the presentation of evidence, Neu laughed and said, "There was great expectation as he opened this box. It contained an auto headlight."[9] Nevertheless, the explanation (apparently turned joke) proved unsatisfactory to the invited skeptics and to Witt him- self. On a returning trip to Alpine, Witt and an assistant recall observing two bright yellow lights "dancing" on the horizon.

"I can't explain what we saw that night," Witt admitted. "It occurred to [8] me that it could be the lights of a locomotive on the Ojinaga-Topolobampo run. Of course, that would have been eighty miles away. I never checked to see if there was a train at that hour."[10]

That same year, postal worker James Mecklin told Gary Painter of Marfa: [9]

> I first came to this country in 1928 to work on a
> newspaper. As soon as we got here we started hearing
> about the Marfa Lights. We saw the Lights several times

and spent a week trying to find them. Later on when World War II came along, I was in charge of the post office at the airbase. One morning I was talking to a Sergeant Robarbe was his name, he was mail orderly, and he was from New York and all he knew was pavement and he thought these antelope were funny looking cows, things like that you know. Anyway we got to talking about this Light, and, boy, that intrigued him a whole lot and some way or another he got to talking to his squadron commander, a Major Davidson, and he was interested in the stars, astronomy. He was an amateur astronomer. So, boy, he comes hot foot'n it down there and wants me to tell him about these Lights.

About a week and he was already het up about it. He'd been out there every night seeing it, and there'd been some talk and he got to listening and they wondered if it was cars or something over there or what.

But me telling him about it, that was what impressed him there was maybe something strange. He investigated and got his maps out and looked at this highway. They had maps of all this country drawn up by the base, and he couldn't locate any ranch houses or anything that would make this light. So he thought maybe, well, there is something out there.

So he asked me, said "Do you think that we could follow it by an airplane or not?"

So I said, "Well I don't know if you could follow it by an airplane or not."

He said, "We got a lot of 'em out here."

They were flying these old twin-engine Cessnas made out of plywood, mostly to train in school there. Those twin-engines they were death traps.

He said, "Well, I can get hold of some planes." Says, "You know, I'm going to check this thing out." Says, "I'm tired of all this stuff I've heard about this."

Meanwhile he talked to other people in Marfa and got the same ideas about the Light as he got from me and heard a bunch of stories about it and said, "We're going to put an end to all this. We're going to check it out."

I wasn't in on this, but they told me that for three nights he set up teams out there of four planes, one behind the other, and that they would follow that Light. When they took off they could see it come and go. After they got to

where they thought it was, it would disappear. Then maybe
it would appear way down ahead of them, and pretty soon
it was ending up in Mexico, where they couldn't go. It
moved ahead of them all the time. It would disappear on
them, then pick up and go.

This man finally gave up on it, this Major Davidson,
and he was mystified. The last time I talked to him before
he left, he said, "Mecklin, I'm leaving you and Marfa and
your Light here. I'd sure like to have found out what it was
but couldn't do it."[11]

Fritz Kahl, who today operates Kahl's Aviation service out of Marfa, also 10
flew in an effort to find the nature of the Marfa Lights. "Whatever they are,
I'd definitely classify them as friendly," says the man who trained pilots at the
air base (on Mitchell Flat) in the forties.[12] Nevertheless, leave him and his
reported adventure in the high dark for a moment and turn to the supernatural.

There are generally two sets of legends about the Marfa Lights. One set 11
serves the older generation, and the other serves the younger. While the
younger generation awaits scientific explanations for the source of the Lights,
old-timers seem to lean toward the supernatural. In fact, they refer to the orbs
as Ghost Lights. Mrs. W. T. Giddens, raised in the Chinati Mountains, told
columnist Ed Syers of a tradition in her family. She said, "I've seen the Ghost
Lights all my life and can't remember their causing any harm other than fright.
They like to follow you out in the pasture at night, seem to be drawn to people
and stock, and animals don't seem to fear them at all."[13] Mrs. Giddens also
told about her father's experience with the Lights. He was lost at night in a
blizzard miles from home. He claimed that the Marfa Lights guided him to a
small cave; he also asserted that they "told" him they were spirits from long
before that wanted to save him. The next morning, the Lights and the blizzard
were gone. He could see the trail back home.

Early settlers would have told you the ghostly illuminations were the spirit 12
of a Chisos Apache warrior left sealed in a cave to guard stolen gold. The
Lights have also been claimed to be Pancho Villa moving supplies across the
Rio Grande. Some think the Marfa Lights are luminous gas, temperature in-
version, static electricity, or even reflections of the Los Angeles freeway lights.
There is, however, a locally accepted story about an Apache chief who became
separated from his tribe and who still lights fires in hopes of finding them.
Many legends, such as this one, tell of Indians in search of their tribes. When
Spaniards rounded up Indians to use as slaves, it is said that they would cut
off the chief's head. According to the tale, the chief picked up his head and
walked away with a lantern to find his tribesmen. It is also said that other

chiefs joined him, and the Lights are the Indian chiefs searching for their captive fellows. Early in this century, Marfa Lights legends told of the pseudo Indians and the stars. One myth is that the Lights are temporary homes of fallen stars in which the Great Spirit stores his thunderbolts.

According to Dr. Elton Miles, professor of English at Sul Ross State University, who has a special interest in folklore research, at least one or more of the Lights appears every night, either in white, green, or blue. They appear, disappear: move diagonally or horizontally.[14] Mrs. Roy Smith, a colleague of Dr. Miles, has also seen them and she claims that the Lights seem to approach quite near.[15] According to her own account, she and her husband stopped to observe them on a clear night. They saw several of the Lights near the ground, moving about. She also claimed that the Lights disappeared in one spot, and reappeared in another. She said that they seemed to move toward the car and remain near the hood.[16]

Even in 1919, cowboys searched for the source of the Lights without any success. It is recorded that in 1900 Roy Stillwell saw the Marfa Lights "dance" on Dead Horse Mountain, in what is now known as Big Bend National Park.[17] Salomon Ramos, a cowboy of the 1930s, working near the Paisano Peak east of Marfa, saw the Lights flickering on the western horizon.[18] They were also spotted in 1927 by Ferdinand Weber.[19] He thought they were spirits of the Chisos Apaches.

Along with the circulation of legends and myths came the inevitable rumors. Mrs. Maria Roberts of Marfa said, "In 1943 during World War II, while working at the Marfa Army Airbase, I overheard two young pilots talking about the strange lights to the south. The boys believed that it (the Marfa Light) was a light used to guide German supply planes in. They were sure that the Germans had a large, well-hidden camp and were getting ready to invade the U.S. by way of Mexico."[20] According to Mrs. Eva Kerr Jones, Mrs. Roberts's mother, in 1918 the tale was similar.[21] She heard that during World War I the Light guided German Cavalry and pack mules in. Even earlier, in 1914, Mrs. E. Kerr, her mother, said the Light (only one appearing) was said to be Pancho Villa moving in supplies and men preparing to attack the United States.[22]

Part of the World War II myth involves Hitler. It was told that German prisoners at the Army Airbase were released when Hitler was killed. They headed for Mexico and were never heard from again, and the Light is Adolf Hitler's ghost searching for them with a lantern. According to another legend, in the latter part of the war, the Marfa Apparitions were supposed to be the remnants of Hitler's Third Reich, joined by escaped POWs from El Paso and the Fuehrer himself.

One legend portrays the shining phantoms as being murderers. By simulating 17
the formation of a landing strip, they have been accused of luring unsuspecting
pilots and crews into the Chinati Mountainside. This was supposedly the cause
for the closing of the airbase. Airport officials sent up a helicopter to locate
the Lights. They could not be seen from the helicopter; and when the pilots
landed the craft where a light was supposed to be, the helicopter exploded,
leaving no trace of the men. Disasters, such as the runway lights incident, as
well as the helicopter incident, made the U.S. Army start an investigation to
try to learn the nature of the Marfa Lights. However, only more stories developed; no documented reports, no official results, nothing evolved.

The military used several jeeps and a plane, equipped with intercommu- 18
nicational devices for the search. One jeep had directions to drive directly into
the Light. According to one of the stories that evolved from the search, when
the jeep reported reaching the Light, contact went dead. The jeep was located,
but the passengers were not. It was found at a place where it was thought that
the rocks drew heat from the sun, radiated it as light at night, and burned up
the men. C. W. Davis of McCamey knows better. He told Charles Nichols
in 1972, "One of the people involved (in the search) was a personal friend of
mine. He told me that him and two of his buddies were sort of drunk and
decided to look for the Lights. They stole a jeep, which they wrecked. They
were afraid of getting caught, so they set fire to the jeep and sneaked back to
the airbase."[23] The record does not bear either incident out.

Once again, returning to aviator Fritz Kahl's account, he once told an 19
interviewer, "What I have to tell you, I could say in five minutes. I chased
them (the Lights) in an airplane, not once but several times, and this was in
1943 and early 1944. My God, there I was, a World War II aviator. Hell, I
was twenty-one years old and didn't have any sense, flying airplanes at night
out in the hills, right down on the ground. You got to be young. You got to
be crazy. But we tried it. Only thing is, you know, you leave the airbase and
you get out on the Presidio Highway a ways, and you run into the hills right
quick."[24] To this day, Mr. Kahl returned to find nothing but flour-covered
brush. Sometimes, not even the flour was found.

If that which is supernatural falls short of explaining the source of these 20
small glowing phantasms, then you might consider siding with scientific interpretation and the younger generation. John P. Kenney and Elwood Wright,
two geologists who prospected for uranium just outside of Marfa in the 1960s,
spent a number of nights on Mitchell Flat investigating the Lights.[25] According
to Marfa Municipal Judge Caroline Rogers, the Marfa Lights became a passion
to her friend John: "Pat (his middle name) did a thorough study on the Lights,

he was determined to discover their source."[26] Mr. Kenney and Mr. Wright recorded their observations in a journal.

On March 19, 1973, according to the handwritten account, the two were 21 sitting in their car near a country road ten miles east of Marfa about 10 P.M. Suddenly, some horses in a field whinnied and bolted. Moments later, they saw a ball of light rapidly moving in from the southwest, with another one behind it. The lights, which "appeared to be about one-half the size of a basketball," moved "behind some bushes and in front of other bushes" and hovered briefly a few hundred feet away before vanishing, Wright and Kenney wrote.[27]

Of course, while viewing the Lights from a clearing on Mitchell Flat, just 22 as Wright and Kenney did, might offer a pleasing view of the glowing spheres, one place also offering a spectacular view is a paved area near the gate of the abandoned airfield. According to the *Lubbock Avalanche-Journal*, it is located nine miles east of Marfa, along U.S. Highway 67/90.[28] However, those wanting a closer view, perhaps to chase the Lights for purposes of investigation, are advised by Municipal Judge Caroline Rogers to request permission from the ranchers to venture on their property. "For this reason," said the honorable Rogers, "a sign indicating the 'Marfa Lights Viewing Site' was erected on the shoulder of a public highway."[29]

Printed in an article written on the Marfa Lights in a March 27, 1975, issue 23 of the *El Paso Herald Post* was a phone number offering interested readers a chance to participate in a club effort to discover the source of the shining apparitions. On March 28, 1975, members of the Big Bend Outdoor Club and a team of engineers from Houston attempted to determine the coordinates of the Marfa Lights.[30] Two nights later, using sophisticated equipment, four-wheel drive vehicles and an airplane to gather data to be fed into a computer, ground teams were stationed at various points near the old airbase to guide the aircraft being used over the area. When the plane reached the right place over the lights, the crew dropped powder over them to mark the spot. Members operating the vehicles then searched for the powder and the source of the Mystery Lights. There were no reports in later issues of the *El Paso Herald Post* either denying the existence or unveiling the source of the Marfa Lights; however, results of this search were mentioned eight days later in the *El Paso Times*.

The March 28 search led observers to believe the Light was a mercury vapor 24 lamp on the Kenneth Mellard Ranch which is located on the plains south of U.S. 90 and between Marfa and Shafter on U.S. 67.[31] Apparently dissatisfied with the results of this search, Don Witt, the Sul Ross University physics instructor previously mentioned, coordinated another hunt for the Presidio County Ghost Light in hopes of finding conclusive evidence of its source. According to Mr. Witt, a former NASA scientist who later analyzed UFO reports for the CIA, a plane was to fly over the Mellard Ranch on Friday the eleventh of April to pinpoint the Light. There were no later reports of this particular search, but Mr. Witt explained the mystery as being "a succession of lights which began with Apache campfires seen by wagon trains passing through to El Paso in the 1850's."[32]

John Derr, a geophysicist with the U.S. Geological Survey in Denver, 25 has his own theory. He thinks that what are seen may be "earthquake lights," softball-size globes such as those reported in places prone to tremors. However, Marfa hasn't had any tremors to prove this theory. In addition, even though Mr. Derr thinks that earthquake lights may be small clouds of charged particles, they themselves need investigation and explanation.[33] Fritz Kahl, our famous flour-dropping aviator, claims that Marfa is in a basin between mountain ranges and has lots of unusual weather.[34] This unusual weather claim is what an astronomer who once worked at the McDonald Observatory 37 miles north of Marfa based his theory on. Looking down toward Marfa from his perch on Mount Locke, Eric Silverberg says he used to see "twinkling lights well above the horizon where there shouldn't have been any. It was one of the most convincing UFO phenomena I've ever seen."[35] He believes that what he saw were light beams bent and carried great distances by what is called the Novaya Zembya effect which is a "tunneling" of light due to adjacent layers of air at sharply different temperatures, the source of light being either car lights or bright stars.[36] This theory is easily dispelled simply because there couldn't have been car lights in the case 100 years ago; and since there have been numerous sightings on cloudy nights, starlight could hardly be a source.

The "scientific" explanations abound; they include mica deposits, gases from 26 the ground, uranium deposits, bat guano in caves, little volcanoes, swamp gas, phosphorus in the rocks, coal deposits, bones in the earth, static electricity, and reflections from a comet or meteor.

Mr. Norman C. Davis, a retired county attorney of Marfa, claims the 27 Chinati Mountains are the starting point for many surveys. Incidentally he was born in 1916, in the same house he presently occupies. "There's been lots of prospecting on these mountains," said Mr. Davis in a recent interview. "Prospectors have looked for ores of many kinds, and they had a perlite mine there at one time. They hauled out quite a bit of perlite from that (Chinati) Mountain," he added.[37] Note that perlite is a volcanic glass, usually appearing as a mass of enamellike globules, formed by concentric fractures.[38] This sounds good enough to solve the mystery of the Marfa Lights phenomenon; however, investigations and reports, again, do not bear this out.

Over the years, the phenomenal specters over Mitchell Flat have been 28 photographed and even captured on videotape. Frank X. Tolbert wrote of his Marfa Light coverage in the *Dallas Morning News*.[39] He claimed that the light was first mistaken for the planet Venus. Proving this theory became difficult, though, because every time Mr. Tolbert stopped the car to take a picture, the light winked out. Joe Shelton, who runs a filling station and lives in Alpine, has also seen the strange lights several times in the area around Marfa. Strange enough to classify them as phenomena? Well, once he and his wife were driving back from the El Paso airport and she had fallen asleep in the front seat. In his rearview mirror, he noticed what he described as "an 18-wheeler lit up like a Christmas tree."[40] Shelton, intimidated by the appearance of this object, turned to look over his left shoulder. "Nothing!" he said, "Gone! Just like that!"[41] Because it seems the actions of the lights depend upon the reactions of their viewers, as the Tolbert and Shelton incidents would prove, it would appear that the Lights interface well with humans.

There is one reported time, however, that the Lights chose not to elude. 29 In January 1980, assigned to pursue the Mountain Light mystery, *Houston Chronicle* newsman Stan Redding and photographer Carlos Antonio Rios were able to obtain the best description, close up, yet recorded.[42] They noted red, white, and blue baseball-sized spheres, darting about the ground, uniting, then separating. They claimed that the Lights seemed unattached, and unsupported, each one illuminating the brush over which it hovered. Photographer Rios backed Redding with his pictures.[43]

Finally, from the Pentagon came succinct instruction—leave the Lights 30 alone.[44] This order was apparently directed at the Army, Air Force, and the many surveyor teams, and reporters that had been flocking to investigate the Marfa Lights since World Wars I and II. The question that arises here is Why did the government issue such an order? It seems quite justifiable to wonder if they had been conducting top-secret experiments near Marfa, especially since documentation of the order and/or any other government intervention, including formal investigations, cannot be found. During the course of my extensive research, I inquired, through several government publications, about the role of government concerning phenomena such as the Marfa Lights. I researched the *Congressional Information Service Four-Year Cumulative Index* under Atmospheric/Meteorological research which led me to publication of prints from the Science and Technology House Committee, which is an interagency coordination of Federal Scientific Research and Development, the Federal

Council for Science and Technology, and found absolutely nothing—no reports, no investigations, nothing. . . .

As Edward Syers, author of *Ghost Stories of Texas*, wrote in his account: 31

> And so—as you see—you may take your choice of explanations. It does seem strange that no thorough scientific probe has ever been . . . I was about to say "undertaken": perhaps the word should be "reported."[45]

Unfortunately, the involvement of science *is* somewhat lower in comparison   32 to the supernatural explanations that have evolved from the Marfa Lights phenomenon. Nevertheless, neither side seems capable of closing the gap. . . .

> We left Marfa Chamber of Commerce at 6:35 P.M. March 14, nineteen hundred and eighty-six. It was me, Thomas Leyba, Mr. Richard Flores, an instructor at Andress High School in El Paso, Texas, and Felipe Soto, a student at Sul Ross State University. We drove east of Highway 90 for about six miles, in search of the Marfa Lights. We turned right off the highway onto a county ranch road that would lead us to the playground of the Marfa Lights. We crossed a cattle guard and found a sign sporting the names of all the ranches found down that particular road. We continued down this dirt road for about 20 minutes. We saw two antelope to our right. They caught a glimpse of the car and ran—by this time dusk had settled in and a few ranch lights appeared in the horizon ahead of us. After turning left at a fork in the road and crossing a cattle guard, we approached a sign that read Barliles Ranches Alta Vista Sampson's Ranch 9 miles. That's when we spotted a light, fluorescent—in the horizon. We drove closer and realized the light that we had spotted belonged to its pole and to the rancher whose land it was on. After a confrontation with a private property sign, we turned back, with great disappointment. However, at 7:44 P.M. we caught sight of what we were chasing, the Ghost Light. At first only one appeared and we could easily distinguish it from the ranch lights sharing the horizon because in contrast, the Mystery Light split in two and both lights danced in the area they had first appeared. Then one Light joined the other and this solitary Light grew dim and diminished. Almost thirty seconds later it reappeared like a star-burst on the Chinati Mountain Peak, only to become separated again. However, what's even more strange is the fact that the Lights seemed

to appear several miles away from their original position. They would vanish and then reappear in some new location. Then they began to bounce. The display seemed as if someone was standing off the highway in back of us shining a high-powered flashlight on the side of the mountain. The Lights then united and became one. Its glow was soft and harmless—it grew brighter, bounced up into the air and vanished. We were not frightened, just satisfied.

Notes

1. Gary Cartwright, "The Marfa Lights," *Texas Monthly* (November 1984): 180.
2. Personal interview with Armando F. Vasquez, 14 March 1986.
3. Elton Miles, "The Marfa Lights," *Tales of the Big Bend* (College Station, TX: Texas A & M University Press, 1976) 150.
4. Ed Syers, "The Mountain Light," *Ghost Stories of Texas* (Waco, TX: Texian Press, 1981) 67.
5. Vasquez interview.
6. Vasquez interview.
7. Ted J. Simon, "Marfa's 'Ghost Lights' Persist," *Lubbock Avalanche-Journal* 27 October 1985: E6.
8. Cartwright 180.
9. Cartwright 180.
10. Cartwright 180.
11. Miles 150.
12. Cartwright 180.
13. Miles 154.
14. Miles 149.
15. Miles 149.
16. Miles 149.
17. Miles 150.
18. Miles 150.
19. Miles 150.
20. Miles 150.
21. Miles 150.
22. Miles 150.
23. Miles 152.
24. Miles 154.
25. David Stipp, "Marfa Texas, Finds a Flickering Fame in Mystery Lights—Curious Glow Out on the Mesa Stirs Curious Theories: Illuminated Jack Rabbits?" *Wall Street Journal* 21 March 1984: 1.
26. Personal interview with Caroline Rogers, 14 March 1986.
27. Stipp 23.
28. Simon E6.
29. Rogers interview.
30. "Club Plans to Find Mystery Marfa Lights," *El Paso Herald Post* 27 March 1975: C2.
31. "Ghost Light Search Resumed," *El Paso Times* 5 April 1975: C1.
32. "Ghost Light Search Resumed" C1.
33. Stipp 23.

34. Stipp 23.
35. Stipp 23.
36. Stipp 23.
37. Personal interview with Norman C. Davis, 14 March 1986.
38. "Perlite," *Random House College Dictionary*, 1980.
39. Dennis Stacy, "Marfa's Mysterious Lights Must Be Seen to Be Believed—And Some People Don't Believe Them When They See Them," *Houston Post* 5 April 1985: E11.
40. Stacy E11.
41. Stacy E11.
42. Syers 68.
43. Syers 68.
44. Syers 67.
45. Syers 69.

Works Cited

Cartwright, Gary. "The Marfa Lights." *Texas Monthly* November 1984: 180+.

"Club Plans to Find Mystery Marfa Lights." *El Paso Herald Post* 27 March 1975: C2.

Davis, Norman C. Personal interview. 14 March 1986.

Flut, Jheri. "Marfa Lights Ancient West Texas Puzzle." *San Angelo Standard-Times* 15 September 1985: E4.

"Ghost Light Search Resumed." *El Paso Times* 5 April 1975: C1.

Miles, Elton. "The Marfa Lights." *Tales of the Big Bend*. College Station, TX. Texas A & M University Press, 1976.

"Perlite." *Random House College Dictionary*. 1980.

Rogers, Caroline. Personal interview. 14 March 1986.

Simon, Ted J. "Marfa's 'Ghost Lights' Still Persist." *Lubbock Avalanche-Journal* 27 October 1985: E6.

Stacy, Dennis. "Marfa's Mysterious Lights Must Be Seen to Be Believed—And Some People Don't Believe Them When They See Them." *Houston Post* 5 April 1985: E11.

Stipp, David. "Marfa, Texas, Finds a Flickering Fame in Mystery Lights—Curious Glow Out on the Mesa Stirs Curious Theories: Illuminated Jack Rabbits?" *Wall Street Journal* 21 March 1984: 1.

Syers, Ed. "The Mountain Light." *Ghost Stories of Texas*. Waco, TX: Texian Press, 1981.

Vasquez, Armando F. Personal interview. 14 March 1986.

Focusing on Thomas Leyba's Techniques and Revisions

1. What is Leyba's *thesis* in this essay? What idea governs the development of his essay? Catalogue the different explanations and stories Leyba offers to account for the existence of the Marfa Lights. What principle of organization does Leyba seem to rely on to create his particular sequence of explanations and anecdotes? Does he seem to favor any explanation(s)? Explain. What conclusion(s), however tentative, does Leyba offer to explain the mystery of the Marfa Lights? What larger issues about contemporary American life does Leyba address— either explicitly or implicitly—in his essay? With what effect(s)?

2. Thomas Leyba has created an ambitious goal for himself in this essay. What

evidence suggests that he enjoys writing about this subject? What evidence is there that Leyba's knowledge of his subject extends beyond library research? What aspect of the Marfa Lights controversy seems to interest Leyba most?

3. How much background information does Leyba provide for those who are unfamiliar with the mystery of the Marfa Lights? How much does Leyba assume his audience knows about the subject? Should he have provided, for example, more background information? More technical details? Anything else? By the end of Leyba's essay, how much more do his readers know about the Marfa Lights? How much closer are either Leyba or his readers to solving the mystery?

4. Leyba explains that he introduced the Marfa Lights in his essay by "reminding the reader of other phenomena, first from space, and then the ocean. As humans, we rely on logic to explain many unnatural phenomena. Science we call it. So when something occurs that we can observe, touch, or smell, yet cannot explain with logic or science, we become fascinated. I drew energy from this fact, and from the fear and astonishment expressed by my personal sources in the essay I created a picture of what can really be seen." As you reread Leyba's essay, point to those moments when he appeals to his reader's sense of sight, touch, and smell. How do the "fear and astonishment" expressed by his "personal sources" help create "a picture of what can really be seen"?

5. One of the many strengths of Leyba's essay is his ability to blend engaging and informative quotations into the flow of detailed explanations in his essay. Select one paragraph from the essay and show how Leyba effectively works into his presentation direct quotations from primary and secondary sources. In this respect, comment on the effectiveness of beginning and ending his essay on a long passage from a secondary source. What writing strategies does Leyba rely on to create a continuous sense of his own intellectual presence in this essay despite the wealth of its citations?

6. One of Leyba's major objectives in writing "The Marfa Lights" was to create an air of authenticity in his sentences: "I knew I wanted an authentic essay— one brought to life by people with a history in Marfa. I wanted to feel what Marfans felt when they spoke of the Lights." What specific strategy does Leyba rely on to create this sense of authenticity in his essay? Point to specific passages to verify your response.

7. Leyba notes that the most difficult aspect of writing for him is "wondering if my words express everything I want my readers to feel. Everything has to be genuine and honest because that is the way I am, so my words must reflect the same. Indeed, it is difficult for the amateur chef to season the soup perfectly; trial and error is time's best companion. And so we stand to be corrected, we stand to be educated." With this statement in mind, reread Leyba's essay carefully and identify the sentences or paragraphs that you think could be made more "genuine and honest." What specific revisions would you propose to strengthen each of those sentences or paragraphs?

8. Leyba reports that when he began writing his essay "everything seemed to fall into place—the quotations, definitions, explanations, everything. . . . As I began to write down all the information I had gathered from books, magazines, and interviews, everything 'melted' together. My note cards were well developed, making the writing process quite smooth. I wrote only one draft, paying high gratitude to my organizational methods." Leyba did create, however, an outline for his essay:

> Thesis Statement:
> In 1833, The Mystery Lights, outside the West Texas town of Marfa, were first reported. To this day in 1986, the Lights remain a puzzle to their observers and to researchers. Although the source of the Marfa Lights stands in need of explanation, they have inspired much folklore, and while some of the legends and myths about their source have supernatural explanations, some have scientific or natural interpretations.
>
>   I. The earliest reported sighting was in 1883. Robert Ellison and his wife had just moved to the Big Bend area of Texas, and on their second night upon settlement, they saw the Marfa Lights on the horizon.
>   A. In 1883, the Marfa Lights were spotted in the Chinati Mountains. Today, they seem to flicker from that very location.
>   B. Some of the townspeople of Marfa can share tales passed on to them by ancestors.
>
> II. From the Cowboys and Indians days to when high technology was being tapped into, the stories and rumors about the Marfa Lights changed with each new generation.
>   A. Since it is not known whether the Marfa Lights were in existence before 1883, Native Americans that occupied the land and roamed the Chinati Mountains previous to that date have become the foundation for many of the supernatural myths and legends in circulation today (1986).
>   B. The post-Indian era saw the birth of many other different myths; this time, World Wars I and II dominated the tales.
>
> III. With the younger generation, science and myth merge.
>   A. Scientific explanations abound.
>   B. Curiosity among the young and old alike brought

about, and still does bring about, significant recent
investigations.

How carefully does Leyba follow this outline? When and how does he deviate
from it? With what purpose? With what effect(s)?

Suggestions for Writing

1. At the beginning of paragraph 11, Leyba observes: "There are generally two
   sets of legends about the Marfa Lights. One set serves the older generation,
   and the other serves the younger. While the younger generation awaits scientific explanations for the source of the Lights, old-timers seem to lean toward
   the supernatural." Select some subject in modern American folklore and write
   an essay using the responses of the "younger generation" and the "old-timers"
   to endorse or to challenge the validity of Leyba's assertion.
2. Thomas Leyba's research paper provides a first-rate illustration of a writing
   maxim: dig up a subject for a research paper in your own backyard. Contact
   your county's or city's historical society. What unusual natural phenomenon
   remains a scientific mystery in your area? Conduct a thorough investigation of
   the primary and secondary sources relating to your subject. Write a research
   paper in which you unravel what is known about the subject and suggest a
   solution, however tentative, to the mystery.

AN EFFECTIVE TECHNIQUE

Sometimes we pick a topic to write on because it intrigues us, because it
seems mysterious; all too often, however, collecting information on the topic
destroys the intrigue before we even start writing. Thomas Leyba shows us a
method for becoming familiar with something mysterious and for introducing
others to it without destroying the mystery that attracted us in the first place.
Instead of trying to find "the right answer" or the definitive view in his research
on the Marfa Lights, he has collected as many different explanations and stories
as he could find, including contradictory ones. He then builds his essay as a
journey through all the fascinating and varied views that people have held
about the subject.

By presenting so many explanations for the Marfa Lights, Leyba creates a

strange effect. As we read along, we do not feel that we are gaining understanding; rather, the Lights seem stranger and stranger and therefore more and
more intriguing. If all these people cannot explain the Marfa Lights, they must
be a truly unusual phenomenon. The essay becomes a pleasant game, as we
watch one person after another step up and foolishly claim to know the right
answer. The author calmly allows everyone a turn on stage, interrupting only
when someone's explanation "sounds good enough to solve the mystery." Then
Leyba simply reminds us that "investigations and reports, again, do not bear
this out." Astronomers speaking of the "Novaya Zembya" effect end up seeming only slightly less absurd than World War II pilots who think they see Adolf
Hitler's ghost holding up a lantern—in Texas! Ultimately the essay astonishes
us with the sheer inventiveness of the human mind as well as the extent of
Leyba's research.

Thomas Leyba has not developed an unusual new form for essays; actually
he is using one of the oldest forms. Michel Montaigne, the sixteenth-century
writer credited with originating the modern essay, often constructed essays by
gathering together all the stories he could find or invent that illustrated one
familiar and simple concept, with the result that the concept became much
more complicated than it seemed at first. In an essay on "drunkenness," for
example, Montaigne includes, besides scenes of the disgusting behavior of
drunks, descriptions of the intoxication of being in love, of writing poetry,
and of having a religious vision. He makes us ponder whether drunkenness is
better or worse than soberness and whether all human activities might at times
lead to some form of drunkenness.

Montaigne points out a significant feature of these kinds of essays: each story
is included because it is fascinating in its own right. He says, "I do esteem [my
stories] solely for the use I derive from them. They often bear, outside of my
subject, the seeds of a richer and bolder material, and sound obliquely a subtler
note, both for myself, who do not wish to express anything more, and for
those who get my drift." The stories and quotations in Leyba's essays similarly
serve as more than simply efforts to pin down the exact explanation for the
Marfa Lights. The stories are engaging enough to make us drift to other topics
as we read; Leyba tantalizes us with hints of insights into such things as the
line between sanity and insanity, the nature of religious experience, and the
dullness of everyday lives. From Leyba (and Montaigne), we can learn how to
build essays that complicate and enrich our understanding of a subject.

Tom Wolfe, in the following excerpt from his book *The Right Stuff*, also
makes an essay out of a series of stories. Each of his stories is an example of
how men with "the right stuff" act; each one seems almost sufficient in itself

to define "the right stuff." But the sum total of all the stories reveals that "the right stuff" is something that exceeds any given story, any given act. As we read, we know more and more what this "stuff" is, and we see more and more that it is indefinable, mysterious.

ANOTHER ILLUSTRATION OF THE TECHNIQUE

TOM WOLFE

The Right Stuff

In the 1960s, Tom Wolfe was one of the inventors of the new journalism, a way of drawing readers into the experiences being reported. He developed a style full of dashes, dots, exclamation points, sentences snaking around a subject for hundreds of words, building and building, finally exploding in a burst of fragments printed in breathless italics—a style especially good for such intense, living-on-the-edge experiences as gambling, ingesting drugs, building exotic cars, and, in the following selection from Wolfe's book about America's first astronauts, testing new jets. Inventing a new style of writing might seem heady intellectual labor, but Wolfe's description of how it happened sounds like a college student's nightmare: he had collected stacks of note cards for a magazine article but had not written anything until the night before his deadline. Hoping that an editor would shape his story for him, he says that he just began typing his notes into a letter. "Inside a couple of hours, typing along like a madman, I could tell that something was beginning to happen. By midnight the memorandum was . . . twenty pages long and I was still typing like a maniac . . . about 6:15 A.M. . . . it was 49 pages long." The magazine published it as Wolfe wrote it, and a new style was christened.

Wolfe's varied background, including a few years playing semipro baseball and a Ph.D. in American studies from Yale University, allows him to arrive "at zonky conclusions couched in scholarly terms," according to the novelist Kurt Vonnegut. After years of writing new journalism, Wolfe published in 1987 his first novel, Bonfire of the Vanities. *Writing fiction might seem to mark the final liberation of his style and his "genius" from any bondage to facts. However, he says that he has grown more respectful of facts as he has matured as a writer. "When I started writing in college, I wanted to think that genius was 95 percent inside your head, and material was 5 percent, the clay that you molded. I now believe that the proportions are more like 65 percent material and 35 percent whatever you've got inside of you. It's very hard starting out to make yourself face up to that fact."*

What an extraordinary grim stretch that had been . . . and yet thereafter   1

Pete and Jane would keep running into pilots from other Navy bases, from the Air Force, from the Marines, who had been through their own extraordinary grim stretches. There was an Air Force pilot named Mike Collins, a nephew of former Army Chief of Staff J. Lawton Collins. Mike Collins had undergone eleven weeks of combat training at Nellis Air Force Base, near Las Vegas, and in that eleven weeks twenty-two of his fellow trainees had died in accidents, which was an extraordinary rate of two per week. Then there was a test pilot, Bill Bridgeman. In 1952, when Bridgeman was flying at Edwards Air Force Base, sixty-two Air Force pilots died in the course of thirty-six weeks of training, an extraordinary rate of 1.7 per week. Those figures were for fighter-pilot trainees only; they did not include the test pilots, Bridgeman's own confreres, who were dying quite regularly enough.

Extraordinary, to be sure; except that every veteran of flying small high- 2 performance jets seemed to have experienced these bad strings.

In time, the Navy would compile statistics showing that for a career Navy 3 pilot, i.e., one who intended to keep flying for twenty years as Conrad did, there was a 23 percent probability that he would die in an aircraft accident. This did not even include combat deaths, since the military did not classify death in combat as accidental. Furthermore, there was a better than even chance, a 56 percent probability, to be exact, that at some point a career navy pilot would have to eject from his aircraft and attempt to come down by parachute. In the era of jet fighters, ejection meant being exploded out of the cockpit by a nitroglycerine charge, like a human cannonball. The ejection itself was so hazardous—men lost knees, arms, and their lives on the rim of the cockpit or had the skin torn off their faces when they hit the "wall" of air outside—that many pilots chose to wrestle their aircraft to the ground rather than try it . . . and died that way instead.

The statistics were not secret, but neither were they widely known, having 4 been eased into print rather obliquely in a medical journal. No pilot, and certainly no pilot's wife, had any need of the statistics in order to know the truth, however. The funerals took care of that in the most dramatic way possible. Sometimes, when the young wife of a fighter pilot would have a little reunion with the girls she went to school with, an odd fact would dawn on her: *they* have not been going to funerals. And then Jane Conrad would look at Pete . . . Princeton, Class of 1953 . . . Pete had already worn his great dark sepulchral bridge coat more than most boys of the Class of '53 had worn their tuxedos. How many of these happy young men had buried more than a dozen friends, comrades, and co-workers? (Lost through violent death in the execution of everyday duties.) At the time, the 1950's, students from Princeton took great pride in going into what they considered highly competitive, aggressive pursuits, jobs on Wall Street, on Madison Avenue, and at magazines such as *Time* and *Newsweek*. There was much fashionably brutish talk of what "dog-eat-dog" and "cutthroat" competition they found there; but in the rare instances when one of these young men died on the job, it was likely to be from choking on a chunk of Chateaubriand, while otherwise blissfully boiled, in an expense-account restaurant in Manhattan. How many would have gone to work, or stayed at work, on cutthroat Madison Avenue if there had been a 23 percent chance, nearly one chance in four, of dying from it? Gentlemen, we're having this little problem with chronic violent death . . .

And yet was there any basic way in which Pete (or Wally Schirra or Jim   5
Lovell or any of the rest of them) was different from other college boys his age? There didn't seem to be, other than his love of flying. Pete's father was a Philadelphia stockbroker who in Pete's earliest years had a house in the Main Line suburbs, a limousine, and a chauffeur. The Depression eliminated the terrific brokerage business, the house, the car, and the servants; and by and by his parents were divorced and his father moved to Florida. Perhaps because his father had been an observation balloonist in the First World War—an adventurous business, since the balloons were prized targets of enemy aircraft— Pete was fascinated by flying. He went to Princeton on the Holloway Plan, a scholarship program left over from the Second World War in which a student trained with midshipmen from the Naval Academy during the summers and graduated with a commission in the Regular Navy. So Pete graduated, received his commission, married Jane, and headed off to Pensacola, Florida, for flight training.

Then came the difference, looking back on it.   6

A young man might to into military flight training believing that he was   7
entering some sort of technical school in which he was simply going to acquire a certain set of skills. Instead, he found himself all at once enclosed in a fraternity. And in this fraternity, even though it was military, men were not rated by their outward rank as ensigns, lieutenants, commanders, or whatever. No, herein the world was divided into those who had it and those who did not. This quality, this *it*, was never named, however, nor was it talked about in any way.

As to just what this ineffable quality was . . . well, it obviously involved   8
bravery. But it was not bravery in the simple sense of being willing to risk your life. The idea seemed to be that any fool could do that, if that was all that was required, just as any fool could throw away his life in the process. No, the idea here (in the all-enclosing fraternity) seemed to be that a man should have the ability to go up in a hurtling piece of machinery and put his hide on the line and then have the moxie, the reflexes, the experience, the coolness, to

pull it back in the last yawning moment—and then go up again *the next day*, and the next day, and every next day, even if the series should prove infinite— and, ultimately, in its best expression, do so in a cause that means something to thousands, to a people, a nation, to humanity, to God. Nor was there *a test* to show whether or not a pilot had this righteous quality. There was, instead, a seemingly infinite series of tests. A career in flying was like climbing one of those ancient Babylonian pyramids made up of a dizzy progression of steps and ledges, a ziggurat, a pyramid extraordinarily high and steep; and the idea was to prove at every foot of the way up that pyramid that you were one of the elected and anointed ones who had *the right stuff* and could move higher and higher and even—ultimately, God willing, one day—that you might be able to join that special few at the very top, that elite who had the capacity to bring tears to men's eyes, the very Brotherhood of the Right Stuff itself.

None of this was to be mentioned, and yet it was acted out in a way that   9 a young man could not fail to understand. When a new flight (i.e., a class) of trainees arrived at Pensacola, they were brought into an auditorium for a little lecture. An officer would tell them: "Take a look at the man on either side of you." Quite a few actually swiveled their heads this way and that, in the interest of appearing diligent. Then the officer would say: "One of the three of you is not going to make it!"—meaning, not get his wings. That was the opening theme, the *motif* of primary training. We already know that one- third of you do not have the right stuff—it only remains to find out who.

Furthermore, that was the way it turned out. At every level in one's progress 10 up that staggeringly high pyramid, the world was once more divided into those men who had the right stuff to continue the climb and those who had to be *left behind* in the most obvious way. Some were eliminated in the course of the opening classroom work, as either not smart enough or not hardworking enough, and were left behind. Then came the basic flight instruction, in single- engine, propeller-driven trainers, and a few more—even though the military tried to make this stage easy—were washed out and left behind. Then came more demanding levels, one after the other, formation flying, instrument flying, jet training, all-weather flying, gunnery, and at each level more were washed out and left behind. By this point easily a third of the original can- didates had been, indeed, eliminated . . . from the ranks of those who might prove to have the right stuff.

In the Navy, in addition to the stages that Air Force trainees went through, 11 the neophyte always had waiting for him, out in the ocean, a certain grim gray slab; namely, the deck of an aircraft carrier; and with it perhaps the most difficult routine in military flying, carrier landings. He was shown films about it, he heard lectures about it, and he knew that carrier landings were hazardous.

He first practiced touching down on the shape of a flight deck painted on an airfield. He was instructed to touch down and gun right off. This was safe enough—the shape didn't move, at least—but it could do terrible things, to, let us say, the gyroscope of the soul. *That shape!—it's so damned small!* And more candidates were washed out and left behind. Then came the day, without warning, when those who remained were sent out over the ocean for the first of many days of reckoning with the slab. The first day was always a clear day with little wind and a calm sea. The carrier was so steady that it seemed, from up there in the air, to be resting on pilings, and the candidate usually made his first carrier landing successfully, with relief and even *élan*. Many young candidates looked like terrific aviators up to that very point—and it was not until they were actually standing on the carrier deck that they first began to wonder if they had the proper stuff, after all. In the training film the flight deck was a grand piece of gray geometry, perilous, to be sure, but an amazing abstract shape as one looks down upon it on the screen. And yet once the newcomer's two feet were on it . . . *Geometry*—my God, man, this is a . . . skillet! It *heaved*, it moved up and down underneath his feet, it pitched up, it pitched down, it rolled to port (this great beast *rolled!*) and it rolled to starboard, as the ship moved into the wind and, therefore, into the waves, and the wind kept sweeping across, sixty feet up in the air out in the open sea, and there were no railings whatsoever. This was a *skillet!*—a frying pan!—a short-order grill!—not gray but black, smeared with skid marks from one end to the other and glistening with pools of hydraulic fluid and the occasional jet-fuel slick, all of it still hot, sticky, greasy, runny, virulent from God knows what traumas—still ablaze!—consumed in detonations, explosions, flames, combustion, roars, shrieks, whines, blasts, horrible shudders, fracturing impacts, as little men in screaming red and yellow and purple and green shirts with black Mickey Mouse helmets over their ears skittered about on the surface as if for their very lives (you've said it now!), hooking fighter planes onto the catapult shuttles so that they can explode their afterburners and be slung off the deck in a red-mad fury with a *kaboom!* that pounds through the entire deck—a procedure that seems absolutely controlled, orderly, sublime, however, compared to what he is about to watch as aircraft return to the ship for what is known in the engineering stoicisms of the military as "recovery and arrest." To say that an F-4 was coming back onto this heaving barbecue from out of the sky at a speed of 135 knots . . . that might have been the truth in the training lecture, but it did not begin to get across the idea of what the newcomer saw from the deck itself, because it created the notion that perhaps the plane was gliding in. On the deck one knew differently! As the aircraft came closer and the carrier heaved on into the waves and the plane's speed did not diminish and the deck did not grow steady—indeed, it pitched up and down five or ten feet per greasy heave—one experienced a neural alarm that no lecture could have prepared him for: This is not an *airplane* coming toward me, it is a brick with some poor sonofabitch riding it (*someone much like myself!*), and it is not *gliding*, it is *falling*, a fifty-thousand-pound brick, headed not for a stripe on the deck but for *me*—and with a horrible *smash!* it hits the skillet, and with a blur of momentum as big as a freight train's it hurtles toward the far end of the deck—another blinding storm!—another roar as the pilot pushes the throttle up to full military power and another smear of rubber screams out over the skillet—and this is nominal!—quite okay!—for a wire stretched across the deck has grabbed the hook on the end of the plane as it hit the deck tail down, and the smash was the rest of the fifteen-ton brute slamming onto the deck, as it tripped up, so that it is now straining against the wire at full throttle, in case it hadn't held and the plane had "boltered" off the end of the deck and had to struggle up into the air again. And already the Mickey Mouse helmets are running toward the fiery monster . . .

And the candidate, looking on, begins to *feel* that great heaving sun-blazing 12 deathboard of a deck wallowing in his own vestibular system—and suddenly he finds himself backed up against his own limits. He ends up going to the flight surgeon with so-called conversion symptoms. Overnight he develops blurred vision or numbness in his hands and feet or sinusitis so severe that he cannot tolerate changes in altitude. On one level the symptom is real. He really cannot see too well or use his fingers or stand the pain. But somewhere in his subconscious he knows it is a plea and a beg-off; he shows not the slightest concern (the flight surgeon notes) that the condition might be permanent and affect him in whatever life awaits him outside the arena of the right stuff.

Those who remained, those who qualified for carrier duty—and even more 13 so those who later on qualified for *night* carrier duty—began to feel a bit like Gideon's warriors. *So many have been left behind!* The young warriors were now treated to a deathly sweet and quite unmentionable sight. They could gaze at length upon the crushed and wilted pariahs who had washed out. They could inspect those who did not have that righteous stuff.

The military did not have very merciful instincts. Rather than packing up 14 these poor souls and sending them home, the Navy, like the Air Force and the Marines, would try to make use of them in some other role, such as flight controller. So the washout has to keep taking classes with the rest of his group, even though he can no longer touch an airplane. He sits there in the classes staring at sheets of paper with cataracts of sheer human mortification over his eyes while the rest steal looks at him . . . this man reduced to an ant, this untouchable, this poor sonofabitch. And in what test had he been found wanting? Why, it seemed to be nothing less than *manhood* itself. Naturally, this was never mentioned, either. Yet there it was. *Manliness, manhood, manly courage* . . . there was something ancient, primordial, irresistible about the challenge of this stuff, no matter what a sophisticated and rational age one might think he lived in.

Perhaps because it could not be talked about, the subject began to take on 15 superstitious and even mystical outlines. A man either had it or he didn't! There was no such thing as having *most* of it. Moreover, it could blow at any seam. One day a man would be ascending the pyramid at a terrific clip, and the next—bingo!—he would reach his own limits in the most unexpected way. Conrad and Schirra met an Air Force pilot who had had a great pal at Tyndall Air Force Base in Florida. This man had been the budding ace of the training class; he had flown the hottest fighter-style trainer, the T-38, like a dream; and then he began the routine step of being checked out in the T-33. The T-33 was not nearly as hot an aircraft as the T-38; it was essentially the old P-80 jet fighter. It had an exceedingly small cockpit. The pilot could barely move his shoulders. It was the sort of airplane of which everybody said, "You don't get into it, you *wear* it." Once inside a T-33 cockpit this man, this budding ace, developed claustrophobia of the most paralyzing sort. He tried everything to overcome it. He even went to a psychiatrist, which was a serious mistake for a military officer if his superiors learned of it. But nothing worked. He was shifted over to flying jet transports, such as the C-135. Very demanding and necessary aircraft they were, too, and he was still spoken of as an excellent pilot. But as everyone knew—and, again, it was never explained in so many words—only those who were assigned to fighter squadrons, the "fighter jocks," as they called each other with a self-satisfied irony, remained in the true fraternity. Those assigned to transports were not humiliated like washouts— *somebody* had to fly those planes—nevertheless, they, too, had been *left behind* for lack of the right stuff.

Or a man could go for a routine physical one fine day, feeling like a million 16 dollars, and be grounded for *fallen arches*. It happened!—just like that! (And try raising them.) Or for breaking his wrist and losing only *part* of its mobility. Or for a minor deterioration of eyesight, or for any hundreds of reasons that would make no difference to a man in an ordinary occupation. As a result all fighter jocks began looking upon doctors as their natural enemies. Going to see a flight surgeon was a no-gain proposition; a pilot could only hold his own or lose in the doctor's office. To be grounded for a medical reason was no

humiliation, looked at objectively. But it was a humiliation, nonetheless!—
for it meant you no longer had that indefinable, unutterable, integral stuff. (It
could blow at *any* seam.)

All the hot young fighter jocks began trying to test the limits themselves 17
in a superstitious way. They were like believing Presbyterians of a century
before who used to probe their own experience to see if they were truly among
the elect. When a fighter pilot was in training, whether in the Navy or the Air
Force, his superiors were continually spelling out strict rules for him, about the
use of the aircraft and conduct in the sky. They repeatedly forbade so-called
hot-dog stunts, such as outside loops, buzzing, flat-hatting, hedgehopping and
flying under bridges. But somehow one got the message that the man who truly
had it could ignore those rules—not that he should make a point of it, but he
could—and that after all there was only one way to find out—and that in some
strange unofficial way, peeking through his fingers, his instructor halfway expected him to challenge all the limits. They would give a lecture about how
a pilot should never fly without a good solid breakfast—eggs, bacon, toast, and
so forth—because if he tried to fly with his blood-sugar level too low, it could
impair his alertness. Naturally, the next day every hot dog in the unit would
get up and have a breakfast consisting of one cup of black coffee and take off
and go up into a vertical climb until the weight of the ship exactly canceled
out the upward pull of the engine and his air speed was zero, and he would
hang there for one thick adrenal instant—and then fall like a rock, until one
of three things happened: he keeled over nose first and regained his aerody-
namics and all was well, he went into a spin and fought his way out of it, or
he went into a spin and had to eject or crunch it, which was always supremely
possible.

Likewise, "hassling"—mock dogfighting—was strictly forbidden, and so 18
naturally young fighter jocks could hardly wait to go up in, say, a pair of
F-100s and start the duel by making a pass at each other at 800 miles an hour,
the winner being the pilot who could slip in behind the other one and get
locked in on his tail ("wax his tail"), and it was not uncommon for some eager
jock to try too tight an outside turn and have his engine flame out, whereupon,
unable to restart it, he has to eject . . . and he shakes his fist at the victor as
he floats down by parachute and his half-a-million dollar aircraft goes *kaboom!*
on the palmetto grass or the desert floor, and he starts thinking about how he
can get together with the other guy back at the base in time for the two of
them to get their stories straight before the investigation: "I don't know what
happened, sir. I was pulling up after a target run, and it just flamed out on
me." Hassling was forbidden, and hassling that led to the destruction of an
aircraft was a serious court-martial offense, and the man's superiors knew that

the engine hadn't *just flamed out*, but every unofficial impulse on the base seemed to be saying: "Hell, we wouldn't give you a nickel for a pilot who hasn't done some crazy rat-racing like that. It's all part of the right stuff."

The other side of this impulse showed up in the reluctance of the young   19
jocks to admit it when they had maneuvered themselves into a bad corner they couldn't get out of. There were two reasons why a fighter pilot hated to declare an emergency. First, it triggered a complex and very public chain of events at the field: all other incoming flights were held up, including many of one's comrades who were probably low on fuel; the fire trucks came trundling out to the runway like yellow toys (as seen from way up there), the better to illustrate one's hapless state; and the bureaucracy began to crank up the paper monster for the investigation that always followed. And second, to declare an emergency, one first had to reach that conclusion in his own mind, which to the young pilot was the same as saying: "A minute ago I still *had* it—now I need your help!" To have a bunch of young fighter pilots up in the air thinking this way used to drive flight controllers crazy. They would see a ship beginning to drift off the radar, and they couldn't rouse the pilot on the microphone for anything other than a few meaningless mumbles, and they would know he was probably out there with engine failure at a low altitude, trying to reignite by lowering his auxiliary generator rig, which had a little propeller that was supposed to spin in the slipstream like a child's pinwheel.

"Whiskey Kilo Two Eight, do you want to declare an emergency?"   20

This would rouse him!—to say: "Negative, negative, Whiskey Kilo Two   21
Eight is not declaring an emergency."

Kaboom. Believers in the right stuff would rather crash and burn.   22

One fine day, after he had joined a fighter squadron, it would dawn on the   23
young pilot exactly how the losers in the great fraternal competition were now being left behind. Which is to say, not by instructors or other superiors or by failures at prescribed levels of competence, but by death. At this point the essence of the enterprise would begin to dawn on him. Slowly, step by step, the ante had been raised until he was now involved in what was surely the grimmest and grandest gamble of manhood. Being a fighter pilot—for that matter, simply taking off in a single-engine jet fighter of the Century series, such as an F-102, or any of the military's other marvelous bricks with fins on them—presented a man, on a perfectly sunny day, with more ways to get himself killed than his wife and children could imagine in their wildest fears. If he was barreling down the runway at two hundred miles an hour, completing the takeoff run, and the board started lighting up red, should he (a) abort the takeoff (and try to wrestle with the monster, which was gorged with jet fuel, out in the sand beyond the end of the runway) or (b) eject (and hope that

the goddamned human cannonball trick works at zero altitude and he doesn't shatter an elbow or a kneecap on the way out) or (c) continue the takeoff and deal with the problem aloft (knowing full well that the ship may be on fire and therefore seconds away from exploding)? He would have one second to sort out the options and act, and this kind of little workaday decision came up all the time. Occasionally a man would look coldly at the binary problem he was now confronting every day—Right Stuff/Death—and decide it wasn't worth it and voluntarily shift over to transports or reconnaissance or whatever. And his comrades would wonder, for a day or so, what evil virus had invaded his soul . . . as they left him behind. More often, however, the reverse would happen. Some college graduate would enter Navy aviation through the Reserves, simply as an alternative to the Army draft, fully intending to return to civilian life, to some waiting profession or family business; would become involved in the obsessive business of ascending the ziggurat pyramid of flying; and, at the end of his enlistment, would astound everyone back home and very likely himself as well by signing up for another one. What on earth got into him? He couldn't explain it. After all, the very words for it had been amputated. A Navy study showed that two-thirds of the fighter pilots who were rated in the top rungs of their groups—i.e., the hottest young pilots—reenlisted when the time came, and practically all were college graduates. By this point, a young fighter jock was like the preacher in *Moby Dick* who climbs up into the pulpit on a rope ladder and then pulls the ladder up behind him; except the pilot could not use the words necessary to express the vital lessons. Civilian life, and even home and hearth, now seemed not only far away but far *below*, back down many levels of the pyramid of the right stuff.

A fighter pilot soon found he wanted to associate only with other fighter pilots. Who else could understand the nature of the little proposition (right stuff/death) they were all dealing with? And what other subject could compare with it? It was riveting! To talk about it in so many words was forbidden, of course. The very words *death, danger, bravery, fear* were not to be uttered except in the occasional specific instance or for ironic effect. Nevertheless, the subject could be adumbrated in *code* or *by example*. Hence the endless evenings of pilots huddled together talking about flying. On these long and drunken evenings (the bane of their family life) certain theorems would be propounded and demonstrated—and all by *code* and *example*. One theorem was: There are no *accidents* and no fatal flaws in the machines; there are only pilots with the wrong stuff. (I.e., blind Fate can't kill me.) When Bud Jennings crashed and burned in the swamps at Jacksonville, the other pilots in Pete Conrad's squadron said: *How could he have been so stupid?* It turned out that Jennings had gone up in the SNJ with his cockpit canopy opened in a way that was expressly forbidden in the manual, and carbon monoxide had been sucked in from the exhaust, and he passed out and crashed. All agreed that Bud Jennings was a good guy and a good pilot, but his epitaph on the ziggurat was: *How could he have been so stupid?* This seemed shocking at first, but by the time Conrad had reached the end of that bad string at Pax River, he was capable of his own corollary to the theorem: viz., no single factor ever killed a pilot; there was always a chain of mistakes. But what about Ted Whelan, who fell like a rock from 8,100 feet when his parachute failed? Well, the parachute was merely part of the chain: first, someone should have caught the structural defect that resulted in the hydraulic leak that triggered the emergency; second, Whelan did not check out his seat-parachute rig, and the drogue failed to separate the main parachute from the seat; but even after those two mistakes, Whelan had fifteen or twenty seconds, as he fell, to disengage himself from the seat and open the parachute manually. Why just stare at the scenery coming up to smack you in the face! And everyone nodded. (He failed—but I wouldn't have!) Once the theorem and the corollary were understood, the Navy's statistics about one in every four Navy aviators dying meant nothing. The figures were averages, and averages applied to those with average stuff.

A riveting subject, especially if it were one's own hide that was on the line. 25 Every evening at bases all over America, there were military pilots huddled in officers clubs eagerly cutting the right stuff up in coded slices so they could talk about it. What more compelling topic of conversation was there in the world? In the Air Force there were even pilots who would ask the tower for priority landing clearance so that they could make the beer call on time, at 4 P.M. sharp, at the Officers Club. They would come right out and state the reason. The drunken rambles began at four and sometimes went on for ten or twelve hours. Such conversations! They diced that righteous stuff up into little bits, bowed ironically to it, stumbled blindfolded around it, groped, lurched, belched, staggered, bawled, sang, roared, and feinted at it with self-deprecating humor. Nevertheless!—they never mentioned it by name. No, they used the approved codes, such as: "Like a jerk I got myself into a hell of a corner today." They told of how they "lucked out of it." To get across the extreme peril of his exploit, one would use certain oblique cues. He would say, "I looked over at Robinson"—who would be known to the listeners as a non-com who sometimes rode backseat to read radar—"and he wasn't talking any more, he was just staring at the radar, like this, giving it that *zombie* look. Then I *knew* I was in trouble!" Beautiful! Just right! For it would also be known to the listeners that the non-coms advised one another: "*Never* fly with a lieutenant. *Avoid* captains and majors. Hell, man, do yourself a favor: don't fly with anybody below colonel." Which in turn said: "Those young bucks shoot dice with death!" And yet once in the air the non-com had his own standards. He was determined to remain as outwardly cool as the pilot, so that when the pilot did something that truly petrified him, he would say nothing; instead, he would turn silent, catatonic, like a zombie. Perfect! *Zombie.* There you had it, compressed into a single word all of the foregoing. I'm a hell of a pilot! I shoot dice with death! And now all you fellows know it! And I haven't spoken of that unspoken stuff even once!

The talking and drinking began at the beer call, and then the boys would 26 break for dinner and come back afterward and get more wasted and more garrulous or else more quietly fried, drinking good cheap PX booze until 2 A.M. The night was young! Why not get the cars and go out for a little proficiency run? It seemed that every fighter jock thought himself an ace driver, and he would do anything to obtain a hot car, especially a sports car, and the drunker he was, the more convinced he would be about his driving skills, as if the right stuff, being indivisible, carried over into any enterprise whatsoever, under any conditions. A little proficiency run, boys! (There's only one way to find out!) And they would roar off in close formation from, say, Nellis Air Force Base, down Route 15, into Las Vegas, barreling down the highway, rat-racing, sometimes four abreast, jockeying for position, piling into the most listless curve in the desert flats as if they were trying to root each other out of the groove at the Rebel 500—and then bursting into downtown Las Vegas with a rude fraternal roar like the Hell's Angels—and the natives chalked it up to youth and drink and the bad element that the Air Force attracted. They knew nothing about the right stuff, of course.

More fighter pilots died in automobiles than in airplanes. Fortunately, there 27 was always some kindly soul up the chain to certify the papers "line of duty," so that the widow could get a better break on the insurance. That was okay and only proper because somehow the system itself had long ago said *Skol!* and *Quite right!* to the military cycle of Flying & Drinking and Drinking & Driving, as if there were no other way. Every young fighter jock knew the feeling of getting two or three hours' sleep and then waking up at 5:30 A.M. and having a few cups of coffee, a few cigarettes, and then carting his poor quivering liver out to the field for another day of flying. There were those who arrived not merely hungover but still drunk, slapping oxygen tank cones over their faces and trying to burn the alcohol out of their systems, and then going up, remarking later: "I don't *advise* it, you understand, but it *can* be done." (Provided you have the right stuff, you miserable pudknocker.)

Air Force and Navy airfields were usually on barren or marginal stretches 28 of land and would have looked especially bleak and Low Rent to an ordinary individual in the chilly light of dawn. But to a young pilot there was an inexplicable bliss to coming out to the flight line while the sun was just beginning to cook up behind the rim of the horizon, so that the whole field was still in shadow and the ridges in the distance were in silhouette and the flight line was a monochrome of Exhaust Fume blue, and every little red light on top of the water towers or power stanchions looked dull, shriveled, congealed, and the runway lights, which were still on, looked faded, and even the landing lights on a fighter that had just landed and was taxiing in were no longer dazzling, as they would be at night, and looked instead like shriveled gobs of candlepowder out there—and yet it was beautiful, exhilarating!—for he was revved up with adrenalin, anxious to take off before the day broke, to burst up into the sunlight over the ridges before all those thousands of comatose souls down there, still dead to the world, snug in home and hearth, even came to their senses. To take off in an F-100F at dawn and cut on the afterburner and hurtle twenty-five thousand feet up into the sky in thirty seconds, so suddenly that you felt not like a bird but like a trajectory, yet with full control, full control of *four tons* of thrust, all of which flowed from your will and through your fingertips, with the huge engine right beneath you, so close that it was as if you were riding it bareback, until all at once you were supersonic, an event registered on earth by a tremendous cracking boom that shook windows, but up here only by the fact that you now felt utterly free of the earth—to describe it, even to wife, child, near ones and dear ones, seemed impossible. So the pilot kept it to himself, along with an even more indescribable . . . an even more sinfully inconfessable . . . feeling of superiority, appropriate to him and to his kind, lone bearers of the right stuff.

From *up here* at dawn the pilot looked down upon poor hopeless Las Vegas 29 (or Yuma, Corpus Christi, Meridian, San Bernardino, or Dayton) and began to wonder: How can all of them down there, those poor souls who will soon be waking up and trudging out of their minute rectangles and inching along their little noodle highways toward whatever slots and grooves make up their everyday lives—how could they live like that, with such earnestness, if they had the faintest idea of what it was like up here in this righteous zone?

But of course! Not only the washed-out, grounded, and dead pilots had been 30 left behind—but also all of those millions of sleepwalking souls who never even attempted the great gamble. The entire world below . . . *left behind.* Only at this point can one begin to understand just how big, how titanic, the ego of the military pilot could be. The world was used to enormous egos in artists, actors, entertainers of all sorts, in politicians, sports figures, and even journalists, because they had such familiar and convenient ways to show them off. But that slim young man over there in uniform, with the enormous watch on his wrist and the withdrawn look on his face, that young officer who is so shy that he can't even open his mouth unless the subject is flying—that young pilot—well, my friends, his ego is even *bigger!*—so big, it's *breathtaking!* Even in the 1950's it was difficult for civilians to comprehend such a thing, but *all* military officers and many enlisted men tended to feel superior to civilians. It was really quite ironic, given the fact that for a good thirty years the rising business classes in the cities had been steering their sons away from the military, as if from a bad smell, and the officer corps had never been held in lower esteem. Well, career officers returned the contempt in trumps. They looked upon themselves as men who lived by higher standards of behavior than civilians, as men who were the bearers and protectors of the most important values of American life, who maintained a sense of discipline while civilians abandoned themselves to hedonism, who maintained a sense of honor while civilians lived by opportunism and greed. Opportunism and greed: there you had your much-vaunted corporate business world. Khrushchev was right about one thing: when it came time to hang the capitalist West, an American business would sell him the rope. When the showdown came—and the showdowns always came—not all the wealth in the world or all the sophisticated nuclear weapons and radar and missile systems it could buy would take the place of those who had the uncritical willingness to face danger, those who, in short, had the right stuff.

In fact, the feeling was so righteous, so exalted, it could become religious. 31 Civilians seldom understood this, either. There was no one to teach them. It was no longer the fashion for serious writers to describe the glories of war. Instead, they dwelt upon its horrors, often with cynicism or disgust. It was left to the occasional pilot with a literary flair to provide a glimpse of the pilot's self-conception in its heavenly or spiritual aspect. When a pilot named Robert Scott flew his P-43 over Mount Everest, quite a feat at the time, he brought his hand up and snapped a salute to his fallen adversary. He thought he had *defeated* the mountain, surmounting all the forces of nature that had made it formidable. And why not? "God is my co-pilot," he said—that became the title of his book—and he meant it. So did the most gifted of all the pilot authors, the Frenchman Antoine de Saint-Exupéry. As he gazed down upon the world . . . from up there . . . during transcontinental flights, the good Saint-Ex saw civilization as a series of tiny fragile patches clinging to the otherwise barren rock of Earth. He felt like a lonely sentinel, a protector of those vulnerable little oases, ready to lay down his life in their behalf, if necessary; a saint, in short, true to his name, flying up there at the right hand of God. The good Saint-Ex! And he was not the only one. He was merely the one who put it into words most beautifully and anointed himself before the altar of the right stuff.

Focusing on Tom Wolfe's Use of Multiple Stories

1. How do Wolfe's stories complicate his initial effort to define "the right stuff" as "bravery"? In other words, what qualities other than bravery seem to be involved in "the right stuff"? In paragraph 30, Wolfe speaks of the pilots as having "titanic" egos and sounding like Communists. In the very next paragraph he speaks of the pilots as "saints." How ironic are these comments? How can you reconcile calling the pilots "saints" and calling them "egotistical"? What is Wolfe's overall view of the pilots?

2. Which phrases are repeated throughout the essay? What effect do the repetitions have? How does Wolfe vary these phrases to keep the essay from seeming dull?

3. In paragraph 8, Wolfe says that "a career in flying was like climbing one of those ancient Babylonian pyramids made up of a dizzy progression of steps and ledges, a ziggurat, a pyramid extraordinarily high and steep; and the idea was to prove at every foot of the way up that pyramid that you were one of the elect and anointed ones who had *the right stuff*." How is Wolfe's essay itself like a ziggurat, a series of steps going higher and higher? What makes the stories dizzying? (Consider, for example, the sentences in paragraph 11.) In paragraph 12, Wolfe says that a student in flight school "suddenly . . . finds himself backed up against his or her own limits." How does Wolfe's prose back the reader up against his or her own limits? How does paragraph 31 add another meaning to the idea of rising higher on the pyramid?

4. Wolfe says that the quality he is going to try to define "was never named . . . nor was it talked about in any way" (paragraph 7). Later, in paragraph 24, he says that "the subject could be adumbrated in *code* or *by example*." What is the difference between "talking about" a subject and using "code" or "examples" to "adumbrate" it? Wolfe certainly writes many words about this quality, and he even seems to give it a name, "the right stuff." In what sense is Wolfe merely using a *code*, giving *examples*, and not defining or talking directly about this elusive quality?

WORKING WITH THE TECHNIQUE IN YOUR OWN WRITING

---

1. Write an essay about something that intrigues and puzzles you, for example, a mysterious phenomenon in your part of the country, a friend's strange behavior, or the way you have changed in the last few years. You might write about a natural phenomenon that has sparked scientific controversy, such as the disappearing ozone layer or the existence of the Loch Ness monster. Collect as many different explanations or stories about your subject as you can, either by

doing research, speaking to various people, or just thinking hard about it. Try to make each anecdote or explanation as interesting and provocative as you can; include contradictory views if you find them. Try to make your readers share your fascination and puzzlement about the subject.

2. Select a word or phrase that intrigues you but whose meaning cannot be summarized in a sentence or two. You might select a word that you hear spoken often by friends (perhaps a part of the slang your friends use) or a word that seems particularly important to you. Develop your essay by creating stories that reveal variations in the meaning of the word. Wolfe collects stories that all illustrate "the right stuff"; Montaigne built an entire essay around various ideas of what constitutes drunkenness. You might collect stories that illustrate the various meanings of "being bad," "having it all together," "being a conservative." To find unusual stories for your essay, you might do some research or talk to people around you.

3. Write an essay defining what it takes to have "the right stuff" in some group to which you belong—perhaps a baseball team, a group that goes to dances together, or just a crowd that gathers every day at lunch to talk about other students. Think about the kinds of behaviors and attitudes your group admires, and see if you can find or invent stories that illustrate these admirable qualities.

BRAD MANNING

Harvard University
Cambridge, Massachusetts
Jack Kimball, instructor

Brad Manning draws much of his personal identity from his southern heritage:

> I am a Southerner. I am very close to my relatives in Ar-
> kansas where I was born, and I am thought to be a bit southern
> in manner and style by my classmates. And though it is some-
> times hard to dispel negative stereotypes that Southerners have
> acquired, I am very willing to let it be a part of my character
> and heritage. While at school, I've studied a good deal of south-
> ern history and southern religion, and I did a paper for my
> freshman writing course on Southerners at Harvard. I guess it's
> more automatic to think about the South and its distinctive char-
> acter now that I'm a fish on dry land. My main goals in writing
> are to be personal, laid-back, and lyrical—three of the more
> pleasant qualities I detect in southern speech. But I won't flatter
> myself to say that I am a "southern writer" (or even a "writer"
> at all), lest I step irreverently on the graves of some of my
> favorite authors.

Born in Little Rock, Arkansas, Brad Manning was raised in the rolling hillside of
Albemarle County, Virginia, near the University of Virginia campus at Charlottesville.
He attended Western Albemarle High School in Croset, Virginia, where he received
numerous scholar/athlete awards. The captain of both the soccer and lacrosse teams,
Manning also served as captain of three school academic teams. An Eagle Scout, he was
the principal bassoonist in the Charlottesville Youth Orchestra and earned that city's
Rotarian Leadership Award. He was selected to receive a Harvard National Scholarship,
which honors the top five percent of the entering class.

At Harvard, Brad Manning is a member of the freshman heavyweight crew team and
plans to major in American history and comparative religion. His career goals include
"politics (particularly in the South), foreign service (in the North or another country),
and journalism." More recently, he was elected to the Harvard-Radcliffe Undergraduate
Council and was awarded the F. Skiddy von Stade prize for the best essay written in a
freshman expository writing course at Harvard. "The only other writing contest I've
won," Manning notes, "was in kindergarten. My story was about a caterpillar who gets
teased by other insects because he looks like a worm; predictably, after the cocoon stage,
he experiences an 'Ugly Duckling' transformation that boosts his popularity. The paper
received second prize and was published in anthologies we all made for ourselves out of
cardboard and cloth."

His prize-winning essay, "Arm-Wrestling with My Father," emerged from three
one-page proposals he was asked to write for a paper on any subject. "My choices were

a portrait of my New York roommate, a discussion of how to pray, and an account of
an arm-wrestling match with my father. I chose the one that was closest to me." Writing
about his family proved especially attractive: "My parents are very important to me.
They affect my writing in that I write best about them. They taught me how to be the
person I am. My father taught me to appreciate sports, nature, and goals (I was an
Eagle Scout in his shadow). My mother helped me more to appreciate people, my faith,
and myself. I'd say the two of them are the best part of me that I have to show."

Asked in a recent interview to identify the response he hoped to elicit from the readers
of his essay, Manning quickly replied: "I'm not sure how I wanted people to feel after
reading the essay. Even though I choke up every time I round the next-to-last paragraph,
I think this is because my emotions are so close to the subject. I would rather readers
finish it with a smile, like the way they smiled after E.T. came back to life."

For an opportunity to analyze the multiple drafts of Brad Manning's essay, see Part II.

Arm-Wrestling with My Father

"Now you say when" is what he always said before an arm-wrestling match. 1
He liked to put the responsibility on me, knowing that he would always control
the outcome. "When!" I'd shout, and it would start. And I would tense up,
concentrating and straining and trying to push his wrist down to the carpet
with all my weight and strength. But Dad would always win; I always had to
lose. "Want to try it again?" he would ask, grinning. He would see my downcast
eyes, my reddened, sweating face and sense my intensity. And with squinting
eyes he would laugh at me, a high laugh, through his perfect, white teeth.
Too bitter to smile, I would not answer or look at him, but I would just roll
over on my back and frown at the ceiling. I never thought it was funny at all.

That was the way I felt for a number of years during my teens, after I had 2
lost my enjoyment of arm-wrestling and before I had given up that same intense
desire to beat my father. Ours had always been a physical relationship, I suppose, one determined by athleticism and strength. We never communicated
as well in speech or in writing as in a strong hug, battling to make the other
gasp for breath. I could never find him at one of my orchestra concerts. But
at my lacrosse games, he would be there in the stands, with an angry look,
ready to coach me after the game on how I could do better. He never helped
me write a paper or a poem. Instead, he would take me outside and show me
a new move for my game, in the hope that I would score a couple of goals and
gain confidence in my ability. Dad knew almost nothing about lacrosse and
his movements were all wrong and sad to watch. But at those times I could

just feel how hard he was trying to communicate, to help me, to show the love that he had for me, the love I could only assume was there.

His words were physical. The truth is, I have never read a card or letter 3 written in his hand, because he never wrote to me. Never. Mom wrote me all the cards and letters when I was away from home. The closest my father ever came, that I recall, was in a newspaper clipping Mom had sent with a letter. He had gone through and underlined all the important words about the dangers of not wearing a bicycle helmet. Our communication was physical, and that is why we did things like arm-wrestle. To get down on the floor and grapple, arm against arm, was like having a conversation.

This ritual of father-son competition in fact had started early in my life, 4 back when Dad started the matches with his arm almost horizontal, his wrist just an inch from defeat, and still won. I remember in those battles how my tiny shoulders would press over our locked hands, my whole upper body pushing down in hope of winning that single inch from his calm, unmoving forearm. "Say when," he'd repeat, killing my concentration and causing me to squeal, "I did, I did!" And so he'd grin with his eyes fixed on me, not seeming to notice his own arm, which would begin to rise slowly from its starting position. My greatest efforts could not slow it down. As soon as my hopes would disappear, I'd start to cheat and use both hands. But the arm would continue to move steadily along its arc toward the carpet. My brother, if he was watching, would sometimes join in against the arm. He once even wrapped his little legs around our embattled wrists and pulled back with everything he had. But he did not have much, and regardless of the opposition, the man would win. My arm would lie at rest, pressed into the carpet beneath a solid, immovable arm. In that pinned position, I could only giggle, happy to have such a strong father.

My feelings have changed, though. I don't giggle anymore, at least not 5 around my father. And I don't feel pressured to compete with him the way I thought necessary for a number of years. Now my father is not really so strong as he used to be and I am getting stronger, it seems. This change in strength comes at a time when I am growing faster mentally than at any time before. I am becoming less my father and more myself. And as a result, there is less of a need to be set apart from him and his command. I am no longer a rebel in the household, wanting to stand up against the master with clenched fists and tensing jaws, trying to impress him with my education or my views on religion. I am no longer a challenger, quick to correct his verbal mistakes, determined to beat him whenever possible in physical competition.

I am not sure when it was that I began to feel less competitive with my 6 father, but it all became clearer to me one day this past January. I was home in Virginia for a week between exams, and Dad had stayed home from work because the house was snowed in deep. It was then that I learned something I never could have guessed.

I don't recall who suggested arm-wrestling that day. We hadn't done it for 7 a long time, for months. But there we were, lying flat on the carpet, face to face, extending our right arms. Our arms were different. His still resembled a fat tree branch, one which had leveled my wrist to the ground countless times before. It was hairy and white with some pink moles scattered about. It looked strong to be sure, though not so strong as it had in past years. I expect that back in his youth, it had looked even stronger. In high school, he had played halfback and had been voted "best-built body" of the senior class. Between college semesters, he had worked on road crews and on Louisiana dredges. I admired him for that. I had begun to row crew in college and that accounted for some small buildup along the muscle lines, but it did not seem to be enough. The arm I extended was lanky and featureless. Even so, he insisted that he would lose the match, that he was certain I'd win. I had to ignore this, however, because it was something he always said, whether or not he believed it himself.

Our warm palms came together, much the same way we had shaken hands 8 the day before at the airport. Fingers twisted and wrapped about once again, testing for a better grip. Elbows slid up and back making their little indentions on the itchy carpet. My eyes pinched closed in concentration as I tried to center as much of my thought as possible on the match. Arm-wrestling, I knew, was a competition that depended less on talent and experience than on one's mental control and confidence. I looked up into his eyes and was ready. He looked back, smiled at me, and said softly (did he sound nervous?), "You say when."

It was not a long match. I had expected him to be stronger, faster. I was 9 conditioned to lose and would have accepted defeat easily. However, after some struggle, his arm yielded to my efforts and began to move unsteadily toward the carpet. I worked against his arm with all the strength I could give. He was working hard as well, straining, breathing heavily. It seemed that this time was different, that I was going to win. Then something occurred to me, something unexpected. I discovered that I was feeling sorry for my father. I wanted to win but I did not want to see him lose.

It was like the thrill I had once experienced as a young boy at my grand- 10 father's lake house in Louisiana when I hooked my first big fish. There was that sudden tug that made me leap. The red bobber was sucked down beneath the surface and I pulled back against it, reeling it in excitedly. But when my cousin caught sight of the fish and shouted out, "It's a keeper," I realized that I would be happier for the fish if it were let go, rather than grilled for dinner. Arm-wrestling my father was now like this, like hooking "Big Joe," the old fish that Lake Ouachita holds but you can never catch, and when you finally think you got him, you want to let him go, cut the line, keep the legend alive.

Perhaps, at that point, I could have given up, letting my father win. But it was so fast and absorbing. How could I have learned so quickly how it would feel to have overpowered the arm that had protected and provided for me all of my life? His arms have always protected me and the family. Whenever I am near him, I am unafraid, knowing his arms are ready to catch me and keep me safe, the way they caught my mother one time when she fainted halfway across the room, the way he carried me, full grown, up and down the stairs when I had mononucleosis, the way he once held my feet as I stood on his shoulders to put up a new basketball net. My mother may have had the words or the touch that sustained our family, but his were the arms that protected us. And his were the arms now that I had pushed to the carpet, first the right arm, then the left.

I might have preferred him to be always the stronger, the one who carries me. But this wish is impossible now; our roles have begun to switch. I do not know if I will ever physically carry my father as he has carried me, though I fear that someday I may have that responsibility. More than once, this year, I have hesitated before answering the phone late at night, fearing my mother's voice calling me back to help carry his wood coffin. When I am home with him and he mentions a sharp pain in his chest, I imagine him collapsing onto the floor. And in that second vision, I see me rushing to him, lifting him onto my shoulders, and running.

A week after our match, we parted at the airport. The arm-wrestling match was by that time mostly forgotten. My thoughts were on school. I had been awake most of the night studying for my last exam, and by that morning I was already back into my college student manner of reserve and detachment. To say good-bye, I kissed and hugged my mother and I prepared to shake my father's hand. A handshake had always seemed easier to handle than a hug. His hugs had always been powerful ones, intended I suppose to give me strength. They made me suck in my breath and struggle for control, and the way he would pound his hand on my back made rumbles in my ears. So I offered a handshake; but he offered a hug. I accepted it, bracing myself for the impact. Once our arms were wrapped around each other, however, I sensed a different message. His embrace was softer, longer than before. I remember how it surprised me and how I gave an embarrassed laugh as if to apologize to anyone watching.

I got on the airplane and my father and mother were gone. But as the plane lifted, my throat was hurting with sadness. I realized then that Dad must have learned something as well and what he had said to me in that last hug was that he loved me. Love was a rare expression between us, so I had denied it at first. As the plane turned north, I had a sudden wish to go back to Dad and embrace his arms with all the love I felt for him. I wanted to hold him for a long time and to speak with him silently, telling him how happy I was, telling him all my feelings, in that language we shared.

In his hug, Dad had tried to tell me something he himself had discovered. 15 I hope he tries again. Maybe this spring, when he sees his first crew match, he'll advise me on how to improve my stroke. Maybe he has started doing push-ups to rebuild his strength and challenge me to another match—if this were true, I know I would feel less challenged than loved. Or maybe, rather than any of this, he'll just send me a card.

Focusing on Brad Manning's Techniques and Revisions

1. What phrase summarizes the nature of Manning's relationship with his father as a youngster? How does the nature of this relationship become represented in the father's choice of language? What metaphor does Manning create for describing his conversations with his father? When and how does their relationship change? With what effects?

2. Manning explains that the goal of his essay was "to portray the rivalry and love that I recognized in my family. I felt this would be most effective if it centered on a specific occurrence or ritual, a defined situation that I could refer to throughout the piece." How is the nature of his father-son relationship expressed in competitive terms? On what forms of language, what parts of speech, does Manning rely to convey the intensity of his competitive urge to defeat his father? How does Manning turn this competition into a "ritual"? Identify each of the components of this ritual and discuss Manning's attitude toward each. Which elements of the ritual does he seem to enjoy? Why?

3. Describe Manning's tone—his attitude toward his subject, as expressed in his word choice and sentence structure—in this essay. How is Manning's attitude toward his father established in the first two paragraphs? How, for example, does Manning respond to his father's laughter at the end of each arm-wrestling match? Does Manning's tone remain consistent or does it change during the course of the essay? Point to specific passages to support your response.

4. What prompts Manning's "changed" feelings toward the ritual of arm-wrestling? Why doesn't he "giggle anymore, at least not around my father" (paragraph 5)? What significance does the narrator attach to his growing stronger? What consequences does that increased strength entail?

5. Reread paragraph 7, in which Manning begins to recount the story of the first time he defeated his father at arm-wrestling. Compare the narrator's

description of his father's arm with his own. What features of each does he emphasize? With what effects? Why does Manning describe the ritual in far greater detail here? What explanation does he offer for his statement in paragraph 8 that "arm-wrestling, I knew, was a competition that depended less on talent and experience than on one's mental control and confidence"?

6. What dramatic function does the phrase "You say when" serve in this essay? What symbolic import does the term bear? What significance do you attach to its being repeated?

7. In the instant that Manning recognizes "that this time was different, that I was going to win," he also realizes that "I was feeling sorry for my father" (paragraph 9). What prompts this realization? What consequences does it produce? In this respect, what dramatic function does paragraph 10 serve? What does Manning mean when he observes there that "arm-wrestling my father was now . . . like hooking 'Big Joe' "? What symbolic significance does the narrator ascribe to the impending defeat of his father?

8. Comment on the departure scene at the airport. How does this moment summarize what Manning had noticed before about his relationship with his father—that "our roles have begun to switch" (paragraph 12)? Point to details in the language and syntax of paragraph 13 that underscore this recognition. What, more generally, does the addition of the scene at the airport add to his essay?

9. Brad Manning wrote several drafts of "Arm-Wrestling with My Father." In each he tried to strengthen his use of symbolic detail: "I got stuck on a dominant image, that of carrying my father on my back, as if this were to be a universal symbol of the changeover of strength and command from father to son." Here is the second draft of what in the final version became paragraph 10:

> Perhaps, at that point, I could have given up, letting him win. But it was so fast and absorbing. How could I have learned so quickly what I know now? I felt like a young hunter who is thrilled, having shot his first buck but upon reaching it as it struggles for life, he is captured in the stare of its very large dark eye and its seeming plea for pity. I, like the young hunter, yearned to see the deer alive once again, sprinting away through the trees, powerful, untamed. But instead, I was compelled to finish it, to stop the pain. In such a situation it would not have been right to walk away claiming victory. Rather, one must sadly lift the deer over his shoulders and carry it out of the woods.

What differences do you notice between this second draft and the final draft of paragraph 10? How does the final version more successfully represent the symbolic importance of this dramatic moment? Be as specific as possible in your analysis.

10. Brad Manning made substantial revisions in the conclusion of his essay. Reprinted here is the final paragraph from his second draft:

> Perhaps, someday I will carry my father, much like the young Aeneas, who lifted his aged father onto his back and carried him to safety out of the burning city of Troy. I must consider now if this will ever become my own role. Today, I feel that I may never be so strong as I see my father to be. When I am near him, I feel protected, knowing he will keep me safe, the way he caught my mother once when she fainted halfway across the room, the way he carried me, full grown, up and down the stairs when I had mononucleosis, the way he would hold my feet as I stood upon his shoulders to put up a new basketball net. I may always wish him to be stronger, to be the one who carries me. In fact, if he were right now working on weights in preparation for our next match, I would feel less threatened than loved. However, it may be that beating him for the first time in arm-wrestling was the first move towards lifting Dad up onto my back. I do not know if I shall ever physically carry my father. I sadly envision, however, one day seeing him collapse onto the floor. In my vision I rush to him and powerfully lift his trembling warm body onto my shoulders. Then, without hesitation, I begin to run fast through the flames, carrying my father out of the burning city, and up into the hills.

Identify and comment on the effectiveness of each change Manning makes between the conclusion of his second draft and final draft. In a recent interview, Manning pointed out: "In the final draft, I was able to retain the Aeneas image." Where does this image appear? Comment on its effectiveness.

Suggestions for Writing

1. One of the overriding points in Brad Manning's essay is that a relationship can be represented in the repetition of a symbolic detail—in this instance, arm-wrestling with his father. Review carefully the nature of your own relationship with someone you are close to. How can this relationship—and especially the changes that have occurred in it—be represented in some symbolic event or object? Write an essay modeled on Brad Manning's in which you use this symbolic detail to unify your paper.

2. During your childhood and youth, what rituals did you and your family participate in each year? Write an essay describing in as much detail as possible the specific occasion for one such ritual. What significance did you or the members of your family attribute to the ritual? Explain why the ritual was important to you then and how you view it today. What did you learn—either positively or negatively—from having participated in the ritual?

3. Write an essay in which you compare and contrast Brad Manning's essay with Barbara Seidel's "A Tribute to My Father." In what specific ways are their respective treatments of their fathers similar? Different? Which essay do you prefer? Why?

AN EFFECTIVE TECHNIQUE

Brad Manning has developed a way to make small details speak volumes. Partly this is a tribute to his writing, but mostly it is a result of his recognizing that some details in the world do have large meaning. When two people meet on the street, the broadness of their smiles reveals much about the precise nature of their relationship. The posture of students in a classroom—whether they are looking out the windows or leaning forward toward the blackboard— is often a more telling commentary on a teacher's effectiveness than their test scores. Smiles and posture in such situations function symbolically, expressing meaning much as words do—to those who know how to read body language. Manning has found an activity—arm-wrestling—that seems to register, like a seismic recorder, the shifting depths of his relationship with his father. By focusing on this one activity, showing how it subtly changed over the years, Brad Manning gives his essay a very tight unity but still manages to make his readers feel that he is reporting everything of importance about nearly twenty years of a complex relationship.

Arm-wrestling reveals so much about Manning's relationship with his father because it was a symbolic means of expression, a "physical language" they used to speak to each other about their "physical relationship." Manning has to teach us how to read this unusual language. He does so by using phrases that can be interpreted as describing either muscular interactions or emotional states. When Manning says his father's arm was "solid, immovable" to a small boy, we can understand how an arm could "speak" of the emotional (and financial) solidity that his father gave him as well as reveal that his father would never be "moved" in public, would never show his emotions. When

Manning describes his own "clenched fists" and "tensing jaw" during his teen-age years, we can similarly see the muscular expression of rebellion.

While establishing that physical acts can communicate like words, Manning uses this means of communication to tell a story: the tale of the reversal of a father-son relationship. When the son finally beats his father, conquering the "immovable" arm, their physical and emotional positions reverse. Manning embodies this reversal in a physical image, a switch of who carries whom: years ago the father carried his small son many times, but years from now the son may have to carry his father—in a coffin. The physical images of one body supporting another carries all the complex meanings of family support; carrying and caring are very close.

Manning's essay shows us both how to discover and how to write about the stages of a relationship. We can think about what activities seem impor-tant in a relationship and are repeated with variations throughout it, espe-cially activities that serve as symbolic forms of communication. For example, we might chronicle the stages of a brief dating relationship by noting differ-ences in the way the couple hold hands or walk down the street together.

We might also use this strategy to write about complex phenomena other than relationships. We might summarize the history of a school in the way its walls are painted—from simple, flat beige as it begins with only a few students to brightly colored walls covered with student murals during the 1960s to gray primer slapped on and never finished when a larger school is built in the 1980s. Political columnists and cartoonists often use symbolic acts and details to rep-resent stages in the history of an event. For example, the history of the talks to end the Vietnam War in the late 1960s and early 1970s was very aptly summarized in a political column that described the various tables at which the diplomats sat. The diplomats kept changing the shape of the table—from a triangle to a square to a circle—as decisions were made about who should be involved in the talks as full participants and who should be present as advisers. At first, the talks involved only North and South Vietnam and the United States, but eventually others were added—the guerrilla group known as the Viet Cong, the Soviet Union, and the People's Republic of China.

The next essay, by Scott Sanders, also is about a man's relationship with his father and also uses a physical activity—working with tools—to define the stages of that relationship. These two essays might perhaps serve to counter the conventional idea that only intellectuals express themselves symbolically: they even suggest that symbols may gain their greatest power among people who are least verbal with each other.

ANOTHER ILLUSTRATION OF THE TECHNIQUE

SCOTT RUSSELL SANDERS

The Inheritance of Tools

Scott Sanders has devoted his life to bridging disciplines usually kept apart: "I have long been divided, in my life and my work, between science and the arts. Early on, in graduate study, this took the form of choosing literary studies rather than theoretical physics. When I began writing fiction in my late twenties, I wanted to ask, through literature, many of the fundamental questions that scientists ask. In particular, I wanted to understand our place in nature, trace the sources of our violence, and speculate about the future evolution of our species." A professor of English at Indiana University at Bloomington since 1971 and the recipient of several awards for his scholarship, Scott Sanders has also written in forms far removed from academic journals—science fiction, folktales, stories for children, historical novels, personal essays.

In contrast to many modern writers, Sanders is not much interested in "the life of isolated individuals" or in experimentation in form and style for its own sake. His writing is "concerned with the ways in which human beings come to terms with the practical problems of living on a small planet, in nature and in communities." He writes of his own life in his essays "only when it seems to have a larger bearing on the lives of others. Thus, I tell what it was like to grow up in a military arsenal because I am convinced we all now live in an armed camp. I tell of my father's death [in the essay reprinted here] because it focused for me lessons about the virtue and fragility of human skill."

At just about the hour when my father died, soon after dawn one February   1
morning when ice coated the windows like cataracts, I banged my thumb with
a hammer. Naturally I swore at the hammer, the reckless thing, and in the
moment of swearing I thought of what my father would say: "If you'd try hitting
the nail it would go in a whole lot faster. Don't you know your thumb's not
as hard as that hammer?" We both were doing carpentry that day, but far
apart. He was building cupboards at my brother's place in Oklahoma; I was at
home in Indiana, putting up a wall in the basement to make a bedroom for
my daughter. By the time my mother called with news of his death—the long
distance wires whittling her voice until it seemed too thin to bear the weight
of what she had to say—my thumb was swollen. A week or so later a white
scar in the shape of a crescent moon began to show about the cuticle, and
month by month it rose across the pink sky of my thumbnail. It took the better

part of a year for the scar to disappear, and every time I noticed it I thought of my father.

The hammer had belonged to him, and to his father before him. The three 2 of us have used it to build houses and barns and chicken coops, to upholster chairs and crack walnuts, to make doll furniture and bookshelves and jewelry boxes. The head is scratched and pockmarked, like an old plowshare that has been working rocky fields, and it gives off the sort of dull sheen you see on fast creek water in the shade. It is a finishing hammer, about the weight of a bread loaf, too light, really, for framing walls, too heavy for cabinet work, with a curved claw for pulling nails, a rounded head for pounding, a fluted neck for looks, and a hickory handle for strength.

The present handle is my third one, bought from a lumberyard in Tennessee, 3 down the road from where my brother and I were helping my father build his retirement house. I broke the previous one by trying to pull sixteen-penny nails out of floor joints—a foolish thing to do with a finishing hammer, as my father pointed out. "You ever hear of a crowbar?" he said. No telling how many handles he and my grandfather had gone through before me. My grand-father used to cut down hickory trees on his farm, saw them into slabs, cure the planks in his hayloft, and carve handles with a drawknife. The grain in hickory is crooked and knotty, and therefore tough, hard to split, like the grain in the two men who owned this hammer before me.

After proposing marriage to a neighbor girl, my grandfather used this ham- 4 mer to build a house for his bride on a stretch of river bottom in northern Mississippi. The lumber for the place, like the hickory for the handle, was cut on his own land. By the day of the wedding he had not quite finished the house, and so right after the ceremony he took his wife home and put her to work. My grandmother had worn her Sunday dress for the wedding, with a fringe of lace tacked on around the hem in honor of the occasion. She removed this lace and folded it away before going out to help my grandfather nail siding on the house. "There she was in her good dress," he told me some fifty-odd years after that wedding day, "holding up them long pieces of clapboard while I hammered, and together we got the place covered up before dark." As the family grew to four, six, eight, and eventually thirteen, my grandfather used this hammer to enlarge his house room by room, like a chambered nautilus expanding its shell.

By and by the hammer was passed along to my father. One day he was up 5 on the roof of our pony barn nailing shingles with it, when I stepped out the kitchen door to call him for supper. Before I could yell, something about the sight of him straddling the spine of that roof and swinging the hammer caught my eye and made me hold my tongue. I was five or six years old, and the world's commonplaces were still news to me. He would pull a nail from the pouch at his waist, bring the hammer down, and a moment later the *thunk* of the blow would reach my ears. And that is what had stopped me in my tracks and stilled my tongue, that momentary gap between seeing and hearing the blow. Instead of yelling from the kitchen door, I ran to the barn and climbed two rungs up the ladder—as far as I was allowed to go—and spoke quietly to my father. On our walk to the house he explained that sound takes time to make its way through air. Suddenly the world seemed larger, the air more dense, if sound could be held back like any ordinary traveler.

By the time I started using this hammer, at about the age when I discovered 6 the speed of sound, it already contained houses and mysteries for me. The smooth handle was one my grandfather had made. In those days I needed both hands to swing it. My father would start a nail in a scrap of wood, and I would pound away until I bent it over.

"Looks like you got ahold of some of those rubber nails," he would tell me. 7 "Here, let me see if I can find you some stiff ones." And he would rummage in a drawer until he came up with a fistful of more cooperative nails. "Look at the head," he would tell me. "Don't look at your hands, don't look at the hammer. Just look at the head of that nail and pretty soon you'll learn to hit it square."

Pretty soon I did learn. While he worked in the garage cutting dovetail 8 joints for a drawer or skinning a deer or tuning an engine, I would hammer nails. I made innocent blocks of wood look like porcupines. He did not talk much in the midst of his tools, but he kept up a nearly ceaseless humming, slipping in and out of a dozen tunes in an afternoon, often running back over the same stretch of melody again and again, as if searching for a way out. When the humming did cease, I knew he was faced with a task requiring great delicacy or concentration, and I took care not to distract him.

He kept scraps of wood in a cardboard box—the ends of two-by-fours, slabs 9 of shelving and plywood, odd pieces of molding—and everything in it was fair game. I nailed scraps together to fashion what I called boats or houses, but the results usually bore only faint resemblance to the visions I carried in my head. I would hold up these constructions to show my father, and he would turn them over in his hands admiringly, speculating about what they might be. My cobbled-together guitars might have been alien spaceships, my barns might have been models of Aztec temples, each wooden contraption might have been anything but what I had set out to make.

Now and again I would feel the need to have a chunk of wood shaped or 10 shortened before I riddled it with nails, and I would clamp it in a vise and scrape at it with a handsaw. My father would let me lacerate the board until my arm gave out, and then he would wrap his hand around mine and help me finish the cut, showing me how to use my thumb to guide the blade, how to pull back on the saw to keep it from binding, how to let my shoulder do the work.

"Don't force it," he would say, "just drag it easy and give the teeth a chance 11 to bite."

As the saw teeth bit down, the wood released its smell, each kind with its 12 own fragrance, oak or walnut or cherry or pine—usually pine because it was the softest, easiest for a child to work. No matter how weathered and gray the board, no matter how warped and cracked, inside there was this smell waiting, as of something freshly baked. I gathered every smidgen of sawdust and stored it away in coffee cans, which I kept in a drawer of the workbench. When I did not feel like hammering nails, I would dump my sawdust on the concrete floor of the garage and landscape it into highways and farms and towns, running miniature cars and trucks along miniature roads. Looming as huge as a colossus, my father worked over and around me, now and again bending down to inspect my work, careful not to trample my creations. It was a landscape that smelled dizzyingly of wood. Even after a bath my skin would carry the smell, and so would my father's hair, when he lifted me for a bedtime hug.

I tell these things not only from memory but also from recent observation, 13 because my own son now turns blocks of wood into nailed porcupines, dumps cans full of sawdust at my feet and sculpts highways on the floor. He learns how to swing a hammer from the elbow instead of the wrist, how to lay his thumb beside the blade to guide a saw, how to tap a chisel with a wooden mallet, how to mark a hole with an awl before starting a drill bit. My daughter did the same before him, and even now, on the brink of teenage aloofness, she will occasionally drag out my box of wood scraps and carpenter something. So I have seen my apprenticeship to wood and tools re-enacted in each of my children, as my father saw his own apprenticeship renewed in me.

The saw I use belonged to him, as did my level and both of my squares, 14 and all four tools had belonged to his father. The blade of the saw is the bluish color of gun barrels, and the maple handle, dark from the sweat of hands, is inscribed with curving leaf designs. The level is a shaft of walnut two feet long, edged with brass and pierced by three round windows in which air bubbles float in oil-filled tubes of glass. The middle window serves for testing if a surface is horizontal, the others for testing if a surface is plumb or vertical. My grandfather used to carry this level on the gun rack behind the seat in his pickup, and when I rode with him I would turn around to watch the bubbles dance.

The larger of the two squares is called a framing square, a flat steel elbow, so beat up and tarnished you can barely make out the rows of numbers that show how to figure the cuts on rafters. The smaller one is called a try square, for marking right angles, with a blued steel blade for the shank and a brass-faced block of cherry for the head.

I was taught early on that a saw is not to be used apart from a square: "If 15 you're going to cut a piece of wood," my father insisted, "you owe it to the tree to cut it straight."

Long before studying geometry, I learned there is a mystical virtue in right 16 angles. There is an unspoken morality in seeking the level and the plumb. A house will stand, a table will bear weight, the sides of a box will hold together, only if the joints are square and the members upright. When the bubble is lined up between two marks etched in the glass tube of a level, you have aligned yourself with the forces that hold the universe together. When you miter the corners of a picture frame, each angle must be exactly forty-five degrees, as they are in the perfect triangles of Pythagoras, not a degree more or less. Otherwise the frame will hang crookedly, as if ashamed of itself and of its maker. No matter if the joints you are cutting do not show. Even if you are butting two pieces of wood together inside a cabinet, you must take pains to ensure that the ends are square and the studs are plumb.

I took pains over the wall I was building on the day my father died. Not 17 long after that wall was finished—paneled with tongue-and-groove boards of yellow pine, the nail holes filled with putty, and the wood all stained and sealed—I came close to wrecking it one afternoon when my daughter ran howling up the stairs to announce that her gerbils had escaped from their cage and were hiding in my brand new wall. She could hear them scratching and squeaking behind her bed. Impossible! I said. How on earth could they get inside my drum-tight wall? Through the heating vent, she answered. I went downstairs, pressed my ear to the honey-colored wood, and heard the *scritch scritch* of tiny feet.

"What can we do?" my daughter wailed. "They'll starve to death, they'll 18 die of thirst, they'll suffocate."

"Hold on," I soothed. "I'll think of something." 19

While I thought and she fretted, the radio on her bedside table delivered 20 us the headlines: Several thousand people had died in a city in India from a poisonous cloud that had leaked overnight from a chemical plant. A nuclear-powered submarine had been launched. Rioting continued in South Africa. An airplane had been hijacked in the Mediterranean. Authorities calculated that several thousand homeless people slept on the streets within sight of the

Washington Monument. I felt my usual helplessness in the face of all these calamities. But here was my daughter, weeping because her gerbils were holed up in a wall. This calamity I could handle.

"Don't worry," I told her. "We'll set food and water by the heating vent 21 and lure them out. And if that doesn't do the trick, I'll tear the wall apart until we find them."

She stopped crying and gazed at me. "You'd really tear it apart? Just for my gerbils? The *wall?*" Astonishment slowed her down only for a second, however, before she ran to the workbench and began tugging at drawers, saying, "Let's see, what'll we need? Crowbar. Hammer. Chisels. I hope we don't have to use them—but just in case."

We didn't need the wrecking tools. I never had to assault my handsome 22 wall, because the gerbils eventually came out to nibble at a dish of popcorn. But for several hours I studied the tongue-and-groove skin I had nailed up on the day of my father's death, considering where to begin prying. There were no gaps in that wall, no crooked joints.

I had botched a great many pieces of wood before I mastered the right angle 23 with a saw, botched even more before I learned to miter a joint. The knowledge of these things resides in my hands and eyes and the webwork of muscles, not in the tools. There are machines for sale—powered miter boxes and radial-arm saws, for instance—that will enable any casual soul to cut proper angles in boards. The skill is invested in the gadget instead of the person who uses it, and this is what distinguishes a machine from a tool. If I had to earn my keep by making furniture or building houses, I suppose I would buy powered saws and pneumatic nailers; the need for speed would drive me to it. But since I carpenter only for my own pleasure or to help neighbors or to remake the house around the ears of my family, I stick with hand tools. Most of the ones I own were given to me by my father, who also taught me how to wield them. The tools in my workbench are a double inheritance, for each hammer and level and saw is wrapped in a cloud of knowing.

All of these tools are a pleasure to look at and to hold. Merchants would 24 never paste NEW NEW NEW! signs on them in stores. Their designs are old because they work, because they serve their purpose well. Like folk songs and aphorisms and the grainy bits of language, these tools have been pared down to essentials. I look at my claw hammer, the distillation of a hundred generations of carpenters, and consider that it holds up well beside those other classics—Greek vases, Gregorian chants, *Don Quixote*, barbed fish hooks, candles, spoons. Knowledge of hammering stretches back to the earliest humans who squatted beside fires, chipping flints. Anthropologists have a lovely name for those unworked rocks that served as the earliest hammers.

"Dawn stones," they are called. Their only qualification for the work, aside from hardness, is that they fit the hand. Our ancestors used them for grinding corn, tapping awls, smashing bones. From dawn stones to this claw hammer is a great leap in time, but no great distance in design or imagination.

On that iced-over February morning when I smashed my thumb with the hammer, I was down in the basement framing the wall that my daughter's gerbils would later hide in. I was thinking of my father, as I always did whenever I built anything, thinking how he would have gone about the work, hearing in memory what he would have said about the wisdom of hitting the nail instead of my thumb. I had the studs and plates nailed together all square and trim, and was lifting the wall into place when the phone rang upstairs. My wife answered, and in a moment she came to the basement door and called down softly to me. The stillness in her voice made me drop the framed wall and hurry upstairs. She told me my father was dead. Then I heard the details over the phone from my mother. Building a set of cupboards for my brother in Oklahoma, he had knocked off work early the previous afternoon because of cramps in his stomach. Early this morning, on his way into the kitchen of my brother's trailer, maybe going for a glass of water, so early that no one else was awake, he slumped down on the linoleum and his heart quit. 26

For several hours I paced around inside my house, upstairs and down, in and out of every room, looking for the right door to open and knowing there was no such door. My wife and children followed me and wrapped me in arms and backed away again, circling and staring as if I were on fire. Where was the door, the door, the door? I kept wondering. My smashed thumb turned purple and throbbed, making me furious. I wanted to cut it off and rush outside and scrape away the snow and hack a hole in the frozen earth and bury the shameful thing. 27

I went down into the basement, opened a drawer in my workbench, and stared at the ranks of chisels and knives. Oiled and sharp, as my father would have kept them, they gleamed at me like teeth. I took up a clasp knife, pried out the longest blade, and tested the edge on the hair of my forearm. A tuft came away cleanly, and I saw my father testing the sharpness of tools on his own skin, the blades of axes and knives and gouges and hoes, saw the red hair shaved off in patches from his arms and the backs of his hands. "That will cut bear," he would say. He never cut a bear with his blades, now my blades, but he cut deer, dirt, wood. I closed the knife and put it away. Then I took up the hammer and went back to work on my daughter's wall, snugging the bottom plate against a chalk line on the floor, shimming the top plate against the joists overhead, plumbing the studs with my level, making sure before I drove the first nail that every line was square and true. 28

Focusing on Scott Sanders's Use of Symbolic Details

1. If you regard Scott Sanders's banging his thumb with a hammer as a way of expressing his feelings about his father's death, what is he saying? What could the scar "in the shape of a crescent moon" that "rose across the pink sky" of his thumbnail represent about his reaction to his father's death?

2. In paragraph 3, Sanders says that the "grain in hickory" is "like the grain in the two men who owned this hammer before" him. How are his father and grandfather like the hammer? What does the hammer symbolize about those men?

3. In paragraph 6, Sanders says the hammer "contained houses and mysteries." What does this mean? What larger meanings are contained in the hammer? As you answer this question, consider also paragraphs 24 and 25, especially the last sentence in paragraph 24.

4. How does Sanders use descriptions of tools to indicate his relationship with his son and daughter in paragraph 13? What does the episode he describes in paragraphs 17–23 show us about his relationship to his daughter?

5. The words "square and true" that end the essay describe literally the way pieces of wood are nailed together. What larger meanings are contained in the phrase? What else besides wood can be "square and true"? As you respond to these questions, you might also look at paragraph 16.

WORKING WITH THE TECHNIQUE IN YOUR OWN WRITING

1. Write an essay describing the history of a relationship you have had with someone. Instead of trying to describe everything of importance in the relationship, select some activity that has been repeated throughout its whole history and describe how that activity has changed or how it has appeared different to you at different times. You might write about something as small as walking to the car, showing, for example, how you and a person you were dating walked along in different ways at different stages in your relationship (a few feet apart at first, looking in different directions; then side by side; then at different speeds, a bit uncertain about who is setting the pace; then . . .). Try to let your readers see how the changes in this activity reflect the changes in the basic character of the whole relationship.

2. Write a brief history of something—a soccer team, a high school, a politician's term in office—by focusing on some detail that changed during the course of that history. You might write about the ways the team celebrated victories, about one wall of the high school, about the tone of the politician's press conferences. Try to let your readers see how the changes in this detail reflect the stages in the history you are constructing.

JOHN E. MASON, JR.

Central Connecticut State University
New Britain, Connecticut
Patricia Lynch, instructor

Like many students, John Mason had to work while attending college. Managing the schedules of both school and work can sometimes prove difficult, as Mason's own memorable experience attests: "I was trying to juggle college with work, and I had to work [installing linoleum] before I went to school on that particular day. I thought I could make it home after the job in order to shower and get a change of clothes, but because the job ran over, I was placed in a rather awkward position. The customer, who had gone shopping, wouldn't be home for an hour. I figured since I couldn't make it home to get cleaned up, maybe I could take a shower at the lady's house before she came back. In any case, I got caught in the act when she arrived home early for some reason. There I was, drying myself off."

Charming anecdotes about family, school, and work punctuate Mason's account of his childhood and adolescence. Born in Hartford, Mason attended elementary school in South Windsor, Connecticut, where, in Mrs. Sullivan's second grade class, he was considered "the king of the 'once upon a time' stories. . . . I don't think anyone knew that I had an interest in writing when I was younger, except for Mrs. Sullivan, who loved my fairy tales." He graduated from South Windsor High School and enrolled in his first writing course in college.

A 1987 graduate of Central Connecticut State University with a degree in communications, Mason values "anything that involves being fearful" and explains that "writing has eased some of that fear by helping me to believe that I have a right to try. . . . Writing, like acting, allows the deprived to express themselves in a way that they were never able to. To see on paper feelings you aren't able to or don't know how to express is sometimes quite a revelation. People can go through their whole lives without being able to express these same feelings, hence depriving themselves of ever finding out who they really are."

When asked to reread and comment on his prize-winning essay several years after having written it, Mason remarked: "I still marvel at how certain sentences can bring me back to that exact moment. . . . I vividly remember teachers barking out orders 'single file under the lights'; I remember how scared I was of school and how secure it actually was in Mrs. Sullivan's lap. I can still see Groove's foot tracks in the snow and see myself trying to keep up with him after hitting a car with a snowball. This story reminds me of how much fun life was. All the places I wrote about were places I'd spent most of my childhood at: Pigsville, Elmore's Stand, the Drive-In, Dell's, all places that kindle fond memories. Part of its success for me as a story is the way these sentences are all filled with so much emotion."

John Mason's goal as a writer has been "to write something good enough to be possibly published in the Northeast Magazine [a local paper] so all my friends could go around saying, 'That can't be the same guy.' . . . I usually write so friends and relatives can *get a thrill out of seeing their name in print. One measure of my writing success would be to have my best buddy, Groove, call me yelling about why I didn't use his first name!"*

Asked to write an essay describing a person in his or her setting, Mason chose to focus on Mrs. Sullivan's funeral and the wealth of memories she inspired.

Shared Birthdays

As usual he had waited until the last minute. Route 5 wasn't a very direct   1
route, but it was free of stop lights and he was already late for the funeral. On the other hand, Ellington Road was more direct, but it was a back road littered with stop lights. He knew he couldn't make as good time on Route 5 and from a distance he saw the miniature golf range, which signaled the fork in the road. At the last possible moment he swerved right, just narrowly missing the curb but managing to cause his wheels to squeal nicely. In spite of the fact that it was the middle of June, the golf course was closed as usual. He momentarily wondered how people could possibly support themselves on such a seasonal business. He quickly remembered from his own experience that, when night rolled around, the place would be packed with teenagers competing for each other's attention. He chuckled as he read the sign on Lucian's Restaurant, which used to be called Lou's Drive-In. He could just imagine the steady customers, mostly truckers, calling Lou by his new name. He wondered if building a new addition, acquiring a liquor license, and widening the parking lot had changed his personality the way it did his name.

He checked his watch and realized that no matter how fast he drove, he   2
would be late as usual. After all, it was his trademark. He was blessed at being able to wait until the last possible moment to do anything. This habit, practiced throughout his life and constantly corrected by his mother, had caused her to parent the saying "Someday you're going to give yourself an ulcer." But now he couldn't really decide whether he wanted to go to the funeral at all. Mrs. Sullivan, his second grade teacher, his favorite teacher, had died, and he was going to pay his respects. But he couldn't for the life of him remember what she looked like. It had only been twenty-five years.

He whipped around a truck that was traveling thirty-five in the thirty-five   3
mile an hour zone. He looked across the field and even from the road he noticed that the drive-in movie screen was in desperate need of a paint job. He shot back to the days as a thirteen-year-old when he and his gang spent many a summer night sneaking in through the back for the pleasure of watching the movie standing outside the concession stand. But the main reason wasn't

to watch the movie; the passionate lovers in the back row were their feature attraction. Pounding on the steamy back windows of young neckers' cars, only to be chased through the potato field, was at that time a thrill and a half. The perilous excitement of being chased through a wet and sticky potato field was comparable to the times when Groove and he would bomb cars with snowballs. It was a systematic process of a snowball crushing against the side of a car, brakes squealing, and swear words filling the winter dark, only to be drowned out by the laughter of kids.

He thought ahead to who would be at the funeral today. Would any of his 4 fellow second graders show? He'd have to run into someone he knew. It was inevitable. "I remember you . . . what are you doing with yourself?" He didn't rehearse what he would say, as he usually did. Instead, he again tried to imagine Mrs. Sullivan, a woman he remembered as nice and kind and sweet . . . everything a girl scout would envy. But he knew there was something more— why else would he take a day off from work and drive thirty miles? Reading the obituary the night before, he racked his brain trying to remember if her first name was Mary. There are so many Sullivans. She seemed so old, even then. Could this be the same Mrs. Sullivan who was his second grade teacher? The same Mrs. Sullivan who shared the same birthday as he?

He slowed down for the newly installed light in front of Elmore's. Although 5 it was not actually Elmore's since a glass company bought it out, he still insisted on calling it Elmore's. In the same way he called Jerry Z's Restaurant, Dell's, after its original owners. He always felt a twinge of guilt on driving past Elmore's. As a fifteen-year-old it became customary for him, after playing basketball, to walk down from the school and steal ice cream sandwiches. It was a cold and calculated ordeal which sometimes caused him to nearly freeze his private parts. This was mainly because Mr. Elmore, who loved kids, loved to talk. Years later when he found Elmore's had gone out of business, he envisioned poor old Mr. Elmore broke with no place to go, mainly because of the loss of his ice cream sales.

"Today is a very special day and we have some special birthdays to cele- 6 brate." Everyone knew it was Mrs. Sullivan's, and he'd tried to tell as many people as possible that it was his. But Al Jankowski's? There Al sat, like a fat cat, purring in the lap of Mrs. Sullivan. He knew that he, and not Al, should have been nestled in that warm and secure lap. Thank God for Al's neighbor who finked that Al's birthday was in September and not in March. In the dignified manner in which she seemed to do everything, she kindly asked Al to return to his seat and not to fib in the future. Seeing fat little Al get caught in the act, he quickly promoted himself to the best seat in the house. From the lap of Mrs. Sullivan, he was able to look down on all the little eyes jealously looking at him. He was also able to shoot Al a "better luck next time" smirk. He crossed his arms, resting his head on her breast, and listened as Mrs. Sullivan explained that even though we're all very different, on our birthdays we're that much more unique, because that's the day that God made us specially. The bell rang telling them that lunch was ready, but he would have gladly missed it for a few more moments of playing king.

He tried to imagine what she would have looked like today. He combined 7 what he remembered of the faces of all his old teachers to construct some sort of imaginary face. Even the sight of Pleasant Valley School, the school where she taught, didn't jog his memory; Pleasant Valley School . . . Pigsville . . . as it was so affectionately called by its devoted students. He slowed down just enough to notice that they had built an addition to the back of the school covering the basketball court. The old blacktop . . . it was on that blacktop that he perfected the dying art of chasing a girl to pull her braids. And of course, there was . . . Kathy . . . his first love. He had had his eyes on her, along with half the boys in school, since they went to kindergarten together at the Little Red School House. The blacktop served as his stage to entertain and amuse Kathy. His antics, long forgotten by most, were filed away in his memory bank, always to be relived when passing "Pigsville." The climactic moment of belting a home run, aided by six errors, crossing the plate to have Kathy tell him she liked him more than Graham . . . Even though it only lasted the length of the recess period, it didn't matter. She liked him! Deliberately tripping and falling, getting his new pants dirty was well worth it to see Kathy laughing. Despite the scoldings by his mother, he loved every minute of it. Probably the deciding factor for his crush on Kathy was the head maintenance man in charge of the whole school. He was her grandfather. Everybody wanted to be on a first name basis with the janitor. Two dreams he had had during those early years were to marry Kathy and to be on the safety patrol . . . "Single file under the lights. . . ."

He stopped abruptly for another damn light. The car before him could have 8 made it. He knew he'd definitely be late and decided to drive straight to the church. It's funny, but it was at this specific light that he set the record for the longest kiss in town. It was mostly caused by peer pressure from his eighth grade friends who seemed to think there was something wrong if you didn't kiss a girl after going with her for eight months. But he loved Anita, he respected her, and what if she slapped his face? On that day, standing at the light waiting for it to change, he again struggled to find a way to say goodbye. "I'll see you in school . . . Call you tonight . . . Going to church tomorrow?" But for some reason unknown to him, he just turned and kissed her. It was a hot and sticky summer day and the sun seemed to melt their lips

together. Despite the honking of the passing cars, they managed to stay glued
together for three changings of the light. He couldn't even look her in the
face as he went to leave, too embarrassed that someone he knew might have
seen him. But as he bounced away, he had never felt so good about being
embarrassed.

What would he talk about if he did run into anybody he knew? He always   9
felt uncomfortable about returning to his hometown. If only they didn't ask
the same basic and boring questions. "What are you doing now? Are you still
working for your father?" He'd always dreaded that twofold question. He
couldn't exactly figure out why. Maybe it was because he didn't enjoy the work
he inherited from his father; maybe because he didn't enjoy only being his
father's son; or maybe because he just didn't enjoy himself. In any case, he
was there to pay tribute to a special teacher; so special he couldn't remember
what she looked like. If anyone inquired about how he knew the deceased, he
could always say they shared the same birthday. He pulled into the church
parking lot, scanning the faces of the few people to see if he knew anyone.
He was surprised, even relieved, to see the familiar face of his good friend
Nurse Files, the high school nurse. Through the years after high school they
had kept in touch. It was only today he was to learn that she was Mrs. Sullivan's sister-in-law.

He took a seat in the last pew, separated from the rest of the mourners.   10
This assured that if he did have to cry, he wouldn't be heard by the others.
The preacher in the middle of his eulogy expounded on the fact that through
the years, Mrs. Sullivan dedicated her life to not only teaching youngsters,
but more importantly, showing love and compassion to people in all walks of
life, including the needy and the less fortunate. As the pastor rattled off the
list of her finer attributes, he wondered to himself what the difference between
teaching youngsters and helping the needy was. For some reason, the way the
reverend worded the differences between youngsters and the needy and less
fortunate struck him as funny. What would he classify himself as? The only
substantial memories he had of her were ones of love that she showed not only
for him, but for all her children (including Al). With each story of accomplishments being recited by the proud preacher, he felt tears burning a path
down his face. He didn't make an effort to wipe his face, even though people
slowly began filing out past him. Farewell tears, because he would miss her,
grateful tears for her being a part of his life, tears because he no longer had
the need to remember what she looked like.

As the weary family members lined up to receive their condolences, Nurse   11
Files made it a point to introduce him to the family—"This boy was a favorite
of your mother's." She was cut short by the pressing line of friends who wanted

their say in the matter. He shook hands with the daughter, dying to say her mother's birthday was the same as his, but judging by the look in her eyes, she too wanted to keep the line moving. He kissed Nurse Files good-bye, promising to keep in touch, knowing he wouldn't. The cold air chilled his face where the tears had covered. He felt a strange sense of accomplishment, the way he felt whenever he pushed himself to do something he didn't want to do. He was happy, not only for having attended the funeral, but for having taken the back road, even if as usual he had waited until the last minute.

Focusing on John Mason's Techniques and Revisions

1. John E. Mason, Jr., explains one of his purposes in writing this essay: "I wanted people to know that Mrs. Sullivan was a special woman, not just to me, but to everyone who was a part of her life." How does he describe Mrs. Sullivan? What does he tell us about her life and her teaching? What memories does thinking about her evoke? Based on what he says in this essay, why do you think Mason regards Mrs. Sullivan as "a special woman"?

2. Reflecting on why he wrote this essay, Mason notes; "As we get older, each of us has a tendency to forget special people who helped us along the way. I originally had questioned my motives for attending the funeral of a teacher I'd known so long ago. But the more I wrote, the clearer I saw our relationship." What explanation does Mason offer for attending Mrs. Sullivan's funeral? What does he describe as the nature of their relationship?

3. Mason explains that in writing his essay, "I wanted people to be able to relate, to be able to remember doing the same thing, to say, 'I felt the same way about that,' to just share feelings about growing up in a small town. I wanted people to feel good about themselves." What specific strategies as a writer does Mason use to elicit an emotional response from his readers? Support your response with detailed references to particular paragraphs and sentences. What do you think he means when he reports, "I think I was saying that the things I seem to find the hardest to do in life are usually the most gratifying"?

4. Characterize Mason's *point of view* in this essay. Is he, for example, detached and objective? Involved and subjective? Some other combination? Support your response with an analysis of specific words and phrases. Consider the way Mason presents the "he" in this essay. Why is or isn't using the third-person point of view appropriate to his overall purpose? How is this person introduced? Show how his character remains consistent or changes as the essay unfolds.

5. Mason's essay seems to be divided into two parts: the driver's reflections as he travels to Mrs. Sullivan's funeral and his thoughts while attending the funeral service in church. Outline the major points Mason makes in each section. How

does each contribute to the overall effect of the essay? How does Mason unify the two parts of the essay?

6. What is the primary function of the series of *anecdotes* about the past? What do these anecdotes have in common? What is the effect of each on the overall unity of the essay?

7. Mason's essay makes skillful use of *irony*, the use of words to suggest a meaning different from their literal meaning. See, for example, paragraph 1, where he ponders the effects of the change in the name of Lou's Drive-In to Lucian's Restaurant. Find other instances in Mason's essay and comment on their effectiveness. How does irony add to or detract from the unity of the essay?

8. Mason wrote several drafts of his essay. In discussing the first draft, he observes: "The difficult part about writing the first draft is getting tangled up in how to phrase the lead sentence. Should I have a delayed lead?" What do you think he means here by a "delayed lead"? What advice would you offer Mason on this question? Consider the first sentence of Mason's first draft: "Like everything in his life, he was waiting until the last minute." Evaluate the effectiveness of this opening sentence. What specific changes does he make in the final draft? Which version is more effective? Why?

9. Here is the opening paragraph of Mason's first draft:

> Like everything in his life, he was waiting until the last minute. Route 5 wasn't a very direct route, but it was free of stop lights and he was already late for the funeral. On the other hand Ellington Road was more direct, but was a back road that was littered with stop lights. He knew he couldn't make as good time and from a distance he saw the miniature golf range, which signaled the fork in the road. At the last possible moment he swerved right, just narrowly missing the curb, but managed to cause his wheels to squeal. Despite being the middle of June the miniature golf range was closed as usual. He momentarily wondered how anyone could support themselves on such a seasonal business, but he knew from personal experience that when night rolled around that place would be packed with teenagers competing for each other's attention. He chuckled as he read the sign of Lucian's Restaurant which used to be called Lou's Drive-In. He could just imagine the faithful customers of truckers calling Lou by his new name. He wondered if adding a new addition, acquiring a liquor license, and widening the parking lot would change his personality the way it did his name.

Contrast this version to Mason's final draft. What specific differences do you recognize? Which version establishes a more effective tone and direction for the essay?

Suggestions for Writing

1. In writing his essay, Mason wanted people "to know that Mrs. Sullivan was a special woman, not just to me, but to everyone who was a part of her life." Recall your own elementary, secondary school, or college teachers. Whom among them could you describe as special? Write an essay in which you explain and *illustrate* this teacher's "specialness." You might want to include a detailed *description* of the teacher and recount one or more *anecdotes* to illustrate the points you make.

2. Mason observes near the end of the first paragraph that Lou's Drive-In has changed its name to Lucian's Restaurant. Describe a similar change in some business establishment you know about. Write an expository essay in which you *compare and contrast* the old place of business with the new, reborn version. How have the physical appearance, the products or services, the staff, and the management changed since the place assumed a new look and identity?

3. You have accumulated more than enough classroom experience by now to warrant speaking and writing publicly about the qualities that distinguish outstanding teachers. Read the following quotations on teachers and teaching:

> A teacher affects eternity; no one can tell where [a teacher's] influence stops.
>
> —Henry Adams

> The mediocre teacher tells. The good teacher explains. The superior teacher demonstrates. The great teacher inspires.
>
> —William Arthur Ward

> The art of teaching is the art of assisting discoveries.
> —Mark Van Doren

> In teaching it is the method and not the content that is the message . . . the drawing out, not the pumping in.
> —Ashley Montagu

Choose one of these statements and make it the focus of an essay in which you use your own experience and that of others to verify or refute it.

AN EFFECTIVE TECHNIQUE

John Mason shows us a method we can use to give structure to essays composed largely of disconnected thoughts: present those thoughts as passing through the mind of a person as he performs a familiar sequence of actions.

Mason strings a series of fragmentary memories together as the daydreams of a man on a long drive. The tale of driving holds little interest in itself: nothing much happens. But because the drive is told as a narrative, in chronological sequence, it serves to create the sense that the essay is moving toward some goal while Mason tells the other story in disconnected fragments. The drive follows a "back road littered with stop lights" and the essay itself moves very much like a car on a road with many stop lights. A short passage describes the man driving, and then the motion stops while the character wanders off in thought; then a bit more driving, and much more daydreaming. The drive provides a structure, a frame that unifies the disparate bits of daydreaming, so that we are not simply lost as the man jumps from one memory to another.

Besides holding the essay together, Mason's framing tale—the drive—serves a secondary function as well. Mason parallels the drive and the memories that arise as the man drives along: as the man physically moves closer to the funeral, he mentally moves closer to the person who died. The drive thereby takes on a symbolic meaning: the man is not only taking a "back road," he is taking a road back to his past. At first, the man is uncertain which road to take, and he is equally uncertain why he is going to the funeral; he does not know where his memories or his car will lead him. When he arrives at the funeral, though, he has traced a path through his memories to Mrs. Sullivan and understands why he needed to make this drive: to reestablish contact with the love and compassion she had provided him as a child.

Even after the man leaves his car, images of traveling and of moving closer fill the essay. In the parking lot, he is worried that he might "run into" people he knew in the past but is happy when the one familiar face he sees is Nurse Files, who has "kept in touch" with him. During the service, the man cries, his "tears burning a path down his face." The tears finish the journey that started back on the road, burning the path he has taken into his mind, sealing the connection he had lost and has reestablished. The essay ends with a return to driving, reminding us that this man still has to drive back to his present life, that the funeral, which seemed the destination of this essay, was itself only a stop along the way.

Mason's technique—structuring an essay as the thoughts accompanying some simple actions—is especially useful for essays that consist largely of reflections on the past or on philosophical issues. Such essays have no movement inherent to them, so building a scene is a way to carry readers along. For example, if we have been speculating in general terms about what people give up to pursue a career, we might arrange our insights into an essay that traces the thoughts of a successful executive as he plays basketball with his fellow executives from the office; his thoughts could reveal that only in sports, and never in his work, has he ever felt real emotional satisfaction. To comment on racism, a writer could present the thoughts of two high school students (one Chicano, one black) as they walk together through the segregated neighborhoods that surround their campus. By carefully arranging such scenes, writers can build suspense and surprise into basically philosophical essays.

In the next selection, Virginia Woolf anchors her abstract speculations on death and fate to a small, everyday scene: she presents the thoughts that pass through her head as she watches a moth slowly grow rigid and die.

ANOTHER ILLUSTRATION OF THE TECHNIQUE

VIRGINIA WOOLF

The Death of the Moth

"In or about December, 1910, human character changed," wrote Virginia Woolf in 1924. This enigmatic statement was partly a declaration of victory, since Woolf spent most of her life actively seeking to change human character. Born in 1882 to an eminent Victorian writer, she was raised to be, as she put it, "an Angel in the House"—a self-sacrificing mother and wife—but she successfully rebelled, joining a group of intellectuals who lived in liberated relationships in London and becoming a feminist, a socialist, and a pacifist.

She also became one of the greatest twentieth-century novelists, changing the shape of characters in fiction. Woolf criticized readers who accepted the simplified characters that previous novelists had created: "You have gone to bed at night bewildered by the complexity of your feelings. In one day thousands of ideas have coursed through your brains; thousands of emotions have met, collided, and disappeared in astonishing disorder. Nevertheless, you allow the writers to palm off upon you a version of all this, an image of Mrs. Brown, which has no likeness to that surprising apparition whatsoever." Instead of giving each person a definite character, Woolf's novels attempt to show that the most ordinary Mrs. Brown is of "unlimited capacity and infinite variety; capable of appearing in any place; wearing any dress; saying anything and doing heaven knows what."

Woolf's success in becoming a writer at all, in escaping her family's plans for her, was partly a result of tragedy: both her parents died when she was very young. As a result of these deaths and of the horrors of World War I, she was haunted by thoughts of death all her life. She often felt her writing kept her alive. As she wrote in her diary, "This insatiable desire to write something before I die, this ravaging sense of the shortness and feverishness of life, make me cling, like a man on a rock, to my one anchor." She committed suicide at the beginning of World War II.

Moths that fly by day are not properly to be called moths; they do not excite 1
that pleasant sense of dark autumn nights and ivy-blossom which the com-
monest yellow-underwing asleep in the shadow of the curtain never fails to
rouse in us. They are hybrid creatures, neither gay like butterflies nor somber
like their own species. Nevertheless the present specimen, with his narrow
hay-colored wings, fringed with a tassel of the same color, seemed to be content
with life. It was a pleasant morning, mid-September, mild, benignant, yet with
a keener breath than that of the summer months. The plough was already
scoring the field opposite the window, and where the share had been, the earth
was pressed flat and gleamed with moisture. Such vigor came rolling in from
the fields and the down beyond that it was difficult to keep the eyes strictly
turned upon the book. The rooks too were keeping one of their annual festivities; soaring round the tree tops until it looked as if a vast net with thousands
of black knots in it had been cast up into the air; which, after a few moments
sank slowly down upon the trees until every twig seemed to have a knot at
the end of it. Then, suddenly, the net would be thrown into the air again in
a wider circle this time, with the utmost clamor and vociferation, as though
to be thrown into the air and settle slowly down upon the tree tops were a
tremendously exciting experience.

The same energy which inspired the rooks, the ploughmen, the horses, and 2
even, it seemed, the lean bare-backed downs, sent the moth fluttering from
side to side of his square of the windowpane. One could not help watching
him. One, was, indeed, conscious of a queer feeling of pity for him. The
possibilities of pleasure seemed that morning so enormous and so various that
to have only a moth's part in life, and a day moth's at that, appeared a hard
fate, and his zest in enjoying his meager opportunities to the full, pathetic.
He flew vigorously to one corner of his compartment, and, after waiting there
a second, flew across to the other. What remained for him but to fly to a third
corner and then to a fourth? That was all he could do, in spite of the size of
the downs, the width of the sky, the far-off smoke of houses, and the romantic
voice, now and then, of a steamer out at sea. What he could do he did.
Watching him, it seemed as if a fiber, very thin but pure, of the enormous
energy of the world had been thrust into his frail and diminutive body. As
often as he crossed the pane, I could fancy that a thread of vital light became
visible. He was little or nothing but life.

Yet, because he was so small, and so simple a form of the energy that was 3
rolling in at the open window and driving its way through so many narrow
and intricate corridors in my own brain and in those of other human beings,
there was something marvelous as well as pathetic about him. It was as if
someone had taken a tiny bead of pure life and decking it as lightly as possible

with down and feathers, had set it dancing and zigzagging to show us the true nature of life. Thus displayed one could not get over the strangeness of it. One is apt to forget all about life, seeing it humped and bossed and garnished and cumbered so that it has to move with the greatest circumspection and dignity. Again, the thought of all that life might have been had he been born in any other shape caused one to view his simple activities with a kind of pity.

After a time, tired by his dancing apparently, he settled on the window 4 ledge in the sun, and, the queer spectacle being at an end, I forgot about him. Then, looking up, my eye was caught by him. He was trying to resume his dancing, but seemed either so stiff or so awkward that he could only flutter to the bottom of the windowpane; and when he tried to fly across it he failed. Being intent on other matters I watched these futile attempts for a time without thinking, unconsciously waiting for him to resume his flight, as one waits for a machine, that has stopped momentarily, to start again without considering the reason of its failure. After perhaps a seventh attempt he slipped from the wooden ledge and fell, fluttering his wings, on to his back on the window sill. The helplessness of his attitude roused me. It flashed upon me that he was in difficulties; he could no longer raise himself; his legs struggled vainly. But, as I stretched out a pencil, meaning to help him to right himself, it came over me that the failure and awkwardness were the approach of death. I laid the pencil down again.

The legs agitated themselves once more. I looked as if for the enemy against 5 which he struggled. I looked out of doors. What had happened there? Presumably it was midday, and work in the fields had stopped. Stillness and quiet had replaced the previous animation. The birds had taken themselves off to feed in the brooks. The horses stood still. Yet the power was there all the same, massed outside, indifferent, impersonal, not attending to anything in particular. Somehow it was opposed to the little hay-colored moth. It was useless to try to do anything. One could only watch the extraordinary efforts made by those tiny legs against an oncoming doom which could, had it chosen, have submerged an entire city, not merely a city, but masses of human beings; nothing, I knew had any chance against death. Nevertheless after a pause of exhaustion the legs fluttered again. It was superb this last protest, and so frantic that he succeeded at last in righting himself. One's sympathies, of course, were all on the side of life. Also, when there was nobody to care or to know, this gigantic effort on the part of an insignificant little moth, against a power of such magnitude, to retain what no one else valued or desired to keep, moved one strangely. Again, somehow, one saw life, a pure bead. I lifted the pencil again, useless though I knew it to be. But even as I did so, the unmistakable tokens of death showed themselves. The body relaxed, and instantly grew stiff.

The struggle was over. The insignificant little creature now knew death. As I looked at the dead moth, this minute wayside triumph of so great a force over so mean an antagonist filled me with wonder. Just as life had been strange a few minutes before, so death was now as strange. The moth having righted himself now lay most decently and uncomplainingly composed. O yes, he seemed to say, death is stronger than I am.

Focusing on Virginia Woolf's Use of a Narrative Frame

1. Describe the stages of the moth's death. Identify the places where Woolf moves from telling what is happening to wandering off into more general thoughts. How do the two opening sentences set up the events she is going to narrate?

2. In paragraph 3, what does Woolf say is "the true nature of life"? Her "point" in this paragraph seems embedded in her descriptions of the motions of the moth and the birds. What do these descriptions make us feel about "life" in general?

3. What does Woolf say about death in the last paragraph? What other deaths— besides the moth's—does Woolf refer to in this paragraph? How do her descriptions make you feel about death?

4. Woolf reports that the dead moth "lay most decently and uncomplainingly composed." Does the essay finally leave you feeling "composed" and calm about death? Why or why not? How did writing this essay serve as a way for Woolf to "compose" her feelings about death?

WORKING WITH THE TECHNIQUE IN YOUR OWN WRITING

1. Write an essay using John Mason's structure: show a person engaged in some activity while at the same time thinking about his past. You probably should choose a familiar activity, such as fishing or packing for a move to a different city, so that your readers know what is likely to happen next. You can, however, make the memories quite fragmented and only gradually reveal their significance. If you select the activity well, you might be able to use it to parallel what is happening in the person's mind. Mason uses driving to a funeral to represent the mental act of moving through memories, getting closer to someone who died. You might similarly use fishing to represent the effort to retrieve something from the depths of your mind.

2. Practice using Virginia Woolf's structure to write an essay that consists largely of reflections on some abstract subject. Organize your essay as the thoughts that pass through your head (or through a character's head) as you (or the character)

watch some event. Try to select an event that is appropriate to the abstract subject you want to write about. Woolf thinks about death in general while watching a moth die. You might write about sitting in a comfortable lawn chair watching a traffic jam develop and then get unsnarled; as you watch, you wander off into thoughts about the results of the American love of individuality—everyone going his own way produces chaos. Make your essay follow the stages of the event, and describe it in enough detail that your readers can see it clearly.

AN-THU QUANG NGUYEN

Yale University
New Haven, Connecticut
George S. Fayen, instructor

Writing for An-thu Quang Nguyen is a fast-paced series of starts and stops. If someone were to observe her hard at work crafting a sentence, that person, she explains, would "see me clutching my hair, staring about the room vaguely from time to time, biting my nails, and sighing a lot. I would start jotting something down furiously, sit back to look at it, then furiously cross it out. I may do this several times until the right word appears, at which time I could force out a couple more sentences until I'm again blocked and need to repeat the process." She also reports that she tries to avoid expository writing "at all costs by trying to twist the assignments to my temperament. I keep thinking that the professors must get quite bored reading such dry styles from everyone."

As her essay "Tâi Con" so readily demonstrates, An-thu Quang Nguyen's life story is as unique—and engaging—as her style. Born in Saigon, Vietnam, in 1967, An-thu Quang Nguyen fled to France with her family before immigrating to the United States and settling in the San Francisco Bay area. While attending Palo Alto Senior High School and earning an award for her writing, Nguyen also worked at Stanford Hospital as a lab assistant, did clerical work in Silicon Valley, and conducted private tutoring sessions in French. A psychology/computer science major at Yale University, her career goals are still unclear.

She credits her parents with being the most significant influence on her writing. They are, as she explains, "the embodiment of my birthplace, race, and religion. . . . In addition to having drawn my plots from life experiences which my parents have controlled (traveling, emigration), I naturally write from my soul which they cultivated. My mentality and temperament have been heavily influenced by the way they chose to raise their family. . . . They, as educated Vietnamese, demand much introspection and self-awareness not only physically but mentally and emotionally as well."

That introspection and self-awareness lie at the center of "Tâi Con." Her essay grew out of what she describes as "the developing kinship between two earlier essays on related topics," the first on "home," the second called "Another Language, Another Self." In a recent interview, she offered the following detailed account of the circumstances that led to her writing "Tâi Con":

> I was dealing with a hard week at that time, so I again succumbed to moping about the question which so often came up in my thoughts. We'd also been studying about memory in my psychology class, so I wondered about memories and their distortion. I called up my parents and talked to them for two hours that evening. As I jotted down notes, the images and emotion which I felt across the phone line overwhelmed me, and I just started putting into words these visualizations. This is the first part of the essay. It came out easily as stream-of-consciousness, and

subsequent revisions only involved minor technical details. Then
I read it through many times and destroyed it. I rewrote it from
memory as a kind of self-test. I figured that if it meant that
much to me, no matter how I wrote technically, the emotional
content and effect should not change. To this day I wonder how
different the two rewrites are from each other. Not very much,
I think.

Tâi Con

I.

My friend says to me: "I want to go back, I *need* to go back." 1
"But it's changed." 2
"Yes . . . but I need my memories." 3
"If you go back, you'll be creating new ones." 4
"I will also be confirming my old ones, their faithfulness. I still see my 5
mother standing at the stove, stirring something. Just stirring. That was eleven
years ago. I might be able to find our house again if I go back. Or the Buddhist
temple where we played. I need to know."
"I'm afraid of returning, I'm afraid for the truth of my memories. I have 6
cherished the ones I do have, though. These very few."

I must write about these memories now. I go back to my "home" to do so. 7
I immerse myself within it to write, I immerse myself in its pain. Pleasure plays
no part in my writing because the pain of melancholia must serve as inspiration.
My words come from the place of memories, and poetry, of the heart and of
the brain. It's a place I must struggle to enter, then struggle to return.
My story emerges not from a visual documentary of my memories, but from 8
the physical sensations which still startle my body, the unnamed emotions
which bring a sudden, surprising smile, or a tear. I start from these senses,
then add the physical details later, the opposite way in which a child will color
in his coloring book. For me the sensations are my colors. They are vague,
moving, indistinct, until the details are drawn about them, forming the defining outline, the shape of my story. I begin thus with the colors of my memories,
because I *cannot* lose the senses, even when I want to forget. They stay with
me: the shrills, the darkness, a descending sky. A thunderstorm.

My father speaks in French to me, his speech punctuated with Vietnamese 9
names and accented English words, December 1985:

"The first awareness was the sound of the bombs, that very distinct sound. 10
Maman and I slept with one eye open, a very shallow sleep, our subconscious
always tuned to *that sound*. It could not be mistaken. It would always start in
a long shrill whistle, then came the explosion. That was when *they* bombed
the city indiscriminately for every night during three weeks. Just to terrorize
us. You know how they are, those bastards. It was in April of 1968—Tết
Mậu Thân. Yes, during the month of Tết Mậu Thân.

"We slept on the upper floor because, you know, the ground floor was too 11
hot, humid, and not well aired. You remember Saigon—it's *really* humid. We
lay up there, taking the risk and hoping that the first bomb would not land
on us. We took that risk. . . . There was usually one minute between the first
and second. As soon as the first whistle came plunging, my only thought was
to get a child downstairs into the shelter. Maman and I had planned it out;
your big brother was old enough to walk, so Maman would take him down
while I would carry you. We had to be alert to that first hiss, and as quickly
as possible run downstairs. We had less than a minute. . . . You see, we had
to be downstairs in less than a minute. . . .

"I sat under the stairs all those nights, thinking, we escaped it again. The 12
first one didn't hit us. The risk had paid off. Yes, during Tết Mậu Thân.

"1975: We were at Tân Sởn Nhất because I was despaired. . . . I didn't 13
know how to get us out, had no usable connections, no one. Tân Sởn Nhất
was the point of departure, it was from there that planes were leaving, taking
people away. That was my only consolation. To hear the engines, the rush of
the winds. But I was waiting for a miracle.

"You, your brothers, and Maman were at Bác Hùng's house. I desperately 14
wandered through the terminal, with no idea of what I seeked. But I am the
father and husband, I had to do *something*. But it was so hopeless, I was so
despaired. . . . And then I ran into your uncle. Being an employee of Pan
Am, he knew about a company flight which was ready to take off very soon
but would only accept their employees or close relatives. He pointed out a
Chinese and told me that I should talk to him, for he was Pan Am's security
officer.

"I posed my problem, to which he answered: 'How many in the 15
family?'

" 'Five.'   16

" 'The plane is leaving in ten minutes.'   17

"The whole thing was done in fifteen minutes. Your uncle drove the van 18
which was supposed to have carried only baggages. A miracle done in fifteen
minutes.

"Only when that Boeing took off, only when I felt the wheels lifting free 19
of the ground, did I think, we have now escaped. Neither the police nor
Việt Cộng bombs can stop us now. We had gotten away from the *Việt Cộng*,
my first priority has been resolved.

"And then I looked out the window, we were still low, heading for the 20
Indian Ocean and I could see very clearly Vũng Tầu. It's the westernmost
boundary of Việt-Nam. At that moment, I knew I was leaving my country,
and that I might never return. I'm old, you know.

"I followed the disappearing land with my eyes, with my body, straining to 21
keep it in sight for as long as possible. And you see, I was right. We've run
away since ten years, and I still can't return. I want to return. Even to the
destruction and poverty, because the Vietnamese *always* come back home.
They may leave their villages to go work elsewhere, to the city, but every
Tết they're home to their molding roofs and sweating walls. It's in the blood,
it's a need, it's a *call*.

"Only when life becomes unbearable to the point of inhumanity do they 22
flee. This has been the first time in the history of Việt-Nam that the people
have wanted or needed to escape in such numbers. Imagine the living conditions which the Communists have created to have forced this migration.
. . . Those bastards.

"We Vietnamese are not happy in foreign countries. The Chinese, Italians, 23
Irish. They left their homelands hundreds of years ago. But not the Vietnamese. Only now. Only now have we left."

                                             *

My mother speaks in her perfect, schoolteacher French to me, December 24
1985:

"When I heard the sound, I felt two simultaneous and completely contra- 25
dictory reactions. The first was a sleepy calmness, a security in knowing that
we had prepared ourselves well. But the other was panic: Where are my children? Where are the bombardments? I would run to your room and carry you
downstairs because you were smaller while Papa took your brother.

"As soon as we were all settled under the stairs behind the sandbags, I felt 26
safer, calmer, but there was some fatalism involved too. I accepted the situation, I prayed and hoped, but there was no revolt, no anger. After two months
of unfailing nightly bombing, we were benumbed. It is strange, but we didn't
even listen to the radio, we did nothing. Inside the house, there was only
silence. But outside, the bombing would rain down upon the city for half an
hour. You heard a whistling, a sinister whistling. And then the explosion,
sometimes you didn't even hear that. Just the whistling. For two months. We

didn't react anymore, our actions were purely automatic, programmed, and we were ready to accept whatever would pass.

"I spent much time upstairs in your room, sewing. There wasn't anything 27 else to do. Just to dramatize the situation. Do you remember the backpacks I sewed? I had to use bedsheets because they were the strongest and most durable material I could find in the house. I used three layers, with the works: zipper, buttons, straps, buckles, everything! They were very, very pretty! An outside loop held a cup, a small pocket had medicine: aspirin, diarrhea pills, some general antibiotics, an American acidic powder which gave you strength. In the inner small pocket I sewed money and in the large one I put a pair of pants, a blouse, socks, sandals, some crackers and water. There was also a notebook with all our pictures with birthdates, birthplaces, full names, . . . just in case we were separated.

"My sister and I chatted, tried to gossip and have fun. What else could we 28 have done? What a waste. We had to leave the backpacks behind when Papa came rushing in at Tân Sơn Nhất telling us to leave for the plane.

"How I prayed, worried about being retained. We were quiet, we tried to 29 shrink, make ourselves as small as possible. Only after having passed the Bangkok frontier did the entire plane burst out in rejoicing. We clapped, we talked, cried.

"I felt the relief and joy of having left, escaped, with my whole family. I 30 was also angry. Angry towards myself for being so vulnerable, helpless. I felt like a marionette, flung, controlled, without power over the conditions which ruled me, without power to turn back the war. . . . I was empty.

"Only the week after, when we had found a sponsor, when we were again 31 eating what we wanted and were secure, did I—could I—look at myself. I found shame, a shame of having been helpless, powerless, of having tried to do nothing. I felt pain. The shame and the pain . . . I felt that in leaving, in running away, I had *abandoned* a mother and father. Việt-Nam is such a part of your body, it's your parent, your child. It's something within yourself, something too valuable, beautiful, brilliant, that you can't but grieve, a racking grief, over its loss. A complete, total loss which you have been powerless to prevent.

"But I've never regretted having left. In face of the past events, the hor- 32 ror stories which have come back to me, I now know that I did correctly.

"I could not return with my pain, I could not return to face the pain of my 33 land, its suffering. *I don't want to return.* I would not be able to help their sorrow. It's egotism and cowardice, I know. It's a wound which can't be opened. . . . But I must not forget."

*   *

I now write what I have been thinking for the last ten years: 34
"Shhh!" 35
"But what are you doing?" 36
It is the middle of night and my father has pulled up the pink mosquito 37
netting from my bed and is gathering me into his arms, blanket too. I think
that it must be a dream. He carries me from our room, past my little brother's
crib, into the hall. He carries me down, bare feet softly thumping against the
wide spiraling wooden staircase. He then turns into the niche under the stairs,
where I played dolls and where I now see my two brothers and mother huddled
on spread blankets. As I feel the hard floor through the sheets, I realize that
this is not a dream but I remain baffled and a little excited at such a game.
"Why are . . . " 38
"Shhhhh. Be quiet. Try to sleep." 39
I lie, drowsy, but am looking at my mother through the dark. She cradles 40
my little brother who is snoring. My big brother has large eyes which stare
around the somber room. Now I am worried because he only stares so when
he's scared; my big brother, to whom I turn for reassurance during a night
storm. We sit in the dark under the silent stairs, five of us in the family.
What are we waiting for? 41
I hear the thunder outside. A large, looming noise is born and expands over 42
our heads to die in a grand crescendo. I think of waves rearing up, building,
then descending in their multitudes of water droplets. That is the most terri
fying moment, when I realize that the curve is going to engulf me, when it is
frozen still just for a second, before crashing. Then it plunges and I feel my
limbs fly out in all directions, turning, turning, in the wet billows. The house
shakes, its timber creaking slowly in secret movements. As I feel the core of
the earth tremble, I realize that it is not raining; a tropical rain is easy to
distinguish, so this is not thunder. The bombs drop from the belly of the plane,
a hiss expanding into screams just before they hit the earth, crashing, sending
out their volleys of fire. I imagine all this, remembering scenes from war movies. I huddle close to my mother.
We wait in the dark, five of us in the family under our staircase. Our house 43
lies in the governmental section of Saigon, which is now Ho Chi Minh City.
It is one of the first sections the Việt Cộng will seek to ravage after their
entrance to the city.

"Where are we going?" 44
"Tân Sởn Nhất." 45

"Are we going to visit Bác Tước there?"   46

"No, we're just going to stay at her house for a few days. She's already left 47
Việt-Nam with your cousins but Bác Hùng is still there."

My uncle's house is located near the Tân Sờn Nhất airport because he is a 48
pilot. In earlier days we would cluster about him, sitting next to his collection
of airplanes. He would take one chopstick, lick the tip, and with this viscosity
capture a hapless ant. It would disappear into his mouth, and we would shriek
with delight as well as disbelief when the end came out empty. We never
learned whether or not this feat had been accomplished by sheer dexterity or
a strong stomach. It would not matter later, however, for his pilot's delicate
touch would be taken off along with a part of his finger while working,
grounded, as a printer in Washington, D.C.

In his three-story house near the airport my parents again wait. My father 49
can catch the phone on the second ring and the door on the first knock. We
play on my aunt's waterbed and on the back porch step with its wide, jagged
crack.

I lie on the cold steel, feeling the rumble of the wheels speeding across the 50
pebbled airstrip. My mother holds my little brother closely, tensely, frightened
that he would wake. But he sleeps peacefully as the van, smelling of fish, races
to pass soldiers and reach the airplane. I only see my mother's hand cradling
my little brother's tousled hair as bullets whistle, grazing the side of the van.

My mother reaches across me and the narrow Pan Am seats to her sister, 51
their tears mixing, running down reddened cheeks. I look up at them and do
not understand. A woman is running about, screaming about her misplaced
wedding dress.

"Mother, where is your wedding dress?"   52

"I had to leave it at home."   53

"But why? She has hers."   54

"Shhh. Don't talk so much."   55

She talks to my aunt, wiping her tears. They cry, then wipe their tears, 56
again.

It suddenly comes to me that my mother and her sister had just cried 57
together, not long ago:

> I wander restlessly through the hot house, feeling the hu-
> midity of Saigon. My brother will not let me play with him
> and I sulk. Stomp, stomp up the hollow wooden steps
> which provide a pleasant resonance to my anger. Oh, re-
> lief. The door to our room is closed which means that the

air conditioner is on. It is the only one in our house, used
for my little brother's afternoon nap. I hear muted voices.
Who could Mother be talking to? I open the door quietly
and sneak in. They're sitting on the cool floor near the
crib. My mother and her sister are bent over their sewing.
I sneak in closer and hide behind the mosquito netting.
They're sewing money into the belts of our pants. But why?
They're talking excitedly, tensely, very quickly in Vietnamese, which I can't understand very well at their speed.

" . . . sending the children ahead . . . "
" . . . I can't . . . plane . . . 188, all the children dead."
My mother pricks her finger as tears start down. The
two sisters cling together and the paper money flutters to
the ground, forgotten.

My mother will talk to me several years later as I bemoan the loss of a 58
favorite ring. She will say, "You should not put such importance on material
possessions. I have lost too much in my life, I now know that nothing is worth
becoming attached to, for it can be taken away just as easily. You should love
that which doesn't disappear on a careless misplacement of shallow memory.
You should love human beings." Later I will understand that she has lost not
only a wedding dress.

Ten years later, I can only grasp a wisp of the pain which she must have 59
felt. I grope for the Việt-Nam my parents knew, for their pain, but it remains
alien to me. I see confusion and frustration, telling myself that I *must* have
loved my mother country and fellow countrymen from whom I now shy away.
A new acquaintance recently asked me about that country in which I have
spent a total of two years, about that country whose language I can hardly
speak:
"How do you feel about America's role in the Vietnam War?" 60
I could only look at him blankly, thinking 61
"I couldn't tell you what I feel, I will tell you what I think. I can think as 62
a Vietnamese, a French, an American, all three combined. I can give you an
analysis of faults in the military strategy, but I cannot cry to you the pain
which you probably expect. You must ask my mother and father for that. My
pain arises from the fact that when the plane took off, we left behind more
than my mother's silk dresses, that the bombs would destroy more than our
wooden staircase but that I couldn't say what it is, or if I miss it."

II.

David jumps from behind the smooth tree trunk and lightly taps me on the 63
shoulder.

"Ah non! Tu n'as pas le droit de faire ça!" I protest his game techniques. 64
We are playing tag together, as with every recess. He and I are usually the
two last ones left in the game for we are the tallest, virtual giants over our
Vietnamese classmates. He is a Eurasian and has inherited his French father's
stature. I am a pure Vietnamese who has been raised in France (my mother
attributes my height to the food she fed me). David is my best friend in the
first grade at Colette, the official French-Vietnamese school in Saigon. He
repeats his complaint once again: "Tại sao mày không nói tiếng Việt-Nam?
Chởi ngoài này chẳng ai nghe thấy dâu!" (Come on, why don't you speak
Vietnamese? It's recess now. The teachers won't hear us anyway!)

"Mais on n'a pas le droit." (But it's against the rules.) I feebly answer. As 65
I race away, I feel my stomach squirm: *And I don't know how to.* In Vietnamese
class my heart aches as it is once again my turn. I stand up and stumble, red
faced, through two pages of oral recitation. The teachers look at my brother
and me with strange, questioning eyes. *They are Vietnamese, why can they not
read such a simple text? They are Vietnamese, why can they not spell such a simple
word?* The classroom is dark. The teachers' faces are vague, hidden in the
shadows and behind long, black hair. One of them writes on the board. Oh
no, I've forgotten how to pronounce that accent. There aren't nearly as many
in French—

Nevertheless, through pure rote recitation, I phonetically learn the tradi- 66
tional sing-songs and delight my relatives at my grandfather's house with per-
formances. Smiling, nodding. They listen to the lilting, wrongly stressed and
accented rhythms coming from my throat. "*Tâi con!*" In their laughing eyes,
I am "the little French kid."

In my grandfather's house I escape to his attic. I cringe as I pass through 67
the cobwebs, making my way to the special section in which he keeps his
French books. I turn on the light as quickly as possible, checking behind for
hairy monsters lurking in the shadows. Satisfied, I then settle myself in the
circle of dim light, squinting to make out the faded print and pictures.

In his youth and especially later, my prideful grandfather had insisted on 68
keeping himself independent from others. His teachers consisted of French
grammar books, simple comic books, and some fat literary texts which I used
as stools. His accent imitates Tino Rossi's famous rolling Italian: he speaks to
me in this musical language which is his French. I finally realize that it is

French, because I detect a few familiar words and he expects me to understand. In those days, my relatives quickly learned that Nga's children, fresh from Paris, could only understand its language. So my grandfather speaks to me, and his tongue conforms to the foreign phonetics. I don't fully understand because of the strange contrast between the music of his speaking and his dry, grammar-book syntax. But the smell of his pipe pleases me as I nod, listening to his rolls. He just talks and talks, seeking my approval—a *tâi con's* approval— of his self-taught language. When he stops, I sneak up to the attic and, sitting on the texts, read his tattered comics.

Vietnamese is not my language. The people are not my people. Outside the 69 family, the Vietnamese language is yet more complicated for me because all the natives speak with the southern accent, whereas I have been raised on my parents' northern dialect. This fluid, melodic learned language immediately identifies them as northern upper class. It is that of the ancient emperors and scholars. It is that of Hồ Chí Minh. It is also that of the evening. When my mother puts us to bed, tucking in the mosquito net, she will then sing to my baby brother. Lying drowsily beside the trembling air conditioner, it seems to me that my mother's songs don't actually have *meaning*. I guess that she simply takes the softest, most undulating sounds of her language and smooths them together. Her voice rises and falls, following sinuous accents, suggesting subtle smells, caresses, visions. It is the language of the night which she speaks to my father. Their voices drift through the thin walls, accompanied by the droning of their fan. The low, relaxed rumbling of my father, an occasional chuckle, and my mother's higher, lighter stream.

After our emigration to the U.S., I conform in language as far as I dare 70 to my American friends and their alien attitudes. I pick up Californian expressions which amuse my parents. I drift toward *America* until the time when every child desires differentiation, rejecting the "norm." In seventh grade I do not perform the pledge of allegiance and sit belligerently, day after day, not listening to the droning classmates as they recite. I was not a U.S. citizen and I had never understood its words. Also in the seventh grade I received this comment: *Your sevens look like backward F's.* Was this a warning?

As I move toward America and its English, I lose my French and forget 71 the Vietnamese which was never mine. I use French riddled by English for explanations to my parents until the topic becomes too complicated for my vocabulary. I talk about Shakespeare, Conrad, Williams. They know about Duras, Hugo, Sartre. I then wave my hands helplessly as if they could somehow convey the idea which so effectively eludes my bastardized foreign lexicon. I struggle against usage of English with my family because it signifies betrayal of the French which gives me so much pride. It signifies a loss of my skill. And my parents may not understand the English words.

My parents, though, also start inserting English into their speech. Its 72 strange sounds explode from the French or Vietnamese, in the middle of a sentence. My parents don't seem to notice. They are used to it because French had earlier been incorporated in the same way into their native Vietnamese. The explosion becomes less noisy, less grating, less painful. I realize that their mix of languages has evolved for efficiency. They simply use whatever part of a language is most convenient and have so accomplished a marriage among their spoken languages. My father often stands with his head cocked, a Bogart twist on his lips, and runs a new word over his tongue, over and over. He will use it the next time it is called for, then flash us a grin. Now when I write school essays and compositions, I struggle with inadequate English words which are perfectly expressed by French ones. Then I give up and hope that my professor knows French.

In the living room at the house in Hằng Sanh my mother and I sit enrap- 73 tured before the screen. A teary woman starts her song and its long, drawn-out notes drag at our hearts because that special Vietnamese style of singing inevitably portrays a character's suffering. The pain rides on the singer's voice as it twists its way through the Vietnamese accents, combining phonetics with a pure humming, accompanied only by wooden drums. The Vietnamese counterpart of the western opera, and just as laborious to master. It is difficult to learn to appreciate the art form, but once you do, you are accepted as a true Vietnamese. The woman grieves, swaying in her tears and latest Parisian dress.

"What is she saying, Maman?"   74

"I have no idea. Besides it being *cải lương*, she's singing it in southern 75 dialect. But it's beautiful, isn't it?"

"Yes. It is beautiful."   76

As the program ends, I look through the window at the shimmering, hu- 77 mid air of Saigon. A lone food vendor drones his usual cry as my mother and I leave the stagnant space of the house for the garden and a clear, blue sky.

                    *   *   *

All memorable places and events contain their own sense of having once 78 existed. Like the gigantic regal tree in our front yard at Hang Sanh, as my mother and I looked up at it, so long ago. I cannot see it anymore, the color of its leaves, the size of its trunk, the number of enormous white flowers which exploded from the foliage. But I feel it behind me, presiding, the pungent smell of the blossoms weaving a heavy blanket overhead. The tropical rain, now gone, evaporates from the dense earth and dilutes its musk. This particular smell, or seeing the way a water drop dangles from a leaf, will activate a certain lobe of the brain, a certain part of the lobe. Certain clues, however faint or transient, will draw out an avalanche of memories and their senses so that I may once again feel that taste in my mouth, feel my heart constricting as it did when my fingertip touched the silk of a white petal. They will call forth a memory, that afternoon with my mother.

Focusing on An-thu Quang Nguyen's Techniques and Revisions

1. In a recent interview, An-thu Quang Nguyen explained the goal of her essay: "to define clearly my memories which had been turning about so vaguely in my mind beforehand and to compare them with my parents' memories." In the first paragraph of "Tâi Con," Nguyen makes it clear that her essay will focus on those memories of her childhood in Vietnam and of her family's escape to France and their immigration to the United States. But does Nguyen seem to be more interested in recalling specific memorable people and events, or does she seem to prefer to focus on the process of remembering? Support your response with a detailed analysis of specific passages.

2. What does the speaker mean when she says, "I'm afraid of returning, I'm afraid for the truth of my memories" (paragraph 6)? What kinds of fear do those memories evoke? What other kinds of fear emerge as the story proceeds? Why does the speaker respond to each? Why does "the friend" say "I *need* to go back"? How does Nguyen develop this notion in the essay? Does the speaker share that conviction? Point to specific words and phrases to verify your response.

3. Nguyen reports that she aimed in her essay "to capture as faithfully as possible the purity of the emotions which I was trying to portray. I wanted [my close friends] to understand me and the way I thought, what I thought, and for my parents, I wanted them to see how I saw them." Identify each of the emotions Nguyen presents in this essay. Which does she treat ironically? With what effect? What, for example, is the dramatic effect of the anecdote about her uncle the pilot? In paragraph 8, Nguyen observes, "My story emerges not from a visual documentary of my memories, but from the physical sensations which still startle my body, the unnamed emotions which bring a sudden, surprising smile, or a tear." How does she follow through on this assertion in the paragraphs that follow?

4. Nguyen does a masterful job of appealing to her readers' senses. Reread the opening pages of her essay and point to those passages in which she appeals to sense experience. On behalf of what larger, more abstract point does Nguyen appeal to her readers' senses?

5. Comment on the structure of Nguyen's essay. What principle of organization governs its development? How, for example, is the essay divided? What is the structural and thematic significance of each section? What function does the white space serve in her essay? What is the effect of her using a single, a double, and then a triple asterisk between sections of her essay? What function does her use of Roman numerals serve? Show how the process of remembering is directly related to the structure of her essay.

6. Nguyen begins each section of her essay *in medias res*, in the middle of things. What writing strategies does she use to orient her reader, however gradually, in each section? How does she eventually make the dramatic function and purpose of each section clear to her readers?

7. Nguyen presents compelling images of what it is like to be a stranger in a strange land as well as a stranger in her own land. How, in section II, does she underscore the painful irony of being ill at ease with other Vietnamese? How does she try to connect with a past from which she has been cut off? How does she stylistically use transitions in her essay?

8. Describe the overall effect of Nguyen's essay. What does the final paragraph contribute to that effect? What is the significance of Nguyen's saying, "This particular smell, or seeing the way a water drop dangles from a leaf, will activate a certain lobe of the brain, a certain part of the lobe"? How might this sentence serve as a metaphor for Nguyen's own efforts in the essay? What does the sentence tell us about Nguyen's purpose in this essay?

9. In Nguyen's third draft, her essay began this way:

> "Home"—"where composed, I am always composing." In this familiar environment, known and accepted, I can write true words; yet for me, the home in which I immerse myself to write must always be slightly painful. Pleasure plays no part in my writing because the pain of melancholia must serve as inspiration. It comes from the place of memories, and poetry, of the heart and finally of the brain. It's a place I must struggle to enter, then struggle to return. I will not write in the real world, it is too obvious.
>
> I then write from "home," from the senses, and add the physical details, the opposite way in which a child will color in his coloring book.

Explain why you think the final version of Nguyen's opening is or is not more effective than the opening of her third draft.

10. Nguyen revised her conclusion several times before she apparently was satisfied with it. Here is the conclusion from her third draft:

> Ten years later, I can only grasp a wisp of the pain which she must have felt. I grope for the Việt-Nam my parents knew, for their pain, but it remains alien to me. I see confusion and frustration, telling myself that I *must* have loved my mother country and fellow countrymen from whom I now shy away. A new acquaintance recently asked me about that country in which I have spent a total of two years, about that country whose language I could hardly speak.
>
> "How do you feel about America's role in the Vietnam War?"
>
> I could only look at him blankly, thinking, "I couldn't tell you what I feel, I will tell you what I think. I can think as a Vietnamese, a French, an American, all three combined. I can give an analysis of faults in the military strategy, but I cannot cry to you the pain which you probably expect. You must ask my mother and father for that. My pain arises from the fact that when the plane took off, we left behind more than my mother's silk dresses, that the bombs would destroy more than our wooden staircase but that I couldn't say what it is, or if I miss it.

What differences do you notice between this conclusion and that of the final draft? Which version is more successful? Why?

Suggestions for Writing

1. Near the end of the first section of her essay, Nguyen recalls an anecdote that makes a graphic point (paragraph 58):

> My mother will talk to me several years later as I bemoan the loss of a favorite ring. She will say, "You should not put such importance on material possessions. I have lost too much in my life, I now know that nothing is worth becoming attached to, for it can be taken away just as easily. You should love that which doesn't disappear on a careless misplacement of shallow memory. You should love human beings." Later I will understand that she has lost not only a wedding dress.

Write a narrative essay in which you recount a story that illustrates this same or a similar point.

2. In *A Thousand-Mile Walk to the Gulf* (1916), the celebrated American environmentalist and writer John Muir observed: "Memories may escape the action of the will, may sleep a long time, but when stirred by the right influence, though that influence be light as a shadow, they flash into full stature and life with everything in place." Consider the wealth of your own memories of childhood. Select several memories and draft an essay in which you create a series of strong, clear images of those memories, using the power of your emotions to unify them.

AN EFFECTIVE TECHNIQUE

An-thu Quang Nguyen's "Tâi Con" has such a strange structure that we might feel we would never try to write an essay like it. However, if we examine what this structure allows Nguyen to accomplish, we might well be inclined to try the same thing. Nguyen begins her essay by speaking of what she is trying to do: to reconnect with a past that she cannot quite remember even though she has strong feelings about it. She reports, "My story emerges not from a visual documentary of my memories, but from the physical sensations which still startle my body" (paragraph 8). She creates in her essay the experience of having memories emerge from strong feelings. She divides her paper into short sections separated by white space. As each section begins, we are uncertain what is happening, but we can very quickly establish the feeling, the tone, of what is being reported. Nguyen gradually makes each scene clear and indicates its connection to other scenes. We could, if we wished, rearrange the tale into strict chronological order, but then we would lose the sense of images surfacing into consciousness. This is not an essay about events; it is an essay about how difficult it is to remember important events.

At the end of the essay, Nguyen speaks again about how memories emerge from various "lobes of the brain"; the image suggests that she does not feel like one single, whole person. We can certainly recognize what has produced her sense of being split into several different persons: Nguyen has been wrenched from one country to another, from France to Vietnam to America, and she has never felt fully immersed in any one culture. Her essay is an attempt to convey to the reader what it is like to feel oneself composed of separate parts that cannot be easily united. Nguyen re-creates the disorder in her mind.

We might not feel our lives have been split up quite as much as Nguyen's, but we all have experienced the disorder of a changing world, perhaps moving from one school to another or living on our own for the first time. Most of us have experienced being torn between two sets of values or two different "sub-cultures," perhaps between friends and parents or between two different sets of friends. At the least, we have felt torn between the thrills promised in advertising and the moral rules established by parents and teachers. If we think about our childhood, we probably find intense, vivid memories that we cannot quite arrange into a proper chronology. If we wanted to try to make sense of the disconnected parts of our past, we could adapt the structure of Nguyen's essay and write a series of short little scenes that encapsulate the especially vivid and emotional memories we have.

Nguyen shows us how to use writing to gain power in a world that seems overpowering, a chaotic world that leaves us feeling that we have been created in separate pieces and are unable to unify ourselves. We can use writing to connect to a past that may seem lost and buried and begin to make sense of the powerful feelings that have shaped us.

In the next selection, Maxine Hong Kingston shows us a slightly different way to write an essay made of disparate pieces, re-creating a slightly different experience of disorder. She uses much smaller pieces than Nguyen and does not use white space to separate them: her scenes blend together, re-creating the general experience of living in a fragmented world. She, too, is writing about the confusion created by having lived in two different cultures, but she has not moved from one to another; she has simply grown up always surrounded by both Chinese and American traditions.

ANOTHER ILLUSTRATION OF THE TECHNIQUE

MAXINE HONG KINGSTON

The Woman Warrior

Maxine Hong Kingston grew up in the tightly knit community of Chinese immigrants in Stockton, a city in central California where her parents owned and operated a laundry. Kingston remembers that "most of the people who worked there passed the time by telling ghost stories. The laundry seemed to be a good place for that." Kingston feels that her writing grew out of "the tradition of storytellers; but I'm different from the others in that I write, whereas the rest of them relied on memory." Her books focus on the role Chinese traditions play in the lives of Chinese Americans. She says her characters are trying to "figure out how what they've been told connects—or doesn't connect—with what they experience." Part of what she finds fascinating and confusing is that modern and traditional views are not simply polar opposites. For example, facing the women's liberation movement in the United States, she realized "that the attitude towards women in China was very puzzling because on the one hand there was this slavery . . . . But at the same time they had these heroic stories about the women warriors, so there were two traditions going at once—about powerful fighters and poets and rulers that were women, and on the other hand, enslavement. So I think that women's liberation was already a tradition in China, too."

In her effort to reproduce the multiplicity of voices that she feels assail Chinese Americans, Kingston developed a distinctive prose style. She studied how other writers have rendered dialects in order to find a way to distinguish persons speaking Chinese in her books from those speaking English with a Chinese accent and those speaking English with a Stockton, California, accent. She decided not to use the "weird spelling and apostrophes and all that" of writers such as Mark Twain; instead, imitating some of Gertrude Stein's experiments, Kingston says she has tried to "play with syntax and rhythm" to "capture some of the power and sounds and rhythms" in both of her native languages.

My American life has been such a disappointment. 1

"I got straight A's, Mama." 2

"Let me tell you a true story about a girl who saved her village." 3

I could not figure out what was my village. And it was important that I do 4
something big and fine, or else my parents would sell me when we made our
way back to China. In China there were solutions for what to do with little
girls who ate up food and threw tantrums. You can't eat straight A's.

When one of my parents or the emigrant villagers said, "Feeding girls is 5
feeding cowbirds," I would thrash on the floor and scream so hard I couldn't
talk. I couldn't stop.

"What's the matter with her?" 6

"I don't know. Bad, I guess. You know how girls are. There's no profit in 7
raising girls. Better to raise geese than girls."

"I would hit her if she were mine. But then there's no use wasting all that 8
discipline on a girl. 'When you raise girls, you're raising children for
strangers.' "

"Stop that crying!" my mother would yell. "I'm going to hit you if you don't 9
stop. Bad girl! Stop!" I'm going to remember never to hit or scold my children
for crying, I thought, because then they will only cry more.

"I'm not a bad girl," I would scream. "I'm not a bad girl. I'm not a bad 10
girl." I might as well have said, "I'm not a girl."

"When you were little, all you had to say was 'I'm not a bad girl,' and you 11
could make yourself cry," my mother says, talking-story about my childhood.

I minded that the emigrant villagers shook their heads at my sister and 12 me. "One girl—and another girl," they said, and made our parents ashamed to take us out together. The good part about my brothers being born was that people stopped saying, "All girls," but I learned new grievances. "Did you roll an egg on *my* face like that when *I* was born?" "Did you have a full-month party for *me*?" "Did you turn on all the lights?" "Did you send *my* picture to Grandmother?" "Why not? Because I'm a girl? Is that why not?" "Why didn't you teach me English?" "You like having me beaten up at school, don't you?"

"She is very mean, isn't she?" the emigrant villagers would say.   13

"Come, children. Hurry. Hurry. Who wants to go out with Great-Uncle?"   14
On Saturday mornings, my great-uncle, the ex–river pirate, did the shopping. "Get your coats, whoever's coming."

"I'm coming. I'm coming. Wait for me."   15

When he heard girls' voices, he turned on us and roared, "No girls!" and 16
left my sisters and me hanging our coats back up, not looking at one another. The boys came back with candy and new toys. When they walked through Chinatown, the people must have said, "A boy—and another boy—and another boy!" At my great-uncle's funeral I secretly tested out feeling glad that he was dead—the six-foot bearish masculinity of him.

I went away to college—Berkeley in the sixties—and I studied, and I   17
marched to change the world, but I did not turn into a boy. I would have liked to bring myself back as a boy for my parents to welcome with chickens and pigs. That was for my brother, who returned alive from Vietnam.

If I went to Vietnam, I would not come back; females desert families. It 18
was said, "There is an outward tendency in females," which meant that I was getting straight A's for the good of my future husband's family, not my own. I did not plan ever to have a husband. I would show my mother and father and the nosey emigrant villagers that girls have no outward tendency. I stopped getting straight A's.

And all the time I was having to turn myself American-feminine, or no   19
dates.

There is a Chinese word for the female I—which is "slave." Break the   20
women with their own tongues!

I refused to cook. When I had to wash dishes, I would crack one or two.   21
"Bad girl," my mother yelled, and sometimes that made me gloat rather than cry. Isn't a bad girl amost a boy?

"What do you want to be when you grow up, little girl?"   22

"A lumberjack in Oregon."   23

Even now, unless I'm happy, I burn the food when I cook. I do not feed   24
people. I let the dirty dishes rot. I eat at other people's tables but won't invite them to mine, where the dishes are rotting.

If I could not-eat, perhaps I could make myself a warrior like the swords- 25
woman who drives me. I will—I must—rise and plow the fields as soon as the
baby comes out.

Once I get outside the house, what bird might call me; on what horse could 26
I ride away? Marriage and childbirth strengthen the swordswoman, who is not
a maid like Joan of Arc. Do the women's work; then do more work, which
will become ours too. No husband of mine will say, "I could have been a
drummer, but I had to think about the wife and kids. You know how it is."
Nobody supports me at the expense of his own adventure. Then I get bitter:
no one supports me; I am not loved enough to be supported. That I am not a
burden has to compensate for the sad envy when I look at women loved enough
to be supported. Even now China wraps double binds around my feet.

When urban renewal tore down my parents' laundry and paved over our 27
slum for a parking lot, I only made up gun and knife fantasies and did nothing
useful.

From the fairy tales, I've learned exactly who the enemy are. I easily rec- 28
ognize them—business-suited in their modern American executive guise, each
boss two feet taller than I am and impossible to meet eye to eye.

I once worked at an art supply house that sold paints to artists. "Order more 29
of that nigger yellow, willya?" the boss told me. "Bright, isn't it? Nigger yellow."

"I don't like that word," I had to say in my bad, small-person's voice that 30
makes no impact. The boss never deigned to answer.

I also worked at a land developer's association. The building industry was 31
planning a banquet for contractors, real estate dealers, and real estate editors.
"Did you know the restaurant you chose for the banquet is being picketed by
CORE and the NAACP?" I squeaked.

"Of course I know." The boss laughed. "That's why I chose it."   32

"I refuse to type these invitations," I whispered, voice unreliable.   33

He leaned back in his leather chair, his bossy stomach opulent. He picked 34
up his calendar and slowly circled a date. "You will be paid up to here," he
said. "We'll mail you the check."

If I took the sword, which my hate must surely have forged out of the air, 35
and gutted him, I would put color and wrinkles into his shirt.

It's not just the stupid racists that I have to do something about, but the 36
tyrants who for whatever reason can deny my family food and work. My job
is my own only land.

To avenge my family, I'd have to storm across China to take back our farm 37
from the Communists; I'd have to rage across the United States to take back
the laundry in New York and the one in California. Nobody in history has
conquered and united both North America and Asia. A descendant of eighty

pole fighters, I ought to be able to set out confidently, march straight down our street, get going right now. There's work to do, ground to cover. Surely, the eighty pole fighters, though unseen, would follow me and lead me and protect me, as is the wont of ancestors.

Or it may well be that they're resting happily in China, their spirits dispersed 38 among the real Chinese, and not nudging me at all with their poles. I mustn't feel bad that I haven't done as well as the swordswoman did; after all, no bird called me, no wise old people tutored me. I have no magic beads, or water gourd sight, no rabbit that will jump in the fire when I'm hungry. I dislike armies.

I've looked for the bird. I've seen clouds make pointed angel wings that 39 stream past the sunset, but they shred into clouds. Once at a beach after a long hike I saw a seagull, tiny as an insect. But when I jumped up to tell what miracle I saw, before I could get the words out I understood that the bird was insect-size because it was far away. My brain had momentarily lost its depth perception. I was that eager to find an unusual bird.

The news from China has been confusing. It also had something to do with 40 birds. I was nine years old when the letters made my parents, who are rocks, cry. My father screamed in his sleep. My mother wept and crumpled up the letters. She set fire to them page by page in the ashtray, but new letters came almost every day. The only letters they opened without fear were the ones with red borders, the holiday letters that mustn't carry bad news. The other letters said that my uncles were made to kneel on broken glass during their trials and had confessed to being land-owners. They were all executed, and the aunt whose thumbs were twisted off drowned herself. Other aunts, mothers-in-law, and cousins disappeared; some suddenly began writing to us again from communes or from Hong Kong. They kept asking for money. The ones in communes got four ounces of fat and one cup of oil a week, they said, and had to work from 4 A.M. to 9 P.M. They had to learn to do dances waving red kerchiefs; they had to sing nonsense syllables. The Communists gave axes to the old ladies and said, "Go and kill yourself. You're useless." If we overseas Chinese would just send money to the Communist bank, our relatives said, they might get a percentage of it for themselves. The aunts in Hong Kong said to send money quickly; their children were begging on the sidewalks and mean people put dirt in their bowls.

When I dream that I am wire without flesh, there is a letter on blue airmail 41 paper that floats above the night ocean between here and China. It must arrive safely or else my grandmother and I will lose each other.

My parents felt bad whether or not they sent money. Sometimes they got 42 angry at their brothers and sisters for asking. And they would not simply ask but have to talk-story too. The revolutionaries had taken Fourth Aunt and

Uncle's store, house, and lands. They attacked the house and killed the grand-father and oldest daughter. The grandmother escaped with the loose cash and did not return to help. Fourth Aunt picked up her sons, one under each arm, and hid in the pig house, where they slept that night in cotton clothes. The next day she found her husband, who had miraculously escaped. The two of them collected twigs and yams to sell while their children begged. Each morning they tied the faggots on each other's back. Nobody bought from them. They ate the yams and some of the children's rice. Finally Fourth Aunt saw what was wrong. "We have to shout 'Fuel for sale' and 'Yams for sale,' " she said. "We can't just walk unobtrusively up and down the street." "You're right," said my uncle, but he was shy and walked in back of her. "Shout," my aunt ordered, but he could not. "They think we're carrying these sticks home for our own fire," she said. "Shout." They walked about miserably, silently, until sundown, neither of them able to advertise themselves. Fourth Aunt, an orphan since the age of ten, mean as my mother, threw her bundle down at his feet and scolded Fourth Uncle, "Starving to death, his wife and children starving to death, and he's too damned shy to raise his voice." She left him standing by himself and afraid to return empty-handed to her. He sat under a tree to think, when he spotted a pair of nesting doves. Dumping his bag of yams, he climbed up and caught the birds. That was when the Communists trapped him, in the tree. They criticized him for selfishly taking food for his own family and killed him, leaving his body in the tree as an example. They took the birds to a commune kitchen to be shared.

It is confusing that my family was not the poor to be championed. They 43 were executed like the barons in the stories, when they were not barons. It is confusing that birds tricked us.

What fighting and killing I have seen have not been glorious but slum 44 grubby. I fought the most during junior high school and always cried. Fights are confusing as to who has won. The corpses I've seen had been rolled and dumped, sad little dirty bodies covered with a police khaki blanket. My mother locked her children in the house so we couldn't look at dead slum people. But at news of a body, I would find a way to get out; I had to learn about dying if I wanted to become a swordswoman. Once there was an Asian man stabbed next door, word on cloth pinned to his corpse. When the police came around asking questions, my father said, "No read Japanese. Japanese words. Me Chinese."

I've also looked for old people who could be my gurus. A medium with red 45 hair told me that a girl who died in a far country follows me wherever I go. This spirit can help me if I acknowledge her, she said. Between the head line and the heart line in my right palm, she said, I have the mystic cross. I could become a medium myself. I don't want to be a medium. I don't want to be a crank taking "offerings" in a wicker plate from the frightened audience, who, one after another, asked the spirits how to raise rent money, how to cure their coughs and skin disease, how to find a job. And martial arts are for unsure little boys kicking away under fluorescent lights.

I live now where there are Chinese and Japanese, but no emigrants from 46 my own village looking at me as if I had failed them. Living among one's own emigrant villagers can give a good Chinese far from China glory and a place. "That old busboy is really a swordsman," we whisper when he goes by, "He is a swordsman who's killed fifty. He has a tong ax in his closet." But I am useless, one more girl who couldn't be sold. When I visit the family now, I wrap my American success around me like a private shawl; I *am* worthy of eating the food. From afar I can believe my family loves me fundamentally. They only say, "When fishing for treasures in the flood, be careful not to pull in girls," because that is what one says about daughters. But I watched such words come out of my own mother's and father's mouths; I looked at their ink drawing of poor people snagging at their neighbor's flotage with long flood hooks and pushing the girl babies on down the river. And I had to get out of hating range. I read in an anthropology book that Chinese say, "Girls are necessary too"; I have never heard the Chinese I know make this concession. Perhaps it was a saying in another village. I refuse to shy my way anymore through our Chinatown, which tasks me with the old sayings and the stories.

The swordswoman and I are not so dissimilar. May my people understand 47 the resemblance soon so I can return to them. What we have in common are the words at our backs. The ideographs for *revenge* are "report a crime" and "report to five families." The reporting is the vengeance—not the beheading, not the gutting, but the words. And I have so many words—"chink" words and "gook" words too—that they do not fit on my skin.

Focusing on the Structure of Maxine Hong Kingston's Essay

1. On first reading, the first three paragraphs of this essay (each one line long) may seem to have little to do with each other. What is the effect of this apparent lack of continuity? How does the fourth paragraph tie the first three together?

2. Through this selection, Kingston jumps from one scene to another; sometimes we cannot even tell where one scene ends and another begins. What is the effect of the lack of transitions?

3. What topic do all the scenes in the first 26 paragraphs deal with? What topics

underlie the collection of scenes in paragraphs 27–36? In paragraphs 37–43? What would the effect have been if Kingston had developed topic sentences that stated her general points and then turned her scenes into lists of examples supporting her topic sentences?

4. In paragraph 26, Kingston says, "China wraps double binds around my feet." To be in a double bind is to feel required to obey two completely opposed rules or to be torn between two completely opposed desires. What is the double bind that she discusses in this paragraph? What other double binds does she discuss? In ancient China, tiny feet were considered an attractive feature of elegant women. The feet of baby girls were sometimes bound up to keep them small. How are the "double binds" that Kingston mentions in her life similar to this practice of foot-binding?

5. In paragraph 47, Kingston says that in the legend of the swordswoman, "the reporting is the vengeance—not the beheading, not the gutting, but the words." How can Kingston's writing of this very chapter be considered an act of revenge? How is she then like the swordswoman?

6. In the last line, Kingston says, "And I have so many words—'chink' words and 'gook' words too—that they do not fit on my skin." How does this essay make us share that experience of having too many words? How does the style and structure of this essay reflect the nature of Kingston's experience living in two cultures at once?

WORKING WITH THE TECHNIQUE IN YOUR OWN WRITING

1. We might think that we could write essays like Kingston's or Nguyen's only if we also come from families that have been transplanted from one culture to another. However, most of us have experienced being torn between differing standards of behavior, say, in a business office and at a party. Certainly we have all felt torn between what advertising tells us about how to live our lives and what schools and parents tell us. Write an essay about the clash between contradictory messages, between differing lifestyles, that you have experienced. Try to bring your reader to experience some of the confusion you have felt; you might want to use some of the sudden jumps and jarring juxtapositions that Nguyen and Kingston use, or you might try to develop other methods.

2. Write an essay in which you try to make sense of your earliest memories of childhood. You might want to write part of your essay in small scenes separated by white space, as Nguyen does. Be careful to prepare your readers so that they do not become too confused by your jumping from one scene to another. Note how carefully Nguyen sets up her disconnected scenes so that her readers can follow them. She tells her readers right at the beginning that she is writing

about memories and that her memories do not add up. Before stating her own memories, she gives her parents' views so that her readers can have some idea of what really happened. You might use these same techniques to help your readers deal with your disconnected memories, or you might invent your own ways of letting readers know what you are doing.

3. Write an essay about something that people around you repeatedly do or say that makes you angry. You might begin your essay with a collection of scenes of people doing or saying these things, as Kingston does, to get your readers to share your frustration at encountering the same attitudes over and over again. Kingston focuses much of her anger on the sexism and racism she sees in "wise old sayings." Similarly, you might want to use proverbs, fairy tales, and clichés as examples of the attitudes that make you angry.

ALLISON ROLLS

San Francisco State University
San Francisco, California
Nancy A. Sours, instructor

Allison Rolls describes herself in elementary school as "an average unmotivated student plastered with the label 'mentally gifted minor.' I considered myself completely and irrevocably ordinary. I never won anything and gave no one any reason to suspect I would." Born in San Francisco, Rolls was raised in Richmond, California, where she graduated from John F. Kennedy High School. Her interest in forensics and drama sustained her during her high school years, and she helped write and produce a number of highly acclaimed skits and historical dramas. She started working "at the tender age of sixteen" and has since earned a living at "renting tuxedos, designing bridal bouquets, making sandwiches, acting at California's Renaissance Faire, running a personnel office in Beverly Hills, selling office machines, and answering the telephone at the Exploratorium, a marvelous science museum in San Francisco."

At the beginning of her junior year, Allison Rolls transferred from San Francisco State University to the University of California, Berkeley, where she earned honors as an English major. Chosen to speak as the covaledictorian of her graduating class, Rolls delivered her commencement address in the form of a parody of literary criticism. Upon finishing her first year as a graduate student in English at the University of Michigan, Allison Rolls was awarded a fellowship to attend Queen's University in Northern Ireland, where she completed the equivalent of another M.A. in Anglo-Irish literature between, as she reports, "pubs and idyllic trips in the country. . . . Having returned from Belfast relatively unscathed, I plan to return to Ann Arbor to continue the long road to my Ph.D., to teach freshman composition, and probably to urge my students to enter essays in the Bedford Prize competition."

Rolls reports that the origins of her satiric essay on Britain's royal couple can be found in both "the absolutely ridiculous amount of coverage the American and British news media give the British royal family—each sneeze and chuckle is reported"—and the "touch of jealousy" that surfaced when Prince Charles finally chose his bride: "I couldn't help but think to myself, 'What's Diana got that I ain't got?' . . . and so an essay was born."

Lady Diana: He Married the Wrong Woman

In light of the recent publicity involving the British Royal Family—the celebration of the Wedding of the Century; the birth of little Prince Willie; the Falklands war; a scandal involving Prince Andrew, Duke of Marlborough (or Randy Andy, as he is also known), and a young porn starlet; and the royal tiffs and spats (heaven knows, it's hard to keep track!)—I think that one very 1 important point has been overlooked. After all the time and deliberation that went into getting Prince Charles, future King of England, hitched, he seems to have wound up marrying the wrong girl. Lady Diana Spencer, now Princess Diana, while outwardly possessing suitable credentials (looks, youth, money, lineage, virginity, etc.), was, in my opinion, the totally wrong choice to fill the position. While youth, looks, money, and family ties do have their advantages, the perfect mate for Charles should transcend all these petty details and rise above all this superficial nonsense. Rather than marrying a member of the idle aristocracy, Charles would have done much better with a sensible, perhaps more experienced, diamond in the rough. The logical choice, when one really examines the issue closely (as I will do here), would have been, of course, me. Along with sharing Diana's youth, beauty, charm, and sparkling personality, I have other down-to-earth qualities which neither vast amounts of money nor centuries of breeding can instill in a person. Unfortunately, Charles lacks the presence of mind to see this fact staring him in the face, so he missed his chance. Instead of choosing a girl whom many would consider the catch of the year, he ended up with the delicate and decorative Lady Diana.

To begin my comparison, I would like to point out that I have known 2 Prince Charles much longer than Diana has. I pasted his picture on my bedroom mirror long before she could even pronounce his name, and, of course, he has all my school photographs, even the one where my hair is sticking out all over. He also received invitations to every party I ever threw, starting with my Sweet Sixteen; although, doubtlessly due to state matters of great importance, he was never able to attend, I know he was there in spirit.

I also think that he displayed rather poor form in marrying one of his own 3 subjects. I feel that a marriage such as this imparts a certain lack of dignity and implies something of a slave-master relationship, which looks bad when a couple are co-ruling a country. Apart from the important international relations breakthrough which would have been accomplished in marrying an American, such as me, Charles could have been assured of a wife who wasn't overly awed by his exalted royal stature.

Another factor in my favor, when compared to the current Princess of 4 Wales, is the large amount of money that I could have saved the British treasury. First of all, I *hate* big weddings and could have done away with all the silly and expensive conceits that I'm sure Lady Diana considered necessary, such as her $10,000 wedding gown with a train longer than the Chattanooga Choo-Choo (complete with three copies should she muss the original), a dozen carriages, hundreds of bagpipers, zillions of guests, and a choir comparable in size to the Mormon Tabernacle, not to mention her honeymoon wardrobe. I hate to think of the cost! Why, her weekly hat budget alone would more than likely feed a dozen Irish coal-mining families for a year! I, on the other hand, prefer to dress unostentatiously and usually make my own clothes. Furthermore, I do not have hordes of hungry relatives flocking to Balmoral Castle for a weekend visit. On the contrary, I am on speaking terms with few, if any, of my relatives, whereas Diana has a family tree whose branches grow for miles in all directions, including her step-aunt, the illustrious Barbara Cartland, of great literary fame. (Anyone who has read one of Miss Cartland's lush, romantic novels knows exactly where Diana got her idea of how to throw a wedding.) Doubtless Diana also has many relatives (especially the imaginative Miss Cartland, who was snubbed at the wedding) who must be bribed with spectacular sums of money to keep them from circulating photos of Diana in braces as a child or unflattering family anecdotes.

It also appears to me that the Princess, to put it delicately, is not possessed 5 of a superior intellect; however, we have little evidence of this since the only time she has ever been allowed to speak out loud in public was while taking her wedding vows. (Unfortunately, the Lady Diana just couldn't seem to remember exactly the order of all Charles's names.) But certainly her batting eyelashes and vacuous expression speak for themselves, while on the other hand all Charles had to do was take a peek at my SAT scores and the doe-eyed Di would have been out of the running. Obviously to anyone who pays attention, she is naught but a silly fluff-head with nothing better to think about than making babies.

Which brings me to my next point—babies. Certainly the British subjects 6 have a right to expect an heir eventually, but for heaven's sake, did it have to be so soon—a scant ten months after the wedding? I suppose that Diana felt that it was important to stay in the international limelight and immediately sought to set the fashion world aflame by introducing her royal maternity wardrobe. However, to simply "lie still and think of England," as Diana certainly did on her wedding night, displays to me a certain lack of character, and to feel that one's role in life (besides that of a worldwide trend-setter) should be as a baby factory seems a sadly outmoded outlook. A reasonable princess, such as I would have made, would have held out for at least five years. Keep the subjects guessing; why rush it all? Imagine Charles proudly looking on as his wife goes out to work for worthy causes, such as dedicating libraries and handing out royal largesse, instead of changing diapers and suffering morning sickness. In addition, my child would have certainly been born perfect, never crying or fussing. And I never could have settled for such an ordinary name as William Charles Phillip for my child, who would be called Balthazar Sidney Caleb or maybe Maud Eliza Shrub.

Another cause for concern for Prince Charles is the behavior of his younger   7
brother, the amorous Andrew, who recently embarrassed and outraged his
family by cavorting around in the company of Miss Koo Stark, a budding nude
actress. Had I been princess, this scandal would have been completely avoided
by keeping Andy (by far the best-looking and most fun of all Queen Elizabeth's
sons) otherwise occupied in the proper and respectable company of his sister-
in-law.

The sad conclusion to all my observation in this matter is that instead of   8
choosing a stimulating, practical, articulate, and independent wife, Charles
(who must have been deliriously desperate when he proposed) decided upon
the first runner-up in a Barbie-doll look-alike contest to be the next Queen of
England, and I am quite positive that he, his country, and the future history
books will be all the more bored for it.

Focusing on Allison Rolls's Techniques and Revisions

1. Allison Rolls explains that she is fascinated with words: "I love the way you
   can string them together and mold them and sculpt with them. Words are a
   very powerful tool and that is why it's very important to have a good rapport
   with them. I usually try to figure out the tone of the paper before I start
   writing. The tone—whether formal, conversational, or just plain off-the-
   wall—determines which words I use and how I shape them around the skeleton
   of my idea." Characterize Allison Rolls's voice in this essay. Point to specific
   words and phrases she uses to sustain that voice.

2. Allison Rolls pokes fun at British royalty by comparing and contrasting herself
   and Princess Diana. List each point in her comparison and contrast. What
   order or sequence does she use? Does she organize her essay point by point?
   Subject by subject? Some combination of the two? Rolls also plays with the
   traditional structure and logic of essays. See, for example, paragraph 2, which
   opens: "To begin my comparison." Explain how Rolls plays ironically with
   the traditional comparison/contrast form of the essay.

3. When is Rolls's attitude toward Lady Diana first expressed? What are Rolls's
   specific objections to Lady Diana and her marriage to Prince Charles? How
   ironically does she treat each of her objections to the princess? What, for
   example, are the implications of the phrases "to fill the position" in paragraph
   1 and "to simply 'lie still and think of England' " in paragraph 6?

4. Rolls reports that "the hardest part of this essay was finding things wrong with
   Princess Diana, who is so secretive about her faults that I had to take some
   liberties with the truth and act on intuition alone." Identify where Rolls may
   have taken "liberties with the truth." Show how these instances strengthen
   or weaken the impact of her essay.

5. Consider the ways in which Allison Rolls presents *herself* in this essay. What do we learn about this writer as her essay develops? What impression, for example, does she create of herself in paragraph 2? How does this image remain consistent—or change—as the essay proceeds? In what specific ways does her voice change in the essay? What risks does she take by using different voices? What effects does each change in voice create?

6. How familiar does Rolls assume her audience is with her subject? How much background information does she provide? With what effects? What risks does Rolls take in possibly misleading her audience? How seriously does Rolls expect her audience to take her? Point to specific words and phrases to validate your response.

7. How do the parentheses function in Rolls's essay? How effective, for example, is her use of parentheses as a way to comment on her subject? Do you think she could have eliminated some (or perhaps even many) of these parentheses and incorporated her points directly into the essay? Explain. What, in effect, does Rolls gain and lose by using as many parentheses as she does?

8. Reread the opening sentence of paragraph 5. Rolls's previous draft of this sentence read, "It also seems to me that the Princess, to put it delicately, is somewhat lacking in the brains department; however, there is not much evidence of this fact due to the fact that the only time she ever has been allowed to speak in public was when taking her marriage vows." Which draft is more effective? Why? How could the final draft be improved?

9. When asked to reread her essay several years after having written it and to comment on its effectiveness, Rolls promptly replied: "Specifically, my response is to let out a very loud groan. I am understandably embarrassed but also slightly surprised that I could have been such a brash, irreverent student. Five years of academia have conditioned me to take my essays slightly more seriously, I suppose. The embarrassment arises mostly out of a change in my attitude toward my subject matter. Nowadays, I think, it is *so uncool* to even pay attention to what the damn royal family does that even to admit that I knew the name of their kids was pretty humiliating. . . . I would also like to correct one glaring factual error that I have been trying to atone for (by being scrupulously careful when dealing with such things as 'facts') since 1983: There are no coal-mining families in Ireland. I would, I suppose, have to change the reference to Welsh coal-mining families or to Irish spud-farming families." Explain why you agree or disagree with her assessment that the voice she used was irreverent?

10. Point to the evidence that suggests that the characteristic voice of that "brash, irreverent student" is present in the quotation cited above, as well as in the following response to a question on how much writing Rolls does now: "I still do as little writing as possible, but at this point there's no way to avoid it. . . . I crank out fifteen or twenty critical papers a year and innumerable letters, I

keep a fairly regular journal, I've got a couple of first chapters of novels on the word processor, I learned the fine art of writing pithy and compelling dust-jacket copy at the University of Michigan Press, and I foresee spending the rest of my life writing encouraging criticism on student essays. My immediate goal is to get a lucrative, cushy job turning out trenchant and witty book reviews for the *New York Review of Books* or the *London Times.*"

Suggestions for Writing

1. Review the major political or social events of the past year that the media have covered extensively—and solemnly. Consider what your own "place" might have been in that "drama" as it unfolded. Write an essay in which you play ironically both with that subject and with your own imagined role in that occasion.

2. Have you ever admired or been infatuated with a public figure? Consider the origin of your admiration or infatuation. To what lengths were you willing to go to cultivate that infatuation? What were the effects of that infatuation? How did you extricate yourself from it? Write an essay in which you explain in detail and play ironically with that infatuation.

3. Allison Rolls notes "all the silly and expensive conceits that I'm sure Lady Diana considered necessary" for her wedding. In many respects, the United States displayed similar extravagance during the last presidential inauguration. Write an essay in which you justify—or criticize—having occasions of state for which the expense would "more than likely feed a dozen . . . families for a year." Depending on your point of view, your essay could be either ironic or straightforward.

AN EFFECTIVE TECHNIQUE

We usually try to write in a voice that is believable and, at the least, consistent. Allison Rolls shows the delightful results a writer can achieve by creating a thoroughly unreliable voice. We are never sure whether or not to take Rolls's narrator seriously, because so many of her sentences are ironic—they seem to mean one thing, but turn out, as we read along, to mean something quite different. Especially disconcerting is our inability to establish what sort of person the narrator is: though she talks about herself incessantly, what she says keeps changing. For example, after the narrator claims that she has "known Prince Charles much longer than Diana has" (paragraph 2), implying that she is something of an international celebrity herself, she immediately proceeds to explain that "knowing" means worshiping his picture and sending him invitations to her high school parties. As readers, we smile as we recognize the speaker as a schoolgirl with a crush on the prince, pretending she is important. Then in the next paragraph she undercuts the image of herself as schoolgirl that she has just created; she declares that she is not "overly awed by his exalted royal stature." Why did she paste his pictures on her mirror if she was not "overly awed" by him? Is she saying that she has outgrown her crush on Charles? Why then does she still wish to marry him? We become uncertain about what sort of person is speaking, and our uncertainty increases as she cavalierly denies most of the reasons we could imagine for her wanting to marry Charles. She even says that she actually prefers Charles's brother Andrew, "by far the best-looking and most fun of all Queen Elizabeth's sons." She tells us that if she were married to Charles, she would save "Randy Andy" from his "friend" the "budding nude actress" by keeping him "otherwise occupied in the proper and respectable company of his sister-in-law" (paragraph 7). It sounds suspiciously as if keeping Andrew "otherwise occupied" actually means having a discreet affair with him. By the end of the essay, the schoolgirl with her hair sticking out has somehow become a worldly woman seeking illicit adult pleasures.

None of the images Rolls creates for herself can truly be believed; they are ironic poses, adopted to be amusing and to satirize the royal family. This is not a serious essay, but it still makes a point—that the royal family are all fools, as are all those who ever admired them, including Allison Rolls herself.

Rolls's essay suggests an unusual way to present ourselves to our readers: as someone not to be trusted. Rolls actually uses three different methods to make her readers doubt her words: she presents herself as foolish (in the beginning of her essay), as immoral (at the end), and as sneakily able to change voices throughout. Because the voices of this essay can never quite be believed, Rolls can explore how silly and even wicked she is without making her readers dislike her.

We can adapt Rolls's methods to write of our own foolishness. For example, we can berate ourselves for some awful quality we honestly have, such as slovenliness, and then make the ironic turn by suggesting that being a slob is of great value (perhaps it saves us from the anxiety of impressing people). We can also build essays by pretending to be foolish or wicked. To criticize a political leader, for example, we could pretend to be his campaign manager and praise him for qualities that are of questionable morality, making ourselves and him seem evil. Or to reveal the immoral behavior of adults at a cocktail party, we could pretend to be a young child naively looking on. The child might describe behavior he or she does not understand but that readers can recognize as despicable.

Creating an unreliable narrator is one way of building ironic essays. Being ironic is risky; people might take what we say at face value, failing to read the cues that we do not really mean it. They may end up believing that we really are the narrators we have created. But if we are willing to give up the clarity of straightforward statements, we can gain some special powers. Using irony, we can make a serious point without preaching; we can express wicked thoughts without being considered immoral; we can accurately convey our uncertainty whether we actually are foolish or intelligent; we can criticize someone powerful and famous without provoking an argument; and we can leave our readers repeating some funny line over and over again, pondering why it seems to sting a bit too much.

In the next selection, Alice Kahn plays with her readers much as Allison Rolls does. Kahn begins her essay by presenting herself as a foolish egotist who imposes her awful singing on everyone around her, but then she defends her music as a cure for the pains of this cold world. We cannot tell which passages of her essay are ironic and which are serious, but at the end we're not so much confused as amused; we have all experienced being simultaneously embarrassed by and pleased with something we have done.

ANOTHER ILLUSTRATION OF THE TECHNIQUE

ALICE KAHN

Pianotherapy: Primal Pop

Alice Kahn says she decided to become a writer "sometime after my mother died or my two daughters were born. Of course, I had always written but I never took it seriously. It was a way of life, not a living." Before turning to writing seriously, she attended the University of Illinois and Columbia University, married, had two children, worked as a high school teacher and as an aide in a women's health collective clinic, and then went back to school for a nurse practitioner degree from the University of California, San Francisco. It took her a long time to feel confident that she could support herself as a writer because, she says, "I didn't really see where the kind of sadder but wise-ass stuff I like to write fit into the landscape of writing for profit. I filled my life with jobs— teacher, nurse, mother—good woman's work. Being a nurse . . . gave me access to the

*human heart and gastrointestinal tract in a manner that few writers, let alone human
beings, get to know."*

In my mind I am Alicia Lamour, the recluse chanteuse. I saunter up to the 1
piano and slowly peel my elbow-length white gloves. A rhinestone bracelet
dangles from my wrist. My white fox wrap (fake! fake animal fur!) falls to the
floor. And in my simple black-velvet, strapless gown I begin to play "Satin
Doll."

Then, switcherooney, I am Patti Page singing "Tennessee Waltz." Segue 2
into Billie Holiday singing "I Cover the Waterfront," then into Barbra Streis-
and singing the slowest, saddest "Happy Days Are Here Again" that you ever
heard. Then I am Linda Ronstadt singing "Blue Bayou," in that opera-singer-
with-gallstones voice.

In the real world, the unjust world, I am a woman in a sweatshirt who can't 3
carry a tune. But in the musical world where dreams come true, I am Tina
Turner in two feet of skirt and 10 feet of legs singing "River Deep, Mountain
High."

My kids scream out, "Oh no, Mom, puh-*leeze*, don't sing." My husband 4
forces them to leave the room so the performance can continue. He has
learned through time that a medley beats an ugly female mood swing any
day.

My Curse

I have always loved to sing and play the piano. Unfortunately, it's my curse 5
to have been given a lousy voice, a tone-deaf ear, and no sense of rhythm.
But play and sing I must because, hey Jude, it's the only thing that will make
things better.

As a child insomniac, I would wait until everyone was asleep and then at 6
midnight take out my Hit Parader magazines and sing "Mockingbird Hill" or
"If I Knew You Were Comin' I'd Have Baked a Cake" or "Till I Waltz Again
with You" or "The Man in the Raincoat" or "The Wheel of Fortune" until
the wee small hours of the morning. My bedroom, my pleasant land of coun-
terpane, became the Club Trocadero, where ladies with gardenia corsages and
men with thin, sterling cigarette cases ate chili con carne and sipped sparkling
champagne.

Later, after I took piano lessons, I discovered that when my parents were 7
fighting, music was my only friend. I would sit there banging the ivories until
they stopped. I really believed my music had charms.

This was confirmed when I worked as a volunteer at the Berkeley Free Clinic 8 in the '60s. Maybe I couldn't bring down the house with my skills, but I could bring down an acid freakout like nobody's business. I'd just relax and let my fingers do the dancing.

And still today, when I'm sad, if I can just get to that piano, I can save my   9 soul. Sometimes I really am Janis singing "Take a Little Piece of My Heart," and sometimes I'm Frank singing "It Never Entered My Mind," and sometimes I'm Frankie singing "Why Do Fools Fall in Love?" so sweetly and happily that you'd swear the whole world was fourteen years old.

Limits

But somehow I am never, ever Little Richard. No matter how hard I try.   10 Imagination has its limits.

Certain songs, like "Wichita Lineman," that I never liked on the radio can   11 sound good to me when performed by Alicia Lamour, while others that I loved, like "I Heard It Through the Grapevine," stink because I'll never be Marvin Gaye. And just because I can't do Jim Morrison, "Come on, Baby, Light My Fire" comes out like "In the Good Old Summertime."

The strange thing is that I can't play around other people at all unless they   12 are blood relatives or are OD'ing on drugs. Every once in a while, when I'm really wailing, I'll think: If my friends could see me now. But the few times I've tried to sing for others, it's been a disaster.

When I learned that my mailman, George C. George, had been a musical-   13 comedy star in his youth, I tried to give him a song and dance for Christmas. As he approached my porch, I came out singing and tapdancing, "It's Mr. George C. George (clap) the mailman . . . bringing me (clap) letters, and maybe (clap) presents, and maybe some (clap) money . . ."

He literally ran away as if he had been attacked by a yelping dog.   14

But I suppose that has always been the goal of Alicia Lamour, a woman   15 and her music—to make the world go away.

Focusing on the Ironic Voice in Alice Kahn's Essay

1. How does the narrator present herself in the first four paragraphs? Why does she sing? In paragraphs 7–9, how does our sense of the narrator's motivation change? She creates images of a world that is rather painful to live in. How does she let us know that she is not completely serious, that she is being at least partly ironic? Point to specific words and phrases to support your response.

2. Primal therapy is a form of psychological therapy in which a person is encour-

aged to "get in touch" with the feelings he or she had as a small child or even as a baby. If the therapy is successful, the person will let out long-repressed feelings of anger, pain, need of love, and fear of abandonment in a "primal scream." How is Alice Kahn's title playing on and mocking this kind of therapy? How is her use of music a kind of therapy?

3. The essay ends with the narrator saying that she sings "to make the world go away." In what ways does the narrator mean this line seriously, and in what ways is she being ironic, making fun of herself? How do you feel about the narrator at the end of this essay?

4. In what ways does the narrator criticize the people around her? How does she criticize the people she has dealt with in the past? In what ways would she like people to change? How serious is she in making these criticisms?

WORKING WITH THE TECHNIQUE IN YOUR OWN WRITING

1. Write an essay about something that you enjoy doing but that makes you feel a bit foolish. You might write about some daydream you enjoy acting out, perhaps a fantasy of being a famous rock star's butler or maid. Try to make your readers share your sense of how foolish you feel, but also try to make them understand why you enjoy the activity.

2. Write an essay in which you comment on a subject by creating a character who is in some way ignorant, foolish, inadequate, or immoral (or all four). Set up a situation in which that character talks about the subject. For example, you might criticize the American dream by creating as your narrator a truly vicious criminal who defends his actions as his version of that dream, of rising out of poverty by his own labor.

3. Write a humorous essay in praise of some quality that is usually considered a vice, such as gluttony, laziness, or dishonesty. Or write a humorous essay in favor of something that is generally considered bad, such as sickness or crime.

JILL A. SAVITT

Yale University
New Haven, Connecticut
George S. Fayen, instructor

"*I tend to stick with things which spurred success,*" reports Jill Savitt. "*Somewhere, sometime in my kidhood, someone told me I was very good at things. Things in general. Maybe it was my parents. I believed it. I attributed my successes to a hard-to-define yet persistent confidence instilled at a young age. No one ever told me risks were scary. By the time I figured an election could be lost and an ego shattered, I'd experienced enough success to cushion any fall and start me over.*"

Evidence of Jill Savitt's self-confidence, fueled by a strongly competitive lifestyle, can readily be discovered in the following account of her youthful years:

> I think I grew up with just about the most normal-seeming American childhood. Lived in New Jersey as a kid while my father commuted to New York. A promotion arrived, we left and moved to the Miami suburbs. I went to a good, affluent public high school and lived a suburban life. In this life there was competition in school, in clothes, in intelligence, and I developed a competitive streak, wide and deep, tainted by a cynicism toward the affluence and glitz of Miami. I don't know if the competition made me or I made the competition—either way, I thrived on it. It pushed me. Grades were never my best thing, except perhaps in English. So positive strokes from that department perpetuated a love for writing and reading. I also concentrated on student government and journalism in high school. Competition again. . . . I was the president of my class six years running. In journalism, I was the co-editor in chief of the school paper.

During her senior year at Miami Palmetto Senior High School, Savitt worked as an intern at the city desk of the Miami Herald. "I served as their house pet. I imagine my two editor-mentors viewed me as replicas of them at eighteen. They coached me and taught me everything I know about newspapers. More important than the teaching, they trusted me and let me write. This, combined with a severe case of senioritis before college acceptances, made work there my life. My Bedford essay originates in this work."

At Yale, Savitt continues to work on a newspaper. "The Yale Herald is the alternative paper. It's almost two years old. As campus news and features editor, I'd like to think we're the Village Voice of Yale while our rival is The New York Times. Most people laugh when I claim this." Jill Savitt divides her academic time between English courses and American studies. "If pressed, I'd say I want to be a journalist because reporting could pay the bills while I write the Universal Novel."

In a recent interview, Jill Savitt explained the circumstances that led to her writing "Decisions" for her first-year composition course:

> I wrote my Bedford essay to discover why I wrote about the event which sparked it. I had been assigned, as an intern for the Miami Herald, to write about a shoot-out, what would become the bloodiest FBI shoot-out in history. They assigned me because I had an in. I knew the supervising agent's daughter. Before the incident, I was a no-holds-barred journalist. At least I thought I was. At nineteen, I hadn't had much of a chance to test this. In theory, though, I was hard-nosed, tough-as-nails, and every other cliché applied to very aggressive people who cover the news.
>
> This incident changed things. It was the first test. The bloody bodies and the shoot-'em up, of course, were heavy sights. More unsettling, though, was seeing the girl I wrote about. That my words, the order I arranged them, and the caution I used in choosing them deeply affected someone who didn't know the subjects of these stories. Or their families. . . . So much to decide. . . .

Decisions

I listened to the car radio. News Bulletin: an FBI stake-out leaves seven   1
men down: two dead, three critically wounded, two less injured, but under
doctors' supervision. As I drive, my mind is less on the road than the radio;
less on the radio than the phone conversation that prompted the drive:

"Do you know a girl at your school with the last name McNeil?" my edi-   2
tor asked when he tracked me down at my father's office before we left for
lunch.

"Yeah. She's in my class at school."   3

"Her father has just been shot in an FBI stake-out," he said. "Go to Baptist   4
Hospital. A team of reporters is already there. See what you can find out."
Click.

So I'm driving to the hospital, wondering why I'm driving to the hospital.   5
As a student intern at the *Miami Herald* I was reserved for parades, festivals,
weather updates, and the occasional murder. This story was one for the senior,
seasoned writers; what did he think I could do there? Sure I knew Carol, but

I knew her as a high school student, not an agent's daughter. We were friendly acquaintances, hardly close friends. Hello-in-the-hall friends. Gossip-in-the-back-of-class friends.

The news bulletin continued—"the bloodiest FBI shoot-out in history," 6 "seven men down," "three men now dead"—I fantasized about what would happen when I arrived. Maybe I could interview Carol, her family, and the agents. Maybe. I thought of the story, the pictures, the layout. Front page. My name at the top. More fantasizing: Accepting the Pulitzer for Ms. Savitt, who is now investigating scandals around the globe, will be. . . .

I arrive at the hospital and feel out of place. Young. I saw the reporters 7 milling about outside the emergency wing. All the local stations and local papers were there as well as an alphabet soup of others: CNN, AP, ABC, CBS, NBC. I continued to ask myself: What did he think I could do here? I found my fellow *Herald* staffers and started talking to them.

We don't know anything more than the radio broadcasts, they told me. 8 We're waiting for a press conference within the hour, they told me. No one is allowed in the hospital, they told me.

They shared what they knew so far. I sat in the grass behind the media 9 huddle and thought about the case. I heard the reporters talking, buzzing around and above me. I sat cross-legged and brushed my hand through the grass, occasionally picking a blade and tearing it. The sun forced my head down, forced me into my own world. Every few seconds I'd make out some words from the reporters. I'd look up, one eye shut and shielded from the sun, to see who was talking. "How many wounded?" "Anyone talked to the doctor?" "How 'bout the agents' families?" Carol. She must feel horrible. Her father. She had spoken of her father before. They were close. My father and I are close. I suddenly felt pained. I knew already that the supervising agent had been shot in the chest. Her father. I wanted to tell Carol I felt for her. Carol. She and I are just kids here. Just kids witnessing this.

"Do you think I could send my friend a note?" I asked one of the reporters. 10 "Just to see how she is." She nodded, more involved in facts and notes, directing me to the hospital press representative. "Carol—Hope your dad is okay. I just wanted to tell you that I'm thinking about you." The press representative disappeared into the hospital. I continued to wait outside and watch. Network television crews filmed updates with the hospital in the background. Reporters compared notes. Photographers focused cameras on trees, cars, each other. I stood in the sidelines. What does my editor think I can do here? How is Carol?

Ten minutes passed. The emergency room door opened and heads turned. 11 Carol. She shielded her eyes, obviously red from crying, with my note. No one knew who she was, but everyone knew she was someone involved with the shoot-out.

She surveyed the crowd. She approached me and hugged me. She asked me 12 to come inside with her. As we walked, I could hear whispering: "Who is the crying girl and who is the kid with her?"

Once inside, the two of us—the crying girl and the kid with her—sit in a waiting area. She starts talking immediately. I should write this down. She tells me about her father's bloody body on the hospital gurney. Emotional, personal details of an as yet unreleased story. My story. My byline. Of course she can see my press pass. It's flashing like a neon sign from my shirt pocket. I should write this down. I'm the only reporter inside. The only one. This is front page material. The *Miami Herald* should have the best coverage of a local story with national significance. I'm here from the *Herald*. She called me inside from the press corps. She knows I work for the newspaper. She knows I'm a reporter. This is a great story. My story. The only reporter inside. She knows this is one hell of a story.

I should write this down.

Once inside, the two of us—the crying 13 girl and the kid with her—sit in a waiting area. She starts talking immediately. Should I write this down? Carol is crying. Crying and hugging me. She tells me about talking to her father as she ran with the orderlies who pushed the gurney. He was bleeding. Carol needs me. I am her friend. Her only friend here. Her father has just been shot in the chest. He is in surgery. He might die. She needs me. Just kids witnessing this. Should I write this down? Should I betray the only confidence this girl, my friend, has? She invited me in to talk to me, to find comfort. She needs a shoulder and a friend. I'd want the same. I can't write this down. These aren't facts to be splashed across the front of the morning paper. They are emotional feelings, private thoughts. Her personal story. Am I the *Herald*'s reporter or Carol's friend? Writing her story would shatter her. I shouldn't write this down.

After five hours of talk, Carol excused herself to the bathroom. I called my 14 editor. Once connected, I heard a proud and excited voice. Another *Herald* reporter had phoned earlier to tell of our success. While I had been talking to Carol, the hospital and FBI press staffs gave two short and standard briefings. But, we, the *Herald* had an in, an assured scoop. We had fresh, original front page material. I knew why my editor sent me.

"Hold on a minute. I'll find someone to take dictation," he said.   15

"Wait," I said.   16

"Didn't you take notes?" he asked. The pressure of an afternoon deadline 17 made both of us uneasy.

"No," I said rather weakly. No. I didn't. I couldn't. But suddenly I didn't 18 remember why. "It didn't feel right," I said. I asked him for coaching guidance. I'm torn, I said. Friend or reporter? I asked. What should I do? I asked.

Go back to her, he said. Tell her people want to know her feelings, he 19 said. Tell her her story will make people feel for the lives of FBI agents and tell her it will lend humanity to the story, he said. Try to get it on the record, he said.

I wanted to scream: "Carol doesn't care about our goddamn story. She's not 20 concerned with our stupid deadline. Her father has just been shot in the chest. Don't you know she doesn't care whether or not this story gets in the paper?" I wasn't sure I really meant Carol. Regardless, I held my thoughts and told him I'd try.

"I'll try." Confused and torn, I went back to Carol in the waiting area.   21

I'll try. Confused and torn, I went back to Carol in the waiting area. I watched her. Her face was now clear. She managed a smile. My editor's words: feelings, lives of agents, humanity, on record. Try to get it on record. Front page. My editor's respect. Why did he send me? To write the story. Write the story.	I'll try. Confused and torn, I went back 22 to Carol in the waiting area. I watched her. Her face was now clear. She managed a smile. She hugged me. She was glad she had a friend. I was glad to be that friend. But was I her friend or a reporter? Friend or reporter. My editor's words: feelings, lives of agents, humanity, on record. Try to get it on record. Why did he send me? Because I knew Carol. I am from the newspaper. Write the story?

"Carol, may I take a few notes?" And even as I said it, I knew the answer. 23 I regretted asking. I then remembered my original reasons. I then remembered what I wanted to tell my editor on the phone. All my reasoning appeared on Carol's face. She shrugged and frowned an answer. She had suddenly lost me as her confidante. I saw she regretted having said so much; she sensed betrayal; she had trusted me, and she no longer could. I was now a reporter and not a friend. I'll have to ask the agents what I can say, she told me. It's the FBI and all, she told me. I'll be right back, she told me. We both knew she would not be coming back.

Feeling guilty, I got in my car to return to the newspaper office. All the 24 way, as I drove, I considered my behavior. I wanted to keep driving. I wished the car ride would not end. I wanted to move further and further from Carol but never reach my editor. I felt I had betrayed them both. I followed my heart, but had I seriously contemplated this? Was I sure? And when I did arrive at the office, how would I explain myself? If the decision was sound, why did I feel like hell? The *Herald* would never trust me and Carol would hate me.

At the office, my editor met me at the door, his eyes questioning. "Did you 25 get it?" I shrugged and frowned an answer. He walked away to edit other stories. I stayed around for a while. It was fascinating to watch the paper come together. The front page. The lead story. I stood toward the back of the newsroom, behind the buzzing of the reporters, the whirr of the wire service telexes, and the frenzy of editors trying to beat the deadline. One reporter approached me: "If I were there, they would have fired me unless I dressed up like a nurse and walked into the emergency surgery room." I went home.

I spent the weekend brooding. Brooding and considering. Did I do the right 26 thing? Yes. Yes, I did. Something in me just felt queer about taking notes there, about writing her story then. Her emotional state persuaded me. With Carol, the facts were inseparable from the emotion. Exploiting her personal pain seemed unfair. I shouldn't have asked her, after the phone call, for permission to take notes. No. No, I shouldn't have even tried. Under pressure though—from my editor and the deadline and my confusion—I reversed myself. True, I was the only reporter inside. However, I was not inside because I was a reporter. She knew I worked for the newspaper, but she invited me in because I was a friend. I knew the *Herald* should have the best coverage of the event, but this was Carol. Carol, my friend. This was Carol's story, not mine. For first day coverage, this teenager's pain didn't seem a priority. I almost wanted to thank her for walking away, for refusing to let me write. However, I had listened to her. I listened for five hours as a friend. I listened when it counted. And I didn't take a single note. I went with my heart. I followed my instinct. At the end of the weekend I concluded I was comfortable with myself and my decision not to write anything down.

When I saw Carol in school the next week, I tried to avoid her. I felt 27 uncomfortable. I didn't want to face her. She found me, though. Immediately, I started to apologize. So did she. "I'm sorry I couldn't come back," she said. "They wanted me to stay." She hugged me. Hugged me and thanked me. Thanked me for not writing the story, for understanding that she could not come back and talk to me, for listening to her at the hospital.

"I really appreciate it," she said. She then invited me to her house to 28 interview her family. She said her father was still in the hospital—he was doing well and recovering—but her mother and sister would be happy to talk with me and describe their experiences and let the *Herald*'s readers know their feelings. She said I could bring a photographer.

The story ran on Page One.   29

Focusing on Jill Savitt's Techniques and Revisions

1. Jill Savitt turns a national news story into a professional—and a personal—dilemma. What question central to ethics in journalism does Savitt raise in her essay? What, in effect, is the nature of the decision she must make? How does she dramatize and then resolve her dilemma?

2. Reread the opening paragraphs of Savitt's essay. From what perspective—from what *point of view*—does she recount these events? What identity does she assume early in the essay? When and how does this point of view change? To what? With what effects? What, for example, is the dramatic function of the refrain "What did he think I could do here?" (paragraph 7)? Where does this line reappear in the essay? With what effect? What is the effect of repeating the phrase "they told me" in paragraph 8?

3. What is the focus of Savitt's thinking once she is in her "own world" in paragraph 9? What and whom is she thinking about? How do the opening sentences of paragraph 9 create a physical and psychological transition to Savitt's retreat into her "own world"? What does she mean when she says at the end of paragraph 9 that "she and I are just kids here. Just kids witnessing this"? What is the significance of the term "witnessing"? How accurate is it? How appropriate is its use in this immediate context?

4. What prompts Savitt to send the note to Carol? From what perspective is the note written? What is the import of the sentence "I stood in the sidelines" at this moment? What does it contribute to the overall impact of the essay?

5. Jill Savitt reports that she had difficulties thinking out a structure for her essay: "This was more or less the topic: 'How people make decisions, formulate options, choose, and then enact. How people deal with the consequences of these decisions.' We had been reading *Hunger of Memory* by Richard Rodriguez. Our papers were supposed to confront decision making as we read in the book. Work from the inside out, we were told." How does the overall structure of her essay suggest that she is working "from the inside out"? What specific passages highlight this successful feature of her essay?

6. In a recent interview, Jill Savitt explained that conveying the tension of decisive moments absorbed her attention: how to create an effective juxtaposition of the dilemma and the options she faced. "I tried one sentence for one option, the next line another option. It turned into a messy, incoherent stream of consciousness. How do I write about thoughts occurring simultaneously? Manipulate the layout. At one point I trashed this idea too, thinking if I had the right words I could say what I meant. I didn't need to play with design. Words alone, if they are the best words, would convey the conflict. Manipulate words, not layout. But then I thought, 'What would *The Sound and the Fury* be without the italicized parts? Or *Absalom, Absalom!*? Or an e. e. cummings poem?' So I did it." How does the visual arrangement of her essay dramatize her thinking? Evaluate the effectiveness of Savitt's use of this format to represent her dilemma.

7. Whose voices dominate the paragraphs after the first use of double columns? What are they saying? Characterize the differences in the nature of these two voices. How do these two voices underscore Savitt's dilemma?

8. Jill Savitt's advice to other writers includes the following cautionary note: "A great sentence stinks unless it fits into the paper as a whole. Remember the whole while working on the parts. Tangents and digressions are dangerous— people threw books and things at Holden Caulfield for digressing." What strategies does Savitt use to control the development of her essay? What techniques does she use to resist lapsing into "tangents and digressions"? Consider, for example, her attention to setting and character development. How much time does she devote to each? How is the dilemma she faces summarized in such lines as "True, I was the only reporter inside. However, I was not inside because I was a reporter" (paragraph 26)? Point to other moments that exemplify Savitt's point that "a great sentence . . . fits into the paper as a whole."

9. Jill Savitt wrote and rewrote "five or six very different drafts" of "Decisions." "Actually, they were not just different drafts but entirely different papers. One was in third person. Another was in first person. Another was in first and third. The rest were variations on these themes. Some drafts sounded like apologies. Some sounded like muckraking. I couldn't decide how to write the paper on decisions. I started cutting and pasting the various versions, producing a paper more on feeling than on thinking. A paper that used instinct as a tool for decision making. So the crux of the paper, deciding whether or not to write the story, reflected the process of decision making in writing." Reread the opening paragraphs of Savitt's essay. What might those paragraphs look like written in the second or third person? Select one and rewrite it in either the second or third person. Compare and contrast your revision with Savitt's final draft. Which version do you prefer? Why?

10. For Jill Savitt, "revising is writing. I can't call the beginning stages of putting words to paper writing. It's spewing. Revising is when all the papers around me are replaced by printouts of what I've spewed. These printouts are cut up and rearranged. The red pen wages war against paper. Arrows. Exes. Carets. Riders are added and taped or clipped. Changes are made. This process goes on and on. Writing, printing, cutting, adding, revising." In the fourth draft of "Decisions," paragraph 24 read this way:

> I drove back to the newspaper, feeling guilty. I had betrayed both Carol and the *Herald*. In the decisive moment, I followed my heart. Had I seriously contemplated this? Was I sure? If the decision was sound, why did I feel like hell? The *Herald* would never trust me and Carol would hate me.

What further revisions did Savitt make to the fourth draft of this paragraph? Comment on the effect of each change.

Suggestions for Writing

1. Each of us makes literally scores of decisions each day; some bear more important consequences than others. Write an essay in which you recount the circumstances that led to a major decision in your life. Describe the dilemma you faced and how you resolved it. Be sure to include adequate attention to your decision-making process. What options did you establish for yourself? What prompted you finally to act in the way you did? Write your essay, in effect, from "the inside out."

2. Jill Savitt's essay raises provocative questions about the ethics of journalists and individual rights to privacy. Write an essay in which you argue for or against establishing an industrywide code of behavior to govern journalists on the matter of interviewing victims or their families. Do such interviews constitute an invasion of privacy, or is it a matter of the public's right to know?

3. Consider the following observation on ethics by Friedrich Nietzsche: "It is the duty of the free man to live for his own sake, and not for others. . . . Exploitation does not belong to a depraved or an imperfect and primitive state of society. . . . It is a consequence of the intrinsic Will to Power, which is just the Will to Live." Write an essay in which you draw on your own personal experience and public events to validate or challenge Nietzsche's claim.

AN EFFECTIVE TECHNIQUE

Jill Savitt shows us a method for bringing readers to think very hard about moral issues: she dramatizes the internal battle she struggled through when she had to make a tough decision. She actually splits her narrator into two opposed voices, representing two parts of her personality vying for sovereignty, and does not let us know until the very end which one will—or should—win out. Reading this essay, we experience what it is like to be torn apart by an impossible-to-resolve dilemma.

Her essay begins smoothly, leading us quickly into an exciting tale of murder and the FBI. However, just when she has primed us for the gory details, she reveals the tough decision she faces: to reveal any more, she has to "shatter" the life of a friend. The story comes to a halt as she is left uncertain how she should continue. Instead of telling us what happens next, Savitt stops and outlines the two possibilities of what could possibly happen next, depending on what she decides. She prints these two possibilities in two parallel columns, literally splitting the text as she is split by her internal conflict. These two possibilities represent two internal voices speaking to her at the same time, battling to be the single voice that will continue telling the story.

Savitt carefully balances the appeal of each alternative, each voice: one promises us the joy and excitement of a "great story"; the other makes us feel the guilt of sacrificing a friend for personal glory. Moreover, each voice inside Savitt is supported by other characters in the essay: the editor on the phone argues for writing the story; Carol's red eyes argue against it. By lining up opposed voices, Savitt intensifies the internal conflict, until we, as readers, feel as paralyzed by the contrary appeals as she does.

Savitt controls her narrative very tightly to keep her readers focused on the issue facing her. She does not succumb to the temptation to develop a short story. She avoids developing her characters in any great detail, because characters in this essay exist only to represent sides of the conflict she faces. She does not repeat any of the five hours of talk with Carol, because Savitt wants us to think only about the dilemma, not about the merits of the particular story she might have written. She leaves settings fairly sketchy; we see more of the huddle of reporters than of the hospital, because the focus of this essay is reporters and their problems, not a particular tragedy. Nothing in the essay gives us any relief from the tense decision Savitt faces—until the very end, when the friend gives permission for the story to be written.

From Savitt we can learn how to build drama, conflict, and suspense into essays about controversial issues. Instead of merely presenting arpense into essays about controversial issues. Instead of merely presenting arguments in the abstract, she demonstrates how to develop characters and voices to express those arguments. By following a similar strategy, we too can make our readers feel the conflict at the heart of a debate. It is usually easier and more effective to make readers feel torn between two persuasive persons than to make them feel torn between two ideas. And by delaying any indication of authorial position until the end of the essay, we leave readers in suspense and free to develop their own responses. We might carry this principle one step further than Savitt does and write an essay in which we never resolve the conflict. These techniques can be adapted to any controversial issue; all we need do is imagine how someone might be brought to the point of paralysis facing a very difficult decision about that issue. We could write an essay like Savitt's about a senator's tough decision on a controversial bill or about a farmer's dilemma whether or not to use a particularly virulent but effective pesticide.

The structure of Savitt's story can also be used in a formal essay, as we can see in the next selection, "The Boston Photographs," by Nora Ephron. Ephron builds suspense and drama into an "objective" discussion of an issue by making her readers listen to many conflicting and compelling voices and delaying to the very end telling us what she thinks is the "right" solution to the issue the voices are discussing.

ANOTHER ILLUSTRATION OF THE TECHNIQUE

NORA EPHRON
The Boston Photographs

Nora Ephron has spent most of her life in the company of other writers. Her parents were both writers who in the early 1960s based their successful play "Take Her, She's Mine" on their daughter's letters home from Wellesley College. After college, Ephron became a reporter and columnist, married a writer, and based a novel, Heartburn, *on her breakup from her second husband, journalist Carl Bernstein. "I've always written about my life," Ephron said in an interview after the release of her novel. "That's how I grew up. 'Take notes. Everything is copy.' All that stuff my mother said to us. I think it would have been impossible for me to go through the end of my marriage and not have written about it, because although it was the most awful thing I've ever been through . . . it was by far the most interesting."*

"I made all kinds of pictures because I thought it would be a good rescue 1 shot over the ladder . . . never dreamed it would be anything else. . . . I kept having to move around because of the light set. The sky was bright and they were in deep shadow. I was making pictures with a motor drive and he, the fire fighter, was reaching up and, I don't know, everything started falling. I followed the girl down taking pictures . . . I made three or four frames. I realized what was going on and I completely turned around, because I didn't want to see her hit."

You probably saw the photographs. In most newspapers, there were three 2 of them. The first showed some people on a fire escape—a fireman, a woman, and a child. The fireman had a nice strong jaw and looked very brave. The woman was holding the child. Smoke was pouring from the building behind them. A rescue ladder was approaching, just a few feet away, and the fireman had one arm around the woman and one arm reaching out toward the ladder. The second picture showed the fire escape slipping off the building. The child had fallen on the escape and seemed about to slide off the edge. The woman was grasping desperately at the legs of the fireman, who had managed to grab the ladder. The third picture showed the woman and child in midair, falling to the ground. Their arms and legs were outstretched, horribly distended. A potted plant was falling too. The caption said that the woman, Diana Bryant, nineteen, died in the fall. The child landed on the woman's body and lived.

The pictures were taken by Stanley Forman, thirty, of the *Boston Herald* 3 *American.* He used a motor-driven Nikon F set at 1/250, f 5.6–8. Because of the motor, the camera can click off three frames a second. More than four hundred newspapers in the United States alone carried the photographs; the tear sheets from overseas are still coming in. *The New York Times* ran them on the first page of its second section; a paper in south Georgia gave them nineteen columns; the *Chicago Tribune,* the *Washington Post,* and the *Washington Star* filled almost half their front pages, the *Star* under a somewhat redundant headline that read: SENSATIONAL PHOTOS OF RESCUE ATTEMPT THAT FAILED.

The photographs are indeed sensational. They are pictures of death in ac- 4 tion, of that split second when luck runs out, and it is impossible to look at them without feeling their extraordinary impact and remembering, in an almost subconscious way, the morbid fantasy of falling, falling off a building, falling to one's death. Beyond that, the pictures are classics, old-fashioned but perfect examples of photojournalism at its most spectacular. They're throwbacks, really, fire pictures, 1930s tabloid shots; at the same time they're technically superb and thoroughly modern—the sequence could not have been taken at all until the development of the motor-driven camera, some sixteen years ago.

Most newspaper editors anticipate some reader reaction to photographs like 5 Forman's; even so, the response around the country was enormous, and almost all of it was negative. I have read hundreds of the letters that were printed in letters-to-the-editor sections, and they repeat the same points. "Invading the privacy of death." "Cheap sensationalism." "I thought I was reading the *National Enquirer.*" "Assigning the agony of a human being in terror of imminent death to the status of a side-show act." "A tawdry way to sell newspapers." The *Seattle Times* received sixty letters and calls; its managing editor even got a couple of them at home. A reader wrote the *Philadelphia Inquirer: "Jaws* and *Towering Inferno* are playing downtown; don't take business away from people who pay good money to advertise in your own paper." Another reader wrote the *Chicago Sun Times:* "I shall try to hide my disappointment that Miss Bryant wasn't wearing a skirt when she fell to her death. You could have had some award-winning photographs of her underpants as her skirt billowed over her head, you voyeurs." Several newspaper editors wrote columns defending the pictures: Thomas Keevil of the *Costa Mesa* (California) *Daily Pilot* printed a

Copyright Boston Herald American, Stanley J. Forman, Boston Newspaper Division of the Hearst Corporation.

ballot for readers to vote on whether they would have printed the pictures; Marshall L. Stone of Maine's *Bangor Daily News,* which refused to print the famous assassination picture of the Viet Cong prisoner in Saigon, claimed that the Boston pictures showed the dangers of fire escapes and raised questions about slumlords. (The burning building was a five-story brick apartment house on Marlborough Street in the Back Bay section of Boston.)

For the last five years, the *Washington Post* has employed various journalists   6
as ombudsmen, whose job is to monitor the paper on behalf of the public. The
Post's current ombudsman is Charles Seib, former managing editor of the *Washington Star;* the day the Boston photographs appeared, the paper received over
seventy calls in protest. As Seib later wrote in a column about the pictures,
it was "the largest reaction to a published item that I have experienced in
eight months as the *Post*'s ombudsman. . . .

"In the *Post*'s newsroom, on the other hand, I found no doubts, no second   7
thoughts . . . the question was not whether they should be printed but how
they should be displayed. When I talked to editors . . . they used words like
'interesting' and 'riveting' and 'gripping' to describe them. The pictures told
something about life in the ghetto, they said (although the neighborhood
where the tragedy occurred is not a ghetto, I am told). They dramatized the
need to check on the safety of fire escapes. They dramatically conveyed something that had happened, and that is the business we're in. They were
news. . . .

"Was publication of that [third] picture a bow to the same taste for the   8
morbidly sensational that makes gold mines of disaster movies? Most papers
will not print the picture of a dead body except in the most unusual circumstances. Does the fact that the final picture was taken a millisecond before the
young woman died make a difference? Most papers will not print a picture of
a bare female breast. Is that a more inappropriate subject for display than the
picture of a human being's last agonized instant of life?" Seib offered no answers
to the questions he raised, but he went on to say that although as an editor
he would probably have run the pictures, as a reader he was revolted by them.

In conclusion, Seib wrote: "Any editor who decided to print those pictures   9
without giving at least a moment's thought to what purpose they served and
what their effect was likely to be on the reader should ask another question:
Have I become so preoccupied with manufacturing a product according to
professional traditions and standards that I have forgotten about the consumer,
the reader?"

It should be clear that the phone calls and letters and Seib's own reaction   10
were occasioned by one factor alone: the death of the woman. Obviously, had
she survived the fall, no one would have protested; the pictures would have
had a completely different impact. Equally obviously, had the child died as
well—or instead—Seib would undoubtedly have received ten times the phone
calls he did. In each case, the pictures would have been exactly the same—
only the captions, and thus the responses, would have been different.

But the questions Seib raises are worth discussing—though not exactly for   11
the reasons he mentions. For it may be that the real lesson of the Boston

photographs is not the danger that editors will be forgetful of reader reaction, but that they will continue to censor pictures of death precisely because of that reaction. The protests Seib fielded were really a variation on an old theme—and we saw plenty of it during the Nixon-Agnew years—the "Why doesn't the press print the good news?" argument. In this case, of course, the objections were all dressed up and cleverly disguised as righteous indignation about the privacy of death. This is a form of puritanism that is often justifiable; just as often it is merely puritanical.

Seib takes it for granted that the widespread though fairly recent newspaper 12 policy against printing pictures of dead bodies is a sound one; I don't know that it makes any sense at all. I recognize that printing pictures of corpses raises all sorts of problems about taste and titillation and sensationalism; the fact is, however, that people die. Death happens to be one of life's main events. And it is irresponsible—and more than that, inaccurate—for newspapers to fail to show it, or to show it only when an astonishing set of photos comes in over the Associated Press wire. Most papers covering fatal automobile accidents will print pictures of mangled cars. But the significance of fatal automobile accidents is not that a great deal of steel is twisted but that people die. Why not show it? That's what accidents are about. Throughout the Vietnam war, editors were reluctant to print atrocity pictures. Why *not* print them? That's what that war was about. Murder victims are almost never photographed; they are granted their privacy. But their relatives are relentlessly pictured on their way in and out of hospitals and morgues and funerals.

I'm not advocating that newspapers print these things in order to teach 13 their readers a lesson. The *Post* editors justified their printing of the Boston pictures with several arguments in that direction; every one of them is irrelevant. The pictures don't show anything about slum life; the incident could have happened anywhere, and it did. It is extremely unlikely that anyone who saw them rushed out and had his fire escape strengthened. And the pictures were not news—at least they were not national news. It is not news in Washington, or New York, or Los Angeles that a woman was killed in a Boston fire. The only newsworthy thing about the pictures is that they were taken. They deserve to be printed because they are great pictures, breathtaking pictures of something that happened. That they disturb readers is exactly as it should be: that's why photojournalism is often more powerful than written journalism.

Focusing on the Ways Nora Ephron Dramatizes a Dilemma

1. How does the opening quotation bring readers into the middle of the photographer's dilemma? What phrases in Ephron's descriptions of the photographs in paragraphs 2–4 suggest that the photographs should not have been printed? What phrases in those paragraphs suggest that the photographs should have been printed?

2. The fifth paragraph is full of quotations. What is the effect of having so many different voices and opinions? From paragraph 6 through 9, Ephron lets one person speak at length—Charles Seib. How do Seib's comments and questions intensify the readers' sense of being faced with an insoluble dilemma?

3. Ephron first brings herself into this essay in paragraph 5, where she says "I have read hundreds of the letters that were printed in letters-to-the-editor sections." What impression of her does this line create? She does not use "I" again to refer to herself until the next to last paragraph when she says, in reaction to the newspaper's policy of not printing certain pictures, "I don't know that it makes any sense at all." Why does she bring herself into this essay, rather than simply stating "objective" arguments?

4. What is the effect of Ephron's not letting the reader know any earlier in this essay that she is going to give her own answers to the questions she has raised? What is the tone of the last two paragraphs? How does the tone of those paragraphs help make Ephron seem capable of resolving the dilemma?

WORKING WITH THE TECHNIQUE IN YOUR OWN WRITING

1. Write an essay about a dilemma you have faced. You might actually set up a scene, as Savitt does, or draw your readers into the drama of a dilemma by describing a difficult situation and then quoting persons who were involved in it, as Ephron does. In either case, use suspense in structuring your essay; set it up so that for most of the essay the reader does not know what you finally did; make the reader experience your uncertainty, the contrary voices tugging at you. If you have trouble thinking up a dilemma you have faced, you might try to recall a time when it seemed that many people were giving you advice. If you feel you have not faced any dilemma worth writing about (even for a humorous essay), you might instead write about a dilemma somebody else, perhaps a public figure, faced.

2. Both Savitt's and Ephron's essays raise the issue of what should and should not be printed in the newspaper. Write an essay in which you try to define what

sorts of stories and pictures should not be printed. Build at least part of your essay as Savitt and Ephron build theirs: bring your readers to face a dilemma about whether or not to print something. You might even use in your essay the dilemma that Savitt faced or the one that Ephron writes about (or both). In other words, you could include in your essay some of the material in Savitt's or Ephron's essays. Be sure, however, that you formulate your own opinion.

BARBARA SEIDEL

Ocean County College
Toms River, New Jersey
Mary Ellen Byrne, instructor

"My upbringing was traditional," reports Barbara Seidel. "We were a close, volatile family and our home was always filled with relatives. I was the oddball from an early age—hot-tempered, rebellious, imaginative. I always loved to listen to the stories of my relatives; who did what, where, and why. I always wanted to understand people's motives, to explain their actions. Even today, I want to lift the lids off people's heads, peek inside, and explain the undercurrents of emotion and thought I often sense but cannot see. Writing is the best way to understand the world around me."

Born in Newark, New Jersey, Seidel grew up in Hillside and now lives in Toms River. She has always received praise and encouragement for her writing from her family and teachers. She served as the features editor of her high school newspaper and has written a cooking column and a column on humor in daily life for a county newspaper. Seidel describes the conditions necessary for writing in the following stark and rather solitary terms: "I want the house to be silent except for the sporadic squawking of my birds. I need to be left alone, without the phone ringing or without anyone asking me questions or needing me at the moment."

Asked to write an essay of tribute to someone, Seidel immediately knew she would write about her father. "I knew this paper would be a very personal essay. I made a promise to myself that I would be open and vulnerable in my writing, that I would speak plainly about Dad. If I did otherwise, this paper would not work. I decided not to worry about the reaction my dad or other family members would have because otherwise I would have been paralyzed with the attempt to please everybody. I wrote what I felt and thought, and I hope anyone who reads this essay will understand that it was written with love."

Several years have passed since "A Tribute to My Father" earned Barbara Seidel a Bedford Prize. During that time, Seidel withdrew from Ocean County College to work full-time, a decision she characterized in a recent interview as "both a choice and a necessity. My original job, on a weekly paper, led to a position there as an assistant editor." She has since moved on to a daily newspaper, the Ocean County Observer, where she is the "lifestyle" reporter. "Feature writing allows me to delve into people and issues and to continue satisfying my need to question and explore human nature." Seidel has also won several awards for her journalism, returned to writing poetry, and has begun, as she reports, "tackling short stories. . . . And I still read constantly. One point winning the Bedford Prize has taught me is to have faith in myself even when it is most difficult, such as after reading The Prince of Tides by Pat Conroy and being left almost breathless by his talent. Winning the Bedford Prize is my reminder that someday, if I persevere, some writer will say, 'Look how she started and how long it took! I can do it, too!' And that's what I would tell other writers: Persevere. Don't give up. Listen to your heart."

For a more detailed study of Barbara Seidel's essay and the drafts that led to it, see Part II.

A *Tribute to My Father*

Thirty years ago, when his father was dying, he would leave his wife and 1
two small children asleep in the square Cape Cod style house, then drive in
the predawn light through the quiet city streets to take his father for outpatient
medical care. Much later in his own life, his daughter puzzled over his devotion
to a man who had divorced his mother, then ignored him and his brother. A
faint look of surprise flickered in his eyes; then he answered concisely, "He
was my father." He has always said that actions speak louder than words.

A soft-spoken man with a frequent low chuckle, he is so slow to anger that 2
some people have been fooled into believing him an easy mark for trickery, a
dangerous mistake. He is just as slow and long in remembering anyone who
violates his strict set of values. He has no textbook education, yet he possesses
an abundance of common sense. He is not religious, yet he is a moral man,
consistent in his values on a daily basis, not only on a Sabbath. The inherent
boundaries of his life, given and expected, have been loyalty, respect, tradition.
Perhaps it is from the wild young hellion who quit school, whose idea of fun
was joyriding in his older brother's car while that brother chased after him,
that this man of caution and habit emerged.

Yet it was not caution, but sharp, clear instincts that twirled him fast and 3
dizzy after the woman he would marry. He was already engaged; his fiancée
made the fatal mistake of introducing her fair-haired, blue-eyed, slender man
to the dark-haired woman whose first sight caused some inner voice to shout
at him, firmly, "yes!" This woman would need him, would nurture him; he
knew it. He broke his engagement, then immediately proposed, waiting a year
before marrying only because of his future mother-in-law's insistence that he
do so. He may have been impulsive, but he was, after all, respectful of his
elders. And he had clearly chosen not only a wife but a family style. Tradition
and warmth, tangled relationships, and rash tempers all spoke of people connecting to one another. His life became one of stability and constancy, of the
same meat loaf served on the same day of each week, of the same conservative
clothes worn year in and year out, of a man and a woman whose lives revolved
around each other, so unlike his own past.

He spoke little about his past. No bitterness over the secondhand shoes 4
stuffed with newspapers, or the hand-me-down clothing several sizes too large,
pushed him to pursue great wealth to power. His dream, he later said, was to
be able to work hard and just provide. He found the greatest pleasure in the
small things—the ability to buy himself new shoes. Nor did he wield his own
meager childhood as a club to inspire guilt or appreciation in his own more
fortunate, more spoiled children. Instead, they learned of him through passing
comments—or from his mother.

Her divorce came in an era when such an act was brazen. She worked long 5
days caring for her two boys, who ate one meal daily at the corner candy store.
The counterman would wait until they entered, then place a sandwich and a
drink in front of them. "Never more or less, and all ordered and paid for in
advance," he once said, a respectful, wondering tone in his voice at the sheer
order of it all. She passed her stern work ethic on to him. He became very
good at being responsible, dependable, at providing.

And the errant, alcoholic, polo-playing father—the womanizer who once 6
told his ladies that this then-nineteen-year-old younger son was his younger
brother—had a few admirable traits of his own left up his sleeve. To his son,
he passed on a love of animals and a fascination with cars, with their sight
and smell and the gas-powered freedom they gave to a man. His son, as a boy,
would drag home one protesting stray after another to a firmly opposed mother.
Years later, a father himself, he would laugh when his own daughter did the
same. After spending forty years selling the mechanical monsters, his love
affair with cars has only dimmed. It is telling of the man that in a profession
where truth is not always a recognizable commodity, he has a staunch reputation for honesty and a loyal following of customers.

If his honesty attracts them, so must his humor, gentle and chiding. And 7
of course, there are the quirks. There are the Hershey chocolate bars hidden
in the night table drawer, the towels folded and placed exactly so in the linen
closet, the sink faucet wiped shiny dry after dishes are washed. If his past did
not create anger or unbridled ambition, it did give him a legacy of sorts:
hoarded candy bars contrast with the giving parent; an obsession with details
fills him with anxiety. He worries over each decision like a dog gnawing on a
bone. He is still the small boy seeking security, the ultimate peacemaker avoiding confrontations, reconciling and rationalizing the good in people and in
issues to the frustration of his children. They, grown, have at last learned to
laugh gently at the habits that once exasperated them. There is the family
favorite—the phone joke. His son speaks to him, hangs up the phone, then
counts, "5-4-3-2—hello, Dad!" He knows his father will hesitate, then call
again. Is everyone happy? Should we talk more?

It is this son who is one of the brief detours on his well-laid road map of 8
life. With his daughter, loving was an easy goal. They shared a silent similarity
of vision, of loving and letting go. With his son, such love was reached only
after struggle; they spoke a different language. His son needed questions answered, challenges met, baseball and other games which had found no place
in his own childhood; he was a man concerned with providing. By the boy's
adolescence, they were like two bucks, antlers locked in a battle of dominance.
Now they are two men, two fathers, who reach gingerly, but often, across the
once-volatile differences of self to touch the love that always existed.

And now, at age fifty-eight, his hair is streaked with gray; his oval face is   9
heavily lined; he is tired. The habits of his lifetime have been altered, a difficult
task for a man who dislikes change, by the death of the woman who needed
and nurtured him. For years, he had watched her slowly die, her illness chipping away small pieces of his own courage, creating small anxieties, worrisome
habits that still linger with him. But he is not a man to live alone; he has
remarried. With his new wife, he can sometimes be found at the cemetery
where their respective first spouses are buried. Flat bronze plaques and high
white headstones stretch across the green fields. He bends down to clear her
grave of grass and dirt. She was, after all, his wife. Actions do, indeed, speak.

Focusing on Barbara Seidel's Techniques and Revisions

1. What is the dominant impression we get of Barbara Seidel's father in her essay?
   How does she create this impression? What kind of man is Seidel's father? How
   does he define the role of a father?

2. It is very easy to be sentimental about our parents, but Seidel writes about her
   father with controlled emotion and restraint. How does she avoid sentimentality? Point to specific passages that highlight that control.

3. What expectations about the writer's *point of view* does she create in the title
   of her essay? When and how does she upset those expectations? What are the
   effects of Seidel's decision to write her essay in the third person? What does
   she gain by having done so? What does she lose? What effect does her decision
   have on your reading of her essay? What would have been some of the appreciable differences had she written her essay in the first person?

4. The speaker in this essay remains surprisingly distant from the people she
   describes. Point to specific passages from which you might infer why she made
   this decision as a writer. What evidence is there to suggest, for example, the
   extent to which the speaker knew about her father from firsthand experience?
   Would you characterize the stories she tells about her father as primary or
   secondary sources? Explain. How much of the essay is devoted to describing
   her father's relationship with his children? To describing herself?

5. Seidel uses details very effectively to catch the nuances of her father's behavior.
   She tells us about his "secondhand shoes stuffed with newspapers" (paragraph
   4) and the "Hershey chocolate bars hidden in the night table drawer." Select
   details and images you find effective and explain how they support the dominant
   impression that she conveys of her father.

6. Seidel reports: "The hardest part of writing this paper was establishing order,
   organizing it so it made sense and did not jump from subject to subject." How
   does Seidel organize her tribute? Describe what holds the essay together so that
   it does not "jump from subject to subject." When asked in a recent interview

to reread her prize-winning essay and identify some of its most successful features, Seidel willingly offered the following response: "The order—the sense of flow to the essay—stands out, perhaps because I worked so hard to achieve it. It's a bit like building a table from scratch and then examining it when done and feeling a sense of hard-won accomplishment." Reread Seidel's essay, focusing on the sense of order, the flow in it. What strategies does Seidel use to achieve these effects? Be as specific as possible.

7. Seidel urges her readers to "read the essay twice. The first time just let yourself be carried along by the rhythm of the words. The second time read the essay just to understand the man." Seidel plays with sentence structure, length, repetition, and rhythm. Which sentences and word choices do you find especially effective? Why?

8. About her introduction, Seidel says: "The lead paragraph in my first rough draft was simply part of the process of pouring words onto paper. I knew it would have to catch my attention if it would be able to catch the attention of a reader. I knew it did not work." Here is Seidel's rough-draft introduction:

> Actions speak louder than words, he often said. If so, then his actions say much about the man. There was that moment, thirty years ago, when his father was dying slowly. He would rise at dawn, leaving his wife and small children asleep in the tiny house, and drive the distance on quiet city streets. Years later, his own daughter, puzzled, would ask why he showed such devotion to the man who divorced his mother and abandoned him and his brother. He answered, with a faint look of surprise at the question, "He was my father."

What are the differences between the rough-draft introduction and the final-draft introduction? How does the revised introduction more successfully introduce and tie together the various ideas in the essay as well as create a far more evocative description?

9. Seidel identified another successful aspect of the essay as "the human frailty of the subject (my dad). He wasn't glorified; people could feel from my words that I obviously love him, yet at the same time see him objectively. Rereading the essay brought that point out very clearly and surprisingly to me." As you reread Seidel's essay, select the passage that best illustrates her ability to balance her love and objectivity. Be as specific as possible in analyzing the success of the passage.

Suggestions for Writing

1. Select someone about whom you would like to write a tribute. It should of course be someone you are close to. Try to describe this person's faults as well as merits to give your readers a complete impression of what he or she is like.

2. Americans ritually celebrate the relationship between children and parents on Mother's Day and Father's Day. Analyze your family's particular way of responding to and celebrating these holidays. What rituals have you created? What do they express about your family?

3. Write an essay in which you explain what you believe are the biggest mistakes parents make in raising their children. Illustrate your *point of view* with convincing examples.

AN EFFECTIVE TECHNIQUE

Barbara Seidel creates an unusual point of view in her essay: though she writes about her own father, she writes as if she were an outsider to the family who has done research to produce a short biography of Mr. Seidel. Instead of referring to herself as "I," she refers to herself as "his daughter"; instead of speaking of "my mother," she speaks of "his wife." We would not even know that the author of this essay is one of the "characters" in it if Seidel had not titled the essay, "A Tribute to My Father." If we try to keep the perspective of that title in mind, to remember that Barbara Seidel is actually writing this essay, we can feel quite disoriented, as if we are trying to look forward and backward at the same time. The narrator writing in the third person seems quite distant from the people she describes, yet we know at the same time that the author behind this narrator is intimately involved with them.

Seidel suggests a possible reason for her unusual point of view in paragraph 4, when she says that her father "spoke little about his past" to his children; "they [including Barbara herself] learned of him through passing comments— or from his mother." She may have felt that her own memories of her father were too limited and would not have added up to a convincing portrait. Even though she lived with the man for years, she herself did not experience most of what she knows about her father's life. In a sense she is being *more* honest by describing her father from an "objective" point of view rather than from her own; she is admitting that the character in this essay is one created from secondhand stories, that she is extrapolating from hints and details, as any biographer or historian would.

This essay is not, in fact, a child's view of her father. Seidel has worked hard to show how her father interacted with his parents, his wife, his customers; only one paragraph is actually devoted to his relationship to his children. She minimizes description of herself.

Usually, we focus in our writing on our personal view of a subject, repeatedly asking ourselves, "What does this subject have to do with me?" Seidel shows us that we may sometimes limit our imagination when we do so. We may find that ignoring our personal involvement in a subject and trying to see it through someone else's eyes (or several persons' eyes) may generate stronger and more interesting emotions than we ourselves have.

We may even find that adopting a perspective other than our own allows us to communicate our *own* emotions about a subject better and more honestly than we could by stating them directly. At times the very strength of our feeling about a subject inhibits our writing; all we want to do is cry or scream, not describe anything in detail. Or we may feel our emotions censoring our best writing; it is hard to include criticism in a loving portrait. To re-create an emotion in words requires a peculiar combination of self-control and self-surrender; feelings often seem to simply "pour" out onto the page, but some part of the mind must be able to stand aside, to shape the outpouring, to decide which words will best enable an uninvolved reader to understand the emotion the author is pouring out. The third-person point of view is a fine tool for establishing the necessary distance. Instead of writing "I love you" over and over again, an author tries "He loved her" and begins to realize that it is no longer clear who "he" and "her" are or what kind of love is involved and so begins to explore and explain his feelings more deeply.

In the next selection, Christopher Nolan carries the same technique a step further. Instead of simply referring to himself as "he," he gives himself a new name. Though the title of this book says it is "The Autobiography of Christopher Nolan," the main character is Joseph Meehan.

ANOTHER ILLUSTRATION OF THE TECHNIQUE

CHRISTOPHER NOLAN

The Knife Used

"Can you credit all of the fuss that was made of a cripple?" is the first line of Christopher Nolan's autobiography. Born paralyzed, unable to speak, Nolan never forgets his body and the heroic struggle he must go through to write, tapping each letter on a typewriter with a "unicorn rod" attached to his forehead. Yet he can mock the "fuss" others make of him because of their surprise that he can write so well. Born in 1965 in Mullingar, Ireland, he early showed his intelligence, developing a language of eye signals to communicate with his family. Even with his system of communication, he felt intensely frustrated and prayed every day for a means of expressing the thoughts "clustered" in his brain. When he was eight, his whole family moved to Clontarf, a suburb of Dublin, so that Christy could attend the Central Remedial School there. For three years he tried to learn to communicate in words and could not. Then, in 1977, a new drug, Lioresal, allowed him sufficient control of his neck that he could learn to type, and he has been writing ever since, winning literary prizes and traveling to England and the United States as a celebrated author.

Nolan's first book was a collection of poems in the styles of the Irish authors James Joyce and Dylan Thomas, full of newly coined words and shortcuts taken through normal grammar. He adapted some of this style to his second book, his autobiography, making the editing process very difficult. The editor explains, "I queried every word he made up. I was narrow-minded at the start, not by the end. His words do mean something, but the dictionary won't tell you that."

One of Nolan's unusual strategies in writing his autobiography is to write as if he is merely the biographer of a fellow named Joseph Meehan. Nolan pretends to write about another person partly to gain some distance because he feels too close to the events he is writing about; he is only twenty-one as he writes his autobiography. He also wants his readers to remain aware of the doubleness of perspective created when any writer writes about himself: the "self" created in words is not quite the same as the "self" writing. Nolan plays with that double perspective. In one scene, for example, Joseph Meehan lies in bed asleep, dreaming that he is a window cleaner outside the bedroom window: "He watched the circular sweep of his cloth; and suddenly he caught sight of the boy asleep in his bed. He noticed his arms flung wide open, hands relaxed; . . . just like a baby he was deeply and happily sleeping. Conscious that he was now looking at himself he stood glued to the ladder. All cleaning stopped abruptly; he even forgot to hold the ladder with his left hand; he was in a trance. How can I see

myself, he questioned in his amazement, how can Boyhood be in two places at the
same time?"
      The selection reprinted here is Chapter 6 of Nolan's autobiography; it tells of the
family's move to Clontarf and the effect on Nolan's life of learning to write. For a more
complete introduction to Christopher Nolan's autobiography, see Patricia Hampl's review,
reprinted on pp. 212–214.

Winter was wonderful in Corcloon. Farming was fun for children but hell 1
for farmers. This was the very last winter on the farm. The Meehans were
moving to the Big Smoke. The rednecks were going to meet the Molly Ma-
lones. It was all Joseph's fault. If he had come into the world head-first, weather
could still be wonderful for kids in Corcloon. But he asked for trouble when
he decided to lie crossways in his mother's womb, not just crossways but all
relaxed on the broad of his back. He wasn't going anywhere, but life demanded
to see him. Stalling, he had to be lifted from his cosy hammock, knife used
to prize him out. Privately, he had decided to choose death, but fate decided
otherwise.

About death there is no secret. Joseph Meehan knows that, after all he has 2
been there and back. He dwelt among the gods for two fobbed hours but life
clawed him back, copperfastened him and called him free.

Christened for his cross-bearing, he chalk-white weathered the avenues of 3
babyhood. But nobody wounded like him could deserve a chance at life. Better
dead said the crones, better dead said history, better jump in at the deep end
decided her strong soul as she heard his crestfallen cry. His mother it was who
treated him as normal, tumbled to his intelligence, tumbled to his eye-signaled
talk, tumbled to the hollyberries, green yet, but holding promise of burning
in red given time, given home.

Quietly Nora sought an expert opinion about her baby. She brought him 4
to Dublin's Fitzwilliam Street. Quietly she entered No. 9 and carrying Joseph
in her arms came face to face with Dr. Ciaran Barry. He listened quietly to a
mother's story of how everything went wrong at her son's birth. It took two
operations to save her, the first was to deliver her of her baby and the second
was carried out to save herself. Such was the cost worked out that brought her
to Dr. Barry.

Watching and listening, the blue-eyed doctor heard of a mother's quiet 5
observations of her son. He watched the inquisitive baby looking at him,
looking all around his surgery, looking as though he could understand what
his mother was saying. The baby was just seventeen months old.

Assessing him, the doctor wisely played games with the child. He blew into 6
his eyes once but when Joseph heard him taking a deep breath he was ready
for him and cutely closed his eyes. Then when the doctor failed to blow the

boy opened his eyes to see what was wrong. The games cutely constructed never found Joseph wanting. Sure of his findings, the doctor agreed with Nora that her son seemed to have normal intelligence. Then the brave doctor advised the mother about the child's treatment. He told her about the Central Remedial Clinic. He suggested that the boy should have attention there for physiotherapy, speech therapy, occupational therapy and in time, schooling.

Now the time was come and Boyblue had to have his education. Fretting 7 for himself, he didn't count the price paid by his family. Now they had to change their whole lifestyle, their whole outlook. Gone would be the great days exploring washed stones in the river or seeing ewes beating tomtom-fashion on the ground with their front legs as they sought to guard their lambs. Gone too the fun gyrating on the swing when the ropes became twisted or singing in concert with the Earley children as they staged outdoor shows on the hay bogey in the haggard. Never again would he witness huge hungry machines bite deep into the bog and then swing wide a great iron arm to drop a long long sausage of shiny wet turf on the ceannbhán-coated[1] bank. Never again the experiences of his childhood for now Dublin City was calling him, calling him to school.

Dull in Corcloon, the weather became milky-blue over Dublin. Their farm 8 lay behind them. Yes, work purpled these dreadful decisive days. But Matthew and Nora Meehan never fostered feeble fear, never looked back, no longer asked life to loosen its hellish hold on their throats for now hurried preparations made grim future join forces with great promise in the hill-long road ahead.

Oil-filled burner replaced turf-burning stove when the Meehans moved up 9 to Dublin. Gone was Sally, gone was the poultry, gone the bold lovely Earleys. Now new neighbors moved in and out of Clontarf, nobody missed them, nobody really knew them.

Time was of the essence in the big busy city. Dublin yelled breezy certainty, 10 told tempting place names and remedied loneliness for Corcloon. But the Meehans were up to it, they settled in, started school, mimed old joys and minimized new problems.

Joseph was familiar with Clontarf. He had been visiting the clinic on Ver- 11 non Avenue ever since his infancy. Three times each week he had traveled the milkyway to the CRC for his sessions of physiotherapy and speech therapy. The family bought their new house near the clinic so that Joseph would be near his school.

Fears of not being understood were quashed before he ever started school 12 when he met the psychologist, Criona Garvey. He gave her a demonstration

1. ceannbhán: Bog cotton.

of his bowing-headed, eye-pointing, foot-peddling language. She smiled and understood his signals. Then she started to test his intelligence.

Holding his breath he watched her lay out her brain posers, but on the 13 instant he found the answers. He was enjoying himself and feeling very much at ease. She eventually cried halt, but he would have liked to go on until he couldn't go any further. Criona Garvey sat back in her chair and smiled. He looked inquiringly at the psychologist. She talked to him about starting school but with a smile she said, "Joseph, if you don't make great progress then you will have to answer to me."

Like the school, the founder was Hector-hearted. Joseph had seen her on 14 one of his visits to the clinic, but when the classroom door flew open one day he failed to recognize the lady who blustered in. She was dressed in a paisley design, mustard-colored dress and flat shoes. "Good afternoon Lady Goulding," chorused the pupils. "Good afternoon children," smiled the visitor. She stood talking with the teacher while Joseph sat looking at none other than Lady Valerie Goulding.

Hesitating at the door she smiled at the class and in a fluster she was gone. 15 Her face remained before his mind's eye, her trestled truth shone from her gaze, her smile came from a soul-burst and he remembered that she had had a ladder in her stocking.

Crying with fear the first few days in school, now here sat the same boy 16 laughing with Alan or Alex. Here he sat demanding to be understood and being eventually interpreted and then understood. Great joy jumped in Joseph's heart as he mastered his subjects, but he was still seeking an outlet for his cubby-holed writings.

Joseph was well used to all the weeping-Jesus comments about his cross. He 17 was now trying to break free from society's charitable mold. He saw how others saw him but he wanted to show everyone how truly wrong they were. Fenced in on all sides he heard things he was never meant to hear and he saw things he was never meant to see. Now could he ever get his chance to let folk see what they never thought existed?

How do I conquer my body, mused the paralyzed boy. Paralyzed I am labeled, 18 but can a paralytic move? My body rarely stops moving. My arms wage constant battle trying to make me look a fool. My smile which can be most natural, can at times freeze, thereby making me seem sad and uninterested. Two great legs I may have, but put my bodyweight on them and they collapse under me like a house of cards. How then can I convey to folk that the strength in my legs can be as normal as that of the strongest man? Such were boy Joseph's taunting posers, but he had one more fence that freezed his words while they were yet unspoken.

But fate was listening and fate it was that had frozen his freedom. Now 19 could fate be wavering in her purpose? Credence was being given to his bowed perceptions—could fate avow him a means of escape?

Writing by hand failed. Typing festered hope. The typewriter was not a 20 plaything. Boy Joseph needed to master it for the good of his sanity, for the good of his soul. Years had taught him the ins and outs of typewriting, but fate denied him the power to nod and hit the keys with his head-mounted pointer. Destruction secretly destroyed his every attempts to nod his pointer onto the keys. Instead great spasms gripped him rigid and sent his simple nod into a farcical effort which ran to each and every one of his limbs.

Eva Fitzpatrick had done years of duty trying to help Joseph to best his body. 21 She told him everything she knew about brain damage and its effects. The boy understood, but all he could do was to look hard into her humble eyes and flick his own heavenwards in affirmation.

"Yes, you may have Joseph," agreed his class teacher each week when Eva 22 came to collect her pupil for his typing lesson. Away down the corridors they sauntered, the young teacher and her disabled student. Eva chatted while Joseph listened. Trying sometimes to have his say, he would mouth his words while looking back into her eyes.

Eva's room was crested by creative drawings. Her manner was friendly, 23 outgoing, but inwardly she felt for her student as he struggled to typewrite. Her method of working necessitated that her pupil be relaxed so she chatted light-hearted banter as she all the while measured his relaxation. The chatting would continue, but when Joseph saw his teacher wheel the long mirror towards the typing table he knew that they were going to play typing gymnastics.

Together they would struggle, the boy blowing like a whale from the huge 24 effort of trying to discipline his bedamned body. Every tip of his pointer to the keys of the typewriter sent his body sprawling backwards. Eva held his chin in her hands and waited for him to relax and tip another key. The boy and girl worked mightily, typing sentences which Eva herself gave as a headline to Joseph. Young Boyblue honestly gave himself over to his typing teacher. Gumption was hers as she struggled to find a very voluntary tip coming to the typewriter keys from his yessing head.

But for Eva Fitzpatrick he would never have broken free. His own mother 25 had given up on him and decided that the typewriter was no help at all. She had put the cover on the machine and stored it away. She felt hurt by defeat. Her foolish heart failed to see breathing destructive spasms coming between her son and the typewriter. But how was a mother to know that hidden behind her cross was a Simon ready and willing to research areas where she strode as a stranger. How could she know that Eva brought service to a head and that science now was going to join forces with her. Now a new drug was being administered to the spastic boy and even though he was being allowed to take only a small segment of Lioresal tablet, he was beginning already to feel different. The little segments of Lioresal tablet seemed harmless, but yet they were the mustard seeds of his and Eva's hours of discovery.

Now he struggled from his certainty that he was going to succeed and with 26 that certainty came a feeling of encouragement. The encouragement was absolute, just as though someone was egging him on. His belief now came from himself and he wondered how this came about. He knew that with years of defeat he should now be experiencing despair, but instead a spirit of enlightenment was telling him you're going to come through with a bow, a bow to break your chain and let out your voice.

At the very same hour fate was also at work on Eva. When it was least 27 expected she sensed that music of which he sampled. She watched Joseph in the mirror as he struggled to find and trip the required keys. Avoiding his teacher's gaze, he struggled on trying to test himself. Glee was gamboling but he had to be sure.

Breathing a little easier, his body a little less trembling, he sat head cupped 28 in Eva's hands. He even noticed the scent of her perfume but he didn't glance in the mirror. Perhaps it won't happen for me today he teased himself but he was wrong, desperately, delightfully wrong. Sweetness of certainty sugared his now. Yes, he could type. He could freely hit the keys and he looked in the mirror and met her eyes. Feebly he smiled but she continued to study him. Looking back into her face he tried to get her response, but turning his wheelchair she gracefully glided back along the corridor to his classroom.

Of the great discovery Nora knew not and Joseph chose not to tell her. 29 Boyblue bested his body but he bragged but to himself.

"Mrs. Meehan, have you seen Joseph at his typing?" innocently inquired 30 Eva Fitzpatrick. "No, Eva, he hasn't been at his typewriter for about eighteen months now," said unwary Nora. Eva smiled in understanding but asked Nora, "Will you come to see him at his next typing lesson?" "Sure," said innocent Nora, "when do you take him again?" "Next Wednesday afternoon at 2:15," said Eva.

Nora sat watching. Spasms ripped through Joseph's body. Sweat stood out 31 on his face. He was trying to let his mother see what he was capable of. She was not impressed. He could see that despite his ordeal. The phone rang and Eva suggested that perhaps Nora would take over from her and hold Joseph's head. The spasms held him rigid but within a couple of minutes he felt himself relaxing. Nora waited, her son's chin cupped in her hands. Then he stretched and brought his pointer down and typed the letter "e." Swinging his pointer to the right he then typed another letter, and another one and another. Eva finished speaking on the telephone and Nora, while still cupping Joseph's chin, turned and said, "Eva, I know what you're talking about—Joseph is going for the keys himself—I could actually feel him stretching for them." Eva, his courageous teacher, clenched her fist and brought it down with a bang on the table. "So I was right, I was afraid to say anything, I had to be sure," she said as she broadly smiled.

Joseph sat looking at his women saviors. They chatted about their discovery 32 while he nodded in happy unbelievable bewilderment. He felt himself float reliably on gossamer wings. He hungered no more. He giggled nervously before he even bespoke his thanks. He cheered all the way up the corridor, said goodbye to dear Eva and giggled and cheered up into Nora's face all the way home.

Feeble Joseph was just eleven years old, but before long he would be taking 33 on Nora, schooling her to see what he could see, instructing her to steady his head for him while he typed beauty from within, beauty of secret knowledge so secretly hidden and so nearly lost forever.

It was by nodding his head then that he bashfully typed green words, frail 34 poems and childish prose. Writing became Joseph Meehan's Word Wold. Brain-damaged, he had for years clustered his words, certain that some Cyclops-visioned earthling would stumble on a scheme by which he could express hollyberried imaginings.

Certain of himself and his word bunting, he was confident enough to feed 35 himself on fame. Nested writing brought him naive belief that he could compete with other writers. Now he was waiting the results of his most recent competition.

Sensing that he might be successful in his attempts to win a prize in the 36 Spastics Society Literary Contest, he waited. He lay in the back garden under the noonday sun. He was wondering how his breathless autobiography would fare in the literary capital of the world.

The sun bore down relentlessly, but Joseph grinned in peculiar mastery. As 37 he looked up through strained eyes he saw seagulls soaring then diving in hungry-voiced hunting. The boy burned and grinned, teeth gritted in defiance. Tumbling yells bullied bold notions as he lay steel-jacketed by fate. Suddenly the scene heard a frantic bell. From inside the kitchen came the urgency of the telephone worrying the life out of Joseph.

Yvonne stirred suddenly, her golden tanned body jerking into life. "I'll get 38 it Mam," she called as she ran up the steps to answer the telephone. Nora didn't stir, she was sitting reading the newspaper in the shade of the clothes-draped line. Sheets billowed and blew on the revolving clothesline, allowing her just a marginal amount of shade. Joseph's pale white shrunken limbs beckoned at the sun. He wanted to be tanned. He wanted to be golden just like his sister.

Yvonne ran down the steps calling, "Mam, it's for you, it's the Spastics 39 Society, Nina Heycock on the line." Nora hurried inside and Yvonne followed her. Joseph lay looking up at the seagulls. He voiced defiance as they soared, wings outspread in flight—to hell with ye showing off up there, my crippled body may fly yet. Can a luckless fellow deny fate? Can he develop wings? Maybe fate will change her mind, bubble mercy, bubble nutshell-hollow beauty. But why doesn't Yvonne come back?

"Hi Joseph, you've won, you've won the Special Prize," hollered Yvonne 40 as she jumped down into the garden. Then throwing herself down beside her brother, she seized his hand and said, "You lucky bugger, I'd a feeling you'd win but was afraid to tell you. I didn't want to build you up for a big letdown." Joseph bowed and bowed at his sister. He felt just like she did but was afraid to tell anyone. Yvonne could feel the tension in his hand so she changed her tactics. "You lucky bugger, off to London again," she said, "but this time don't bring me back cheap jewelry," she advised. "It's gold this time, or maybe silver is more suitable for my age." Joseph burst out laughing and with the laugh came lovely temporary ease.

Yet they circled, circled, circled, those albatross-winged gulls. They flew up 41 high then swept eyescavingly low. Joseph eyed them, but now sure of himself he scoffed in merry laughter. Nora ran back to play fairy godmother. "He's done it again, that's the verdict from London," she said. Joseph looked up at his seagulled scenario and craning his neck he locked his body into beauty by pressing on the ground with his heels. Now he was able to glance to the north, south, east and west and follow each gull with his eyes. "Ah wait till you hear what the judge said, Joseph," enthused his mother. "They're comparing you with Joyce and Yeats and even Dylan Thomas too. Imagine. Ah, but you're very young. Very young yet."

Joseph was very excited, very numb with happiness, very full of secret 42 premonitions and very great gratitude. Mesmerized, he anointed vivid-voice love. Nocturnal messages budded now, budding his withered stalk in buds of rosy-tipped shoots. He heard his mother and sister expressing their happiness for him, but he hesitated before joining them in glad-glanced mouthings. Nothing could change his crippled body but now he languished in literary shadows and he liked the view in the Market Place ahead.

Talking excitedly, Nora knelt on the ground looking into her son's eyes 43 while Yvonne lay prone, still holding her brother's hand and snapping numb the spasms which ricocheted through his body. Her glance met his imploring glance as he directed her to his chariot. "Mam," she said, picking up his clue, "Joseph wants to get back into his wheelchair." Nora and Yvonne lifted him from the rug and eased him back into his seat. The telephone rang again, ringing ringing despite the business of the scene. "I'll bet it's Dad," said Yvonne as she ran again to answer it.

Nora brought Joseph's chair into the kitchen by dragging it up the two steps 44 on its back wheels. Yvonne was chatting with her dad, telling him about Joseph's great news. Nora wheeled her son out into the dark, cold, dim hall and taking the phone from her daughters she held it to Joseph's ear. He heard his dad in mid-sentence but let out a wild cheer. Matthew stopped short and laughing said, "Oh, it's yourself Joseph, you're a great lad. I'm very proud of you." Then he asked, "Are you very pleased with yourself?" But he couldn't see his son nodding furiously. Joseph glanced up at smiling Nora and indicated that it was time that she took over.

Sadness was gone out with the tide, Dollymount Strand was silent save for 45 the family and their black and white collie dog. Restfully they strolled along the beach with Joseph now center-stage and the *cause célèbre* for this nighttime outing. The signals flashed from the Bailey Lighthouse in Howth, challenging sailors to beware of the cased, hidden rocks. Joseph bragged to his family. He bowed and nodded towards England. They understood his signals and rejoiced for him. Even his adopted city seemed to cheer his success, for Dublin twinkled its lights in horseshoe shape around him, framing the story of Joseph Meehan in watercolors tinted with blue, green, white and gold. Water shimmered on the bay, the sound of the sea golloped his voiced thanks but he nodded towards the horizon. God, forgive me for chiding Why, he prayed, but how was a small fella like me to know that a bested prayer from me can move God to fling open the floodgates of heaven.

In the company of his family he boyishly bragged but in the silence of the 46 night he ducked his comforter in seas of creature-cradled gratitude. Communion too brought his comforter within his grasp and in close body contact he crested silent desperate credence. Communion served grand purpose, serving to bring God to him and him to servile God.

Focusing on Christopher Nolan's Point of View

1. In the first paragraph, the narrator says that the Meehan family moved to Dublin, and "It was all Joseph's fault." How do you think Christopher Nolan feels, knowing that his family gave up their life in the country to help him? How would the effect of the passage be different if it were written in the first person, and the writer said, "It was all my fault"?

2. What does the word "Boyblue" (paragraph 7) suggest to you? We cannot tell whether this is a nickname the family gave Joseph or one of the narrator's inventions. In either case, how does the narrator's calling Joseph "Boyblue" make us feel about Joseph? What would you think of someone who referred to *himself* in an essay this way?

3. In paragraph 17, the narrator describes what Joseph hoped to accomplish by learning to use words: "to let folk see what they never thought existed." How does this whole book accomplish this purpose? How does the third-person technique help in accomplishing this purpose?

4. How do you visualize the narrator? As mentioned in the headnote, the narrator later retells a time when Joseph dreamed he was a window washer, looking in at himself lying in bed. As part of the dream, Joseph asks in amazement, "How can I see myself . . . how can Boyhood be in two places at the same time?" How does this passage help explain Nolan's unusual point of view in this book?

5. In paragraph 45, the narrator says, "Even his adopted city seemed to cheer his success, for Dublin twinkled its lights in horseshoe shape around him, framing the story of Joseph Meehan in watercolors tinted with blue, green, white and gold." How do you feel about Joseph at this moment of success? How would you feel if the narrator said that the city was "framing *my* story in watercolors"?

6. How do the other unusual elements of Nolan's style, besides his point of view, contribute to putting some distance between the events and us readers as we read? How might developing this style have helped Christopher Nolan gain some distance on his own life?

WORKING WITH THE TECHNIQUE IN YOUR OWN WRITING

1. Write an essay trying to summarize the life of a person with whom you have a strong relationship. Include in your essay a description of how that person sees you—but do not refer to yourself as "I" or "me." Make yourself a character in the story of this other person. If you are writing of your mother, you would speak of yourself as "her daughter"; if you are writing of a girlfriend, you would speak of yourself as "her boyfriend." You might even refer to yourself by name. Try to make your role in the essay fit the other person's view of your importance in his or her life. You might find it difficult to avoid thinking of yourself as "I," but you might also discover that you gain a new perspective on yourself in doing so.

2. Write a section of your autobiography as Christopher Nolan writes his: give yourself a new name and write about this newly named person in the third person. Instead of saying, "I always like telling people that I came from Paris,"

you might write, "Edgar Flint always liked telling people that he came from Paris." See if you can establish some distance from your own experiences by writing this way; you might find that you discover things about the character you create that you never noticed before about yourself. For example, Edgar's snobbery in speaking of Paris may bother you, and you may therefore begin to think about your own snobbery.

JAMES M. SEILSOPOUR

Riverside City College
Riverside, California
William F. Hunt, instructor

James Seilsopour was born in Anaheim, California, but spent most of his childhood and adolescence living in Teheran, until the Iranian revolution forced his family to return to the United States in 1979. He graduated from high school in Norco, California, in 1982 and enrolled in Riverside City College, where he worked toward a degree in English.

James Seilsopour says he did not plan "I Forgot the Words to the National Anthem" as a response to a specific course assignment but as a means "to talk about that part of my life." When he returned to the United States from Teheran, he was alienated from many of his American peers and ridiculed at times for his Iranian heritage, and he decided to write some poetry about these experiences. But then, as he explains, "I had fallen behind in my English class and needed a paper to turn in." Encouraged by his instructor to "write for publication," Seilsopour revised his essay several times. ("Revisions are painful—like cutting yourself with a hot blade," he says.) Eventually he satisfied himself with the knowledge that his story "will finally get told."

"When people read my essay, I want them to imagine themselves in my place for just a moment—then never think about it again."

I Forgot the Words
to the National Anthem

The bumper sticker read, "Piss on Iran." 1

To me, a fourteen-year-old living in Teheran, the Iranian revolution was 2 nothing more than an inconvenience. Although the riots were just around the corner, although the tanks lined the streets, although a stray bullet went through my sister's bedroom window, I was upset because I could not ride at the Royal Stable as often as I used to. In the summer of 1979, my family— father, mother, brothers, sister, aunt, and two cousins—were forced into exile. We came to Norco, California.

In Iran, I was an American citizen and considered myself an American, 3 even though my father was Iranian. I loved baseball and apple pie and knew the words to the "Star-Spangled Banner." That summer before high school, I was like any other kid my age; I listened to rock and roll, liked fast cars, and thought Farrah Fawcett was a fox. Excited about going to high school, I was looking forward to football games and school dances. But I learned that it was not meant to be. I was not like other kids, and it was a long, painful road I traveled as I found this out.

The American embassy in Iran was seized the fall I started high school. I 4 did not realize my life would be affected until I read that bumper sticker in the high school parking lot which read, "Piss on Iran." At that moment I knew there would be no football games or school dances. For me, Norco High consisted of the goat ropers, the dopers, the jocks, the brains, and one quiet Iranian.

I was sitting in my photography class after the hostages were taken. The 5 photography teacher was fond of showing travel films. On this particular day, he decided to show a film about Iran, knowing full well that my father was Iranian and that I grew up in Iran. During the movie, this teacher encouraged the students to make comments. Around the room, I could hear "Drop the bomb" and "Deport the mothers." Those words hurt. I felt dirty, guilty. However, I managed to laugh and assure the students I realized they were just joking. I went home that afternoon and cried. I have long since forgiven those students, but I have not and can never forgive that teacher. Paranoia set in. From then on, every whisper was about me: "You see that lousy son of a bitch? He's Iranian." When I was not looking, I could feel their pointing fingers in my back like arrows. Because I was absent one day, the next day I brought a note to the attendance office. The secretary read the note, then looked at me. "So you're Jim Seilsopour?" I couldn't answer. As I walked away, I thought I heard her whisper to her co-worker, "You see that lousy son of a bitch? He's Iranian." I missed thirty-five days of school that year.

My problems were small compared to those of my parents. In Teheran, my 6 mother had been a lady of society. We had a palatial house and a maid. Belonging to the women's club, she collected clothes for the poor and arranged Christmas parties for the young American kids. She and my father dined with high government officials. But back in the States, when my father could not find a job, she had to work at a fast-food restaurant. She was the proverbial pillar of strength. My mother worked seventy hours a week for two years. I never heard her complain. I could see the toll the entire situation was taking on her. One day my mother and I went grocery shopping at Stater Brothers Market. After an hour of carefully picking our food, we proceeded to the cashier. The cashier was friendly and began a conversation with my mother. They spoke briefly of the weather as my mother wrote the check. The cashier looked at the check and casually asked, "What kind of name is that?" My mother said, "Italian." We exchanged glances for just a second. I could see the pain in her eyes. She offered no excuses; I asked for none.

Because of my father's birthplace, he was unable to obtain a job. A natu- 7 ralized American citizen with a master's degree in aircraft maintenance engineering from the Northrop Institute of Technology, he had never been out of work in his life. My father had worked for Bell Helicopter International, Flying

Tigers, and McDonnell Douglas. Suddenly, a man who literally was at the top of his field was unemployable. There is one incident that haunts me even today. My mother had gone to work, and all the kids had gone to school except me. I was in the bathroom washing my face. The door was open, and I could see my father's reflection in the mirror. For no particular reason I watched him. He was glancing at a newspaper. He carefully folded the paper and set it aside. For several long moments he stared blankly into space. With a resigned sigh, he got up, went into the kitchen, and began doing the dishes. On that day, I know I watched a part of my father die.

My father did get a job. However, he was forced to leave the country. He   8
is a quality control inspector for Saudi Arabian Airlines in Jeddah, Saudi Arabia. My mother works only forty hours a week now. My family has survived, financially and emotionally. I am not bitter, but the memories are. I have not recovered totally; I can never do that.

And no, I have never been to a high school football game or dance. The   9
strike really turned me off to baseball. I have been on a diet for the last year, so I don't eat apple pie much anymore. And I have forgotten the words to the national anthem.

Focusing on James Seilsopour's Techniques and Revisions

1. What is the function of the opening line in James Seilsopour's essay? Seilsopour quotes the bumper sticker again in paragraph 4. Does his use of it at the beginning of the essay strengthen or weaken its impact later? Explain why. At what point in his essay does Seilsopour reveal the significance of the imperative "Piss on Iran"? At what point does Seilsopour clarify the importance of the title of his essay?

2. Reread the first two paragraphs of James Seilsopour's essay. In what country is the scene in the first sentence located? In the second sentence? What is the effect of this geographical and chronological leap?

3. Comment on the relationship—thematically and stylistically—between paragraphs 3 and 9. In what specific ways does that final paragraph clarify the significance of what he says in paragraph 3? In what ways does the final paragraph complicate the issues presented earlier?

4. Seilsopour explains that the only problem he had writing this essay was "toning the paper down from an angry commentary to a straightforward personal essay." How does he maintain control of his anger? Consider, for example, paragraph 5. How does he restrain his emotions? What is the effect of the final sentence in this paragraph?

5. What does James Seilsopour tell us about himself in paragraphs 2 and 3? Why

do these two paragraphs make the rest of his essay more powerful? What kind of relationship does Seilsopour establish with his audience? Point to specific words and phrases to support your response. How does he elicit his readers' sympathy for himself and his family?

6. Outline the three *anecdotes* in this essay (paragraphs 5, 6, and 7). What point does each anecdote make? Explain how Seilsopour uses these anecdotes to unify his essay. Consider the overall organization of this essay. Explain why you think Seilsopour's essay would or would not have been more effective had he ended it with his mother's denial that Seilsopour is an Iranian name? What do the final three paragraphs add to his essay?

7. In his first draft, Seilsopour ended paragraph 7 with the following sentence: "To this day we have never spoken of that incident." Does Seilsopour's decision to omit this line from his final draft improve or damage the effect of this paragraph?

8. James Seilsopour and An-Thu Quang Nguyen describe in detail their struggles to deal with the consequences of the contrast between their current and former "homes." Compare and contrast their current situations, their approaches to their past, and their responses to their future. What inferences can you draw about the American character from their stories?

9. Reread Seilsopour's and John Clyde Thatcher's essay ("On Killing the Man"), paying particular attention to the specific ways in which each writer clarifies the significance of his essay's title. At what point in each essay does the writer make the title's significance clear? What are the effects of doing so in each case?

10. Compare and contrast the use of suspense in James Seilsopour's and Celeste Barrus's essays. What specific stylistic strategies does each employ to heighten suspense? Which writer does so more effectively? Why?

Suggestions for Writing

1. Imagine that you are a diplomatic representative of the United States government responsible for writing a letter to James Seilsopour in response to his essay. In writing the letter, you must decide whether you should explain, justify, or apologize for the treatment he and his family received since their return to the United States. What action, if any, will you take on behalf of the United States government? Or imagine that you are a student at the high school Seilsopour attended. Write an essay in response to Seilsopour's paper. Will you explain, justify, or apologize on behalf of other students for the ways in which Seilsopour and his family have been mistreated? What action, if any, will you take on behalf of your peers?

2. A particularly painful episode in James Seilsopour's narrative is the humiliation

he suffers in his high school class. Write an essay in which you use either the
first or the third person to recount a humiliating or embarrassing incident in
high school or college. Account for the motives and the responses of those
involved. What lasting effects did the incident have?

3. Americans have been accused of being quick to label others, especially during
   times of national crisis or when our national pride is at stake. Consider, for
   example, our treatment of Japanese Americans during World War II or the
   recent parodies of the Soviets in television advertising. Write an essay in which
   you examine the implications of some ways in which the call to patriotism has
   caused Americans to treat other people with disregard.

AN EFFECTIVE TECHNIQUE

James Seilsopour begins his essay in a surprising way: he creates a carefully
controlled confusion—just enough to be intriguing, but not enough to make
us stop reading. Seilsopour's opening leaves us in suspense; it forces us to ask
many questions and to wonder what is going to come next. From this essay
we can learn of the power to be gained from surprising readers and even making
them uncomfortable.

Seilsopour refuses to cater to our expectations. We do not expect the word
"piss" in the first sentence of an essay. Seilsopour wants us to be puzzled about
the connection between the vulgar slang of "Piss on Iran" and the high ideals
of the national anthem. And instead of explaining the connection, he jumps
around from scene to scene in the first four paragraphs. We expect a writer at
least to let us know where his scenes are set, but Seilsopour leaps back and
forth from Iran to America in ways that leave us repeatedly uncertain about
where we are. Seilsopour re-creates the experience he has had: he thought he
was an American when he was in Iran, but he discovers he must be an Iranian
when he is in America. He has learned to live warily, in suspense, waiting for
revelations that things are not as they seem. He has developed a form for his
essay that puts us in that same frame of mind. He jumps from one kind of
langue to another, and from one scene to another, because his essay is about
how he has been jarred out of the comfortable worlds of his childhood, and
he wants to lead his readers through some of his experience, to share the
uncertainty and questioning that led him to write his essay.

Seilsopour carefully limits how long he leaves his readers confused; after the
jarring introductory passages he moves to a clearer style. But the introduction

haunts the rest of the essay; we remain wary, ready for further jarring moments. After the fourth paragraph, we are no longer confused about what is happening, but we are still a bit uncertain about how to react to the tone of the essay. We share in the suffering of Seilsopour's family, but the villains who are so cruel to them seem uncomfortably close to "us," the American readers of this essay. We expect Seilsopour to let us off the hook, to recognize that some parts of America are decent and admirable. However, as the essay comes full circle and returns to the anger and ideals of the opening, Seilsopour seems to want to deflect that anger onto the most sacred of American institutions; he seems to be saying, in a polite way, "Piss on America."

This essay demonstrates several ways to raise questions in our readers' minds as well as some ways to break free of our readers' expectations. Jarring, surprising introductions and suspense are often thought of as simply tricks to capture readers' attention, ways of making essays entertaining. They can do much more than that in an essay whose purpose is to make its readers suspend their conventional judgments. If you want to present an unconventional view of something—of school, of parents, of America—you might find it useful to shock or even confuse your readers a bit in the beginning of the essay, to make them ask questions that you can slowly answer in ways they would not anticipate. If you feel limited by the assumptions your readers are apt to make about you (for example, that you are a typical student writing a typical college paper), then you can attack those assumptions by violating some of the rules of "proper" essay decorum. Or if you want to write about surprising twists that have occurred in your life, you might make your readers share your surprise.

Of course, you take a risk by disorienting your readers—the risk that they will dismiss the essay as a confusing mess and will not bother reading far enough to see that the confusion is cleared up. Writers have to know how far they can stretch their suspense, how long they can leave the reader in doubt about something. A surprising, suspenseful essay usually has to be tested on readers, to see if the essay delays too long clearing up the mysteries it creates.

The next selection presents an example of a longer and more complex introduction designed to disrupt readers' expectations: the prologue to Richard Rodriguez's autobiography, *Hunger of Memory*. Rodriguez is concerned that his readers will come to his book with many assumptions because before writing it he had gained fame as a Hispanic American who opposed bilingual education and affirmative action. Because he wants to disrupt his readers' assumptions, Rodriguez's introduction is, like Seilsopour's essay, full of surprises and sudden jumps. We have reprinted part of the first chapter of his book as well as his prologue, so you can see how different the prologue is from the autobiography itself.

ANOTHER ILLUSTRATION OF THE TECHNIQUE

RICHARD RODRIGUEZ
Hunger of Memory

Richard Rodriguez was raised in San Francisco and Sacramento, California, the son of working-class Mexican immigrant parents. He entered school barely able to speak English and twenty years later completed a doctoral dissertation on English Renaissance literature at the University of California, Berkeley. He wrote his autobiography, Hunger of Memory, *to describe his transformation; Rodriguez calls the book a "meditation on education—the way it shaped me into a very public man, an American of the middle class." He derives political conclusions from his experience: he is irrevocably opposed to bilingual education and affirmative action programs.*

Rodriguez's controversial conclusions have drawn most of the attention given his book. But the book is much more than a political tract. Richard Rodriguez says that he sees himself "straddling two worlds of writing: journalism and literature. There is Richard Rodriguez, the journalist—every day I spend more time reading newspapers and magazines than I do reading novels and poetry. I wander away from my desk for hours, for weeks. I want to ask questions of the stranger on the bus. I want to consider the political and social issues of the day.

"Then there is Richard Rodriguez, the writer. It takes me a very long time to write. What I try to do when I write is break down the line separating the prosaic world from the poetic word. I try to write about everyday concerns—an educational issue, say, or the problems of the unemployed—but to write about them as powerfully, as richly, as well as I can."

Prologue: Middle-Class Pastoral

I have taken Caliban's advice. I have stolen their books. I will have some 1
run of this isle.

Once upon a time, I was a "socially disadvantaged" child. An enchantedly 2
happy child. Mine was a childhood of intense family closeness. And extreme
public alienation.

Thirty years later I write this book as a middle-class American man. Assim- 3
ilated.

Dark-skinned. To be seen at a Belgravia dinner party. Or in New York. 4
Exotic in a tuxedo. My face is drawn to severe Indian features which would
pass notice on the page of a *National Geographic*, but at a cocktail party in Bel

Air somebody wonders: "Have you ever thought of doing any high-fashion modeling? Take this card." (In Beverly Hills will this monster make a man.)

A lady in a green dress asks, "Didn't we meet at the Thompsons' party last 5 month in Malibu?"

And, "What do you do, Mr. Rodriguez?" 6

I write: I am a writer. 7

A part-time writer. When I began this book, five years ago, a fellowship 8 bought me a year of continuous silence in my San Francisco apartment. But the words wouldn't come. The money ran out. So I was forced to take temporary jobs. (I have friends who, with a phone call, can find me well-paying work.) In past months I have found myself in New York. In Los Angeles. Working. With money. Among people with money. And at leisure—a weekend guest in Connecticut; at a cocktail party in Bel Air.

Perhaps because I have always, accidentally, been a classmate to children 9 of rich parents, I long ago came to assume my association with their world; came to assume that I could have money, if it was money I wanted. But money, big money, has never been the goal of my life. My story is not a version of Sammy Glick's.* I work to support my habit of writing. The great luxury of my life is the freedom to sit at this desk.

"Mr.? . . . " 10

Rodriguez. The name on the door. The name on my passport. The name I 11 carry from my parents—who are no longer my parents, in a cultural sense. This is how I pronounce it: *Rich-heard Road-ree-guess.* This is how I hear it most often.

The voice through a microphone says, "Ladies and gentlemen, it is with 12 pleasure that I introduce Mr. Richard Rodriguez."

I am invited very often these days to speak about modern education in 13 college auditoriums and in Holiday Inn ballrooms. I go, still feel a calling to act the teacher, though not licensed by the degree. One time my audience is a convention of university administrators; another time high school teachers of English; another time a women's alumnae group.

"Mr. Rodriguez has written extensively about contemporary education." 14

Several essays. I have argued particularly against two government programs— 15 affirmative action and bilingual education.

"He is a provocative speaker." 16

I have become notorious among certain leaders of America's Ethnic Left. I 17 am considered a dupe, an ass, the fool—Tom Brown, the brown Uncle Tom, interpreting the writing on the wall to a bunch of cigar-smoking pharaohs.

---

*Title character in the novel and Broadway play *What Makes Sammy Run?* Sammy runs on greed and power in the fast-paced life of Hollywood.

A dainty white lady at the women's club luncheon approaches the podium 18
after my speech to say, after all, wasn't it a shame that I wasn't able to "use"
my Spanish in school. What a shame. But how dare her lady-fingered pieties
extend to my life!

There are those in White America who would anoint me to play out for 19
them some drama of ancestral reconciliation. Perhaps because I am marked by
indelible color they easily suppose that I am unchanged by social mobility,
that I can claim unbroken ties with my past. The possibility! At a time when
many middle-class children and parents grow distant, apart, no longer speak,
romantic solutions appeal.

But I reject the role. (Caliban won't ferry a TV crew back to his island, 20
there to recover his roots.)

Aztec ruins hold no special interest for me. I do not search Mexican grave- 21
yards for ties to unnamable ancestors. I assume I retain certain features of
gesture and mood derived from buried lives. I also speak Spanish today. And
read García Lorca and García Márquez at my leisure. But what consolation
can that fact bring against the knowledge that my mother and father have
never heard of García Lorca or García Márquez? What preoccupies me is immediate: the separation I endure with my parents in loss. This is what matters
to me: the story of the scholarship boy who returns home one summer from
college to discover bewildering silence, facing his parents. This is my story.
An American story.

Consider me, if you choose, a comic victim of two cultures. This is my 22
situation: writing these pages, surrounded in the room I am in by volumes of
Montaigne and Shakespeare and Lawrence. They are mine now.

A Mexican woman passes in a black dress. She wears a white apron; she 23
carries a tray of hors d'oeuvres. She must only be asking if there are any I want
as she proffers the tray like a wheel of good fortune. I shake my head. No.
Does she wonder how I am here? In Bel Air.

It is education that has altered my life. Carried me far.   24

I write this autobiography as the history of my schooling. To admit the 25
change in my life I must speak of years as a student, of losses, of gains.

I consider my book a kind of pastoral. I write in the tradition of that high, 26
courtly genre. But I am no upper-class pastoral singer. Upper-class pastoral can
admit envy for the intimate pleasures of rustic life as an arrogant way of reminding its listeners of their difference—their own public power and civic
position. ("Let's be shepherds . . . Ah, if only we could.") Unlike the upper
class, the middle class lives in a public world, lacking great individual power
and standing. Middle-class pastoral is, therefore, a more difficult hymn. There
is no grand compensation to the admission of envy of the poor. The middle

class rather is tempted by the pastoral impulse to deny its difference from the lower class—even to attempt cheap imitations of lower-class life. ("But I still *am* a shepherd!")

I must resist being tempted by this decadent solution to mass public life. It 27 seems to me dangerous, because in trying to imitate the lower class, the middle class blurs the distinction so crucial to social reform. One can no longer easily say what exactly distinguishes the alien poor.

I do not write as a modern-day Wordsworth seeking to imitate the inti- 28 mate speech of the poor. I sing Ariel's song to celebrate the intimate speech my family once freely exchanged. In singing the praise of my lower-class past, I remind myself of my separation from that past, bring memory to si- lence. I turn to consider the boy I once was in order, finally, to describe the man I am now. I remember what was so grievously lost to define what was necessarily gained.

But the New York editor is on the phone and he can't understand: "Why 29 do you spend so much time on abstract issues? Nobody's going to remember affirmative action in another twenty-five years. The strength of this manu- script is in the narrative. You should write your book in stories—not as a series of essays. Let's have more Grandma."

But no. Here is my most real life. My book is necessarily political, in the 30 conventional sense, for public issues—editorials and ballot stubs, petitions and placards, faceless formulations of greater and lesser good by greater and lesser minds—have bisected my life and changed its course. And, in some broad sense, my writing is political because it concerns my movement away from the company of family and into the city. This was my coming of age: I became a man by becoming a public man.

This autobiography, moreover, is a book about language. I write about 31 poetry; the new Roman Catholic liturgy; learning to read; writing; political terminology. Language has been the great subject of my life. In college and graduate school, I was registered as an "English major." But well before then, from my first day of school, I was a student of language. Obsessed by the way it determined my public identity. The way it permits me here to describe myself, writing . . .

Writing this manuscript. Essays impersonating an autobiography; six chap- 32 ters of sad, fuguelike repetition.

Now it exists—a weight in my hand. Let the bookstore clerk puzzle over 33 where it should be placed. (Rodriguez? Rodriguez?) Probably he will shelve it alongside specimens of that exotic new genre, "ethnic literature." Mistaken, the gullible reader will—in sympathy or in anger—take it that I intend to model my life as the typical Hispanic-American life.

But I write of one life only. My own. If my story is true, I trust it will 34
resonate with significance for other lives. Finally, my history deserves public
notice as no more than this: a parable for the life of its reader. Here is the
life of a middle-class man.

Chapter One: Aria

1

I remember to start with that day in Sacramento—a California now nearly 1
thirty years past—when I first entered a classroom, able to understand some
fifty stray English words.

The third of four children, I had been preceded to a neighborhood Roman 2
Catholic school by an older brother and sister. But neither of them had revealed very much about their classroom experiences. Each afternoon they returned, as they left in the morning, always together, speaking in Spanish as
they climbed the five steps of the porch. And their mysterious books, wrapped
in shopping-bag paper, remained on the table next to the door, closed firmly
behind them.

An accident of geography sent me to a school where all my classmates were 3
white, many the children of doctors and lawyers and business executives. All
my classmates certainly must have been uneasy on that first day of school—as
most children are uneasy—to find themselves apart from their families in the
first institution of their lives. But I was astonished.

The nun said, in a friendly but oddly impersonal voice, "Boys and girls, this 4
is Richard Rodriguez." (I heard her sound out: *Rich-heard Road-ree-guess.*) It
was the first time I had heard anyone name me in English. "Richard," the nun
repeated more slowly, writing my name down in her black leather book.
Quickly I turned to see my mother's face dissolve in a watery blur behind the
pebbled glass door.

Many years later there is something called bilingual education—a scheme 5
proposed in the late 1960s by Hispanic-American social activists, later endorsed by a congressional vote. It is a program that seeks to permit non-English-
speaking children, many from lower-class homes, to use their family language
as the language of school. (Such is the goal its supporters announce.) I hear
them and am forced to say no: It is not possible for a child—any child—ever
to use his family's language in school. Not to understand this is to misunder-
stand the public uses of schooling and to trivialize the nature of intimate life—
a family's "language."

Memory teaches me what I know of these matters; the boy reminds the 6
adult. I was a bilingual child, a certain kind—socially disadvantaged—the son
of working-class parents, both Mexican immigrants.

In the early years of my boyhood, my parents coped very well in America. 7
My father had steady work. My mother managed at home. They were nobody's
victims. Optimism and ambition led them to a house (our home) many blocks
from the Mexican south side of town. We lived among *gringos* and only a block
from the biggest, whitest houses. It never occurred to my parents that they
couldn't live wherever they chose. Nor was the Sacramento of the fifties bent
on teaching them a contrary lesson. My mother and father were more annoyed
than intimidated by those two or three neighbors who tried initially to make
us unwelcome. ("Keep your brats away from my sidewalk!") But despite all
they achieved, perhaps because they had so much to achieve, any deep feeling
of ease, the confidence of "belonging" in public was withheld from them both.
They regarded the people at work, the faces in crowds, as very distant from
us. They were the others, *los gringos*. That term was interchangeable in their
speech with another, even more telling, *los americanos.*

I grew up in a house where the only regular guests were my relations. For 8
one day, enormous families of relatives would visit and there would be so many
people that the noise and the bodies would spill out to the backyard and front
porch. Then, for weeks, no one came by. (It was usually a salesman who rang
the doorbell.) Our house stood apart. A gaudy yellow in a row of white bun-
galows. We were the people with the noisy dog. The people who raised pigeons
and chickens. We were the foreigners on the block. A few neighbors smiled
and waved. We waved back. But no one in the family knew the names of the
old couple who lived next door; until I was seven years old, I did not know
the names of the kids who lived across the street.

In public, my father and mother spoke a hesitant, accented, not always 9
grammatical English. And they would have to strain—their bodies tense—to
catch the sense of what was rapidly said by *los gringos*. At home they spoke
Spanish. The language of their Mexican past sounded in counterpoint to the
English of public society. The words would come quickly, with ease. Conveyed
through those sounds was the pleasing, soothing, consoling reminder of being
at home.

During those years when I was first conscious of hearing, my mother and 10
father addressed me only in Spanish; in Spanish I learned to reply. By contrast,
English (*inglés*), rarely heard in the house, was the language I came to associate
with *gringos*. I learned my first words of English overhearing my parents speak
to strangers. At five years of age, I knew just enough English for my mother
to trust me on errands to stores one block away. No more.

I was a listening child, careful to hear the very different sounds of Spanish 11
and English. Wide-eyed with hearing, I'd listen to sounds more than words.
First, there were English (*gringo*) sounds. So many words were still unknown
that when the butcher or the lady at the drugstore said something to me,
exotic polysyllabic sounds would bloom in the midst of their sentences. Often,
the speech of people in public seemed to me very loud, booming with confidence. The man behind the counter would literally ask, "What can I do for
you?" But by being so firm and so clear, the sound of his voice said that he
was a *gringo;* he belonged in public society.

I would also hear then the high nasal notes of middle-class American speech. 12
The air stirred with sound. Sometimes, even now, when I have been traveling
abroad for several weeks, I will hear what I heard as a boy. In hotel lobbies or
airports, in Turkey or Brazil, some Americans will pass, and suddenly I will
hear it again—the high sound of American voices. For a few seconds I will
hear it with pleasure, for it is now the sound of *my* society—a reminder of
home. But inevitably—already on the flight headed for home—the sound fades
with repetition. I will be unable to hear it anymore.

When I was a boy, things were different. The accent of *los gringos* was never 13
pleasing nor was it hard to hear. Crowds at Safeway or at bus stops would be
noisy with sound. And I would be forced to edge away from the chirping chatter
above me.

I was unable to hear my own sounds, but I knew very well that I spoke 14
English poorly. My words could not stretch far enough to form complete
thoughts. And the words I did speak I didn't know well enough to make into
distinct sounds. (Listeners would usually lower their heads, better to hear what
I was trying to say.) But it was one thing for *me* to speak English with difficulty.
It was more troubling for me to hear my parents speak in public; their high-
whining vowels and guttural consonants; their sentences that got stuck with
"eh" and "ah" sounds; the confused syntax; the hesitant rhythm of sounds so
different from the way *gringos* spoke. I'd notice, moreover, that my parents'
voices were softer than those of *gringos* we'd meet.

I am tempted now to say that none of this mattered. In adulthood I am 15
embarrassed by childhood fears. And, in a way, it didn't matter very much
that my parents could not speak English with ease. Their linguistic difficulties
had no serious consequences. My mother and father made themselves understood at the county hospital clinic and at government offices. And yet, in
another way, it mattered very much—it was unsettling to hear my parents
struggle with English. Hearing them, I'd grow nervous, my clutching trust in
their protection and power weakened.

There were many times like the night at a brightly lit gasoline station (a 16 blaring white memory) when I stood uneasily, hearing my father. He was talking to a teenaged attendant. I do not recall what they were saying, but I cannot forget the sounds my father made as he spoke. At one point his words slid together to form one word—sounds as confused as the threads of blue and green oil in the puddle next to my shoes. His voice rushed through what he had left to say. And, toward the end, reached falsetto notes, appealing to his listener's understanding. I looked away to the lights of passing automobiles. I tried not to hear anymore. But I heard only too well the calm, easy tones in the attendant's reply. Shortly afterward, walking toward home with my father, I shivered when he put his hand on my shoulder. The very first chance that I got, I evaded his grasp and ran on ahead into the dark, skipping with feigned boyish exuberance.

But then there was Spanish. *Español:* my family's language. *Español:* the 17 language that seemed to me a private language. I'd hear strangers on the radio and in the Mexican Catholic church across town speaking in Spanish, but I couldn't really believe that Spanish was a public language, like English. Spanish speakers, rather, seemed related to me, for I sensed that we shared— through our language—the experience of feeling apart from *los gringos*. It was thus a ghetto Spanish that I heard and I spoke. Like those whose lives are bound by a barrio, I was reminded by Spanish of my separateness from *los otros, los gringos* in power. But more intensely than for most barrio children—because I did not live in a barrio—Spanish seemed to me the language of home. (Most days it was only at home that I'd hear it.) It became the language of joyful return.

A family member would say something to me and I would feel myself spe- 18 cially recognized. My parents would say something to me and I would feel embraced by the sounds of their words. Those sounds said: *I am speaking with ease in Spanish. I am addressing you in words I never use with* los gringos. *I recognize you as someone special, close, like no one outside. You belong with us. In the family.*

(*Ricardo.*)   19

At the age of five, six, well past the time when most other children no 20 longer easily notice the difference between sounds uttered at home and words spoken in public, I had a different experience. I lived in a world magically compounded of sounds. I remained a child longer than most; I lingered too long, poised at the edge of language—often frightened by the sounds of *los gringos*, delighted by the sounds of Spanish at home. I shared with my family a language that was startlingly different from that used in the great city around us.

For me there were none of the gradations between public and private society 21
so normal to a maturing child. Outside the house was public society; inside
the house was private. Just opening or closing the screen door behind me was
an important experience. I'd rarely leave home all alone or without reluctance.
Walking down the sidewalk, under the canopy of tall trees, I'd warily notice
the—suddenly—silent neighborhood kids who stood warily watching me.
Nervously, I'd arrive at the grocery store to hear there the sounds of the *gringo*—foreign to me—reminding me that in this world so big, I was a foreigner.
But then I'd return. Walking back toward our house, climbing the steps from
the sidewalk, when the front door was open in summer, I'd hear voices beyond
the screen door talking in Spanish. For a second or two, I'd stay, linger there,
listening. Smiling, I'd hear my mother call out, saying in Spanish (words): "Is
that you, Richard?" All the while her sounds would assure me: *You are home
now; come closer; inside. With us.*

"*Sí,*" I'd reply.   22

Once more inside the house I would resume (assume) my place in the family. 23
The sounds would dim, grow harder to hear. Once more at home, I would
grow less aware of that fact. It required, however, no more than the blurt of
the doorbell to alert me to listen to sounds all over again. The house would
turn instantly still while my mother went to the door. I'd hear her hard English
sounds. I'd wait to hear her voice return to soft-sounding Spanish, which
assured me, as surely as did the clicking tongue of the lock on the door, that
the stranger was gone.

Plainly, it is not healthy to hear such sounds so often. It is not healthy to 24
distinguish public words from private sounds so easily. I remained cloistered
by sounds, timid and shy in public, too dependent on voices at home. And
yet it needs to be emphasized: I was an extremely happy child at home. I
remember many nights when my father would come back from work, and I'd
hear him call out to my mother in Spanish, sounding relieved. In Spanish,
he'd sound light and free notes he never could manage in English. Some nights
I'd jump up just at hearing his voice. With *mis hermanos* I would come running
into the room where he was with my mother. Our laughing (so deep was the
pleasure!) became screaming. Like others who know the pain of public alienation, we transformed the knowledge of our public separateness and made it
consoling—the reminder of intimacy. Excited, we joined our voices in a celebration of sounds. *We are speaking now the way we never speak out in public. We
are alone—together,* voices sounded, surrounded to tell me. Some nights, no
one seemed willing to loosen the hold sounds had on us. At dinner, we invented new words. (Ours sounded Spanish, but made sense only to us.) We
pieced together new words by taking, say, an English verb and giving it Spanish

endings. My mother's instructions at bedtime would be lacquered with mock-urgent tones. Or a word like *sí* would become, in several notes, able to convey added measures of feeling. Tongues explored the edges of words, especially the fat vowels. And we happily sounded that military drum roll, the twirling roar of the Spanish *r*. Family language: my family's sounds. The voices of my parents and sisters and brother. Their voices insisting: *You belong here. We are family members. Related. Special to one another. Listen!* Voices singing and sighing, rising, straining, then surging, teeming with pleasure that burst syllables into fragments of laughter. At times it seemed there was steady quiet only when, from another room, the rustling whispers of my parents faded and I moved closer to sleep.

2

Supporters of bilingual education today imply that students like me miss a 25 great deal by not being taught in their family's language. What they seem not to recognize is that, as a socially disadvantaged child, I considered Spanish to be a private language. What I needed to learn in school was that I had the right—and the obligation—to speak the public language of *los gringos*. The odd truth is that my first-grade classmates could have become bilingual, in the conventional sense of that word, more easily than I. Had they been taught (as upper-middle-class children are often taught early) a second language like Spanish or French, they could have regarded it simply as that: another public language. In my case such bilingualism could not have been so quickly achieved. What I did not believe was that I could speak a single public language.

Without question, it would have pleased me to hear my teachers address 26 me in Spanish when I entered the classroom. I would have felt much less afraid. I would have trusted them and responded with ease. But I would have delayed—for how long postponed?—having to learn the language of public society. I would have evaded—and for how long could I have afforded to delay?—learning the great lesson of school, that I had a public identity.

Fortunately, my teachers were unsentimental about their responsibility. 27 What they understood was that I needed to speak a public language. So their voices would search me out, asking me questions. Each time I'd hear them, I'd look up in surprise to see a nun's face frowning at me. I'd mumble, not really meaning to answer. The nun would persist, "Richard, stand up. Don't look at the floor. Speak up. Speak to the entire class, not just to me!" But I couldn't believe that the English language was mine to use. (In part, I did not want to believe it.) I continued to mumble. I resisted the teacher's demands.

(Did I somehow suspect that once I learned public language my pleasing family life would be changed?) Silent, waiting for the bell to sound, I remained dazed, diffident, afraid.

Because I wrongly imagined that English was intrinsically a public language 28 and Spanish an intrinsically private one, I easily noted the difference between classroom language and the language of home. At school, words were directed to a general audience of listeners. ("Boys and girls.") Words were meaningfully ordered. And the point was not self-expression alone but to make oneself understood by many others. The teacher quizzed: "Boys and girls, why do we use that word in this sentence? Could we think of a better word to use there? Would the sentence change its meaning if the words were differently arranged? And wasn't there a better way of saying much the same thing?" (I couldn't say. I wouldn't try to say.)

Three months. Five. Half a year passed. Unsmiling, ever watchful, my 29 teachers noted my silence. They began to connect my behavior with the difficult progress my older sister and brother were making. Until one Saturday morning three nuns arrived at the house to talk to our parents. Stiffly, they sat on the blue living room sofa. From the doorway of another room, spying the visitors, I noted the incongruity—the clash of two worlds, the faces and voices of school intruding upon the familiar setting of home. I overheard one voice gently wondering, "Do your children speak only Spanish at home, Mrs. Rodriquez?" While another voice added, "That Richard especially seems so timid and shy."

That Rich-heard!   30

With great tact the visitors continued, "Is it possible for you and your 31 husband to encourage your children to practice their English when they are home?" Of course, my parents complied. What would they not do for their children's well-being? And how could they have questioned the Church's authority which those women represented? In an instant, they agreed to give up the language (the sounds) that had revealed and accentuated our family's closeness. The moment after the visitors left, the change was observed. "*Ahora,* speak to us *en inglés,*" my father and mother united to tell us.

At first, it seemed a kind of game. After dinner each night, the family 32 gathered to practice "our" English. (It was still then *inglés,* a language foreign to us, so we felt drawn as strangers to it.) Laughing, we would try to define words we could not pronounce. We played with strange English sounds, often overanglicizing our pronunciations. And we filled the smiling gaps of our sentences with familiar Spanish sounds. But that was cheating, somebody shouted. Everyone laughed. In school, meanwhile, like my brother and sister, I was required to attend a daily tutoring session. I needed a full year of special attention. I also needed my teachers to keep my attention from straying in class by calling out, *Rich-heard*—their English voices slowly prying loose my ties to my other name, its three notes, *Ri-car-do*. Most of all I needed to hear my mother and father speak to me in a moment of seriousness in broken— suddenly heartbreaking—English. The scene was inevitable: One Saturday morning I entered the kitchen where my parents were talking in Spanish. I did not realize that they were talking in Spanish however until, at the moment they saw me, I heard their voices change to speak English. Those *gringo* sounds they uttered startled me. Pushed me away. In that moment of trivial misunderstanding and profound insight, I felt my throat twisted by unsounded grief. I turned quickly and left the room. But I had no place to escape to with Spanish. (The spell was broken.) My brother and sisters were speaking English in another part of the house.

Again and again in the days following, increasingly angry, I was obliged to 33 hear my mother and father: "Speak to us *en inglés*." (*Speak*.) Only then did I determine to learn classroom English. Weeks after, it happened: One day in school I raised my hand to volunteer an answer. I spoke out in a loud voice. And I did not think it remarkable when the entire class understood. That day, I moved very far from the disadvantaged child I had been only days earlier. The belief, the calming reassurance that I belonged in public, had at last taken hold.

Shortly after, I stopped hearing the high and loud sounds of *los gringos*. A 34 more and more confident speaker of English, I didn't trouble to listen to *how* strangers sounded, speaking to me. And there simply were too many English-speaking people in my day for me to hear American accents anymore. Conversations quickened. Listening to persons who sounded eccentrically pitched voices, I usually noted their sounds for an initial few seconds before I concentrated on *what* they were saying. Conversations became content-full. Transparent. Hearing someone's *tone* of voice—angry or questioning or sarcastic or happy or sad—I didn't distinguish it from the words it expressed. Sound and word were thus tightly wedded. At the end of a day, I was often bemused, always relieved, to realize how "silent," though crowded with words, my day in public had been. (This public silence measured and quickened the change in my life.)

At last, seven years old, I came to believe what had been technically true 35 since my birth: I was an American citizen.

But the special feeling of closeness at home was diminished by then. Gone 36 was the desperate, urgent, intense feeling of being at home; rare was the experience of feeling myself individualized by family intimates. We remained a loving family, but one greatly changed. No longer so close; no longer bound tight by the pleasing and troubling knowledge of our public separateness. Neither my older brother nor sister rushed home after school anymore. Nor did I. When I arrived home there would often be neighborhood kids in the house. Or the house would be empty of sounds.

Following the dramatic Americanization of their children, even my parents 37 grew more publicly confident. Especially my mother. She learned the names of all the people on our block. And she decided we needed to have a telephone installed in the house. My father continued to use the word *gringo*. But it was no longer charged with the old bitterness or distrust. (Stripped of any emotional content, the word simply became a name for those Americans not of Hispanic descent.) Hearing him, sometimes, I wasn't sure if he was pronouncing the Spanish word *gringo* or saying gringo in English.

Matching the silence I started hearing in public was a new quiet at home. 38 The family's quiet was partly due to the fact that, as we children learned more and more English, we shared fewer and fewer words with our parents. Sentences needed to be spoken slowly when a child addressed his mother or father. (Often the parent wouldn't understand.) The child would need to repeat himself. (Still the parent misunderstood.) The young voice, frustrated, would end up saying, "Never mind"—the subject was closed. Dinners would be noisy with the clinking of knives and forks against dishes. My mother would smile softly between her remarks; my father at the other end of the table would chew and chew at his food, while he stared over the heads of his children.

My *mother!* My *father!* After English became my primary language, I no 39 longer knew what words to use in addressing my parents. The old Spanish words (those tender accents of sound) I had used earlier—*mamá* and *papá*—I couldn't use anymore. They would have been too painful reminders of how much had changed in my life. On the other hand, the words I heard neighborhood kids call *their* parents seemed equally unsatisfactory. *Mother* and *Father*; *Ma, Papa, Pa, Dad, Pop* (how I hated the all-American sound of that last word especially)—all these terms I felt were unsuitable, not really terms of address for *my* parents. As a result, I never used them at home. Whenever I'd speak to my parents, I would try to get their attention with eye contact alone. In public conversations, I'd refer to "my parents" or "my mother and father."

My mother and father, for their part, responded differently, as their children 40 spoke to them less. She grew restless, seemed troubled and anxious at the scarcity of words exchanged in the house. It was she who would question me about my day when I came home from school. She smiled at small talk. She pried at the edges of my sentences to get me to say something more. (What?) She'd join conversations she overheard, but her intrusions often stopped her children's talking. By contrast, my father seemed reconciled to the new quiet.

Though his English improved somewhat, he retired into silence. At dinner he spoke very little. One night his children and even his wife helplessly giggled at his garbled English pronunciation of the Catholic Grace before Meals. Thereafter he made his wife recite the prayer at the start of each meal, even on formal occasions, when there were guests in the house. Hers became the public voice of the family. On official business, it was she, not my father, one would usually hear on the phone or in stores, talking to strangers. His children grew so accustomed to his silence that, years later, they would speak routinely of his shyness. (My mother would often try to explain: Both his parents died when he was eight. He was raised by an uncle who treated him like little more than a menial servant. He was never encouraged to speak. He grew up alone. A man of few words.) But my father was not shy, I realized, when I'd watch him speaking Spanish with relatives. Using Spanish, he was quickly effusive. Especially when talking with other men, his voice would spark, flicker, flare alive with sounds. In Spanish, he expressed ideas and feelings he rarely revealed in English. With firm Spanish sounds, he conveyed confidence and authority English would never allow him.

The silence at home, however, was finally more than a literal silence. Fewer 41 words passed between parent and child, but more profound was the silence that resulted from any inattention to sound. At about the time I no longer bothered to listen with care to the sounds of English in public, I grew careless about listening to the sounds family members made when they spoke. Most of the time I heard someone speaking at home and didn't distinguish his sounds from the words people uttered in public. I didn't even pay much attention to my parents' accented and ungrammatical speech. At least not at home. Only when I was with them in public would I grow alert to their accents. Though, even then, their sounds caused me less and less concern. For I was increasingly confident of my own public identity.

I would have been happier about my public success had I not sometimes 42 recalled what it had been like earlier, when my family had conveyed its intimacy through a set of conveniently private sounds. Sometimes in public, hearing a stranger, I'd hark back to my past. A Mexican farmworker approached me downtown to ask directions to somewhere. "*¿Hijito . . . ?*" he said. And his voice summoned deep longing. Another time, standing beside my mother in the visiting room of a Carmelite convent, before the dense screen which rendered the nuns shadowy figures, I heard several Spanish-speaking nuns— their busy, singsong overlapping voices—assure us that yes, yes, we were remembered, all our family was remembered in their prayers. (Their voices echoed faraway family sounds.) Another day, a dark-faced old woman—her hand light on my shoulder—steadied herself against me as she boarded a bus.

She murmured something I couldn't quite comprehend. Her Spanish voice came near, like the face of a never-before-seen relative in the instant before I was kissed. Her voice, like so many of the Spanish voices I'd hear in public, recalled the golden age of my youth. Hearing Spanish then, I continued to be a careful, if sad, listener to sounds. Hearing a Spanish-speaking family walking behind me, I turned to look. I smiled for an instant, before my glance found the Hispanic-looking faces of strangers in the crowd going by.

Today I hear bilingual educators say that children lose a degree of "individ- 43 uality" by becoming assimilated into public society. (Bilingual schooling was popularized in the seventies, that decade when middle-class ethnics began to resist the process of assimilation—the American melting pot.) But the bilingualists simplistically scorn the value and necessity of assimilation. They do not seem to realize that there are *two* ways a person is individualized. So they do not realize that while one suffers a diminished sense of *private* individuality by becoming assimilated into public society, such assimilation makes possible the achievement of *public* individuality.

The bilingualists insist that a student should be reminded of his difference 44 from others in mass society, his heritage. But they equate mere separateness with individuality. The fact is that only in private—with intimates—is separateness from the crowd a prerequisite for individuality. (An intimate draws me apart, tells me that I am unique, unlike all others.) In public, by contrast, full individuality is achieved, paradoxically, by those who are able to consider themselves members of the crowd. Thus it happened for me: Only when I was able to think of myself as an American, no longer an alien in *gringo* society, could I seek the rights and opportunities necessary for full public individuality. The social and political advantages I enjoy as a man result from the day that I came to believe that my name, indeed, is *Rich-heard Road-ree-guess*. It is true that my public society today is often impersonal. (My public society is usually mass society.) Yet despite the anonymity of the crowd and despite the fact that the individuality I achieve in public is often tenuous—because it depends on my being one in the crowd—I celebrate the day I acquired my new name. Those middle-class ethnics who scorn assimilation seem to me filled with decadent self-pity, obsessed by the burden of public life. Dangerously, they romanticize public separateness and they trivialize the dilemma of the socially disadvantaged.

My awkward childhood does not prove the necessity of bilingual education. 45 My story discloses instead an essential myth of childhood—inevitable pain. If I rehearse here the changes in my private life after my Americanization, it is finally to emphasize the public gain. The loss implies the gain: The house I returned to each afternoon was quiet. Intimate sounds no longer rushed to the door to greet me. There were other noises inside. The telephone rang. Neighborhood kids ran past the door of the bedroom where I was reading my schoolbooks—covered with shopping-bag paper. Once I learned public language, it would never again be easy for me to hear intimate family voices. More and more of my day was spent hearing words. But that may only be a way of saying that the day I raised my hand in class and spoke loudly to an entire roomful of faces, my childhood started to end.

Focusing on Richard Rodriguez's Use of a Surprising Opening

1. The first fifteen paragraphs of the prologue cite many images that people have of Rodriguez and expectations they have of his writing. What do the people at the party mentioned in paragraphs 4 and 5 think of him? What kind of book do the quotations in paragraphs 9–16 imply he will write? What do the people in "White America" (paragraph 19) want him to write? How does his editor want him to write his book (paragraph 29)? How does Rodriguez respond to all these expectations? What is the effect of spending so much of the prologue discussing what people expect of him and of his book?

2. Rodriguez switches from one kind of language to another in the first few sentences. In the first sentence, Rodriguez refers to Caliban, a character in Shakespeare's play *The Tempest*. What expectations about the rest of the book and about Rodriguez as a writer are created by his starting with allusions to Shakespeare? In the third sentence, Rodriguez uses the phrase "once upon a time." What kind of book does this phrase come from? What kind of book would speak of "socially disadvantaged" children? What is the effect of Rodriguez's shifting *diction*—word choice—in these first few sentences?

3. Caliban is half man, half monster, living on an island under the control of a magician, Prospero. Caliban repeatedly tries to steal Prospero's books to free himself and to rule the island. What does Rodriguez seem to be saying by comparing himself to Caliban in paragraphs 1 and 20? At the end of the prologue, what questions are left in your mind about how Rodriguez is like Caliban? How does Chapter One, "Aria," help explain the Caliban quote that begins the prologue—what books do we see Rodriguez "stealing" in this chapter and from whom? Why would a writer begin his prologue with sentences that do not become fully understandable until a chapter later?

4. Rodriguez writes in very short paragraphs in the prologue, and he sometimes jumps from one scene to another quite abruptly. What is the effect of this lack of transitions? How would the effect of the prologue be different if it moved more smoothly? He also uses some rather short sentences (including sentence fragments) and disrupts his sentences with frequent parentheses. He continues

using this style in Chapter One. How does this style reflect his life, as he describes it in the prologue?

5. You probably found the first chapter much easier to read than the prologue, and much more like an autobiography. Rodriguez actually wrote and published that chapter before he wrote the prologue. Why would Rodriguez want to add a confusing prologue to fairly clear chapters?

6. Rodriguez said in a recent interview that he feels he is "straddling two worlds of writing: journalism and literature," that he wants to "break down the line separating the prosaic world from the poetic word." Several elements in the prologue point to his desire to mix literature and journalism in this book. He says in paragraph 26, for example, that he considers his book "a kind of pastoral." A pastoral is a poem or song written by a person in a royal court praising the life of poor shepherds. Rodriguez says that he is a middle-class man who is "singing the praise of my lower-class past" (paragraph 28). How does calling this book a poem or a song clash with our expectations of an autobiography? What features of Rodriguez's writing, in the prologue or in Chapter One, seem "poetic"? The first chapter is titled "Aria"; an aria is a song in an opera. In what ways is the first chapter like a song? Later in the book, Rodriguez says that when a person sings, he can break out of "public language" and reveal private, intimate feelings such as love. How do these comments on song help explain why Rodriguez names his chapter "Aria"?

WORKING WITH THE TECHNIQUE IN YOUR OWN WRITING

1. Write an essay about a time in your life when you were shocked or surprised by the behavior of people you thought you knew well. Or write about some institution or group (school, family, a sports team, a hospital) that did not live up to your expectations. You might try to re-create for your readers some of the disorientation you experienced by using a suprising opening.

2. Seilsopour and Rodriguez are angry that people react to them according to false images and assumptions. Write an essay about the false assumptions others have of you that have made you angry or irritated. You might even want to challenge the assumptions your readers would be likely to have about you based on their knowledge that you are a college student writing an esay for a college class. Use a surprising or disorienting opening in your essay to lead into your topic about false assumptions and expectations.

3. Write an essay presenting an unconventional view: you might demonstrate the negative effects on people of something that is conventionally assumed to be good (such as American democracy, a first-rate education, or a happy family) or you might demonstrate the positive effects of something that is conventionally assumed to be negative (such as having a family that argues all the time or being below average). Try to disrupt your readers' expectations about this subject by using a surprising opening.

PAULA SISLER

Kings River Community College
Reedley, California
David Borofka, instructor

Paula Sisler describes herself as a woman with a multifaceted identity and a hectic schedule: "I am a homemaker and wife, a college student, a writer, a piano student, a Sunday school teacher, and editor of the church newsletter. I play volleyball in two different leagues. My children play soccer and football, and I am a chauffeur to their various practices and games. Yet I find time to read. I have an extensive library of over 2,000 books. . . . My mailman hates me because of the extensive list of magazine subscriptions I receive: The New Yorker, Esquire, Harper's, the Atlantic, Omni, Good Housekeeping, Redbook, McCall's, the Ensign, Discover, the Writer's Market, Vanity Fair, Saturday Evening Post, Reader's Digest, Organic Gardening. (No, I don't find time to do much gardening—but I think about it a lot.) I don't require very much sleep."

Given the circumstances of her childhood, it is not surprising to hear that reading continues to occupy so much of her attention. She reports that in the household in which she grew up "there was only one way to get to stay up any later than 7:30 in the evening— summer included—and that was by reading. I can remember having a book in my hand as early as kindergarten, but my memories of enjoying my reading start around the third grade. By the fourth grade, unbeknownst to my mother, I would read with a flashlight under my covers until as late as 2:00 A.M. During the summers, the school librarian would fill a box for me, of books she had selected—sometimes as many as fifteen books— to be returned the following Wednesday. I read from the time I finished my chores in the morning until I fell asleep, finishing one or two books a day. One of my most miserable memories is having the twelve-day measles, lying in a darkened room with nothing to read."

Sisler regards reading as essential to writing. "Reading shows a person—especially an aspiring writer—how to break down an event and analyze it. It gives the reader the opportunity to compare the experiences found on the pages of books with the personal experiences and observations of his own life. The adversities of life, whether childhood, bad marriages, difficulty raising children, getting fired from a job, etc., give us something to act upon or react to. I've always had the ability to spread life out and examine it, to come to conclusions, to forgive, to push forward." *And, as she reports, she speaks from experience:*

> My childhood was rough. My father was negligent and over time
> my mother became abusive. During my senior year in high
> school, at the age of seventeen, I moved from my parents' home
> into my own apartment. I continued my education, going to
> school from 8:00 A.M. to 11:00 A.M. At 11:00, I went to
> my first job as a clerk in a finance company. I worked until

> 4:00 P.M., at which time I traveled to my second job as a
> cashier in a furniture store. I worked 4:30 to 9:00 P.M. five
> days a week and 9:00 to 5:00 on Saturdays. On Sundays, I
> worked from 6:00 A.M. to 4:00 P.M. as a hostess in a restau-
> rant. When I wasn't working, I did homework. I maintained a
> 3.75 grade point average.

After high school graduation, Sisler married and started a family. Over the next ten years, she and her husband raised four of their own children as well as a total of sixteen foster children who lived with them for varying lengths of time. She also did volunteer work for the Social Services Agency, "teaching new and potential foster parents how to parent these children, what to do in a certain crisis, and to always, always wait just one more day before giving up on a child."

In December 1986, the Sislers relinquished their foster-parent license, and Paula started college part-time, at night. For her first assignment in her first class—a four-to-six page paper "detailing a personal experience in dramatized fashion"—Sisler wrote "The Water Lily." She recalled that "it had to be a personal experience at a specific moment in time and was not to cover days, weeks, or months. . . . Our instructor begged us, for the sake of his 'gag reflex,' not to write about anything on 'meeting our true love or our senior prom.' In other words, write about something interesting." She realized, of course, that her instructor would read her essay but said, "In my mind I could see the faces of my parents as they observed their actions through their daughter's eyes. The goal of my essay was to have the reader experience, as closely as possible, the same feelings I experienced. But instead of a boat and water and angry parents, my only tools were words. With these words, I had to make my reader taste the gasoline and grit, experience the sunburn, remember what the bottom of a lake felt like. And since I was an adult interpreting a childhood memory, I wanted to leave the reader with a taste of wistfulness— for what could have been. My essay reminds people that our actions affect other people's lives."

The Water Lily

"Lily" was not the normal hobby: she was my father's mistress and my mother's source of jealousy. Every day after work, and all day Saturdays and Sundays, my father doted on her, taking her engine apart and putting it back together again, polishing the already-gleaming chrome, dusting the turquoise seats and bathing her pearl sides and top with cool water before buffing her polished finish dry.

My father wasn't the only man in love with The Lily. Arnie, an ex-marine whom my father met in Korea during his tour-of-duty, was my father's best friend. Arnie, a sliver of a man, stood well over six feet. His face, a perpetual shade of red, was crowned with a flattop haircut of the whitest hair imaginable. My father was a perfect opposite of his friend: fifteen pounds overweight, dark complected, and barely reaching five foot ten with his shoes on. But like Arnie, he sported a flattop hair style, his the color of ebony. Arnie practically lived at our house on the weekends, usually bringing his twittering wife Twilah for my mother to entertain, freeing his time to work on his white and turquoise Chevy with the tail fins. The two men enjoyed racing their motors, simultaneously filling the carport with acrid blue smoke and the neighborhood with the echoes of a racecourse.

Christened "The Water Lily," she was not the ordinary kind of boat one buys from the want ads (those boats rarely running the way they're supposed to) or the shiny new floor room model that takes seven years to pay for. This boat was his masterpiece, built piece by piece with loving hands from ordered parts—fiberglass, marine polyurethane, Naugahyde—and every spare cent my mother's and father's combined incomes could spare.

Lily was housed beneath the redwood carport on the side of the house. It was here that the conversations of our household took place, from my three-year-old sister's baby banter and my important six-year-old chatter about what happened in kindergarten that day, as well as my mother's monumental announcements to my preoccupied father who could never be found anywhere else but in the belly of his beloved, plying her with tender loving care. It was here, in the long shadows of weekday dusk or the sweltering heat of a late spring weekend that my mother announced her raise, her pregnancy, and her mother's impending death due to cancer. It was here that her announcements were met with a shrug or a grunt, a rev of the motor, or a request for a tool or a piece of sandpaper.

There was only one thing I could think of that my father loved more than The Lily and that was my mother's beautiful waist-length hair. And on this particular Saturday, late in May while handing tools to my father when he motioned and grunted, I watched my mother get out of her new white Thunderbird without her long, lovely tresses; in their place a bevy of short-cropped curls, fluffed and ratted into the fashion of the day—a "Bubble." Gasping, I dropped the wrench into the hull of the boat, just missing my father's bare toes as I took off to greet my mother and help her carry in the groceries for our trip to the lake that afternoon. He never noticed as we went back and forth with the packages. He never heard us as we talked about her new hairdo and how much cooler it would be in the hot, humid weather we'd had so much of. And she could save time each morning now that she didn't have to pile her hair up into a neat bun for work! I helped her make lunch and load the Coleman. We packed the car and still he didn't notice.

Sending me into the house to change, my mother walked my sister across 6
the street to the sitter. I could hear Fern's loud exclamations through her open
windows as I came back outside to the carport, climbing behind The Lily's
great steering wheel, impatient to go. My father spotted the missing hair as
my mother came back across the street.

"What the hell have you done to your hair?" my father shouted, loud enough 7
for the whole neighborhood to hear.

"What? You don't like it?" my mother asked innocently. "Everyone has a 8
'do like this, even Twilah. I thought I could wear a scarf in my hair like she
does," said my mother, knowing my father hated Twilah's gaudy scarves which
were tied in a bow on the top of her head. I swallowed and scrunched down
into the seat.

"Like Twilah?" he snorted. "Twilah has to wear a scarf to keep her brains 9
in her head. Jesus Christ, Jessie, why didn't you ask me before you did this?"

"I did. You didn't answer, James. You never answer my questions. In fact, 10
you don't listen to anything I say," returned my mother, her chin held up
defiantly as she tried to control the shrillness of her soprano replies. Perspiration dotted her lip as the flame of her anger rose to match the heat of the
102 degree noon hour. Across the street, Fern was looking out the window
towards the carport.

"Someone could die and it would be days before you'd notice. All you notice 11
is this boat. I hate this stupid boat!" screeched my mother as she stomped into
the house, slamming the door with all of her 105 pounds.

"Damn it, Jessie, get back here," yelled my father as he threw the last of 12
his tools into the toolbox under the turquoise seat before rushing into the
house after her.

Uneasily, I sat there considering their argument. Fern moved away from 13
the window and my sister took her place. My swimsuit was starting to stick to
me and my legs squeaked against the Naugahyde as I sat up straight. While
counting abandoned wasp nests in the rafters of the carport, rubbing my arm
at a remembered sting, I listened to the muffled sounds of my parents' argument. It was drowned out by Arnie, honking and revving, the radio blaring,
pulling into the driveway in the familiar Chevy. Twilah was dressed in a steel-
gray one-piece swimsuit that came a quarter of the way down her thighs, the
shape of the suit reminding me of a suit of armor I'd seen in a movie. Her
hair, windblown and wild, was tied in a bright pink bow that matched her
glasses; the lenses green, the wings set with silver rhinestones. She wore gold
sandals studded with ruby red and sapphire blue stones that I thought were
the most marvelous shoes I'd ever seen, as I glanced at my bare feet and wished
I had a pair.

"Going with us today, Sweetie? It's your first time, huh?" she asked, an- 14
swering her own question while she nodded her head up and down, the pink
bow bobbing wildly on top of her head.

My parents came out of the house dressed and smiling, carrying bunches of 15
blankets and towels and acting as if nothing were the matter. They greeted
their friends, laughed, and made jokes as they hitched the boat to the car and
loaded it with skis. We headed towards Millerton Lake for a day of sun and
skiing, Arnie and Twilah following behind our white caravan. My father
smoked a stub of a cigar, its stench mingling with the new car smell. He smiled
with pleasure as he crushed it out in the unused ashtray, my mother's mouth
dropping open in disgust. Quickly she shut it, choosing not to say anything.
Taking advantage of my parents' hostile silence, I asked my mother endless
questions.

"How come some mountains are round and some are flat? Where do lakes 16
come from? Are lakes deep? What is a dam?" My mother patiently answered
my questions and explained about the dam, and then told me a story about
a man falling into the wet cement and being buried alive while it was being
built. I listened in awe, my excitement mounting. When the dam finally
came into sight I searched in vain for some sign of the poor buried man,
before rounding a curve toward the boat ramp. Expecting the lake to be like
a big blue swimming pool, I was disappointed that I'd have to wade to get to
the floating vehicle. Dragonflies buzzed, their iridescent blue-green skins
frightening me as they darted back and forth among the tules and marsh
grasses. I was sure their long tails were used for stinging, and I didn't plan
on becoming their next victim. Ducking and flinching, I carefully tried to
avoid the jagged edges of broken beer bottles, rusty cans, cockleburs, and
any creatures that might be living in the mud which oozed over my ankles
as I inched myself towards the boat. The water waist high, the waves picking me up and setting me back, I ignored my father's sharp commands to
hurry. The grownups loaded the boat with ice chests, ignoring me as I mum-
bled and grumbled about the yuckiness of lakes and how I wanted to go
home. Finished with his loading, Arnie caught me around the waist and
dumped me into the back of the boat, chiding me for being afraid of a little
water.

The Lily started without a hitch, the loud cla-clugs of her cold engine 17
turning into the high-pitched whir of a precision ski boat. With a jolt we
moved forward, the wind whipping my hair into my face a thousand stings a
minute. Noticing my discomfort, Mother tied my hair back, then lifted my
seat to pull out several ski belts and the bright orange life vests. Vests littered
the deck and still she couldn't find what she was looking for, a new child-size

vest recently purchased for this trip. Obviously it had been left behind. She picked up the smallest adult vest, trying to make it fit me, to no avail.

"Sit here. Don't go near the sides of the boat," she warned me. For two 18 hours I watched the adults ski, stuffing myself with sandwiches and strawberry soda, reveling in the exhilaration of the ride, loving the damp mist that kept me cool, watching the antics of the different skiers as they hopped wakes and skied on one ski.

Every half hour or so, Twilah, her rhinestone glasses flashing in the sun, 19 would turn to me and say in her high-pitched, "for children only" voice, "Are you having fun, Sweetie?" She never waited for my reply, since something else would have her attention already. She squealed and waved at other boaters. She squealed when we hit a wake. She squealed when Arnie put his arms around her and tweaked her on the bottom. Arnie didn't say much, he was more interested in the Water Lily's performance and in the amount of blue-black smoke she was emitting. Arnie's normally red face was crimson, his white hair glistening with perspiration that ran down his sideburns in a constant trickle.

Signaling to come in, Mom dropped into the water as my father circled 20 back to retrieve her. The boat sputtered and coughed, then wouldn't start. The two men put their heads together, clinking tools and trying to restart it while the women, red as cherry Jell-O, stretched out on their towels to even their tans. Without the wind and the spray to keep me cool, I chafed around the neck from the bulging life jacket, rivulents of perspiration streaming down my small body. Still we waited while the men tinkered; The Lily, a bobbing patch of white and green upon the murky water. While the women dozed, I worked feverishly on the buckles of my vest. Loosening it slightly after long minutes of work, I gave up and went to the side of the boat, glancing at my mother to see if she'd object. Her eyes were closed when I leaned over the side, the rocking motion allowing me to scrape my fingertips over the iridescent rainbow film of petroleum on the surface of the water. On the other side, a speedboat raced by as my father got the boat started, his hoots of success joined by the others'. The wake hit as my father pulled the throttle forward, tossing me over the side by the violent, contrasting motion.

Slipping through the life jacket, I sank into the dark recesses of icy water, 21 filling ears, eyes, and nose, a violent scream of rushing air drowned in the thrashing, swallowing, clawing of thick darkness, holding me down, surrounding me, filling me; the shock making me gasp and choke. I struggled to reach the surface, the orange vest somewhere above me, no longer in sight. It was my mother who heard the splash as my father accelerated over her screams to stop, unnoticed until she jumped overboard. Long minutes passed before my father managed to turn the boat around and maneuver it near us, in which time I nearly drowned my mother as I frantically struggled to climb on top of her.

It was Arnie who jumped in and lifted me to Twilah before helping my 22 mother on board. Shivering, I sat huddled on the floorboard possessed by the uncontrollable trembling of terror past, still choking, the taste of grit and gasoline gagging me between pants. I tried not to cry as Twilah, squatting down in front of me, wiped my running nose, doing her best to comfort me.

"That sure wasn't any fun, was it, Sweetie? Were you scared?" I nodded in 23 reply as the first surge hit me, my stomach convulsing from lake water, sand-wiches, strawberry soda, grit, and gasoline, the warm liquid splattering Twilah's feet and covering the gold sandals with the ruby red and sapphire blue stones. She didn't squeal. She didn't move. Holding my shoulders, she supported me until I was finished and then cleaned me up. Going to the side of the boat, she threw her shoes in the water.

"They didn't match anything I had anyway," she said, giving me a warm 24 smile before she slipped over the side to wash off.

Nothing was fun anymore. The wind was no longer exhilarating, but frigid. 25 Wrapped in a towel that felt like sandpaper, I became aware of my sunburn; the pain intense, my misery accented by my mother's angry accusations.

"Stupid idiot! I knew this would happen. You nearly drowned us both!" she 26 screamed at my father, though at first I thought she meant me. Trying to be heard over The Lily's coughing cla-clugs, she continued the berating.

"When are you going to grow up and watch what you're doing? You didn't 27 even look to see where she was. You knew she didn't have a life jacket that fit her!" Tears glistened in my mother's eyes, her fury checked by the re-membrance that there were other people in the boat besides us. Arnie filled the silence as he stood and stretched.

"Let's call it a day. I've had about all the sun I can take." 28

The ride back to the dock was subdued. Huddled on the turquoise seat, 29 wrapped in an old beach blanket, I shivered, partly from the cold and partly from the fear of the punishment I expected to receive. I felt guilty about the shoes and falling over the side and causing my mother to cry and yell at my father in front of others. I drowned myself in self-pity, wishing I had sunk to the bottom of the lake, imagining myself buried in the endless mud and muck along with the refuse of discarded cans and bottles and a pair of gold shoes, the stones ruby red and sapphire blue.

The ignored announcements, the hair incident, the accident, the never 30 hearing, the never answering, slowly dissolved my parents' marriage. The boat was sold at the end of the summer and was soon replaced with a flesh and blood version. My parents alternated between bouts of shouting and freezing silence, the hull of the family drifting towards destruction. I've often wondered how it would have been to float across the wakes of life, knowing our roots were anchored securely in the depths of a firm foundation, floating in family love, floating across still waters like a lovely water lily.

Focusing on Paula Sisler's Techniques and Revisions

1. What specific functions does the boat, "The Water Lily," serve in the family's daily life? How does it literally and figuratively become the center of the family members' lives? How does the symbolic significance of the boat broaden as the essay develops?

2. Characterize Sisler's *tone*—her attitude toward the subject—in describing the boat in paragraph 3. Does her voice in these sentences sound neutral and dispassionate? Involved and resentful? Some other combination? Explain. How does she convey a memorable sense of the extent to which her father "loved" "The Lily"? Point to specific passages to support your response.

3. One of the most successful strategies in this essay is Sisler's use of seemingly ordinary details for their dramatic effect. Consider, for example, the details in paragraph 10. Explain how Sisler uses them effectively. For what purpose? How does she employ details in paragraph 13 to reinforce her own unease at witnessing her parents argue? Consider her earlier use of details in paragraph 2. What is the effect of her detailed comparison of her father with Arnie, his "ex-marine" best friend? To what point of comparison does she pay special attention in these descriptions? With what effects? How does Sisler use this image of Arnie to heighten the sense of conflict she recounts?

4. What strategies does Sisler use to create and then reinforce the pervasive sense of tension and hostility in the opening scenes of her essay? Virtually everything in the environment Sisler describes seems to harbor hostile intentions. Consider, for example, the details she introduces in paragraphs 13 and 15. How does each detail and anecdote reinforce the narrator's sense of "being afraid"? Show how she relies on similar writing strategies in the paragraphs that follow.

5. In marked contrast, Sisler also introduces comic elements into her essay. Identify as many as possible and comment on the effectiveness of each. What comic scenes does Sisler create? With what effects? What specific writing strategies does she use to intensify these effects? Be as specific as possible.

6. Examine Sisler's description of Twilah. What details does Sisler accentuate in her description of Twilah's grand entrance in paragraph 13? How are these effects reinforced by the way Sisler characterizes Twilah's voice? How does Sisler use Twilah's voice as an increasingly unpleasant reminder of the "hostile

silence" embedded in the lives of these characters? What, more generally, is the symbolic import of Twilah's voice? Her clothes? Her personality?

7. What standards does the mother invoke to justify her decision to cut her waist-length hair? What purpose does she seem to have in mind for offering this explanation? How does her husband respond? How does his response spark a broader argument? What writing strategies does Sisler employ to convert the car ride to Millerton Lake into an exploration of "hostile silence"?

8. Reread paragraph 21, in which Sisler presents an account of "slipping through the life jacket . . . into the dark recesses of icy water." What strategies does she use to accelerate the projection of her fear? What parts of speech does she rely on to accomplish that effect? Sisler reports that she worked especially hard on this scene, rewriting it many times "to get the words right. . . . I wanted to convey the feeling of suffocation and panic I was experiencing. Just to read that section out loud, one runs out of breath and must come back up for air because of the complexity of the sentence structure." What, exactly, is the nature of the "complexity" in these sentences?

9. Reread the final paragraph of Sisler's essay. How does the second sentence return her readers to the opening sentence of the essay? What specifically does Sisler mean when she announces that the boat was "soon replaced with a flesh and blood version"? What do you make of the last line of the essay? What metaphor dominates it? Identify the components of that metaphor. In what specific ways might this be a "mixed metaphor"? What revision(s) could Sisler make to render the image more consistent?

10. Paula Sisler reports that at the time she wrote "The Water Lily," "we had been studying sentence structure (absolutes, participles, appositives, etc.) in descriptive narrative pieces, including George Orwell's 'Shooting an Elephant,' Isaac B. Singer's 'A Day of Pleasures,' and Langston Hughes's 'Saved from Sin.' " In proofreading her final draft, Sisler made a few changes in her essay, all in the opening sentence of paragraph 3. Here is the uncorrected version:

> Christened "The Water Lily," I was reminded many times by my father, that she was not the ordinary kind of boat one buys from the want ads (these boats rarely running the way they're supposed to) or the shiny new floor room model that takes seven years to pay for.

What principal change did Sisler make in this sentence in her final version? Why? What does this change suggest she learned about sentence structure and participles?

Suggestions for Writing

1. Paula Sisler's essay demonstrates the evocative power of symbolic detail. Using Sisler's essay as a model, write an essay in which you use an object to symbolize a relationship. Be sure to invest this object with symbolic importance comparable to that of the boat in Sisler's "The Water Lily."

2. Among the writers Paula Sisler had been reading at the time she wrote "The Water Lily" was George Orwell. Read his essay "Shooting an Elephant" (reprinted on pp. 82–88), paying special attention to its pattern of organization: a précis of current conditions, a précis of preceding events, a dramatic narrative, and a précis of succeeding events. Write an essay, using the pattern of organization evident in Sisler's and Orwell's essays as models, in which you re-create a dramatic personal experience. Follow Sisler's and Orwell's lead here: work in symbolic details to express your interpretation of the significance of the events you recount.

AN EFFECTIVE TECHNIQUE

Paula Sisler's story grips us from the beginning, even though little happens in the early scenes except trivial discussions of a boat. There is a thick, tense atmosphere about the relationship of the mother and father in the story that makes us think that every time they interact something else is going on behind the words they are saying. The climactic event, the narrator falling into the water, seems much more than a boating accident, and the ending confirms that suspicion, finally identifying what the whole story is really about: the end of a marriage. The last line pulls together all the oddly powerful moments in this essay, revealing why they affect us so strongly: Sisler has been using the story of a boating accident to speak symbolically about something else. At the end, we see that the boat and the accident are symbols of the family: a secure family would have supported the narrator, floating her in "family love"; her actual family was like a boat out of control, tossing the narrator overboard into the muck of the horrible emotions of discord and divorce.

From Sisler's essay we can learn a technique for infusing small details with broad, symbolic significance. Sisler does this by describing ordinary objects and events using words that are much too powerful, that would more aptly apply to something else. Consider, for example, Sisler's opening description of the boat: "Lily . . . was my father's mistress and my mother's source of jealousy."

She directly identifies the boat as representing something destroying a marriage, something drawing the father away from the mother. This description alone, though, is not sufficient to establish the symbolism of the boat. The opening line could be read simply as a humorous way of saying her father spent too much time with his boat. But when we put this line together with others like it and with the revelation that divorce is the end of this tale, we can see that the boat indeed is a symbolic mistress.

That we have to wait to the end of the essay to realize precisely how elements are symbolic is not a result of our failure to be clever readers. It actually matches our experience in life. When we go through something as powerful as a divorce, we often realize that little events and actions that occurred months or years before were far more significant than we thought at the time: they "symbolized" the impending breakup. In this story, as in real life, we often have only a sense that some small action has too much emotional power attached to it, but we cannot quite see what the act really means, what it symbolizes, until much later. We feel that the action has symbolic weight, but we cannot interpret it.

If we pay attention to moments in real life when we react too strongly to some minor event, we can probably discover details that are symbolic for us, ordinary objects and events that evoke powerful emotions deriving from their association with important parts of our lives. Gail Godwin, a contemporary American novelist, describes the memory as "rigged with thousands of little landmines, waiting for you to step on the right place and blow yourself up on a long-suppressed grief or terror or mortification." To illustrate her point, she creates a scene of a boy looking at a magnolia tree and "wondering what it was about the dark, waxy leaves . . . that made him queasy and afraid," until he is told by others that when he was three, he went to his father's funeral, where the table was decorated with magnolia leaves from a "grand old tree." Cut leaves from an old tree can effectively symbolize death for a three-year-old and can convey to him years later emotions he cannot remember.

Symbols can also be used quite consciously. In Sisler's story, the mother's cutting her hair in a style that the father dislikes is clearly a conscious symbolic act of rebellion and anger. We often dress for certain occasions to purposely and symbolically express opinions about those occasions—consider the symbolism of traditional wedding outfits and what a couple is "saying" if they marry in blue jeans. Everyday acts and objects may acquire complex meanings when placed in unusual contexts, as the boat in Sisler's tale acquires meaning because of its role in the emotionally charged life of the family preceding a divorce.

In the next selection, James Joyce tells a tale about a boy who watches a girl, goes to buy her a gift, and then doesn't buy it. Very little actually happens in Joyce's tale, yet Joyce gives such emotional weight to the events, through his descriptions, that this insignificant tale seems to reveal the essence of first love and every young boy's fall from innocence.

ANOTHER ILLUSTRATION OF THE TECHNIQUE

JAMES JOYCE

Araby

As a young man in Ireland in the 1890s, James Joyce felt stifled by the injustice of English colonial rule and the weight of Catholic dogma. When he became convinced that no movement would free Ireland, he fled to Europe in 1904, living the rest of his life in Trieste, Paris, and Zurich. Though he could not live in Ireland, all Joyce ever wrote about was his birthplace, Dublin. He published very few works—a collection of short stories, a play, two slim volumes of poems, and three novels—but his stories and novels established him as one of the greatest writers of the twentieth century. His success was tempered by his sense that his art never accomplished what he dreamed of doing when he left Ireland—helping create a new Ireland and redeem its failures and his own. As he wrote in his autobiographical novel, A Portrait of the Artist as a Young Man, he hoped while in exile "to forge in the smithy of my soul the uncreated conscience of my race."

Joyce's first book, the short-story collection Dubliners, in which "Araby" appears, was based on notes he had taken before he left Ireland. During his teens, he had been collecting vignettes of ordinary life that he felt provided surprising insights; he called them "epiphanies." In his uncompleted first novel, Stephen Hero, he defined an epiphany as "a sudden spiritual manifestation, whether in the vulgarity of speech or of gesture or in a memorable phase of the mind itself . . . the most delicate and evanescent of moments." While living in Europe, he slowly transformed his collected epiphanies into short stories and assembled them into a book that he called "a moral chapter of the history" of Ireland. Joyce described the stories as revealing the "paralysis" that engulfed anyone living in Dublin; he arranged the stories to trace the progression of this disease from the first infection of children's private worlds to the corruption of all of adult life.

North Richmond Street, being blind, was a quiet street except at the hour   1
when the Christian Brothers' School set the boys free. An uninhabited house of two storeys stood at the blind end, detached from its neighbours in a square ground. The other houses of the street, conscious of decent lives within them, gazed at one another with brown imperturbable faces.

The former tenant of our house, a priest, had died in the back drawing-   2
room. Air, musty from having been long enclosed, hung in all the rooms, and
the waste room behind the kitchen was littered with old useless papers. Among
these I found a few paper-covered books, the pages of which were curled and
damp: *The Abbot*, by Walter Scott, *The Devout Communicant* and *The Memoirs
of Vidocq*. I liked the last best because its leaves were yellow. The wild garden
behind the house contained a central apple-tree and a few straggling bushes
under one of which I found the late tenant's rusty bicycle-pump. He had been
a very charitable priest; in his will he had left all his money to institutions
and the furniture of his house to his sister.

When the short days of winter came dusk fell before we had well eaten our   3
dinners. When we met in the street the houses had grown sombre. The space
of sky above us was the colour of ever-changing violet and towards it the lamps
of the street lifted their feeble lanterns. The cold air stung us and we played
till our bodies glowed. Our shouts echoed in the silent street. The career of
our play brought us through the dark muddy lanes behind the houses where
we ran the gauntlet of the rough tribes from the cottages, to the back doors
of the dark dripping gardens where odours arose from the ashpits, to the dark
odorous stables where a coachman smoothed and combed the horse or shook
music from the buckled harness. When we returned to the street light from
the kitchen windows had filled the areas. If my uncle was seen turning the
corner we hid in the shadow until we had seen him safely housed. Or if
Mangan's sister came out on the doorstep to call her brother in to his tea we
watched her from our shadow peer up and down the street. We waited to see
whether she would remain or go in and, if she remained, we left our shadow
and walked up to Mangan's steps resignedly. She was waiting for us, her figure
defined by the light from the half-opened door. Her brother always teased her
before he obeyed and I stood by the railings looking at her. Her dress swung
as she moved her body and the soft rope of her hair tossed from side to side.

Every morning I lay on the floor in the front parlour watching her door.   4
The blind was pulled down to within an inch of the sash so that I could not
be seen. When she came out on the doorstep my heart leaped. I ran to the
hall, seized my books and followed her. I kept her brown figure always in my
eye and, when we came near the point at which our ways diverged, I quickened
my pace and passed her. This happened morning after morning. I had never
spoken to her, except for a few casual words, and yet her name was like a
summons to all my foolish blood.

Her image accompanied me even in places the most hostile to romance.   5
On Saturday evenings when my aunt went marketing I had to go to carry some
of the parcels. We walked through the flaring streets, jostled by drunken men

and bargaining women, amid the curses of labourers, the shrill litanies of shop-
boys who stood on guard by the barrels of pigs' cheeks, the nasal chanting of
street-singers, who sang a *come-all-you* about O'Donovan Rossa, or a ballad
about the troubles in our native land. These noises converged in a single
sensation of life for me: I imagined that I bore my chalice safely through a
throng of foes. Her name sprang to my lips at moments in strange prayers and
praises which I myself did not understand. My eyes were often full of tears (I
could not tell why) and at times a flood from my heart seemed to pour itself
out into my bosom. I thought little of the future. I did not know whether I
would ever speak to her or not or, if I spoke to her, how I could tell her of
my confused adoration. But my body was like a harp and her words and gestures
were like fingers running upon the wires.

One evening I went into the back drawing-room in which the priest had   6
died. It was a dark rainy evening and there was no sound in the house. Through
one of the broken panes I heard the rain impinge upon the earth, the fine
incessant needles of water playing in the sodden beds. Some distant lamp or
lighted window gleamed below me. I was thankful that I could see so little.
All my senses seemed to desire to veil themselves and, feeling that I was about
to slip from them, I pressed the palms of my hands together until they trembled,
murmuring: "O love! O love!" many times.

At last she spoke to me. When she addressed the first words to me I was so   7
confused that I did not know what to answer. She asked me was I going to
Araby. I forgot whether I answered yes or no. It would be a splendid bazaar,
she said she would love to go.

"And why can't you?" I asked.   8

While she spoke she turned a silver bracelet round and round her wrist.   9
She could not go, she said, because there would be a retreat that week in her
convent. Her brother and two other boys were fighting for their caps and I
was alone at the railings. She held one of the spikes, bowing her head towards
me. The light from the lamp opposite our door caught the white curve of her
neck, lit up her hair that rested there and, falling, lit up the hand upon the
railing. It fell over one side of her dress and caught the white border of a
petticoat, just visible as she stood at ease.

"It's well for you" she said.   10

"If I go," I said, "I will bring you something."   11

What innumerable follies laid waste my waking and sleeping thoughts after   12
that evening! I wished to annihilate the tedious intervening days. I chafed
against the work of school. At night in my bedroom and by day in the classroom
her image came between me and the page I strove to read. The syllables of
the word *Araby* were called to me though the silence in which my soul luxu-

riated and cast an Eastern enchantment over me. I asked for leave to go to
the bazaar on Saturday night. My aunt was surprised and hoped it was not
some Freemason affair. I answered few questions in class. I watched my master's
face pass from amiability to sternness; he hoped I was not beginning to idle. I
could not call my wandering thoughts together. I had hardly any patience with
the serious work of life which, now that it stood between me and my desire,
seemed to me child's play, ugly monotonous child's play.

On Saturday morning I reminded my uncle that I wished to go to the bazaar   13
in the evening. He was fussing at the hallstand, looking for the hat-brush, and
answered me curtly:

"Yes, boy, I know."   14

As he was in the hall I could not go into the front parlour and lie at the   15
window. I left the house in bad humour and walked slowly towards the school.
The air was pitilessly raw and already my heart misgave me.

When I came home to dinner my uncle had not yet been home. Still it   16
was early. I sat staring at the clock for some time and, when its ticking began
to irritate me, I left the room. I mounted the staircase and gained the upper
part of the house. The high cold empty gloomy rooms liberated me and I went
from room to room singing. From the front window I saw my companions
playing below in the street. Their cries reached me weakened and indistinct
and, leaning my forehead against the cool glass, I looked over at the dark
house where she lived. I may have stood there for an hour, seeing nothing but
the brown-clad figure cast by my imagination, touched discreetly by the lamp-
light at the curved neck, at the hand upon the railings and at the border below
the dress.

When I came downstairs again I found Mrs. Mercer sitting at the fire. She   17
was an old garrulous woman, a pawnbroker's widow, who collected used stamps
for some pious purpose. I had to endure the gossip of the tea-table. The meal
was prolonged beyond an hour and still my uncle did not come. Mrs. Mercer
stood up to go: she was sorry she couldn't wait any longer, but it was after
eight o'clock and she did not like to be out late, as the night air was bad for
her. When she had gone I began to walk up and down the room, clenching
my fists. My aunt said:

"I'm afraid you may put off your bazaar for this night of Our Lord."   18

At nine o'clock I heard my uncle's latchkey in the halldoor. I heard him   19
talking to himself and heard the hallstand rocking when it had received the
weight of his overcoat. I could interpret these signs. When he was midway
through his dinner I asked him to give me the money to go to the bazaar. He
had forgotten.

"The people are in bed and after their first sleep now," he said.   20

I did not smile. My aunt said to him energetically: 21

"Can't you give him the money and let him go? You've kept him late enough   22
as it is."

My uncle said he was very sorry he had forgotten. He said he believed in   23
the old saying: "All work and no play makes Jack a dull boy." He asked me
where I was going and, when I had told him a second time he asked me did
I know *The Arab's Farewell to his Steed*. When I left the kitchen he was about
to recite the opening lines of the piece to my aunt.

I held a florin tightly in my hand as I strode down Buckingham Street   24
towards the station. The sight of the streets thronged with buyers and glaring
with gas recalled to me the purpose of my journey. I took my seat in a third-
class carriage of a deserted train. After an intolerable delay the train moved
out of the station slowly. It crept onward among ruinous houses and over the
twinkling river. At Westland Row Station a crowd of people pressed to the
carriage doors; but the porters moved them back, saying that it was a special
train for the bazaar. I remained alone in the bare carriage. In a few minutes
the train drew up beside an improvised wooden platform. I passed out on to
the road and saw by the lighted dial of a clock that it was ten minutes to ten.
In front of me was a large building which displayed the magical name.

I could not find any sixpenny entrance and, fearing that the bazaar would   25
be closed, I passed in quickly through a turnstile, handing a shilling to a weary-
looking man. I found myself in a big hall girdled at half its height by a gallery.
Nearly all the stalls were closed and the greater part of the hall was in darkness.
I recognised a silence like that which pervades a church after a service. I walked
into the centre of the bazaar timidly. A few people were gathered about the
stalls which were still open. Before a curtain, over which the words *Café
Chantant* were written in coloured lamps, two men were counting money on
a salver. I listened to the fall of the coins.

Remembering with difficulty why I had come I went over to one of the stalls   26
and examined porcelain vases and flowered tea-sets. At the door of the stall a
young lady was talking and laughing with two young gentlemen. I remarked
their English accents and listened vaguely to their conversation.

"O, I never said such a thing!"   27

"O, but you did!"   28

"O, but I didn't!"   29

"Didn't she say that?"   30

"Yes. I heard her."   31

"O, there's a . . . fib!"   32

Observing me the young lady came over and asked me did I wish to buy 33
anything. The tone of her voice was not encouraging; she seemed to have
spoken to me out of a sense of duty. I looked humbly at the great jars that
stood like eastern guards at either side of the dark entrance to the stall and
murmured:

"No, thank you."   34

The young lady changed the position of one of the vases and went back to 35
the two young men. They began to talk of the same subject. Once or twice
the young lady glanced at me over her shoulder.

I lingered before her stall, though I knew my stay was useless, to make my 36
interest in her wares seem the more real. Then I turned away slowly and walked
down the middle of the bazaar. I allowed the two pennies to fall against the
sixpence in my pocket. I heard a voice call from one end of the gallery that
the light was out. The upper part of the hall was now completely dark.

Gazing up into the darkness I saw myself as a creature driven and derided 37
by vanity; and my eyes burned with anguish and anger.

Focusing on James Joyce's Use of Symbolism

1. Which words in the first paragraph are normally used to describe people rather
   than a street or houses? If the narrator is really telling us about the people who
   live on this street in his description of the street, what does he say about these
   people?

2. What do words like "chalice," "strange prayers and praises," and "adoration"
   have in common? What do they suggest about the quality of the narrator's
   feeling for Mangan's sister? Considering this, is there anything ironic about his
   "press[ing] the palms of [his] hands together" and murmuring "*O love! O love!*"?
   How does the narrator suggest, through the details of the girl's appearance in
   paragraph 9, that the boy's love is not merely spiritual?

3. In paragraph 12, what does the bazaar represent in the boy's imagination? How
   does the description of the bazaar in paragraph 25 show that it is different from
   what he imagined? What do men counting money make you think of?

4. The conversation between the two gentlemen and the young lady seems to
   have almost no significance, yet it affects the boy greatly, apparently changing
   his views of himself and Mangan's sister. How does the language in this conversation contrast with the language the boy has used to describe his relationship with Mangan's sister? The conversation seems to be about what a girl did
   or did not say. How could this conversation represent to the boy an image of
   his relationship to Mangan's sister?

5. Where does the word "dark" appear in the story? Where are things or people

described as brightly lit? What could Joyce be saying about the narrator's world by describing so much of it as dark, with only a few brightly lit contrasts?

6. The last line has perplexed critics, who have proposed numerous interpretations. If you think about the line as "symbolically" expressing something, you might find your own distinctive way of understanding it. Some things you might consider: If you described a person as "gazing into the darkness" but did not mean it literally, what would you be saying about him or her? What possible meanings could you attach to the image of eyes "burning"? Why would a person describe himself as a "creature"?

7. This story is clearly told by an adult looking back on his life. Why is this story, in which little happens, important enough for the narrator to want to retell it years later? How are the events in this story symbolic of something that is very important to the narrator as an adult? One way to answer this question is to consider how the events in this story might have changed the narrator's way of understanding his life.

WORKING WITH THE TECHNIQUE IN YOUR OWN WRITING

1. Paula Sisler tells of a period when her life underwent a major change, when her parents divorced. Instead of directly telling us about all the family problems that led up to her parents' decision to divorce, she focuses on a small incident that seems to represent everything that was going wrong in her family. Her essay suggests a way to provide some focus in writing about a period when much of life seems unclear and unstable. Think about a decision that you or people around you made that changed your life. Examine the period before the decision was made, and see if you can identify an incident that seems to show the problems or tensions that led up to the decision. The incident may not at the time have seemed very important, but looking back you can recognize that it revealed that something had to change. Write an essay about that incident, letting your readers see how it is symbolic of the problems that eventually led up to the decision to change.

2. Often a story about something a person did in childhood ends up being repeated over and over again, by parents, friends, and even by the individual himself or herself. Such a story might seem to describe some ordinary thing that all children do, but the fact that the story continues to be told suggests that it is symbolic, that is, that it has greater significance than simply being funny or memorable. Reciting the story has become a way to "say" something: the story may seem to rather magically predict the future, or it may seem to reveal personality traits that have become much more prominent than they were in childhood. Sometimes a story about a person reveals more about the people who tell it than about that person, especially stories that parents like to repeat

about their children (a story that a girl's parents repeatedly tell about how she hoarded pennies behind the toy chest might suggest that her parents want her to be rich, or it might express their fear that they never gave her enough). Select one story that you remember being told about you and write an essay explaining what you think that story reveals about you, about your childhood, or about those who told it.

3. Styles of clothing often function symbolically; people dress a certain way to make a statement. Even when the symbolism seems obvious (for example, punk styles representing rebellion), subtle details might suggest complex meanings (punks often wear styles from the 1950s, suggesting, in contradiction to their seeming rebellion, a desire to return to a stabler, more sedate, more conformist era). Write an essay about one or more styles of dress, and explain the symbolic significance of the details that make up the style or styles.

JOHN CLYDE THATCHER

Otterbein College
Westerville, Ohio
Sylvia Vance, instructor

"I am a famous procrastinator. I had put off writing my essay until the night before it was to be turned in," John Thatcher reveals. *"This, however, is not unusual, for it seems I can write only under tremendous pressure. I seem to take perverse delight in watching the time slip by until it is almost too late to begin writing. It is like a game of literary Russian roulette. The hammer clicks as the cylinder revolves and time rushes by. And I pray that inspiration will come before the occupied cylinder snaps into place and the hammer poises above the pin. This essay was begun at 11:00 P.M. and finished around 4:00 A.M. I by no means endorse this method, but that is what works for me. So far."*

Born in Galion, Ohio, Thatcher was raised in his family's five-generation home outside Mt. Liberty, Ohio. He has worked part-time as an assistant in both a nursing home and his father's electrical engineering business. He credits his parents and teachers for nurturing his interest in writing and reading, and he recalls that as a child *"books were more important than toys."* Thatcher graduated from Otterbein College with degrees in political science and history and several college writing prizes. He is now a law student at Capital University in Columbus, Ohio, where he is involved in several student legal activities and works part-time as a law clerk at a local firm. Although he enjoys all facets of the law, he reports that he will probably specialize in *"plaintiff personal injury law."*

Thatcher reports that he wrote "On Killing the Man" *"during my first term of college and first long period away from home. I didn't get as homesick as the rest of my freshman friends because if I wanted to go home all I had to do was sit down and write about things that happened when I was at home and what it was like to be there."* In his essay, Thatcher records the impact of what he calls his *"brief trapping career."*

For an extended discussion of John Thatcher's essay, see Part II.

On Killing the Man

I wanted to trap! All of the other boys did. Certainly that was reason enough   1
for me. And what about the stacks of money to be made through this time-honored trade? Why, boys had been known to make a small fortune in one season. Boys that wished to become young men required inordinate amounts of money, and for those that live out of town, on a farm with a woods and small creek, trapping during the winter is a most convenient means to an end. The end being, in most cases, the all-important automobile. So I began trapping in the winter of my seventeenth year. I felt as if I were pleasing generations

of woodsmen; the pioneer spirit raged in my blood. I would soon be a man. Whose man?

One goes about trapping in this manner. At the very outset one acquires a   2
"trapping" state of mind. This entails several steps. The purchase of as many traps as one might need is first. A pair of rubber gloves, waterproof boots, and the grubbiest clothes capable of withstanding human use come next to outfit the trapper for his adventure. A library of books must be read, and preferably someone with experience is needed to educate the novice. The decision has to be made on just what kinds of animal to go after, what sort of bait to use, and where to place the traps for highest yield. Finally, the trapper needs a heavy stick. Often a trap set to drown the animal once caught fails to do so. Then it is necessary to club the animal and drown him. A blow with a club will not damage the pelt the way a gunshot would. A club is a most necessary piece of equipment for the trapper.

So I set out on my wilderness adventure. My booted feet scarred the frosted   3
grass. The traps slung over my shoulder tolled a death knell as they slapped against my back, and the oaken club rapped a steady drumbeat on my thigh. I had my chance to become a man, a real man in the old sense of the word. I was the French voyageur trapping lands no white man had ever seen before. I was Dan'l Boone about to catch my famous coonskin cap. I was the Hudson Bay Company trapper, trading axes and blankets with the Indians and sending beaver pelts to London for a gentleman's top hat. I was my father too. I was he and he was me as the two of us set out together for the great woods. This was truly the way men should live.

The actual work of trapping can be completed only after the trapper has   4
suffered as much as possible. It is cold, tedious, backbreaking, finger- and toe-numbing, infuriating torture often described as exciting and fun by someone who really enjoys trapping. In my case the traps were mostly set in the water. This is done in the hopes of catching muskrats, raccoons, and possibly a mink or two. It is also done to enhance the feeling of already numb fingers by immersing them in freezing water. It is a most difficult task becoming a man, even more difficult to enjoy doing it.

Once the animal is caught it must be skinned. This involves cutting the   5
pelt away from the body, scraping off the fatty deposits from the underside, and stretching the skin on a board until it is dry. All in all a great amount of work for a twenty-five-dollar pelt. Twenty-five dollars, that is, if the pelt is large for a raccoon, if it is in good condition, and if the dealer you go to is a generous man. But who can deny the sense of accomplishment a man feels when he sells his pelts? Only he can know the great satisfaction felt by out-smarting small animals through catching and killing them in traps they could

not smell or see. What joy is felt when a man can say he has beaten nature with only his quick mind, traps of spring steel, rubberized gloves that leave no betraying scent, scientifically tested lures and baits, and clever sets that catch the animals and sink them to their deaths as they struggle to get away while water fills their small, gasping lungs.

But often the novice does not succeed in making a "water set" that quickly 6 drowns the animal.

One cold morning I stayed home from school, and though sick with a cold 7 I checked my trapline like any humane trapper. My "water sets" had not worked the night before. I walked in the direction of a trap anchored to a fallen log that was intended to encourage a trapped animal to escape by swimming across the creek and thus drown itself. As I neared the trap I immediately saw that it had been disturbed but didn't see an animal. "Drowned," I thought. When I was very close to the set I realized the animal was not drowned and underwater; hopelessly entangled around a limb of the log was a large male raccoon.

Now I had a problem. The raccoon must be knocked senseless and drowned. 8 The club that hung around my wrist had grown very heavy all of a sudden and my stomach knotted at the thought of what I had to do. I was torn between wanting to absolve myself by setting him free (although I knew he would suffer a horrible death) and doing what it was I had worked so hard to come to. I wanted to be a man but also wanted to run away from what I'd done and cry into my mother's breast. My hand, however, was forced by my earlier actions, and now I had to take this creature's life to end the suffering I had caused it. The bile rose in my throat as I raised the club.

At that moment I knew what an awful thing it is to be hated, violently 9 hated by another living thing. He looked at me and not the club. He looked at me with his trap-torn flesh bleeding away his fear, leaving only raging hate. He barely paused in his screamed hiss as the club came down, again and again, on his skull. I didn't kill him well because he was my first murder, and the hot tears that burst from me blinded my eyes, making the blows poorly aimed.

Once that hideous screaming stopped and the despising, damning eyes rolled 10 back into their sockets, I drowned him. As I watched the water fill him up and the bubbles and blood float up from his nostrils, I wondered if I was now the man I had wanted to be. Whose man? I decided then that the boy who was responsible for this wretched thing was not ready to be a man because he had aspired to be someone else and not himself. I knew then that I would never do this despicable thing again and never have since. To reach manhood is a wonderful thing, but this happens only when the man can look at himself and recognize what he sees. A boy must kill "the man," the one he has dreamed for himself in his head, in order to let out the one inside that patiently bides his time until the boy is ready to accept what he is. It takes a significant event to make the change. In my case it took the murder of an animal. Life is not always clean and bloodless. If I could have killed my "man" with a swift rapier thrust I would have done it. Instead I am left with the memory of blow after blow on a tiny head. I still see the bared teeth and still hear the wild snarling. My "man" died especially hard in bloody frothing waters. I have learned from that and will never forget.

Focusing on John Clyde Thatcher's Techniques and Revisions

1. John Clyde Thatcher casts his essay in the form of two stories. The first recounts a traditional American rite of male initiation: the myth of how a boy becomes a man by killing an animal. The second dramatically changes the first: he revises the myth to express his revulsion at his own brutality. What, more specifically, does Thatcher learn about being a man from his brief trapping career? What does he mean, for example, when he writes: "A boy must kill 'the man,' the one he has dreamed for himself"?

2. How does Thatcher describe "a real man in the old sense of the word" (paragraph 3)? In what tradition does he place himself when he talks in these terms? What variation does he create for this mythic identity? Define what constitutes a " 'trapping' state of mind" (paragraph 2). What did trapping represent before his venture into the woods? How does he revise that vision after his experience there?

3. What *point of view*—relation to the subject—does Thatcher establish in the opening paragraph? Does this point of view remain consistent throughout the essay? If so, with what effects? If not, when and to what does it shift? With what effects?

4. How would you characterize Thatcher's *tone*—his attitude toward his subject— in this essay? Consider, for example, his first paragraph. Point to specific words and phrases that reveal his tone of voice. More specifically, how do you read the tone of the final two sentences in this paragraph? Do you detect any irony or sarcasm in them? Explain. Show how the tone of these sentences is consistent or inconsistent with his tone earlier in the same paragraph. Identify other instances of irony or sarcasm in Thatcher's essay and comment on the effectiveness of its use in each instance.

5. From paragraph 7 to the end of the essay, Thatcher relies on narrative techniques to tell us about killing his first animal. What features of his narration make it particularly effective? What is his purpose in relating this incident? What specific writing strategies does Thatcher use to make it so fast-paced and

convincing? What are the effects of shifting between personal narration and impersonal process analysis? Because Thatcher's personal narrative does not extend beyond killing the raccoon, explain why you think he does or does not need to include the process analysis on skinning and selling pelts in paragraph 5. In a similar vein, comment on the function and evaluate the necessity of paragraphs 2, 4, and 5, which analyze the process of trapping. How effectively, for example, do they introduce the narrative of killing the raccoon?

6. Thatcher's essay is solidly grounded in personal experience. What details indicate that he is writing forcefully about an experience of great significance to him? In this respect, which words and phrases—which aspects of his description—do you find especially powerful and compelling?

7. Comment on the ending of Thatcher's essay. Did it surprise you? If not, how did Thatcher prepare his readers for the ending? What does he mean when he reports, "My 'man' died especially hard in bloody frothing waters"? To whom or to what does "My 'man' " refer? How does Thatcher succeed at the end of the essay in "killing" the images and fantasies people have of being a "man"?

8. Asked in a recent interview to discuss the risks he took when he wrote his essay and to indicate what changes, if any, he would now make—several years later—Thatcher noted: "The only risks I feel I took were personal. I was putting a private experience on paper and knew the experience was now public. I suppose every writer does that, but I was only eighteen at the time and not invulnerable. . . . As for changes, I would try to delete some of the wry humor I put in when I wrote my essay. The essay would be a more serious piece if I had not tried to be funny. Now I see that the subject matter would have been served better without humor." Do you agree with Thatcher's assessment? Point to specific passages that you regard as humorous and use them to justify your endorsing or challenging his view that his essay "would have been served better without humor."

Suggestions for Writing

1. Choose an incident in your own life or the life of someone you know well that marked the turning point between childhood and adulthood. In an essay, describe the incident and explain its significance.

2. Think of an ideal image you cherished as a child (the ideal mother or father, the ideal friend, the ideal family, the ideal wife or husband). Write an essay describing how that image is similar to and different from your view of the ideal today. Try to focus on one incident that will demonstrate how and why your view has developed to its present form.

3. When John Thatcher set out to trap, he saw himself as "Dan'l Boone" and

"the Hudson Bay Company trapper" until that myth was dispelled by reality. Have you ever been in a similar situation where reality intruded on fantasy? Describe the fantasy, why you believed in it, and how it was dispelled. Did you come to any better understanding as a result?

AN EFFECTIVE TECHNIQUE

Revision is not only a process for developing a paper; it is also a process we use throughout our lives. We all have revised ideas that we have been taught, adapting them to fit our particular situation. A writer can build an essay around such an act of revision, as John Clyde Thatcher does. He tells how he tried to live out a story he had been told and how his experience forced him to revise that story. In the beginning of his essay, Thatcher takes us through his careful, detailed plans to reenact a myth we all know—the myth of "Dan'l Boone," of "generations of woodsmen," of the "pioneer spirit." Thatcher intends to become a man by going into the woods and killing a wild creature on his own. He convinces us that he has the expertise to live out this myth; he essentially teaches us how to trap animals, just as his father taught him.

Halfway through Thatcher's essay, however, he stops telling us what he intends to do and starts recounting a different story—his actual experiences. Reality does not follow the myth. Instead of joy accompanying Thatcher's first real kill, he feels "awful" at having committed "murder"; instead of expressing manly pride, he bursts into tears. But Thatcher does not simply give up the myth he has been trying to follow, declaring it a fraud; he revises it, discovering a different kind of killing that a boy has to perform in order to become a man. Instead of killing some wild creature, the boy has to kill a part of himself, "the man" that "he has dreamed for himself in his head," in order to finally "accept what he is."

Thatcher's essay consists of two stories, one a revision of the other: two "drafts" of Thatcher's life. The first five paragraphs tell us what should happen when the boy goes out to become a man; the last five tell us what does happen. But even in the beginning of his essay, Thatcher lets us know that something is wrong; he presents his boyhood dreams ironically. From the first few sentences, the essay does not have the right tone for an adventure tale. Daniel Boone went into the woods to escape civilization and establish himself as an independent person. In contrast, the boy in Thatcher's tale wants to go trapping because "all the other boys did" and to make "stacks of money" to buy "the all-important automobile." This boy clearly is not trying to escape civilization. The mocking tone lets us know from the beginning of this essay that myth and reality are in conflict and prepares us for the explosion that eventually destroys the boy's mistaken dreams.

Thatcher's essay presents a particularly vivid example of a process that everyone goes through. We all spend much of our lives trying to live out myths we have been taught or have picked up from books, TV, or movies. Our experiences often contradict those myths. Sometimes we simply discard a myth and go on. But if the myth embodies some dearly held beliefs that we do not want to give up, we have to find a way to revise it. For example, a youth might feel he has to be the strongest athlete but repeatedly injure himself lifting weights. He may finally realize that it takes strength to give up lifting weights, to resist the taunts of his athletic friends, and so he may revise his image of the strong man from Hercules with bulging muscles to, perhaps, Martin Luther King, Jr., standing alone against a crowd of hecklers.

We can write powerful essays if we focus, as Thatcher does, on the tension between dearly held beliefs and the pressures of reality. Our myths may not seem as colorful and dramatic as Thatcher's, but we have all had to kill "the man" or "the woman" we dreamed of becoming, and such deaths are rarely painless or quick. For example, one woman writer, Virginia Woolf, spoke of the years it took her to "kill the Angel in the House," to escape the image of the always cheerful, self-sacrificing mother she was expected to become. She wrote an essay much like Thatcher's about her struggle with false sweetness. The drama in such essays derives from the battle between two stories and from the torment we imagine in the mind of the person caught between those two stories. Woolf battled an Angel trying to control her mind and body; Thatcher fought free of Daniel Boone. We can write essays about our efforts to escape Casanova, Marilyn Monroe, Ivanhoe, Joan of Arc, Snow White, Peter Pan, Albert Einstein, Madame Curie, or whatever mythic selves we carry inside our minds and measure ourselves against.

In the next selection, Doris Lessing presents two views of Africa, one impersonal and mythic, one the experience of a fourteen-year-old girl. In the change from one story to another, Lessing shows us the terrible difficulty of revising oneself completely out of one's cultural heritage; her heroine has to escape her father, her government, her textbooks, even her own dreams.

ANOTHER ILLUSTRATION OF THE TECHNIQUE

DORIS LESSING

The Old Chief Mshlanga

"There is a kind of cold detachment at the core of any writer or artist," states Doris Lessing. She believes her own detachment arose from growing up feeling like an "exile" in a small white settlement in Africa: "My father went to Southern Rhodesia on an impulse (which is how he ran his life), to farm. He had never been a farmer, but he took a very large tract of land—thousands of acres, in American terms—to grow maize. Thus I was brought up in a district that was populated sparsely, very sparsely. . . . I spent most of my childhood alone in a landscape with very few human beings to dot it. At the time it was hellishly lonely, but now I realize how extraordinary it was, and how very lucky I was."

Lessing left Africa after two failed marriages, settling in England, a place she regards as a "paradise" for a writer because it is "not an exciting place to live, it is not one of the hubs of the world, like America, or Russia or China." Lessing feels the need for distance from important political events precisely because she feels a writer must react to them, and up close they are overwhelming. She reports, "I have always observed incredible brutality in society. My parents' lives and the lives of millions of people were ruined by the First World War. But the human imagination rejects the implications of our situation. War scars humanity in ways we refuse to recognize." A writer has to stand back from these scars to be able to make his or her own "personal and private judgments," without falling into despair or taking refuge in the standard political myths about how problems will be solved: "I believe that the pleasurable luxury of despair, the acceptance of disgust, is as much a betrayal of what a writer should be as the acceptance of a simple [political theory]; both are aspects of cowardice, both fallings-away from a central vision, the two easy escapes of our time into false innocence."

They were good, the years of ranging the bush over her father's farm which,   1
like every white farm, was largely unused, broken only occasionally by small
patches of cultivation. In between, nothing but trees, the long sparse grass,
thorn and cactus and gully, grass and outcrop and thorn. And a jutting piece
of rock which had been thrust up from the warm soil of Africa unimaginable
eras of time ago, washed into hollows and whorls by sun and wind that had
traveled so many thousands of miles of space and bush, would hold the weight
of a small girl whose eyes were sightless for anything but a pale willowed river,

a pale gleaming castle—a small girl singing: "Out flew the web and floated wide, the mirror cracked from side to side. . . ".

Pushing her way through the green aisles of the mealie[1] stalks, the leaves arching like cathedrals veined with sunlight far overhead, with the packed red earth underfoot, a fine lace of red-starred witchweed would summon up a black bent figure croaking premonitions: the Northern witch, bred of cold northern forests, would stand before her among the mealie fields, and it was the mealie fields that faded and fled, leaving her among the gnarled roots of an oak, snow falling thick and soft and white, the woodcutter's fire glowing red welcome through crowding tree trunks.

A white child, opening its eyes curiously on a sun-suffused landscape, a gaunt and violent landscape, might be supposed to accept it as her own, to take the msasa trees and the thorn trees as familiars, to feel her blood running free and responsive to the swing of the seasons.

This child could not see a msasa tree, or the thorn, for what they were. Her books held tales of alien fairies, her rivers ran slow and peaceful, and she knew the shape of the leaves of an ash or an oak, the names of the little creatures that lived in English streams, when the words "the veld" meant strangeness, though she could remember nothing else.

Because of this, for many years, it was the veld that seemed unreal; the sun was a foreign sun, and the wind spoke a strange language.

The black people on the farm were as remote as the trees and the rocks. They were an amorphous black mass, mingling and thinning and massing like tadpoles, faceless, who existed merely to serve, to say "Yes, Baas,"[2] take their money and go. They changed season by season, moving from one farm to the next, according to their outlandish needs, which one did not have to understand, coming from perhaps hundreds of miles north or east, passing on after a few months—where? Perhaps even as far away as the fabled gold mines of Johannesburg, where the pay was so much better than the few shillings a month and the double handful of mealie meal twice a day which they earned in that part of Africa.

The child was taught to take them for granted: the servants in the house would come running a hundred yards to pick up a book if she dropped it. She was called "Nkosikaas"—Chieftainess, even by the black children her own age.

1. Mealie: Corn, maize.
2. Baas: Boss, sir.

Later, when the farm grew too small to hold her curiosity, she carried a gun 8
in the crook of her arm and wandered miles a day, from vlei[3] to vlei, from
kopje[4] to kopje, accompanied by two dogs: the dogs and the gun were an armor
against fear. Because of them she never felt fear.

If a native came into sight along the kaffir[5] paths half a mile away, the dogs 9
would flush him up a tree as if he were a bird. If he expostulated (in his
uncouth language which was by itself ridiculous) that was cheek.[6] If one was
in a good mood, it could be a matter for laughter. Otherwise one passed on,
hardly glancing at the angry man in the tree.

On the rare occasions when white children met together they could amuse 10
themselves by hailing a passing native in order to make a buffoon of him; they
could set the dogs on him and watch him run; they could tease a small black
child as if he were a puppy—save that they would not throw stones and sticks
at a dog without a sense of guilt.

Later still, certain questions presented themselves in the child's mind; and 11
because the answers were not easy to accept, they were silenced by an even
greater arrogance of manner.

It was even impossible to think of the black people who worked about the 12
house as friends, for if she talked to one of them, her mother would come
running anxiously: "Come away; you mustn't talk to natives."

It was this instilled consciousness of danger, of something unpleasant, that 13
made it easy to laugh out loud, crudely, if a servant made a mistake in his
English or if he failed to understand an order—there is a certain kind of
laughter that is fear, afraid of itself.

One evening, when I was about fourteen, I was walking down the side of 14
a mealie field that had been newly ploughed, so that the great red clods showed
fresh and tumbling to the vlei beyond, like a choppy red sea; it was that hushed
and listening hour, when the birds send long sad calls from tree to tree, and
all the colors of earth and sky and leaf are deep and golden. I had my rifle in
the curve of my arm, and the dogs were at my heels.

In front of me, perhaps a couple of hundred yards away, a group of three 15
Africans came into sight around the side of a big antheap. I whistled the dogs
close in to my skirts and let the gun swing in my hand, and advanced, waiting
for them to move aside, off the path, in respect for my passing. But they came

3. Vlei: A shallow lake or a low-lying swamp ground.
4. Kopje: Knoll, hill.
5. Kaffir: Native Bantu.
6. Cheek: Impudence, arrogance.

on steadily, and the dogs looked up at me for the command to chase. I was angry. It was "cheek" for a native not to stand off a path, the moment he caught sight of you.

In front walked an old man, stooping his weight on to a stick, his hair 16 grizzled white, a dark red blanket slung over his shoulders like a cloak. Behind him came two young men, carrying bundles of pots, assegais,[7] hatchets.

The group was not a usual one. They were not natives seeking work. These 17 had an air of dignity, of quietly following their own purpose. It was the dignity that checked my tongue. I walked quietly on, talking softly to the growling dogs, till I was ten paces away. Then the old man stopped, drawing his blanket close.

" 'Morning, Nkosikaas," he said, using the customary greeting for any time 18 of the day.

"Good morning," I said, "Where are you going?" My voice was a little 19 truculent.

The old man spoke in his own language, then one of the young men stepped 20 forward politely and said in careful English: "My Chief travels to see his brothers beyond the river."

A Chief! I thought, understanding the pride that made the old man stand 21 before me like an equal—more than an equal, for he showed courtesy, and I showed none.

The old man spoke again, wearing dignity like an inherited garment, still 22 standing ten paces off, flanked by his entourage, not looking at me (that would have been rude) but directing his eyes somewhere over my head at the trees.

"You are the little Nkosikaas from the farm of Baas Jordan?"   23

"That's right," I said.   24

"Perhaps your father does not remember," said the interpreter for the old 25 man, "but there was an affair with some goats. I remember seeing you when you were. . . ." The young man held his hand at knee level and smiled.

We all smiled.   26

"What is your name?" I asked.   27

"This is Chief Mshlanga," said the young man.   28

"I will tell my father that I met you," I said.   29

The old man said: "My greetings to your father, little Nkosikaas."   30

"Good morning," I said politely, finding the politeness difficult, from lack 31 of use.

" 'Morning, little Nkosikaas," said the old man, and stood aside to let me 32 pass.

---

7. Assegais: Spears.

I went by, my gun hanging awkwardly, the dogs sniffing and growling, 33 cheated of their favorite game of chasing natives like animals.

Not long afterwards I read in an old explorer's book the phrase "Chief 34 Mshlanga's country." It went like this: "Our destination was Chief Mshlanga's country, to the north of the river; and it was our desire to ask his permission to prospect for gold in his territory."

The phrase "ask his permission" was so extraordinary to a white child, 35 brought up to consider all natives as things to use, that it revived those questions, which could not be suppressed: they fermented slowly in my mind.

On another occasion one of those old prospectors who still move over Africa 36 looking for neglected reef, with their hammers and tents, and pans for sifting gold from crushed rock, came to the farm and, in talking of the old days, used that phrase again: "This was the Old Chief's country," he said. "It stretched from those mountains over there way back to the river, hundreds of miles of country." That was his name for our district: "The Old Chief's Country"; he did not use our name for it—a new phrase which held no implication of usurped ownership.

As I read more books about the time when this part of Africa was opened 37 up, not much more than fifty years before, I found Old Chief Mshlanga had been a famous man, known to all the explorers and prospectors. But then he had been young; or maybe it was his father or uncle they spoke of—I never found out.

During that year I met him several times in the part of the farm that was 38 traversed by natives moving over the country. I learned that the path up the side of the big red field where the birds sang was the recognized highway for migrants. Perhaps I even haunted it in the hope of meeting him: being greeted by him, the exchange of courtesies, seemed to answer the questions that troubled me.

Soon I carried a gun in a different spirit; I used it for shooting food and not 39 to give me confidence. And now the dogs learned better manners. When I saw a native approaching, we offered and took greetings; and slowly that other landscape in my mind faded, and my feet struck directly on the African soil, and I saw the shapes of tree and hill clearly, and the black people moved back, as it were, out of my life; it was as if I stood aside to watch a slow intimate dance of landscape and men, a very old dance, whose steps I could not learn.

But I thought: this is my heritage, too; I was bred here; it is my country as 40 well as the black man's country; and there is plenty of room for all of us, without elbowing each other off the pavements and roads.

It seemed it was only necessary to let free that respect I felt when I was 41 talking with Old Chief Mshlanga, to let both black and white people meet gently, with tolerance for each other's differences: it seemed quite easy.

Then, one day, something new happened. Working in our house as servants 42
were always three natives: cook, houseboy, garden boy. They used to change
as the farm natives changed: staying for a few months, then moving on to a
new job, or back home to their kraals.[8] They were thought of as "good" or
"bad" natives; which meant: how did they behave as servants? Were they lazy,
efficient, obedient, or disrespectful? If the family felt good-humored, the phrase
was: "What can you expect from raw black savages?" If we were angry, we
said: "These damned niggers, we would be much better off without them."

One day, a white policeman was on his rounds of the district, and he said 43
laughingly: "Did you know you have an important man in your kitchen?"

"What!" exclaimed my mother sharply. "What do you mean?" 44

"A Chief's son." The policeman seemed amused. "He'll boss the tribe when 45
the old man dies."

"He'd better not put on a Chief's son act with me," said my mother. 46

When the policeman left, we looked with different eyes at our cook: he was 47
a good worker, but he drank too much at weekends—that was how we knew
him.

He was a tall youth, with very black skin, like black polished metal, his 48
tightly growing black hair parted white man's fashion at one side, with a metal
comb from the store stuck into it; very polite, very distant, very quick to obey
an order. Now it had been pointed out, we said: "Of course, you can see.
Blood always tells."

My mother became strict with him now she knew about his birth and 49
prospects. Sometimes, when she lost her temper, she would say: "You aren't
the Chief yet, you know." And he would answer her very quietly, his eyes on
the ground: "Yes, Nkosikaas."

One afternoon he asked for a whole day off, instead of the customary half- 50
day, to go home next Sunday.

"How can you go home in one day?" 51

"It will take me half an hour on my bicycle," he explained. 52

I watched the direction he took; and the next day I went off to look for 53
this kraal; I understood he must be Chief Mshlanga's successor: there was no
other kraal near enough our farm.

Beyond our boundaries on that side the country was new to me. I followed 54
unfamiliar paths past kopjes that till now had been part of the jagged horizon,
hazed with distance. This was Government land, which had never been cultivated by white men; at first I could not understand why it was that it appeared, in merely crossing the boundary, I had entered a completely fresh type
of landscape. It was a wide green valley, where a small river sparkled, and

8. Kraals: Tribal villages.

vivid waterbirds darted over the rushes. The grass was thick and soft to my calves, the trees stood tall and shapely.

I was used to our farm, whose hundreds of acres of harsh eroded soil bore 55 trees that had been cut for the mine furnaces and had grown thin and twisted, where the cattle had dragged the grass flat, leaving innumerable crisscrossing trails that deepened each season into gullies, under the force of the rains.

This country had been left untouched, save for prospectors whose picks had 56 struck a few sparks from the surface of the rocks as they wandered by; and for migrant natives whose passing had left, perhaps, a charred patch on the trunk of a tree where their evening fire had nestled.

It was very silent: a hot morning with pigeons cooing throatily, the midday 57 shadows lying dense and thick with clear yellow spaces of sunlight between and in all that wide green parklike valley, not a human soul but myself.

I was listening to the quick regular tapping of a woodpecker when slowly a 58 chill feeling seemed to grow up from the small of my back to my shoulders, in a constricting spasm like a shudder, and at the roots of my hair a tingling sensation began and ran down over the surface of my flesh, leaving me goose-fleshed and cold, though I was damp with sweat. Fever? I thought; then uneasily, turned to look over my shoulder; and realized suddenly that this was fear. It was extraordinary, even humiliating. It was a new fear. For all the years I had walked by myself over this country I had never known a moment's uneasiness; in the beginning because I had been supported by a gun and the dogs, then because I had learnt an easy friendliness for the Africans I might encounter.

I had read of this feeling, how the bigness and silence of Africa, under the 59 ancient sun, grows dense and takes shape in the mind, till even the birds seem to call menacingly, and a deadly spirit comes out of the trees and the rocks. You move warily, as if your very passing disturbs something old and evil, something dark and big and angry that might suddenly rear and strike from behind. You look at groves of entwined trees, and picture the animals that might be lurking there; you look at the river running slowly, dropping from level to level through the vlei, spreading into pools where at night the buck come to drink, and the crocodiles rise and drag them by their soft noses into underwater caves. Fear possessed me. I found I was turning round and round, because of that shapeless menace behind me that might reach out and take me; I kept glancing at the files of kopjes which, seen from a different angle, seemed to change with every step so that even known landmarks, like a big mountain that had sentineled my world since I first became conscious of it, showed an unfamiliar sunlit valley among its foothills. I did not know where I was. I was lost. Panic seized me. I found I was spinning round and round, staring anxiously at this tree and that, peering up at the sun which appeared

to have moved into an eastern slant, shedding the sad yellow light of sunset.
Hours must have passed! I looked at my watch and found that this state of
meaningless terror had lasted perhaps ten minutes.

The point was that it was meaningless. I was not ten miles from home: I 60
had only to take my way back along the valley to find myself at the fence;
away among the foothills of the kopjes gleamed the roof of a neighbour's house,
and a couple of hours walking would reach it. This was the sort of fear that
contracts the flesh of a dog at night and sets him howling at the full moon. It
had nothing to do with what I thought or felt; and I was more disturbed by
the fact that I could become its victim than of the physical sensation itself: I
walked steadily on, quietened, in a divided mind, watching my own pricking
nerves and apprehensive glances from side to side with a disgusted amusement.
Deliberately I set myself to think of this village I was seeking, and what I
should do when I entered it—if I could find it, which was doubtful, since I
was walking aimlessly and it might be anywhere in the hundreds of thousands of acres of bush that stretched about me. With my mind on that village, I realized that a new sensation was added to the fear: loneliness. Now
such a terror of isolation invaded me that I could hardly walk; and if it were
not that I came over the crest of a small rise and saw a village below me, I
should have turned and gone home. It was a cluster of thatched huts in a
clearing among trees. There were neat patches of mealies and pumpkins and
millet, and cattle grazed under some trees at a distance. Fowls scratched
among the huts, dogs lay sleeping on the grass, and goats friezed a kopje
that jutted up beyond a tributary of the river lying like an enclosing arm
round the village.

As I came close I saw the huts were lovingly decorated with patterns of 61
yellow and red and ocher mud on the walls; and the thatch was tied in place
with plaits of straw.

This was not at all like our farm compound, a dirty and neglected place, a 62
temporary home for migrants who had no roots at all.

And now I did not know what to do next. I called a small black boy, who 63
was sitting on a log playing a stringed gourd, quite naked except for the strings
of blue beads round his neck, and said: "Tell the Chief I am here." The child
stuck his thumb in his mouth and stared shyly back at me.

For minutes I shifted my feet on the edge of what seemed a deserted village, 64
till at last the child scuttled off, and then some women came. They were
draped in bright cloths, with brass glinting in their ears and on their arms.
They also stared, silently; then turned to chatter among themselves.

I said again: "Can I see Chief Mshlanga?" I saw they caught the name; they 65
did not understand what I wanted. I did not understand myself.

At last I walked through them and came past the huts and saw a clearing 66
under a big shady tree, where a dozen old men sat cross-legged on the ground,
talking. Chief Mshlanga was leaning back against the tree, holding a gourd in
his hand, from which he had been drinking. When he saw me, not a muscle
of his face moved, and I could see he was not pleased: perhaps he was afflicted
with my own shyness, due to being unable to find the right forms of courtesy
for the occasion. To meet me, on our own farm, was one thing; but I should
not have come here. What had I expected? I could not join them socially: the
thing was unheard of. Bad enough that I, a white girl, should be walking the
veld alone as a white man might: and in this part of the bush where only
Government officials had the right to move.

Again I stood, smiling foolishly, while behind me stood the groups of 67
brightly clad, chattering women, their faces alert with curiosity and interest,
and in front of me sat the old men, with old lined faces, their eyes guarded,
aloof. It was a village of ancients and children and women. Even the two
young men who kneeled beside the Chief were not those I had seen with him
previously: the young men were all away working on the white men's farms
and mines, and the Chief must depend on relatives who were temporarily on
holiday for his attendants.

"The small white Nkosikaas is far from home," remarked the old man at 68
last.

"Yes," I agreed, "it is far." I wanted to say: "I have come to pay you a 69
friendly visit, Chief Mshlanga." I could not say it. I might now be feeling an
urgent helpless desire to get to know these men and women as people, to be
accepted by them as a friend, but the truth was I had set out in a spirit of
curiosity: I had wanted to see the village that one day our cook, the reserved
and obedient young man who got drunk on Sundays, would one day rule over.

"The child of Nkosi Jordan is welcome," said Chief Mshlanga.   70

"Thank you," I said, and could think of nothing more to say. There was a 71
silence, while the flies rose and began to buzz around my head; and the wind
shook a little in the thick green tree that spread its branches over the old men.

"Good morning," I said at last. "I have to return now to my home."   72

" 'Morning, little Nkosikaas," said Chief Mshlanga.   73

I walked away from the indifferent village, over the rise past the staring 74
amber-eyed goats, down through the tall stately trees into the great rich green
valley where the river meandered and the pigeons cooed tales of plenty and
the woodpecker tapped softly.

The fear had gone; the loneliness had set into stiff-necked stoicism; there 75
was now a queer hostility in the landscape, a cold, hard, sullen indomitability
that walked with me, as strong as a wall, as intangible as smoke; it seemed to

say to me: you walk here as a destroyer. I went slowly homewards, with an empty heart: I had learned that if one cannot call a country to heel like a dog, neither can one dismiss the past with a smile in an easy gush of feeling, saying: I could not help it, I am also a victim.

I only saw Chief Mshlanga once again. 76

One night my father's big red land was trampled down by small sharp 77 hooves, and it was discovered that the culprits were goats from Chief Mshlanga's kraal. This had happened once before, years ago.

My father confiscated all the goats. Then he sent a message to the old Chief 78 that if he wanted them he would have to pay for the damage.

He arrived at our house at the time of sunset one evening, looking very old 79 and bent now, walking stiffly under his regally draped blanket, leaning on a big stick. My father sat himself down in his big chair below the steps of the house; the old man squatted carefully on the ground before him, flanked by his two young men.

The palaver was long and painful, because of the bad English of the young 80 man who interpreted and because my father could not speak dialect, but only kitchen kaffir.

From my father's point of view, at least two hundred pounds worth of 81 damage had been done to the crop. He knew he could not get the money from the old man. He felt he was entitled to keep the goats. As for the old Chief, he kept repeating angrily: "Twenty goats! My people cannot lose twenty goats! We are not rich, like the Nkosi Jordan, to lose twenty goats at once."

My father did not think of himself as rich, but rather as very poor. He spoke 82 quickly and angrily in return, saying that the damage done meant a great deal to him, and that he was entitled to the goats.

At last it grew so heated that the cook, the Chief's son, was called from 83 the kitchen to be interpreter, and now my father spoke fluently in English, and our cook translated rapidly so that the old man could understand how very angry my father was. The young man spoke without emotion, in a mechanical way, his eyes lowered, but showing how he felt his position by a hostile uncomfortable set of the shoulders.

It was now in the late sunset, the sky a welter of colors, the birds singing 84 their last songs, and the cattle, lowing peacefully, moving past us towards their sheds for the night. It was the hour when Africa is most beautiful; and here was this pathetic, ugly scene, doing no one any good.

At last my father stated finally: "I'm not going to argue about it. I am 85 keeping the goats."

The old Chief flashed back in his own language: "That means that my 86 people will go hungry when the dry season comes."

"Go to the police, then," said my father, and looked triumphant.   87

There was, of course, no more to be said.   88

The old man sat silent, his head bent, his hands dangling helplessly over   89
his withered knees. Then he rose, the young men helping him, and he stood
facing my father. He spoke once again, very stiffly; and turned away and went
home to his village.

"What did he say," asked my father of the young man, who laughed un-   90
comfortably and would not meet his eyes.

"What did he say," insisted my father.   91

Our cook stood straight and silent, his brows knotted together. Then he   92
spoke. "My father says: All this land, this land you call yours, is his land, and
belongs to our people."

Having made this statement, he walked off into the bush after his father,   93
and we did not see him again.

Our next cook was a migrant from Nyasaland, with no expectations of   94
greatness.

Next time the policeman came on his rounds he was told this story. He   95
remarked: "That kraal has no right to be there; it should have been moved
long ago. I don't know why no one has done anything about it. I'll have a
chat to the Native Commissioner next week. I'm going over for tennis on
Sunday, anyway."

Some time later we heard that Chief Mshlanga and his people had been   96
moved two hundred miles east, to a proper native reserve; the Government
land was going to be opened up for white settlement soon.

I went to see the village again, about a year afterwards. There was nothing   97
there. Mounds of red mud, where the huts had been, had long swathes of
rotting thatch over them, veined with the red galleries of the white ants. The
pumpkin vines rioted everywhere, over the bushes, up the lower branches of
trees so that the great golden balls rolled underfoot and dangled overhead: it
was a festival of pumpkins. The bushes were crowding up, the new grass sprang
vivid green.

The settler lucky enough to be allotted the lush warm valley (if he chose   98
to cultivate this particular section) would find, suddenly, in the middle of a
mealie field, the plants were growing fifteen feet tall, the weight of the cobs
dragging at the stalks, and wonder what unsuspected vein of richness he had
struck.

Focusing on Doris Lessing's Use of Revision Within Her Story

1. Identify the narrator's *point of view*—her relation to the subject—in the first thirteen paragraphs. Where have you heard the kind of language used in these paragraphs? Lessing says that the child "could not see a msasa tree, or the thorn, for what they were." What does the child see when she looks at a msasa tree, or any part of the African landscape?

2. How and to what does the point of view shift after paragraph 13? What is the effect of this shift? If the voice of the narrator is the voice of "I," who (or what) is speaking in the first thirteen paragraphs?

3. How were young whites trained to respond to blacks? When does the young girl first question that training? Why does her first meeting with old Chief Mshlanga disturb her ideas so completely? What is her first "revision" of her understanding of the way whites and blacks should get along with each other (to answer this question you might look at paragraphs 40 and 41)?

4. How does her experience of panic and fear, told in paragraphs 60 and 61, affect her ideas about Africa? How does her visit to the Chief's village cause her to revise her views of the relations of whites and blacks a second time?

5. How are young whites trained to think of themselves? How has the young girl revised her understanding of whites by the end of the essay? In particular, how has her view of her father changed?

6. What is ironic about the language of the last two paragraphs? How does it mock the language of the first section of this story? How does this change of language match the revision of the views of the young girl?

WORKING WITH THE TECHNIQUE IN YOUR OWN WRITING

1. Write an essay about a legend, a fairy tale, or some other story or myth that you have tried to use as a model for your life, even if only for a short time. You might have a clear memory of modeling yourself on some mythic character, of trying to become Snow White or Albert Einstein. You might also write about a time when you followed a myth without really knowing it; you could realize in looking back on your life that you always thought of yourself as a perfectly innocent girl hated by her wicked stepmother (like Snow White) or as an absent-minded genius, misunderstood by all around him (like Albert Einstein). See if you can explain the ways that the myth came into conflict with reality, forcing you to develop a revised version. For example, someone who tried to be Snow White may finally have decided that she could never be perfectly innocent and so have begun to think of herself as a combination of Snow White and the stepmother.

2. Write an essay about some myth that you see many people trying to reenact, to their detriment. Instead of simply advocating that people give up the myth, see if you can develop a revised version that they could adopt. It is much easier to persuade people to revise their ideas than to persuade them to abandon them.

TODD UNRUH

Oklahoma State University
Stillwater, Oklahoma
Don McDermott, instructor

Todd Unruh reports that he enjoys "reading, running, playing drums, and participating in all types of sports. I'm a member of FarmHouse fraternity at OSU. I'm involved in various campus relations committees organizing homecoming festivities and fundraising projects, and I compete in all kinds of intramurals." Born in Pampa, Texas, Unruh attended high school in Guymon, Oklahoma, where he worked summers operating his own lawn-mowing business and launching various projects for that city's Parks Department. Currently a physiology/pre-med student at Oklahoma State University, he hopes to attend medical school and "eventually become an orthopedic surgeon." Unruh acknowledges his family's support and encouragement: "I was raised to be very independent and became very accustomed to making my own decisions. I think my writing reflects this independence. I like to write—with strong feeling expressing new ideas."

Todd Unruh explains that he needs "complete silence, a well-lighted room, and a solitary area" to write. "I like to write in the late evenings (after 9:00 P.M.) in my room, where I've set up a secluded, partitioned area. . . . I have a hard time writing a first draft because I can't really get involved with the paper at this point. That's why an outline is imperative to my completion of a first draft. Also, I've always got to have a snack available."

Unruh wrote five drafts of "No Respecter of Persons." Asked to "narrate an experience which in retrospect has grown in significance," Unruh decided to draw on his experiences working in a cemetery during the summer. He aimed in the essay at "trying to make a philosophical statement about the value of life and the frivolity of death.

No Respecter of Persons

The backhoe groaned and rattled as it took ravenous bites from the earth. 1
I watched with the rest of the grave crew while the machine lifted the newly
exposed soil into the dump truck, and I couldn't help but notice the stale odor
of the moist, oily dirt which seemed to hover above the excavation. Then,
we lowered a cement vault which would contain and protect the casket from
the weight of the dirt. Rubbing wet dirt from my hands, I thought about the
burial I was about to perform. I guess I felt unworthy of burying another human
body, but because this would be my first burial, I wanted to do a good job.
The other workers, I thought, lacked this same reverent attitude, and I won-

dered how they could be so uncaring. I thought it was possible too that after I had more experience, I might also assume the same attitude of insensitivity. Maybe later, burials would actually seem commonplace and insignificant to me, but before that day came, I would ponder more than a little the significance of life and death.

I put the lowering device on top of the open grave after checking the position of the vault at the bottom of the pit. Ironically, I thought, caskets are lowered into graves in much the same way that lifeboats are lowered. Artificial turf was laid, a tent was erected; chairs were positioned. The site was ready, and we left to wait for the graveside services to begin. 2

The other members of the grave crew and I waited in the cemetery maintenance building, and we talked about the ceremony in progress. Looking through a dirty and cracked window, I watched the deceased's relatives and friends gathering under the tent and around the gravesite. One of the guys who worked with me said that his dad had been a friend of the man we were going to bury. The eighty-five-year-old retired postman had raised his two grandchildren. Beyond this, what else was there to say? He had had a "full life," and his "time was up." Within a few minutes, the brief service was ended. I guess I expected to see signs of mourning as the family was escorted away from the grave. But there was little more than a few comforting, but brief, embraces. It is hard to explain how insignificant it all seemed. There was a certain dutifulness among the mourners—this was true and we too had our duty that day towards the deceased—but there was no real sorrow. I saw this too in the faces of the men I worked with. 3

We left the building and paced down the green to the grave. The casket was in place, and my boss, flicking a burning cigarette butt into the fresh grave, said, "Todd, grab that handle and lower the casket real slowlike. But be careful because those damned things slip sometimes and dump the caskets straight down." 4

We had lowered the casket about three feet into the grave when the gears jammed due, no doubt, to the tremendous weight of the walnut casket. Even if there had been room in the grave for one of us to stand, the casket was too heavy to lift. I was exasperated, but my boss knew what to do. "Get down there, Todd. Stand on the casket—jump around on it. See if you can knock the damned thing loose by rocking it." 5

I felt funny jumping around on it, soiling the glossy walnut finish with my muddy hightops. Then, with a sudden jerk, the casket was free. I climbed back out of the grave, my hands and knees caked with mud, and finished lowering the casket. The three other workers and I then lifted the vault's cement lid and not so carefully lowered it till it fit snugly over the smudged casket. My 6 boss motioned for the dump truck to back up and fill in the grave. Then, to my astonishment, the falling dirt crushed the cement vault as if it were made of eggshells. Oh gawd, I thought, thinking that we would now have to dig the dirt, broken vault, and casket out.

"Nah," my boss said. "Go ahead and fill it up. Those damned boxes always   7 crush, and we could never get it out anyway."

I don't know what stunned me more. My jumping around on the casket and   8 then seeing the vault crushed, or just realizing that we didn't intend to do a thing about it.

We moved the tent and chairs, and rolled up the turf. I began my next job   9 of mowing surrounding plots, but my thoughts remained with the burial. Admittedly, I would want those close to me to be buried with care and reverence. This burial, which was supposed to be a memorial to the old man's life, only seemed to mock the significance of his life through our disgraceful mismanagement.

Several weeks later, I was again sitting in the maintenance building with   10 the rest of the grave crew. Looking through the same dirty window, I noticed that this day's ceremony was proceeding much differently. By this time I had performed fifteen or more burials, and they were all much like the old man's ceremony. However, with this ceremony there seemed to be a greater feeling of tragedy among the family as they reluctantly left the gravesite. Recalling the old man's interment a few weeks earlier, I remembered that there was almost no sorrow. Why was this burial so different? Whom were we going to bury? When I found out that she was a little, ten-year-old girl who had been hit by a car, a feeling of grief swept over me, and I understood why this ceremony seemed so different.

In fact, we all agreed, as we walked towards the gravesite, that it was a   11 terrible tragedy, but I felt that I was the only one who truly felt sadness. While I lowered the girl's casket, I noticed how much more carefully we handled the whole affair, and I was sincerely hoping, as though it was really important to me, that the dirt didn't crush the vault as it covered it. Well, it didn't and this was perhaps because of our concern.

Why had the old man's death seemed so insignificant compared to the girl's   12 death? Don't the old value their lives as much as the young? Certainly they do. I wondered if our grave crew, like society, hadn't treated the old man's death just as those around him had treated the old man's last few years. Had he been forgotten and neglected long before his funeral? At the child's funeral I felt a new sorrow for the old man's death.

As I arranged the flowers on the girl's grave, I looked up at one of the guys   13 and said, "You know, life is no respecter of persons."

"You mean, death is no respecter of persons, don't you?" he replied.   14
I thought for a moment and said, "No, I mean life."   15

Focusing on Todd Unruh's Techniques and Revisions

1. Todd Unruh's essay focuses on his first day on a new job—as a gravedigger. What perspective does he establish immediately on his new work? Summarize the nature of his initial reaction to his work (paragraph 1). What does the phrase "I guess" tell his readers about how clearly he sees himself in relation to his work? What other evidence can you point to in this paragraph that expresses his state of mind? How does his attitude toward his work change as the essay proceeds? Point to specific words and phrases to clarify your response.

2. How does the narrator see himself in relation to the other workers? What initial attitude does he express toward the people he works with? Where and how does his attitude toward them change? With what effects?

3. How does the line "life is no respecter of persons" summarize Unruh's mixed emotions toward his work, his fellow workers, and toward the mourners he observes through the "dirty and cracked window"? What, exactly, do you think Unruh means when he says this? What clarification of his meaning does he offer when he rejects the proposed substitution of "death" for "life"?

4. Consider the nature of his generalization that "life is no respecter of persons." Might the statement also be read as an aphorism, a concise statement of a truth? Explain. In what specific ways is an aphorism similar to and different from a generalization?

5. One of the principal satisfactions readers can gain from reading Unruh's essay carefully is that he continually surprises us—and himself—as he proceeds. His essay might well be read as a series of defeats of the expectations he creates, expectations about gravediggers as well as their work, about burial rites as well as their sponsors, about people's deaths as well as their lives. As you reread Unruh's essay, identify each instance when he defeats his readers'—and/or his own—expectations. In what ways, for example, does his opening paragraph appear to be a relatively traditional introduction? How does he quickly undermine that appearance? Find similar examples. What does each contribute to the overall effect of his essay?

6. What dramatic function(s) do paragraphs 2–6 serve? How do we suspect that the narrator will react to this scene? How are his readers expected to respond? Describe the narrator's *tone*—his attitude toward the subject—in these paragraphs. How does that tone change in paragraph 9? To what? With what effect? Show how the phrase "our disgraceful mismanagement" summarizes his thinking at this point.

7. How does Unruh further complicate his story in paragraphs 10 and 11? How does the last line in paragraph 11 balance the final line in paragraph 9? What is the effect of this "balance"? How do the last line in paragraph 11 as well as all of paragraph 12 prepare for the final generalization? How does Unruh use that generalization to comment on life and the ways people treat each other as much as on death and the ways people bury each other? What overriding point does Unruh make in the essay about *life* in juxtaposing the stories of the old man's and the young girl's burials? How, in effect, does Unruh demonstrate that death is as complicated as life?

8. Todd Unruh wrote five drafts of this essay. Reprinted below is the third draft of paragraph 9:

> We moved the tent and chairs and rolled up the turf. I then began my next job of mowing surrounding plots. Thoughts of the burial still weighed heavily on my mind because it was not at all as I had envisioned. The burial was not neat, clean, or even careful; it was crude, rough, and completely uncaring. Most people out of a basic expectation for reverence would be appalled at such treatment of their loved ones. And admittedly, I would want those close to me to be buried with care and reverence as well. This burial, which was supposed to be a memorial to the old man's life, only seemed to mock the significance of his life through its disgraceful mismanagement.

What changes does Unruh make in his final revision. Which version do you think is more effective? Explain why.

9. Here is the fourth draft of paragraph 12:

> Why had the old man's death compared to the girl's seemed so insignificant? Don't the old value their lives as much as the young value theirs? Certainly they do. Furthermore, we would all concede that life is an equal act of living no matter how old or young a person may be. I realized that our grave crew like society had treated the old man's death just as his life was treated. He had been forgotten and neglected. After pondering this realization about the "equality of life," I felt a new sorrow for the old man's death.

Identify the substance and the spirit of the revisions Unruh makes in the final draft of this paragraph. Evaluate the impact of each revision.

Suggestions for Writing

1. Write an essay in which you twist a proverb to gain new insight into your own experience or that of others. If you have some difficulty thinking of an appropriate proverb, consider one of the following:

> Our last garment is made without pockets.
>
> —Italian proverb

> Death cancels everything but truth.
>
> —Anonymous

> To die is poignantly bitter, but the idea of having to die without having lived is unbearable.
>
> —Erich Fromm

2. Read the following poem by the American writer Wallace Stevens:

The Emperor of Ice-Cream

Call the roller of big cigars,
The muscular one, and bid him whip
In kitchen cups concupiscent curds.
Let the wenches dawdle in such dress
As they are used to wear, and let the boys
Bring flowers in last month's newspapers.
Let be be finale of seem.
The only emperor is the emperor of ice-cream.

Take from the dresser of deal,
Lacking the three glass knobs, that sheet
On which she embroidered fantails once
And spread it so as to cover her face.
If her horny feet protrude, they come
To show how cold she is, and dumb.
Let the lamp affix its beam.
The only emperor is the emperor of ice-cream.

Write an essay analyzing the attitude toward death and life that Wallace Stevens expresses in this poem.

AN EFFECTIVE TECHNIQUE

Unruh uses an effective method to bring his readers to appreciate an unusual insight: he tells us the story of the mental struggle he went through to discover the insight. He arranges his essay to allow us to share his surprise at the unexpected conclusions he drew from his experiences working as a gravedigger.

Unruh begins his essay by putting us in the frame of mind that he had when he first joined the grave crew. The first paragraph lulls us as Unruh was lulled into thinking that all the insights to be gained from working in a cemetery would be about death. This paragraph looks like a standard introduction, ending on a general statement of what the essay will show us: "the significance of life and death." The title's allusion to an old proverb about death and the somber tone of the opening paragraph make us overlook the word "life": we think we have a good idea of what is coming in this essay—a chilling vision of death's indifference to human concerns. We expect, and dread, that the essay will show how Unruh eventually came to share the "insensitivity" of the experienced burial workers, how he learned that nothing really matters in the face of death.

However, the story develops in an unexpected way: in paragraphs 2–6, Unruh does not show us the somber triumph of death, but rather a grotesque black comedy—burial as farce. We become rather unsure how to react, as is Unruh: should we be outraged at the destruction of the concrete vault holding the elegant coffin or laugh at the people who pay for walnut and concrete in the deluded hope that it will somehow make a difference to a rotting corpse?

In paragraph 9, Unruh returns to the serious tone of the opening, to state his views in a straightforward way: the "disgraceful mismanagement" of the old man's burial "only seemed to mock the significance of his life." The essay seems over, Unruh's conclusion clear: people are callous, uncaring, especially those who make a living by dealing with death all the time.

But the essay continues, with a scene showing precisely what Unruh has led us to believe would never occur: the burial crew being properly reverential and grief-stricken. Unruh's original conclusion does not hold up, and he eventually has to revise it. He makes us realize how far he has come from his (and our) initial expectations of what he would learn from burying people by using as his final generalization an ironic reversal of the proverb we expected would be the point of the essay. When Unruh says, "life is no respecter of persons," he changes our perspective on the whole essay, making us realize finally that he has only incidentally been writing about death. He has been using burial scenes to comment on the callous way we treat people all our lives. His final point is complicated: he is not saying, as he did in the middle, that we are always callous, but rather that we are unfair in our choice of whom to care about. Moreover, he seems to suggest that little can be done about this unfairness; it is part of "life" that we cannot care about everyone equally. Life is as difficult to comprehend and accept as death.

Unruh's way of leading up to his final conclusion enables us to share his surprise at what he learns from his experiences and to share in the pleasure he has in finding the right words to state his insight. He shows us an unusual way to develop an essay centered on a generalization. Instead of presenting our main idea as a fully formed whole and then including only those stories and facts that best support our idea, we can re-create for our readers the circuitous mental paths we followed to settle on that idea. For example, we might begin an essay by describing our experience watching a dull Ping-Pong match and then wander off into thoughts about how our lives are equally dull: we do the same thing over and over again, proud of our skills, ignoring everything beyond the carefully marked boundaries of the proper games we play. We could take this structure a step further, as Unruh does, and include a second experience that then causes us to revise our conclusions. We might continue our essay by describing a day when we tried to play Ping-Pong in a truly nonconformist way, ending up feeling rather foolish. We might then end the essay wondering whether it is at all possible to exist outside of the games society dictates we play.

Phyllis Rose, in the next selection, takes her readers on a truly circuitous mental journey. She visits a museum of torture implements and a beauty parlor and from these two experiences leads us to some remarkable and unexpected generalizations about politics.

ANOTHER ILLUSTRATION OF THE TECHNIQUE

PHYLLIS ROSE

Tools of Torture:
An Essay on Beauty and Pain

"A life is as much a work of fiction—of guiding narrative structures—as novels and poems," writes Phyllis Rose. Her own life has been spent in the company of fiction, from her college days as an English major at Radcliffe to her current tenure as professor of English at Wesleyan University. She has specialized in the study of the way fictions entwine with life, her major "enthusiasms" being biography and women's literary history. She has written an acclaimed literary biography of Virginia Woolf and a study of five Victorian marriages. She has also published essays, often exploring the way she and others she knows create their own "personal mythologies" from everyday events. She believes that "each of us, influenced perhaps by one ideology or another, generates his or her own symbolic landscape, with its individual twists and curves, so that one person's fork in the road—to take a crude example, the fork between family and career—is no fork at all to another, but a two-lane highway."

In a gallery off the rue Dauphine, near the *parfumerie* where I get my mas- 1
sage, I happened upon an exhibit of medieval torture instruments. It made me
think that pain must be as great a challenge to the human imagination as
pleasure. Otherwise there's no accounting for the number of torture instruments. One would be quite enough. The simple pincer, let's say, which rips
out flesh. Or the head crusher, which breaks first your tooth sockets, then your
skull. But in addition I saw tongs, thumb-screws, a rack, a ladder, ropes and
pulleys, a grill, a garrote, a Spanish horse, a Judas cradle, an iron maiden, a
cage, a gag, a strappado, a stretching table, a saw, a wheel, a twisting stork,
an inquisitor's chair, a breast breaker, and a scourge. You don't need complicated machinery to cause incredible pain. If you want to saw your victim down
the middle, for example, all you need is a slightly bigger than usual saw. If
you hold the victim upside down so the blood stays in his head, hold his legs
apart, and start sawing at the groin, you can get as far as the navel before he
loses consciousness.

Even in the Middle Ages, before electricity, there were many things you 2
could do to torment a person. You could tie him up in an iron belt that held
the arms and legs up to the chest and left no point of rest, so that all his

muscles went into spasm within minutes and he was driven mad within hours. This was the twisting stork, a benign-looking object. You could stretch him out backward over a thin piece of wood so that his whole body weight rested on his spine, which pressed against the sharp wood. Then you could stop up his nostrils and force water into his stomach through his mouth. Then, if you wanted to finish him off, you and your helper could jump on his stomach, causing internal hemorrhage. This torture was called the rack. If you wanted to burn someone to death without hearing him scream, you could use a tongue lock, a metal rod between the jaw and collarbone that prevented him from opening his mouth. You could put a person in a chair with spikes on the seat and arms, tie him down against the spikes and beat him, so that every time he flinched from the beating he drove his own flesh deeper onto the spikes. This was the inquisitor's chair. If you wanted to make it worse, you could heat the spikes. You could suspend a person over a pointed wooden pyramid and whenever he started to fall asleep, you could drop him onto the point. If you were Ippolito Marsili, the inventor of this torture, known as the Judas cradle, you could tell yourself you had invented something humane, a torture that worked without burning flesh or breaking bones. For the torture here was supposed to be sleep deprivation.

The secret of torture, like the secret of French cuisine, is that nothing is unthinkable. The human body is like a foodstuff, to be grilled, pounded, filleted. Every opening exists to be stuffed, all flesh to be carved off the bone. You take an ordinary wheel, a heavy wooden wheel with spokes. You lay the victim on the ground with blocks of wood at strategic points under his shoulders, legs, and arms. You use the wheel to break every bone in his body. Next you tie his body onto the wheel. With all its bones broken, it will be pliable. However, the victim will not be dead. If you want to kill him, you hoist the wheel aloft on the end of a pole and leave him to starve. Who would have thought to do this with a man and a wheel? But, then, who would have thought to take the disgusting snail, force it to render its ooze, stuff it in its own shell with garlic butter, bake it, and eat it?

Not long ago I had a facial—only in part because I thought I needed one. It was research into the nature and function of pleasure. In a dark booth at the back of the beauty salon, the aesthetician put me on a table and applied a series of ointments to my face, some cool, some warmed. After a while she put something into my hand, cold and metallic. "Don't be afraid, madame," she said. "It is an electrode. It will not hurt you. The other end is attached to two metal cylinders, which I roll over your face. They break down the electricity barrier on your skin and allow the moisturizers to penetrate deeply." I didn't believe this hocus-pocus. I didn't believe in the electricity barrier or in the ability of these rollers to break it down. But it all felt very good. The cold metal on my face was a pleasant change from the soft warmth of the aesthetician's fingers. Still, since Algeria it's hard to hear the word "electrode" without fear. So when she left me for a few minutes with a moist, refreshing cheesecloth over my face, I thought, What if the goal of her expertise had been pain, not moisture? What if the electrodes had been electrodes in the Algerian sense? What if the cheesecloth mask were dipped in acid?

In Paris, where the body is so pampered, torture seems particularly sinister, 5 not because it's hard to understand but because — as the dark side of sensuality — it seems so easy. Beauty care is among the glories of Paris. *Soins esthétiques* include makeup, facials, massages (both relaxing and reducing), depilations (partial and complete), manicures, pedicures, and tanning, in addition to the usual run of *soins* for the hair: cutting, brushing, setting, waving, styling, blowing, coloring, and streaking. In Paris the state of your skin, hair, and nerves is taken seriously, and there is little of the puritanical thinking that tries to persuade us that beauty comes from within. Nor do the French think, as Americans do, that beauty should be offhand and low-maintenance. Spending time and money on *soins esthétiques* is appropriate and necessary, not self-indulgent. Should that loving attention to the body turn malevolent, you have torture. You have the procedure — the aesthetic, as it were — of torture, the explanation for the rich diversity of torture instruments, but you do not have the cause.

Historically torture has been a tool of legal systems, used to get information 6 needed for a trial or, more directly, to determine guilt or innocence. In the Middle Ages confession was considered the best of all proofs, and torture was the way to produce a confession. In other words, torture didn't come into existence to give vent to human sadism. It is not always private and perverse but sometimes social and institutional, vetted by the government and, of course, the Church. (There have been few bigger fans of torture than Christianity and Islam.) Righteousness, as much as viciousness, produces torture. There aren't squads of sadists beating down the doors to the torture chambers begging for jobs. Rather, as a recent book on torture by Edward Peters says, the institution of torture creates sadists; the weight of a culture, Peters suggests, is necessary to recruit torturers. You have to convince people that they are working for a great goal in order to get them to overcome their repugnance to the task of causing physical pain to another person. Usually the great goal is the preservation of society, and the victim is presented to the torturer as being in some way out to destroy it.

From another point of view, what's horrifying is how easily you can persuade 7 someone that he is working for the common good. Perhaps the most appalling psychological experiment of modern times, by Stanley Milgram, showed that ordinary, decent people in New Haven, Connecticut, could be brought to the point of inflicting (as they thought) severe electric shocks on other people in obedience to an authority and in pursuit of a goal, the advancement of knowledge, of which they approved. Milgram used—some would say abused—the prestige of science and the university to make his point, but his point is chilling nonetheless. We can cluck over torture, but the evidence at least suggests that with intelligent handling most of us could be brought to do it ourselves.

In the Middle Ages, Milgram's experiment would have had no point. It 8 would have shocked no one that people were capable of cruelty in the interest of something they believed in. That was as it should be. Only recently in the history of human thought has the avoidance of cruelty moved to the forefront of ethics. "Putting cruelty first," as Judith Shklar says in *Ordinary Vices*, is comparatively new. The belief that the "pursuit of happiness" is one of man's inalienable rights, the idea that "cruel and unusual punishment" is an evil in itself, the Benthamite notion that behavior should be guided by what will produce the greatest happiness for the greatest number—all these principles are only two centuries old. They were born with the eighteenth-century democratic revolutions. And in two hundred years they have not been universally accepted. Wherever people believe strongly in some cause, they will justify torture—not just the Nazis, but the French in Algeria.

Many people who wouldn't hurt a fly have annexed to fashion the imagery 9 of torture—the thongs and spikes and metal studs—hence reducing it to the frivolous and transitory. Because torture has been in the mainstream and not on the margins of history, nothing could be healthier. For torture to be merely kinky would be a big advance. Exhibitions like the one I saw in Paris, which presented itself as educational, may be guilty of pandering to the tastes they deplore. Solemnity may be the wrong tone. If taking one's goals too seriously is the danger, the best discouragement of torture may be a radical hedonism that denies that any goal is worth the means, that refuses to allow the nobly abstract to seduce us from the sweetness of the concrete. Give people a good croissant and a good cup of coffee in the morning. Give them an occasional facial and a plate of escargots. Marie Antoinette picked a bad moment to say "Let them eat cake," but I've often thought she was on the right track.

All of which brings me back to Paris, for Paris exists in the imagination of 10 much of the world as the capital of pleasure—of fun, food, art, folly, seduction, gallantry, and beauty. Paris is civilization's reminder to itself that nothing leads you less wrong than your awareness of your own pleasure and a genial desire to spread it around. In that sense the myth of Paris constitutes a moral touchstone, standing for the selfish frivolity that helps keep priorities straight.

Focusing on the Surprising Conclusions in Phyllis Rose's Essay

1. What is the effect of Rose's detailed descriptions of torture implements? The general point she seems to be proving in the first three paragraphs is that humans are very imaginative and inventive. Why does this seem a strange conclusion to draw from looking at torture implements?

2. What does Rose say about cuisine and beauty treatments in paragraphs 3, 4, and 5? How are these things similar to torture? How does her view of these sources of pleasure in paragraphs 9 and 10 differ from what she seems to say about them in paragraphs 3–5?

3. In what specific ways does the essay change after paragraph 5? How does Rose make it easy for us to follow her wandering essay?

4. Rose draws two surprising conclusions in paragraph 9, defending things that most people condemn: fashion accessories that look like instruments of torture and Marie Antoinette's famous line in response to the clamor of starving poor people demanding bread—"Let them eat cake." How does Rose defend these seemingly frivolous responses to the horrors of the world?

5. In the last sentence, Rose says that "selfish frivolity" is the best basis for morality. We usually think of "selfishness" and "frivolity" as worthless and immoral qualities. How does she defend these qualities? Do you agree with her arguments? Why or why not? Since she is defending frivolity, we might suspect that some parts of her essay are not meant to be taken seriously. What parts, if any, of her essay strike you as expressing a frivolous attitude?

WORKING WITH THE TECHNIQUE IN YOUR OWN WRITING

1. Describe in about a page an object, an event, a person, an argument, or anything else. You should probably pick something that you can describe fully in a page, so anything as complicated as your strange little brother or that endless night when you altered your brain's chemistry and went to a rock concert is probably too complicated. Try instead, say, one of your little brother's strange habits or your reaction to the presence of large numbers of chemically altered people at that rock concert. Whatever you pick, look at it in minute detail, and do not give up your description until you've exhausted the subject and filled about a page with nonrepetitive prose. Now speculate about that thing or event, moving to general thoughts that may be only indirectly connected to it. How has your description touched on other objects and events? Does your close look at whatever it is bring you to any conclusions about other things? Phyllis Rose looks at objects in a museum and wanders off to reflections about the nature of politics and fanaticism. Such odd and unexpected connec-

tions will come only if you give your attention not to making connections but to examining the original object of reflection in some detail.

2. Todd Unruh tells a story of how he developed increasingly complicated insights as he worked at his job. Write an essay about a time in your life when you found your ideas about something becoming increasingly complicated. You might write an essay about your reactions to a news story that developed for several weeks or months—perhaps revelations of scandal in government. Or you could write about something that you were involved in for a long time, such as a job, a class, or a neighborhood gang. You could begin your essay, as Unruh does his, by showing your readers how you started out with fairly clear expectations of what insights you would gain from reading about the government scandal, taking the job, or being in a gang and then go on to show how you had to repeatedly change your ideas. Try to bring your readers to share your experience of being surprised by the unexpectedness and complexity of your insights.

TOR VALENZA

Middlebury College
Middlebury, Vermont
John Elder, instructor

Tor Valenza believes that the most useful advice he could give to other student writers is "the same advice that every writing teacher has given me: if you want to write well, then you must practice as much as you can without becoming so obsessed that it is the only thing you do. Writing is living and observing and manipulating those experiences and observations. You can't observe the world from your dorm room. Know yourself. Don't attempt to do what you can't do; otherwise you'll never finish it or, if you do, it will be a giant pile of pretentious caca."

Valenza's father encouraged him to write, even though, as he reports, "before the eleventh grade I wanted to go into engineering. Taking physics and calculus changed my mind. I always took my grades in English for granted, except in eleventh grade. My English teacher gave me annoying grades, such as B+ + +/−, which meant 'almost, but not quite A−.' This inspired me to try for that A−, and by the end of the semester I finally did it with an essay entitled 'Prostitution in McBurney School.'"

Tor Valenza was born and raised in New York City and graduated, A− in hand, from the McBurney School. "I am eight minutes younger than my twin sister, Tasia. My brother, D. Greg, is two and a half years older than us. . . . I think that the fact that my parents were divorced when I was two has given me a certain degree of independence. When I was ten, I was diagnosed as having diabetes. This is also a factor in my independence. New York has given me a wide background for people, places, stereotypes, original characters, and independence. (I like that word.) Not having protective parents, I was allowed to explore on my own." Valenza has worked at various jobs "since twelve, from dog walker to waiter to New York City bicycle messenger." Cycling and cross-country skiing are his favorite sports. A film major at Middlebury College, Valenza hopes to pursue a career as "a screenwriter-director, and maybe write a book or two."

Tor Valenza explains that he wrote "At Diane's" to encourage the reader "to think about his or her group of friends and where they hung out, etc., and how they perhaps thought they 'knew it all' when they still had much to learn—as most people, including myself had, and still have, too much to learn about ourselves and others. I'm not sure of the reaction to my essay from those who didn't grow up in a big city. But I thought that as long as there was a burger joint 'just like any other burger joint' any reader could relate."

At Diane's

When Diane's burgers were only a buck and change, Columbus Avenue was   1
only Columbus Avenue and Mayor Koch was only Ed Koch. Diane's was a

little burger joint, just like any other burger joint, where we met for dinner before going to see a flick at the 83rd St. Quad, or hanging out at Alisa's house, listening to tunes and lying on her floor while Brian did one-armed push-ups, Tanya took pictures of me tossing roasted cashews in Martin's mouth, and Aria just sat on Alisa's couch wondering why we had left Diane's.

When Diane's burgers went to $1.85 we had just entered high school, 2 Columbus Avenue had the makings of a mini–Madison Avenue, and Mayor Koch had won his second term, having run on both the Democratic and Republican tickets. What used to be only a gray, cracked, dusty, New York sidewalk had been garnished with a sapling tree, which would become my usual spot for waiting until the others showed. I could always count on Martin to come next and take his place behind me, sitting on the car that's always parked in the reflection of Diane's window. Alisa and Tanya seemed to always stroll across the street together with Brian strategically following them close behind. We walked into Diane's knowing well that somewhere in the distance, Aria was running past a pedestrian and he would sit down, thirsty and out of breath, just as we gave our drink order.

With the price of Diane's burgers soaring to $2.05, Columbus Avenue had 3 opened its first Benetton and Mayor Koch had published his first autobiography. The five of us were huddled in one of Diane's dark-brown, wooden booths, waiting for a girl in a green Diane's tee-shirt to take our order. Although the burgers were not a buck and change, the menu was still the same: burgers, burgers on an English muffin, bacon burgers and mushroom burgers, cheese burgers and chili burgers. They were all delicious. We forgot about the ome- lettes, or we didn't care about them. It went without saying that we'd have a few side orders of fries and onion rings to munch on between sips of Cokes and Tabs. The waitresses who would take our order were all beautiful young girls working their way through college or waiting for their big break. In a sense, we were waiting for our own big break but weren't aware of it. Though we were only fifteen, the waitresses would still treat us like adults, which was fine by us since we thought we were.

Two weeks before Diane's announced that it would be renovating to keep 4 up with the rest of Columbus Avenue, the price of a burger jumped to $2.45. Meanwhile, Mayor Koch's best-seller was being produced as a successful off- Broadway musical, and we ate our burgers with the conversation running in five different directions—as usual. Alisa wondered how she would ever break a thousand on the SATs while Tanya, bloated from being on the pill, talked about Andy in between bites of a plain burger with no fries. As Martin tried to explain to Tanya the medical reasons why she was gaining weight, I was breaking the news to Aria that I didn't think I wanted to be a solar engineer any more. That was OK, because Brian thought he would have an athletic scholarship and would apply to Tufts with Aria.

As Mayor Koch won another landslide victory and Columbus Avenue saw 5 yet another sushi restaurant open, Diane's burgers were up to $2.65. That was cool; we could splurge now that we had our acceptances behind us. We could even afford dessert, always a giant extravaganza. The only thing Diane's served were these massive ice cream sundaes. How could we refuse? We all knew when Alisa scored 1500 on her SAT that she would get into Yale and then celebrate by eating a whole "Death by Chocolate" sundae all by her lonesome, enjoying every calorie she devoured. Tanya began her new life without Andy by first cutting her extraneous daily supplements, then by replacing them with a new sundae fetish. At Bennington, she declared, things would be different. Martin, the aspiring physician, warned us of the evils of sugar, as he swallowed a cancer-causing red maraschino cherry, as if it were a goldfish. Aria just ate his scoop of Rum Raisin with quiet delight. I think that's what he thought Tufts was like, without the quiet. I guess Brian was the most excited of all of us. He literally picked up the waitress who brought him his "Banana Rocky Road Bonanza Split." We gave him a few forks to bend and he eventually settled down.

Not having a sweet tooth, I sat with a cup of coffee and enjoyed the 6 company. I started to think about when we'd meet at Diane's next. I figured by Christmas break Koch would be president, Columbus would look like Rodeo Drive, and Diane's burgers would be five bucks. Alisa, Tanya, Martin, Brian, and I would still meet in front of the sapling, which would no longer be a sapling, but a tree, and we'd walk in just as Aria was maneuvering around the crowds of people idly walking by Diane's—a burger joint, just like any other burger joint, where we met for dinner before going to see a flick at the 83rd St. Quad or hanging out at Alisa's house lying on her floor while Brian did one-arm push-ups, Tanya took pictures of me tossing roasted cashews in Martin's mouth, and Aria just sat on Alisa's couch wondering why we had ever left Diane's.

Focusing on Tor Valenza's Techniques and Revisions

1. Tor Valenza's essay presents a series of vignettes highlighting the changing lives of a group of high school friends. Each paragraph functions as a figurative snapshot of their individual and collective lives. What strategies does Valenza use to unify the paragraphs? What, for example, do you notice about the syntax, the rhythm, and the diction of the opening sentence of each section? How are these stylistic features used in a similar manner in each opening sentence?

2. Consider the overall sequence of the paragraphs in this essay. Chart the chronology Valenza establishes in this sequence. Identify the principal events that signify the group's advances in experience and consciousness. To what end does the sequence of paragraphs seem to lead? What conclusion(s), if any, does Valenza draw in the final paragraph of the essay? What overriding point, in effect, does Valenza seem to make in the essay? How is that point reflected in his decisions about the essay's structure, syntax, and diction?

3. Consider the nature and the purpose of Valenza's depiction of the students. To what extent does Valenza distinguish one student from another? How individualistic are their hopes and aspirations, their fears and anxieties? What do you remember about their individual lives? What purpose, what compositional end, does this strategy seem to serve? Point to specific passages to support your response.

4. The price of burgers at Diane's serves as a controlling metaphor in the essay. How, for example, does the ever-increasing price of burgers come to represent something important about these students' lives? What kinds of figurative equations does Valenza establish between, on the one hand, either Koch and the White House or Columbus Avenue and New York City's gentrification and, on the other, these students and the colleges they'll attend?

5. As each student gets ready to pursue his or her own vision of success, what does Valenza do to suggest that somehow these people will still remain a group? In this respect, reread the first and final paragraphs of the essay. What similarities do you notice in their overall organization, sentence structure, syntax, and diction? What reasonable inferences might you draw about Valenza's purpose from these similarities?

6. Reread the final paragraph. What kinds of limitations, if any, does Valenza build into his final vision of both the group's identity and each member's individual success? Does the essay, in effect, bring to closure its optimistic, future-oriented view of the lives of these students, their hometown, or its mayor?

7. One of the remarkable features of Valenza's essay is his ability to create effective and memorable similes and metaphors. Consider, for example, paragraph 5, where Martin, "the aspiring physician," warns of "the evils of sugar, as he swallowed a cancer-causing red maraschino cherry, as if it were a goldfish." Locate other examples of successful similes and metaphors. What does each contribute to the overall effect of the essay?

8. When invited to identify the most successful features of Tor Valenza's essay, his instructor, John Elder, offered these observations: "Tor Valenza's work has a nice sense of *situation*. He wants to write movies, and I think that this piece shows his ability to evoke physical surroundings and social chemistry. I also like very much his ability to combine a New Yorker's tough, satirical perspective

with a warm, caring voice." As you reread Valenza's essay, point to those moments that warrant each of his instructor's specific points of praise.

9. From what point of view does the narrator present the details and events? Does that perspective remain unchanged throughout the essay? Consider the final paragraph. Does the narrator provide any indication that he is distancing himself—either physically or in tone—from the other members of the group? What evidence can you point to that might suggest that Valenza treats the group wryly, if not satirically?

Suggestions for Writing

1. Recall your own high school years, especially those anxious times when you considered the merits of attending one college or another. Write an essay in which you lead your readers through the confusions and uncertainties of that period. Using Valenza's essay as a model, create a unifying device for your essay.

2. Consider the nature of the changes that are occurring in your hometown. Write an essay in which you describe a particular location in detail and use it to symbolize the town's transformation.

AN EFFECTIVE TECHNIQUE

Tor Valenza takes the unusual tack of relying entirely on the structure of his essay to convey his point, a point he never states directly. His essay is like a song whose effect depends more on how its melody sounds than on what its lyrics say. Like a song, Valenza's essay is held together by its repetitions and its rhythms. Each paragraph is an independent scene, like a stanza, presenting an episode in the life of a group of high school friends. The paragraphs are held together by their opening sentences, which are so similar that they act like a refrain running throughout this song. No matter what happens to these friends in a particular paragraph, we know the next one will once again mention Diane's burgers, Columbus Avenue, and Mayor Koch. As in a ballad, we follow a story through the stanzas/paragraphs, but this story has only the most delicate climax and resolution. The point of this essay is not contained in the plot or the actions of the main characters, but rather in the rhythms and the repetitions that structure the details of the essay, making us feel a part of the flow of life that seems to cause everything and everyone to change together.

The individual decisions, hopes, and fears of this group of friends are presented as merely part of the changes affecting everything else in New York. Valenza makes us feel that the rising hopes of these high school students are part of a general inflation pushing everything up; these students will gain glory in elite colleges only because they are carried on the same rising tide that will send Koch to the White House and Diane's prices beyond the range of a typical "burger joint." We can barely tell the friends apart; mostly we let ourselves flow along as we read, enjoying being part of such a happy group with such great hopes for the future.

Even when it seems that the group must disband, as each member goes to a different college, the essay simply ends with a dream of their returning to Diane's sometime in the future. Valenza makes us share the hope that everyone's independent success will not break apart the flow of the group. The last few lines of the essay return to the last few lines of the first paragraph and make us hope that the pleasures of hanging out together will last longer than the glory of individual success.

Valenza shows us how to use elements of essays that we usually overlook—rhythms, repetitions—to re-create a certain kind of experience and communicate a "point" about that experience. Writers often use repetitions and rhythms in small parts of their essays, usually in climactic moments, where emotions become very strong. Strong emotions have strong rhythms and are often well expressed in repeated phrases—repeated curses or repeated shouts of joy, for instance. When a writer uses repetition throughout a work, as Valenza does, something else happens: instead of one intense moment of emotion, we feel instead a muted and extended emotion that seems to permeate everything. The sense that the way one is feeling will last forever and be shared by everyone can be delightful, as it is in Valenza's essay, a dissolving of the individual in a warm and friendly environment where all acts turn out happy.

On the other hand, the sense of unchangingness, of the irrelevance of individual actions, that derives from constant repetition can also be used to create a nightmare, as we see in the next selection. Valenza shows the joy of people constantly rising on an economic boomtide; Jo Goodwin Parker shows the horror of people endlessly falling, caught up in an economic mudslide.

ANOTHER ILLUSTRATION OF THE TECHNIQUE

JO GOODWIN PARKER

What Is Poverty?

Who is Jo Goodwin Parker? We don't know. She made her unusual first appearance as a writer when George Henderson, a professor at the University of Oklahoma, was preparing his book America's Other Children: Public Schools Outside Suburbia *(1971). Henderson received the following essay in the mail from West Virginia with Parker's name on it; he decided to include it in his book even though he could not make contact with the author. Whether Parker wrote it out of personal experience or as a spokesperson for America's rural poor, we will never know.*

You ask me what is poverty? Listen to me. Here I am, dirty, smelly, and with no "proper" underwear on and with the stench of my rotting teeth near you. I will tell you. Listen to me. Listen without pity. I cannot use your pity. Listen with understanding. Put yourself in my dirty, worn-out, ill-fitting shoes, and hear me. 1

Poverty is getting up every morning from a dirt- and illness-stained mattress. The sheets have long since been used for diapers. Poverty is living in a smell that never leaves. This is a smell of urine, sour milk, and spoiling food sometimes joined with the strong smell of long-cooked onions. Onions are cheap. If you have smelled this smell, you did not know how it came. It is the smell of the outdoor privy. It is the smell of young children who cannot walk the long dark way in the night. It is the smell of the mattresses where years of "accidents" have happened. It is the smell of the milk which has gone sour because the refrigerator long has not worked, and it costs money to get it fixed. It is the smell of rotting garbage. I could bury it, but where is the shovel? Shovels cost money. 2

Poverty is being tired. I have always been tired. They told me at the hospital when the last baby came that I had chronic anemia caused from poor diet, a bad case of worms, and that I needed a corrective operation. I listened politely— the poor are always polite. The poor always listen. They don't say that there is no money for iron pills, or better food, or worm medicine. The idea of an operation is frightening and costs so much that, if I had dared, I would have laughed. Who takes care of my children? Recovery from an operation takes a long time. I have three children. When I left them with "Granny" the last 3 time I had a job, I came home to find the baby covered with fly specks, and a diaper that had not been changed since I left. When the dried diaper came off, bits of my baby's flesh came with it. My other child was playing with a sharp bit of broken glass, and my oldest was playing alone at the edge of a lake. I made twenty-two dollars a week, and a good nursery school costs twenty dollars a week for my three children. I quit my job.

Poverty is dirt. You say in your clean clothes coming from your clean house, "Anybody can be clean." Let me explain about housekeeping with no money. For breakfast I give my children grits with no oleo or cornbread without eggs and oleo. This does not use up many dishes. What dishes there are, I wash in cold water and with no soap. Even the cheapest soap has to be saved for the baby's diapers. Look at my hands, so cracked and red. Once I saved for two months to buy a jar of Vaseline for my hands and the baby's diaper rash. When I had saved enough, I went to buy it and the price had gone up two cents. The baby and I suffered on. I have to decide every day if I can bear to put my cracked, sore hands into the cold water and strong soap. But you ask, why not hot water? Fuel costs money. If you have a wood fire it costs money. If you burn electricity, it costs money. Hot water is a luxury. I do not have luxuries. I know you will be surprised when I tell you how young I am. I look so much older. My back has been bent over the wash tubs for so long, I cannot remember when I ever did anything else. Every night I wash every stitch my school-age child has on and just hope her clothes will be dry by morning.

Poverty is staying up all night on cold nights to watch the fire, knowing one spark on the newspaper covering the walls means your sleeping children die in flames. In summer poverty is watching gnats and flies devour your baby's tears when he cries. The screens are torn and you pay so little rent you know they will never be fixed. Poverty means insects in your food, in your nose, in your eyes, and crawling over you when you sleep. Poverty is hoping it never rains because diapers won't dry when it rains and soon you are using newspapers. Poverty is seeing your children forever with runny noses. Paper handkerchiefs cost money and all your rags you need for other things. Even more costly are antihistamines. Poverty is cooking without food and cleaning without soap.

Poverty is asking for help. Have you ever had to ask for help, knowing your children will suffer unless you get it? Think about asking for a loan from a relative, if this is the only way you can imagine asking for help. I will tell you how it feels. You find out where the office is that you are supposed to visit. You circle that block four or five times. Thinking of your children, you go in. Everybody is very busy. Finally, someone comes out and you tell her that you need help. That never is the person you need to see. You go see another person, and after spilling the whole shame of your poverty all over the desk between you, you find that this isn't the right office after all—you must repeat the whole process, and it never is any easier at the next place.

You have asked for help, and after all it has a cost. You are again told to 7 wait. You are told why, but you don't really hear because of the red cloud of shame and the rising black cloud of despair.

Poverty is remembering. It is remembering quitting school in junior high 8 because "nice" children had been so cruel about my clothes and my smell. The attendance officer came. My mother told him I was pregnant. I wasn't, but she thought that I could get a job and help out. I had jobs off and on, but never long enough to learn anything. Mostly I remember being married. I was so young then. I am still young. For a time, we had all the things you have. There was a little house in another town, with hot water and everything. Then my husband lost his job. There was unemployment insurance for a while and what few jobs I could get. Soon, all our nice things were repossessed and we moved back here. I was pregnant then. This house didn't look so bad when we first moved in. Every week it gets worse. Nothing is ever fixed. We now had no money. There were a few odd jobs for my husband, but everything went for food then, as it does now. I don't know how we lived through three years and three babies, but we did. I'll tell you something, after the last baby I destroyed my marriage. It had been a good one, but could you keep on bringing children in this dirt? Did you ever think how much it costs for any kind of birth control? I knew my husband was leaving the day he left, but there were no good-byes between us. I hope he has been able to climb out of this mess somewhere. He never could hope with us to drag him down.

That's when I asked for help. When I got it, you know how much it was? 9 It was, and is, seventy-eight dollars a month for the four of us; that is all I ever can get. Now you know why there is no soap, no needles and thread, no hot water, no aspirin, no worm medicine, no hand cream, no shampoo. None of these things forever and ever and ever. So that you can see clearly, I pay twenty dollars a month rent, and most of the rest goes for food. For grits and cornmeal, and rice and milk and beans. I try my best to use only the minimum electricity. If I use more, there is that much less for food.

Poverty is looking into a black future. Your children won't play with my 10 boys. They will turn to other boys who steal to get what they want. I can already see them behind the bars of their prison instead of behind the bars of my poverty. Or they will turn to the freedom of alcohol or drugs, and find themselves enslaved. And my daughter? At best, there is for her a life like mine.

But you say to me, there are schools. Yes, there are schools. My children 11 have no extra books, no magazines, no extra pencils, or crayons, or paper and the most important of all, they do not have health. They have worms, they have infections, they have pink-eye all summer. They do not sleep well on the floor, or with me in my one bed. They do not suffer from hunger, my seventy-eight dollars keeps us alive, but they do suffer from malnutrition. Oh yes, I do remember what I was taught about health in school. It doesn't do much good. In some places there is a surplus commodities program. Not here. The county said it cost too much. There is a school lunch program. But I have two children who will already be damaged by the time they get to school.

But, you say to me, there are health clinics. Yes, there are health clinics 12 and they are in the towns. I live out here eight miles from town. I can walk that far (even if it is sixteen miles both ways), but can my little children? My neighbor will take me when he goes; but he expects to get paid, *one way or another*. I bet you know my neighbor. He is that large man who spends his time at the gas station, the barbershop, and the corner store complaining about the government spending money on the immoral mothers of illegitimate children.

Poverty is an acid that drips on pride until all pride is worn away. Poverty 13 is a chisel that chips on honor until honor is worn away. Some of you say that you would do *something* in my situation, and maybe you would, for the first week or the first month, but for year after year after year?

Even the poor can dream. A dream of a time when there is money. Money 14 for the right kinds of food, for worm medicine, for iron pills, for toothbrushes, for hand cream, for a hammer and nails and a bit of screening, for a shovel, for a bit of paint, for some sheeting, for needles and thread. Money to pay *in money* for a trip to town. And, oh, money for hot water and money for soap. A dream of when asking for help does not eat away the last bit of pride. When the office you visit is as nice as the offices of other governmental agencies, when there are enough workers to help you quickly, when workers do not quit in defeat and despair. When you have to tell your story to only one person, and that person can send you for other help and you don't have to prove your poverty over and over and over again.

I have come out of my despair to tell you this. Remember I did not come 15 from another place or another time. Others like me are all around you. Look at us with an angry heart, anger that will help you help me. Anger that will let you tell of me. The poor are always silent. Can you be silent too?

Focusing on Jo Goodwin Parker's Use of Repetition

1. How do the repeated commands to "listen" in the first paragraph make you feel? How does the last line in the essay recall the opening paragraph? What is the effect of this circular structure?

2. What is the effect of the repetition of the word "poverty" throughout the essay? What kind of progression do the "Poverty is . . ." sentences show over the course of the essay? How would the effect be different if Parker began with the long-term impact of poverty on her family (see paragraphs 10 and 11) instead of with the sight and smell of herself and her house? The word "poverty" disappears from the last two paragraphs. What is the effect of her leaving the word out of those paragraphs?

3. What words and phrases besides "poverty" does Parker use repetitively, either within a paragraph or over the course of her essay? What are the effects of such repetition? How does it suit Parker's subject?

4. How does Parker keep us from becoming bored even though she repeats words and phrases so often? Both Valenza's essay and Parker's are fairly short. How could an author write an effective essay that is much longer than these two and still rely on repetitions to structure it?

WORKING WITH THE TECHNIQUE IN YOUR OWN WRITING

---

1. Practice using Valenza's unusual structure: write an essay describing the changes in a group of persons to which you belonged by showing a series of brief scenes of the group at different times. You might use one paragraph for each scene, as Valenza does. You can write about a short or a long time period—a few weeks or many years. Try to give your readers a sense of things being repeated over and over again, but a little bit differently each time. You might use similar settings or actions in each scene. For example, you could show people going to class in each scene, and vary the way they walk and what they say about their classes; or you might show several kids arguing with their parents in each scene, first arguing about toys, then about clothes, then about car keys, then . . . . Use a sentence or two at the beginning of each scene to identify the date of each scene, but do so by describing how some part of the neighborhood, the city, or the country appeared at each date. See if you can make your readers feel that there is a general flow carrying everything along during this period.

2. Write an essay about something that seemed to color everything in your life for a long time—and perhaps still does. You might write about such things as being caught in the throes of adolescence, being in a wheelchair, being very attractive, or being on a football team. Structure at least part of your essay as Jo Goodwin Parker structures hers. She builds her paragraphs around sentences beginning "Poverty is . . ."; you could develop sentences like those, beginning "Adolescence is . . ."; "Living in a wheelchair is . . ."; or "Being pretty is . . . ." Use repetition to create the feeling that what you are writing about affects almost everything in your life.

STUDENT WRITERS
AT WORK

Part II

1.

REVISING DRAFTS

MOST PEOPLE WRITE without consciously thinking about what they are doing. There are as many writing habits as there are writers. Some people can write anywhere—riding on buses, waiting in line, sitting in restaurants—while others need special conditions. Barbara Seidel, for instance, reports: "I want the house to be silent except for the sporadic squawking of my birds. I need to be left alone, without the phone ringing, or without anyone asking me questions or needing me at the moment. I sit at my desk, running my fingers through my hair, reaching for pieces of chocolate, or grabbing for a drink of ice water. I move around a lot in my chair, sigh deeply, and stare at the wall. Finally, I put pen to paper and write."

This chapter observes Barbara Seidel at work—getting started, drafting, and revising—and considers writing from her point of view. Seidel talks about her concerns as she worked through her pile of notes and six drafts to a final, prize-winning essay. Even though all writers need to find the conditions and circumstances that work best for them, we can still learn a great deal about the stages of the writing process by studying how one writer made important decisions and revisions as she progressed through these stages.

Too often when a piece of writing is successful, readers do not have the opportunity to see how it was written; the writing carries them along so that they are not concerned with the writer's process. The writing reads smoothly and logically and readers assume, if anything, that it must have flowed equally smoothly from the writer's pen. What readers don't see are the scratch-outs and the drafts, the decisions and conversations that went on in the writer's mind to produce such writing.

Seidel's notes and drafts show that her carefully conceived and balanced essay required a great deal of work. She began with fragments—notes to herself.

Her ideas did not spring full-blown from her mind in clear, coherent prose. Rather, they tumbled out in unformed, fragmented ways that she developed in draft after draft as she made decisions, evaluated those decisions, and adjusted her writing so that the new decisions were consistent with what she had already written. Guiding Seidel throughout the process were the concerns of subject, audience, and purpose.

This chapter begins with a detailed look at how Seidel wrote her essay "A Tribute to My Father." It concludes with Brad Manning's drafts for his essay "Arm-Wrestling with My Father," which is presented as an exercise. The drafts of these writers reveal how writing evolves from tentative beginnings to become effective writing. What clearly emerges is the power and possibility of writing.

Getting Started

In her freshman writing class, Barbara Seidel was given the broad assignment of writing a tribute to someone. She reports that she decided immediately to write about her father: "My first reaction to this assignment, though, was a feeling of slight panic. I knew I wanted to write about my dad and I thought the assignment would give me a chance to further understand him and our relationship. But I kept thinking, This is going to be tough; I will have to be open and vulnerable if I am going to write plainly about Dad. I knew if I did otherwise, the essay would not work."

For a writer, having a subject to write about is only the beginning. Seidel knew her subject—she knew she had a strong interest in writing about her father—but she didn't know specifically what she wanted to say about him. She needed to get her thoughts down on paper to see what she wanted to write. Seidel's method of getting started was brainstorming, a strategy that helps a writer think as quickly and broadly as possible about a subject by writing down everything about the subject that springs to mind. Brainstorming usually takes the form of an unstructured list with words and phrases written as quickly and uncritically as possible. Brainstorming helps Seidel to get involved with any subject quickly. "I jot down words, ideas, and images to give me a way of remembering what I know; the more I brainstorm, the more I have to work with." Here are copies of Seidel's brainstorming sheets for her essay.

Barbara Seidel's Brainstorming Notes

```
--58 years old
--parents divorced when he was young
--1 older brother, Arthur, mom's favorite
```

--young--white hair, pale skin, blue eyes

--young--brother had darker skin, brown
eyes, black hair

--grew up--wore hand-me-down clothes and
shoes--used to fold newspapers into
shoes

--Mother worked early morn til after dinner

--went to corner store for meal--Mother
paid $ in advance to store

--hell-raiser as teen; didn't like
school, dropped out (car and Uncle Art)

--Navy man during WWII; never overseas

--loved animals; always bringing home
strays

--saw little of his father who was alcoholic, til age of 19 (father dating)

--great common sense, wise man, folk sayings

--not an intellectual; doesn't read; not
"learned"

--patient; calm in crisis; resigned

--very hard worker; in car business since
hung around father's car lot in late
teens

--family man; loyal, devoted, dependable

--instinctive, yet never called it that
(marrying Mom)

--extremely honest

--non-confronter: peace within family at
all costs, sometimes to detriment of
people

--not religious

--worrier; drives people crazy (5 countdown humorous quirk)

--obsessive about details; perfectionist:
towels just so, etc.

--5'7"

--sandy blond hair, reddish gold, curly,
short

--blue eyes, glasses

--long oval face with slightly square jaw

--conservative dresser

```
--man of habits; does not like change
--homebody; needs family warmth and love;
  gravitated to Mom's family
--dependable (Uncle Art; Mom--illnesses)
--loves candy (would hide his choc. in
  night table drawer and diet sundae--
  humorous quirks)
--strong sense of traditional values (his
  father ill, etc.; his mom driving him
  crazy yet he's there; grave)
--slow to anger but doesn't forget;
  stubborn
--drives around corner in car to cool
  down
--horseback riding when younger with
  daughter
--closer to daughter than son thru child-
  hood years; able to talk with son when
  grown
--likes to talk things out
--Mother said he and his daughter very
  alike
```

Seidel spent a half-hour brainstorming, letting her mind roam, and generating details and information. Her brainstorming sheets are rich with possibilities; it is clear that she knows her subject well. To an outside observer, these notes might look rather disorganized and idiosyncratic. We might ask: What does "5 countdown humorous quirk" mean or what about "perfectionist: towels just so, etc."? Yet this is how notes at this stage might well look. Seidel is writing these notes for herself, an audience of one, and it is important only that she can read and interpret them. What outside observers can see in these notes, however, is that Seidel asked herself important questions as she brainstormed in order to collect her thoughts and to see what she wanted to write. She asked, for instance, What does Dad look like? What can I say about his family—his background—his growing up poor? What are his values? One thought suggested another.

These brainstorming sheets offered Seidel enough information to write a first draft. She had collected a stock of materials to work with, and this helped her feel confident that she knew where she was headed. As she reports: "My brainstorming served as a road map, pointing me where I should focus my attention and helping me to see how I wanted to view my subject."

Getting started is often the most difficult stage for writers. They stare at the blank page, waiting for inspiration, expecting to write a perfect opening sentence. Or they write something down, strike it out, crumple up the paper, mumble to themselves, "This isn't what I wanted to say," and begin again—and again. Having no sense of direction to guide them, they are forced to improvise, attempting to find ideas at the same time they are developing and organizing them. The time spent in getting started is time well spent. Writers write with more confidence and ease if they have developed a focus for their first drafts. Such a focus shows writers where they are headed and leads them to a more developed and organized draft.

Seidel's brainstorming notes offered her numerous details, but these details were unsorted and unfocused. She spent some time thinking about her notes and asking herself: Which details seem most interesting? Which details can be developed? How can these details be grouped to provide a focus? As she reports, "Before I wrote my first draft, I read and reread my notes. They clearly pointed me in the direction of *contrasts, honor,* and *principles.* These were factors about my father I intuitively knew were important to me, but I had never before identified or singled out. I realized these factors could be used as a focus to write about my father with both objectivity and compassion."

Drafting

Having reread and thought about her notes, Seidel wrote her first draft. She reports: "As I wrote my first draft, I was excited about my essay. I knew I had something important to say about my father. I just let loose in writing this draft so that I could connect all my notes and the ideas that were still rushing through my head. If I try to be too orderly in the first draft, then I am stymied. A first draft is always an experiment; I am still testing and exploring what I want to write. I was still trying to describe my father, make me see and understand him, so that my readers could. My lead sentence, 'Actions speak louder than words, he often said,' kept jumping into my head. I found it to be a very telling phrase and I knew it gave me a good sentence with which to start writing."

The following is Seidel's first draft.

Seidel's First Draft

A Tribute to My Father

Actions speak louder than words, he often said. If so,   1
there are actions that say much about the man. There was
that moment, thirty years ago, when his father was dying
slowly of cancer. In order to take his father to and from
the hospital for medical care, he would arise at dawn, leaving his wife and small children asleep in the tiny house, and
drive the distance on deserted city streets. Years later,
his own daughter, puzzled, would ask why he showed such devotion to the man who had divorced his mother and almost abandoned him and his brother. He answered, with a faint look
of surprise at the question, "He was my father."

As though such an answer explains it all . . . he is   2
still not a man to say more when less will do. Soft-spoken,
slow to anger but long in remembering, he has his own set of
values. The towels in the linen closet were always folded
just so. The lights in an unused room turned off, to the
exasperation of children lectured to do likewise. One's
word is one's bond, he said. Loyalty, respect, tradition,
honesty . . . these were the basic tenets of his life, unspoken but inherent. Perhaps it is because of the young hellion who quit school, tired of being caught napping, who
trailed after his older brother while his mother worked, that
the older man of rigid values emerged. Nonreligious, unschooled by textbooks, he is a man of enormous common sense,
ready folk wisdom, and stubborn, instinctive notions. He
has always been a man of instincts, though never introspective enough to notice their presence.

Such instincts propelled him, fast and dizzy, toward his   3
future wife. He was engaged to her friend, who introduced
him to the dark-haired, pale-skinned woman, about whom his
inner voice said, firmly, yes. He broke the engagement,

proposed to Marilyn, then reluctantly waited a year before
marrying at the insistence of his future mother-in-law.   He
chose a family of traditions and closeness, of gnarled inter-
dependencies and rash tempers, so unlike his own past.   He
knew this woman would need him, nurture him.

　　But then, he never shared much about his own past.   No   4
bitterness over the shoes stuffed with newspapers, or the
hand-me-down clothes several sizes too large.   No club of
guilt-inspiring comparisons was wielded over his more fortunate, and often unappreciative, children.   Instead they
learned of him in casual answers to direct queries, or from
his mother, a woman divorced in an era when such action was
hardly respectable.   She worked long, tiresome days, leaving
him and his older brother Arthur to fetch a meal at the corner candy store.   The counterman, waiting, would place a
sandwich and a drink before them.   "Never more or less, and
all paid for in advance," he once said, a tone of wonder in
his voice just at the sheer order of it all.   She passed her
stern work ethic on to him; he became a good provider, obsessed with being responsible.

　　And the errant, alcoholic, polo-playing father--the   5
womanizer who told girlfriends his then-nineteen-year-old
younger son was a younger brother--passed on some traits of
his own.   A love for animals and a love for cars that would
last a lifetime.   The former caused the young boy to drag
home a succession of dirty pets to an emphatically opposed
mother, and the young man to smile when his own daughter did
the same thing to his wife.   The latter prompted an affair
with cars that forty years of selling automobiles has only
dimmed, not ended.   It is telling of the man that in a
profession where truth is not a known commodity, he has a
reputation of such staunch honesty that customers return,
year after year.

　　Perhaps it is his subtle humor, his ability to enjoy   6
people that attracts them as well.   Such humor takes the

form of quirks and annoyances in his home.   There is the
"diet" dessert of ice milk over bananas and Hershey chocolate
bars, eaten nightly with an innocent smile.   Or the chocolate bars hidden in his night table drawer.   There is the
obsession over details, prompting him to worry over each decision.   And the peacemaker, the small boy within him still
seeking approval and love, who avoids confrontation, attempting to reconcile people and issues, provoking frustration in
his daughter.   And laughter in his son, who at the end of a
phone conversation over any issue, hangs up the phone, then
counts "5-4-3-2-hello, dad," knowing his father will immediately re-call to be certain everyone is pleased.

        If there is a failure in his values, it has been, until   7
recently, with this son.   It has taken them until now, when
the boy is a father himself, to see the love that exists beneath their opposite personalities.   With his daughter,
being needed and revered was easy; she idolized him.   With
his son, there were questions, wants, swirling energy and demands.   And he, working to provide for his children, had not
time for the baseball or other games that were no part of his
own childhood.   Now, two men, two fathers, they reach across
the distance with love.

        And now, at age fifty-eight, his blond hair has become a   8
gray-brushed reddish gold.   His long, oval, square-jawed
face is heavily lined.   The habits of his lifetime have been
altered, a difficult task for a man who dislikes change, by
the death of the woman who needed and nurtured him, and bore
his children.   Years of chronic illness and possible loss of
her created little anxieties, worrisome habits that, he admits, remain with him still.   But he has remarried, and with
his new wife, can often be found walking at the cemetery
where their respective spouses are buried.   He bends down to
clear the grave of grass and dirt.   She was, after all, his
wife.   And his actions continue to speak.

There is quite a jump between Seidel's rough, disorganized notes and this rough but organized first draft. The details are beginning to make sense, and the essay is beginning to take shape. Seidel's strategy in writing her first draft was to refer to her notes and establish her purpose by grouping details from these notes. Consider, for instance, a few of her brief sketchy notes:

—grew up—wore hand-me-down clothes and shoes—used
    to fold newspapers into shoes
—Mother worked early morn til after dinner
—went to corner store for meal—Mother paid $ in advance
    to store

She developed these details about her father's boyhood into paragraph 4 of her first draft. Seidel also combined and grouped details from different places in her notes. Details such as "hell-raiser," "slow to anger," "not religious," and "perfectionist," scattered throughout her notes, all are grouped together in paragraph 2, where she writes about her father's values.

As she wrote her first draft, Seidel found that she needed to go beyond her notes to define her purpose. New ideas came out in writing as one idea stimulated another and new possibilities emerged. She added the details about her mother in paragraph 3, for example, when she realized that she needed this information to illustrate her father's complex set of principles. Seidel was open and receptive, as writers need to be while drafting, discovering new ideas and following her writing where it took her. Because she spent so much time brainstorming and developing her ideas, and because her notes were so well developed, Seidel was able to write a detailed, focused first draft. Her first draft was indeed a very promising beginning.

Revising

Seidel put her draft aside for one day before beginning to revise. With time, she reports, she gains the necessary distance to rethink what she has written and to see her writing more objectively. "Most of my time 'writing' is really revising. I first revise by reading my draft from start to finish. Next, I begin scribbling changes on the draft—additions, deletions, arrows, circles, notes to myself, and ideas for moving paragraphs around. The draft really looks chewed over at this point. Then I type a new draft, make more changes on the draft, and continue and continue. I have often felt alone and very strange because I write so many drafts, but I can rarely complete even a very short piece of writing without multiple drafts. It is only through revising that I can keep refining my writing and hope to reach my readers."

Seidel's major concern as she read her first draft was that she had not captured her father and achieved her purpose in writing about him. She recalls her thinking at this point: "I was very uneasy about my tribute to my father. I saw too many of my opinions of his actions and realized that I had not distanced myself emotionally from my subject. I had to take my emotional likes and dislikes out of my essay and try to see my work more objectively. In the third paragraph of my first draft, for instance, I described my mother's physical appearance, not my father's. I was getting carried away with my memories. I began to ask myself, 'Well, what is it I want to say? What is my purpose in writing this essay?' I knew I was trying to achieve a sense of flowing movement from one idea to another, so the man I was writing about would just seem to 'appear' to be 'real' the way he was in my mind's eye. I wanted my father to tell his own story; I wanted to show that his actions do speak louder than his words. One of my goals in revising was to remove myself from the essay. I shortened my sentences to let simple statements and my father's actions speak for themselves. I recognized that the more I interjected ME into describing HIM, the less of HIM could be seen."

To revise means, literally, "to see again," and that is what Seidel was able to do. While getting started, she could see her writing only as parts and pieces, but having written an entire draft, she could see from the perspective of the whole if her draft were consistent with her purpose. As she moved from draft to draft, Seidel revised by adding, deleting, and reordering. She refined her writing, searching for a precise word or a more descriptive phrase, rearranging sentences, and tightening her writing. As Seidel tells us: "My sentences were just too wordy. The essay, in fact, was so bloated with words that my father's actions could not speak for themselves. Wordiness is always a first-draft problem because it is part of the process of pouring out ideas and discovering a purpose. In revising, I work for a rhythm and mood in my writing that is possible only by removing every excess word and phrase."

Seidel maintained the basic structure of her essay throughout her drafts, but the focus on her father's personality, his contrasts, his honor, and his principles became more vivid. Accumulating small changes from draft to draft—so that each sentence, phrase, and word fit her purpose—made the difference in Seidel's prize-winning essay. Seidel reports: "I knew my essay was finished when I saw a clear pattern. I had created a logical transition from paragraph to paragraph. It no longer mattered if I wanted to add anything else; I could 'hear' the essay was complete."

It was through revising that Seidel was able to "reach the hearts of her readers" and achieve the essay she wanted—a vivid and memorable tribute to her father. As we learn from her, the best reason for putting anything down on paper is to allow a writer to see it, understand it, and know how to change it. In revising, Seidel patiently brought her ideas and her imagination together.

On the following pages Seidel's final draft appears alongside her first draft so that you can study the major decisions and changes she made. New sentences or phrases in the final draft have been underlined.

Seidel's First Draft

A Tribute to My Father

    Actions speak louder than words, he often said. If so,   1
there are actions that say much about the man. There was
that moment, thirty years ago, when his father was dying
slowly of cancer. In order to take his father to and from
the hospital for medical care, he would arise at dawn, leaving his wife and small children asleep in the tiny house, and
drive the distance on deserted city streets. Years later,
his own daughter, puzzled, would ask why he showed such devotion to the man who had divorced his mother and almost abandoned him and his brother. He answered, with a faint look of
surprise at the question, "He was my father."

    As though such an answer explains it all . . . he is   2
still not a man to say more when less will do. Soft-spoken,
slow to anger but long in remembering, he has his own set of
values. The towels in the linen closet were always folded
just so. The lights in an unused room turned off, to the exasperation of children lectured to do likewise. One's word
is one's bond, he said. Loyalty, respect, tradition, honesty
. . . these were the basic tenets of his life, unspoken but
inherent. Perhaps it is because of the young hellion who quit
school, tired of being caught napping, who trailed after his

Seidel's Final Draft

A Tribute to My Father

Thirty years ago, when his father was dying, he would   1
leave his wife and two small children asleep in the square
Cape Cod style house, then drive in the predawn light through
the quiet city streets to take his father for outpatient medical care.   Much later in his own life, his daughter puzzled
over his devotion to a man who had divorced his mother, then
ignored him and his brother.   A faint look of surprise
flickered in his eyes; then he answered concisely, "He was my
father."   He has always said that actions speak louder than
words.

1. The phrase "actions speak louder than words" functioned as a touchstone for Siedel's ideas, a way of getting at what she wanted to say about her
father and finding the words to express her central idea about his values. In
revising, Seidel moved this phrase from her lead sentence to the last sentence.
She wanted to make her lead sentence more specific, to draw her readers into
her essay by showing one of her father's most telling actions. The last sentence
of the paragraph in the final draft, "He has always said that actions speak
louder than words," unifies the paragraph and summarizes Seidel's dominant
impression of her father. In revising, Seidel has also condensed six sentences
into four to create a more forceful impression of her father.

A soft-spoken man <u>with a frequent low chuckle</u>, he is so   2
slow to anger <u>that some people have been fooled into believing him an easy mark for trickery, a dangerous mistake</u>.   He
is just as slow and long in remembering anyone who violates
his strict set of values.   He has no textbook education, yet
he possesses an abundance of common sense.   He is not religious, yet he is a moral man, consistent in his values on a
daily basis, <u>not only on the Sabbath</u>.   The inherent boundaries of his life, given and expected, have been loyalty, respect, tradition.   Perhaps it is from the wild young hellion

older brother while his mother worked, that the older man of
rigid values emerged.   Nonreligious, unschooled by textbooks,
he is a man of enormous common sense, ready folk wisdom, and
stubborn, instinctive notions.   He has always been a man of
instincts, though never introspective enough to notice their
presence.

        Such instincts propelled him, fast and dizzy, toward his   3
future wife.   He was engaged to her friend, who introduced
him to the dark-haired, pale-skinned woman, about whom his
inner voice said, firmly, yes.   He broke the engagement,
proposed to Marilyn, then reluctantly waited a year before
marrying at the insistence of his future mother-in-law.   He
chose a family of traditions and closeness, of gnarled inter-
dependencies and rash tempers, so unlike his own past.   He
knew this woman would need him, nurture him.

```
who quit school, whose idea of fun was joyriding in his older
brother's car while that brother chased after him, that this
man of caution and habit emerged.
```

2. In revising, Seidel took what was essentially a list of details from her brainstorming notes that she had strung together into sentences in her first draft and focused them by reorganizing and deleting. She decided to develop this paragraph around her father's values as a man of caution and habit. Thus she moved the detail about the towels in the linen closet to paragraph 7 and cut the last sentence of the first draft about instincts and introspection. She deleted the phrase "to the exasperation of children" to shift the focus of the sentence to her father. She added the important detail that "he is so slow to anger that some people have been fooled into believing him an easy mark for trickery" to establish her father's values.

```
       Yet it was not caution, but sharp, clear instinct that       3
twirled him fast and dizzy after the woman he would marry.
He was already engaged; his fiancée made the fatal mistake of
introducing her fair-haired,blue-eyed, slender man to the
dark-haired woman whose first sight caused some inner voice
to shout at him firmly, "yes!"  This woman would need him,
would nurture him; he knew it.  He broke his engagement, then
immediately proposed, waiting a year before marrying only be-
cause of his future mother-in-law's insistence that he do so.
He may have been impulsive, but he was, after all, respectful
of his elders.  And he had clearly chosen not only a wife
but a family style.  Tradition and warmth, tangled relation-
ships and rash tempers all spoke of people connecting to one
another.  His life became one of stability and constancy, of
the same meat loaf served on the same day of each week, of
the same conservative clothes worn year in and year out, of a
man and a woman whose lives revolved around each other, so
unlike his own past.
```

3. Seidel realized in revising that she could use the story in this paragraph about her mother to show us more about her father's principles. She shortened her sentences, allowing her father's actions to speak for themselves, and added

But then, he never shared much about his own past.   No   4
bitterness over the shoes stuffed with newspapers, or the
hand-me-down clothes several sizes too large.   No club of
guilt-inspiring comparisons was wielded over his more fortunate, and often unappreciative, children.   Instead they
learned of him in casual answers to direct queries, or from
his mother, a woman divorced in an era when such action was
hardly respectable.   She worked long, tiresome days, leaving
him and his older brother Arthur to fetch a meal at the corner candy store.   The counterman, waiting, would place a
sandwich and a drink before them.   "Never more or less, and
all paid for in advance," he once said, a tone of wonder in
his voice just at the sheer order of it all.   She passed her
stern work ethic on to him; he became a good provider, obsessed with being responsible.

And the errant, alcoholic, polo-playing father--the   5
womanizer who told girlfriends his then-nineteen-year-old

an effective detail: "His life became one of stability and constancy, of the same meat loaf served on the same day of each week."

He spoke little about his past. No bitterness over the   4
secondhand shoes stuffed with newspapers, or the hand-me-down
clothing several sizes too large, pushed him to pursue great
wealth or power. His dream, he later said, was to be able
to work hard and just provide. He found the greatest
pleasure in the small things--the ability to buy himself new
shoes. Nor did he wield his own meager childhood as a club
to inspire guilt or appreciation in his own more fortunate,
more spoiled children. Instead, they learned of him through
passing comments --or from his mother.

Her divorce came in an era when such an act was brazen.   5
She worked long days caring for her two boys, who ate one
meal daily at the corner candy store. The counterman would
wait until they entered, then place a sandwich and a drink in
front of them. "Never more or less, and all ordered and
paid for in advance," he once said, a respectful, wondering
tone in his voice at the sheer order of it all. She passed
her stern work ethic on to him. He became very good at
being responsible, dependable, at providing.

4–5. Seidel divided paragraph 4 of her first draft into two paragraphs, giving her father's mother a separate paragraph, which emphasizes her influential role. In paragraph 4 of the final draft, Seidel added the two sentences on her father's adult ambition and his pleasure in buying himself new shoes. These sentences resonate for us, as readers, because we remember the earlier detail about his secondhand shoes stuffed with newspaper. Seidel cut out unnecessary words in her lead sentence in paragraph 4, again allowing her father's actions to speak for themselves. In the new paragraph 5, we see how small changes make the difference, reinforcing Seidel's purpose.

And the errant, alcoholic, polo-playing father--the   6
womanizer who once told his ladies that this then-nineteen-

younger son was a younger brother--passed on some traits of
his own.   A love for animals and a love for cars that would
last a lifetime.   The former caused the young boy to drag
home a succession of dirty pets to an emphatically opposed
mother, and the young man to smile when his own daughter did
the same thing to his wife.   The latter prompted an affair
with cars that forty years of selling automobiles has only
dimmed, not ended.   It is telling of the man that in a
profession where truth is not a known commodity, he has a
reputation of such staunch honesty that customers return,
year after year.

        Perhaps it is his subtle humor, his ability to enjoy peo- 6
ple that attracts them as well.   Such humor takes the form
of quirks and annoyances in his home.   There is the "diet"
dessert of ice milk over bananas and Hershey chocolate bars,
eaten nightly with an innocent smile.   Or the chocolate bars
hidden in his night table drawer.   There is the obsession
over details, prompting him to worry over each decision.
And the peacemaker, the small boy within him still seeking
approval and love, who avoids confrontation, attempting to
reconcile people and issues, provoking frustration in his
daughter.   And laughter in his son, who at the end of a
phone conversation over any issue, hangs up the phone, then
counts "5-4-3-2-hello, dad," knowing his father will immediately re-call to be certain everyone is pleased.

year-old younger son was his younger brother--had a few admirable traits of his own left up his sleeve. To his son, he
passed on a love of animals and a fascination with cars, with
their sight and smell and the gas-powered freedom they gave
to a man. His son, as a boy, would drag home one protesting
stray after another to a firmly opposed mother. Years
later, a father himself, he would laugh when his own daughter
did the same. After spending forty years selling the mechanical monsters, his love affair with cars has only dimmed.
It is telling of the man that in a profession where truth is
not always a recognizable commodity, he has a staunch reputation for honesty and a loyal following of customers.

6. Here it is the small changes—details added, excess words deleted—that make this paragraph more effective. Seidel added the phrase "with their sight and smell and the gas-powered freedom they gave to a man" to emphasize her father's fascination with cars.

If his honesty attracts them, so must his humor, gentle   7
and chiding. And of course, there are the quirks. There
are the Hershey chocolate bars hidden in the night table
drawer, the towels folded and placed exactly so in the linen
closet, the sink faucet wiped shiny dry after dishes are
washed. If his past did not create anger or unbridled ambition, it did give him a legacy of sorts: hoarded candy bars
contrast with the giving parent; an obsession with details
fills him with anxiety. He worries over each decision like
a dog gnawing on a bone. He is still the small boy seeking
security, the ultimate peacemaker avoiding confrontations,
reconciling and rationalizing the good in people and in issues to the frustration of his children. They, grown, have
at last learned to laugh gently at the habits that once exasperated them. There is the family favorite--the phone joke.
His son speaks to him, hangs up the phone, then counts,

    If there is a failure in his values, it has been, until   7
recently, with this son.   It has taken them until now, when
the boy is a father himself, to see the love that exists beneath their opposite personalities.   With his daughter, being
needed and revered was easy; she idolized him.   With his son,
there were questions, wants, swirling energy and demands.
And he, working to provide for his children, had not time for
the baseball or other games that were no part of his own childhood.   Now, two men, two fathers, they reach across the distance with love.

"5-4-3-2--hello, Dad!"   He knows his father will hesitate,
then call again.   <u>Is everyone happy?   Should we talk more?</u>

7. Seidel's skill as a writer is evident in her revisions of this paragraph. She has revised every sentence, cut out every excess word, and removed every unnecessary detail so that her father's idiosyncrasies become real to us. Paragraph 7 of her first draft was baggy and lacked a clear focus. In revising, Seidel shows how her father's quirks have been shaped by the legacy of his childhood: "hoarded candy bars contrast with the giving parent; an obsession with details fills him with anxiety. He worries over each decision like a dog gnawing on a bone." Seidel dropped the detail about the diet dessert because it didn't fit in, inserted the example from paragraph 2 about the folded towels, and added the new detail about "the sink faucet wiped shiny dry." Her sentences become much more direct: instead of "Such humor takes the form of quirks and annoyances in his home," Seidel's revision says, "And of course, there are the quirks." The phone joke also becomes more concrete as we hear the father's voice saying, "Is everyone happy? Should we talk more?"

<u>It is this son who is one of the brief detours on his</u>   8
<u>well-laid road map of life</u>.   With his daughter, loving was
an easy goal.   <u>They shared a silent similarity of vision, of</u>
<u>loving and letting go</u>.   With his son, such love was reached
<u>only after struggle; they spoke a different language</u>.   His
son needed questions answered, challenges met, baseball and
other games which had found no place in his own childhood; he
was a man concerned with providing.   <u>By the boy's adoles-</u>
<u>cence, they were like two bucks, antlers locked in a battle</u>
<u>of dominance</u>.   Now they are two men, two fathers, who reach
gingerly, but often, across the <u>once-volatile differences of</u>
<u>self</u> to touch the love <u>that always existed</u>.

8. Seidel developed this paragraph to make the conflict between father and son more real to us. She straightened out the chronology of the paragraph so that she first describes the conflict and then explains its resolution, by moving the second sentence to the end. Her revision of the lead sentence is important. In the first draft, she wrote of the conflict as a "failure in [the father's] values," but "failure" was inexact, Seidel realized, because the conflict has since been

        And now, at age fifty-eight, his blond hair has become a   8
gray-brushed reddish gold.   His long, oval, square-jawed face
is heavily lined.   The habits of his lifetime have been altered, a difficult task for a man who dislikes change, by the
death of the woman who needed and nurtured him, and bore his
children.   Years of chronic illness and possible loss of her
created little anxieties, worrisome habits that, he admits,
remain with him still.   But he has remarried, and with his
new wife, can often be found walking at the cemetery where
their respective spouses are buried.   He bends down to clear
the grave of grass and dirt.   She was, after all, his wife.
And his actions continue to speak.

resolved. In her first draft, she described this conflict between father and son in vague language: "With his son, there were questions, wants, swirling energy and demands." In revising, Seidel was much more precise: "With his son, such love was reached only after struggle; they spoke a different language. . . . By the boy's adolescence, they were like two bucks, antlers locked in a battle of dominance."

And now, at age fifty-eight, his hair is streaked with 9 gray; his oval face is heavily lined; <u>he is tired</u>. The habits of his lifetime have been altered, a difficult task for a man who dislikes change, by the death of the woman who needed and nurtured him. For years, he had watched her slowly die, <u>her illness chipping away small pieces of his own courage</u>, creating small anxieties, worrisome habits that still linger with him. <u>But he is not a man to live alone; he has remarried</u>. With his new wife, he can sometimes be found at the cemetery where their respective first spouses are buried. <u>Flat bronze plaques and high white headstones stretch across the green fields</u>. He bends down to clear her grave of grass and dirt. She was, after all, his wife. Actions do, indeed, speak.

9. Seidel removed all excess words from this paragraph so that her father stands before us in his final actions. In the first draft, she wrote about his first wife by saying: "Years of chronic illness and possible loss of her created little anxieties." In the final draft, her father becomes the actor in the sentence: "For years, he had watched her slowly die, her illness chipping away small pieces of his own courage." Finally, we see Seidel's father in the cemetery, bending down to clear the grass and dirt from his first wife's grave and honoring her memory. In revising, Seidel brings her essay full circle by connecting the beginning and ending.

Exercise: Three Drafts by Brad Manning

This exercise looks at Brad Manning's first, second, and final drafts to understand the decisions and changes Manning made as he developed what would become his prize-winning essay.

Brad Manning's "Arm-Wrestling with My Father" evolved early in the semester in his freshman English course. During the first week of classes, Jack Kimball, the course instructor, asked his students to write 10 or more pages of what Kimball calls "experimental writing (mapping, list-making, freewriting, and so forth)" on their choice of topics. The students were then asked to write "three one-page proposals, again on their choice of topics, for a 'formal' paper due in a couple of weeks."

Manning reports that his three choices were "a portrait of my New York roommate, a discussion of how to pray, and an account of an arm-wrestling match with my father. I chose the one that was closest to me." Manning also reports that he found the idea of written proposals "really helpful. I felt that I could think through a potential piece without feeling committed to it." In his original proposal for his prize-winning essay, he explains, "I planned to develop a theme in the father-son relationship that I had discovered through the ritual of arm-wrestling. That was all I had at the time, this idea of a son sadly accepting dominance over his father."

Reprinted here is a copy of that one-page proposal:

```
Proposal Number Three: "Arm-Wrestling"
     This is an autobiographical story.
It centers on an occurrence that is true,
recent, and common.  As soon as a boy
reaches physical maturity, he begins to
challenge the previous dominance that his
father held over him for so many years.
At last, after all that struggle against
the father, all that competition and
demand for independence from the influen-
tial model, the son can prove a superior-
ity in strength.  However, if my
situation is not singular, the son may
wish to lose.  In January, the last time
I was home, I challenged Dad to an arm-
wrestling match, our first in almost a
year.  All during the fall, I had been
rowing freshman crew.  My arms were
larger and nearer their potential
```

```
strength.  My father's arms were still
larger but had weakened over the years.
I could remember times when my brother
and I combined were no match for his arm,
but this time I won.  After the competi-
tion had begun, however, and I began to
sense my advantage, I believe I felt in-
side a combination of pity, disillusion,
and sadness. . . . I have determined
since then that the day a son first beats
his own father in arm-wrestling is a sad
one:  I have not determined why.  This
is a problem I will address in the writ-
ing of this paper.  My method will in-
volve a sense-related description of the
match and my feelings.  I will then ask
questions as to why I felt sad and why I
did not choose to lose the competition.
Hopefully, I will touch on my impressions
of the father-son evolution.  It is hard
to predict what I will discover in this
writing.  I may find a "universal," a
weakened Priam falling to the sword of
young Pyrrhus (ha, ha).  I may find that
my relationship with my father has
changed more than I could have guessed.
He could be lifting weights right now in
preparation for our next match.  If he
were, I think I would fool less threat-
ened than loved.
```

Soon after Brad Manning submitted his three proposals, he met with his instructor to "talk over his proposals and ways for developing his ideas." As Jack Kimball recalls, "It was obvious to us both that he wanted to work on the piece about arm-wrestling with his father. This proposal was the most fully realized, packed with anecdotal specifics. I asked Brad if he thought he might learn something new in writing about the wrestling match. He said he was 'pretty sure' he would, because he had not yet figured out how he felt about the incident—it had happened so recently."

The following is Brad Manning's first draft.

Manning's First Draft

```
                    Arm-Wrestling
```

"Now you say when." It's what he always said before an   1
arm-wrestling match. He liked to put the responsibility on
me, knowing that he would always control the outcome.
"When!" I'd shout, and it would start. I would tense up,
concentrating, straining, trying to push his wrist down to
the carpet with all my weight and strength. But Dad would
always win. I always had to lose. "Want to try it again?"
he would ask, grinning. Then he would look into my downcast
eyes, seeing my reddened, sweating face, sensing my intensity. And he would laugh at me, a high laugh, through his
very wide mouth. But I would just roll over on my back to
frown at the painted ceiling. I never thought it was funny
at all.

This ritual of father-son competition had started early   2
in my life, back even when Dad could start off with his wrist
just an inch from defeat and still win the match. I remember how my tiny shoulders would press over our locked hands,
my whole upper body pushing down to win that inch from his
calm, unmoving forearm. "Say when," he'd repeat. That
would always kill my hope. "I did, I did!" So he'd grin
and the arm would slowly begin to rise from its starting position. No great effort on my part could slow it down. I'd
start to cheat and use both hands. My brother, if he was
watching, would sometimes join in against the arm. He once
even wrapped his legs around the embattled wrists and pulled
back with everything he had. But the man would win, and I
could only giggle, happy to have such a strong father.

My feelings have changed, however. I don't giggle any-   3
more. My father is not so strong as he was years ago and I
am stronger, it seems, than he. This change in strength
comes at a time when I am growing mentally faster than any-

time before. I am becoming more myself and less them. However there is no more of that competition I felt it necessary
to have against my father, especially. There is no longer
that feeling I had for a while, to rebel and make myself different from him, to stand up to him with spiteful tensing
jaws, to correct his verbal mistakes and to beat him in physical games whenever I could. It was not obvious to me when
this transition of feeling occurred, but it became clearest
to me one day this past January. That day, I was home after
college exams with the house snowed in deep. And it was
then that I discovered something I never could have pre-
dicted. I discovered that the day a son first beats his
father at arm-wrestling is a sad one.

I'm not sure how the idea came up. It had not come up   4
for a long time, for months. But my father and I, after exchanging words of prediction, were soon flat on the carpet,
facing one another. We extended our right arms. As I recall, his still resembles a fat tree branch, one which had
leveled my wrist to the ground countless times before. It
is hairy and white with some of those pink moles scattered
across the skin. It is strong to be sure, though not so
strong as it had been in the past. He had played halfback
during high school and had been voted "best-built body" of
the senior class. I envied him for that. The power in his
aging arm could still be seen. My arm, on the other hand is
lanky and featureless, although at college I have begun to
row crew and it has produced some small buildup along the
muscle lines. My body is now in its supposed prime while my
father is nearing fifty years. I thought at the particular
time that I could sense an advantage over him.

He insisted that I would win this match. That's some-   5
thing he would always say, though, whether or not he believed
it himself. Our warm palms came together, much like when we
shake hands at the airport. Fingers twisted and wrapped
around palms once, again, again, testing for a better grip.

Elbows slid up and back across the itchy carpet making inden-
tations.   Eyes pinched closed in concentration as we tried
to center as much of our thought as possible on the match.
Arm-wrestling is one of those competitions, in fact, that
depends less on talent and experience than on one's mental
control.   Often, if a person can convince himself that he'll
win, then it's a lot easier to accomplish.   I looked up into
his eyes, and was ready when he said (somewhat nervously?),
"You say when."

     I had expected him to be stronger, faster.   I was con-   6
ditioned to lose and would have accepted defeat.   However,
his arm began to yield and move unsteadily toward the carpet.
It was all the strength I could produce.   He was straining,
breathing heavily.   Then something occurred to me, something
unexpected.   I discovered that I was feeling sorry for my
father, and that really I did not want to see him lose.

     Perhaps, at that point, I could have given up, letting   7
him win.   But it was so fast and absorbing.   How could I
have learned so quickly what I know now?   I felt like a
young hunter who is thrilled, having shot his first buck and
upon reaching it as it struggles for life, he is captured by
the stare of the large dark eye and its seeming plea for
mercy.   The young hunter, if he feels as I did then, will
yearn to see his prize trophy alive once again, sprinting
away through the trees, elusive.   Without this possibility,
he will be compelled to place it out of its pain.   But he
will not walk away claiming victory, instead he will sadly
lift the deer over his shoulders and carry it out of the
woods.   Virgil wrote of a father and son tale that pictured
the young Aeneas lifting the very aged Anchises, his father,
onto his back and carrying him to safety out of the burning
city of Troy.   I must consider now if this will become my
own role.

     It is almost incredible to me that the relationship with   8
my father could change so much.   There are recent hints,

however, that this might become the case. He has always
wanted me to do well, to feel good within. Sometimes,
though, his help was given to me as admonitions or as unwanted counsel. I remember during my slump in lacrosse, he
tried so hard, though knowing little about the game, to teach
me a new move so that I could score. I felt terrible watching him carry the lacrosse stick incorrectly and make a spinning, blind release. I felt sad, knowing he couldn't teach
me anything of worth despite his desire to help. Now, he
gives me less help. He listens more closely to what I say.
And he says things to me on the phone that sound so foreign.
It used to be that I only felt that I returned his love when
I made him proud of me. Now, he says things like how impressed he is with things I try to accomplish in school and
how proud I make him feel for no reason except for my simple
self. Reflecting on past years and how difficult conversation had been and how seldom the word "love" was said between
us, I discover that I can love him more openly now and that I
wish to stand up for him rather than against him. Finally,
I have found a responsibility to protect him in his later
life and to make him live within and through me. The arm-
wrestling match may have been the first move toward lifting
Dad up onto my back. Perhaps I will never physically carry
him as he used to carry me. I sadly envision, however,
seeing him collapse onto the floor. In my vision, I rush to
him and powerfully lift his trembling warm body onto my
shoulders. Then without hesitation I begin to run swiftly
through the flames, carrying my father out of the burning
city.

Questions on Manning's First Draft

1. Manning's one-page proposal provided him with a good place to begin developing his ideas about his arm-wrestling match with his father. Outline the major points he makes in the proposal.

2. Which of these points does Manning introduce in his first draft? To what extent does he develop each? With what effects?

3. What "theme" does Manning announce in the opening of his proposal? On what generalization does he base it? How does he adapt that generalization to his own circumstances?

4. What does Manning's proposal declare will be the goal of his first draft? How successful is he in accomplishing that goal?

5. In his proposal, Manning expresses the hope that "I will touch on my impressions of the father-son evolution." How does Manning develop his own interest in "the father-son evolution"? Chart Manning's depiction of the evolution of his relationship with his father. What images does he use to underscore the changes in their relationship?

6. Manning reports in his proposal that it is "hard to predict what I will discover in this writing." What does he discover—both in specific and in general terms—as a result of writing his first draft?

7. In his proposal Manning notes, "I may find a 'universal,' a weakened Priam falling to the sword of young Pyrrhus (ha, ha)." What, finally, can be said to be "universal" about his first draft? When and how efficiently is the image of Priam presented in his first draft?

8. What is the importance of the last line of his proposal? How does this point surface in the first draft?

9. In what specific ways do Manning's proposal and his first draft move beyond the limits of personal experience? How, in effect, does he manage to blend personal experience and scholarship?

In describing his writing, Manning underscores the importance of a first draft: "I have taken the route of writing about the topic first in my journal, pouring out thoughts and ideas all over the page without much clarity. Then, after making a list of ideas I want to cover in the paper, I turn on the computer, strap myself to the chair, and work completely through the first draft. I remember how frustrating it was in high school when I used to write and edit one sentence at a time, trusting eventually that a theme or thesis would emerge.

"I don't mind writing badly and digressively in my first draft; I even look forward to it. Therefore, it is easy to get at least something started on paper. Only after I begin to type will the choice words and ideas come out of hiding. I can't sit back and organize in my head. I would take too long, and I would forget it all before I started." Here is Brad Manning's second draft.

Manning's Second Draft

Arm-Wrestling

"Now you say when." It's what he always said before an   1
arm-wrestling match. He liked to put the responsibility on
me, knowing that he would always control the outcome.
"When!" I'd shout, and it would start. I would tense up,
concentrating, straining, trying to push his wrist down to
the carpet with all my weight and strength. But Dad would
always win. I always had to lose. "Want to try it again?"
he would ask, grinning. Then he would look into my downcast
eyes, seeing my reddened, sweating face, sensing my intensity. And he would laugh at me, a high laugh, through his
very wide mouth. But I would just roll over on my back to
frown at the colorless ceiling. I never thought it was
funny at all.

That was my feeling for a number of years during my   2
teens, after I had lost my enjoyment of it and before I had
given up that intense desire to win. This ritual of father-
son competition in fact had started early in my life, back
when Dad could start off with his wrist just an inch from defeat and still win the match. I remember in those matches
how my tiny shoulders would press over our locked hands, my
whole upper body pushing down in hope of winning that single
inch from his calm, unmoving forearm. "Say when," he'd repeat. That would kill my concentration and I would squeal,
"I did, I did!" So he'd grin, his eyes fixed on mine, not
seeming to notice the arm which would slowly begin to rise
from its starting position. No great effort on my part
could slow it down. Losing hope, I'd start to cheat and use
both hands. The arm would keep rising. My brother, if he
was watching, would sometimes join in against the arm. He
once even wrapped his little legs around our embattled wrists
and pulled back with everything he had. But despite the

opposition, the man would win, and I could only giggle, happy
to have such a strong father.

My feelings have changed, however. I don't giggle any-   3
more. My father is not really so strong as he was years ago
and I am becoming stronger, it seems, than he. This change
in strength has come at a time when I am growing mentally
faster than anytime before. I am becoming less my father
and more myself. As a result, there is no more of that need
to be set apart, that competition I felt it necessary to have
against my father. There is no longer a rebel in the household, wanting to stand up against the master with clenched
fists and tensing jaws, always correcting his verbal mistakes
and trying to beat him in physical games whenever possible.
I am not certain when this transition of feeling occurred,
but it became clearest to me one day this past January when I
was home after college exams and the house was snowed in
deep. It was then that I discovered that the day a son
first beats his father at arm-wrestling is a sad one, though
I am not sure why.

I do not recall how the idea came up. It had not come   4
up for a long time, for months. But there my father and I
were, exchanging words of prediction, laying flat on the carpet, face to face. We extended our right arms. His still
resembled a fat tree branch, one which had leveled my wrist
to the ground countless times before. It was hairy and
white with some of those pink moles scattered across the
skin. It looked strong to be sure, though not so strong as
it had been in the past. In high school, he had played
halfback and had been voted "best-built body" of the senior
class. Between college semesters, he worked on road crews
and on Louisiana dredges. I admired him for a lot of that.
My arm, on the other hand, was lanky and featureless, although I had begun to row crew in college and it accounted
for some small buildup along the muscle lines. He insisted

that I would win the match.   That's something he always
said, though, whether or not he believed it himself.

Our warm palms came together, much the same way we shake   5
hands at the airport.   Fingers twisted and wrapped about
once, again, again, testing for a better grip.   Elbows slid
up and back on the itchy carpet making indentions.   My eyes
pinched closed in concentration as I tried to center as much
of my thought as possible on the match.   It is true that
arm-wrestling is one of those competitions that depends less
on talent and experience than on one's mental control.   I
looked up into his eyes, and was ready when he said (did he
sound nervous?), "You say when."

It was not a long match.   I had expected him to be   6
stronger, faster.   I was conditioned to lose and would have
accepted defeat easily.   However, his arm yielded to my efforts and began to move unsteadily toward the carpet.   I
worked with all the strength I could give.   He was straining, breathing heavily.   It was evident that this time was
different.   Then something occurred to me, something unexpected.   I discovered that I was feeling sorry for my
father.   I wanted to win but really I did not want to see
him lose.

Perhaps, at that point, I could have given up, letting   7
him win.   But it was so fast and absorbing.   How could I
have learned so quickly what I know now?   I felt like a
young hunter who is thrilled, having shot his first buck but
upon reaching it as it struggles for life, he is captured in
the stare of its very large dark eye and its seeming plea for
pity.   I, like the young hunter, yearned to see the deer
alive once again, sprinting away through the trees, powerful,
untamed.   But instead, I was compelled to finish it, to stop
the pain.   In such a situation, it would not have been right
to walk away claiming victory.   Rather, one must sadly lift
the deer over his shoulders and carry it out of the woods.

    Perhaps, someday I will carry my father, much like the   8
young Aeneas who lifted his aged father onto his back and
carried him to safety out of the burning city of Troy.   I
must consider now if this will ever become my own role.   Today, I feel that I may never be so strong as I see my father
to be.   When I am near him, I feel protected, knowing he
will keep me safe, the way he caught my mother once when she
fainted halfway across the room, the way he carried me, full
grown, up and down the stairs when I had mononucleosis, the
way he would hold my feet as I stood upon his shoulders to
put up a new basketball net.   I may always wish him to be
stronger, to be the one who carries me.   In fact, if he were
right now working on weights in preparation for our next
match, I would feel less threatened than loved.   However it
may be that beating him for the first time in arm-wrestling
was the first move towards lifting Dad up onto my back.   I
do not know if I shall ever physically carry my father.   I
sadly envision, however, one day seeing him collapse onto the
floor. . . . In my vision, I rush to him and powerfully lift
his trembling warm body onto my shoulders.   Then, without
hesitation I begin to run fast through the flames, carrying
my father out of the burning city, and up into the hills.

Questions on Manning's Second Draft

1. Brad Manning's second draft provided him with an opportunity to develop his ideas. Describe the strengths and weaknesses of this draft. Be as specific as possible.

2. Describe the overall revisions Manning makes as he moves from the first to the second draft. Which anecdotes, for example, does he expand? Which does he delete? With what effect?

3. Reread the final sentence in paragraph 3 of the second draft. What specific revision does Manning make here? What is the effect of this change? Describe the relation of this change to the focus and impact of the rest of his second draft.

4. Reread paragraph 4 in Manning's second draft. Identify the revisions he makes there and evaluate the effectiveness of each.

5. Manning makes several substantial revisions in paragraphs 7 and 8 of his second draft. What, for example, are the effects of substituting the references to mononucleosis and the basketball net for the examples of his father's "admonitions" and "unwanted counsel"?

6. How do the conclusions, however tentative, that Manning draws in the final paragraph of each draft differ? Which version do you find more effective? Explain why.

7. Identify the revisions in tone and diction that Manning makes in his second draft. Explain how these changes contribute to improving his essay.

8. Consider the effectiveness of Manning's allusion to Greek mythology near the end of both drafts. What does this image contribute to his essay? How does Manning introduce the allusion? Where and how does he return to it in the essay? How does Manning extend the allusion in the second draft? With what effect?

9. Brad Manning identifies the crucial ingredients of a first draft: "A completed journal entry, a list of important points, a large mug of water, and Crazy Glue on the seat." He also explains that the easiest thing for him to do in writing a first draft is "to digress. This is fun and potentially valuable, but it carries me far past the page limit and requires much stamina. The hard thing is to keep at it. If I stop, I get lost and forget. This happens invariably if I try to stop and edit as I go along." As you reread the first draft of his essay, do you notice any sections where he seems "to digress"? If so, how does he deal with the problem in the second draft?

Manning continued to make major revisions as he worked on his essay. He recalls, for example, that "in the first drafts I handed in, I had come up with many of the images and scenes that I would use later, but I did not go beyond my own revelation that I was stronger; I would later include my father's own realization—that he could express his love for me."

"I got stuck on a dominant image, that of carrying my father on my back, as if this were to be a universal symbol of the changeover of strength and command from father to son. I thought it worked nicely with the deer metaphor, though it was not expressed clearly. But I took it too far, I think, when I universalized the action by invoking the image of Aeneas bearing his father, Anchises, on his back.

"It made some sense, but it did not fit the story about me and my father. So I changed it in a later revision. The buck metaphor became the first story. This was so much more effective, my teacher and I thought, because it was a true happening. It was a shorter jump. The problem was that you can't easily carry fish on your back. Even though I really liked my concluding image of Aeneas running with his father out of the flames, up into the hills, I discovered that it was not going to work thematically. And looking back now, I agree with my teacher that it seemed like a little too much high drama for a story about my home life. I am glad I stuck with things I knew; I'm more comfortable that way. Anyway, in the final draft, I was able to retain the Aeneas image in the imagined scene of my father's collapse on the floor ('I see me rushing to him, lifting him onto my shoulders, and running').

"One sentence about 'Old Joe' gave me trouble. I was trying to be different by using a string of verbal clauses like 'cut the line, let him go, cut the line. . . .' But I determined with my teacher's help that a simple statement worked best.

"Finally, as I straightened out images and details, I came across something new that would work well in the piece—that being my father's perspective, his own feelings or discoveries. This I conveyed in the description of the last hug. I'm glad this occurred to me, because now I see it as essential to bringing out the full emotion and to finishing the piece."

Reread the final version of Manning's essay (Part I, pp. 369–374) before answering the following questions.

Questions on Manning's Final Draft

1. How does Manning resolve his problem of being "stuck on a dominant image, that of carrying my father on my back"?

2. How does he handle the issue of his father's "own realization—that he could express his love for me"? In what specific ways is adding his father's perspective "essential to bringing out the full emotion and to finishing the piece"?

3. Manning talks of the risks—and the satisfactions—of trying to "universalize" the action of his narrative. How does his story remain universalized in the final draft? Identify its universal elements. How does Manning make them more effective in his final draft?

4. What did Manning gain and lose by replacing the buck metaphor with the fish story?

5. Manning observes that he "straightened out images and details" in his final draft. What images and details—in addition to the buck and fish stories—does Manning straighten out in his final draft?

6. When asked in a recent interview to describe the response he hoped to elicit from the readers of his essay, Manning responded, "I'm not sure. . . . Even though I choke up every time I round the next to last paragraph, I think this is because my emotions are so close to the subject. I would rather readers finish it with a smile, like the way they smiled after E.T. came back to life." What specific strategies does Manning use to evoke an emotional response in his readers similar to his own?

7. Comment on the nature of the revisions Manning makes in the final two paragraphs of his essay. How do those changes strengthen the overall impact of his essay?

8. Write an explanation of what you have learned about revising from studying Brad Manning's drafts.

2.

PEER EDITING

T HE PREVIOUS CHAPTER EXAMINED the composing process from the
writer's point of view. In Chapter 1, "Revising Drafts," Barbara Seidel
and Brad Manning reconstructed the different approaches they used to get
started, write, and then revise their essays. This chapter studies the composing
process from the points of view of both the writer and the reader by focusing
on how writers can work with their peers to improve one another's essays. Like
their professional counterparts (see Chapter 4, "Responding to Professional
Editing"), peer editors serve as supportive readers, ready to understand a
writer's purpose and to assist the writer in achieving that purpose. In such
circumstances, a writer can sense the immediacy of an audience—other students who are willing to read his or her work thoughtfully and offer detailed
comments on how effectively a particular draft expresses the writer's intentions.
As a peer editor you can provide both specific praise and practical advice about
how to strengthen the already successful features of an essay and how to revise
its weaknesses. And by responding to and evaluating your peers' writing, you
will be better able to write, read, revise, and edit your own essays.

Peer editors and writers can work one on one, in small groups, or within
the class as a whole to help one another get started, draft, revise, and edit
essays that will satisfy themselves as well as their course requirements. Although the principles and procedures of peer editing can be applied to any
stage of the composing process, peer editing usually works best after writers
have produced a first draft of an essay, when they can benefit most from detailed
and supportive responses to what they have written. By working collaboratively
with peer editors, writers are not limited to their own perspective on the
composing process; they can see how other writers—the peer editors—would
deal with exactly the same circumstances and challenges.

This chapter examines the most effective techniques peer editors can use when responding to the writing of other students. The chapter first presents an example of peer editing: several students offer detailed responses to and recommendations for Patrick Kinder Lewis on how he might improve his essay "Five Minutes North of Redding." The chapter then considers in general terms how a writer might work most productively with the peer editors' responses to plan more effective revisions based on their comments and recommendations. More specifically, the chapter presents Lewis's explanations of how and why he incorporated, modified, and occasionally rejected the peer editors' suggestions in working on his revision. A revised draft of Lewis's essay follows, along with several peer editing exercises in which you can apply the principles and procedures of peer editing, first to Johnna Lynn Benson's "Rotten at the Core" and then to your own writing.

If you have little or no experience with peer editing, you may be somewhat anxious about or even skeptical of its principles and procedures. Try to be patient with yourself. Remember, peer editing, like writing, is a skill that develops best over time with frequent practice. The more you work at peer editing, the more thoughtful and specific—and therefore the more helpful—your responses will be.

The Peer Editor's Response to Writing

The most effective peer editor is an interested and sensitive reader. To be a sympathetic and helpful critic of another student's writing, you should be willing to work diligently to understand the writer's purpose and to offer thoughtful and specific advice about how the writer might best achieve that purpose. You need to be interested in helping other students write better—not by suggesting ways to avoid error but by assisting them to articulate their ideas fully.

When approaching another student's writing, you should think, talk, and write about it seriously and respectfully; any writer will respond more appreciatively and energetically to criticism—be it positive or negative—that has been tactfully worded. Judicious comments also signal that you are genuinely interested in helping another writer improve; the most helpful comments are specific, direct, and encouraging. A peer editor who says simply that he or she "liked" or "disliked" an essay doesn't help the writer understand either the essay's strengths or its weaknesses. But noting, for example, that the writer has emphasized a particular point by developing a striking metaphor in the third sentence of the second paragraph makes that achievement more appreciable—and the skill more repeatable—for both the writer and the peer editor. And it is, after all, the ability to repeat success that can make writing so satisfying and enduring an intellectual enterprise.

As a peer editor, you can respond in innumerable ways to another student's writing. The most typical and widely used strategies for peer editing fall into two categories: specific comments in the margin of the essay and a general statement, usually at the end of the essay. These specific and general comments most often serve two functions: to describe what the writer has actually said in the essay and to evaluate the essay's strengths and weaknesses.

Perhaps the most valuable service that you, as a peer editor, can perform for a writer is to return a clear and, at least initially, nonjudgmental description of what the writer has written. One of the best ways to do that is to write as many specific observations as possible about the essay, either directly on the manuscript or on a separate sheet of paper to be given to the writer. In peer editing, an *observation* is a statement about which there can be no disagreement. In this sense, an observation is concrete, limited, verifiable, and often fairly obvious. It is also nonjudgmental. The purpose of your observations is to help the writer understand and appreciate a reader's perceptions of what he or she has actually written. Many peer editors, especially those who are relatively unpracticed at it, resist pointing out what they think is most obvious about an essay. They apparently do so to avoid embarrassing themselves by talking about what is obvious; they somehow seem to feel obliged to begin with what their peers will perceive as a subtle, sophisticated, or highly refined comment. Don't hesitate to start by noting what may strike you as an obvious observation about another writer's essay. An ostensibly obvious comment can be of great help to a writer. Consider, for example, that such a seemingly obvious observation as "I notice that you begin the first five sentences in your essay with 'It is' and 'There are' " may lead the writer to reread the essay with an eye to varying its verbs and sentence structure. So too, your observation might also address such larger issues as fundamental problems in logic and organization: "You mention the same point about the effects of nuclear weapons in paragraphs 4 and 7." Whatever the precise nature of your observation, the decision to revise, and in fact the authority to do so, remains where it belongs—solely with the writer.

Evaluative comments shift the emphasis in peer editing from describing what the essay says to assessing its specific strengths and weaknesses and suggesting particular revisions. In making evaluative comments, the peer editor writes detailed marginal notations about such elements of composition as word choice, tone, use of examples, logic, and organization. You identify both what the writer does well in the essay and what the writer needs to spend more time and intellectual energy developing. The more honest your assessments are, the more helpful they will be.

A particularly useful kind of evaluation is one in which you as a peer editor summarize as succinctly as possible the thesis of the essay and note specifically how the writer develops that controlling idea in each paragraph. The aim of this kind of evaluation is to assist the writer in expressing, clarifying, and developing completely the main point of the essay as well as the assertions in each paragraph that support it.

As a peer editor, you usually write a general evaluation at the end of the essay based on the specific marginal notations made throughout the paper. Your goal in this general evaluation is to give a balanced overview of the essay's strengths and weaknesses, not simply a summary of its flaws. You should also include suggestions to help the writer develop a detailed and achievable plan for revision. These suggestions should be selective rather than exhaustive and should help the writer set clear priorities for revising. These general comments are also the most appropriate place to review the essay with an eye to helping the writer make it as concise, engaging, and elegant as possible. Your suggestions are also quite likely the last ones the writer can draw on before revising the essay and submitting it to the instructor for an additional reading and eventually a grade.

Student writers who serve as peer editors will become both practiced writers and practiced readers, since the skills of writing and reading are truly integrated. What peer editors learn about the interaction between reading and writing will help them a great deal when they turn to their own writing.

Peer Editing Patrick Kinder Lewis's Essay

To demonstrate how a writer can improve an already successful essay with the help of peer editors, this section presents several peer editors' responses to Patrick Kinder Lewis's essay "Five Minutes North of Redding." We have chosen this essay because of its complexity and ambition. Lewis writes knowledgeably and dramatically about a youthful adventure "riding the rails" in northern California. Aboard a freight train traveling north from Sacramento, Lewis discovers a great deal about himself and his relation to the world around him.

Lewis spent roughly a year on the road, trying "to figure out what made life tick—and whether there was really anything that made one's life worth all the pain. What I came back with was the beginnings of something more than simple self-worth. That was there too. But that year, more than any other, assured me that life is really only as absurd as we choose to make it. . . . I also came back with a new realization of the value God has placed on every human life. The hobos and mixed-up kids I met were no less worthy of the meager amount of grace that I was able to show them than any others I might meet under other circumstances. Nothing in this life comes cheaply—nothing of value anyway—but none of us pays anywhere near the face value for what we get either: what we have, we have been given on loan. I began to live in the midst of that antinomy, to be liberated by it. The world of others around me continues to be bathed in that strange light for me."

With this recognition in mind, Lewis set out to write an essay about the chain of events that led to his realization about the profound dignity of each human life, "to create the snapshot which I never took of that epiphanic moment. And I wanted to create the peace of that moment. . . . The experience about which I wrote was a brief but meaningful excerpt from a much longer story I hope to write about learning from life-lived-on-the-edge. 'Five Minutes North of Redding' was in a way the fulfillment of a youthful dream and the beginning of a more mature vision."

Soon after Patrick Kinder Lewis's essay had been selected to receive a Bedford Prize in Student Writing, we invited four writing students at Queens College in the City University of New York to respond as peer editors to "Five Minutes North of Redding." At that time, the students—Nicholas Balamaci, Jason Eskenazi, Nelson Farias, and Fran Osborne—had accumulated nearly a semester's worth of peer editing experience. These students read and responded to Lewis's essay as though he were a classmate. Then Lewis responded in writing to their comments and suggestions and planned and wrote a revision based on their recommendations.

Here are both the specific marginal notations the peer editors made on Lewis's essay and their general comments at the end of the essay. Read the essay as it appears on pages 320–323 without any comments on it. Then reread it as it appears below, this time considering the peer editors' responses.

Lewis's Edited Essay

This title puts the incident in both time and place. You tell us where we are immediately. (NF)

Five Minutes North of Redding

I notice you use a technical term. Is this the language of hobos? of railroad people? both? (JE)

I rolled out of the weeds into the
crisp daylight of that late September
morning to catch the north train out of
Roseville. The herder had said it would
leave about 3:00 A.M.; so I had huddled

Is this necessary? (NF)

Powerful description of your state of mind. (FO)

in my coat for at least three hours,
wishing in the predawn chill for a cup of
hot anything. But the noise and lights
of the train yard had filtered through

You transform wishes to dreams here. (FO)

You create a strong sense of anticipation at the end of the first paragraph. (NB)

the tall grass and disturbed even those
harmless dreams.

I notice that you equate wishing and dreaming here. Your equation is very indirect, however. Make it clearer? (JE)

Finally she came. Forty cars were
in sight before the engines passed me.

Who is "she"? (NB)

How about: "As I moved down"? I think it reads better that way. (NB)

Moving down to the rail bed, I noticed
for the first time that I had not slept
alone on this stretch of tracks. Three
figures were coming down to claim a rail
car 150 yards up the line, and even as I
cautiously watched them, two other groups
of riders were claiming cars behind me.
I bounded onto a flatcar, concerned that
the line of empties would soon pass me

I notice that you use many participial phrases. (JE)

What is this other thought? Is it the next sentence? (JE)

by--then thought again. A solitary
presence on that flat deck, instinct
shouted within me warnings about such a
vulnerable position. I crossed the ten-
foot width and dropped down onto the
ground on the other side of the car.

This is a dangling modifier. (NB) (JE) (FO) How about: "I was a solitary presence on that flat deck, and within me instinct..."? (NB)

You make me feel how sensitive you are to your own vulnerability here. (NB)

This time I watched until everyone was on
board before I picked out one of the last
empty boxcars. And still there were some
fifty closed cars behind mine. This

All references to the journey between Rockville and Sacramento are left out. Can we assume that you got on board, the train started, and you travelled? (FO)

train was surely big enough, I imagined, for all of us.

    The line of cars came to its first   3
stop on a siding three hours up the Sac-
ramento Valley as we allowed another
train to pass.   Groves of plum trees
lined the track on either side.   Even so
late in the season, the trees to the
train's right were still full of hard
purple fruit.   I laid down in a splash of
sun on the deck of my car.   For the first
time that morning I was warm and relaxed,
but the startling sound of shouts out the
east door caused me to retreat into the
shadows again.   I peered out to find six
men playing among the trees like kids as
they picked plums only to pelt each other
with them.   I watched intently, as if it
were some elaborate social experiment,
until the sound of boots on gravel
brought me back around.   Looking to the
shadow behind me, I suddenly realized
that it was too late to conceal myself.
The man whose crunching boots had just
announced his approach was somehow already at my back door looking me over.
    "There you are.   I've been lookin'
for you.   You're travelin' alone ain't
you?"   All the wrong questions to ask
someone who is already scared of you.
[Luckily the voice betrayed nothing but a
desire for friendship]
    "That's right, I am.   What . . . are
you alone, too?"   I sized him up coolly

I notice that you refer to your-self and the train collectively. (JE)

There are lots of details here. They work well. (NP)

If they are playing, then this should be fun. "Experiments" are for rats. (NF)

There is an innocence here that fights against the alienation you say you feel. (NB)

By whom? You seem to want to generalize here. Why? (JE)

Whose shadow? Your participial phrase keeps me guessing. (JE)

Excellent aural and visual description. (NB)

You make this sound ominous. It works! (NB)

I like how you showed friendship with his voice instead of simply telling us about it. (JE)

Is this word necessary? What does it add to your sentence? (NB)

But only one is asked. (JE)

4

5

It seems to me that this phrase reduces the relief caused by the discovery. (NF)

It would be interesting for a reader to know why you would need to carry a knife. It would create tension if the danger was dramatically present. (NF)

You give your audience lots of detail here. You make it easier for us to see the knife. (NF)

as I moved toward my knapsack in the far corner. In its open front pocket I had a knife if I needed it. He had an eight inch Bowie knife strapped frontier-style to his right shin.

There's a real sense of voice, of personality here. These lines back up your point that the stranger is friendly. (FO) (JE)

You separate the dialogue with lines of description. That gives the effect of coolness, of distance, between the speakers. (FO)

"No. Couple of beaners and me pick up together in Stockton; but they ain't speakin' nothin' but Spanish, man. You want sumpum to eat? They're gettin' some plums. We got cukes and tomatoes still that they picked in the Valley yesterday. And I got a box of saltines in Roseville."

6

Is this necessary? It doesn't seem like essential information to me. What does it add? (NF)

There is excellent control in here. The tension begins to grow, but it's reduced by the following sentence. ("If I planned...") (NF)

He had a ruddy face that was roughly pocked, probably from adolescence, and a scraggly mustache that only became noticeable when he looked right at you. I had reached my pack, but simply turned toward him in a crouch to look for my next move.

7

Can "standing" be a time? (NB)

Do we "look out" for our next move? Don't we get "ready" for it? (FO)

"This is a concise description. (FO)

This is an unusual way of saying this and the phrase works well. (NB)

If I planned to turn down his offer, standing four feet up in a boxcar was the time to do it. His bony frame and large hands gave away his height: I would be at a three- to four-inch disadvantage once down on level ground. And he just looked tough. Shoulder-length, muddy blond hair he had tied back with a lace of dark buckskin; it laced the seams of his chamois pants too. (He was fond of buckskin and wore it well.) Very tough but somehow gentle. He seemed all in all an atavism, a confusing mixture of General Custer with a sixties flower child.

8

You repeat this word later. (NF)

Do you need this? Isn't this understood? (NF)

Move to beginning of sentence? (NF)

This is a sentence fragment. (NF)

How do you know this unless he told you? And if he did, then why not let him speak here? (JE)

How? The contrast needs to be developed. (NF)

I decided to trust my second inclination.

9 "Sounds good," I said closing my pack. "What's your name?" I grabbed my jacket and hopped down onto the loose shale bed. The train was just pulling away with a halting rumble as we neared his car. On quickening our pace, I noticed he was limping from his hip down. I was in the car before him and offered him a hand. But he ignored it and managed an agile roll into the car by catching hold of a break in the floor.

10 Alex and the beaners were the first hobos I was to travel with. For the space of a couple days we ate, drank, slept, and fought like brothers. I learned their pasts and their plans in that short time together and laid awake to think what it would be like to live their lives. At one point, left behind by our train somewhere south of Red Bluff, we hiked together most of the way to the next railhead, ducking many a curious sheriff en route. Finally Alex found us a ride out of a truck stop with an ex-Harley biker. Ambling over the gunwales of his pickup, we rode it all the way to Redding.

11 That night, we caught the last train out still on its dinner break. Ducking into a store nearby, I quickly bought enough sardines, crackers, and canned sausages for ten men. While the train sat idle we found a boxcar that was open

I think it's a good idea to let us figure out what that was. It's more fun for your readers. (NB)

Where else would he limp from? Sounds like he kicked the door! (JE)

This is an excellent sentence.

I notice that you use the word "him" twice in one sentence. (JE)

You show his experience in action. This is filled with great details! (JE)

Was seems out of place here. It's like looking back on something you're looking back on? (JE)

Use "in" here instead? (JE)

I'm not sure that this is the right word. If you meant "fought" literally, then that seems like a cliché. You need to work harder here on your language. (NB)

You need to give some examples here. (NB) (FO)

Same train? New train? (JE)

I notice that you use the word "their" three times in one sentence. (JE)

This paragraph confuses me. I've lost a clear sense of time and place. (FO)

Which night? (FO) (NB)

This is ambiguous. Can a train be on a dinner break? (JE)

Why ducking if you are a legitimate customer? (JE)

Nearby what? (NB)

only on its east side. (For the cold
trip into the mountains ahead, warmth was
a more important concern than a view of
the scenery to the west.) We had just
finished off the sardines as the train at
last began to lumber out of the yard.

This implies that you're impatient for it to move. If so, why? (NF)

Our bodies exhausted, our hunger (at last)
abated, we sat on the dirty floor of our
boxcar [enjoying the last warm breath of
the evening.] We were now at the northernmost end of California's fertile
basin. From here on the land would climb
more steeply. Only the Sacramento River
lay between us and the Cascade mountains.
As we approached the trestle, the track
took only one slow curve to the northwest. On ahead, I was sure it would begin a series of slow switchbacks to climb
Mt. Shasta's side. But for now, because
dead ahead, Shasta was out of sight.
I leaned tiredly against the back
door and watched as the scene in front of
me began to change. Low on the horizon,
a nearly full moon was rising slowly to
take its place in the center of our
stage. Mt. Lassen's distant volcanic
head joined (it) as we rounded the last
turn before the river, showing mutely
through a carpet of velvet green peaks.
Inside the car, Alex stood up to blow the
smoke of his cigarette out into the crystal air. He propped himself like a caryatid supporting the right border of our
window on the world. My (Mexican) (com-

Show us, don't tell us. (JE)

Why? (FO)

You make me feel this sentence! Well done. (JE)

I notice that you use another technical term. (SE)

Something missing? (NF)

Why? (FO)

Is there such a word? (NB)

You shift here from the concrete to a metaphor. (NF)

Your use of this metaphor from drama is very effective.

It's almost poetic! (FO)

This simile seems out of place. (FO)

You move back to being more specific here. That's very effective. (FO)

Read this aloud. Doesn't it sound awkward? (NF)

The naming of places does not fully produce a feeling of movement. 12

This is especially true for readers unfamiliar with the geography of California. (NF)

I'm not sure what "it" refers to. (JE)

This sentence sounds awkward. (JE)

I think it would have been more effective to mention their origin earlier. (NF)

Excellent word choice, suggesting oneness with each other and emphasizing the feeling of the paragraph (FO)

Your words grow more affectionate here, and that seems appropriate. (JE)

padres sat nearly motionless at the door's left side. Mesmerized, I dug blindly into my pack to find the harmonica which I had saved for just such an inspiring moment. I sucked in a chord or two of "This Train Is Bound for Glory," laughing inside. Suddenly, another actor entered from stage left and I came up to a squatting position to get a better vantage. The wild Sacramento below us had begun to snake its way into view, illumined only by the bright moonlight. It was all I could do to keep from walking out our door onto that stage. Like something from a dream, it seemed too fantastically beautiful to be real. And finally, unexpectedly, the train itself emerged as a player. The trestlework not only poised the line of cars two hundred feet above the river's surface but managed as well to bend it into a slow arc midway in the crossing. The sweep of that northward arc turned our view to the south. And just for that instant both the front and rear of the train were visible at once. The engines at our head disappeared slowly into the shadow of Mt. Shasta while the cars that trailed our coach paraded behind us across the massive trestle. And on it all was poured the stark quiet of the moonlight reflected in the river below. The trestle, from south to north, could not have been over a mile long.

Why? (JE)(NF) Are you using this phrase ironically or talking about pure pleasure? (FO)

You make us figure this out for ourselves. I like that. (NB)

What is "it"? (JE)

This is an overused word, but here you use it effectively. (FO)

You return here to talking about yourself and the train in collective terms. (JE)

This seems like a peacocky word to use here. (FO)

This verb makes it sound a little melodramatic. (NB)

But you don't develop the metaphor of the stage until six sentences after it is introduced. (NF)

The Sacramento? (FO) The river? If not, who? (JE)

Your essay picks up momentum in these past few sentences, and the momentum increases with each new sentence. (JE)   13

What is "it"? (JE)

Excellent! You reinforce your metaphor of the stage nicely. (JE)

This is wonderful! The train has been a silent player all along, and here you finally see it too, and consciously. (FO)

I love the idea of quiet being "stark". It's really a good example of how you control your language in the last two paragraphs so that it sounds greeting-card like. (FO)   14

This sounds philosophical and therefore a little risky for some readers. Would something like "Time stood still" work here? (NB)

These are very powerful images. You handle them well! (JE)

The metaphor of Birth doesn't work as well as your others. It seems inappropriate. (FO) (NF)

The entire panorama played before us for less than two minutes. Yet, in a very real way, it has run in my mind's eye ever since.

As that team of Southern Pacific diesels pulled us out of Redding, eternity sat captive for a moment. Like a stolen glimpse of childbirth, I shared in that peaceful feeling of something both beginning and ending at once. And like a mother smiling at her child born at last, I found myself smiling with a similar relief. It was joy without euphoria. I hunted again for the insights of the moment before but found them fading with the darkness of the mountains ahead.

These sentences seem to contrast, if not contradict each other. (JE) 15

But what were they? (NB)

I'm not sure that you explained them clearly. (NF)

What race had I run to earn such rest? What was born in that moment? I looked to my companions for an answer but found it instead full-formed in the darkness between us. There was the sudden realization of the only bond that we all shared: our passion for life. We were living life moment by moment. That was our race well run. As our halos began to fade I picked up my harmonica and found myself playing "Bound for Glory" in a different key.

The problem of this last paragraph is — unlike the rest of your essay — you tell me this. I want you to show me. I want to experience what you're talking about here so that I can also feel it. (JE)

I don't understand this. How does an appreciation for beauty show a passion for life? (FO)

General Comments at the End of the Essay

The four peer editors added these general comments, in addition to their marginal notes, to the end of Lewis's essay.

NICHOLAS BALAMACI   — This is even-keeled, controlled writing. It is also vivid; I "saw" the story. Your essay is also philosophical and, because of that, risks being sentimental. Yet I feel that you avoid this problem very well, although there are just a few lapses (for example "tough but gentle," and "ate, drank, slept, and fought like brothers"). You narrate an important experience in your life, and you emphasize the particular with lots of concrete details. You also use those details to make more general and abstract statements. That's why the essay is so well-crafted.

The only part of your essay that seems a little shaky is the ending. Your words there seem mostly abstract, and you run the risk of letting your essay slide off into important-*sounding* talk. You should think about saying this more simply or less abstractly. Also, there's one repeated mechanical problem: you allow loose connections at times between your modifiers and their referents and between your subjects and the participial phrases that modify them. But I want to say that I could have written beside every paragraph: This essay comes ALIVE! It really makes the experience come to life for the reader. I feel as if I had been there. It's vivid and yet matter-of-fact writing. I look forward to reading it again and owning my own copy of it!

JASON ESKENAZI

— When writing for others, we sometimes write more elaborately than we need to, changing sentences for complexity, for example. I think you need to watch out for this. Sometimes you exchange complexity for clarity. I think you should be clear first.

This essay approaches being a short story. You have the main character come to a moment of insight, and that moment seems to change him at the conclusion. Why did you decide to write an essay? What makes this an essay and not a short story?

If you're going to revise this essay, I'd suggest thinking more about the opening paragraphs. You seem to be much more indirect in the opening paragraphs than you are in the final ones. I think you should be more consistent about this.

The momentum of your essay builds up nicely to the conclusion. Your realization about how the train became a "player" is terrific! Your realization became mine! In moments like that you use a good deal of poetic language. I hear you! The chances you've taken are worth it! You've created many intriguing images and ideas, and you make me want to think more about your story and what it means.

NELSON FARIAS

— Your story has lots of fine word choices and effective metaphors. And these choices give your essay its tone. In this respect, your word choices are appropriate to the mood you want to create. But your sentences are sometimes incomplete and your metaphors aren't developed fully. The way to improve these weaknesses is to place metaphors and ideas that are connected closer together.

You also seem to use lots of proper nouns in your story. That's both effective and ineffective. It's effective because you really draw the reader into your experience, but it's ineffective when the nouns are obscure or confusing. For example, what is a "herder"? Also much of the terminology of the trains is hard to understand. What and where is the "east door"? Is a "closed" car the opposite of an "empty" car? What are "switchbacks"? How can you be sure that your reader will understand what these terms mean? I think your essay could be improved if you'd concentrate on who your audience is. If these railroad terms aren't essential to the overall point you're making in your essay, then maybe you should eliminate them. They distracted me. I guess they'll distract other readers. How important are these terms to what you really want to say in your paper? Maybe you should write another paper on the technical parts of railroading! I'm just not sure that these terms contribute anything to your essay. Besides, I'm more interested in reading about what happens to you than I am about what happens to the train! I'd suggest eliminating some of what you say about the train and adding more about yourself and your experiences with Alex and the beaners.

FRAN OSBORNE

— Up to this point [paragraph 9], there's a real caution in your word choices. (See all the words marked by +.) But when you come to the end of this paragraph, that caution seems to disappear. Did you intend to do that?

This essay has real power to move your audience, power which stems from your ability to communicate "the magic of a moment." It seems to me that paragraphs 12 and 13 capture that moment very effectively. But these paragraphs also contribute much more to your essay. The metaphor of the "stage" that you introduce in paragraph 11 brings all the elements ("the players") of the essay together into a powerful moment of recognition for you. And you have prepared your audience well for that moment—even from the very beginning of your essay. You express the basic idea of your essay in a beautifully understated way in the title.

If the moment of recognition in your essay is presented in paragraphs 12 and 13, then I think you should consider eliminating most, if not all, of your final paragraph in your revision. The metaphor of the childbirth, for example, seems inappropriate to the context you have created. Also, your tone changes in the last paragraph. You seem to want to summarize, but you do that in a very different voice. Perhaps you should leave out most of the final paragraph and end by returning to "playing 'Bound for Glory' in a different key."

The essay needs some "fixing" in a purely technical sense. I need to understand better the architecture of the train more clearly (What does it look like?). I also need to understand better the passing of time more clearly (How much time elapses while you're on the train?). Finally, I also need to understand better the relationships between you, Alex, and the beaners more clearly (How much more can you tell us about them that will strengthen your story?).

All in all, though, I think your essay borders on the poetic, and it is all the more effective for it. I enjoyed reading it and thinking about what you accomplished.

Questions on Lewis's Edited Essay

1. Reread the peer editors' statements about Patrick Lewis's essay. On which aspects of the essay does Nicholas Balamaci focus his attention? Jason Eskenazi? Nelson Farias? Fran Osborne? What overall advice does each offer? What specific changes in focus, tone, and word choice do you notice between the peer editors' general concluding statements and their marginal comments? Which parts of the essay does each regard as most successful? Least successful? Why?

2. Review the peer editors' detailed marginal notations. Which of the comments are observations (statements about which there can be no disagreement)? Which are evaluations that try to summarize the main idea of the essay and then show the relation between specific paragraphs and this idea?

3. Examine Fran Osborne's comments at the end of the essay. What is her response to the overall structure of Lewis's essay? To his use of diction and figurative language? To the speaker's voice? Which of these aspects of composition does Osborne think Lewis handles best? Why? Point to specific words and phrases to support your response.

4. List the points the peer editors agree on; disagree on. On what points do you agree with them? On what points do you disagree?

5. Reread Nicholas Balamaci's final comments. Sketch out what Lewis would need

to do in a revision to respond adequately to what Balamaci says. Then reread Jason Eskenazi's concluding statement. What specific plan for revision could Lewis extrapolate from it? In what ways do Balamaci's and Eskenazi's final recommendations differ? Which plan do you find more useful? Explain why.

The Writer's Response to Peer Editing

As a writer, you will benefit most from peer editing when you listen attentively to what your peer editors have to say about your essay and then examine with them the implications of their observations and recommendations. But it is important to remember that peer editing and writing are skills that take time and frequent practice to develop. So you and your peer editor need to remind each other, at least occasionally, that even the most well intentioned efforts at peer editing—and especially the first few tries at it—may not bring immediate improvement. Be patient with your own intelligence and with the intelligence of others. There are few quick fixes in the world of ideas. Remember to keep an open mind when responding to your peer editors' comments, especially if you as a writer are new to peer editing and are more experienced with responding exclusively to what an instructor says about a draft of your essay.

As a writer about to work with peer editors, you can anticipate receiving a good deal of generous and supportive criticism from readers who are familiar with and sympathetic to your purpose. And the presence of a real audience, who will read and respond to what you have written, may well be all you need to reassure yourself that writing is worth the effort involved, especially when you face moments, as nearly every writer does, when ideas seem hard to discover and energy and interest falter.

To make the best possible use of the peer editors' responses and advice, you need to listen thoughtfully to their observations and recommendations and take advantage of them when you write the final draft of your essay. By listening purposefully, you are less likely to be distracted from examining the strengths and weaknesses of your essay by what may occasionally be a peer editor's poorly phrased comment or an ill-advised judgment.

When done rigorously, peer editing is as much a writing exercise as a reading exercise. When your peer editors are searching quickly for the best way to convey their responses to your essay, they too may occasionally slip into awkward or even inappropriate phrasing. But such moments, however uninstructive they may appear at first glance, can be opportunities for you to reciprocate by helping your peer editors express themselves more effectively. Sometimes their comments may not be entirely clear, and in such cases you should not hesitate to press for clarification. This process often results in a dialogue in which you have a chance to explain more fully your purpose or sense of audience and the peer editors have an opportunity to clarify and develop some of their comments and suggestions. But whatever the particulars of such dialogue, writing is clearly the source—and the result—as well as the arbiter of productive conversation.

Writing should be at the center of peer editing. You should leave a peer editing session with more than the impression of your peer editors' response. You should carry away, and later evaluate and act on, their detailed written responses to your essay, responses that have been amplified in your discussion with them. Having all the peer editors' comments in writing not only makes particular points of the discussion recoverable later, it also enables you to more easily evaluate their comments and enumerate your priorities for revision.

With the benefit of peer editors' responses, you should improve—perhaps dramatically so—your ability to evaluate the reactions of many different readers, each of whom may read your essay in a slightly different way. You ought to pay special attention to any comments about strengths and weaknesses pointed out by more than one peer editor. In each instance, you as the writer must decide what to change and what to retain in your new draft. Although the peer editors can help, the authority and the responsibility for those decisions remain yours, and yours alone, as the writer.

Discussing and then evaluating peer editors' comments should help you develop a clear sense of how to improve your essay. Your detailed plan for revision should include the peer editors' recommendations you have decided to accept and act on as well as your own ideas about how to reinforce your essay's strengths and eliminate its weaknesses. The peer editing process encourages you to treat your essay as a work-in-progress, to understand your specific strengths and shortcomings as a writer, and, eventually, to produce stronger writing at every phase of the composing process.

One Writer's Response to Peer Editing

In this section we present Patrick Kinder Lewis's response to the peer editing of Nicholas Balamaci, Jason Eskenazi, Nelson Farias, and Fran Osborne. Lewis's comments explain his decisions to include, adapt, and sometimes reject their recommendations in the revised version of his essay. Lewis's reactions to the peer editors' final general comments and then to their specific marginal notations are followed by his overall response to peer editing itself—its principles and practices and its value in the composing process.

ON THE PEER
EDITORS' FINAL
COMMENTS

— The final comments gave me a general idea of the temperament of my audience. Did they like me and the paper, or did they think I was from another planet? I wanted to know about any big gaps that I needed to bridge. I have taken four general guidelines for revision from the peer editors' end notes:

1. Nicholas comments about my tendency to philosophize to the point of sentimentality. I knew exactly the passages in which I made the offenses. The question I had to ask was "Is that so bad?" After talking things over with my writing teacher, I came away feeling that, whatever I did—as in so many things—it was always going to be better to use silver polish than a sandblaster. A little philosophy never hurt anyone, so long as it isn't overblown—"important-*sounding* talk" as Nicholas calls it. Since some kind of expository essay seems to be my natural mode, I guess I had better learn to do it well if I can.

2. The same question in my mind comes up in Jason's query about whether I hadn't really wanted to write a short story. The truth is that I would have liked to write one, but that was not the assignment. I decided that, if I hope to really "assay" my thoughts on the story I want to tell, then I should do it engagingly, and without resorting to any abrupt mood shifts.

3. Nelson asked for more development of the "I" character. That in fact prompted the most obvious change in the paper, that is, its opening. Nelson made me realize that the central character was the only thing that made the story coherent. So I worked myself into every line in a more conscious way. Enough said! This begins to sound self-aggrandizing, which is not my intent at all.

4. Fran made me see more clearly that it was the "magic of the moment" which needed to be the telos of the work. I am glad that she liked it, because I was beginning to lose sight of why I felt I *had* to write this paper in the first place. She also agreed with the haunting feeling I had that the last paragraph was somehow overkill.

Fran also raises a very interesting question for me. She wanted to understand better the relationship between me and the other characters. In fact, she went through and marked words [with a + sign] that seemed to indicate my isolation from them up to the point where I met Alex.

In the revision I have tried to make that theme more consistent and the transition more obvious. I *was* afraid and then resolved not to live in that unfounded fear. So, as to the basics of human friendship, I wanted to show that change as one that was/is evident to even me. But there is another distance that separated us, which is not as central.

It was interesting to find Fran in a marginal note assuming that we (that is, the travelers) were all in the same boat. There is a barely legible note on my "General Directions" outline where I ask myself (to explain) where the ignorant and illiterate fit into my scheme of the world. I see quite a distance separating me from the fellows that I am writing about. But it is not the same sort of distance I mentioned above (fear), nor the sort I mentioned in the paragraph about hobo life (ignorance and uncaring). I am not isolated from them by my choice as much as by "our choice." I feel for and with them, but there is no less a real distance of understanding. But I resolve that it not be a distance of appreciation. My empathy, born in our exposures (and the sometimes palpable misunderstanding that exposure brought), affords them a very special place in my world—perhaps akin to the place which Jesus intimates in the beatitudes (and in fact throughout his teaching ministry). The poor in spirit *are* blessed. Not simply because of their ignorance nor in spite of it. It is for both of these reasons and more. And somehow, it makes them my *superiors*, in a realm that I don't understand well, but respect very much. The uncomfortable distance which I feel between the "ignorant" and the "enlightened" is the result of *our* misunderstanding—both sides are guilty. It is bridged, then, by admission of our own ignorance. The bridge seems intensely spiritual.

ON THE PEER
EDITORS' MARGINAL
NOTATIONS

— I am not a detail person, so I guess it shouldn't surprise me that the big things worked in my essay, while, often as not, the sentences struggled to make themselves even coherent. I took Jason's comments about "exchanging complexity for clarity" and "writing too elaborately" to heart. I hope that most of the sentences in the new version are at least readable. . . . Let me quickly mention no more than a dozen marginal comments that got me thinking.

What is so mystifying about the relationship between wishing and dreaming? I added the phrase "half-awake" to a sentence from the old paragraph 1 to clarify the point. I hope it works. I think that more than likely, the heavy opposition was due to first paragraph overzealousness. Anyway, it does read better.

I am truly indebted to Nicholas (my tongue is *not* in my cheek this time!) for two very specific suggestions which I think improve paragraph 2 immensely: just the kind of cleaning up that Jason drew to my attention in his general comments—a misplaced participial phrase and a predicate with a (mis)understood subject.

At the end of the same paragraph, I dropped the last two sentences because they were a weak attempt at developing the "fear" theme. The more direct reference two paragraphs later made them superfluous.

All the editors got their wishes in paragraph 3 when I interrupted a very difficult sentence (again with a misunderstood subject) to make a detour for Fran and Nelson's benefit. Actually, I had wanted to put more of the hobo's eye-view description in my original, but couldn't seem to make it fit. I hope the addition gives new insights, though I suspect it has a few difficulties of its own.

I was disappointed that everyone seemed to concur with Nelson's remark that "experiments are for rats," a little later in the same paragraph (old number 3). The sense of observer-observed isolation is exactly what I had felt up to that time. And it is what I tried to convey by that word choice.

Again in the same paragraph, Fran made a practical, seemingly obvious, suggestion that vastly improved the feel of the prose. I substituted the simple Anglo-Saxon verb "hide" for a difficult Latin reflexive phrase "conceal myself."

Both Nelson and Jason helped me clean up the next paragraph (that is, number 4 in the original).

I was trying all along to keep Alex down to a "manageable size." Several of the peer editors, in the paragraph describing Alex's appearance, wanted me to somehow expand on "tough but gentle." Though Alex was a real person, I really wanted him, for the purposes of this essay, to stand for a character type: the good guy, gentleman-of-the-rails. Having to develop *two* characters to everyone's satisfaction threatened to diffuse the overall direction of the essay and add an unnecessary dimension.

The old paragraph 10 has a whole new look for the same sort of reason: too much detail with not enough direction.

Both to introduce a paragraph that contains what I consider to be some "important talk" and to satisfy the urgings of Nicholas and Fran (that is, to expand the somewhat sappy line about "fighting like brothers"), I cut out much of that paragraph and some of the next. Most of the next paragraph in the revision (as well as parts of the new introduction and conclusion) came from the material that I cut from the original for lack of space.

I thought the question about technical terms perplexing. Anyone who has grown up around mountains should have encountered "switchbacks" as the only practical way for a road or a trail (or a railroad track) to climb a steep grade. Words like "herder" and "beaners" I assumed would be obvious by their contexts (who else in California speaks "nothing but Spanish, man"?).

For the rest of the story, I had spent great pains in getting a very difficult picture in my mind's eye on paper. So I felt comfortable about the generally favorable comments and leaving it much the same. I made one very specific change suggested by Nelson, shifting the first sentence of paragraph 13 with the last one of 12.

ON PEER EDITING
AND WRITING

— I certainly hope that the peer editors like the new look and feel of the essay. It took a while to get started after the preliminary notes I made on everyone's ideas. I didn't really hit a groove until a few hours of working on the revision. Then, and only then, did I start to enjoy what I was doing again. The final product seems more focused than before, moving with a kind of concerted effort it didn't have before. And I also came to feel a lot more comfortable with the distinct voice that an essay should have. It just sounds more controlled than before, less rambling and storylike.

When I began the process of this revision, after reading through both the peer editors' final comments and their marginal notes, I was ready to make a broad statement about the greater relative value of the end-type comments. I thought I would reject 90 percent of the marginal stuff. Now that I have finished, I can no longer make that statement. I ended up weighing every comment carefully, and I would guess that 90 percent of them have affected the new essay in some way or other. I hope the peer editors can see the extent of each of their contributions to the new version. And I very much appreciated the strongly personal approach each took. It made their recommendations "stand apart" with much less overlapping than I anticipated. What's more, they wrote very lucidly about rather difficult subjects. All that said, I am glad there were no more than four peer editors—even five would have been overwhelming.

As a new writer, I suppose it is natural that I am a rather unself-conscious writer. I enjoy writing. I suppose that there is a similar feeling in the neophyte painter. If nothing else, writing always seems to sharpen my perception of what I have seen. The peer editing process has rushed me into the world of the conscious. There is an almost unimaginable benefit in simply the suggestion that someone is taking something I have written seriously enough to respond to it personally. That feeling of "someone watching," if not allowed to dominate our mind, can probably be the greatest single factor in encouraging seminal talent. But you must, I think, enjoy writing first.

Now that you have had the opportunity to read Patrick Kinder Lewis's responses to the peer editors' observations and recommendations, examine the revised version of his essay, which he prepared after considering their reactions and advice.

Lewis's Revised Essay

Five Minutes North of Redding

My twenty-fifth year was a mixed-up time for me, full up   1
with broken relationships and lost hope, all-day school and
all-night jobs.   I was "living in the shade of a freeway"
(as Jackson Browne so aptly put it) in a worn-out mobile home
with a Siamese cat on loan from a friend, and a primer gray
Datsun 110 with a bad transmission: the whole thing was
rather comical for a while, but I was slowly becoming more
desperate for whatever was next.   And so it was that I began
to notice the routine of a work train that daily came out of
a cement yard over on the other side of the throughway fence.

"Riding the rails" had wooed me for several years, from   2
the time I had first seen three modern hobos jump off their
"coach" on the outskirts of Las Vegas.   From that moment on,
the romance of life seen from the door of a boxcar had captured my imagination.   I even resurrected an old harmonica
that I had used in high school and began playing woeful tunes
late at night, while the open road sang along in a familiar
voice. The words of the ballad promised to tell a tale yet
untold, but then they drifted off into the soft stillness
outside my door.

I left the L.A. basin with only one change of clothes, a   3
bedroll, and a little bit of money hidden so well that it
took me ten minutes to get to it.   I waited until I heard
the train pulling into the cement plant and locked the door
of my trailer behind me as I ran to meet it.   Twenty minutes
later I was riding my first freight.   Alone.   And that was
just fine.   I had heard too many stories about shifty bums
who would kill for a pair of shoes.   I stayed wide of their
campfires and always traveled by myself.

Two weeks later found me near Sacramento, waiting for   4
another train on the outskirts of the biggest rail yard in

northern California. This time I was bound for Seattle. I
rolled out of the weeds into the crisp daylight of that late
September morning to catch the north train out of Roseville.
The herder had said it would be leaving about 3:00 A.M. So
I had huddled half-awake in my coat for at least three hours,
wishing in the predawn chill for a cup of hot anything. But
the noise and lights of the train yard had filtered through
the tall grass and disturbed even that harmless dream.

Finally she came. Forty cars were in sight before the 5
engines passed me. As I moved down to the rail bed, I noticed for the first time that I had not waited alone on this
stretch of tracks. Three figures were coming down to claim
a rail car 150 yards up the line, and even as I cautiously
watched them, two other groups of riders were claiming cars
behind me. With what looked like seasoned confidence, I
bounded onto a flat car, concerned that the line of empties
would soon pass me by—then thought again. I was a solitary
presence on that flat deck, and, within me, instinct shouted
warnings about such a vulnerable position. I crossed the
ten-foot width of the car and dropped down onto the ground on
the other side. This time I watched until everyone was on
board before I picked out one of the last empty boxcars.

The line of cars came to its first stop on a siding 6
three hours up the Sacramento Valley as we allowed another
train to pass. Groves of plum trees lined the track on
either side. Even so late in the season, the trees to the
train's right were still full of hard purple fruit. I lay
down in a splash of sun on the deck of my car. For the
first time that morning, I was warm and relaxed. The world
of the hobo seemed at the moment to be everything I had hoped
for. Maybe more. For one thing, I hadn't figured on the
dust, but there was plenty of it to go around. My first
hour reclining against the wall of a boxcar left me smudged
with enough soot to convince anyone that I had been hoboing
all my life. Nor had I counted on the noise. The crashing

clatter, especially of start-ups, made me wish often enough
for the luxury of earplugs.   Even the click of the rails inside this car (with both doors pushed open wide) was less
than soothing after an hour or so.   Still, all that seemed
to make stops like this one the more enjoyable.   The view
and the solitude of such regular pauses lured me into the
kind of romantic reverie that had inspired this adventure.
Later, after a nap, I would get out to step away from the
train far enough to see what was up ahead.   But for now,
what I could see through my door was all the world I had
wished for.

Suddenly, the startling sound of shouts out the east   7
door caused me to retreat into the shadows again.   I peered
out to see six men playing among the fruit trees like kids as
they picked plums only to pelt each other with them.   I
watched intently, as if it were some elaborate social experiment, until the sound of boots on gravel out the other door
brought me back around.   Looking back to the shadows of the
car's interior, I suddenly realized that it was too late to
hide.   The man whose crunching boots had just announced his
approach was already at the west door looking me over.

"There you are.   I've been lookin' for you.   You're   8
travelin' alone ain't you?"   The wrong question to ask someone who is already scared of you.   Luckily the tone of his
voice betrayed only a desire for friendship.

"That's right, I am.   What . . . are you alone, too?"   9
I sized him up coolly as I moved toward my knapsack in the
far corner.   In its open front pocket I had a knife if I
needed it.   He had an eight-inch Bowie knife strapped frontier-style to his right shin.

"No.   Couple of beaners and me pick up together in   10
Stockton; but they ain't speakin' nothin' but Spanish, man.
You want sumpum to eat?   They're gettin' some plums.   We got
cukes and tomatoes still that they picked in the Valley yesterday.   And I got a box of saltines in Roseville."

He had a ruddy face that was roughly pocked, probably 11
from adolescence, and a scraggly mustache that only became
noticeable when he looked right at you.   I had reached my
pack, but simply turned toward him in a crouch to look for my
next move.

If I planned to turn down his hospitality, standing 12
there four feet up in a boxcar was the moment to do it.   His
bony frame and large hands gave away his height.   He would
be three to four solid inches taller than me on level ground.
He had tied his shoulder-length, muddy blond hair back with a
lace of dark buckskin; it laced the seams of his chamois
pants too. (He was fond of buckskin and wore it well.)   But,
tough as he looked, there was an obvious gentleness to him as
well.   He seemed all in all an atavism, a confusing mixture
of General Custer with a sixties flower child.   I decided to
trust my second inclination.

"Sounds good," I said closing my pack.   "What's your 13
name?"   I grabbed my jacket and hopped down onto the loose
shale bed.   The train was just pulling away with a halting
rumble as we neared his car.   As we quickened our pace, I
noticed he was limping from his hip down.   I was in the car
before him and offered him a hand. But he ignored it and managed an agile roll into the car by catching hold of a break
in the floor.

Alex and the beaners were the first hobos I was to 14
travel with.   Their friendship wore away the edge of the
fear I had felt since hearing my first hobo story.   Over the
space of a few days we ate, drank, slept, and fought like
brothers.   I shared my rations, and at one point, even my
bedroll, with my Mexican companions who had come less prepared, while Alex laughingly looked on and told story after
story.   I learned something of their pasts and their plans
in that short time together, and lay awake to think what it
would be like to live their lives.

Life in a downtown rail yard is much farther away from   15
most of us than simple distance suggests.   The bums, drying
out from damp nights by fires built under the bridges, rarely
venture into our world from their environs plaited out of
steel and wood.   Sometimes they make the trip to downtown
skid rows for the social interaction offered at missions and
overnight shelters.   But hobos are really in a class by
themselves.   Not quite as permanently debilitated as the
downtown drunks, they generally live their private lives
without panhandling, building a world of their own in the
hobo jungles that spring up among the weeds and warehouses
surrounding train yards.   Few of them have anything resembling a year-round home.   Transience and seasonal migrations
are the more general rule.   Some do venture in and out of
institutional life: missions, dry-out centers, acute psychiatric wards.   Paranoid schizophrenia is surely their most
common syndrome; alcohol is their drug of choice.   But there
are also, of course, many exceptions.   Alex and the beaners
were three of them.

While the train sat idle in Redding, we found a boxcar   16
that was open only on its east side.   (For the cold trip
into the mountains ahead, warmth was a more important concern
than a view of the scenery to the west.)   We had just finished off several tins of sardines as the train at last began
to lumber out of the yard.   Our bodies exhausted, our hunger
at last abated, we sat on the dirty floor of our boxcar, enjoying the last warm breath of the evening.   We were now at
the northernmost end of California's fertile basin.   From
here on the land would climb more steeply.   Only the Sacramento River lay between us and the Cascade mountains.   As we
approached the river's trestle, the track took only one slow
curve to the northwest.   On ahead, it was sure to begin a
series of slow switchbacks to climb Mt. Shasta's side.   But
for now, because dead ahead, Shasta was out of sight.

I leaned tiredly against the back door and watched as   17
the scene in front of me began to change.   Low on the horizon, a nearly full moon was rising slowly to take its place
in the center of our stage.   Mt. Lassen's distant volcanic
head joined it as we rounded the last turn before the river,
showing mutely through a carpet of velvet green peaks.   Inside the car, Alex stood up to blow the smoke of his cigarette out into the crystal air.   He propped himself like a
caryatid supporting the right border of our window on the
world.   My Mexican compadres sat nearly motionless at the
door's left side.   Mesmerized, I dug blindly into my pack to
find the harmonica which I had saved for just such an inspiring moment.   I sucked in a chord or two of "This Train Is
Bound for Glory," laughing inside.   Suddenly, another actor
entered from stage left and I came up to a squatting position
to get a better vantage, as the river below came into view.
It was all I could do to keep from walking out our door onto
that stage.

The wild Sacramento below us had begun to snake its way   18
into view, illumined only by the bright moonlight.   Like
something from a dream, it seemed too fantastically beautiful
to be real.   And finally, unexpectedly, the train itself
emerged as a player.   The trestlework not only poised the
line of cars two hundred feet above the river's surface, but
managed as well to bend it into a slow arc midway in the
crossing.   The sweep of that northward arc turned our view
to the south.   And just for that instant, both the front and
rear of the train were visible at once.   The engines at our
head disappeared slowly into the shadow of Mt. Shasta while
the cars that trailed our coach paraded behind us across the
massive trestle.   And on it all was poured the stark quiet
of the moonlight reflected in the river below.

The trestle, from south to north, could not have been   19
over a mile long.   The entire panorama played before us for
less than two minutes.   Yet, in a very real way, it has run

in my mind's eye ever since.   As that team of Southern-
Pacific diesels pulled us out of Redding, eternity sat
captive for a moment.

Later that night, I found out that Alex wasn't running   20
away as I had supposed.   He was "tired of all that" and
thought it was time to head home and help out his mother.
Maybe he would even settle down with a waitress who had been
chasing him for years.   At thirty-eight, the traveling
seemed to be wearing him away little by little.   I wondered
what crisis had brought him to his decision, but decided not
to ask.   For it seemed that a similar moment had just passed
in my life--one which no words could explain.   The open road
had told me its tale, and now I too was ready to walk into
whatever was next.   I closed my eyes for the night, humming
"Bound for Glory" in a different key.

Questions on Lewis's Revision

1. In his responses to the peer editing (pages 617–621), Lewis discusses some of his plans for revising his essay. What did he decide to focus on in his revision? Which points does he accomplish most successfully? Point to specific words and phrases in both his responses and his revision to support your answer.

2. Which of Lewis's responses to the peer editors' comments do you agree with? Which do you disagree with? Why? Which points in his plan for revision would you like to see expanded? Dropped? Altered slightly? Why?

3. Which aspects of Lewis's essay would benefit from additional attention and revision? Why? Point to specific places where he could make further changes and indicate what those changes might be.

4. Lewis reports that he made substantial revisions in the opening and closing of his essay. How, specifically, has he done this, and with what effect?

5. Write as many observations as you can about the specific differences between Lewis's original essay (pages 320–323) and his revised essay. In what ways is his *purpose* clearer? How does each paragraph relate more clearly to the main point of the essay? How is his handling of Alex and the beaners stronger? How does he consider his audience's knowledge of hobos, trains, and life "on the rails"? How does his choice of words reflect a different consideration for his *audience*? Point to specific words and phrases in the essay to support your responses.

6. In a recent interview, Patrick Kinder Lewis was invited to reread both his prize-winning essay and the subsequent revision prompted by the responses of the peer editors. We asked Lewis to comment not only on the specific strengths and weaknesses of both versions but also, more generally, on the peer editing process. Here is his response: "I still enjoy the essay, especially the peer edited revision. It actually refreshes me to read it because I have forgotten so much about the episode. I held the memory in check. But since then, I have not reviewed those memories to keep them fresh. So much is happening every day; I will need to collect my thoughts for a period before I am able to write again with the same intensity. Also, the essay is technically better than I could do now without a good bit of practice.

"Its successful features? Well, I like the flow of the essay. It moves from wishes to wish-fulfillment—in both versions really. I like the feeling it has that the writer begins very green and ends less so.

"The descriptive attempts I made seem very successful. I especially like paragraph 7 in the original version where I turn to Alex. Also, paragraph 15 in the revised version about hobo life is succinct but evocative—at least for me.

"I guess I like the introductory paragraph of the revised version, though I am still not sure if that enjoyment doesn't come from introspective indulgence.

"I had a chance, of course, to completely rework my first essay with the help of peer editors. . . . I wanted 'Five Minutes North of Redding' to capture the reader like a good short story, but still to remain an essay by virtue of its singular focus. I think that happened in the peer edited version.

"Having enjoyed the peer editing process, I would encourage others to write as if they were writing for a critical friend or two—whether or not they will actually read it. Or at least after the first draft is created, revise with an audience in mind."

What insights into the writing process and into peer editing does Patrick Kinder Lewis provide in this detailed response? Comment on the significance of each insight.

Practicing Peer Editing

In this section you have an opportunity to practice applying the principles and procedures of peer editing, first to Johnna Lynn Benson's "Rotten at the Core" and then to your own writing.

The following checklist points out many of the concerns peer editors keep in mind as they work on an essay. Your instructor may add others.

1. *Purpose.* What is the writer trying to do in the essay? What is the main idea, the essay's thesis or overriding point? What intention or promise does the essay state or imply? Where and how well does the writer act on that intention or promise? What specific examples, ideas, or information would help clarify or reinforce the writer's purpose?

2. *Organization.* How is the essay organized? What is its basic structure? Comment on the logic and effectiveness of the sequence of paragraphs. How well does each paragraph support and develop the essay's main idea? In which paragraphs is the main idea most effectively supported by details and examples?

3. *Choice of Words.* Is the language of the essay primarily abstract or concrete? If it is abstract, do you understand what each abstraction means? Does the writer use special terminology or colloquial terms? How effective is such language? How well does it support the writer's purpose?

4. *Point of View.* Point of view means the point or perspective from which the essay is written or the story is told. From what perspective does the writer approach the subject of the essay? Where is this point of view stated or implied? Does the writer maintain the point of view consistently throughout the essay? Point to those places where the writer's point of view is most clearly stated, where it seems uncertain, and where it is consistent or inconsistent.

5. *Audience.* Characterize the audience the writer seems to have in mind. What does the writer expect the audience to know about the subject? Point to specific words and phrases that reveal the writer's assumptions about the audience's familiarity with the subject.

From your own experience and your study of peer editors at work, what other aspects of composition should peer editors attend to as they read another student's writing? Prepare sets of questions for each aspect.

Exercises in Peer Editing

1. Apply the principles of peer editing to "Rotten at the Core" by Johnna Lynn Benson (pages 63–66), following the peer editing procedures outlined in this chapter. Read the essay several times and write your observations, evaluations, and recommendations in the margin.

   —Write as many observations as you can about the essay (remember, an observation is a statement about which there can be no disagreement).

   —Summarize the essay's main idea and note how the writer supports and develops that idea in each paragraph.

   —Identify both the strengths and the weaknesses of the essay. In this respect, pay particular attention to Benson's sentence structure and variety, her verb tenses and voice, her paragraph transitions, and her concluding paragraph.

   —Prepare a general final statement noting the essay's overall strengths and weaknesses and offering some specific recommendations for revision.

   After you have completed your work as a peer editor on "Rotten at the Core," write Johnna Lynn Benson a letter in which you analyze the strengths and weaknesses of her essay and offer her as much reasonable, practical, and detailed advice as you can about what she might do in another draft to improve her essay.

2. After you have completed your peer editing of Benson's essay, you might find it instructive to compare and contrast your marginal notations and final comments with those prepared by Nicholas Balamaci, Jason Eskenazi, Nelson Farias, and Fran Osborne. Here are both the specific marginal notations that these peer editors made on Benson's essay, along with their general reactions and recommendations for revision at the end of her essay. Reread Benson's essay, which begins on the next page, this time paying special attention to the other peer editors' responses.

Benson's Edited Essay

Rotten at the Core

> *Your title seems inconsistent with the outcome of your essay. (JE)*

George A. Kelly's Theory of Personality has scrubbed me on a washboard and put me through the wringer. Discovering what I actually am under the dirt and debris has been bewildering and has left me wondering if I would be better off blissfully ignorant. I had thought "to know thyself" an admirable pursuit, especially since I believed truth was beauty. Now I see I have been beautifully wrong about who I am and who everybody else is. 1

> *You use a cleaning metaphor to begin with: neat because you're going to clean yourself off and start over. (FO)*
>
> *Cleansing metaphor works well here. (JE)*
>
> *This word repeats "better off," and it can be considered a cliché. Remove? (NB)*
>
> *Shakespeare! (JE)*
>
> *Reference to Keats's "Ode to a Grecian Urn." But are you searching for "beauty"? (JE)*
>
> *Your use of "blissfully" and "beautifully" worries me because you do not explain how your ignorance was either. (FO)*

When the colloquium introduced me to Theory of Personality, I was sure we would get along great. I have always loved dabbling in psychology. My friends and I would make Freudian jokes or play shrink-games, using those little tests in women's magazines designed to save on psychoanalysis costs. You could say I won those games; my free associations were always more bizarre than anyone else's. I wasn't even trying to be shocking or clever. That is just a bad habit. My only feud with psychology was that I aspired to be more than a product of my environment, a multiplication of Mormonism by a materialistic middle-class suburb. Theory of Personality eliminated that limitation for me. 2

> *You personify the colloquium. (FO)*
>
> *Colloquial language. (FO)*
>
> *Combine this sentence with the one before it for the sake of clarity. (FO)*
>
> *But you do try to be "shocking" and "clever." Why not say so? (And they are not necessarily bad habits.) (NF)*
>
> *You change tenses here. (NB)*
>
> *I don't understand your point here. (JE)*

I loved it instantly. Kelly's treatise holds that people create their 3

> *Your point of view is now clear. (JE)*

own personalities. As a person tries to
make sense of the circus around him, he
picks up on recurring themes in his life

I notice that you go to the source for a dab of objectivity.

Do you mean inferences here? (FO)

and makes deductions about what is going
on. The individual creates these explanations, called "constructs," for his
convenience in anticipating what the
world is going to hit him with next. As
a person construes, he builds an inner
road map of himself, of life, and of what
he can expect from it. The psychology I
had been exposed to before treated man
like an organism poked and prodded into
reactions. I found the concept of deciding for yourself who you are and what
you can expect from life far more palatable. Claiming total responsibility for
my outlook on life filled me with satisfaction.

I like how you work Kelly in here. (JE)

This is an effective metaphor. (JE)

 Theory of Personality created a little (garden paradise) in the corner for me,
but it also (unearthed) something upsetting. As part of our colloquium study of
constructs, we were asked to write about
our core roles, or how we viewed ourselves. I kept putting the assignment
off because every time I started it, my
query led me down the same path. [If you
do not want to go to Rome, finding that
all roads go there is rather dismaying.]
Suddenly it was the day to hand in the
assignment, and I discovered, as I frantically wrote the thing in the Harris
Fine Arts Center for an hour before
class, that I had spent enough time

The essay really seems to gel under way here. (FO)

4

Your tone changes here. Is that what you intend? Do you both love and fear the book and what it reveals? (JE)

Going anyway shows deter-mination and strength of character. (NF)

This is an innovative and pleasant way to turn around the old cliché, and to make a point besides. (NB)

What a
concise way
to put this!
Excellent!
(NB)
You return us here
to the idea
of shocking
and clever in
paragraph
one. (FO)

This way of
talking about
yourself seems
unwarranted.
(FO)
But you haven't
explained how
you are
"rotten at the
core," only
slightly
arrogant.
(NB)

You sound
a little
snobbish and
egotistical
in here. (JE)

This is
unclear. Did
the three
colors alter-
nate as your
favorite
over the
years? Aren't
you certain
which was
your
favorite?
(NB)

trying not to think about it that I knew exactly what I didn't want to know.

This could be a
sentence
by itself.
(NF)

With Fresh, Original, and Bizarre as my highest ideals, my core role seems to be that I must be different. And I am different, which makes me exceptional, though not in a way the general population appreciates. This arrogant idea actuates my every thought and emotion, a realization that makes me shudder. Exploring the fact that I'm rotten at the core reduced me to tears.

"Different"
is not a
quality word.
(FO)
I don't
see why being
different
makes you
exceptional.
(FO)
"Exceptional"
implies better
than average.
(FO)

Yet I can't seem to get around it. I look at how I hate get-acquainted parties. To adhere "Hello, my name is . . ." on my lapel is to assume common ground exists between these strangers and me. But my core role says my lifeline runs geometrically askew to theirs. Kelly defines guilt as an awareness of contradicting one's core role structure, and guilty well describes the uncomfortable feeling I get pretending such parties aren't futile. I forget that I actually do share significant parallels and intersections with family and friends. I like the differences. By the time I was six I introduced myself by saying, to the consternation of my playmates, that I did not like chocolate cake or sodapop. For years my favorite color was chartreuse, sienna, or puce. My favorite number is 3.02875×10^{14}. I took up origami because I thought no one had heard of it. In short, anything popular was not worth

This is an
innovative,
clear, and
artful way of
putting this.
(NB)

Can
parallels
be "shared"?
Can
"intersections"?
(JE)

my time, while anything obscure or new
was mine by right.

These paragraphs Moreover, I felt unique enough to   *This para-*
enumerate assume that although rules were necessary *graph gives*
differences to keep the regulars in line, they did *examples of*
but they also *how you "break"*
enumerate not apply to me. Because rules were *rules without*
similarities necessary, I never quite broke them but *breaking*
too. You, found interpretations to suit me. For *them! (FO)*
like most example, when an elementary class punish-
people, do ment to copy five pages from the dictio-
have a nary was handed down, my paper always in-
favorite cluded a few words outside the assigned
color, number, alphabetical range, like "despot," "tou-
etc. And you pee," "maltreatment." Lights-out at camp
do "obey" meant it was dark enough to leave the
rules. The cabin unnoticed and go for a moonlight
"differences" walk. Going to parties where friends
appear to be were too drunk to really notice my absti-
semantic nence was showing my love and understand- *The idea*
rather than ing for people with problems, not to *about the*
substantial. mention making them aware of the Mormon *Mormon Church*
(FO) Church. And of course, as long as my *seems unrelated*
Do you see the boyfriend and I didn't go all the way, *to the rest of*
contradiction whatever we wanted to do was fine. We *the sentence.*
here? If were toying with the idea of marriage *It would*
friends are anyway. Other people needed rules. I *help if you*
"too drunk did not. *gave an ex-*
to really *ample of*
notice" how I have been carried away with my own *what the*
can you be individuality enough to hypothesize that *Mormons*
"showing"? when I was a zygote, some stray cosmic *have to*
(FO) ray zapped my DNA, making me a daughter *offer such*
This seems to say of chance and not of Terry and Dianna *troubled*
"Before I was Benson. On a similar note, I latched *people.*
spiritual, I onto the idea that I have always existed, *(NF)*
was physical." that before I was a spirit I was an en-
(FO)

7

8

Without the religious aspect, your essay still makes sense. Is the sole purpose of your talking about religion to account for your differences? I think not. (JE)

It would be a lot easier on your readers if you simply spelled it out. (NB)

You sound like you're condemning yourself in here. (FO)

The problem you elucidate concerning your faith is never resolved. Is it convenient or is it based on something more? (FO)

tity, an intelligence bobbing out somewhere like a chartreuse soap bubble. I
did not want to be someone else's crea-
tion. I figured God recognized the spe- *Colloquial (FO)*
cial and distinctive thing I was and *This is a cliché,*
handpicked me to be his child. *and judging from your use of language elsewhere,*

Being Mormon has been convenient in *you can do a*
other ways. It is a guaranteed way to *lot better*
stick out like a sore thumb. I always *than this. (NB)*
felt a swell of pride as I answered astonished cries of "You've never done such
and such?" I could spend hours elabor-
ating on LDS precepts with the sole in- *There is something*
tent of blowing an innocent Protestant *arrogant in this: 1) in*
mind. I have had so much fun being Mor- *the impli-*
mon that I have to wonder how much of my *cation that*
testimony is based on faith and how much *you are*
on the attention it garners. I created *sophisticated (and so can*
my outlook on life according to my con- *blow an*
venience, says Kelly. My convenient *"innocent mind")*
testimony thus becomes as meaningful as *and 2) in*
my green argyle earrings; I would proba- *your focus on Protestant*
bly join any group that boasted of being *rather than*
a peculiar people. *other religious sects. (FO)*

Yet my testimony of the gospel encapsulates some of my strongest emotions
and most important rational convictions.
I founded my belief on study, contemplation, and prayer, not whim. If such a
testimony is invalid, there is little I
think or feel that is valid. But I must
consider I may have forced my personality
to grow in unnatural and indirect ways
because I wanted to be different, cultivating a taste for mustard on my french

9

10

How do you make the break here from Kelly's theory being merely possible to its being true? (NB)

The problem of looking at yourself in a new way begins here. (FO)

Is Kelly dead? (FO)

Is this necessary? I don't see what it adds. Remove? (NB)

I like your realization here. Maybe those previous comments made the necessary contrast. (JE)

This is a very sensitive question to ask. (NF)

fries and a taste for LDS doctrine. (I) have created my personality and maybe I could have done a better job. Yet the thought of supplanting myself with a new and improved model based on different criteria scares me. It would be person- ality suicide; although someone would be here named Johnna, I would cease to exist.

And what about all these other peo- ple? I always pictured my intelligence as a chartreuse bubble in contrast with their monochromatic assembly of lemon yellow bubbles. If Kelly gives me the right to be self-made, he also extends that right to all those dumb slobs. Be- sides, I doubt Kelly was lemon yellow.

If he and I can be different, then proba- bly everyone else [is on a slightly dif- ferent wavelength,] can be a slightly dif- ferent color. This means I probably don't stand out at all. I have always understood why people were worried that God might not know them specifically. There was no reason for him to bother when they were all the same. But if everyone is a unique individual, how does Heavenly Father remember which finger- print I am? In my place in the sun, I did not notice all those stars out there, each one shining bright for someone. I do not feel important or special while gazing at billions of stars.

For the first time in my life I feel truly lost, an electron carrying practi-

This is the heart of your essay. It is clear, thought- ful, and very meaningful. (NF)

Is there another way to convey that you looked down on them without resorting to such coarse words? They seem inappropriate because the rest of your essay is artful and innovative. (FO)(NB) (JE)(NF)

Don't be insecure here. Take a stand! (NF)

You have used the word "probably" several times. (NF)

Capitalize? (NB)

You cannot stand under the sun and see the stars! (NF)

11

12

This is an excellent verb here. (NB)

You have taken the road to Rome! (NF)

This is very honest. Now you are not afraid to draw definite conclusions. (NF)

You use the image of the soap bubble in a new way by reference to substance rather than color. (FO)

I feel like I've gone through hell with you and come up a winner! (JE)

cally no weight, fairly indistinguishable
from any other electron, whose orbit is
an unknown in a probability cloud. I am
looking at life in a new and startling
way, and this is the ultimate test of my
taste for the new and startling. I find
myself attempting to straddle the importance of my uniqueness and the existence
of 4.5 billion other unique individuals.
I do not like wondering who I am. I
could always tell before by the stark
contrast between me and anyone else. I
had three dimensions and the other person
only had two. Now I see that I just had
no depth perception.
    How everyone can be different intim-
idates and amazes me. Without its former
base, my sense of identity has become as
fragile as the chartreuse soap bubble I
imagine as its beginnings. I fear the
existence of all the variegated personalities that might crowd and pop it. Yet
in returning to that sense of fragile
newness, I see the world freshly. I have
bemoaned the fact that no one could appreciate my special outlook. Now I see
there are countless other outlooks for me
to explore, each a world as strange and
wonderful as mine. For the first time
there is an impetus for me to get to know
people. This potential soothes my battered psyche and fills me with wonder in
proportion to my fear.

What does this phrase mean? (NB

Yes, and we are not "dumb slobs." It's an inconsistent metaphor, but it's also a strong way to show what you feel. (NF)

Before you were talking about people in general. Now you're talking about one other person. (FO)

13

You use this image well. It helps to unify your essay. (NF)

The fear is minimized by wonder: you have the equipment now with which to move forward. (FO)

General Comments at the End of the Essay

NICHOLAS BALAMACI

— I thought that the overall structure of your essay was excellent. There is a clear beginning, middle, and end. Your paragraphs and transitions flow well. You seem to be in control of what you want to say and how you want to say it.

— Your essay seems tightly reasoned, yet it also seems spontaneous—straight from your mind and heart.

— The title of your essay is clever (and therefore tempting to use), but it struck me as inappropriate. "Rotten" is too strong a word and is never really shown or proven.

— Your writing is lean and easy to read. Your use of language is innovative and artful.

— This is an honest and mature essay, and it works in a way that most of us, I think, would have a hard time *ever* achieving. I admire it!

JASON ESKENAZI

— This is an effective essay, but I feel it needs to go through the same wringer you described in order to get at its core.

— Your essay is filled with understatement, which makes my view of your essay sway. But there is a vitality to it that keeps me on the edge of my seat. I'd almost lost my faith that words (books) could transform people, and then you introduce me to Kelly.

— The core of your essay is great, but I needed to read what you wrote two or three times to get it. I think that was because of its complexity. You fill up your sentences with many complex and tenuous ideas. You need to develop them and make the relationship between the sentences and ideas clearer.

— Please invent a word that's ten times better than "fantastic," and I'll use it. The ideas flow and are inspiring. Your emergence into the human community is glorious! Welcome to your life!

NELSON FARIAS

— You really do take a meaningful conflict in your life and discuss its implications without fear, which is a very difficult thing to do. This essay is at its strongest when you look into yourself.

— Your writing is loaded with colorful metaphors, which are the result of a creative play on words and ideas. However, they are overshadowed by the reality at which the essay arrives.

— Finding that all individuals are unique should not prevent you from experiencing your own individuality. You have accomplished this extremely well in the essay.

FRAN OSBORNE — The essential idea in this essay seems to me to be about the uniqueness/commonness of each human being. It is an enormous topic, and you deal with it lucidly and intelligently.

— The idea that you are rotten at the core seems incompatible with the honesty that pervades the essay. How can such frankness/honesty be rotten? The title bothers me as a result.

— The religious issues you introduce are so big that they could be looked at again in a separate essay. Is your religion a convenience?

— As for the structure of the essay, I found it to be well organized, with a good, strong beginning, and a strong, optimistic conclusion.

— The introduction seems slightly overdone: you take five paragraphs before getting into the meat of your essay. From there on, the reading is fast, entertaining, and informative. I particularly like the fact that you use specific examples to show how you tried to be different, but I am slightly bothered by the fact that these differences seem superficial.

— I thought the last four paragraphs were particularly strong: you have a core identity (being different), but you are frightened of giving it up (in spite of its arrogance) because such relinquishing might result in a kind of personality suicide. You find a way around this by looking at yourself in a "new and startling way" that straddles individuality and common humanity. Finally, you find in the wonder of looking at—and exploring—yourself a way of overcoming fear.

Exercises in Peer Editing

1. Reread the general statements at the end of Benson's essay. How is each similar to and different from the final general comment you have written about her essay? What does each focus on, and how consistent is the overall advice with yours? Review the four peer editors' marginal notations on Benson's essay. Which are observations? Which are evaluations? Which aspects of composition does each focus on? List the points you and the other peer editors agree on; disagree on. Finally, sketch out what Benson would need to do in a revision to respond adequately to what you and the other peer editors have recommended.

2. Your own writing is the focus for this exercise. Prepare a draft of an essay according to your instructor's directions. Then review the various peer editing

activities described on pages 601–603. Bring your own essay to class and present it to your peer editors. After you have received their written observations and recommendations on the essay, their assessment of its specific strengths and weaknesses, and their recommendations for improving it, prepare a detailed plan for revising your essay. Consult with your peer editors about your plans, and then draft a new version of the essay.

3. Review the peer editing process. Write an essay in which you offer a clear sense of what you think you have learned about writing and reading as a result of your experiences with it. How has peer editing helped you improve your writing? In what specific ways has it strengthened your reading? What new insights have you developed about the processes of writing and reading? How will peer editing affect the ways in which you prepare your next essay? What do you see as the limitations of peer editing? How would you suggest improving or extending the peer editing process? Be as specific as possible. The emphasis in your essay should reflect either your reservations about peer editing or your enthusiasm for it.

3.

MOVING FROM
PERSONAL EXPERIENCE
TO EXPOSITION
AND ARGUMENT

THE POET ROBERT FROST ONCE OBSERVED, "All thought is a feat of association: having what's in front of you bring up something in your mind that you almost didn't know you knew. Putting this and that together. That click." Frost's description of "that click" may well remind you that one of the most appreciable pleasures of writing is recognizing the connections between one of your ideas and another. This recognition usually comes at the most unexpected moments, often after you have struggled for hours trying to express your thoughts clearly in writing. Yet part of the enduring satisfaction of writing is precisely that element of surprise, that life-long pleasure of discovering your own resourcefulness with language, of finding new ways to explore your own intelligence and to contribute in some original and visible way to improving the world of ideas. And as Frost's remark implies, one useful way to approach mastering the art of thinking in writing is to learn how to multiply connections—between the ideas you have and between the essays you write.

How is one essay connected with another? No paper you write is ever a unique, self-contained task; each is a step in the learning process. Any subject you write about involves two important types of connection: building on what you already know and linking your ideas into a coherent presentation. Suppose you are asked to write an essay for your history class on the post–Civil War South. You may have personal memories of the South or a sense of the post–Civil War era from course reading that will help you to approach the topic with greater confidence and authority. Once you have written your essay, you may be able to adapt the research and thinking you have already done when you are asked to write, say, an essay on William Faulkner for your English class. Professional writers very often follow this strategy, choosing a single subject—congressional lobbyists, microcomputers, public education budgets—that they can write about from several different angles for different publications. The crucial point, as Robert Frost suggested, is to be attuned to the connections between ideas. The work you do in a freshman composition course can sharpen your awareness of such connections and give you valuable practice at building related ideas into a lucid essay. So too, the effort to recognize and develop productive connections between one essay and another is very much akin to the process of revising your ideas within the boundaries of a single essay. In both instances, you re-see (re-vise) your thinking from a fresh perspective. More generally, frequent practice in recognizing and developing the productive connections between the ideas you generate and the essays you write will also better prepare you to discover the intellectual connections between the courses you take.

We have designed *Student Writers at Work and in the company of other writers* to encourage you to recognize and develop the abundant resources of your own intelligence by practicing your skills as a writer—one who is able to connect and extend ideas both within an essay and from one essay to another. The discussion questions following each of the thirty-two student essays in this book focus on analyzing how each writer has developed an essay governed by a powerful idea. The ability of these writers to create clear and convincing relationships, both between and among the ideas in the sentences they write in an essay, has earned them the special recognition of a Bedford Prize in Student Writing. Their explanations of the strategies they used to come up with ideas, draft, and revise offer accessible models for every student writer, whether practiced or inexperienced. In Chapter 1, two student writers—Barbara Seidel and Brad Manning—explained in even greater detail the specific strategies they used to plan, draft, and rewrite their essays. This chapter extends those same principles and strategies to a larger issue: How can student writers most successfully connect the controlling idea and its supporting, subordinated ideas in one essay form to the intellectual demands of working in another essay form?

Comparing the Personal Essay
with Exposition and Argument

Our correspondence and conversations with teachers and students across the country underscore what we have noticed in our own composition classes: many student writers find it difficult to move from writing personal-experience essays to writing expository and argumentative ones. For most first-year students, personal essays seem easier to write because they focus on what we think we know best. Expository and argumentative essays can also focus on what we know. The difference in essay forms lies less in the subject matter than in the way the writer approaches and organizes each.

All writing fundamentally expresses an idea about a subject, but the purpose, the language and forms used, the evidence summoned, the point of view adopted, and the audience imagined may vary greatly. Personal experience essays most often narrate an event (report what occurred) or describe a person, place, or object (record appearance in sensory terms). For example, you could write an essay in which you describe in detail a favorite hometown hangout that is now gone. Or you could write a narrative essay in which you recount a memorable incident of your adolescence that occurred at that hangout. In both descriptive and narrative essays, the perspective or point of view from which you write is usually first person. The evidence you present to convey a clear sense of that place (description) or a vivid rendition of what happened there (narration) is normally bounded by the limits of your own experience. The audience writers envision for personal-experience essays can be either themselves or others as well. And because the emphasis in personal-experience essays is usually on narration and description, such writing does not necessarily assert an explicit idea about the subject rendered.

What distinguishes expository and argumentative writing from personal-experience essays is the nature of and the critical prominence given to asserting an idea about a subject. *Exposition* is a form of nonfiction prose that puts forth facts and ideas about a subject. But more importantly and specifically, expository writing *asserts and explains an idea about a subject*. That subject can be a person, place, object, or an event, or an abstraction such as *justice* or *liberty*. Because exposition asserts and explains an idea about a subject, it often involves *generalizing*; that is, it moves beyond personal experience to make a statement about a group or class based on the collective knowledge or experiences of some or all of its members. In effect, exposition requires a greater distance between the speaker and the subject than would occur in a personal essay. And since its purpose is to explain, exposition assumes an audience beyond the speaker.

Consider again the example of the favorite hometown hangout. A descriptive essay about the hangout would emphasize what the place looked like several years ago. A narrative essay might recount a memorable incident that occurred there. In contrast, an expository essay about the hangout might assert the following idea about it: the hangout has changed a great deal in the years since you last spent some time there. Given the fact that the purpose of the exposition is to explain an idea about a subject, you might well want to explain how (comparison and contrast) or why (cause and effect) the hangout has changed. The audience imagined by writers of expository essays always includes other readers.

Argumentation is another form of nonfiction prose in which the speaker attempts *to convince an audience that a specific claim or proposition is true.* What makes the claim or proposition true is that it is supported by a body of logically connected statements that are true. Argumentation is, in effect, a form of theorizing, of speculating, proposing that a specific claim or proposition would be true if certain statements proved to be true. When writers move from personal-experience essays to exposition and argumentation, they broaden considerably their point of view, their range of evidence, and their conception of the real or imagined audience to whom they are writing.

Return to the example of the hangout once again. An argumentative essay on this subject might address the issue of whether urban redevelopment displaces more people than it helps. Or the writer of an argumentative essay might formulate the following proposition or claim: urban renewal programs destroy the architectural character indigenous to a neighborhood in favor of governmentally sanctioned standards. The purpose of such an essay would be to convince an audience of the validity of the proposition or claim by citing evidence, which might range from personal anecdote to research reports. The writer of an argumentative essay wants to do more than explain an idea; he or she wants to convince an audience of the truth of a proposition or claim.

The purpose of this chapter is to help you apply the range of options available to you as a writer. It is not meant to suggest that expository and argumentative essays are somehow "better" or more "advanced" forms than personal-experience essays. We do not want to imply, in effect, either that one essay form is preferable to another or that there is some unannounced hierarchy of essay forms. Practicing your skills in moving from personal-experience essays to expository and argumentative ones will increase your repertoire of aptitudes as a writer.

As a starting point, let's observe how two student writers—Beverly Dipo and Curtis Chang—discovered ample resources in their original prize-winning essays for writing other papers. Because Dipo's "No Rainbows, No Roses"

(p. 116) and Chang's "Streets of Gold: The Myth of the Model Minority" (p. 91) are both strongly felt personal accounts of topics with broad implications, each writer derived a second essay from the first, using the original paper as a springboard into a different structural pattern. The following sections trace Dipo's and Chang's respective progress—from carefully rereading their personal essays to generating ideas and then to formulating and ultimately writing a new composition.

Beverly Dipo: From Narration to Argument

Beverly Dipo is a licensed practical nurse who enrolled at Utah State University to "try to get my R.N." In her work as a nurse, she sees "human suffering, weaknesses, triumphs, and tragedies on a daily basis. It provides a unique perspective that many do not have." Asked to write a narrative essay focusing on a personal experience in which she gained some insight, Dipo responded with a compelling account of the death of one of her patients, Mrs. Trane. "I was asked to write about a moving experience, and Mrs. Trane's death was just that. I felt I could give an accurate account of the situation. . . . As a nurse, I frequently observe *things* before I ever speak to patients or get to know them as human beings. Right or wrong, it's the way we are trained. . . . All I did in this paper was to describe in detail a situation that really happened and my reactions to it."

When asked to describe herself as a writer, Beverly Dipo observed that "I am not a 'natural' at anything, including writing. . . . In fact, my writing process may be unique. I can, and have, written an entire outline and the first paragraphs of a work at night, in bed, in my head. The next time I sit down at the typewriter, I put my rough draft on paper. I will make a second rough draft to redo spelling, punctuation, basic structure, and make revisions as needed. . . . Then I will proceed to thoroughly mess up the rough draft with slashes, exclamation points, secret codes, doodles, medical shorthand, and assorted expletives. . . . I will then retype what is left and repeat the procedure until I produce a whole essay without one single red mark!" In writing her essay "No Rainbows, No Roses," Dipo notes that "the final draft practically ended up word for word the same as my first rough draft"—a testament to the emotional intensity of her narrative as well as to her own dictum that writers ought to "keep it simple."

Beverly Dipo's claim that she is not a natural at writing seems overly modest in view of her impressive work in "No Rainbow, No Roses" (p. 116). As you reread that essay, watch how Dipo uses the skills of observation she has developed as a nurse. "All I did in this paper was to describe in detail a situation that really happened and my reactions to it," she says. In writing down her observations, Dipo shows a strong sense of what details to include, how to translate sensory images into verbal ones, and how to balance setting, char-acters, action, and emotion. To do this requires skills that almost every be-ginning writer finds elusive, but that improve markedly with practice. As Dipo notes, the innate simplicity and intensity of the incident she chose to write about counted heavily in her favor.

Picking a subject for her second essay proved more difficult than Dipo had hoped. In a journal she kept track of her efforts to identify and explore ideas for a new essay based on "No Rainbows, No Roses." After rereading her original essay several times, Dipo was able to note little progress: "Somewhere in my mind I have the general idea of what is expected of me. An 'expository or argumentative essay.' They make it sound so easy. Do I make it a more difficult task than it should be? Yes, I do. I want it to be a good paper." After several more readings, Dipo reports: "I'm still stuck for a subject. I've put it aside—thinking it will 'come to me' in a brilliant flash of light. Well I was hoping. Now I must sit down and do some brainstorming." Here is Dipo's record of the results of that effort:

1. Avoid death; it's too morbid.
2. Nursing the terminally ill—good possibility—a subject dear to me, but still too morbid.
3. Why do I want to avoid it? Doesn't everybody?
4. How about rainbows? That's as far as I can get from death and still be considered part of my original essay. But what on earth could I contribute to the subject?
5. Obituaries? Back to the death thing again.
6. Am I going to be able to avoid it?
7. Families of patients as a subject comes to mind. A pos-sibility. Families of the terminally ill?
8. Nursing in general? Too broad!
9. Nursing the elderly—a good possibility—something I really love. They can be so special: the gray, thinning hair, a twinkle in the eye, some with such a sense of humor. It's a joy but it can be painful. I find old folks more afraid of living than dying, especially if they're ill. This may be the choice. I will have to think about it.

Several days of preparing for summer school examinations intervened before Dipo could find adequate time to return to thinking about an appropriate subject for a new essay. When she did, her ideas developed quickly:

I have been studying for exams; had little time to think about writing an essay. At work this morning, I found a patient's chart on which the Dr. had written: "patient to be allowed to die with dignity, only supportive care to be given at the pt.'s request." I wondered: how many times have I seen this actually written on a chart? Once, maybe twice before. And from this same physician. Why are doctors so reluctant to do this? "The God Syndrome" we nurses call it. Doctors do not actually believe that they are God; they just try to act like Him. What is it that is taught in medical school that tells these people that they can *save everybody*?? It is so foolish, because *everybody* dies, sooner or later!! I admire the few who know when they have done enough, the few who are honest enough to give their patients realistic expectations. I remember Judy, whom you will meet in my essay, and I remember Mrs. Trane. They both died of the same disease. And my essay is pouring out into my brain. I sat down and scribbled out the first two pages before being summoned elsewhere and having to put it aside. My subject: Does a patient have the right to die the way *he* chooses? Is he informed enough to be able to choose? If not, why not? Is it the physician's responsibility to give his patient *informed* choices? These are questions my paper should include. So, I have my subject. The paper is started. Some research is needed.

Several days later, Dipo made the following entry in her journal: "I wish writing were easy! I wonder if I'm making myself understood. The essay is developing—my thoughts ramble, though. This will take some organization. An outline may have been of some help, but the first five or six paragraphs came so easily; but now I seem stuck. Will plunge onward!"

Later that same day, Dipo made the following notations in her journal:

— Euthanasia: "A painless *putting* to death of persons having an incurable disease; an easy death. Also mercy killing."
— Suicide: "One who *intentionally* takes one's own life. The intentional taking of one's own life; to kill oneself."
— Murder: "The act of unlawfully killing a human being by another human with premeditated malice; to commit murder." (Not applicable.)
— Ethical: "Pertaining to morals or morality; right and wrong in conduct."

The final entry in Dipo's journal, made a few days later, reads: "Received articles from library. Wow! So *many* different arguments—some good, some bad. I will be very limited in how much of the subject I can present. My first draft is done. Think—as time is limited—I will have to stick with what I've already done."

Beverly Dipo eventually wrote three drafts of her new essay. The final version follows. Notice as you read it that although Dipo opens with a specific case, as she did in "No Rainbows, No Roses," her thesis this time is a general one. She uses the concrete examples of Judy and Mr. Syms to illustrate the abstract principle of "dying with dignity." To do this, she gives up the central character's point of view for that of a narrator writing mainly in the third person. Dipo thereby draws on her nursing experience for illustrations and information rather than for characterization. Her language and organization show that she is less concerned now with setting a mood—appealing to her readers' emotions—and more concerned with building a case based on claims, evidence, and logic. Although the issue itself is highly emotional, and so is some of Dipo's supporting evidence, her tactics are not. She is still writing for a general audience, but her purpose has changed significantly.

Dipo's Argumentative Essay

A Time to Die

Judy had been looking awfully tired recently. Her hus-   1
band, Clair, had been in and out of the hospital over the
last six months following his heart attack, and Judy had been
naturally concerned about his failing health. She had managed to continue working at her full-time job as a registered
nurse, but the effort was beginning to show. There were now
creases in her once smooth brow, dark circles under dull
eyes, and an ashen hue seemed to dim not only her complexion,
but her personality as well. The vigor which she had once
applied to all her tasks was gone. A number of her friends
began encouraging her to get a checkup, but she claimed she
just did not have the time.

Three months passed, and Judy began to lose weight, have   2
bouts of nausea, and back pain. She finally decided to find
the time for a physical examination. After numerous tests,
X rays, scans, and an admission to the hospital for a biopsy,
Judy's doctor told her she had pancreatic cancer. He informed her that with chemotherapy and radiation, the probability of her living another year, maybe two, was pretty
good. As a nurse, Judy was well informed about her disease,
its treatments, and her prognosis. She knew her doctor was
being optimistic and kind. She talked to Clair at length
about what her future would be, and then weighing her options
carefully, she chose to refuse treatment. Both Clair and
her doctor pleaded with her to accept the treatments, but she
remained adamant. She knew she might have extra time with
the help of the drugs and radiation, but she also knew that
the extra time would be a time in and out of the hospital,
nausea, vomiting, weakness, emaciation, and, to Judy the
worst side effect of all, the loss of control of her life.
Finally, as a person whose life was spent in concern for

others, typically, her concern was now for Clair. Since his
heart attack, their income and savings had dwindled, and she
seriously doubted Clair's ability, either physically or emotionally, to handle her prolonged illness. It was not the
way she wanted to die. To Judy, her death was the natural
and inevitable consequence of living, and she accepted it
with grace and dignity.

Judy went home from the hospital, arranged her affairs,   3
painted her last landscapes, and died within five months.

Was Judy's decision a right one? Did she have the   4
right to determine how she was going to die?

Her husband never agreed with her but finally came to   5
accept it as her decision. Her doctor, on the other hand,
maintained that she did not have the right to refuse treatment. As a matter of fact, he refused to support her
choice. Judy, as a nurse, knew a doctor who would, and it
was easy for her to seek him out. Other patients are not
that lucky. Most patients do whatever is recommended to
them by their doctors, without question and without the
knowledge that they do have a right to refuse treatment because the doctor never gives them that option. A doctor
will explain a terminal illness to his patient by telling him
of the medicines and procedures that are available to combat
the disease. Doctors believe, and it is sometimes true,
that this is what the patient wants to hear and that this is
the treatment the patient expects to receive. Some doctors
will explain to the patient that while there are side effects
to the treatments, they can be controlled by changing the
chemotherapy or by giving more medications to counteract the
effects of the chemotherapy. An occasional physician will
tell his patient he has "a 50/50 chance of living another two
years or so with treatment." Rarely is a patient told that,
even after the chemotherapy, radiation, surgery, and the "two
years or so" of extended life, he is going to die anyway. A
doctor is trained to treat illness and cure the patient. To

him, by not acting to prevent death, he is allowing his patient to die.   To a doctor, death is an enemy and failure.
Every measure is taken to ensure that the patient does not
become a "failure."   When his patient dies, the doctor feels
personal failure.

With today's technology, a patient's appointment with   6
death, while still inevitable, can be rescheduled according
to the arbitrary wishes of the physician.   If a patient's
lungs fail, put him on a ventilator to do his breathing for
him; if his kidneys fail, start dialysis; even if his heart
fails, he can be maintained mechanically.   Here again, patients are rarely given information about the effects, the
costs, or the benefits of these treatments, let alone informed of the potential harm they may cause.   Often the institution of these treatments by the physician are afterwards
explained to the patient or family as "necessary to prevent
death." Should not the patient be allowed to decide if and
when and which treatments he wants to have, prior to their
use?   Some physicians will argue that their patients do not
have sufficient knowledge to be able to determine whether or
not they need to be put on a respirator or started on dialysis or receive any other medical treatment that might be
necessary.   I will counter that such a physician has a responsibility to educate his patients in such matters.   The
patient does not need a medical degree to make decisions
about his own care.   He needs only the information pertaining to his specific condition, and all the options that are
open to him, including his right to refuse any or all of
those options.

What about the patient who is unable to make informed   7
decisions?   Is it possible that medical treatment could become medical abuse?

Mr. Syms was a 73-year-old gentleman who, while walk-   8
ing home from visiting his wife at a local nursing home,
was struck by a car.   Besides a shattered left femur, a

fractured pelvis and a ruptured bladder, and fractured ribs
and abdominal bleeding, he suffered head injuries, the extent
of which could not be determined on admission.   An emergency
operation removed his lacerated spleen and repaired his abdominal injuries and the ruptured bladder.   His left leg was
set as best as it could be, but useful function of the leg
would be doubtful.   He lay in the intensive care unit, his
leg in a cast from hip to toe; a catheter drained his still
bloody urine from his bladder out through his abdomen; he had
a nasogastric tube draining his stomach contents out through
his nose; two IV lines were running, one in each arm, to provide him with fluids.   He remained comatose and an electro-
encephalogram showed only minimal brain activity.   His wife
had Alzheimer's disease and was not even aware that he was
missing from her life.   He had no other family.

Mr. Syms remained in critical condition for two days.   9
On the third day after the accident he had a heart attack,
but with resuscitation was revived.   Within twenty-four
hours, he had two more heart attacks and was again revived
each time.   In the following three days, he had two more
heart attacks and was twice again revived and placed on a
respirator to keep him alive.   Finally, on the tenth day
after the accident and after developing pneumonia, he died
even while attempts to resuscitate him continued.

Here was a body trying desperately to die.   Who among   10
the medical profession would step up and say "enough is
enough"?   None did.   Was Mr. Syms's medical treatment medical abuse?

In my opinion it was.   Had efforts to keep Mr. Syms   11
alive succeeded, he would have been eventually transferred to
a nursing home to be "maintained" in a vegetative state until
he died, a silent reminder of miraculous medicine.

Besides the obvious ethical issues in Mr. Syms's treat-   12
ment, there are two questions I feel need to be asked.
First, what about the cost of Mr. Syms's care, not only his

hospital care, but what about the care he would have needed
should he have survived?   His hospital bill was over
$46,000, which was paid for by Medicare (you and me).
Should cost be a factor in anyone's care?   Mr. Syms's early
treatment, right after the accident, was certainly justified,
but when it was known that he would not ever recover, continued efforts to keep him alive were highly questionable.

What about his age?   If Mr. Syms had been a six-year-   13
old hit by a car while playing in the street would his treatment be justified, even when there was no hope of recovery?
While most children have parents or guardians to make decisions for them, it is still the physician who has the responsibility to inform those decision makers about reasonable
expectations of recovery and the options they have concerning
treatment, including the right to stop or refuse treatment.

Physicians are devoted to a moral duty to heal their   14
patients.   They are also faced with an ethical dilemma which
invariably involves taking some risks in making judgments.
In making life-or-death decisions, they must employ wisdom
and judgment.   They cannot act on whims or prejudices, and
decisions must be supportable with the desires and well-being
of the patient in the forefront, even when those desires
counter the physician's own beliefs, and even when they may
constitute death to his patient.   Conflict arises when
the doctor's moral duty to heal impedes the patient's right
to die.

Euthanasia is a term defined by the dictionary as "a   15
painless putting to death of persons having an incurable disease; an easy death." The medical profession has conveniently
broken that definition down into two: "active euthanasia" or
the hastening of death by deliberate action, and "passive
euthanasia" or the alleviating of symptoms, even though life
may be shortened and nature be allowed to take its course.
This was the course Judy chose.   Was Judy's decision a right

one? It was for her. She made her choice based on a knowledgeable foundation.

There are not any hard and fast rules within the medical 16 community concerning euthanasia. It is a word never spoken in hospitals even though passive euthanasia is practiced by some physicians like the one Judy found. The right to die is basically a decision now made by doctors based on their own morals and beliefs, even though it is a decision that should be based on the patient's morals and beliefs. Some doctors are thoughtful and reasonable about their expectations of a patient's course of disease. They are considerate of the desires of the patient and discuss openly all options open to the patient, including what will happen should the patient elect to refuse treatment. That is as it should be. Other physicians, however, never give in to that old enemy death. These doctors will frequently confuse patients and families by offering hope through medications and treatments that are only temporary measures to prolong life. To them, the quality of life is not even a matter that needs consideration or discussion. They fully believe they are doing their best for the patient by saving him from death, even for a short while, even in misery.

The right to die has been slow in being brought forth 17 for open discussion. Gradually, medical schools are beginning to recognize that the life of a dying patient becomes steadily less rich and less worth living, and that as the pain and suffering involved in maintaining what is left of life are mounting, there comes a point when decisions must be made. These decisions must be made by a knowledgeable patient and family, clergy and physician, all together.

There are no absolute rules that will resolve all the 18 questions with the same answer. Each case and each patient are different and need to be considered on an individual basis. I cannot advocate active euthanasia or mercy killing.

That involves one person ending the life of another. I do not advocate patients refusing all treatments, when there are certainly patients who can benefit. I am saying that all of us are going to die sooner or later. I am saying that the medical profession has a duty to accept that fact, that it be given to the patient as an alternative to all other treatments he may be asked to consider, and that his wishes in the choices he makes be accepted gracefully. I do hope that in the near future the medical profession allows that to each individual there is a time to die and that that time is the patient's rightful choice.

As it is written in Ecclesiastes: "To everything there is a season, and a time to every purpose under heaven: a time to be born, and a time to die; a time to plant, and a time to pluck up that which is planted." [19]

Amen! [20]

When Beverly Dipo completed the final draft of "A Time to Die," she wrote the following commentary on the process of writing the essay:

> It's done! It is always a great relief to get something that is difficult finished. I did find writing an argumentative essay difficult. A personal-experience essay requires only that you describe something and report your responses to it. An argumentative essay requires some thought and research. Also, I suppose I had some difficulty because I am basically a passive and introverted person. While I may have some strong feelings and opinions, I do not usually publicize them.
>
> Medical abuse is one subject I do have strong feelings about. I work with it daily, and it is so very frustrating. Nurses are somehow caught in the middle of a great dilemma between the medical hierarchy on one side and just wanting to help people on the other. As for my paper, I am sure I stated that position as well as it could have been. I hope I gave some good examples and expounded on some of the problems that confront the dying patient. But—being my own worst critic—I feel it probably could have been said better by someone else.
>
> The most difficult aspect of the assignment was to restrain and contain the subject. I did do some research on it and found it to be much more involved than I could possibly cover in one paper. My theme could have covered "codes" or the lack of them, "slow codes," living wills, malpractice, families, or hospice care, among other things. I did feel at times a certain limitation and at other times that I had picked a subject which was more than I could handle.
>
> During the process of writing this essay, my mind frequently wandered back to Mrs. Trane and to so many other dying patients I have taken care of over the years. I wonder, had they really known what their remaining time would be like after a terminal diagnosis was made, how many of them would have agreed to treatment? Would they have refused treatment if they had been given all the facts? I remember one man being so angry about not being told what would happen to him that, much against his family's wishes, he ordered that his remains be cremated, without funeral services. He had shunned every friend and all but his closest family. He did not want to have them see him, during his illness or after his death. He not only blamed his

doctors, but the nurses as well. He died an angry and hostile man. One of his last remarks to me was, "This disease
didn't kill me, my fellow man did." Well, his disease may
have killed his body, but it probably was his fellow man
who killed his spirit.

It is people like this that I thought about when writing
this essay. It is my argument for them and to them. They
are the ones who need to be educated about their rights.
They are the ones who need to realize that doctors are only
humans, not gods, and that medicine cannot keep everyone alive forever. This argumentative essay let me make
that point, whereas the one on Mrs. Trane did not.

Thinking about it now, after the essay is done, I find I
like the idea of being able to say right out loud how I feel
about the issue. It is not such a bad thing to be able to do.
That is probably the thing I enjoyed most about this paper.

In my personal-experience essay, I suffered Mrs. Trane's
death silently and alone. In this argumentative essay, I gave
the burden of sharing death over to those who are experiencing it. Maybe someone will learn something from it,
or think about death differently than they had before, or
discover that they do indeed have control over their own
lives—and deaths.

Questions on Dipo's Two Essays

1. Beverly Dipo's journal entries include "some brainstorming." What relation
   does this brainstorming exercise have to "A Time to Die"? Which notations,
   if any, provide an early indication of the eventual focus and direction of "A
   Time to Die"?

2. At what point in her journal entries does Dipo seem to settle on a subject for
   her new essay? What specific thoughts trigger her decision to write about a
   patient's "right to die in the way he chooses"?

3. Once Dipo has begun to write her essay, what concerns does she express about
   finishing it? Based on your reading of her final draft, how did she resolve those
   "problems"? Support your response by pointing to specific words and phrases.

4. Dipo's journal entries include several definitions. In what specific ways does
   Dipo incorporate these definitions, either explicitly or implicitly, in "A Time
   to Die"? Where and how does she include information from the library research
   she has done?

5. Reread Dipo's explanation of her goal in writing this essay. Assess as specifically
   as possible the extent to which she achieves that goal. Outline Dipo's argument

in "A Time to Die." What are the specific strengths of her argument? In what ways do you think she might strengthen it?

6. What specific thematic connections can you identify between "No Rainbows, No Roses" and "A Time to Die"? What stylistic features link both essays? What evidence can you point to in the word choice, phrasing, sentence structure, and overall organization that would verify Dipo's authorship of both?

7. Review the brainstorming notes and journal entries exploring possible subjects that resulted when Dipo reread her original essay. What other possibilities for writing a new essay can you identify in "No Rainbows, No Roses"?

Curtis Chang: From Narration to Exposition and Argument

With this next example, we have an unusual opportunity: to trace the origins of Curtis Chang's prize-winning essay "Streets of Gold: The Myth of the Model Minority" back through its earlier drafts to its original form—as a personal-experience essay entitled "Ni Hao Ma?"

Curtis Chang reports that near the end of the first section meeting of his freshman expository writing course at Harvard, his instructor, Judith Beth Cohen, announced the first formal writing assignment: "Define a problem and discuss its social and ethical dimensions." After considerable deliberation, Chang decided to write a narrative account of an occasion highlighting the social and cultural implications of a dilemma he faced about his own identity as an immigrant to and an ethnic minority in the United States.

Curtis Chang emigrated from Taiwan in 1971 with his parents and two older sisters. His family settled in the Chicago area, and he attended public schools there. He decided to draw on his experiences as a high school student there to create the following personal essay.

Chang's Personal-Experience Essay

"Ni Hao Ma?"

"You speak Chinese?   Neat!   Say somethin', willya?"   1

Ever since I immigrated to the United States, I have in-   2
termittently heard that plea from curious classmates.   So
shivering by the bus stop two weeks ago, I wearily prepared
myself for the standard ritual.

"What do you want me to say?"   I asked.   3

"I dunno, just say something!"   4

"I can't just say 'something'," I explained slowly,   5
"it's like asking you to say 'something' in English?"

"OK, OK, say 'how are you' in Chinese."   6

For all their inquisitiveness, these people are singu-   7
larly concerned with being able to find out how the Chinese
speaking world is feeling.   Like a kindergarten teacher pronouncing the first three letters of the alphabet for the hun-
dredth time, I articulated, "Ni hao ma?" and then braced myself to hear the mutilations sure to follow.

This particular person, however, was not easily satis-   8
fied.   "How do you say 'This bus stand is terribly cold'?"

Like a kindergarten teacher suddenly being asked about   9
special relativity from a child, I stammered, "Um . . . Huo
Che . . . uh . . . uh . . . I kinda forgot how to say 'bus
stand.'"   Undaunted and obviously beginning to enjoy himself
in a sick sort of way, he flipped open a tattered U.S. history textbook and began impertinently peppering me with
phrases.   "How do you say this . . . how do you say
that . . .?"   I struggled, scratched my head, wiped the
beads of sweat from my neck, but could not completely answer
even one of his questions.   I was finally saved from the
interrogation by the arrival of the bus.

I wish I could blame my ineptitude on a massive mental   10
block.   But I knew I had simply lost my grasp of Chinese.

Beyond a fixed set of very common phrases, I was forgetting
what had once come easily.   The previous few months, my
mother began using more Chinese in the house, and it was
sounding, well, rather foreign.   Lately, she began mentioning in passing the local Chinese Language School.   After the
bus stop incident, I could no longer nod appreciatively,
thinking my Chinese was fine.

I knew the decision to attend Chinese School would al-   11
ways be up to me.   I suppose it seems like a rather simple
decision.   Go and learn Chinese, or stay at home and deteri-
orate into a morass of "Chinglish" (a dialect of those
Chinese Americans who know only a smattering of Chinese).
However, I was strangely reluctant to start attending Chinese
School.

The Saturday after the bus stop incident, I met my   12
friend Duane for my regular weekend game of basketball at the
high school gym.   Duane and I come from similar backgrounds.
We both immigrated from Taiwan when we were young, we both
were losing fluency in Chinese, and we both were lousy basketball players.

During a break we squatted courtside, resting our heads   13
against the water fountain.   I mentioned I was thinking
about Chinese School.

"You what?" he asked incredulously, his head jerking   14
forward.   "Why do you want to go to Chinese School?"

"Well, I don't know," I responded hesitantly, "to keep   15
my Chinese I suppose."

"Why is it so important to keep your Chinese?" he shot   16
back.   He jumped up and began pacing back and forth, his
sneakers squeaking on the wooden floor.   "That's what all
the parents say and it sounds nice, but what's the big deal?
When do I ever use Chinese?   Not at home, not at school, and
I don't want to go into any job that requires another language.   Why do I need Chinese?"

17

I stood there toweling myself and nodding in seeming agreement. But I was wondering why it was true that we both never used Chinese. I could perhaps understand why we never absolutely needed to speak Chinese, but why did we never choose to use it? For instance, we had known each other since childhood and never even once exchanged a "Ni hao ma?"

". . . I'm just 100 times more fluent in English," Duane 18 continued. "That's just the way it turned out. . . ."

But our loss of our original language was "not just the 19 way it turned out." Not being able to say "bus stand" was not a result of fate, I thought, there was a choice involved.

For young immigrants in the United States, learning 20 English is like surviving one of those desert scenes in the movies. It is a struggle and to keep going you have to de-cide to carry only what is absolutely necessary. You shed everything else. For myself and for Duane, Chinese charac-ters, idioms, and pronunciations littered the trail to fluency in English. In that headlong dash, we used English at every opportunity--at school, at home, and even with each other. We rejected Chinese children's books and chose Superman comic books. We rejected local Chinese cultural presentations and chose The Electric Company. We rejected "Ni hao ma?" and chose "What's up?"

"Knowing Chinese is nice but it's not that important, 21 it's just no big deal." By now Duane was vigorously bounc-ing the ball against the floor. "I mean, I know lots of Chinese that can't speak anything but English!"

Yes, that's true, I thought. But it is quite obvious 22 there is such a difference. If you can't speak the lan-guage, it is very difficult to understand the culture. Lan-guage is an integral part of any cultural heritage, and I knew that speaking Chinese and being Chinese were very closely connected.

Ironically, I believe that was the very reason I was so 23 hesitant about returning to Chinese School. When I aban-doned speaking Chinese, I abandoned a large part of my ethnic

identity. Going to Chinese School would force me to acknowledge that uncomfortable fact. It would force me to decide whether or not I wanted to reclaim a certain part of myself.

Duane was rambling on, ". . . and don't forget, Curtis, 24
all that extra work, school on Saturday, it's too much. . . ."

Indeed, I nodded in silence, it is not easy to go back 25
on that desert trail and slowly pick up all that you had left
along the way. But could I keep rationalizing that I didn't
need my heritage? I was born Chinese first and no amount of
assimilation could change that. Uncomfortable or not, I
knew I had to at least make an attempt to regain my ethnic
identity. Duane would have to find someone else to play
basketball with next Sunday.

Duane was staring at me curiously. The gymnasium was 26
all empty now and shadows were creeping along the floor.

"Curtis! Hello? Say somethin', willya?" 27

Questions on Chang's Personal-Experience Essay

1. Identify the focus of Curtis Chang's essay. Characterize the tone of this essay. What attitude, for example, does Chang express toward himself? Toward his mastery of Chinese? What is his initial reaction to the notion of attending Chinese Language School? What alternative does he propose to attending? What is his attitude toward that alternative?

2. What point of view does Chang's friend Duane express toward the problem that Chang defines? Characterize Chang's attitude toward Duane. Point to specific words and phrases to support your response. What function does Duane serve in this essay? What does he contribute to its overall impact?

3. Comment on the importance of the "regular weekend game of basketball at the high school gym." What, in addition to serving as a location for the discussion between the narrator and Duane, does this scene contribute to the essay?

4. Identify the moment in this essay when Curtis Chang begins to broaden the focus of his essay beyond his own personal experience. Where does he begin to generalize in the essay? With what effects?

5. What does Chang see as the broader consequences of losing his fluency in Chinese? What more serious, personal consequences does he envision?

6. Consider the image of the "desert trail" in paragraph 20. What, exactly, is the nature of this metaphor? What response does it elicit from you as a reader? How does this image consolidate many of the narrator's thoughts at this point? How does the image speak to the issue of assimilation?

7. Comment on the effectiveness of the essay's ending. What general point does it dramatize? What irony does it underscore?

8. Based on your reading of this personal experience essay, what do you think will be the subject—the focus—of Curtis Chang's next essay?

As Curtis Chang settled into his new life as an undergraduate at Harvard, he continued his long-standing interest in reading history, playing what he describes as "incredibly mediocre basketball," as well as public speaking and debate. He also served as an "investigative Bible studies coordinator" for the Harvard-Radcliffe Christian Fellowship, contributed to the *Harvard Political Review,* served as a member of the Harvard Parliamentary Debate Society, and volunteered in the university's Lutheran homeless shelter. During this period, he also became increasingly involved in minority student issues on campus. He helped found, for example, the Harvard Minority Student Alliance, a coalition of the different campus minority organizations, and served as a steering committee member of the Asian-American Association. His interest in religious experience and issues of racial identity gradually merged into a personal commitment: "I am committed," he reports, "to developing the biblical notion of justice, a justice that—by the world's standards—is radical, all-encompassing, and is intellectually truthful. As a member of a nonwhite minority, I know how much the issue of justice in the American racial spectrum strikes home. The evolvement of my racial identity is complex and long, but many of its intellectual roots were developed at Harvard. . . . I view my writing skills as a tool to work for justice, especially in matters of race. In certain situations, this view leads to moralistic rhetoric that does not appeal to the wider populace. Thus, I consciously attempt to base my writings on analytical and empirical arguments which work from certain common assumptions."

Judith Beth Cohen, the instructor in his expository writing course, provided Curtis Chang with an opportunity to write about and to develop his interest in racial justice. Her sixth writing assignment in that course asked students to "write an eight-page paper on a controversial issue based on at least six sources, including an interview." Chang decided to expand on the original essay he had written for the course. His goal in this new essay, as he explained in a recent interview, was "both educative and stimulative. I wished to explain to everyone the true socio-economic condition of Asian-Americans and to expose how we are being used for ideological reasons. I also hoped to stimulate further thought on Asian-American issues, to interest others in subjecting our situation to intellectual scrutiny." He also reports on the more immediate circumstances that led to taking a different approach to writing about racial identity: "The subject stemmed mostly from my personal dealings with black, radical Christians at Harvard. As I listened to them discuss the issue of race in America, I realized that it wasn't clear to them (or to me) where Asian-Americans fit into the picture." With this general purpose in mind—to explain "where Asian-Americans fit into the picture"—Chang set out to write a new essay, one with a broader and more ambitious purpose. Here is the first rough draft of that new essay.

Chang's Rough Draft

The Myth of the Model Minority

"Take a look at this." My Caucasian friend handed me   1
the latest copy of a Fortune magazine. "Not bad, huh?" He
pointed to a headline story titled "Asian-Americans: America's Super Minority." It was just the latest congratulatory
addition to the media image of Asian-Americans as the "Model
Minority." In the last several years, major publications
like Time, Newsweek, US News, Fortune, the New Republic, the
Wall Street Journal, and The New York Times Sunday Magazine
have published headline stories with such titles:

> "America's Super Minority"
> "An American Success Story"
> "A Model Minority"
> "Why They Succeed"
> "The Ultimate Assimilation"
> "The Triumph of the Asian-Americans"

As an Asian-American, it appears that I, in the politi-   2
cian's lingo, have been getting "great press." The idea is
that we are an ethnic minority that is finally "making it in
America" (Time, July 9, 1985). This idea seems happily im-
planted in the minds of universities, government officials,
and the general populace. But the Model Minority is a myth.
It is a falsity that engenders neglect of Asian-Americans'
serious handicaps and problems, both among the government and
ourselves. Finally, and perhaps most importantly, it subtly
reveals how the American majority views the entire issue of
minorities.

The Model Minority image is the belief that here is an   3
ethnic minority who has "made it" by "laying claim to the
American dream" (Fortune, Nov. 24, 1986). The media gives
three basic reasons for its optimistic view: Asian-Americans'
success in the workplace, the schoolroom, and in the social
arena. All of those reasons, however, are either completely

false or at least distorted.   It is also important to note
that all three reasons are directly related to success as defined as material wealth.

In proving that "Asian-Americans present a picture of   4
affluence and economic success" (<u>The New York Times Sunday
Magazine</u>, Nov. 30, 1986), 9 out of 10 of the major Model Minority stories of the last four years relied heavily on one
statistic: the family median income.   The median Asian-American family income, according to the U.S. Census Survey of
Income and Education data, is $22,713 compared to $20,800 for
white Americans.   Armed with that figure, national magazines
have trumpeted our "remarkable, ever-mounting achievements"
(<u>Newsweek</u>, Dec. 6, 1982).   Some, like <u>Fortune</u> of May 17,
1982, have even used it to complain that Asian-Americans are
in fact "getting <u>more</u> than its share of the pie."   (Funny,
10 years ago, when white Americans were leading the nation in
every single economic measure, I don't remember <u>Fortune</u> magazine editorializing that whites were getting more than <u>its</u>
share of the pie.)

When I see such assertions, I am reminded of an old say-   5
ing that "Statistics are like a bikini.   What they reveal is
suggestive, but what they conceal is vital."   What the family median income figures conceal is that Asian-American families generally (1) are larger than white families and thus
have more mouths to feed (exact quote to be obtained); (2)
are often forced by necessity to have their children work and
thus average more than two income earners in the family,
while whites only have 1.6 (Cabezas); and (3) live disproportionately in high cost of living (and correspondingly high
dollar income) areas like New York, Chicago, Los Angeles, San
Francisco, and Honolulu (Mariano).   Dr. Robert S. Mariano,
Professor of Economics at University of Pennsylvania, has
calculated that:

> When such appropriate adjustments and
> comparisons are made, a different and

> rather disturbing picture emerges, show-
> ing indeed a clearly disadvantaged group.
> . . . Filipino and Chinese men are no
> better off than black men with regard to
> median incomes in standard metropolitan
> statistical areas (Mariano/see Endnote
> 1).

Like all the other minorities, Asian-Americans are still getting the crumbs of the American economic pie.

Furthermore, in outlining the Asian-Americans' alleged   6
economic success, the media makes two crucial assumptions:
First, we are viewed as a monolithic, homogeneous, yellow
skinned mass.   Such a view ignores the existence of an incredibly disadvantaged Asian-American underclass.   Recent
Vietnamese refugees in California are living like the poor in
Appalachia.   While going to his Manhattan office, multimillionaire architect I. M. Pei's car passes Chinese restaurants
and laundries where 72% of all New York Chinese men still
work (Cabezas).

The media's second assumption is much more significant   7
to the broader question of race in America.   It is the belief that our alleged material success is proof that racial
handicaps are no longer significant.   Citing the venerable
family median income figure, the media often assumes Asian-
Americans are "obviously non-disadvantaged folks" (Fortune,
May 17, 1982).   The wider implications of this claim will be
discussed later; for now, suffice to say that it is patently
false.   A study on Asian-Americans by the United States
Equal Employment Opportunity Commission "found discriminatory
patterns in overall level of employment as well as in occupational distribution in industries" (Cabezas).

Tied very closely to the media's claim of Asian-American   8
success in the workplace is the media's stress on our success
in the schoolroom, "to the top of the class" (Newsweek, On
Campus, April 1984).   Asian-Americans' "march into the ranks
of the educational elite" (US News, April 2, 1984) is also

usually discussed in the context of material success.   More
importantly, the same media assumptions plague this "whiz
kids" view of Asian-Americans.

The media again downplays the fact that class division   9
accounts for much of the educational success.   Until 1976,
the U.S. Immigration Department would only admit Asian immigrants that were termed "skilled" workers--which generally
meant college educated (usually in the sciences since language would not be a problem).   The result was that the vast
majority of pre-1976 Asian immigrants came from already well
educated, upper class backgrounds--the classic "brain drain"
syndrome (Hirschman and Wong).

The immigrants after 1976, however, come generally from   10
the lower, less educated classes (Kim).   A study by Professor Elizabeth Ahn Toupin of Tufts University matched similar
Asian and non Asian students along class lines and found that
Asian-Americans "did not perform at a superior academic level
to non-Asian students.   Asian-Americans were more likely to
be placed on academic probation than their white counterparts
. . . twice as many Asian-American students withdrew from the
university" (Toupin).

Thus, it is doubtful whether the perceived, widespread   11
educational success will continue as the Asian-American population continues to balance out along class lines.   When
11.1% of all Chinese lack _any_ formal education (versus 3.3%
for blacks and .9% for whites), it seems many future Asian-
Americans will be worrying more about being able to
read a newspaper rather than a Harvard acceptance letter
(Azores).

Besides assuming continued educational success, the   12
media again dangerously assumes the lack of racial barriers.
It is widely accepted throughout all the Model Minority stories that "as a result of their academic achievement, Asians
are climbing the economic ladder with remarkable speed"
(_Time_, July 8, 1985). Yet, almost all of the academic studies

on the returns Asians are getting on their education point
out:

> Discrimination on this level is highly
> institutionalized . . . in the profes-
> sional, technical, and managerial occupa-
> tions in complex bureaucratic systems of
> employment, there is modern racism--the
> subtle, sophisticated, systemic patterns
> and practices which may have no indica-
> tion of malevolent intent, nonetheless,
> function to effect and to obscure the
> discriminatory outcomes (Nishi).

A striking example of this was found in a CUNY research study
which constructed equivalent resumes, and then sent to employers one group under an Asian name and a similar group under a Caucasian name.   Whites received interviews 5 times
more than Asians (Nishi).   The media never headlines even
more shocking data that can be easily found in United States
Census data.   Chinese and Filipino males only earned respectively 74 and 52 per cent of the salaries similarly educated
white males earned.   Asian females fared even worse, earning
only 44 to 54 per cent of the salaries equivalent males gar-
nered (Cabezas).   These figures are the same or worse for
blacks.   We Asian-Americans are indeed a Model Minority--a
perfect model of racial discrimination in America.

Another type of this "modern racism" involves exclusion   13
to "positions of institutional power and in political influence" (Kuo).   Professor Harry Kitano of UCLA has written extensively on the plight of Asian-Americans as the "middleman
minority," a minority materially successful but forever
barred from true participation in society.   In other words,
while the education of the upper class Asians prevents them
from the breadlines, their race still prevents them from the
boardroom.   (Note for example, that out of Fortune magazine's list of top 1,000 corporate officers, only 5 had Asian
surnames, many of whom started their own companies.)   This
type of "employment discrimination is prevalent among Asian

American professionals" (Kahng). Far from having "all
that education paying off spectacularly" (Fortune, Nov. 24,
1986), Asian-Americans still face significant racism (see
Endnote 2).

The perpetuation of this myth in the workplace and the   14
classrooms causes two major problems. First, our real problems get neglected. In 1979, while the President was praising Asian-Americans' "successful integration into American
society," his administration was revoking Asian-Americans'
eligibility for small business loans. This particularly
hurt the struggling Korean and Chinese small businessmen in
New York, Chicago, and San Francisco. But no matter, they
were "self-sufficient." Furthermore, with all the hype of
our "astonishing record of achievement" (Time, July 8, 1985),
it is not surprising that "the myth that poverty does not
touch Asian/Pacific communities . . . is a view that per-
meates many social service and public agencies" (Hirano).
Thus, the pressing needs of Asian-Americans are never recognized and never met.

The second danger caused by the Model Minority myth is   15
in some ways more crucial. It is the creation of the general belief that we no longer should be identified as a minority. In its attack on affirmative action, the Boston
Globe (Jan. 14, 1985) pointed out that universities, like
many people, "obviously feel that Asian-Americans, especially
those of Chinese and Japanese descent, are brilliant, privileged, and wrongly classified as minorities." Harvard Dean
Henry Rosovsky, hardly an expert on Asian-Americans, has
stated that "Disadvantaged is the key concept . . . in that
sense, Asian-Americans appear to be an . . . it does not seem
to me that as a group, they are disadvantaged."

Since others do not view us as a minority that faces   16
serious racial handicaps, we begin to agree with the dominant
view. We start believing the Model Minority image's definition of success and its attainability.

As I have pointed out, the media defines our "success"   17
in the workplace and the classroom by how it relates to material wealth.   In a speech given at Boston University, Professor Shirley Hune presented the results from a nationwide
survey of Asian-American first-year college students taken
from 1976 to 1986.   Respondents who said financial well
being was "essential or highly important" increased steadily
from 51% to 73% over the 10 years.   This increase coincided
with the steady increase of Model Minority stories over the
same period of time.   Now, I am sure there are other factors
involved (such as the general trend among all groups in that
direction and even our own family's pressure); but when the
dominant culture preaches a gospel of success so strongly to
minority youth who are struggling to be accepted, the effect
is overwhelming.   As an Asian-American growing up during
that period, I am personally convinced of a connection.

Having bought this imposed definition of success and the   18
fact that fellow Asian-Americans everywhere are attaining it,
we also buy into Rosovsky's belief that we are in an "odd
category among other protected minorities."   In that same
abovementioned poll, Asian-American students were also asked
how essential racial understanding was.   From 1976 to 1986,
the number plunged from 36% to 27%, dipping 5 points in the
last year alone (which again, was marked by a torrent of
Model Minority stories).

Our lack of self-identification as a minority and with   19
other minorities can be further seen in the media's portrayal
that the "Asian-American success story . . . impressive and
increasingly conspicuous" (Time, July 8, 1985) extends into
the broad social arena.   Many Model Minority articles give
an undefinable tone that Asian-Americans are beginning to be
socially accepted by the American mainstream.   Newsweek of
November 24, 1986 ran a story titled the "Ultimate Assimilation" which stated the increasing number of Asian-White
marriages as evidence of Asian-Americans' "acceptance into

American society." These stories give a hint at where this
alleged social acceptance stems from: identification with the
white majority.

The New Republic article titled "America's Greatest Suc- 20
cess Story" (July 15, 1985) pointed out that "all the various
explanations of the Asian-Americans' success do tend to fall
into one category: self-sufficiency." Other articles, like
The New York Times Sunday Magazine article titled "Why They
Succeed" have similarly praised Asian-Americans' "Puritan-
like" traits that have disdained governmental welfare en
route to gaining the "American" dream of material success.
Besides not bothering the government (and the rest of the majority population) with welfare, we are also widely perceived
as "well-behaved" (Newsweek, April, 1984). In other words,
our parents work hard and collect their paychecks, the kids
quietly study their textbooks, as a group, we don't have too
many problems. And most importantly, we don't cause problems like other minorities. We are America's new techno-
coolies, and a "model" for all other minorities.

This ideology behind the Model Minority image is best 21
seen when we examine the first Model Minority story that US
News of Dec. 26, 1966 published. It is important to note
that the period was one of growing black militancy and racial
instability:

> At a time when it is being proposed that
> hundreds of billions be spent to uplift
> Negroes and other minorities, the na-
> tion's 300,000 Chinese Americans are mov-
> ing ahead on their own--with no help from
> anyone else. . . . few Chinese-Americans
> are getting welfare handouts--or even
> want them . . . they don't sit around
> moaning.

It also praises how well behaved Chinese youth are and that
"delinquency" in Chinatown is minor compared with what goes on

around it. [my note: which was generally black ghettoes]
After mentioning past discrimination (but failing to speak at
all of present discrimination), the article notes, "It is a
story of adversity and prejudice that would shock those now
complaining about the hardships endured by today's Negroes."

And what about today? In response to newfound, al-   22
though very limited, Asian-American activism, the influential
Washington Monthly (May 1986) came out with a long article
which began, "Watch out, here comes another group to pander
to . . ." and interestingly enough, argued for political action based on class, not race. The New Republic (July 15,
1985) pointed out that "the most important thing for Asian-
Americans is not any particular combination of issues, but
simply 'being part of the process.' Unlike blacks or Hispanics, Asian-American politicians have the luxury of not
having to devote the bulk of their time to an 'Asian-American
agenda,' and thus escape becoming prisoners of such an
agenda." The article further quotes Thomas Sowell, author
of Race and Economics, who has argued "those minorities that
have pinned their greatest hopes on political action--the
Irish and the Negroes, for example--have made some of the
slower economic advances." The New Republic then goes on to
praise the fact that "rather than search for a solution to
their problems through the political process, Jewish,
Chinese, and Japanese immigrants developed self-sufficiency."

We Asian-Americans must remember that much of what they   23
gained came on the backs of black activism that led to the
Civil Rights Act of 1964 (which benefited all minorities).
We cannot escape the fact that, despite the media's rosy
claims to the contrary, we are a minority and will be treated
as one. If we accept the "model minority" status, we are
accepting a lie.

Endnotes

1. The picture may in reality be even more disturbing if researchers finally begin to consider other factors that

also <u>specifically</u> inflate Asian-American family median incomes. For instance, language difficulties may cause the census (which median income data are based on) to undercount Asian-Americans by as much as 25 percent (Sung). Most of the uncounted are extremely poor immigrants. Furthermore, the immigrants that are counted have been known to report "nonexistent incomes" due to "apprehension about an immigration crackdown" (Dutta). Finally, the media also forgets that high income or low does not necessarily translate into a higher quality of life. For instance, in New York Chinatown, 29 percent of the employed work more than 57 hours per week, 43 percent of the elderly work; 1 out of 5 of those working elderly work more than 55 hours per week (Nishi).

2. A significant fact also forgotten when viewing Asian-American educational success is that "Asians invest heavily in education as a means of upward mobility since other primary mobility strategies are not available" (Yun). They are not available primarily because of racism. For instance, Asian-Americans until recently were barred from unions and traditional lines of credit because of systemic, historical racism. Other "white" avenues to success, such as influential contacts, are also unavailable to Asian-Americans.

Bibliography

Azores, Fortunata M., "Census Methodology and the Development of Social Indicators for Asian and Pacific Americans," <u>U.S. Commission on Civil Rights: Testimony on Civil Rights Issues of Asian and Pacific Americans</u> (1979), pp. 70–79.

Cabezas, Dr. Armado, "Employment Issues of Asian Americans," <u>U.S. Commission on Civil Rights: Testimony on Civil Rights Issues of Asian and Pacific Americans</u> (1979), pp. 70–79, 389–399.

Dutta, Manoranjan, "Asian/Pacific American Employment Profile: Myth and Reality—Issues and Answers," <u>U.S. Commission on Civil Rights: Testimony on Civil Rights Issues of Asian and Pacific Americans</u> (1979), pp. 445–489.

Hirano, Irene, "Poverty and Social Service Perspectives," <u>U.S. Commission on Civil Rights: Testimony on Civil Rights Issues of Asian and Pacific Americans</u> (1979), pp. 125–132.

Hirschman, Charles, and Wong, Morrison, "Trends in Socioeconomic Achievement among Immigrant and Native-Born Asian-

Americans, 1960–1976," The Sociological Quarterly 22 (Autumn 1981), pp. 495–513.

Kahng, Dr. Anthony, "Employment Issues," U.S. Commission on Civil Rights: Testimony on Civil Rights Issues of Asian and Pacific Americans (1979), pp. 411–413.

Kim, Illsoo, "Class Division among Asian Immigrants: Its Implications for Social Welfare Policy," Asian American Studies: Contemporary Issues, Proceedings from East Coast Asian American Scholars Conference (1986), pp. 24–25.

Kuo, Wen H., "On the Study of Asian-Americans: Its Current State and Agenda," Sociological Quarterly (1979), pp. 279–290.

Mariano, Dr. Robert S., "Census Issues," U.S. Commission on Civil Rights: Testimony on Civil Rights Issues of Asian and Pacific Americans (1979), pp. 57–59.

Nishi, Dr. Setsuko Matsunaga, "Asian American Employment Issues: Myths and Realities," U.S. Commission on Civil Rights: Testimony on Civil Rights Issues of Asian and Pacific Americans (1979), pp. 495–507.

Sung, Betty Lee, Chinese American Manpower and Employment, 1975.

Toupin, Dr. Elizabeth Ahn, "A Model University for a 'Model Minority,' " Asian American Studies: Contemporary Issues, Proceedings from East Coast Asian American Scholars Conference (1986), pp. 10–11.

Yun, Grace, "Notes from Discussions on Asian American Education," Asian American Studies: Contemporary Issues, Proceedings from East Coast Asian American Scholars Conference (1986), pp. 20–23.

Questions on Chang's New Essay

1. Identify the general subject of Curtis Chang's new essay. What specific idea does he assert and then explain about that subject? What specific evidence and explanations does he offer to support his assertion about that subject?

2. What specific thematic connections can you identify between "Ni Hao Ma?" and "The Myth of the Model Minority"? In what ways does "The Myth of the Model Minority" build on the issues expressed in "Ni Hao Ma?"? Show, for example, how Chang turns a repeated phrase in the conversation between the narrator and Duane in "Ni Hao Ma?" into one of the bases for his second essay.

3. What specific differences can you point to between Chang's strategies and accomplishments as the writer of both "Ni Hao Ma?" and "The Myth of the Model Minority"? In what specific ways do you think Chang might be able to strengthen the expository qualities of "The Myth of the Model Minority"?

4. Curtis Chang reports that the most difficult aspect of writing a first draft is "resisting the urge to perfect each sentence as I am writing. One is especially vulnerable when working on a word processor. I often have to force myself to continue getting the basic facts out first." What are "the basic facts" Chang presents in this essay?

5. Chang also observes that he composes "the basic outline of a paper in my head. But after that point, I must see my thoughts on the computer screen. I find it difficult to manipulate thoughts unless I can physically manipulate the words that represent them." In this respect, what specific stylistic consistencies link these two essays? Analyze the word choice, phrasing, and sentence structure of Chang's two essays. Point to specific evidence that would verify the fact that these two essays were written by the same person.

6. Review Chang's explanation of his purpose in writing "The Myth of the Model Minority." Explain in detail how he achieved that purpose. What aspects of his new essay do you think would benefit from additional work? Explain why.

7. What purpose and emphasis does Chang establish in his new essay? Does he, for example, seem most interested in explaining the nature of "the myth of the model minority"? In documenting the existence of "the myth of the model minority" in both the American media as well as in the general American public's collective consciousness? In establishing a cause-and-effect relationship between "the myth of the model minority" perpetuated in the American media and the Asian-American population in this country? Some combination of these? Explain.

8. Characterize the tone of Chang's essay. Does his voice in the new essay sound, for example, neutral and objective? Impassioned and involved? Something else? Support your response with detailed references to specific evidence in the essay. Does his tone remain consistent throughout this new essay? If not, where and how does it change? With what effects?

9. Comment on Chang's use of secondary sources in this first draft of "The Myth of the Model Minority." Evaluate his range of sources. Which does he seem to cite more frequently? With what effects? How successfully does he work these secondary sources into his essay? What other primary and secondary sources might he have consulted for stereotypical images and discussions of Asian-Americans?

10. Identify the specific changes that Chang has made as he moves from a personal-experience essay to an expository one.

Curtis Chang reports that he wrote three drafts of "The Myth of the Model Minority" and that his original conception of his audience changed. He explains that he eventually had two distinct audiences in mind: "(1) Asian-Americans who were unaware of their own people's condition and (2) the wider, white audience who may have unknowingly accepted the ideology inherent in the Model Minority image. I approached both audiences as skeptics, since many Asian-Americans are just as ignorant and just as 'white' in attitude as Caucasians. Thus, I knew that I had to avoid the rhetoric and catch phrases which often typify my end of the political spectrum. . . . Thus, I tried to work from their beginning assumptions and avoid alienating the reader from the outset."

As he began to work on developing his new essay, he discovered that the most arduous task was to gather research material. But, as he explains, his rapidly expanding research file created new and unexpected compositional issues: "As my folder grew bigger, I also became more convinced of my analysis and also more angry. . . . From my reading of black writers of the '70s, I understood how rage (no matter how justified) erects a barrier to the skeptical audience. I face a dilemma in this process because one of my major complaints was that White America had encouraged the Asian-American nonmilitancy. I wondered if it would have been better for myself, as an Asian-American, to be as forceful as possible. Finally, however, I decided to try to work a careful balance between my anger and the sensibilities of my audiences. Thus from my first to my third draft of the new essay I worked with my instructor to 'soften up' the tone without 'softening up' the essential message."

The final draft of Curtis Chang's essay appears in Part I, pp. 91–99.

Questions on Chang's Final Draft

1. Is this draft of Chang's essay governed by an assertion or a proposition? Where is it expressed most clearly? In what specific ways is this assertion or proposition different from the governing idea in the rough draft?

2. Chang reports that he envisioned two distinct audiences for this essay. Identify

each. What strategies does Chang use to address each group? Does he seem to be more interested in addressing one group? If so, what devices does he use to do so? Comment on the effectiveness of each.

3. Chang notes that he felt he "had to avoid the rhetoric and catch phrases which often typify my end of the political spectrum. . . . Thus I tried to work from their beginning assumptions and avoid alienating the reader from the outset." Does Chang accomplish this goal? If so, what does he do to avoid the pitfalls he describes?

4. Characterize the speaker's tone in the final draft. In what specific ways is it similar to or different from the speaker's tone in the rough draft? Point to specific words and phrases to support your response. When commenting on his essay, Chang observed: "I decided to try to work a careful balance between my anger and the sensibilities of my audiences. Thus from my first to my third draft of the new essay I worked with my instructor to 'soften up' the tone without 'softening up' the essential message." Comment on the extent to which you think Chang succeeded at this. Use specific passages from the essay to validate your reading.

5. What is the "essential message" of "Streets of Gold: The Myth of the Model Minority"? How is that message similar to or different from the message in Chang's first draft? In what specific ways has the emphasis in Chang's drafts shifted from exposition to argumentation? Locate the moves Chang makes to produce that shift in emphasis. Comment on the effectiveness of each move.

6. Compare and contrast Chang's use of metaphors as a unifying device in all three versions of his essay on racial identity. Which version is most effective? Explain why.

7. When asked to comment on the revisions he made in this final draft, Chang responded: "I think perhaps in the end that I used a bit too many empirical arguments (to convince the audience of the Asian-Americans' true situation) at the expense of further developing the ideological implications of the Model Minority." Reread Chang's final draft and explain why you agree or disagree with his assessment.

8. Chang defines revising as "more than just the usual forms of correcting grammar and spelling and using one adjective instead of another. For myself, revising means acting as a devil's advocate and trying to pick apart my paper's argument. Then, I have to answer to those criticisms." Show how Chang anticipates as well as includes and refutes opposing arguments. In this respect, comment on the differences between Chang's incorporation of secondary sources in his first and final drafts. Which version do you think is more effective? Why?

9. Based on the differences between Chang's rough and final drafts, what would you identify as the principal distinctions between exposition and argumentation? Point to specific passages to support your response. Based on your reading

of these two drafts, list as many as possible of the characteristic moves that writers make when they proceed from exposition to argumentation. In a similar fashion, identify the characteristic moves writers make when they turn a personal-experience essay into an expository or argumentative one.

Turning a Personal-Experience Essay
into Exposition or Argument

Now that you have observed how two student writers developed new essays from personal-experience essays, you can practice the procedures they followed by applying them to your own writing. The whole process, from start to finish, consists of five basic steps:

1. Reread your personal-experience essay carefully several times and generate as many new subjects as possible.
2. Generate as many ideas about each of these subjects as possible.
3. Decide on a new subject to write about.
4. Assert a specific idea about that subject.
5. Write a new essay in which you explain (exposition) or verify a claim or proposition about that new subject (argumentation).

You have probably noticed that both Beverly Dipo and Curtis Chang devoted a large proportion of their efforts to steps 1 and 2. For these writers, as for many others, steps 3 and 4 happened together as step 2 progressed. That is, once you have come up with a list of subjects and are thinking about how you might approach each of them, you may well find that a *thesis*—an interesting idea to assert about a workable subject—occurs to you almost spontaneously. Very often steps 1 and 2, generating possible subjects and ideas, are the most daunting and time-consuming steps in the process. Let's look at them closely.

As Beverly Dipo's and Curtis Chang's examples indicate, the personal-experience essays you have already written contain rich and ready resources for writing other types of essays. Chang moved from narration to exposition and argument, while Dipo moved more directly from narration to argument. It is clear, however, from her freewriting and brainstorming that Dipo's original paper might just as well have led her to an expository essay. The choice of which kind of essay may depend on your assignment or on the combination of subject and idea that strikes you as the most promising thesis. Keeping an open mind is wise. Recall Beverly Dipo's initial reluctance to write an argumentative essay; once she did it, however, she commented: "I find I like the idea of being able to say right out loud how I feel about the issue. . . . This is probably the thing I enjoyed most about this paper."

Step 1 involves rereading your original personal-experience essay carefully, several times, and listing every subject that comes to mind as you think about what you are reading. When you return to your earlier work after a lapse of time, you are better able to see it from a fresh perspective. Ask yourself questions: What made me feel strongly enough about my original topic to write about it? What controversies does it suggest? What broader subjects does it relate to that would allow me to generalize (exposition) or theorize (argumentation) about my experience? Your goal at this point is simply to list as many new subjects to write about as possible.

After completing step 1, you may conclude that only one of your possible subjects is worth pursuing or that one subject is significantly stronger than the others. If so, go on to step 2 and ask yourself: What idea can I assert about this topic? Focus your thinking about the subject or issue until you are reasonably confident you can assert a specific idea about it. Now consider what information, what data, you can provide to support and clarify your idea about this subject or issue. Explaining that idea will become your new expository essay. Or, when you have narrowed your list of possible topics to one, ask yourself: What claim or proposition can I assert about this topic? Presenting logically related statements in support of your claim or proposition will lead to a new, argumentative essay.

In most cases, more than one subject on your list will have good potential as an essay topic. Step 2, then, is to generate as many ideas as you can about each of your "finalists." Some possible theses or approaches to a thesis probably will have occurred to you while you were considering topics. Even if these do not look promising, write them down; they may suggest other possibilities later. As when you thought of subjects, you can try brainstorming, as Beverly Dipo did. Let ideas swirl around in your head and write down everything that might lead to a thesis.

Another Bedford Prize winner, Judy Jennings, has described the kind of chain of associations from which she gleans ideas. (See "Student Writers on Writing: An Overview," p. 10). Jennings's essay "Second-Class Mom" is the result of looking at ordinary personal experience from as many angles as possible. Cultivating this kind of "writer's eye" not only generates a continual supply of ideas but suggests ways of asserting those ideas in an essay.

It sometimes happens, however, that even after rereading your original essay and listing possible subjects and ideas, you still have no workable thesis for an expository or an argumentative essay. If so, you may find the following additional questions helpful. Consider all four sets of questions and then choose one set to guide you as you develop your new essay.

1. *Move from the specific to the general.* A narrative or descriptive essay focuses on a specific event, person, place, or object. Beverly Dipo's "No Rainbows, No Roses" related the death of Mrs. Trane; Curtis Chang's "Streets of Gold: The Myth of the Model Minority" initially recounted his own doubts and anxieties as he grappled with the personal implications of the pervasive image of Asian-Americans as the "model minority." Every specific case can be viewed as an example of a generality: people dying in hospitals, people being presented in stereotypical terms in the media. To move from the specific subject of your personal-experience essay to a more general topic, think about how your experience can be considered representative of many people's experience, as, for example Curtis Chang has done so successfully. The goal here is to broaden your point of view, to extend your thinking to take in that of others besides yourself. Once you have done this, you may want to choose one segment within that general topic, as Beverly Dipo chose "people dying in hospitals *with dignity.*" Or your first generalization may lead you to others: people dying at home; the value of funerals; the importance of making a will.

Questions: What general topic is implied in your specific personal experience? What general subject does your personal experience exemplify? What general issue or issues does your experience raise? What other general subjects or issues emerge from rereading your original essay and thinking about its larger implications?

2. *Move from autobiography to biography.* Another way to move from personal experience to exposition and argumentation is to shift the focus of your original essay from autobiography to biography, from a first-person to a third-person point of view. The shift from a subjective to an objective perspective carries you beyond the limitations of your own experience. It also enables you to distance yourself from your own experience as well as to understand and participate in a multiplicity of cultures and life experiences that in turn may help to illuminate your own life.

Questions: As you reread your personal-experience essay, pay special attention to whether you talk about anyone else during the course of your essay. Consider each such person carefully. What aspects of this person's life do you think are worth writing about? Consider beliefs, attitudes, accomplishments, or perhaps an incident or an anecdote in which he or she figures prominently. What ideas can you assert about this person? Of what general concept is this person's life a specific example? What proposition or claim can you make on the basis of this person's views or behavior?

3. *Move from the concrete to the abstract.* Narrative and descriptive essays are based in large part on concrete information: sensory details about how something looked, felt, or sounded; actions that occurred; the writer's response to those details and actions. In Patrick Kinder Lewis's essay "Five Minutes

North of Redding" (p. 320), we feel the predawn chill of a railway roadbed, and we share the author's tension as he bounds onto a flatcar. But Lewis's essay also alludes to such abstract concepts as freedom, risk-taking, and friendship. As you reread your own personal-experience essay, look for the abstractions it suggests.

Questions: What abstract nouns come to mind as you reread your essay? You may very well think of several abstractions that are associated with your specific, concrete experience. Choose one of these and work at developing its potential as the subject of another essay. Why did this particular abstract noun surface in your mind as you reread your essay? What aspects of your essay suggested it? How does it summarize the point of your essay or indicate what your essay is about? What idea, claim, or proposition might you assert that conveys your thoughts regarding this abstract concept?

4. *Move from observation to inference.* Yet another way to find a suitable subject to develop into a new essay is to move from observation to inference. (For our purposes, an "observation" may be defined as a statement about the visible facts in a specific situation, a statement about which there can be no disagreement. An "inference" is a conclusion based on a premise drawn from observations, a statement about what is still uncertain made on the basis of what is certain. For additional information about observations and inferences, see Chapter 2, "Peer Editing.") In one sense, your original essay might be considered a series of observations about your experience.

Questions: What inferences about experience in general can you draw from your essay? What theory or pattern of behavior seems to govern the experience you wrote about? Consider that theory or pattern carefully and list as many observations as you can about it. Based on your observations, what inferences can you draw about this theory or pattern? To what conclusion about experience, however tentative, do these observations and inferences lead you? Turn this tentative conclusion into the thesis—the controlling idea—for either an expository or an argumentative essay. How can you use the evidence of your own experience, or your inferences about experience in general, to support this thesis?

Having considered these four broad sets of questions aimed at helping you move from writing personal experience essays to expository and argumentative ones, you need next to decide which cluster seems most appropriate to the purpose of your new essay. Once you have made that determination, you might want to work with the following summary of useful procedures. As you reread your personal experience essay, what new "angles," what new approaches to this subject, can you think of? What broader subjects does this essay suggest?

Keep track of these subjects in note form and develop each by following your usual methods of developing an idea about a subject: brainstorm, freewrite, and so on. Narrow your list of possible subjects to one and examine it further. Then ask yourself: What idea can I assert about this subject? Explaining that idea will become your new, expository essay. Or, when you've narrowed your list of possible subjects to one, ask yourself: What claim or proposition can I assert about this subject? Presenting logically related statements in support of your claim or proposition will lead to a new, argumentative essay.

Discovering and learning how to develop the connections between the ideas in one successful essay and another are important skills to master, especially for writers who are not only respectful of the richness of their own intelligence but also committed to exploring that richness fully. Learning to explore the connections between one idea and another, between one essay and another, and between one course and another also helps every writer to recognize and strengthen both the interrelations of writing and reading and the common thread that weave together the seemingly disparate verbal elements of our lives into a practiced, confident, and unique intellectual identity.

Three Exercises for Moving from Personal Experience to Exposition and Argument

1. Reread Ann Louise Field's essay "The Sound of Angels" (p. 147). Here are some possible subjects and ideas asserted about those subjects that Field prepared after rereading her essay:

    —Paper routes
      1. Early jobs build responsibility.
      2. Forcing children to work at too early an age robs them of their youth.

    —Sibling relationships
      1. A little bit of rivalry can be a good thing.
      2. Traditions of childhood; experiences common to all kids.
      3. Love-hate feelings between siblings.

    —Orange groves
      1. The rise and fall of the Southern California citrus industry.
      2. The pros and cons of growing oranges for Minute Maid.
      3. The art of tree-climbing.
      4. Linus Pauling and the vitamin C/cancer controversy.

—Childhood pranks
  1. Lead to delinquency.
  2. Encourage imagination and creativeness in youth.
—Christmas
  1. Holiday traditions.
  2. The evolution of commercialism at Christmas.
—Loss of innocence
  1. The effects of economic stress on the contemporary American family.
  2. The need for everyone to recognize reality.
  3. The nature of adolescent rebellion.
  4. The increase in teenage suicide—the inability to function in an adult world?

Based on your reading of Field's essay, which of these possible subjects and assertions for expository and argumentative essays do you think Field would handle best in a new essay? Why? Point to specific passages in "The Sound of Angels" to support your response. Which seems to offer the least potential as the subject and the assertion for a new essay? Why?

2. Write an expository or argumentative essay based on a personal-experience essay you have written. Follow the questions and procedures outlined above.

3. Write as detailed a commentary as possible on how you wrote your new essay. For instance, how did the idea or claim you chose to assert about your new subject develop and change as you wrote the essay? What particular problems did you have to work out from one draft to the next? What was the goal of your new essay? Whom did you see as the readers of your new essay? How did you try to appeal to those readers? What did you want them to think or feel after they read your essay? What advice would you offer your readers on how to respond to and understand your new essay?

4.

RESPONDING TO
PROFESSIONAL EDITING

I N PREVIOUS CHAPTERS we have seen how students revise their work, first on their own and then with the help of peer editors. In this chapter we have the opportunity to see a professional editor, Jane Aaron, make suggestions for revisions as she shapes the essay by John Clyde Thatcher as if for professional publication.

Observing a professional editor at work teaches several lessons about the place of revision in the composing process. First, all writing, even effective writing, can be improved. Writing effectively takes time, effort, and patience and often requires further revision, or editing, even after a "final" draft. At this point in the process, the professional editor's goal is to preserve the writer's intentions while suggesting changes to improve the accuracy, emphasis, specificity, and consistency of the text. The process, though, is not predictable, as Jane Aaron tells us, because "each writer's process is unique, and the barriers to clear, effective expression are many."

Second, professional editing provides a model of close and careful reading that we can translate to our reading of our own and another writer's work. The job of the professional editor, like that of a peer editor or an instructor, is to provide an objective view; by standing in for the audience, the editor becomes a collaborator who shows the writer whether he or she has communicated effectively with the intended audience. Jane Aaron's editing of John Clyde Thatcher's essay shows how a revised sentence or paragraph, a change in emphasis or tone can allow the writer's intentions to become even clearer to his readers. We see the power and possibility of revising as Thatcher's essay moves from being a strong essay to a polished piece.

Third, observing the professional editing process also shows what happens when a piece of writing goes public. For those who publish their work, whether in a commercial publication or a school newspaper or literary magazine, editing is the final step in the composing process. As readers, we are not aware of this stage—of the extensive editing that goes on—because the printed page does not reveal how each piece of writing was created. We see only the polished words and are not privy to the suggestions and changes, the additions and deletions that constitute the important work of editing.

Gary Goshgarian, a professor of English at Northeastern University and a novelist, textbook author, and freelance writer, is one of the many writers with whom Jane Aaron has worked. In the following passage, the fourth paragraph from Goshgarian's essay "Zeroing in on Science Fiction," we see the suggestions and changes Aaron offered him.

> Science fiction is that branch of
> literature that imaginatively speculates
> on the consequences of living in a scien-
> tific or technological world.

OK to include conditions here? It's used twice below. A closer look at ~~our~~ *the* definition will help ~~us to understand~~ *outline* some SF prerequi-sites. The word "speculates" implies the future. Therefore, a writer who "imag-inatively speculates" is one who creates *and conditions* experiences ∧that ~~may or may not~~∧yet ~~have~~ *have not yet* *seems more accurate, given what you go on to say. See also opposite margin.* occurred in the real world. Certainly

You might consider cutting the human ∧experience ~~of~~ love, hate, and *the Wells exam-ple here: it may not be familiar enough to readers to make it use-ful. The inter-vening points (besides Wells) are really covered in the earlier sentence Therefore... real world.* fear ~~are real~~ however, the writer may create unreal conditions out of which those experiences evolve, as H. G. Wells did in his War of the Worlds. The point *Here, and later, OK to delete* is that SF speculates about some tomorrow ~~conditions and circumstances.~~ ~~Such~~ may *circumstances, The same redundant with conditions?* be said of any non-historical fiction that presumes some general future time. *— and* But∧this is where ~~the rest of our defini-tion separates~~ SF∧ from non-SF∧ ~~Those~~ *differs — the future* *experiences* and *conditions* ~~conditions and circumstances~~ are categor- *Dashes OK to help empha-size shift in focus?*

And Wells is introduced in more detail at the end of the paragraph.

ically scientific or technological~~, by na-~~
~~ture.~~   In other words, SF is about ~~what~~
~~it is like to~~ be(ring) human in ~~a future of~~
some imagined technological ~~advances.~~ future.
The
~~Our~~ definition does not specify locale,
so SF stories can be set on earth, in   *Note that if*
                                          you cut the
                                    Nor   *earlier*
space, or on worlds galaxies away. ~~Like-~~ *Wells example*
does the   *you need to*
~~wise, our~~ definition ~~does not~~ specify ✓ *add Wells*
whose technology.   In War of the Worlds, ~~it*add Wells*
Changes OK   the   -   of   *name to this*
to simplify/ ~~is Martian~~ know-how ~~that permits~~ the bug- *sentence.*
strengthen   Martians transports them
phrasing?   eyed ~~invaders to journey the~~ millions of
               miles ~~of space~~ to earth ~~which it~~ nearly
                                        and then
                      the planet
               devastates, with deadly gases and heat
               rays.

Aaron's specific suggestions show Goshgarian how to strengthen his paragraph so that his message and purpose are clearer. Her editing suggestions help to simplify his sentences, clarify parts of the paragraph that might be confusing to readers, and improve the accuracy and emphasis of his word choice. Because the interaction between a professional editor and writer demonstrates vividly the very process a writer must follow in preparing a final draft, we invited Jane Aaron to edit the essay by John Clyde Thatcher in the same way she worked with Gary Goshgarian. In nearly twenty years as a professional editor, Jane Aaron has worked with the authors of magazine articles, of books for general audiences, and of college textbooks in almost every discipline, including freshman composition. She is the editor of *The Compact Reader*, an anthology of essays for composition courses, and co-author of *The Little, Brown Handbook*, a best-selling composition textbook.

Aaron's editing procedure was similar to the standard editing process used by most professional publications. Aaron edited Thatcher's essay by making some changes, suggesting others, and questioning the writer in places about his meaning and intended effect. Along with the edited version of his essay, she sent him a covering letter in which she explained her general response to his essay and offered an analysis to support her comments on his manuscript. Thatcher was asked not only to revise his essay by considering Aaron's suggestions but also to describe how it felt to have his work professionally edited. As Jane Aaron wrote to Thatcher, she hoped that he would find her suggestions helpful, but he, as a writer, would have the final word; all decisions on revision were his to make. Before reading the edited version of the essay, read the unedited essay as it appears on pages 515–518.

We begin with Jane Aaron's description of a professional editor at work.

A Professional Editor Describes Her Work

In his comments on being edited (page 698), John Thatcher describes his initial feelings of insecurity, fear, and indignation that would sound familiar to any editor. Like most writers who have poured themselves into their work, Thatcher had good reason to believe that his essay was successful. And indeed it was. But, like most manuscripts received by publishers, the essay also had the potential to be better—clearer, more convincing, and more enjoyable for his readers.

An editor is a kind of messenger between writer and reader, representing each to the other. On the one hand, the editor helps the writer state his or her message as effectively as possible. On the other hand, the editor represents the typical reader for whom the piece of writing is intended, anticipating his or her needs for information, clarity, and readability. At the practical level this dual representation works itself out in one process, as the editor helps shape the writer's work for the reader's maximum understanding and enjoyment.

The goal of the editing process is thereby to preserve all the strengths of the manuscript while removing whatever impedes communication between writer and reader. Such a broad goal can encompass any feature of the work, including development, organization, emphasis, pace, specificity, conciseness, consistency, and accuracy. The process is not predictable, however, for each writer's purpose is unique, and the barriers to clear, effective expression are many. From one writer's work to another's, or even from one paragraph to the next in the same work, fresh problems arise to demand fresh solutions. And always the solutions must be conceived in the context of the writer's intentions and the reader's needs.

To understand the writer's intentions, diagnose the weaknesses of the manuscript, and conceive appropriate solutions, the editor may read the work as closely and as often as the writer has. Usually the first reading is a quick one to get the gist of the author's ideas and the sound of the author's voice. Then slower readings follow, during which the editor notes any problems in organization, gaps in the development of ideas, shifts in tone, or unnecessary repetitions. These readings require a kind of peripheral vision of the mind, an ability to recall the entire work while concentrating on a bit of it in order to see the connection—or lack of connection—between the part and the whole.

The actual editing is the most time-consuming part of the process, as the editor tries to resolve the larger problems and also weighs every sentence against the author's intentions and the reader's likely response. It is during this stage that the dialogue between editor and writer occurs. The writer's part in the dialogue consists of the words on the page. The editor's consists of changes, questions, comments, and suggestions, either on the manuscript, in the margins, or on separate sheets of paper. Sometimes the editor changes the manuscript without explanation if the need for change seems obvious enough; most corrections of grammatical, spelling, and typographical errors fall into this category. Sometimes the editor explains changes that reflect interpretations of the author's meaning. And sometimes the editor relies solely on suggestions or questions if the meaning cannot be safely assumed or if passages seem to require rewriting that the author is best equipped to handle. (All three approaches appear on John Clyde Thatcher's essay.) The explanations and suggestions may be lengthy, seemingly out of proportion to the problem being addressed, so that the author will understand why the manuscript is not clear or what impairs its readability. An editor quickly learns that a simple comment like "Not clear" usually prompts the natural response "It's clear to me"—and no revision.

When the editing is completed, the editor returns the manuscript to the author with a covering letter that includes a general response to the piece—both strengths and any overall weaknesses that will provide some context for the specific comments on the manuscript. (See the letter on page 691.) Usually the author's revision is the final round in the process, as it was with John Clyde Thatcher's essay. But occasionally the editor may negotiate last-minute changes with the author before the manuscript is set in type.

Editing requires a certain amount of mind-reading to discern the writer's intentions as well as a sense of the possible solutions, an ear for language, and a firm grounding in the conventions of grammar, punctuation, mechanics, and spelling. It also requires an ability to work "silently," suspending one's own ideas instead of pushing them on the author. Of course, editors sometimes overstep their bounds. Beyond grammar and spelling, few matters in writing are clear-cut: almost everything is a question of choice and of judgment, and judgment calls are endlessly debatable. Although authors have the final word, the good ones, from an editor's standpoint, will always suspend their initial feelings of insecurity, fear, and/or indignation to engage in the debate. By that criterion alone, John Clyde Thatcher is an outstanding author.

John Clyde Thatcher: "On Killing the Man"

The following example of a student writer's response to professional editing begins with Jane Aaron's letter to John Clyde Thatcher and her editing of his essay. We then see Thatcher's comments about Aaron's editing and the essay as he revised it in response to her recommendations.

Editor to Author:
Jane Aaron's Letter to John Clyde Thatcher

Dear Mr. Thatcher:

Your essay is insightful and moving. It is also quite complex, so many of the attached suggestions for revising it are necessarily complex as well. The second half of the essay—the detailed narration of the raccoon experience—is fast-paced and powerful. It is effective in itself, but it is even more dramatic because of the buildup it receives in the first half of the essay. I imagine that this earlier section was difficult to write. It combines an explanation of trapping with an expression of your initial, conventional feelings about trapping—all in an ironic tone that keeps hinting, "This is not the full story; something important is going to happen." As complicated as this first half is, some passages understandably succeed less well than others. As you will see, several of my comments concern the sequencing of information, some shifts away from the first person ("I"), and an inconsistency in tone. In both halves of the essay, I have also queried other passages and made occasional changes for clarity and emphasis.

I hope that all my suggested revisions interpret your intentions accurately and that you agree they will strengthen the essay's capacity first to suspend and then to move the reader. The decisions on whether and how to implement the suggestions are, of course, yours to make.

Sincerely,
Jane E. Aaron

Thatcher's Edited Essay

On Killing the Man

I wanted to trap! All of the other
boys did. Certainly that was reason
enough for me. And what about the stacks
of money to be made through this time-
honored trade? Why, boys had been known
to make a small fortune in one season.

verbs shift from past to present tense

Boys ~~that~~ *who* wished to become young men required inordinate amounts of money, and
for those ~~that~~ *who* live*d* out of town, on a
farm with a woods and small creek, trapping during the winter ~~is~~ *was* a most convenient means to an end: ~~The end being, in~~
~~most cases,~~ the all-important automobile
So I began trapping in the winter of my
seventeenth year. I felt as if I were
pleasing generations of woodsmen; the
pioneer spirit raged in my blood. I
would soon be a man. ~~Whose man?~~ ⟵

a colon seems to emphasize the car's importance just as effectively as the sentence fragment and eliminates repetition ("end... end") and an apparent contradiction ("an end... in most cases"). 2

This paragraph is hard to read because most sentences do not have human actors as subjects (see underlining) and few sentence subjects pick up either the subject or the object of the preceding sentence (thus forcing readers to refocus their attention on each new sentence).

One goes about trapping in this manner. At the very outset one acquires a
"trapping" state of mind. This entails
several steps. The purchase of as many
traps as one might need is first. A pair
of rubber gloves, waterproof boots, and
the grubbiest clothes capable of withstanding human use come next to outfit
the trapper for his adventure. A library
of books must be read, and preferably
someone with experience is needed to educate the novice. The decision has to be
made on just what kind of animals to go

The reader doesn't yet understand the implications of this question, and it is repeated more effectively later. OK to cut?

The problem may occur because you start with "one" as the subject of the first two sentences and then (naturally) want to avoid it. Why not rewrite the paragraph using the first person ("I")? That would make you the actor (removing the unnecessary distance between you and the paragraph content), and it would probably smooth the flow of sentences almost automatically.

after, what sort of bait to use, and *Your later explanation of what animals you were trying to catch (p.3, 1st paragraph) and how/why you set traps in water (p.4, middle) would be more helpful here.*
where to place the traps for highest yield. Finally, the trapper needs a

heavy stick. Often a trap set to drown *Assuming that the raccoon experience was your first clubbing, you might also indicate that your knowledge of how a club was used was secondhand. That would set up the transition on p.4.*
the animal once caught fails to do so.
Then it is necessary to club the animal and drown him. A <u>blow</u> with a club will

not damage a pelt the way a gunshot would. A <u>club</u> is a most necessary piece of equipment for the trapper.

I gather from later paragraphs that you went trapping several times (at least), but this paragraph seems to describe a single experience and so leads the reader to expect a continued emphasis on one experience. Could you reword the first couple of sentences as suggested or in some other way to indicate that you did this more than once?

Properly outfitted and informed,
~~So~~ I set out on my wilderness adven- *is on each foray,*
ture. ∧My booted feet scarred the frosted

grass. The traps slung over my shoulder tolled a death knell as they slapped

against my back, and the oaken club rapped a steady drumbeat on my thigh. I

had my chance to become a man, a real man in the old sense of the word. I was the

French voyageur trapping lands no white man had ever seen before. I was Dan'l

Boone about to catch my famous coonskin cap. I was the Hudson Bay Company trap-

per, trading axes and blankets with the Indians and sending beaver pelts to Lon-

don for a gentleman's top hat. I was my father too. I was he and he was me̱ as

the two of us set out together for the great woods. This was truly the way men

should live.

3

These images give a real sense of your feelings at the time.

I soon learned that becoming a man is a most difficult task, and enjoying the work is even harder.
~~The actual work of trapping can be completed only after the trapper has suf-~~
~~fered as much as possible.~~ It is cold,

tedious, backbreaking, finger- and toe-numbing, infuriating torture often de-

I moved this sentence from the end of the paragraph 4 because it seems a better transition from the previous paragraph and a better lead-in to what follows. OK?

Placing the "fun" view before your view would emphasize your view more.

scribed as exciting and fun by someone who really enjoys trapping. In my case the traps were mostly set in the water. This is done in the hopes of catching

See p. 2, top: more information there? (The next sentence will then need a new beginning.)

If you accept moving this material to the beginning of the paragraph these 2 paragraphs could be combined.

muskrats, raccoons, and possibly a mink or two. It is also done to enhance the feeling of already numb fingers by immersing them in freezing water. ~~It is a most difficult task becoming a man, even more difficult to enjoy doing it~~.

a new transition would be needed; for instance: "and catching the animal does not finish the work: it must be skinned by cutting [etc.]"

Once the animal is caught, it must be skinned. This involves cutting the pelt away from the body, scraping off the fatty deposits from the underside, and stretching the skin on a board until it is dry. All in all, a *single pelt requires a substantial* great amount of *effort* work for a twenty-five-dollar ~~pelt~~ *return—*

5

The two sentence fragments here make reading difficult. I've suggested one way to work them into one complete sentence.

It isn't clear here whether you felt the sense of accomplishment and satisfaction. If you did, then perhaps you should say so directly: the reversal in your attitude when you kill the raccoon would then be that much more dramatic.

Twenty-five dollars, that is, if the pelt is large for a raccoon, if it is in good condition, and if the dealer *(shift in person)* ~~you go to~~ is a generous man. But who can deny the sense of accomplishment a man feels when he sells his pelts? Only he can know the great satisfaction ~~felt by~~ *of* outsmarting small animals ~~through~~ *by* catching and killing them in traps they could not smell or *a man feels* see. What joy ~~is felt~~ when ~~a man can say~~ he has beaten nature with only his quick

The heavy sarcasm in these 2 sentences seems to jump the gun on the powerful raccoon experience. Presumably the feelings underlying this sarcasm were aroused by the raccoon experience. (If you had them before the experience, would it have been so shattering?) I

mind, traps of spring steel, rubberized gloves that leave no betraying scent, scientifically tested lures and baits, *and hold* and clever sets that catch the animals ~~and sink them to their deaths as they~~

suggest cutting this to a single sentence phrased in the same ironic tone you've used so successfully before. For example: "Only a man can know the great satisfaction of outsmarting wary animals with his quick mind and clever equipment."

~~struggle to get away~~ while water fills
their small gasping lungs.

This is an excellent transition, but can you make it more personal by indicating that this was your first failure? (You've already mentioned the general problem of un-drowned animals.)

But often the novice does not succeed in making a "water set" that quickly
drowns the animal.

6

I suggest deleting these 2 sentences. The first is not yet clear, and the information in the second would be more useful on p.2 (see note there). Perhaps save part of the second sentence so that the next sentence begins: "As I neared one trap anchored to a fallen log, ..." — or some such?

One cold morning I stayed home from
school, and though sick with a cold I
checked my trapline like any humane trapper. [My "water sets" had not worked the
night before. I walked in the direction
of a trap anchored to a fallen log that
was intended to encourage a trapped animal to escape by swimming across the
creek and thus drown itself] As I neared
the trap I immediately saw that it had
been disturbed, but didn't see an animal.
"Drowned," I thought. When I was very
close to the set, I realized the animal
was not drowned and underwater; hopelessly entangled around a limb of the log
was a large male raccoon, still alive.

7

OK to add this so the point is unmistakably clear?

I suggest reversing the conflicting emotions in this sentence (as shown) for 2 reasons: (1) the sentence is easier to read if the longer part comes second; and (2) the next sentence starts with "I wanted to be a man," as the 2 sentences are now parallel in content. The sentence would be even easier to read if you phrased the inserted emotion more clearly — perhaps "wanting to achieve what I had worked for"?

Now I had a problem. The raccoon
must be knocked senseless and drowned.
The club that hung around my wrist had
grown very heavy, ~~all of a sudden~~ and my
stomach knotted at the thought of what I
had to do. I was torn between wanting to
absolve myself by setting ~~him~~ free (although I knew he would suffer a horrible
death, ~~and doing what it was I had worked
so hard to come to~~. I wanted to be a man,
but also wanted to run away from what I'd
done and cry into my mother's breast. My
hand, however, was forced by my earlier

8

suddenly

wanting to do what I had worked so hard to come to and

the raccoon ← *Occasionally, it seems necessary to repeat "raccoon" instead of using a pronoun.*

actions, and now I had to take this creature's life to end the suffering I had
caused it.   The bile rose in my throat as
I raised the club.

At that moment I knew what an awful   9
thing it is to be hated, violently hated
by another living thing. *The raccoon* ~~He~~ looked at me
and not *at* the club.   He looked at me with
his trap-torn flesh bleeding away his   *Rewording*
fear, leaving only raging hate. ~~He~~   *focuses atten-*
Barely let up ~~barely paused in~~ his screamed hiss, as *the* *tion on the*
                                                      hiss — OK?
club came down, again and again, on his
skull.   I didn't kill him well because he
was my first murder and *because* ~~the~~ hot tears   *The tears seem*
~~that burst from me~~ blinded my eyes, mak-   *to be a second*
                                              reason for
ing the blows poorly aimed.   *killing poorly—*
                                               hence changes
Once the hideous screaming stopped   *—OK?*   10
and the despising, damning eyes rolled
back into their sockets, I drowned *the raccoon.* ~~him.~~
As I watched the water fill him up and
the bubbles and blood float up from his
nostrils, I wondered if I was now the man
I had wanted to be.   Whose man?   I decided then that the boy who was responsible for this wretched thing was not ready *Perhaps*
                                          start a new
to be a man because he had aspired to be *paragraph*
someone else and not himself.   I knew   *here to set*
                                         off your
Rewording then that I would never do this despica- *reflections*
seems more   *on the in-*
emphatic. ble thing again; and *never have ~~since~~.* ✓ *To cident from*
reach manhood is a wonderful ~~thing~~, but *the incident*
                                                 itself?
it ~~this~~ happens only when the man can look
                                          a more
at himself and recognize what he sees.   *A precise word*
                                         is needed here
boy must kill "the man," the one he has *because "thing"*
dreamed for himself; ~~in his head.~~ in order *appears in*
   the 2 preceding sentences with a different meaning;
      "achievement" perhaps?

to let out the one inside ~~that~~ *who* patiently ~~bides his time~~ *waits* until the boy ~~is ready to~~ *can* accept what he is. It takes a signifi-cant event to make the change. In my case it took the murder of an animal.

This sentence is complicated, and fewer words help make it more readable.

→ Life is not always clean and bloodless. If I could have killed my "man" with a swift rapier thrust I would have done it. Instead I ~~am left with the memory~~ *remember* of blow after blow on a tiny head. I still see the bared teeth and still hear the wild snarling. My "man" died especially hard in bloody frothing waters. I have learned from that and will never forget. ⟶

Neither of these sentences seems necessary: you make the points clearly and concretely in the surrounding material. The last sentence, especially, seems a weaker ending than the sentence preceding it.

The Author Responds:
Commentary from John Clyde Thatcher

When I read Ms. Aaron's comments, I was at the same time greatly flattered and scared to death of her changes. I had never been edited by someone who edits other people's work for a living. I didn't know where to start. Somewhere in my mind I thought I should play the temperamental young author and fight the suggestions of the mad-slashing editor who wanted me to compromise my writing. Once I started, however, I found all of Ms. Aaron's comments helpful, clear, and perfectly logical. Ms. Aaron helped me polish my essay so that it is now meaningful to anyone who may read it.

It has been a bad practice of mine to feel mild indignation while being edited. In the past I thought I personally was being edited, not the thing I'd written. After this experience I have learned that I am not being told that I am inadequate but that my writing isn't as good as it might be. It's not a good idea to treat one's writing as if it were carved in stone. Now I welcome an outside opinion to point out something I might have missed. Often I am too close to my writing and miss many things that could be strengthened.

From studying Ms. Aaron's comments, I learned that I need to treat writing as a craft. My writing has always been an outlet for great emotion with little conscious thought toward form, balance, timing, and the things that make writing aesthetic. I also discovered that in order to create the desired effect on my reader, I need to be careful with correct introduction of information, suspense, and climax. I feel that too often I have been bowling my reader over with emotion and often have not been clear in an effort to be a better writer. Writing is like building a house of cards; you've got to be patient and careful.

Before I began rewriting I decided that I would accept most of Ms. Aaron's suggested changes. I knew they were all in my best interest, and the only disagreement arose where a word or short phrase that I liked was being deleted. When I was through rewriting I was surprised that my essay was not an empty shell as I had feared. The suggested changes even inspired some new thoughts. My essay is now more polished and satisfying. I knew it had rough edges; I just needed Ms. Aaron to show me where they were.

Thatcher's Revised Essay

On Killing the Man

I wanted to trap! All of the other boys did. Cer- 1
tainly that was reason enough for me. And what about the
stacks of money to be made through this time-honored trade?
Why, boys had been known to make a small fortune in one season. Boys who wished to become young men required inordinate amounts of money, and for those who lived out of town,
on a farm with a woods and small creek, trapping during the
winter was a most convenient means to an end: the all-important automobile. So I began trapping in the winter of my
seventeenth year. I felt as if I were pleasing generations
of woodsmen; the pioneer spirit raged in my blood. I would
soon be a man.

I went about trapping in this mannor. At the very out- 2
set I acquired a "trapping" state of mind. This entailed
several steps. I purchased the traps I thought I would need
first. Next, to outfit myself for my trapping adventures I
collected a pair of rubber gloves, waterproof boots, and the
grubbiest clothes capable of withstanding human use. I read
a library of books and was educated by an experienced trapper, my father. I then made the decision on just what kinds
of animals to seek, what sort of bait to use, and where to
place my traps for highest yield. Finally, I found a heavy
stick: a souvenir Indian war club from Cherokee, North Carolina. I had decided to set my traps in the water. I had
hoped to catch water animals such as muskrats, raccoons, and
possibly a mink or two. My traps were anchored to something
heavy on the bank to encourage trapped animals to swim away
from their torment, into deeper water, where they would drown
from the weight of the trap pulling them down. The club was
a precautionary measure to stun and drown animals that might
inconveniently choose not to follow my plan. I knew my club
would not damage a pelt the way a gunshot would. My club

was my most necessary piece of equipment as I began my passage into manhood.

With a storehouse of woodland lore and all the trappings, as it were, dangling from me, I set out early every morning on my wilderness adventures. The brilliantly cold eye of the winter sun looked on morosely each brittle dawn as my booted feet scarred the frosted grass. The traps slung over my shoulder tolled a death knell as they slapped against my back, and the hickory club rapped a muffled drumbeat on my thigh. I had my chance to become a man, a real man in the old sense of the word. I was the French voyageur trapping lands no white man had ever seen before. I was Dan'l Boone about to catch my famous coonskin cap. I was the Hudson Bay Company Trapper, trading axes and blankets with the Indians and sending beaver pelts to London for a gentleman's top hat. I was my father too. I was he and he was I as the two of us set out together for the great woods. This was truly the way men should live.

I soon learned that becoming a man is a most difficult task, and enjoying the work is even harder. What someone who really enjoys trapping would call exciting and fun was for me cold, tedious, backbreaking, finger- and toe-numbing, infuriating torture, and my "water-set" traps served only to enhance the feeling of my already numb fingers by immersing them in freezing water. And once you've been successful in catching an animal, your work begins again. The animal's pelt must be cut away from its body. The layer of subcutaneous fat must be scraped from the underside, and the skin must be stretched on a board designed for the purpose and left to dry. All in all, a single pelt requires a substantial effort for a twenty-five-dollar return--twenty-five dollars, that is, if the pelt is large for a raccoon, if it is in good condition, and if the dealer is a generous man. But I believed a man could feel no greater sense of accomplishment than when he sold his pelts. I wanted to know the

3

4

great satisfaction of outsmarting animals by catching them in
traps they could not smell or see. I wanted to know the joy
a man must feel when he has beaten nature with only his quick
mind, traps of spring steel, rubberized gloves that leave no
betraying scent, and scientifically tested lures and baits.
I wanted my water sets to succeed in catching, holding, and
drowning my prey.

Being a novice, I had not counted on the possibility   5
that my water sets might fail to pull down a captured animal
while water filled its small, gasping lungs.

One cold morning I stayed home from school, and though   6
sick with a cold I ran my trapline like any humane trapper.
As I neared the last trap on my line, a water set anchored to
a fallen log, I immediately saw that it had been disturbed.
But I didn't see an animal. "Drowned," I thought. When I
was very close to the set, I realized the animal was not
drowned and underwater; hopelessly entangled around a limb of
the log was a large male raccoon, very much alive.

Now I had a problem. The raccoon must be knocked   7
senseless and drowned. The club that hung from a thong on
my wrist had suddenly grown very heavy, and my stomach knotted at the thought of what I had to do. I was torn between
wanting to do what I had worked so hard to come to and wanting to absolve myself by setting the raccoon free (although I
knew he would suffer a horrible death). I wanted to be a
man, but I also wanted to run away from what I'd done and cry
into my mother's breast. My hand, however, was forced by my
earlier actions, and now I had to take this creature's life
to end the suffering I had caused it. The bile rose in my
throat as I raised the club over my head.

At that moment I knew what an awful thing it is to be   8
hated, violently hated by another living thing. The raccoon
looked at <u>me</u> and not at the club. He looked at me with his
trap-torn flesh bleeding away his fear, leaving only white,
raging hate. His screamed hiss barely let up as the club

came down, again and again, on his skull.   I didn't kill him
well because he was my first murder and because hot tears
blinded my eyes, making the blows poorly aimed.

Once that hideous screaming stopped and the despising,   9
damning eyes rolled back into their sockets, I drowned the
raccoon.   As I watched the water fill him up and the bubbles
and blood float up from his nostrils, I wondered if I was now
the man I wanted to be.   Whose man?   I decided then that the
boy who was responsible for this wretched thing was not ready
to be a man because he had aspired to be someone else and not
himself.   I knew then that I would never do this despicable
thing again, and I never have.

To reach manhood is a natural progression, but it hap-   10
pens only when the new man can look at himself and recognize
what he sees.   A boy must kill "the man," the one he has
dreamed for himself, in order to free the one inside who patiently bides his time until the boy can accept what he is.
It takes a significant event to make the change.   In my case
it took the murder of an animal.   If I could have killed my
"man" with a swift rapier thrust I would have done it.   Instead I remember blow after blow on a small head.   I still
see the bared teeth and still hear the wild snarling.   My
"man" died especially hard in bloody frothing waters.

Questions on Thatcher's Essay

1. John Thatcher remarked in his response to Jane Aaron's editing: "It has been a bad practice of mine to feel mild indignation while being edited. In the past I thought I personally was being edited, not the thing I'd written." What is it about the process of editing that makes writers feel indignant? Why do writers need the outside opinion that an editor can provide?

2. In her letter, Aaron states Thatcher's intention as she sees it. Do you agree with her evaluation? Do her suggested changes maintain this intention?

3. In his response, Thatcher says that his revised essay is "not an empty shell" but that Aaron's suggestions "inspired some new thoughts" and the essay "is now more polished and satisfying." Do you agree? How does Thatcher keep his enthusiasm for and involvement with his subject in revising?

4. Aaron shows Thatcher that some passages in his essay succeed less well than others. From her comments, decide which passages in the essay she thinks are most successful and which are least successful. Do you agree with her?

5. Locate Aaron's comments in the first part of the essay that ask Thatcher to rewrite a paragraph or sentence using the first-person pronoun ("I") rather than the third person ("one" or "he"). Why do these comments help Thatcher's purpose?

6. In her letter, Aaron mentions problems with "sequencing of information." Which of her specific comments deal with this problem? How did she think Thatcher should revise the essay? Did Thatcher make the changes she asked for?

7. Aaron questions Thatcher's inconsistency in tone. In paragraph 5 in particular she feels that Thatcher's sarcasm anticipates too early the narrative that follows. Do you agree with her? Why or why not? Has Thatcher answered her criticism in his revision? Has he toned down the sarcasm? Is the revision more effective here than the original? Can you suggest other ways of revising?

8. Aaron likes the images Thatcher uses in paragraph 3 because they give a sense of his feelings at the time. Do you agree that they are successful? Why are they important for making the narrative more meaningful?

9. Aaron made occasional changes, as she says, for "clarity and emphasis." Find places where her changes make Thatcher's meaning clearer. Why does her rewording make the meaning clearer in each case? How has she improved the emphasis? What has been emphasized more effectively in the revised essay?

10. Study paragraph 2 of Thatcher's original essay, with Aaron's comments. Do you agree with Aaron's comments? Why? Then look at paragraph 2 of Thatcher's revised essay. Has he used all of Aaron's suggestions? What has he accepted and what has he rejected? Describe the differences between the original and revised essays. What further revisions would you suggest?

11. Which of Aaron's comments did you find most helpful? What did you learn

about reading and writing from studying Aaron's comments on Thatcher's essay?

12. Imagine that you are a professional editor preparing one of the student essays in this book for publication. What changes would you recommend that the writer make? Annotate that student's essay, as Aaron did with Thatcher's essay, explaining the changes you think are necessary and offering possible solutions. Also write a letter to that student pointing out the strengths of his or her essay and telling what still needs to be done to improve it.

The 1985 Bedford Prizes in Student Writing

Student, (Instructor), *School, State*

Johnna Lynn Benson, (Brian S. Best), *Brigham Young University, Utah*
Terry L. Burns, (Robert Durante), *Canisius College, New York*
Barbara J. Carter, (Mary Slayter), *Rogue Community College, Oregon*
Sandra Casillas, (Alicia Gaspar de Alba), *University of Texas at El Paso, Texas*
David A. Christman, (Tony Giffone), *New York University, New York*
Ravenel Boykin Curry, (Fred Strebeigh), *Yale University, Connecticut*
Beverly P. Dipo, (Joyce Kinkead), *Utah State University, Utah*
Ann Louise Field, (Nancy Jones), *University of Iowa, Iowa*
Erik Field, (Patricia L. Cagwin), *Iowa State University, Iowa*
Petrea Galloway, (Timothy May), *Yuba College, California*
Pamela Garrettson, (Wallace Shugg), *University of Maryland, Baltimore County,*
  Maryland
Matthew J. Holicek, (John Ruszkiewicz), *University of Texas at Austin, Texas*
Brenda Jacobs, (Nelda J. Lott), *Mississippi Gulf Coast Junior College, Mississippi*
Judy Jennings, (Rica Garcia), *Richland College, Texas*
Monika Jerabek, (Swen Birkerts), *Harvard University, Massachusetts*
Earnestine Johnson, (Lois Cucullu), *George Mason University, Virginia*
Amber Kennish, (Claire Gleitman), *New York University, New York*
Karen L. Kramer, (Joan Griffin), *University of Nebraska at Lincoln, Nebraska*
Linda Lavelle, (Edward McCarthy), *Harrisburg Area Community College, Pennsylvania*
Patrick Kinder Lewis, (Sharon Ewert), *Wheaton College, Illinois*
William G. Malley, (Holly Weeks), *Harvard University, Massachusetts*
John E. Mason, Jr., (Patricia Lynch), *Central Connecticut State University,*
  Connecticut
Nelsy Massoud, (Rebecca Mlynarczyk), *Hunter College, New York*
Kelly J. Mays, (Jerome Beaty), *Emory University, Georgia*
Thu Hong Nguyen, (Donald S. Pratt), *Palomar College, California*
Carol A. Oberhaus, (Gerald W. Morton), *Auburn University at Montgomery,*
  Alabama
Max Ramsey, (Joy M. Barnes), *University of Richmond, Virginia*
Julie A. Reardon, (Mary Beth Lake), *Normandale Community College, Minnesota*
Jonathan A. Schilk, (Luke M. Reinsma), *Highline Community College, Washington*
Barbara Seidel, (Mary Ellen Byrne), *Ocean County College, New Jersey*
John S. Siegrist, (Holly Westcott), *Florence-Darlington Technical College, South*
  Carolina
Kim Sport, (Sister Rose Elizabeth Brown), *Our Lady of Holy Cross College, Louisiana*
Frances E. Taylor, (Louise A. DeSalvo), *Hunter College, New York*
Greg Weekes, (Gerald Schiffhorst), *University of Central Florida, Florida*
Steve West, (Laura Novo), *Columbia University, New York*